The Psychoanalytic Study of the Child

VOLUME FIFTY–ONE

New Haven and London
Yale University Press
1996

Designed by Sally Harris
and set in Baskerville type.
Printed in the United States of America by
Vail-Ballou Press, Inc., Binghamton, N.Y.

Library of Congress catalog card number: 45-11304
International standard book number: 0-300-06579-5
A catalogue record for this book is available from the British Library.

The paper in this book meets the guidelines for
permanence and durability of the Committee on
Production Guidelines for Book Longevity of the
Council on Library Resources.

2   4   6   8   10   9   7   5   3   1

Contents

APPLIED PSYCHOANALYSIS

Introduction

ALBERT J. SOLNIT, M.D.

IN THIS FIFTY-FIRST VOLUME OF *The Psychoanalytic Study of the Child,* we commemorate scientifically and clinically the one-hundredth birthday of Anna Freud, who, with Ernst Kris and Heinz Hartmann, founded this annual repository of writings on child psychoanalysis and child development. (The voice and legacy of Heinz Hartmann were acknowledged in Volume 49 [1994], and we are contemplating a commemorative volume to rediscover the voice and legacy of Ernst Kris on his centenary, in the year 2000.) The editor-founders, all three of them originally from Vienna, were an endowment from the diaspora created by the Nazis to the United Kingdom and to the United States. In the first volume, published in 1945, they defined the field: "The contributions of psychoanalysis to the study of the child cover many areas. In therapy the range extends from child analysis to child guidance and group work; in theory, from the basic problems of genetic psychology to those concerned with the interrelation of culture and the upbringing of the child" (p. 9). They also noted: "The annual is an Anglo-American venture. We hope that in following volumes we may include contributions from other countries."

On December 2, 1995, one day before the hundredth anniversary of her birth, Anna Freud was remembered at Yale University by a daylong scientific meeting ("Anna Freud at Yale") devoted to aspects of her contributions to psychoanalytic child development and their applications. The program of that meeting constitutes the first section of this book. I had the privilege of introducing this meeting with the following speech.

Sterling Professor Emeritus of Pediatrics and Psychiatry and senior research scientist at the Yale University School of Medicine and Child Study Center; commissioner, Connecticut Department of Mental Health and Addiction Services.
The Psychoanalytic Study of the Child 51, ed. Albert J. Solnit, Peter B. Neubauer, Samuel Abrams, and A. Scott Dowling (Yale University Press, copyright © 1996 by Albert J. Solnit, Peter B. Neubauer, Samuel Abrams, and A. Scott Dowling).

1

Setting this program in New Haven acknowledges Anna Freud's work at Yale during month-long visits over a seven-year period and her continuing collaboration with colleagues and friends at Yale, including Marianne and Ernst Kris, Milton Senn, Joseph Goldstein, Jay Katz, Seymour Lustman, and Sally Provence.

We have elected to remember Anna Freud's lasting contributions to our intellectual history and to psychoanalysis and child development selectively, because what she left for us from the more than sixty years of her work cannot be encompassed in one day. Her legacy constitutes more than the sum of her published writings; the students she taught; her productive collaborations with several generations of psychoanalysts, educators, pediatricians, legal scholars, psychologists, nurses, and social workers; and, above all, the children she served directly and indirectly.

Born in Vienna on December 3, 1895, the youngest of six children of Sigmund and Martha Freud, Anna Freud was the only one to become a psychoanalyst. She began her professional career as an elementary school teacher, stimulated by the contributions of Maria Montessori. She was educated at the College Lyceum, a Viennese girls' school, where she later taught for many years, exercising a strong influence on teacher training and directly on many of the teachers. During this period (1919–1925) she also began a training analysis, and in 1922, at 26 years of age, she became a member of the Vienna Psychoanalytic Society. She practiced and taught psychoanalysis and took a leading role in the Vienna society until the Nazis forced her and her family to leave in 1938.

Elisabeth Young-Bruehl's *Anna Freud: A Biography* (1988) confirms that Anna Freud was (1) guardian, advocate, and enriching contributor to the work of her father, the creator of psychoanalysis—that is, she was his true psychoanalytic heir; (2) a pioneer in establishing child psychoanalysis; and (3) an original clinical scientist and psychoanalyst.

In this third domain, as Peter Neubauer's article (below) documents, Anna Freud's contributions were always as readily understood by educators, pediatricians, and the courts—those who were concerned with the child's development and external life—as by psychoanalysts and others who concentrated on the child's inner life.

The Young-Bruehl biography offers substantial evidence that Anna Freud's leadership in psychoanalysis was well established before she and her family moved to England and that her creativity flowered in England after her father's death in 1939.

To mention but two of her accomplishments:

It was during her life in London that she created what Clifford Yorke (below) has called her greatest achievement—the development of the Hampstead Child-Therapy Course and Clinic. Also during this period she sponsored the care and treatment of six children who had been abandoned at Theresienstadt when they were between six months and one year old and who for the next three years had been cared for by many different exhausted adults as they clung together in a refugee camp. The children became a gang who learned to count on one another because there was no adult they could count on. When they were brought to England, "It was evident that they cared greatly for each other and not at all for anybody or anything else" (Young-Bruehl, p. 320). A home called Bulldogs Bank became their residence, and Anna Freud's Hampstead colleagues Sophie and Gertrude Dann, with help from others, notably Alice Goldberger, reared them, making systematic recordings of their observations. Anna Freud converted an early draft of Sophie Dann's observations into "An Experiment in Group Up-bringing" (1951). This "experiment" confirmed what Anna Freud had discovered in theory and practice in her Hampstead War Nurseries about children who were without their parents.

Responding to experiments of nature or of man, Anna Freud developed models of service for children in need—the poor, the blind, the abandoned, the neurotically and developmentally impaired—from which she organized systematic observations, theory-building explorations, training programs, and the world-famous Hampstead Child-Therapy Course and Clinic training program (which after her death was renamed The Anna Freud Centre).

In collaborative scientific work, Anna Freud's love of truth was evident. She enjoyed sustained arguments about significant disagreements. Often she would bring in just the right folktale or parable to illustrate her point. Such discussions were intense but civil, with no acknowledgment of discrepancies in experience or status. At the same time, these exchanges were serious; Anna Freud insisted on a full exploration of the question involved in order to achieve clarity and on the avoidance of the use of ten words when one carefully selected word would do.

Her *Writings* in eight volumes provide us with a rich legacy of her scientific, clinical, and educational contributions. Her accomplishments were widely acknowledged and formally expressed through the many honorary doctorates and awards she received in the United States and Europe.

All of Anna Freud's teaching, research, and clinical work demonstrated her belief in the unity of the human personality. Her individual papers and books have documented this view in a scholarly way with a special emphasis on the developing child. In her style of writing and teaching, she was unfailingly lucid, incisive, and persuasive. Her hallmark was an integration of this style and scientific rigor. Her spoken presentations were often salted by a wonderful sense of humor in which she used her gift as a storyteller to dramatize and illustrate theoretical and educational issues.

It is fitting to conclude this introduction with Anna Freud's own words. In her Doctoral Award Address at Jefferson Medical College, on June 12, 1964, she commented:

> One more personal addition: when I was a young girl and dissatisfied with my appearance—as girls often are—I felt comforted by a saying then popular in Vienna: "After a certain age every woman gets the face that she deserves"—that is, the face she creates for herself. Today, I want to apply this assertion to the work of every psychoanalyst: I think it is true that after a certain age and point in his career, every psychoanalyst creates for himself the type of work that he deserves. In Professor Castle's Commencement Speech this morning, we heard how wide a choice there is for the medical man, how many fields to select from, and how difficult it is in the beginning to predict whether the individual persons will turn into clinicians or theoreticians or administrators—that is, which fate they will carve out for themselves in medicine. What is true for the medical graduate is applicable to the analytic graduate. Some become analytic practitioners; some apply psychoanalysis only to psychiatry; some even restrict themselves to psychotherapy; some enter a field of application and remain there; some turn to theory, etc. So far as I am concerned, I feel I have been well treated by fate and have been given more than I deserved. At present, I am lucky enough to be organizer of an institution which combines in itself almost all the aspects of psychoanalysis: teaching, therapy, techniques, theory, research, application to prevention, education, pediatrics, etc. There is no better life for the analyst than to be able to be in constant contact with all the facets of human behavior, from childhood to adulthood and from normality to the severest forms of pathology.
>
> And one final remark. When I return home tomorrow, as a new Sc.D., people not familiar with university usage may ask in which of the sciences I received my doctorate. I hope I have your agreement if I answer: "The science of psychoanalysis, of course."

BIBLIOGRAPHY

FREUD, A. (IN COLLABORATION WITH SOPHIE DANN). "An Experiment in Group Upbringing," *The Psychoanalytic Study of the Child,* New York: IUP, Vol. V, 1951, pp. 127–168.

FREUD, A. "Doctoral Award Address," *Writings, Vol. V, 1956–1965,* New York: IUP, 1967, pp. 515–516. First published in *Journal of the Amer. Psychoanal. Assn.,* Vol. 15:833–840, 1967.

FREUD, A., KRIS, E., & HARTMANN, H. "Preface" *The Psychoanalytic Study of the Child,* New York: IUP, Vol. I, 1945.

YOUNG-BRUEHL, E. *Anna Freud: A Biography,* New York: Summit Books, 1988.

"ANNA FREUD AT YALE"
SYMPOSIUM

Anna Freud's Contributions to Our Knowledge of Child Development

An Overview

CLIFFORD YORKE, FRC PSYCH. DPM

Anna Freud's contribution to our understanding of child development, normal and abnormal, is so substantial, extensive, diverse, and rich in its implications that its summary is beyond the scope of a single presentation. Accordingly this paper concentrates on some contributions that have especially influenced the author, on later, comparatively neglected writings, and on works that looked at what had gone before as well as what lay ahead. But, it is argued, Anna Freud's contributions cannot be assessed simply in terms of her writings. The creation of the Hampstead Child Therapy Course and Clinic, along with its leadership and the stimulation it gave to others both there and world wide, is regarded as her greatest achievement.

A FEW WEEKS BEFORE WRITING THIS PAPER, I ATTENDED A CONFERENCE that must be unique in the history of psychoanalysis, certainly in Great Britain and perhaps elsewhere. The conference, by invitation, was attended by some thirty judges in family law, including four of the five Lords of Appeal, the Official Solicitor to the High Court and his Deputy, some academics in jurisprudence, guardians ad litem, and a num-

---

Honorary consultant psychiatrist to The Anna Freud Centre, London; formerly psychiatrist-in-charge.

The Psychoanalytic Study of the Child 51, ed. Albert J. Solnit, Peter B. Neubauer, Samuel Abrams, and A. Scott Dowling (Yale University Press, copyright © 1996 by Albert J. Solnit, Peter B. Neubauer, Samuel Abrams, and A. Scott Dowling).

7

ber of child psychiatrists and psychoanalysts. Eight papers were precir-
culated: two by judges, six by psychoanalysts. (Three of the latter,
including my own, were written by former members of the Anna Freud
Centre.) Because the conference was residential and held over an extended weekend, there was a good deal of informal as well as formal
discussion. We got on well together, and the successful meeting led to a
demand for continuing association. The judges wanted to know about
child psychoanalysis and how its better understanding could help them
and those who advised them in their work. All were united in this
common aim.[1]

I do not know how much that meeting owed historically to Anna
Freud and her collaboration with Joe Goldstein of the Yale Law School
and Albert Solnit of the Child Study Center. She would have been
delighted by the very existence of such a conference and, had she been
alive, would have inspired the gathering with the eloquence, sanity, and
sound analytic thinking that so many from the different disciplines to
which she contributed remember with pleasure and gratitude.

On this special occasion (Anna Freud at Yale University, the Centenary Celebration of her birth, held December, 1995) I emphasize the
long-standing links between Anna Freud and the Yale Child Study
Center, the Yale Law School, and the Hampstead Child Therapy
Course and Clinic (now the Anna Freud Centre), which she founded
with Dorothy Burlingham and ran with such distinction for many
years. But the joint contributions to applied psychoanalysis in respect
to family law go far beyond the subject matter of the three books
published through that collaboration: *Beyond the Best Interests of the
Child, Before the Best Interests of the Child,* and *In the Best Interests of the
Child.* This work could not have been undertaken without the background knowledge of children's needs at each stage of development; of
the support and circumstances necessary to promote healthy maturation; of the roles of mothers and fathers in relation to their children, of
the possible effects of atypical families, fostering, adoption, and residential care; of physical maturation; and of the ways in which disabilities, illnesses, and physical traumata may interfere with normal development, stunt it, or force it into pathways that challenge adaptation to

1. The Darlington Conference on Dynamic Practitioners—The Family Law System
was held 23–25 September 1995, Tornes, Devon. It was preceded by a meeting the year
before initiated by Lord Lloyd of Berwick (an appeal judge) and members of the Institute
for the Study and Treatment of Delinquency, in which psychoanalysts met with judges in
criminal law. This successful encounter led to the decision to organize the present one,
arrangements for which were largely in the hands of Mr. Justice Thorpe (now Lord
Justice Thorpe), and Drs. Anne Zachary and Donald Campbell of the Institute.

its very limits. References in the books I have mentioned give ample evidence of the force of such considerations behind the wisdom they disseminate.

Anna Freud's contributions to this knowledge were beyond measure, and the analytic understanding she brought to the applied fields of education and pediatrics was unrivaled. But I cannot hope to justify the title of this talk and offer an adequate survey of her work. I thought it better to concentrate here on contributions that I have found of special interest, and I include some of her later work that seems to me comparatively neglected.

Following the Anschluss, Anna Freud came with her father and family to England and first extended work already started in Vienna.[2] Her interest in education was continued through her association with the distinguished schools inspector J. C. Hill (who attended every open meeting at Hampstead until shortly before his death at the age of 90).[3] It was at his instigation that Anna Freud gave public lectures on pedagogy that echoed those she had given years before (in 1930) to teachers and parents in Vienna. More importantly, however, she established the War Nurseries, which also had roots in Vienna, in the Edith Jackson Nursery. Set up by herself and Dorothy Burlingham, it was an experimental day nursery for the poorest city toddlers providing psychological and physical care under the guidance of pediatrician Josefine Stross. That work is documented in two books written by Burlingham and Anna Freud: *Young Children in Wartime* (1942) and *Infants Without Families* (1944),[4] which showed inter alia the detrimental effect of family separation on a young child's development. And although ways of minimizing the impact of enforced separation and dealing with some of the upsets derived from it are now well known, some other lessons to be learned from it are not.[5] Anna Freud once said, in a talk televised for a meeting in the United States, which she was then unable to attend, that someone had recently said of her father's *Three Essays* (S. Freud,

2. Anna Freud's arrival in London rather than elsewhere was not welcomed by everyone; and Melanie Klein found the part played by Ernest Jones in arranging it difficult to forgive. But I shall not, include anything about the Freud/Klein controversies: they have been dealt with elsewhere by others as well as myself (e.g., Yorke, 1971; 1994) and are fully documented in the scholarly records meticulously edited by Pearl King and Riccardo Steiner.

3. John C. Hill became a lasting friend of Anna Freud's, and she wrote the foreword to one of his fine books (Hill, 1971).

4. Books are available, together with hitherto unpublished Monthly Reports, in Volume III of the *Collected Writings* (1973).

5. A great deal about child development to be learned there was elaborated later and is of permanent value.

1905): "But, of course, *everyone* knows all that! There's nothing *new* in it." "Well," said Anna Freud, with a resigned shrug, "that is the fate of such books!" Well, perhaps that is the fate of the two books written by Anna Freud and Dorothy Burlingham. But there are some differences. In the *Three Essays,* what was "universally known" was radically modified later by analysts of different persuasions; but, in the books on the War Nurseries, much that was written *is* taken for granted today by many who know nothing of its origins. In some ways the wartime books recall the meticulous observations that lie behind the case histories of the *Studies on Hysteria* (Breuer and Freud, 1895). The careful, detailed records made in the War Nurseries and the intellectual vigor brought to bear on them are not nowadays readily found. Case histories have become condensed and desiccated, that is, reduced to bare essentials that deprive their subjects of any real semblance of life.

For those unacquainted with the bulk of Anna Freud's works *The Ego and the Mechanisms of Defence* (1936) is all too often the only one that springs to mind, as if the work she did in England can safely be ignored. Even a major work like *Normality and Pathology in Childhood* (1965a) is rarely mentioned: the view of child development presented there is rarely discussed and is regarded, if at all, as conventional and "old hat." Even *The Ego and the Mechanisms of Defence* is widely misunderstood. "Yes," people infer, "she has added a good deal to our knowledge of defence"; but in making this concession they fail to recognize that the gravamen of her argument is the need to draw a distinction between drive derivatives and representatives that threaten the child with basic danger situations (Freud, 1926), and defenses against affects that threaten the child with psychic pain and, until that time, were largely neglected by psychoanalysts.

The foundation of the War Nurseries established the vital role that painstaking observation and precise recordkeeping brought to our knowledge of child development, and the work was greatly extended, clarified, and vitally reinforced by the extension of child analysis made possible by the training course founded in 1947 and by the Hampstead Child Therapy Clinic five years later. I regard the development of the course and clinic as Anna Freud's greatest achievement, bringing together her unique gifts in furthering investigation and discovery. In many ways *Normality and Pathology in Childhood* (A. Freud, 1965a) represents a culmination of her accomplishment, work that sprang not only from Anna Freud's personal achievements but also from those she inspired in others. She had the capacity to bring people together in pursuit of a common purpose, while allowing each one to make his mark on the discipline, often through skills not always known to their possessor.[6] She gave everyone guidance when sought, showed unflagging interest, acted as exemplar and, when asked, was an auxiliary thinker, but she never interfered with their discovery of their own lines of interest. She and the colleagues she inspired offered both a service for children and a training that was unmatched. The service extended beyond treatment and included a well-baby clinic and a nursery school for children under five, which was later devoted largely to the socially disadvantaged. It was the clinical research fostered by both service and training that is seen as the major source of her extension of our knowledge of child development. Even an incomplete list of some of the study groups that came into being proves the point. The diagnostic group was one in which Anna Freud always took special interest, but the formulation of the profile Schema called for a Profile Study Group as well. There were groups for the study of borderline children, children with atypical disorders, children with physical disabilities, adopted children, adolescents, a clinical concept group, a theoretical concept group, and groups that came together for varying periods to study special subjects such as mainline heroin addiction, pseudo-intellectual backwardness, and the development of language. Anna Freud also strongly supported Dorothy Burlingham in founding a nursery school and study group for the blind, as well as in founding the Index project, later under the care of Joseph Sandler; she was also responsible for a number of detailed conceptual studies. In addition, she supported Dorothy Burlingham's project on the simultaneous analysis of mother and child as well as her work on twins. The list is not exhaustive.

It was Anna Freud's policy that the clinical records of every case be made available for purposes of clinical research. Thus the groups themselves were able to draw on far more information than their own members could offer from their personal experiences. This was a central principle on which Anna Freud insisted. Wherever a child came into treatment, the clinic files contained: (1) detailed referral material and the provisional diagnostic profile based on it; (2) weekly treatment reports and twice yearly summaries; and (3) in a great many instances index cards, in which clinical examples pointing to drive organization, defenses, superego operation, relation to self and objects, and the like, were recorded for ready access.

There is a clear link between this intensive work at the clinic, with its staff and student presentations (recorded), regular discussions and case conferences (minuted), and the distillation of the essentials of normal and abnormal child development suggested by the title *Nor-*

6. "He," "his," and "him" are used generically throughout this paper.

mality and Pathology in Childhood (A. Freud, 1965a). It came at a time
when detailed annual reports were sent to the National Institute of
Mental Health in Washington, and applications for further support
had to be made at regular intervals. One such application (in 1961) had
secured a grant for an investigation under the title *Assessment of Pathology in Children* (completed in 1965). Anna Freud's applications were
models of clear analytic thinking, and this one forms the core of substantial sections of the book. At this point psychoanalytic diagnostic
assessment had taken a revolutionary turn following Anna Freud's
(1962) formulation of the diagnostic profile schema and its routine
application to the assessment of every accepted referral. The concept
of developmental lines, which in my view is complementary to the
profile (Yorke, 1980), soon followed (Freud, A., 1963). This concept
demonstrated its value not only for the assessment of pathology but
also for assessing the suitability and readiness of a child, within the
normative range, to undertake fresh tasks and take new steps such as
entry into nursery school. Here the practical results of the clinic's nursery school were clearly evident. Both normality and pathology feature
in the comprehensive psychoanalytic assessments that the tools provided by Anna Freud's formulations were designed to assist. It is not
the diagnostician's task to direct his attention only to what strikes him
as obviously *wrong* with the child he has to assess. He must be every bit
as concerned with what is *right* with the child, with his psychological
strength as well as weaknesses. Some people wrongly suspected that
when Anna Freud devised the Profile, she was somehow advocating the
consideration of a child in terms of a collection of *mental bits,* a common
allegation by some so-called "object relations" theorists. But although,
for example, one may look at the organization, level of development,
and effectiveness of the superego complex; at the state of ego functioning, defenses, adaptiveness, intellectual functioning and the like; and
at the level of drive development and the question of arrests and regressions, it is the *relations* between these agencies, both internally and
in connection with the outside world, their functioning within the
context of the total personality, which the profile (and its complement,
the gains and losses along the lines of development) articulates, that
facilitates rather than hinders a picture of a child at a given moment in
development. One starts with the clinical data of the case history, the
clinical interviews, and information gained elsewhere; one turns to
metapsychology to give a theoretical understanding, at a higher level of
abstraction than the clinical data in themselves afford; and, armed with
a greater awareness of internal strengths and handicaps and their

internal and external interactions, one can clothe the picture the child now presents in terms of clinical flesh and blood.[7] No profile presented at the clinic was ever complete without a record of the discussion that followed. No one who read the minutes of those meetings could be in any doubt that, although many theoretical questions were discussed, a living child was at the heart of the deliberations.

The assessment of pathology, discussed so illuminatingly in *Normality and Pathology,* was not confined to the investigations of the infantile and childhood neuroses but addressed the pre-stages in childhood of adult psychopathology. As Sigmund Freud (1918) once said,[8] the study of childhood neuroses "afford us . . . as much help towards a proper understanding of the neuroses of adults as do children's dreams in respect of the dreams of adults" (p. 9); but the study of possible pre-stages of later disturbances is a proper concern of the child analyst. So Anna Freud looked at such searching questions as whether, to what extent, and at what point in a child's development one can speak of dissocial behavior, delinquency, criminality, homosexuality, other perversions, and addictions. But *Normality and Pathology in Childhood* essentially records, not the detailed results of the Clinic's investigations up to that date, but the principles on which its findings were based.

The fertile thinking behind *Normality and Pathology* led to another burst of productivity. If, in her work with children, Anna Freud looked back at the developmental processes that had led to any given state, she also looked forward to the possible outcome as the child moved toward adulthood. She was well aware that even rough prediction was rarely possible, but development did not end with childhood and it was necessary to put the findings of child analysis at the disposal of the analyst working with adults. This was reflected in an address to the Menninger Clinic (Freud, A., 1966) in which she observed that the extensive facilities found there offered the psychiatric residents "the full range of human problems as they arise from the cradle to the grave." Her interest in psychiatry went back to the days when she regularly attended the ward rounds at the Psychiatric Clinic in Vienna, then under the direction of Wagner-Jauregg (the discoverer of malarial treatment for syphilitic general Paresis). The two assistants were Heinz Hartmann and Paul Schilder, and it was from Schilder that she learned so much about adult psychiatry, an interest which eventually led to her encouragement of comparisons between psychotic disorders in adolescents and

7. For a more general discussion of the issues raised here see Yorke (1996).
8. Quoted by Anna Freud in the book under discussion.

adults and "borderline" disorders in children. A great deal of work came out of this, including *Childhood Psychopathology and Adult Psychoses* (1976) by Thomas Freeman.

She was intrigued by such comparisons: her interest in development extended across the whole range of human behavior. The profile schema was adapted for use with adolescents (Laufer, 1965), adults (Freud, A., Nagera, H., and Freud, W. E., 1965), and it was the encouragement she gave to Thomas Freeman to produce no fewer than twenty profiles on adult psychotic patients that influenced eventually the book mentioned here as well as others to follow. Still from the standpoint of pathology, she was influenced by the differences and similarities between the sweet addictions of childhood and the more ominous addictions of later onset, and she encouraged the use of the profile on some ten "mainline" heroin addicts that formed the basis for other studies.

In 1968, Anna Freud's *Indications and Contraindications for Child Analysis* revisited her findings of 1945 and discussed its eponymous subject with customary clarity. She drew attention to some comparisons between analytic difficulties encountered in adults, examined by her father in *Analysis Terminable and Interminable* (1937), and conditions that adversely affected analysis in children, some of them surprisingly resembling each other. Whereas, for example, one would hesitate to take into analysis an adult who was in the middle of a tempestuous love affair, one did not always give comparable consideration to a child fighting his way through the oedipus complex. And, while one might hesitate to take an adult who had just sustained a major bereavement into treatment, one did not always bear in mind that a child whose mother had just produced a sibling had suffered a significant object loss. She returned to the subject more fully later that year,[9] adding to her father's account some special factors militating against success in child analysis.

This important address is finely crafted, elegant in expression, and it draws together in one seemingly simple outline a whole group of related if different ideas; and it puts before the reader a survey of fertile territory ready for further cultivation. Its title is borrowed from Freud's paper of 1917—"A difficulty in the path of psychoanalysis" in which, like the later paper "The resistances to psychoanalysis" (1925), the obstacles to psychoanalysis encountered in the outside world pro-

9. *Difficulties in the Path of Psychoanalysis: A Confrontation of Past With Present Viewpoints* (Freud, A., 1969 [1968])—the Freud Anniversary Lecture at the New York Psychoanalytic Society.

vided the basic material for discussion. "Analysis terminable and inter-minable," on the other hand, was concerned with internal forces acting against a successful outcome for analytic work. Anna Freud, accord-ingly, discussed the adverse factors from three sources: the public, the patients, and the analyst. The first included changes in the public attitude toward psychoanalysis since 1905. At that time the *Three Essays* were regarded by many as shamelessly prurient, while in the 1960's the work of Masters and Johnson aroused mass interest but raised few eyebrows. The myth of the innocence of childhood had also disap-peared. Two world wars had made the theory of aggression, in both adults and children, more tenable for the general public. Infantile sexuality was now broadly accepted. The child was seen by parents and teachers, far more readily than formerly, as a creature of impulse, dominated by emotions and the search for pleasurable experiences. About the *dynamic unconscious,* on the other hand, she was rather more cautious: the law, for example, still put its faith in the notion of a "reasonable man," though there are some welcome signs of change. Academic psychology, with some exceptions, still clung to methods of rigorous investigation, evaluation, and mensuration that ignored the role of the dynamic unconscious in mental life. For the general public, however, the notion of unconscious motivation was, she thought, much more widely accepted, though, thirty years later, I am less convinced of this. As for dreams, their investigation would no longer be attributed to misguided eccentricity.

The third danger she mentioned is unquestionably still with us. Psychoanalysts tried to contest the charge that their approach was "un-scientific" by overtly or covertly agreeing with it, aping the methods of the academics, trying to measure the immeasurable, rejecting the fact that the mind is the true explorer of the mind, and falling into what many of us today would regard as a spurious "scientism," a malady, which does not lend itself readily to cure. Lastly, the attitude of the young has changed: psychoanalysis, once seen as part of a revolution, is too often regarded, not as a danger to the existing social order, but rather as something to which only those left behind by social change still cling with spurious nostalgia. Anna Freud's response to these atti-tudes showed, I believe, her wisdom: we should, she insisted, scrutinize the obstacles and learn from them; the belief that the enthusiast, the eloquent, and the proselyte could change things was not only wrong—it ran the risk that the analyst ended up changing himself rather than his opponents.

Opposition from *patients* still provided opportunities to learn, just as they did in 1937. Then, as now, the difficulties for analysis could be increased by imbalance between id and ego—the strength of instinct reinforced by puberty or menopause, perhaps, or ego strength diminished by illness or exhaustion. These *quantitative* disequilibria were matched by *qualitative* factors: by ego alterations arising from whatever source *including the struggles of early years* that might, for example, favor primitive rather than more sophisticated defenses; by excessive adhesiveness or mobility of libido; by "psychical inertia" or "depletion of plasticity" leading to fixity and rigidity of attitude and mitigating against change; by the intractability often encountered in the *negative therapeutic reaction;* by the intensity of moral masochism; by the excessive intervention of free aggressiveness; and by the undoing of defenses in circumstances where there was too little to replace them, so that an increase, rather than a decrease, in maladaptive behavior followed. And, among many others, bisexual struggles that led to intractable opposition to the man's recognition of his femininity or the depression that sometimes followed the woman's unchanged and stubborn wish for a longed-for penis when she realized that analysis couldn't give it to her. All these, to greater or lesser extent, could be found in later childhood and adolescence, though the forward push of maturation favored their modification.

To her father's list of difficulties Anna Freud added four, all of which appear in her child profile schema. First, a low threshold of tolerance for the frustration of instinctual wishes was in opposition to the child analyst's attempts gradually to modify and to "tame" the peremptory need for pleasure. Second, a low threshold for the tolerance of anxiety could increase defensive measures or intensify symptoms. Third, a low sublimation potential meant that fewer pathways were available for substitute gratification or could be made so by analysis. Lastly, a preponderance of regressive over progressive tendencies was not a hopeful sign. Finally, without the child's wish to push forward in development, analysis could be used by the child as a license to "return to earliest levels of id satisfaction and ego expression" (1968, p. 32).

Anna Freud pointed out that suggestions for improvement in analytic efficiency following Freud's paper fell into two broad groups: first, therapeutic normalization of the ego—in Bibring's terms (1937), to change the relations of the ego to id and superego, and, second, attempts to deal with the earliest defensive struggles against unpleasure. The first put increased emphasis on analysis of the ego, for which, in any case, Hartmann's studies in the thirties and his extensions of the scope of metapsychology had given new impetus, and to which Anna Freud's own studies of *The Ego and the Mechanisms of Defence* (1936) had made important contributions. It did not introduce anything fundamentally new, but it did underline the need to analyze as thoroughly as possible those derivatives of the preoedipal phases that could be made accessible. Anna Freud did not subscribe to the belief, held by many analysts of otherwise widely divergent opinions, that the *preverbal* phase and the archaic interactions between mother and child could be reached by unmodified analytic technique. This was not to say that many of the difficulties already enumerated did not indeed have roots in very early life; and in this respect she quoted with approval from a paper by her friend Jeanne Lampl-de Groot (1967) who went through Freud's list and traced their pre-stages in early development.

But Anna Freud held firmly to the view that these factors were not accessible to memory and verbal recall but revealed themselves through repetition and reenactment. It was precisely this, she maintained, that led to the emphasis put on transference interpretation as the exclusively effective avenue of communication, and led to a controversy that continues to this day. Anna Freud questioned whether the transference really had the power accorded it in respect of these early roots: it was, she contended, almost magical thinking to expect the patient to change back into a pre-psychological, undifferentiated, and unstructured state. Her view is even more strongly contested today by some who put great emphasis on the implications of infant observational research for therapeutic work (a dispute well documented in Dowling and Rothstein [1989] and which I have discussed elsewhere [Yorke, 1995]). And certainly, Anna Freud emphasized the dissimilarities rather than the similarities between the mother/baby and the analyst/patient relationship. And, even if some early features were acquired and not exclusively innate, the assumption that everything that is acquired is reversible is seriously open to doubt.

Anna Freud then turned her attention from the patient to the analyst. The analyst's personality, abilities, and handicaps, such as analytic blind spots and lack of sensitivity to the unconscious, have a bearing on the analysability of any given patient. Freud (1937) thought the analyst should possess a "considerable degree of mental normality" and a "basic love of truth" (p. 248). Lampl de-Groot (1967) followed Spitz (1965) in emphasizing the analyst's need for "receptive empathy" and traced its roots in the mother/child relationship. Unchecked countertransference had been stressed by many authors and could be countered only by the analyst's own further analysis.

Had anything new emerged to add to these concerns? Some analysts looked for improved measures of selection, better training, and sought to encourage creative candidates. Anna Freud, in sympathy with these general aims, nonetheless thought that the analyst's task was not to *create*, not to *invent*, but "to observe, to explore, to understand." In these respects, an important quality was in danger of being lost.

What she had in mind was metapsychology. Psychoanalytic thinking demanded that every clinical fact be understood *genetically* (in terms of origin); *dynamically* (the interplay of forces that lay behind it); *economically* (in terms of energy charge [and distribution]); and *topographically/structurally* (in terms of location in the mental apparatus). But in recent times, she averred, metapsychology had been increasingly regarded as a speculative exercise from which the clinician often felt alienated, resulting in a divorce of theory from clinical practice to the detriment of both.

The *dynamic* point of view was least contentious: the notion of conflict within the mind seemed so central to psychoanalysis that the discipline was often referred to as "dynamic psychology." But the notion of conflicting forces makes little sense without information about the *location* of forces within the mental apparatus, whether their physical qualities (unconscious, preconscious, conscious) are the same or different, whether they can engage with each other and enter into compromise, or whether they are isolated from each other by defensive maneuvers. But if location (*topography*) was largely ignored before the formulation of the *structural* model, the *genetic* factor was always recognized, and still occupies analysts who wish to dig forever deeper, ignoring other viewpoints on the way. Mental *economics* gave many analysts more trouble than anything else: the concept of mental energy, with force and distribution, was anathema to them, even though, as Freud pointed out, the outcome of psychoanalysis—the theme of Anna Freud's paper—depended on quantitative factors such as the strength of resistances and negative reactions compared with the strength of the forces (i.e., in Anna Freud's terms, the *progressive* forces) on which the analyst can draw.

It may seem strange to summarize at such length a single work, emphasizing as it does technique. In doing so I had four purposes. I wanted (1) to stress Anna Freud's emphasis on the unity of theory and practice; (2) to catch the flavor of her thinking in a way that might be lost in a formal survey; (3) to point to her conviction that the developmental point of view can only be understood in terms of the changing relationships between structure, dynamics, and economics; and (4) to give prominence to a paper that, in the development of our discipline, looks both forwards to the future and backwards to the past.

This "then and now" quality—and its implied question, "where are we going?"—lends a historical perspective to her address, but it does more than make a comparison between the difficulties of thirty years before and those prominent at the time she spoke. It underlines the relevance for the present of much of the past, including her own contribution to the understanding of the ego in 1936. And in turning to Hartmann's studies of the ego, culminating in his monograph of 1939, she leads us to her address of 1964 (Freud, A., 1965b) on the links between Hartmann's ego psychology and the child analyst's thinking. She regarded his contributions as more revolutionary and less restricted at the time than her own, and considers with care such concepts as the conflict-free ego sphere, intrasystemic conflict, the problems of psychic health, of morality, and other matters bearing on child development. A further tribute to Hartmann on his seventieth birthday (1965c, [1964]) skillfully and economically summarizes the manner in which he had widened the frontiers of analytic investigation and laid the foundations for a general psychology. It is important to remember, on Anna Freud's centenary, what she had to say about celebratory occasions during which hostile criticism and polemics were set aside, while they were still inclined to resurface once the special occasion was past.

There is a place for the discussion of conflict-free ego functions in Anna Freud's profile schema, but this paper also looks back to the profile in other respects. This approach to assessment falls into four phases. The first gathers together the available referral data. On the basis of this, the second teases out the metapsychology, as far as incomplete information allows, with any clearly designated speculation. The third section assesses the factors militating against the possible success of analytic treatment and consists of those four items Anna Freud added to her father's list of difficulties. The fourth section is the psychoanalytic diagnosis itself, informed, as it has to be, by the metapsychological thinking that has gone before.

In an inspired burst of activity over a single weekend, Anna Freud (1970a) turned her attention to *The Symptomatology of Childhood* and set out what she described as "a preliminary attempt at classification."[10] She put childhood disturbances into a broad perspective, and emphasized that, since these were much less structured than adult disorders, they were even less suited to traditional taxonomy than their grown-up counterparts. While aware of "the misleading quality of manifest symptomatology" in children, she believed that analysts who attached too little importance to surface presentations might well be doing a disservice to diagnosis. She distinguished between symptoms proper and "other signs of disturbance" or "other reasons for a child's clinical

10. Freud, A., 1970a. I have discussed this paper at greater length elsewhere (Yorke, 1996).

referral." The first category included symptoms resulting from inadequate differentiation between somatic and psychological processes—the "psychosomatics of early life in which psychic distress could be discharged through bodily channels, and bodily distress through psychic pain; symptoms resulting from compromise formations between id and ego so that, for example, in a childhood neurosis a paralyzed leg might symbolically gratify a wish for a penis while, at the same time, its uselessness satisfied the defense against that wish; symptoms resulting from the eruptions of id derivatives into the ego; and other important groups of symptoms including those resulting from undefended regression and those with an underlying organic basis. In the second category—other signs of disturbance—she included a number of nonspecific pointers to *underlying* disturbances such as the manifold fears and anxieties of childhood; delays or failures in development; school failures and failures in social adaptation; and those various aches and pains that had psychological origins of varying type and severity. In concluding, she again drew attention to the value of the profile in assessing these various disorders.

During the next ten years all these contributions were subject to elaboration in a variety of contexts. In the same year she had already discussed, against a historical background, the infantile neurosis from the points of view of genetics and dynamics (Freud, A., 1970b), but enlarged on the subject in 1972 in what she called *The Widening Scope of Child Psychology, Normal and Abnormal.* In some unscripted remarks made during a meeting of the Association for Child Psychoanalysis in London she spoke with wit and cogency of the *Fears, Anxieties, and Phobic Phenomena* (Freud A., 1976a) of childhood, telling some hilariously illustrative stories that lose some of her sense of fun in the printed version. Above all, it was during these years that, concerned as she was with the *practical* aims of diagnosis in respect of prognosis, treatment, and management, she sought to clarify the distinction between what might loosely be called the childhood neurosis on the one hand, and, on the other, developmental disturbances where the pathology appeared of a different order. She recognized that these disturbances were protean in their presentation and that each case needed careful diagnostic scrutiny, but her own studies and those of her colleagues ultimately led her to put forward a concept that still calls for wider attention. In a major addition to this work Anna Freud (1979a) gave an account of *Mental Health in Terms of Internal Harmony and Disharmony.*[11] She was concerned with the degree of harmonious interaction between

11. Specially written for chapter 2 of Yorke et al., 1989.

the inner agencies themselves—between the id, ego and superego—and between these agencies and the external world. Such harmony can only be achieved if, at any particular time, the agencies themselves have reached and maintained comparable levels of development, and if the external influences with which they interact reflect an "average expectable environment" (Hartmann, 1939). She was always aware, however, that development was never really harmonious except in a maturational sense—that is, in terms of both quantitative and qualitative progress. Once adequate structuralization has taken place, the agencies are always in latent or actual dispute.

What Anna Freud had in mind was not *absence* of conflict but *inner equilibrium*. What called for integration with each other were "the potentialities inherent in the inherited constitution; the vicissitudes connected with the gradual structuralization of the personality; and the influences emanating from the parental environment which is responsible for the atmosphere in which development proceeds." In the late sixties and seventies, she was well aware but did not mention publicly that this environment was increasingly less expectable with the rise in divorce rates, in the number of one parent families, and with other accelerating changes in social structure.

While Anna Freud considered that the task of integrating contending mental agencies was always a difficult one, it could be managed if all or most of the responsible factors fell within a normal range in respect of "momentum and quality" and did not differ greatly from each other in terms of onset and rate of progression. All too often, however, constitutionally determined deviations, aberrant modes of structuralization, and deviant environmental factors, led to a disharmonious result. This could be a basis for later neurosis: for example, a disparity between advanced ego and superego development on the one hand and retarded instinctual progress on the other, with an attendant failure to negotiate the anal phase at all adequately, could lay the ground for a later obsessional neurosis. But it could also lead to deviations and arrests in development that could not necessarily be reached by analysis and called for what she termed "developmental help." Exactly what she meant by this, and the theories behind it, had long been a source for discussion at the Clinic and antedated the paper under discussion by some years.[12] But what she added here was something *new*, something often forgotten, or even perhaps ignored on account of its pessimistic implications. Developmental disharmonies were not, for her, simply a

12. It was a matter of considerable debate at the recent Colloquium at the Anna Freud Centre.

matter of imbalances between the agencies themselves, or the failure of the outside world to foster proper equilibrium. A *developmental dishar-mony was integrated into the personality by the synthetic function of the ego.* Once full structuralization had taken place, the developmental dishar-mony was established *"for better or for worse."* If there was no possibility of intervention *before* such disharmonies were established for good, any neurotic superstructures might yield to analytic intervention, but the underlying disharmony would not.

It seems fitting that the final volume of Anna Freud's collected writ-ings concludes with a number of papers on applied psychoanalysis that reflect her interest in physical illness in relation to psychological development and thus to the interaction between pediatrics and psy-choanalysis, thus recalling her own attention to this important matter when a teacher at the Lyceum in Vienna, and the later joint leader of the Jackson Nursery, and with further contributions to the psy-choanalytic approach to education (1976b) and the nursery school (1979b). It rounds off so appropriately the record of her professional lifetime and service to children both then and now. She has left a fine legacy.

BIBLIOGRAPHY

BIBRING, E. (1937). On the theory of the therapeutic results of psycho-analysis. *Int. J. Psycho-Anal.,* 18:170–189.

BREUER, J., & FREUD, S. (1895). *Studies on Hysteria. S.E.,* II.

BURLINGHAM, D., & FREUD, A. (1942). *Young Children in War-time.* London: George Allen & Unwin.

——— (1944). *Infants Without Families.* London: George Allen & Unwin.

DOWLING, S., & ROTHSTEIN, A. (1989). *The Significance of Infant Observational Research for Clinical With Children, Adolescents, and Adults.* Madison, Conn: Int. Univ. Press.

FREEMAN, T. (1976). *Childhood Psychopathology and Adult Psychoses.* New York: Int. Univ. Press.

FREUD, A. (1936). *The Ego and the Mechanisms of Defence. Writings,* II.

——— (1945). Indications for child analysis. *Writings,* IV.

——— (1962). Assessment of childhood disturbances. *Psychoanal. Study Child.,* 17:149–158.

——— (1963). The concept of developmental lines. *Psychoanal. Study Child.,* 18:245–265.

——— (1965a). Normality and Pathology in Childhood. *Writings,* VI.

——— (1965b). Links between Hartmann's ego psychology and the child an-alyst's thinking. *Writings,* V.

——— (1965c), [1964]. Heinz Hartmann: a tribute. *Writings,* V.

—— (1966). Some thoughts about the place of psychoanalytic theory in the training of psychiatrists. *Writings*, VII.

—— (1968). Indications and contraindications for child analysis. *Writings*, VII.

—— (1969). Difficulties in the path of psychoanalysis: a confrontation of past and present viewpoints. *Writings*, VII.

—— (1970a). The symptomatology of childhood: A preliminary attempt at classification. *Writings*, VII.

—— (1970b). The infantile neurosis: Genetic and dynamic considerations. *Writings*, VII.

—— (1972). The widening scope of psychoanalytic child psychology, normal and abnormal. *Writings*, VIII.

—— (1976a). Fears, anxieties, and phobic phenomena. *Writings*, VIII.

—— (1976b). Dynamic psychology and education. *Writings*, VIII.

—— (1979a). Mental health and illness in terms of internal harmony and disharmony. *Writings*, VIII.

—— (1979b). The nursery school from the psychoanalytic point of view. *Writings*, VIII.

FREUD, A., & BURLINGHAM, D. (1973). *Writings*, III.

FREUD, A., NAGERA, H., & FREUD, W. E. (1965). Metapsychological assessment of the adult personality. *Psychoanal. Study Child* 20:9–41.

FREUD, S. (1905). *Three Essays on the Theory of Sexuality. S.E.*, VII.

—— (1909). Analysis of a Phobia in a five-year-old Boy. *S.E.*, X.

—— (1917). A difficulty in the path of psycho-analysis. *S.E.*, XVII.

—— (1918). From the history of an infantile neurosis. *S.E.*, XVII.

—— (1925). The resistances to psycho-analysis. *S.E.*, XIX.

—— (1926). Inhibitions, Symptoms, and Anxiety. *S.E.*, XX.

—— (1937). Analysis Terminable and Interminable. *S.E.*, XXIII.

GOLDSTEIN, J., FREUD, A., AND SOLNIT, A. J. (1973). *Beyond the Best Interests of the Child*. New York: Free Press.

—— (1979). *Before the Best Interests of the Child*. New York: Free Press.

GOLDSTEIN, J., FREUD, A., SOLNIT, A. J., AND GOLDSTEIN, S. (1980). *In the Best Interests of the Child*. New York: Free Press.

HARTMANN, H. (1939). *Ego Psychology and the Problem of Adaptation*. New York: Int. Univ. Press, 1958.

HILL, J. C. (1971). *Teaching and the Unconscious Mind*. New York: Int. Univ. Press.

LAMPL-DE GROOT, J. (1967). On obstacles standing in the way of psychoanalytic cure. *Psychoanal. Study Child*. 22:20–35.

LAUFER, M. (1965). Assessment of adolescent disturbances: The application of Anna Freud's diagnostic profile. *Psychoanal. Study Child*. 20:99–123.

SPITZ, R. A. (1965). *The First Year of Life*. New York: Int. Univ. Press.

YORKE, C. (1971). Some suggestions for a critique of Kleinian psychology. *Psychoanal. Study Child*. 26:129–155.

—— (1980). The contributions of the diagnostic profile and the assessment of developmental lines to child psychiatry. *Psychiat. Clinics North America.* 3:593–603.

——— (1994). Freud or Klein: Conflict or Compromise. *Int. J. Psycho-Anal.,* 75:375–385.

——— (1995). Freud's psychology: Can it survive? *Psychoanal. Study Child.,* 50:3–31.

——— (1996). Diagnosis in clinical practice: Its relationship to psychoanalytic theory. *Psychoanal. Study Child.,* 51:190–214.

YORKE, C., WISEBERG, S., AND FREEMAN, T. (1989). *Development and Psychopathology: Studies in Psychoanalytic Psychiatry.* New Haven: Yale Univ. Press.

Differentiation and Integration

SAMUEL ABRAMS, M.D.

The purpose of this paper is to propose a clinical approach to coordinating the psychoanalytic process with the developmental process in treating children. The paper is constructed as a dialogue between the spirit of Anna Freud and myself; a vignette brings together the principal traditional features Ms. Freud understood as "psychoanalytic" with her innovative propositions about the "developmental."

JUST BEFORE PREPARING THIS PAPER, I DREAMED I WAS VISITED BY THE spirit of Anna Freud.

Why me? I wondered.

We spoke only three times in her lifetime. Once occurred over a cup of tea; the second was a whimsical chat about her knitting; and the third was an educationally stimulating exchange. However, they all seemed too brief and inconsequential to warrant a spiritual visit to me. So I concluded that in this, the one hundredth year since her birth, Ms. Freud was researching the status of the discipline she had left behind and that I had been selected to participate in the survey.

I have always admired her capacity to precisely differentiate complex elements and then put them together productively. This was especially true in the way she dealt with the traditional and novel features in our enterprise—the old and the new. If there are two contributions that spring to mind when thinking of Anna Freud, they are her comprehensive descriptions of defense, which enhanced classical psychoanalysis (the "old" that had been handed down to her), and her innova-

Clinical professor, The Psychoanalytic Institute at the New York University School of Medicine.

Prepared for the symposium "Anna Freud at Yale," in celebration of the one hundredth birthday of Anna Freud, New Haven, December 2, 1995.

The Psychoanalytic Study of the Child 51, ed. Albert J. Solnit, Peter B. Neubauer, Samuel Abrams, and A. Scott Dowling (Yale University Press, copyright © 1996 by Albert J. Solnit, Peter B. Neubauer, Samuel Abrams, and A. Scott Dowling).

tive proposals about developmental lines, which ushered in an entirely "new" area of interest. The psychoanalytic process that had been willed to her by her father and the developmental process that she infused with new vigor are astonishingly complex processes; yet she was able to distinguish them effortlessly, implement each skillfully, and coordinate them fruitfully. Perhaps it was my open admiration for her ability to differentiate and integrate so adeptly that accounted for my having made her survey list.

Having assumed that Ms. Freud was in my dream to ask about the status of these two regions of interest—the psychoanalytic process and the developmental process—I prepared myself for a lengthy theoretical exposition when I felt her silent discomfort. I filled it with an imploring query: could I please delay a discourse into abstractions and begin with some clinical data instead?

I told her about the treatment of a boy named Leslie. He was almost four when he was brought for help, principally because he insisted that he was a girl. Leslie had been laying claims to girlish things like jewelry and high heels from the early part of his second year. His first year had been characterized by intense outbursts of temper, which intimidated his family. His parents indulged his many peculiar demands rather than endure Leslie's fury. They catered to certain food idiosyncrasies and to his insistent claims of ownership. (He regularly walked away with items that belonged to others, and by the time he came to treatment he was often shoplifting cheap jewelry from local merchants.)

The treatment began with Leslie testing the limits of the therapeutic setting. Could he take home whatever he liked from the office, and was I prepared to endure the consequences of frustrating him? The answers were "No, he could not take whatever he fancied," and "Yes, I could endure the resultant flailing and outbursts." He struggled with these unexpected answers, but they had the happy, although not entirely unexpected, effect of promoting the therapeutic relationship.

Ms. Freud nodded. I continued my presentation.

After a year of treatment dominated by his testing the limits of the one-to-one exchange, the setting underwent a remarkable transformation. He had become friendly with one of the puppets I kept in my office, which often served as a somewhat innocuous intermediary between us. Once this period began, the puppet became a distinctive character, a participant in a kind of three-person drama with roles for a hero, a villain, and a vulnerable girl. Leslie readily shifted these roles among himself, the puppet, and me. The hero was generally an adventurer with a weapon, the villain often a voracious monster with an appetite for people, and the distressed damsel was a somewhat less clearly defined creature who was regularly in trouble with the monster. After several months of playing and replaying this piece, while insisting on my accepting whatever roles he assigned, Leslie began to rework the scene with even greater specificity. The hero became Robin Hood, the girl Maid Marian, the villain still vaguely monstrous, although occasionally the wicked Sheriff of Nottingham. The shifting of roles among the three of us continued, however, emphasizing a trait of fluidity in Leslie that had previously drawn my attention. The extent of Leslie's fury generated in these battles was as impressive as the rapid shifts.

In one session, something precipitated out of that fluidity, giving me an opportunity to intervene in a useful way. Leslie had cast himself as Robin Hood, I was a monster villain, and the puppet was Maid Marian. Leslie laid hold of a large decorative willow branch in a vase in my office, raised the branch, geared himself for battle, but then paused. I asked about the delay. He said that he was undecided about whether to pretend that the branch was a sword or a witch's broomstick. Either weapon might be successful in the encounter, but he was uncertain which was preferable. I said that he couldn't be sure that a sword alone would work; he had to have a woman's secret magic power to win such a battle. He reflected on my comment and then pretended that the willow was a sword. The villain was defeated, the damsel was freed, and for the moment, Robin and Marian lived happily ever after.

I paused at this point in my presentation, indicating to Ms. Freud that the designated session was complete. She remained silent. I interpreted her silence to mean that I should describe my view of the hour in general and account for my intervention in particular.

I took a deep breath. I said that this session demonstrated a way of coordinating the developmental process and the psychoanalytic process, two of her favorite things. Her face assumed a contemplative expression. My understanding of the developmental process, I went on, was that it is a normal part of human growth. Biologically based, it is fueled by an underlying maturational program that becomes actualized in the form of a progressive sequence of hierarchical organizations—of minds, of emergent systems. In the months preceding the session, Leslie had been caught up in the sweep of that special hierarchical organization often labeled the oedipal phase. For an underlying maturational program to become actualized as psychological systems, I continued, felicitous interactions with stimuli from the surround are required. Systems are constructed around more or less coherent narratives. An effective normal narrative usually brings together object relations, drives, and available equipment. Once the new organization is consolidated, some features of that narrative may persist as unconscious informing fantasies while others become transformed into novel structures within the emergent system. Your father, I added, said it more simply when he noted that the superego is heir to the Oedipus complex.

She listened.

I continued. The growth of these three subordinate realms of object relations, drives, and equipment is accelerated or retarded by internal and external factors. This may result in serious disparities, yielding a variety of unusual psychopathologic conditions. I was referring to the potential for disharmonies in development, an issue that had not escaped Ms. Freud's attention.

Still she listened in silence.

I added that each new hierarchical level also brings together antecedent experiences and organizations as well as the three subordinate realms. This contributes to the fact that development is both continuous (linear) and discontinuous (involving transformational leaps). It is no wonder the developmental process is so difficult to understand.

Ms. Freud nodded again, this time approvingly, I thought, but I also read in her silence the request that I try to link this complex conceptualization to the clinical data I had just offered.

I said that I thought Leslie had had serious difficulties in his first years of life, difficulties that corrupted some subordinate realms within the earlier hierarchies as well as the hierarchies themselves. All this left pathologic residues in object relations, drives, and equipment. I was not able to clearly designate the sources of the difficulties, either in the surround or in the dispositional pool. The figures in his environment could not be characterized as abusive, neither by way of impoverishment nor excess, but they were not exemplary figures either. There was some evidence of idiosyncratic equipmental features. For example, Leslie possessed a curious sensitivity to the subtleties of colors before he was one year old. In addition, he had always been intolerant of limit setting, and then, of course, there was the volume of his rage. I had also long recognized that there was more than the usual fluidity between and within the objects in his representational world and had even hypothesized that this may have contributed to a preponderance of externalizations over transferences in the treatment transactions.

Ms. Freud smiled; I think she liked my having preserved her distinction between transference and externalization, a distinction sadly lost in our blurred contemporary psychoanalytic language. I think she also recognized that I was trying on an extended diagnostic profile within the clinical situation modeled after her own, appraising sequences of development of object relations, drives, and varieties of ego equipment.

From the standpoint of the developmental process, I continued, Leslie was being pulled forward into the oedipal organization, creating a coherent narrative that involved three persons in a setting of passion and rivalry. However, I added quickly, he was putting together residues of earlier pathologic organizations, residues that had been held back from participating in the normal developmental march, principally, I suspected, by defense. Referring to the Robin Hood drama, I cited the implicit problem of boundaries between self and other, the clinging to the earlier cognitive commitment to magic, the lure of power, and some unrecognized but informing fantasies about the anatomy of women.

I immediately read her next question in her continuing silence. I had satisfactorily described what was *developmental* about the designated session, but what was *psychoanalytic* about it? I took another deep breath. I replied that I viewed the psychoanalytic process as that specially induced setting that is established in the attempt to bring into new organizations past pathological features that had been excluded from the progression by defense. This conceptualization, I noted, worked equally well with adults as with children, although the issues are far more complex with children.

She remained silent, but I thought it was a validating silence, so I became more emboldened. The technique of psychoanalysis, I went on, is designed to establish a setting so that those antecedent conflicts and archaic self and object representations can be revived, freshly engaged within the analytic interaction—principally but not exclusively as transferences—so that they can be integrated within the more mature prevailing or emerging organization. I noted that the features of revival, the centrality of transference, and the integrative aspects of analysis were all matters that had also systematically attracted her attention and I cited some of her references. My remark to Leslie about choosing between sword or witch's broom was an attempt to interpret those trailing residues of disordered object relations, power, cognition, and adaptation that had been so condensed in his imagery. I had hoped the displaced awareness of them would help shift the balance toward the more advanced features of these categories and help move forward an organization committed to values of right and wrong rather than strong and weak. My comment was differentiating, I explained; it was intended to promote integration and facilitate organization.

Ms. Freud listened; her attention even more fixed, I thought.

The problem of *coordinating* the developmental process and the psychoanalytic process in children, I went on, is this: They are very different ways of effecting change. The developmental process is a naturally occurring event, especially vivid during childhood and adolescence. It induces change by interacting with new stimuli within the environment to actualize the inherent maturational potential. The novel hierarchies that are brought together have a transformational impact on the features of the evolving subordinate realms: new ways of relating, new orders of drive organization, new ways of feeling, thinking, defending, and adapting arise along with each emergent system. The critical features in the developmental process are the underlying maturational pull forward, the availability of new objects and things to actualize the maturational potential, and the resultant transformational yield in the emergent system. The psychoanalytic process, by contrast, is not naturally occurring. It is actively induced and requires a practiced technique. In psychoanalysis, the change is achieved by facilitating the revival of past objects and drives and conflicts and equipment, so that they may be reengaged within the therapeutic interaction. In this way, a new integration of hitherto excluded features becomes possible. Because the developmental process uses the analyst as a *new* object for the emerging hierarchy while the psychoanalytic process uses the analyst as an *old* (revived) past figure, the treatment of children is invariably burdened with complexities and likely to tax the technical know-how of even the most experienced practitioner.

Ms. Freud smiled and nodded in agreement.

Practitioners vary as much as the needs of children, and this further enhances the complexities, I went on. Some clinicians find an ease with techniques that favor revival and others prefer approaches that facilitate novelty. By insisting that one or the other is always preferable with children, many analysts avoid opportunities to coordinate the potential of these disparate processes. I added that there are other mutative elements, independent of the old and the novel that are part of every treatment situation. People get better because the setting provides a transaction that promotes identifications, buttresses affect tolerance, sustains limit setting, elicits mourning, promotes the articulation of unrecognized affects and unconscious fantasies, and provides caring characterized by regard and the encouragement of a sense of agency. These are powerful healing factors, factors that are activated when analysts are tapped as real here-and-now objects and subjects in addition to being experienced as past objects and sources of new future-building experiences. This differentiation among old, real, and new, I added, has the potential of broadening our therapeutic equipment by integrating what are otherwise quite different modes of therapeutic action. I reminded Ms. Freud that this followed similar lines of inquiry of her own. Surely she remembered her famous smorgasbord metaphor where child therapy was depicted as a buffet of possibilities.

Now it was my turn for silence, a somewhat sullen silence. This alerted Ms. Freud. I responded to her inquiring glance.

I explained that while what I had just described as a reasonable derivative of her work was received in a congenial way by many analysts, the majority would view these formulations as either unnecessarily complex or just plain anachronistic. For the first time, she frowned.

Much of that proposed conceptual framework, I went on, depends on honoring differentiation over global thinking. However, as a cognitive mode, differentiation entails an effort, while global thinking has a seductive lure. I noted that what I had been describing was an attempt to distinguish *different* ways of change. The therapeutic action of psychoanalysis leans on revival: a past object becomes centered in the analytic relationship, and a resultant new integration follows. The developmental mode of change relies on the natural pull forward, a new object relationship centered in the analytic interaction, and an inherent organizing function that yields transformations in structures and functions. The real here-and-now transaction produces modifications in the representations of self and object and buttresses different dispositional weaknesses. I briefly summarized how each of these factors had been components of Leslie's treatment.

A cognitive leaning in favor of differentiation, I continued, also leads to distinguishing the nature of the therapeutic interactions— past, real, and new—and the technical endeavors necessary to promote each in addition to sorting out the resultant modes of therapeutic action. Regrettably, I added, the contemporary psychoanalytic scene favors global thinking and diffuse generalizations rather than differentiation and integration. If there ever was a time when the concept of the psychoanalytic process was clearly delineated, that time has long since passed. As the first century of our discipline draws to a close, virtually anything is designated psychoanalysis, and use of the term is justified by arguments that are either ludicrous or fallacious. A close reading of many clinical publications these days shows that many practitioners are engaged in very different activities yet calling them all by the same term: psychoanalysis.

Ms. Freud seemed more resigned than surprised.

You recall how drive theory once dominated the psychoanalytic marketplace, I went on, momentarily forgetting whom I was talking to. Everything, including normal development, psychopathology, the arts, myth, and culture, was accounted for on the basis of the vicissitudes of instincts. Analysts could find their preferred drive phase in any painting, novel, social group, and certainly in all their patients. It took some decades for that enthusiasm to be tempered, and, of course, you, Ms. Freud, played no small part in the tempering. Today it seems as if object relations theory has become the heir to such unconstrained enthusiasm. And you are well aware of how big a net object relations casts: separation-individuation, attachment, self psychology, representational structures all are part of the expanding realm of object relations. If instinct theory once eclipsed object relations, object relations now eclipses instinct theory, and sometimes enthusiasts of both tend to obscure the necessary attention to dispositional variants as well as to each other's preferred interests. It seems to me that your point of view, Ms. Freud, placed the developmental process as the ground and instincts, object relations, and the ego and its equipment as the interweaving figures positioned on that ground. Yours was a bold undertaking as it meant uprooting the notion that instincts constituted ground and that everything else—human relationships, dispositions, and development—were mere vicissitudes, mere figures. Today, the claim seems to be that object relations are ground, that development and dispositions are simply vicissitudes of the object-interaction system, and that instincts are altogether superfluous. The concept of progressive developmental hierarchies, a concept that is indispensable for comprehending normal and abnormal growth and development as far as you were concerned, has disappeared from many training centers. It has been replaced by the dominance of varying subsets of preferred object relations theories burnished by the excitement about intersubjectivity.

Ms. Freud gave me a glance, quizzically responding to the word *intersubjectivity.*

I gave a hurried explanation. Intersubjectivity is one of the concepts that is currently in fashion, I said. The term highlights the features of the subject-to-subject interaction both in the course of growth and within the therapeutic situation. The person-as-subject offers a contrast to the original psychoanalytic perspective of person-as-object. As is evident, intersubjectivity and all the other subsets of object relations theory are important areas for extensive research. These subsets can be looked on as more differentiated lines of development within the object-interactional realm of mental growth. Regrettably, partly out of the enthusiastic passion of discovery, collectively or individually, the subsets have come to be viewed as superordinate to the other mental realms. To make matters even more complex, many students of object relations theory have co-opted the term developmental as well and apply it as an encompassing label to their work, as if the term contributes an inherent validating valence. In doing so, they further confound the study of the developmental process itself and interfere with the research activities that might logically be applied to learning more about it and where it fits into clinical efforts. Such terminological diffuseness has made the word *developmental* cease to mean anything specific because it means too many different things to too many different people. Note that this is precisely what has happened in our profession to the word *psychoanalytic*. And here's the strangest irony, the ultimate in global thinking: in some circles the words *psychoanalytic* and *developmental* are regarded as synonyms, irreducibly interwoven. The myth of the Tower of Babel emphasized how different languages interfered with people's ability to understand one another. Now the myth has been wryly modified: enthusiasts devoted to our discipline cannot cooperate with one another to construct the psychoanalytic edifice because they are all confounded by the *same* language.

I had anticipated shock or dismay, but Ms. Freud's expression was somewhat bemused; she seemed entirely familiar with the phenomenon I found so discouraging.

I was not certain how much longer she could remain with me so I decided to succinctly summarize my statements. I said that the concept of development has become a center of confusion and controversy. The word *developmental* is sometimes used as a modifier, sometimes as a substantive noun, and has become so valued that it means too many different things to many different people. One of your legacies, Ms. Freud, was to reserve the term for features of the biologically based developmental process. Another legacy was your insistence that the developmental process be regarded implicitly as the ground around which the figures of instincts, object relations, and equipment constantly interplay. Among other things, I believe that attunement to this developmental process enhances the opportunities for helping distressed children inside and outside the consulting room. As for the psychoanalytic process, I went on, it faces equivalent ambiguities and controversies. Many clinicians are doing different things and calling them by the same word. The differences encompass such diverse matters as technique, views of the treatment process, and modes of therapeutic action; yet such broad differences are alleged to yield the same effect. To be sure, the expanded corpus of psychoanalytic facts and theories provides a weighty leverage for many different treatment actions, and therefore each can be legitimately called psychoanalytically informed. But differentiating each from the others and determining which are complementary and which are incompatible would surely yield a greater scientific prize than lumping them together. You took a stand in favor of regarding the psychoanalytic process as implying revival, the representation of the revived past within the transferred present, and a treatment relying on tapped integrative tendencies to promote the cure. That is a reasonably clear view and one that I comfortably embrace, but for the time being that view has few adherents. Instead, endless territorial battles go on. Those who prefer global thinking suggest that homogenization is the preferred approach for promoting communal peace among restive societies. So, here we are: your psychoanalytic process is threatened with the same fate as your developmental process. The new Babel is firmly entrenched.

Despite my somewhat despairing tone, Ms. Freud appeared unperturbed, albeit a bit less bemused. After another extended period of silence, she quietly left. I searched for the meaning of her last protracted silence. I found three things. From her silence I inferred that the problems facing our discipline may not be so very different from the ones she herself had encountered. I also found a suggestion that the position of a beleaguered minority might not necessarily be only strategically disadvantageous. And, finally I found a reminder of her special gift of bringing together the valued past and the precious new. She seemed to be saying: ignore the enthusiastic excess and focus instead on the substantive contributions of the current corps of psychoanalytic researchers and clinicians. You may find that the facts and theories they discover and invent can be readily integrated within the distinguished past frameworks of the psychoanalytic process and the developmental process.

Anna Freud's unexpected visit could have been a nightmarish apparition; instead, it turned out to be just an old-fashioned dream of wish fulfillment.

Current Issues in Psychoanalytic Child Development

PETER B. NEUBAUER, M.D.

This paper addresses Anna Freud's propositions about the significance of the developmental point of view. Beyond the role of genetic reconstruction, the developmental dimension demands our investigation of developmental reorganization, which leads to new structures with new priorities and new hierarchies.

This paper also attempts to explore the difficulties and resistances in the path that forwards the developmental point of view.

References are made to object relations and intersubjectivity theories, which seem to give relatively little attention to the structure and the history of pathology. Moreover, we have outlined areas of development and maturation that need further investigation in order to achieve a better understanding of the complex evolvement of the mind.

I AM QUITE CERTAIN ANNA FREUD'S LEGACY, AMONG MANY OTHER CONTRIBUtions, rests on her emphasis on the developmental dimension. This dimension was never elevated to a metapsychological point of view, for it was always linked to the observable data and to clinical processes. As early as 1965, in *Normality and Pathology in Childhood*, she stated: "It is this mixed psychopathology of childhood for which the comprehensive method of child analysis is needed. Only in child analysis proper is the whole range of therapeutic possibilities kept available for the patient, and all parts of him are given the chance on the one hand, to reveal, and on the other, to

Clinical Professor of Psychiatry at the Psychoanalytic Institute, New York University; Chairman Emeritus at the Columbia University Psychoanalytic Center.

Presented at the Anna Freud Symposium at Yale University, New Haven, on December 2, 1995.

The Psychoanalytic Study of the Child 51, ed. Albert J. Solnit, Peter B. Neubauer, Samuel Abrams, and A. Scott Dowling (Yale University Press, copyright © 1996 by Albert J. Solnit, Peter B. Neubauer, Samuel Abrams, and A. Scott Dowling).

cure themselves" (p. 232). Thus, in considering the conditions that influence our technique, she added developmental dimension to neurotic conflict and defenses. She assumed that interpretations should lift repressed feelings and that the contents of neurotic conflicts need an analytic process that leads to a corrective emotional experience.

It was expected that this widening scope would challenge and encourage child analysts to explore additional clinical interventions. Indeed, the psychoanalytic literature, particularly papers written by child psychoanalysts, favors the impression that the developmental dimension has gained increasing significance. There are frequent references to developmental disorders, developmental conflicts, deviations, regression, and arrests. But if we study case presentations, we rarely find a construction or a reconstruction of the developmental progression of the patient. Specific developmental stages or phases may be described, but these are only genetic reconstructions. If we look for descriptions of the transformations of earlier developmental organization, of processes of differentiation, of discontinuities, and of changes toward a new organization and synthesis, we find fewer examples.

We cannot avoid asking why resistances or difficulties in incorporating developmental considerations into our theory and clinical work remain so pervasive. Edgcumbe discusses this question in her clarifying paper on "The History of Anna Freud's Thinking on Developmental Disturbances" (1995), and I shall rely on her account of the factors that contribute to these resistances and difficulties.

From the beginning, psychoanalytic investigation focused on dynamic conditions, compromise formations, and unconscious fantasies that maintained continuity and interfered with change and developmental progression. The search for the genetic roots of the pathology confirmed the power of childhood experiences and references to developmental stages and the notion of critical periods.

The analyst feels at home when he explores the ego's defensive maneuvers, he lifts the repressed, interprets unconscious fantasies that determine later malfunction, or disengages those psychic factors that lead to regression and arrest. Traditionally, the analyst's concern was with the removal of developmental interferences, and he judged his success by the reinstatement of developmental progression.

The earlier assumption was that uncovering the unconscious neurotic conflicts allows the ego by itself to exercise its synthesizing and integrative functions. Today preoedipal conditions are given more attention. Thus the child in the adult, and then the infant in the child, are considered to be the primary areas of investigation.

Historically, strategies that served to treat the various layers of psychoneurotic pathologies formed the basic core of psychoanalytic therapy. Analysis of the defenses of the ego resulted in support for ego functions, which strengthened the secondary processes. Considerations about the developmental processes, however, led to new propositions. To Freud's shorthand "where id was, there shall ego be" was added the new aim that where there is developmental regression or arrest, there shall again be progression, as interferences are removed. But other developmental disorders revealed the limitations of the traditional technique.

Edgcumbe's paper shows Anna Freud's attempts to coordinate the traditional psychoanalytic technique with clinical intervention on the basis of her insight into the demands of the developmental processes. Anna Freud formulated it this way:

> So far as the developmental process itself is defective or unbalanced due either to innate or environmental conditions, we cannot expect interpretation to undo the damage, even if it clarifies the past and may help the child toward better ways of facing and coping with its consequences. If, in spite of that, children also profit from analysis in this respect, such success may be due not to the analytic work but to admixtures to the technique such as new positive object attachment, new superego identification, suggestive influence, or even corrective emotional experience, which with the very young can set arrested developmental lines going again (1974, p. 72).

Anna Freud's formulation raises the problem of how to define defective or uneven development and to distinguish between pathologies that rest on innate and on environmental causes. This requires us to differentiate primary developmental disorders from secondary ones. Primary developmental disorders are caused by a deviant innate blueprint of developmental unfolding and thus are not based on environmental interferences. We recognize that it is difficult to arrive at a secure differentiation between nature and nurture, particularly as the developmental process unfolds over a long period of time. But infant studies and the history of individual disorders allow us to observe those conditions that determine precocious or delayed development and those in which the primary structure formation is faulty, where we find a restriction of the ego and also of development.

The definition of primary developmental disorders implies that they are not the result of environmental interferences but are linked to dispositional factors that co-determine the strength of the developmental pull. Clinical case histories have documented the slowness or precocity of development, the capacity to achieve phase dominance, or the absence of phase differentiation, and the coexistence of phases throughout childhood. Explorations of the dynamics of conflicts must be placed within the overall individual developmental blueprint to be more fully understood.

The interactive experience with the object, from infancy on, makes it impossible to distinguish the dispositional from the experiential factors, because nature and nurture forever co-determine each other; thus we need to pay attention to the clearly observable individual differences among infants from birth on. One has to define these differences as characteristic not only of adaptive capacity but also of the infant's shaping of his selective environment. From a developmental point of view, they have to be seen in the context of unfolding, changing, and differentiating processes in each individual timetable. We must hold in check the tendency to explain any deviation from the norm by searching for the environmental influences that caused it.

Analysts are much more familiar with and have accepted the power of the environment to derail development. Either developmental regression or fixation on the level of unresolved neurotic conflicts then leads to the deviations of the developmental process. Change alone does not signify development. There can be change in psychic structure at any stage of development, but in order to have a developmental dimension, it must rest on a transformation followed by a new structural organization. Integration and reorganization may occur within a given structure without developmental progression based on differentiation and new or expanded structure formation.

I do not wish here to pursue the issue of nature-nurture but to point to the psychoanalytic assumption that drives and maturation lean on the biological matrix, whereas some ego functions emerge as a result of environmental influences.

As Mayes and Cohen (1996) suggest: "Each of the models of development closely related to one another suggested that the process of development reflected the maturational taming and shaping of basic instincts. Drives were the fuel, and the biological developmental imperative was to deal with the drives" (p. 126).

It is not sufficient to refer to developmental disorder as a definable unit. It appears logical to differentiate primary from secondary developmental disorders. Primary developmental disorders do not refer to structural faults or to ego disorders, which affect the developmental program. This includes deviant development, developmental retardation, or precocity and the coexistence of unresolved phase conflicts that are not determined by experiential (environmental) conditions. The category of primary developmental disorder still deserves further exploration. We should differentiate between developmental disorders based on maturational unfolding whether in the area of the ego apparatus—speech, motility, perception, memory—and those based on drive deviations that affect the successive phase organization.

As analysts, we are more secure in assessing the secondary developmental disorders in which various environmental and internally conflictual conditions interfere with developmental progression. Traumatic experiences, unresolved preoedipal and oedipal conflicts, inappropriate stimulation, lack of continuity in care—these and other experiences can derail development.

I shall not continue along this path, because considerations that outline differential diagnosis under the heading of developmental disorders are not favored by analysts. Nevertheless, I have pointed to it because diagnostic clarity should guide our intervention program and help us to fill in the various steps that constitute developmental lines.

To return to the focus of this presentation, I should like to explore the difficulties we face when we include developmental propositions in our theory and practice. Anna Freud wished that "a more or less comprehensive developmental psychology could be added to the existing body of psychoanalytic metapsychology" (1978, p. 343). As I have stated before, the developmental dimension was never elevated to the status of metapsychological proposition, for it is clearly limited to observational and clinical data. Anna Freud was well aware of the problems of expanding the theory to include additional developmental propositions. The difficulties are both in our system of theory and in our clinical work—that is, in the technique of analytic intervention.

Freud's construction of and pathbreaking insights into early childhood opened a new vista that linked adult pathology to developmental phases. His outline of libidinal phases of development established the basis for a psychoanalytic theory of development. Beyond this, he guided us to link neurotic disorders to specific phase conflicts which, if unresolved, explain symptom formation and characterological disorders. These conflicts emerge from the demands of drive expressions as they confront the taming influences, that is, the regulatory function of the ego. Thus, oral, anal, phallic, and oedipal conflicts were described and clinically confirmed. The latency period did not reveal a similar conflict constellation, as the term "latency" indicates, but that does not mean that the latency years are entirely free of conflict or impulses. The drive demands are then in retreat, allowing for the rapid expansion of the ego. With the renewed strength of the drives, preadolescence and adolescence again allow a clear view of the reemergence of specific conflict formation and solution, resulting in a new structure formation and new developmental organizations.

As analysts, we feel comfortable in exploring those conflicts, the developmental regressions and arrests and the concomitant unconscious fantasies. The psychoanalytic technique of intervention is specifically tailored to address these unresolved developmental conflicts. Freud's linkage of neurotic disorders to developmental conflicts constituted a totally new view of the causation of pathology and shaped the evolution of psychoanalytic technique. As long as the analyst rests his theoretical and clinical convictions on those generic assumptions, he feels reasonably secure in his work. But this was changed by the widening scope, which required an expansion of earlier views and additional technical instrumentation in making interventions.

Edgcumbe (1995) has clearly recorded Anna Freud's intention of exploring the significance of the developmental point of view for the widening scope. She quotes from Anna Freud's 1974 paper:

> If we accept the view that childhood psychopathology has a twofold causation, one rooted in the conflicts defense, and compromise formation, the other in the developmental processes, we have no reason to believe that the same therapeutic measures will be equally effective for both. . . . As far as the developmental progress itself is defective or unbalanced due to innate or environmental conditions, we cannot expect interpretations to undo the damage. Even if it clarifies the past and may help the child toward better ways of facing and coping with its consequences" (p. 72).

This leads us more clearly to define and differentiate the developmental process based on innate conditions from that process based on reactions to experience. The psychoanalytically oriented treatment by which we attempt to correct the one or the other will also differ. Anna Freud's understanding that the child analyst is not only a transference object but also a new object qualifies our interpretive formulations. She put the new object function *outside* analysis ("due not to the analytic work but to admixtures"), whereas Loewald and Schafer, and now everyone, put it within analysis.

While maintaining the genetic and developmental point of view that Freud had introduced, Anna Freud enlarged it considerably by her proposals of developmental lines. The historical realities of the developmental lines encompass the interaction between drive and ego, maturation and development, adaptation and structure formation. Thus the line from egocentricity to companionship, from body to toy, play, and work, from dependency to self-reliance, considers factors beyond the traditional phase conflicts. Each of the developmental lines includes a wide range of ego functions operative in the developmental progression that build new mental organization or new structure.

Thus, it is not enough to remove past interferences; we must also make use of the child's compelling need to prepare for the future, the next step in his development. This view tests the limits of psychoanalytic technique, for not all factors that contribute to the developmental process are equally accessible by the psychoanalytic method.

It is not surprising that these considerations have created a disequilibrium in some analysts and have disturbed the historical developmental line of psychoanalytic theory and practice. It has raised questions about what is psychoanalysis proper and how is it to be distinguished from psychoanalytically oriented therapy. Can one widen psychoanalytic intervention without losing the core position of psychoanalysis? These questions remind us of Anna Freud's view that "the analyst's task is not to create, that is to invent anything, but to observe, to explore, to understand and to explain" (1969, p. 153).

Clearly, she means that we should not impose theoretical propositions beyond those that are clinically justified and beyond the tested psychoanalytic position. Mayes and Cohen formulate it this way: "Developmental lines, rooted in direct observation of infants and children, afforded a rethinking of a stage-theory based on the unfolding of instinctual life. . . . Experience might constrain, slow, or accelerate the maturational necessity, but maturation was the presumed constitutional block" (1996, p. 127). This directs us toward the difference between development and maturation, as the latter is closely tied to biological constitutional factors.

After describing the traditional analytic aims of uncovering unconscious motivation, reconstructing past events, and interpreting transference manifestations, Anna Freud (1978) defined the issues for the analyst: "to the extent to which developmental harm can be undone belatedly, child analysis may accept it as its next duty to devise methods for the task. In the interim, the best that can be done is to identify developmental defects wherever they are located and to pinpoint their differences from neurotic sympatomatology. If we help the child patient at least cope with their consequences, this may be the first step towards a more basic therapy." Anna Freud did not appear to have a problem in her hope that new methods will be developed to address the understanding of observable clinical conditions.

There is always a tension in science between the search for the generalizable and attention to the specific. In regard to locating the factors that contribute to the multiple determinants of the mind, Anna Freud's seminal contribution, *Ego and the Mechanisms of Defense* (1936), is a good example of the probing toward specificity. There is now a tendency in psychoanalysis to minimize differences and to read the message of our data in such a way as to protect us from the consequences of disagreement. There is a danger in doing so because we may substitute bland generalizations for lively specifics and sacrifice new findings to the purpose of uniting analysts.

We recognize Anna Freud's extension of the developmental dimension, which asked for further modification of our intervention strategies and raises questions about the borders of psychoanalysis. We also recognize that today many psychoanalysts are interested in a different area, in some ways leading in the opposite direction. Attention to mother-infant interaction has increased our awareness of the object's regulatory influence on the infant's psychic equilibrium. With it, there is a shift from the function of the ego to the role of the object, from exploration of the changing nature of the developmental organizations to the powerfully shaping effect of the early mother-child relationship. Attachment theories, separation-individuation processes, were seen in the context of the dimension of self-object relationship. It was then a logical step to transfer this view, with equal attention, to the analyst-patient dialogue and thereby to extend the range and depth of the self-object interaction in the psychoanalytic situation. I can summarize this by quoting the "principal components of tactical moves" set forth in Ehrenberg's book *The Intimate Edge,* as quoted in John Gedo's review:

> 1. Do not confine attention to verbal association alone; carefully monitor the affectivity of both participants as well as their other [wordless] activities, particularly in terms of their reactions to each other.
> 2. Give priority to analyst-patient interactions in the here and now.
> 3. Take responsibility for devising a tailor-made solution for any obstacle in the way of therapeutic progress.
> 4. While doing the work, use your subjective reactions as clues about the patient's attitudes within the transference. . . .Do not hesitate to communicate in an affectively charged manner.

I quote this passage because it clearly shows the replication of mother-child interaction in the therapeutic setting. These assumptions are to be understood not as corrective object relations but as the pivotal therapeutic agents. One can esteem the wish to maximize the therapeutic dialogue, but it is also important to see the sacrifice of the therapeutic task to the aim of intersubjectivity, with patient and analyst as equal partners. This is clearly stated by Samuel Abrams in his article in this collection (Offerings and Acceptances): "The non-hierarchical partnership is a novel feature, it is not a necessary ingredient for a new organization. (p. 76) . . . The therapeutic alliance [the dyadic exchange] is conceptualized within a model of process that is principally used to generate interpretation and yield insight." (p. 77) The dyadic model leans on the exploration of normal development. Thus Fonagy and his colleagues (1993, p. 983) write: "Our capacity to conceive our subjective state may be the consequence of being active observers of the functioning of other minds as well as being the subject of their observations, the mind, or more specifically our theory of mind and the reflective part of the self, should be thought of as inherently interpersonal." This view of the non-hierarchical dialogue in many respects places the developmental-maturational sequences in a subordinate position.

The study of object interaction has yielded many significant contributions; we are reminded of those by Mahler, Winnicott, Loewald, Kohut, and many others. At present this orientation places Anna Freud's contributions outside the center of psychoanalytic interest. The history of the evolution of psychoanalytic theory and practice reveals the shift from the examination of one aspect of the mind to another. I suppose it was Anna Freud's intent to eliminate this one-sidedness by proposing the metapsychological profile, which should help us to maintain an equidistant position between various mental agencies. The object relations model gives clear and overriding preference to the interactive process by which health and pathology can be understood.

It seems clear to me that the quotes about the dyadic unit as the field of observation alert us to recognize the transference-counter-transference experiences and the various modes of relatedness between analyst and patient. But it does not pay equal attention to the built-in transformations that occur by the progression of maturation and development. Maturation relies on biological growth involving the ego apparatuses, perception, language, motility, and cognition, which enhance the ego, shifting dependency toward independency. The need to secure autonomy, to establish separation and individuation, runs parallel to the longing for identification and the search for object and self-constancy. Moreover, we have to observe the individual child's disposition, his selective reaction to the environmental influences, the genetic givens without which we are unable to gain a complete understanding of the object relations. Attention to the assessment of the pathology, the disease entities and symptoms and their history, should not be derailed. In this respect the non-hierarchical dyadic interaction fails to recognize the professional knowledge, the objectivity, the therapist has to exercise, for which the patient comes to him. Anna Freud (1970) addresses these issues when she refers to the analyst's metapsychological thinking and the analyst as a diagnostician: "The attempt seems worthwhile to bridge the gap between the two contrasting approaches and to use the vast array of overt symptoms themselves for the purpose of forging links between them . . . and why probing into dynamic clashes and genetic antecedents should be excluded from it, to be reserved for scrutiny within the analytic procedure."

I attempt here to understand the difficulties and resistances in the path that forwards the developmental point of view. Thus, I have referred to some aspects without exploring in detail the sources of differences. Fortunately, we have the paper by Yorke (1995), which gives us an excellent view of the theoretical and clinical issues. He confirms Anna Freud's position as he writes: "Metapsychology is a theoretical model of the mind and to that extent is basic to further psychological constructions. It is closely related to, but by no means identical with, a model of illness on which a model of treatment has to be based" (p. 26).

It is not by neglect that the emphasis on intersubjectivity does not include the study of the illness or its history except as it interferes with the interactive process. Thus, psychopathology is conceived to be caused by an interruption of the mother-child relationship and is seen as a reenactment in the analyst-patient interaction. This view excludes the primary genetic disorders, imbalances, and deviations that enter into the mother-child unit but are not caused by it. It implies that the infant has to be seen as a *unique* entity; as such he interacts with the environment seeking a secure relationship for the unfolding of his potential space or his individuation. Emde's studies outline basic motivations for each infant leading to specifically experienced environments which then in turn determine development, health, or mental disorder.

It may be of interest to refer here to the four basic motivations described by Emde for they can be linked to Anna Freud's developmental lines: the infant-child activity as a motivation, his self-regulation, his social fitness, and his affective monitoring. These are components that motivate the child to seek attachment and later to loosen it in order to establish his autonomy and equilibrium. They address the uniqueness of each child as part of motivational coordinates. One also has to follow each through the stages of developmental change.

It is my purpose not to present a critical review of the direction taken by propositions of object relations theory, but rather to understand the divergent views which, on the one hand, stem from Anna Freud's model of the developmental progression and, on the other, are based on exploration of the dyadic system.

I discuss here that part of Anna Freud's legacy that rests on adherence to the developmental point of view. This has always been a basic and orienting part of psychoanalysis. The expansion of our knowledge of developmental disorders demands new theoretical and clinical considerations. The developmental-maturational propositions link psychoanalysis to biology, genetics, and the neurosciences. Additional technical tools should not divert us from the basic psychoanalytic approach. The outline of developmental lines leads in many directions and gives us the choice to explore new territories of the mind. As Anna Freud said, "The study of purely developmental aspects has not been taken very seriously in child analysis so far" (1978, pp. 108–09). I have tried to understand some of the difficulties in the way. From a developmental point of view, psychoanalysis has enriched our ability to reconstruct the past, to inform us about development, regression fixation, and arrest. As we follow Anna Freud's work, we are directed to study the power of the developmental transformations of the child and thereby to contribute to the future of psychoanalysis.

BIBLIOGRAPHY

ABRAMS, S. (1996). Offerings and acceptances: Technique and therapeutic action. *Psychoanal. Study Child.* 51.

EDGCUMBE, R. (1995). The history of Anna Freud's thinking on developmental disturbances. *Bulletin of the Anna Freud Centre.* V. 18. part L.

EMDE, R. (1988). Risk, intervention and meaning. *Psychiatry,* 51:254–260.

EHRENBERG, D. B. (1995). The Intimate Edge. Extending the Reach of Psychoanalytic Interaction. Gedo, John, Review of Ehrenberg: The Intimate Edge. *Psychoanal. Q.* 64, 2.

FONAGY, P., MORAN, G. S., EDGCUMBE, R., KENNEDY, H. & TARGET, M. (1993). The roles of mental representation and mental processes in therapeutic action. *Psychoanal. Study Child.* 48:9–48.

FREUD, A. (1970). The symptomatology of childhood. *The Writings of Anna Freud.* New York: Int. Univ. Press. 1971. Vol. 7:157–188.

———— (1969 [1968]). Difficulties in the Path of Psychoanalysis. *The Writings of Anna Freud.* New York: Int. Univ. Press. 1971. Vol. 7:124–156.

———— (1978 [1977]). The Principal Task of Child Analysis. *The Writings of Anna Freud.* New York: Int. Univ. Press. 1981. Vol. 8:69–109.

———— (1936). *The Ego and the Mechanisms of Defense.* London: Hogarth.

———— (1965). *Normality and Pathology in Childhood.* London: Hogarth.

———— (1974). A Psychoanalytic View of Developmental Psychology. *The Writings of Anna Freud.* New York: Int. Univ. Press. 1974. p. 72.

MAYES, L. C., & COHEN, D. J. (1996). Anna Freud and Developmental psychoanalytic psychology. *Psychoanal. Study Child.* 51:117–141.

YORKE, C. (1995). Freud's Psychology: Can it Survive? *Psychoanal. Study Child.* 50:26.

"Put Yourself in the Skin of the Child," She Said

JOSEPH GOLDSTEIN, PH.D., LL.B.
SONJA GOLDSTEIN, LL.B.

Two Native American children were adopted by a non-Indian family. Following a legal challenge under the provisions of the Indian Child Welfare Act, the case became before both the United States Supreme Court and an Indian Tribal Court. In this paper we analyze the procedure and outcome of this transcultural adoption case from the point of view of the children involved and compare it with the intracultural "Baby Richard" case.

Anna Freud believed that continuity of care is vital for each child's healthy growth and development. Transcultural adoptions highlight questions that characterize contested placements, whether or not they cross cultural boundaries and whether or not they place children across lines of race, color, religion, or national origin.

IN THE COURSE OF OUR WORK WITH ANNA FREUD WE LOOKED AT THE child-placement process—contested proceedings involving divorce, neglect and abuse, foster care, and adoption—with a view to determine what would be the best outcome (or rather, since we believed that "best" was already compromised when there was state intrusion into the life of

Joseph Goldstein is Sterling Professor of Law Emeritus and Ruttenberg Professorial Lecturer at Yale Law School and professor at the Yale Child Study Center. Sonja Goldstein is of counsel to the law firm of Eric I. B. Beller, P. C., New Haven, visiting lecturer at Yale Law School, 1995–1996, and lecturer at Yale Child Study Center.

An earlier version of this paper was presented at the 13th International Congress of the International Association for Child and Adolescent Psychiatry and Allied Professions on "Violence and Vulnerability" on July 7, 1994, in San Francisco.

The Psychoanalytic Study of the Child 51, ed. Albert J. Solnit, Peter B. Neubauer, Samuel Abrams, and A. Scott Dowling (Yale University Press, copyright © 1996 by Albert J. Solnit, Peter B. Neubauer, Samuel Abrams, and A. Scott Dowling).

a family, the "least detrimental" outcome) for the child who was caught up in this process.

Over and over, as we examined both substantive and procedural aspects of individual cases, Anna Freud would admonish us: "Put yourselves in the skin of the child." She made us realize that a child's interest could not be adequately served by legislators, social workers, judges, or academics like ourselves who look at a child's experiences in the child-placement process through adult eyes; rather, they—and we—must try to transcend the adult persona and to look through the eyes of a child. This is not easy, precisely because adults are adults and not children. But adults can learn enough from child-development theory and practice and, perhaps, from drawing on their own childhood memories, to make the attempt.

In this paper we focus on an adoption case involving two Native American children, Roy and Thelma—where decision-makers had to resolve a potential conflict between the best interest of these children and the interest of their tribe, the Choctaws, in preserving its heritage. The case arose in the context of the United States Indian Child Welfare Act of 1978, which was enacted to stop the practice of separating large numbers of Indian children from their families and tribes through adoption or foster-care placement, usually in non-Native American homes.

The Act declares that "it is the policy of this Nation to protect the best interests of Indian children and to promote the stability and security of Indian tribes and families by the establishment of minimum Federal standards for the removal of Indian children from their families and the placement of such children in foster or adoptive homes which will reflect the unique values of Indian culture."[1] The Act's twin goals of safeguarding the child's well-being and the tribe's cultural interest are potentially incompatible. Put another way, to preclude or to promote "transcultural" placements tends to introduce stereotypes in a setting—any child-placement proceeding—where individual decisions ought to serve each *individual* child's needs. This is not meant to downplay the issues and concerns surrounding transracial and transethnic adoptions; it is only to place them in the broader context of what it means to any child to be placed with a new family. Thus, transcultural adoptions highlight questions that characterize all contested placements, whether or not they cross cultural boundaries and whether or not they place children across lines of race, or color, or religion, or national origin.

1. 25 U.S.C.A. sec. 1902 (1982).

With this in mind, and emphasizing that we take it as a fundamental given that the law of child placement should make each individual child's interest paramount and not allow it to be subordinated to the interests of any individual adults or of any community, we now turn to an examination of the controversy involving the placement of twins whom we call Roy and Thelma and its resolution by the United States Supreme Court and subsequently by an Indian tribunal, the Choctaw Tribal Court. The name of the case is *Mississippi Band of Choctaw Indians v. Holyfield*.[2]

At the end of December 1985, Roy and Thelma were born to Ms. B. and Mr. J., who were members of the Choctaw tribe of Mississippi. They had left the tribal reservation on which they had been living in time for Ms. B. to give birth to the twins and to arrange for their adoption outside the tribe.

In January 1986, when the twins were one month old, a lower Mississippi state court issued a final decree granting the adoption petition of Orrie and Vivian Holyfield, a non-Indian couple. Two months later, the Chocktaw tribe urged the state court to vacate its adoption decree. In July 1986 the court rejected the tribe's claim that the children were "domiciled" on the reservation. Under the Indian Child Welfare Act, if the claim were accepted, it would have required that their placement be decided by a tribal and not a state court. In 1987 the Supreme Court of the State of Mississippi affirmed the lower court's decision, emphasizing that the twins had never been physically present on the reservation and that they had been "voluntarily surrendered" by their parents, who had deliberately seen to it that they were born away from the Choctaw reservation.

In April 1989, by which time Roy and Thelma had been members of the Holyfield family for three years, the Supreme Court of the United States held that the Mississippi Supreme Court was wrong—that the twins' placement was for a tribal and not a federal or state court to decide. Justice Brennan, speaking for the Supreme Court, observed that the Court's task was to decide "the legal question of *who* should make the custody determination concerning [the twins], not *what* the outcome of the determination should be. The law places that decision in the hands of the Choctaw tribal court" (p. 53).

The Court reasoned that "Congress was concerned not solely about the interests of [individual] Indian children and families, but also about the impact on the tribes themselves of the large numbers of children adopted by non-Indians" (p. 42). "In addition," the Court said, "it is

2. 490 U.S. 30 (1988).

clear that Congress's concern over the placement of Indian children in non-Indian homes was based in part on evidence of the detrimental impact on the children themselves of such placements outside their culture" (pp. 49–50). The Court explained that the Indian Child Welfare Act was the "product of rising concern in the mid-1970s over the consequences . . . of abusive child welfare practices that resulted in the separation of large numbers of Indian children [25–35 percent of all Indian children] from their families and tribes through adoption or foster care placement, usually in non-Indian homes. . . ." [p. 32]. "[I]n the state of Minnesota, for example . . . during the year 1971–1972 nearly one in every four [Indian] infants under one year of age was placed for adoption" (pp. 32–33)—an adoption rate eight times that of non-Indian children.

Justice Brennan observed, using the language of the Supreme Court of the State of Utah in the 1986 case of *In re Adoption of Halloway:*[3] "The protection of [the] tribal interest [in its children] is at the core of the [Indian Child Welfare Act] which recognizes that the tribe has an interest in the child which is distinct from but on a parity with the interest of the parents. *This relationship between Indian tribes and Indian children domiciled on the reservation finds no parallel in other ethnic cultures found in the United States.* . . . It is precisely in recognition of this relationship . . . that the [Indian Welfare Act] designates the tribal court as the exclusive forum for the determination of custody and adoption matters for reservation-domiciled Indian children and the preferred forum for nondomiciliary Indian children" (pp. 52–53, emphasis added). As Justice Thurgood Marshall explained in an earlier Supreme Court decision, *Santa Clara Pueblo v. Martinez,*[4] Indian tribes retain a substantial measure of sovereignty; they "remain a 'separate people with the power of regulating their internal and social relations.'"[5] "In contrast to many of the states," Professor Judith Resnik has written, "Indian tribes are arguably truly distinct sovereigns, which did not cede sovereignty with the adoption of the Constitution."[6]

Justice Brennan closed his opinion by referring for the first and only time to the interests of children generally and of Roy and Thelma specifically: "It is not ours to say whether the trauma that might result from removing these children from their adoptive family should outweigh the interest of the Tribe—and perhaps the [twins] themselves]—

---

3. 732.P2D 962, 969–970 (1986).

4. 436 U.S. 49 (1978).

5. As reported in Judith Resnick, *Dependent Sovereigns: Indian Tribes, States, and the Federal Courts,* 56 *U. of Ch. L. Rev.* 671, 674 (1989).

6. *Id.* at 679.

in having them raised as part of the Choctaw community." That would be for the Tribal Court to determine. He noted that the Choctaw Tribal Court had authority under the tribal code to permit adoption by the present adoptive family. At the same time, however, he recognized that the Supreme Court "must defer to the experience, wisdom and compassion of the [Choctaw] tribal courts to fashion an appropriate remedy" (p. 54).

Before turning to the Tribal Court's decision and before discussing whether the Indian Child Welfare Act's goal of protecting the best interest of Indian children can be compatible with its goal of promoting the stability and security of Indian families and tribes, we propose general guidelines for processing and substantively resolving disputes in law about the placement of children.

GUIDELINES—CONTINUITY AND A CHILD'S SENSE OF TIME

As you think about the interest of Roy and Thelma in the *Holyfield* case, we urge each of you to heed Anna Freud's admonition to "put yourself in the skin of the child" from adoption at birth until shortly after your third year, when the tribal court must decide whether to place you in a new setting or to allow you to remain a member of the Holyfield family.

Our guidelines for making child-placement decisions, first developed in *Beyond the Best Interests of the Child*,[7] rest on a theory that interconnects the wide array of child-rearing practices in which children may thrive. We draw on a body of generally applicable knowledge about child development that recognizes that the law must be respectful of what families of different social and economic classes, of different religions and races, of different colors and cultures, and of different lifestyles believe to be best for their own children. Though each child placement case may be described as culture-specific, our guidelines and underlying principles for decision-making are not.

From psychoanalytic theory, as well as from the common experience that all of us have had as children (and many of us have had as parents), we single out continuity of care—continuity of a child's relationships with adult caregivers—as a universal essential to the child's well-being and a common denominator of healthy growth and development. With Anna Freud we said: "Continuity of relationships, surroundings, and environmental influences is essential for a child's normal development. . . . Growth—physical, emotional, intellectual, social, and

7. Goldstein, Freud, and Solnit, *Beyond the Best Interests of the Child*. Free Press (New York, 1973).

moral—does not happen without causing the child inevitable internal difficulties. The instability of all mental processes during the period of development needs to be offset by stability and uninterrupted support from external sources. Smooth growth is arrested or disrupted when upheavals and changes in the external world are added to the internal ones."[8]

Our second guideline is that the process and substance of placement should accord with the child's sense of time. It is

an integral part of the continuity concept. . . . Unlike adults, who have learned—at least in theory—to anticipate the future and thus to manage delay, children have a built-in time sense based on the urgency of their instinctual and emotional needs. As an infant begins to incorporate the way in which parents satisfy wishes and needs, either directly or by distraction, as well as the experience of the reappearance of parents after their disappearance, a child gradually develops the capacity to anticipate the future and to postpone gratification. For example, that interval of separation between parent and child which would constitute a break in continuity for an infant would be of no or little significance to a school-age youngster. The time it takes to break an old or to form a new attachment will depend upon the different meanings time has for children at each stage of their development. . . .

The significance of parental absences depends upon their duration, frequency, and developmental stage during which they occur. The younger the child, the shorter is the interval before a leave-taking will be experienced as a permanent loss accompanied by feelings of helplessness, abandonment, and profound deprivation. Since a child's sense of time is directly related to her capacity to cope with breaches of continuity, it becomes a factor in determining if, when, and with what urgency the law should act.

We urge, therefore, that placements and the procedures for placement maximize a child's opportunity for being wanted and for maintaining on a continuous, unconditional, and permanent basis a relationship with at least one adult who is, or is capable of becoming, the child's psychological parent. By "psychological parent" we mean "one [or more] adults who, on a continuing, day-to-day basis, through interaction, companionship, interplay, and mutuality, fulfills the child's psychological . . . as well as physical needs. Psychological parents may be biological, adoptive, foster, or common-law parents, or any other [adults]."[9] We ask to what extent was this standard met in placing Roy and Thelma?

8. *Id.* at 31–32.
9. *Id.* at 98.

First we describe and assess what the Choctaw Tribal Court decided about the placement of Roy and Thelma. Tribal Court Judge Roy Jim appointed a guardian for the twins, obtained proof of Mr. J.'s paternity—presumably to verify his entitlement to consent or to deny consent to the adoption, and conducted a thorough home investigation of Ms. Holyfield. Mr. Holyfield had died some time previously, and the death of their adoptive father was already an interruption of continuity in the lives of Roy and Thelma. Nine months later, in February 1990, Judge Jim decided that it was in the children's best interest to remain with Ms. Holyfield and granted adoption to her.[10] We do not know whether this decision took the same shape as the agreement approved by the Navajo tribal court in the *Halloway* case. There, the adopting non-Indian parents, the Carters, were granted permanent guardianship—"a status that enables them to retain custody and to act in most respects as if they are . . . lawful parents. . . . Unlike a standard adoption, for which there is no precedent in Navajo law, the permanent guardianship is consistent with tribal customs. [The child's] legal ties to his parents and the Navajo are not severed."[11] In any event, Choctaw custom and practice apparently do not and did not in the *Holyfield* case preclude Judge Jim from focusing on the interests of the twins—from recognizing and acting on the knowledge that it would be contrary to their best interests to break the bonds that tied them to Ms. Holyfield, even though she was not a Native American.

We can conclude, therefore, that the Indian Tribal Court's decision, the final outcome of the legal proceedings in the Holyfield case, was in accord with the continuity guideline.

Second, we look—once again from the point of view of Thelma and Roy—at the over-all legal process of the *Holyfield* case, from the moment of their birth until they were more than three years old. Our continuity and child's sense-of-time guidelines would demand that, as soon as possible after their birth, they would be placed with a parent or parents who wanted them and whose parental authority was not, in the absence of neglect, abuse, or abandonment, subject to legal intervention of any kind. Our guidelines would mandate that the Choctaw tribe's claim of jurisdiction over the placement of Thelma and Roy be made and finally adjudicated within at most a few months after their birth. Whatever appellate process was allowed should have been given priority as an emergency procedure.

This did not happen, however. From the initial intervention of the

10. *National Law Journal*, February 25, 1991, *After the Gavel Comes Down*, by Marcia Cole.
11. Hollinger, *Beyond the Best Interests of the Tribe. . . .* 66 U. of Det. L. Rev. 451, 498 (1989).

Choctaw tribe in the Mississippi state court to the decision by the U.S. Supreme Court that the Choctaw tribe had authority to decide the placement of the twins, the case seems at no stage to have been expedited. And after the U.S. Supreme Court's ruling, nine months elapsed before the Tribal Court made its decision. But it should be noted that Judge Jim did not, as review and appellate courts often do, turn the clock back to ask whether it was in the best interests of the twins to have been originally placed in a non-Indian family. He recognized that his court had to determine their *present* interest. Other than this, there was no apparent recognition by anyone that the development of growing children was involved—a non-judicial process that could not be put on hold. Having said that, it should be noted that had it not taken so long (three years) to decide that the tribal court had authority to decide the adoption question; had the Holyfields' petition for adoption been before the Tribal Court when Thelma and Roy were newborns; and had there been an Indian family available and qualified to adopt them, the Tribal Court might have, and probably should have, placed the twins within the tribe to protect their and the tribe's cultural continuity. But had no Indian family been available, the court should not—if its decision was to be in Thelma and Roy's best interests—have delayed placing them for adoption with an available and qualified non-Indian family.

What parent-less Indian children, like all children, need most are loving parents who will provide them with a nurturing environment. For any court, state or tribal, not to place them in such an environment when one is available, would be to commit an act of violence against them.

As we said earlier, the issues presented by the *Holyfield* case are not restricted to intercultural adoptions. The Choctaw tribe's intervention was made possible by the jurisdictional provisions of the Indian Child Welfare Act. But such interventions in adoption proceedings by competing adults, as well as jurisdictional questions as to which court has the right to decide placement, are often, and unfortunately, characteristic of child-placement proceedings in general. Opportunities, or even incentives, are provided for delay in making final placements or for calling into question and disturbing ongoing relationships.

In the widely publicized "Baby Richard" case,[12] the highest court of the State of Illinois ordered that three-year-old Richard be removed from his adoptive parents, who had cared for him since birth, and that

---

12. *In the Matter of the Petition of John Doe and Jane Doe, Husband and Wife, To Adopt a Baby Boy, A Minor*, 254 Ill. App. 3rd 405, 627 N.E. 2nd 648 (Ill. App. 1993), rev'd 638 N.E. 2nd 181 (Ill. 1994), cert Den'd 115 S. Ct. 499 (1994), subsequent habeas corpus pet. Den'd 115 S. Ct. 891 (1995). John and Jane Doe are fictitious names used to refer to the adopting parents. The court also uses the name Richard to refer to the child. We follow both conventions.

he be placed with his biological parents, with whom he had never lived and whose touch he had never known. The reason for the decision was that the adoption was "invalid" because the biological father had been told by the biological mother that the baby had died at birth and therefore he did not have the opportunity to withhold his consent to the adoption.

The Baby Richard case exemplifies not only the failure of the judicial system to treat contested child-placement cases as the emergency that, given the child's sense of time, they always are for the child; it also exemplifies another aspect of such proceedings which, fortunately for Roy and Thelma, was not part of the *Holyfield* case. Richard was treated by the Illinois State Supreme Court like chattel rather than as a human being. He was used as the remedy for the wrong that had been done to his biological father. By judicial order, Richard was wrenched from the only parents he had ever known and delivered to adults who were strangers to him.[13] The decision of the Choctaw Tribal Court, on the other hand, respected the twins' need for continuity of care and allowed them to remain with their adoptive mother who had become their psychological parent. This in spite of the fact that the Choctaw tribe had been "wronged" by the erroneous jurisdictional decision of the Mississippi state court and perhaps also by the loss of yet another Indian child as an integral member of the tribe.

It is important not to attribute to the tribal courts the policy goals that motivated Congress to enact the Indian Child Welfare Act. Congress sought to promote the best interests of Indian children and to end state and national policies and practices that promoted the "wholesale removal of Indian children from their homes" and their separation from "their families and tribes through adoption or foster-care placement in non-Indian homes." Congress sought, by the Act, to empower Indian tribes to follow their own practices with regard to placement. The tribal courts, however, are free, once they have jurisdiction, to subordinate that policy goal to the well-being of the individual child. To the extent that tribal courts are vehicles (in Judith Resnik's words) or reflections of culture, one might speculate, on the basis of comparing the *outcome* in Thelma and Roy's case with the *outcome* in Richard's case, that the Choctaw tribal culture, more than Illinois culture, allows decision-makers to place themselves in the skin of the child before they make rulings about the placement of the child.

13. Justice James D. Heiple of the Illinois Supreme Court is reported to have written: "The law is simple and straightforward. The boy will get over his initial shock of being taken from the family he has lived with since he was four-days-old. It will work itself out in the fullness of time." (*New Haven Register,* July 14, 1994, B 15).

In this discussion we have not addressed whether and to what extent it is in the best interests of children to be placed with families of the same culture, religion, race, or color if such placement can be accomplished within the parameters of the continuity and child's-sense-of-time guidelines. Certainly, as is spelled out in the description of the purposes of the Indian Child Welfare Act, discouraging the placement of children outside their own Indian culture can be made official policy. And policy-makers may also believe that if a child is placed with a family of a different culture, that child may feel, as she grows up, a sense of not belonging, a sense of something lost, or, more positively, a sense of a tie to and appreciation for her heritage.

We believe that, as exemplified by another guideline to child placement that we have proposed—namely "least detrimental alternative" (rather than "best interest")—policy-makers must recognize that children caught up in the child-placement process have already been deprived of their "best interests." The law can best salvage the interests of such children by ensuring their placement as quickly and permanently as possible with a family that wants them. Prevention of eventual feeling of alienation due to loss of cultural heritage is consistent with "least detrimental alternative" only if decision-makers do not attempt to implement this long-term goal by encouraging instability or by promoting obstacles to immediately meeting each parentless child's need for physical and emotional nurture as a permanent member of a family.

If decision makers in the child-placement process can, as Anna Freud urged, place themselves "in the skin of the child," there is hope that "least detrimental" will move closer to "best."

Anna Freud as a Historian of Psychoanalysis

ELISABETH YOUNG-BRUEHL, PH.D.

This article explores a series of papers Anna Freud wrote in the 1970s, which constitute her history of child psychoanalysis. It notes her purposes—theoretical, clinical, and institutional—for reviewing this history and then focuses on three themes that she stressed. First, she emphasized that the "widening scope of psychoanalysis" had been both tremendously fruitful and perplexing as it revealed areas—such as the developmental pathologies—for which theory and technique lag. Second, she underscored the way child analysis had been extended from pathology to the theory of normal development, particularly by adding child observation to its research methods. Third, she noted how child analysis has often been hampered by reductionist thinking, and she made a plea for complexity: for considering all metapsychological frameworks and all developmental lines, and for articulating a complexly grounded diagnostic.

1

COUNTING FROM 1908, WHEN FREUD'S FIRST DISCIPLES BEGAN TO MEET IN Vienna, and allowing fifteen years for each generation, there have been six generations of psychoanalysts. The history of psychoanalysis has been written, as it were, on their persons, for it is, of course, a characteristic of this science that it is transmitted from one generation to the next by a unique means—the training analysis. Psychoanalysis is practiced on its future practitioners, altering them in its terms, struc-

Professor, Haverford College; on staff of the outpatient clinic, Institute of Pennsylvania Hospital; and candidate at the Philadelphia Association for Psychoanalysis.

The Psychoanalytic Study of the Child 51, ed. Albert J. Solnit, Peter B. Neubauer, Samuel Abrams, and A. Scott Dowling (Yale University Press, copyright © 1996 by Albert J. Solnit, Peter B. Neubauer, Samuel Abrams, and A. Scott Dowling).

turing into them a relationship with an analyst and, by this peculiar descent, with the first analyst, Freud. Until recently, psychoanalysis has hardly had a history or a historiography of the conventional textual sort, although since the 1950s it has had an outpouring of biographical—predictably, psychobiographical—studies devoted to Freud.[1] What textual writing there has been of the history of psychoanalysis has largely been biographical. Freud's first small circle and the outstanding early trainees have been the subjects of biographies, most of them focused on the subjects' relationships with Freud and on the schisms in psychoanalysis.

Freud's early followers were not historians of their science, but when Hitler's rise to power in Germany forced many European analysts to emigrate, they—the first generation of trainees, Anna Freud's generation—decided to survey the state of their science and prepare it for export, even, perhaps, for its survival, and they thus became its first textbook writers. They tried to show what in psychoanalysis was considered secure knowledge, what was still tentative, and what was unexplored. Otto Fenichel's *The Psychoanalytic Theory of the Neuroses* is perhaps the best work in this genre and time. Soon afterward, with Jones's research on his biography of Freud and with the completion of Strachey's monumental *Standard Edition*, including its invaluable apparatus, the materials and means allowing the next generation to write the history of the psychoanalytic theory of neuroses became available. But a turn in the study of psychoanalysis suddenly occurred; it had two dimensions, each of which was detrimental to psychoanalysis as a science. The first dimension was the cultural hostility toward psychoanalysis (interpreted as a conservative or counter-reformist enterprise) in the late 1960s. The second was a rash of fractures that split psychoanalytic organizations into rivalrous camps battling for dominance. The cultural hostility was reflected in the many biographies of Freud, each of which linked him to some kind of repressiveness. The internal fissuring reinforced an existing tendency in training programs—that is, the programs were aimed at teaching a given school's technique and gave little attention to training in the history of psychoanalytic con-

1. There have been books purporting to be *A History of Psychoanalysis*, the title of one by Reuben Fine (New York: Columbia Univ. Press, 1979), which is a bibliographic tour. Edith Kurzweil's *The Freudians: A Comparative Perspective* (New Haven: Yale Univ. Press, 1989) is a helpful survey, taking into account what has been written nation by nation historically. Nathan Hale's *The Rise and Crisis of Psychoanalysis in the United States: Freud and the Americans, 1917–1985* (New York: Oxford Univ. Press, 1995), the sequel to his *Freud and the Americans: The Beginnings of Psychoanalysis in the United States, 1896–1917*, is a good history of American psychoanalysis in its cultural setting, which contains in its notes a guide to recent historical writing.

cepts, theory-construction, or the collective enterprise of building up the science qua science, for which historical consciousness is key.[2]

One of the most interesting ways to take stock of these developments is to consider Anna Freud's reaction to the embattled state of psychoanalysis. In 1965, she had, of course, completed her important and synthetic book *Normality and Pathology in Childhood*, which contains the most complete history of child analysis—a history in the Fenichelian manner, one that maps what can be considered secure knowledge about child development and then indicates which areas are in need of investigation and which are unexplored. But over the next ten years, while she continued to initiate many important research projects at her Hampstead Clinic, Anna Freud grew uneasy. And the result was a series of papers in the mid-1970s in which she wrote more and more frequently as a historian.[3] She clearly felt the need to prepare and present a general historical assessment, and the papers she wrote repeatedly opened with variations on the following sentence (written in 1976): "It is the privilege of age to view present happenings in the light of past experience" (VII, 193). But she also had a political purpose. Thinking that institutional psychoanalysis might finally be ready to reconsider the second-class status conferred from the beginning on child analysis, and more generally to remedy the bifurcation of analytic training into adult training and child training, she presented the history of psychoanalysis and child analysis as what she thought it was—an institutional travesty.[4]

2. In 1966, Anna Freud summarized this complex training issue, which has so much to do with why psychoanalysts do not write their own history well: "Thus candidates are guided how to extract the maximum of information from transference, resistance, dreams, other id derivatives, or ego mechanisms; how to time their interpretations; in short, how to cure their patients. They receive no guidance in such important matters as how to record their material, or sift and summarize it, or verify their findings, or pool them with others; how to trace the history of psychoanalytic concepts, to inquire into their definitions, and to clarify and unify their technical terms; how to select specific areas for their research interests or to become alerted to the gaps in our knowledge." (VII, 57) (In this note and others, as well as in my text, I will refer to Anna Freud's writings by citing volume and page number to *The Writings of Anna Freud* (New York: International Univ. Press, 1966–1981).)

3. Particularly important among these papers (in volumes VII and VIII of Anna Freud's *Writings*) are "A Short History of Child Analysis" (1966), "The Ideal Psychoanalytic Institute: A Utopia" (1966), "Difficulties in the Path of Psychoanalysis: A Confrontation of Past with Present Viewpoints" (1969), "Child Analysis as a Subspecialty of Psychoanalysis" (1970), "The Widening Scope of Psychoanalytic Child Psychology, Normal and Abnormal" (1972), "Beyond the Infantile Neurosis" (1974), "The Principal Task of Child Analysis" (1978), "Changes in Psychoanalytic Practice and Experience" (1976), and "A Study Guide to Freud's Writings" (1978).

4. See especially "Child Analysis as a Subspecialty of Psychoanalysis," prepared in 1970 (VII: 204–219).

I want to offer here an interpretation of these historical papers of Anna Freud's because they are, I think, a neglected resource for understanding what psychoanalysis has become in the past several decades. But before I do that I want to make a few remarks about Anna Freud as a historian of psychoanalysis in order to consider how it came about that Anna Freud, of all the figures in her generation, emerged as the most historically minded. (I should note, however, that these remarks are not going to be psychobiographical, because the psychobiographical issues involved are too complex for this setting.)

2

Anna Freud was, of course, not just the daughter of the founder but the daughter analyzed by the founder, bound uniquely in this recapitulatory process that was unique to psychoanalysis among the sciences. She was grounded in her father's life and work more completely, more emblematically than any other psychoanalyst, and she had to play—particularly after his death—the role of his representative, his intellectual executor, his living shrine, his museum-keeper, his vestal. But she was skeptical about biographies of her father; indeed, she considered all biographies, even Jones's, which she aided in so many ways, to be intrusions into his—and her—privacy. Her loyalty protected her from becoming fixated on the biography genre while it kept her attention on the future. She wrote history only for the sake of the future, with the conviction that the only kind of memorialization her father would have approved was the continued health and growth of psychoanalysis. Her attitude sometimes led her to use her own work as a historian of psychoanalysis defensively, to keep up her father's tradition of pointing to the true path and naming the schismatics, a practice that might have made her not so much a historian as an apologist, or even a catechist. But defensiveness was not her usual mode in print—even though she was a conservator, in the deepest meaning of the word—and it is interesting to consider why this is so.

In the first place, Anna Freud had the advantage of viewing herself as working in a field different from her father's, something which no analyst of adults has done or can do.[5] And she had the sanction for this view right from her father, who in 1925, as part of the preface to August Aichhorn's *Wayward Youth*, divided the history of psychoanalysis into two parts—his part and her part: "Children have become the main subject of psychoanalytic research and have thus replaced in

---

5. In terms of the defense mechanisms that Anna Freud had explored so brilliantly earlier in her career, the one at work here was "altruistic surrender," her elaboration of the maneuver to which Freud himself had originally given the name "retiring in favor of another."

importance the neurotics on whom its studies began." As far as she was concerned, her father had laid down what there was to know about adults and particularly about adult neurotic (although not psychotic) psychopathology; all innovations in his domain she viewed merely as adjustments, refinements. But child and adolescent analysis was another matter. From her analytic field she anticipated and helped bring about two achievements that could be described as novel, as innovations in psychoanalysis. One was delineation of childhood pathologies in their own terms—that is, not as infantile neuroses that might be rewritten or reedited in adulthood. And the second was a full descriptive framework for normal development. She noted:

> Reconstruction from adult analysis inevitably is weighted toward pathology to the neglect of normal developmental happenings; [for] it is always the conflictual and unsolved which does not come to rest in an individual's mind, which welcomes the opportunity to re-establish itself in the transference situation and thus captures and monopolizes the analyst's attention. In contrast, the satisfied impulses, the successful adaptive conflict solutions disappear by entering the fabric of the personality. They are outgrown with little incentive left for revival at a later date.
>
> Thus, while the analysts of adults become expert in tracing psychopathology back to its earliest roots, only the child analysts appear to hold the key to the description of the course taken by normal adult development (VIII, 85)

It is interesting to note how frequently Anna Freud conceded to analysts of adults (and over topics in the domain of the psychoses, to medical practitioners) the territories of debate about adult psychopathology and histories of those debates. For example, when she was asked to comment on a discussion between Leo Rangell and Andre Green that took place in 1975, the topic of which was how and to what extent classical psychoanalytic technique should be altered to deal with psychotic patients, she contented herself with framing the issue so that her hearers could, as she said, "construct their own personal picture of the future of psychoanalysis, following either one or the other of the two protagonists." She wanted to convey, subtly but firmly, that any discussion of whether to adjust psychoanalytic technique should be thought about with the whole future of psychoanalysis in mind. She was trying to train her hearers to think "in the best interests of psychoanalysis" (if I may borrow her well-known maxim "in the best interests of the child").

Anna Freud's position here was, again, a function of her conviction about the centrality of child and adolescent analysis to the present and future of psychoanalysis. This conviction also allowed her to maintain the excitement and curiosity—the sense of pioneering—that she had

had since her youth and that she attributed to her generation in general. In 1975, when she was beginning to write her historical papers, Anna Freud offered a description of the satisfied and excited attitude toward psychoanalysis that she thought had become so difficult for younger analysts to find in their own terms and times[6]:

> We {of the initial generation} felt that we were the first who had been given a key to the understanding of human behavior and its aberrations as being determined not by overt factors but by the pressure of instinctual forces emanating from the unconscious mind; that we were the first, therefore, to see mental illness as a battle between rationality and irrationality; that we also were the first to possess a method, namely, free association, for breaking down the barrier between consciousness and the unconscious; that this method was applicable to ourselves as well as to our patients, thus reducing the difference between the mentally ill and the mentally healthy and altering the relationship between therapist and patient from one of dominating authority to one of shared endeavor; that our new technique of inquiry and exploration of resistance and transference was identical with our technique of cure; and, finally, that, apart from suggestion and hypnosis, we had no rivals in the field of mental treatment. (VIII, 177)[7]

3

As a perpetual pioneer, Anna Freud stood for psychoanalytic history as a map of territory traversed and to be traversed. Her map is not complicated, in fact, it has only three regions or, as I call them, themes.

6. In 1976, Anna Freud attended a symposium on "The Identity of the Psychoanalyst," where she felt herself to be something of a token, a "representative of the past," and where she wanted to make it clear that she did not have a personal relation to the topic. Allowing herself a little sarcasm, she said: "[About] the question of the identity of the analyst, I really have no justification to speak: I have never gone through a crisis of identity as an analyst. I can remember that during my analytic life I have met several crises, in the external world and in the internal world, but what I have missed out on evidently is that I felt my own identity shaken . . . With me [social identity, professional identity and personal identity] fell together into one." (VIII, 189–190).

7. At the end of this paragraph, Anna Freud was clearly responding to the then current charge (of which there are many echoes in the last few years) that the "orthodox" analytic stance was too authoritarian: she presents the founding generation as anti-authoritarian, particularly in comparison to the psychiatric attitude Freud battled. She knew very well that the ideal of analysis as a "shared endeavor" between analysts and patients had emerged as a consensus among her colleagues especially under the challenge of Ferenczi and his "active technique." Only in the next generation, so replete with medical people and men with military psychiatry experience, did school-bound authoritarianism flourish, particularly in hospital settings—producing, of course, a countertrend among the more independent and innovative, like the best of the Middle Group in Britain or Hans Leowald in America.

The first of her themes always went under the title "the widening scope of psychoanalysis." Here she tracked how her father had widened his scope over the entire course of his work, including work done with his first collaborators: "from the neuroses to the psychoses; from sexual inhibitions to the perversions; from character disorders to the delinquencies; from adult psychopathology to adolescence; from adolescence to childhood" as she once put the catalog (VIII, 83). Then she tracked how the scope of psychoanalysis had continued to widen. On the unambiguously positive side of this continued widening, she included developments in child and adolescent analysis. But she also noted difficulties. For example, the widening of scope had, eventually, produced a condition in which analytic understanding was greater in scope than analytic therapy—that is, that many of the mental conditions that could be explored could not be cured. In this category, for example, she placed many childhood developmental pathologies, adult psychoses, and borderline cases (VIII, 183).

Anna Freud's second theme—which is referred to above—bore the title "from psychopathology to theory of normal development." And this was the historical theme that most emphasized the pioneering role of child and adolescent analysis. In connection with this theme, she argued frequently and forcefully for giving child and adolescent analysis institutional parity with adult analysis—which would at least eliminate the anomalous condition of the avant-garde area of research being staffed by the second class citizens. Similarly, she argued strongly that psychoanalysis had done itself a great damage by contradicting Freud in its policy toward nonmedical practitioners; and she was quite aware that the hostility toward lay analysis cast a deep shadow over child analysis, where so many nonmedical people worked. In many papers on questions of training, Anna Freud always tried to bind together what others had historically tried to put asunder—psychopathology and normality, adult and child analysis, medical and nonmedical practitioners.

It was in connection with this theme "from psychopathology to theory of normal development" that Anna Freud constructed a history of methods within child analysis. She came forward in 1957 to acknowledge Ernst Kris as the first historian of child analysis, and to accept his claim that child analysis up to 1950 had had two periods—one before Freud broached the structural theory, the second anxiety theory, and the dual instinct theory, and one after the 1920s when observation emerged as a source of knowledge along with analytic research based on reconstruction in the analysis of adults and children.[8] Anna Freud

8. See "Child Observation and Prediction of Development," V 8: 104.

herself had been skeptical about direct observation as a research method and about the contribution that direct observation could make to knowledge of normal development, but she took the occasion of the 1957 memorial lecture for Kris to correct herself and, further, to set herself in opposition to a then emergent trend of considering as analytic data only indirect and direct manifestations of transference. Her sense in 1957, confirmed in her later 1970s retrospections, was that a third methodological period in the history of child analysis was beginning, one marked by innovatory combinations of analytic reconstruction and observation in research focused toward normal development.

At about the same time in the late 1950s, Anna Freud articulated a second idea about normal development that became crucial to her later work and central in subsequent historical reflections. Viewing development as a process extending from birth through late adolescence to the phase of character consolidation that is the transition from late adolescence to adulthood will show, she argued in her 1958 classic "Adolescence," that adolescence is a "second chance." She opposed conceptions of development that featured the preoedipal phenomena as all-determinative, no matter whether oriented toward preoedipal instinctual drive and object relations "positions" or separation-individuation issues or attachment behaviors. She thought that the various debates among schools of psychoanalysis about what happens preoedipally all neglected adolescence (as well as latency), underestimating critically the degrees and kinds of psychic alterations that can and do come about in adolescence. In her 1970s historical reflections, she repeatedly stressed both what advances in understanding had resulted from focusing analytically and observationally on the preoedipal period mother-child dyad and how truncated the image of "normal development" had become as the first two years of life dominated all else.

Interestingly, as she reflected on the ideal of a theory of child-adolescent normal development, and as research on developmental issues proceeded in the 1970s at the Hampstead Clinic, Anna Freud shifted her own research focus—and provided a brilliant example of how historical reflection can shape a view of what needs doing. Targeting normal development had helped her bring into focus pathologies *of development,* which are pathologies of arrest, as distinguished from infantile neuroses, which are pathologies of unconscious conflict producing regression. The developmental pathologies—arrests, traumatic interruptions, unevennesses on different developmental lines, organic or environmental defects or deficits—require special and specific analytic techniques, and discovering them emerged in Anna Freud's mind as a key challenge before child and adolescent analysis.

Late in her life, she envisioned two kinds of child and adolescent analysis—one for the infantile neuroses and one for the developmental pathologies, that is, one that had been created, and one that needed creating.

The third and most complex theme Anna Freud pursued required her to sketch the main psychoanalytic interpretive frameworks or views—the dynamic, the genetic, the economic, and the topographical-structural—and to argue that good practitioners and theoreticians use them in combination, each complementing the others. Historically, however, these frameworks have not, she noted, received equal attention either in practice or in theoretical writing. She was convinced that the genetic view, and particularly its object relations strand, had, by the early 1970s, eclipsed the others in theoretical work, and that the instinctual drive theory, for which the dynamic and economic views particularly account, had fallen into neglect. Even more generally, she felt that psychoanalysis had fissured into two camps, the clinical practitioners and the theoretical researchers, precisely because the metapsychological frameworks had come to be considered so widely and wrongly as *merely* theoretical, not as the very essence of therapy as well.

One particular consequence of this distorted view of metapsychology frequently received her attention: namely, the failure of analysts to develop diagnosis into a metapsychologically grounded practice. She argued against considering diagnosis as cataloging of symptoms but also against refusing to diagnose because symptom cataloging is non-analytic (mere DSM application in the American context).[9] Her stance was related to the one she took towards distinguishing infantile neuroses from developmental pathologies—without a good diagnosis, a child's disorder cannot be assessed, and thus the right type of treatment cannot be recommended. In historical terms, Anna Freud had summarized the situation in 1965, just as she was beginning to articulate her own distinction between infantile neuroses and developmental pathologies:

> to date, [the] revolutionary and adventurous spirit of the child analyst has exhausted itself in the areas of technique and theory, and has stopped short of the important question of the classification of disorders. Here a wholly conservative policy has been pursued, i.e., diagnostic categories have been taken over wholesale not only from the field of adult analysis but, beyond this, from adult psychiatry and criminology.

9. "As in the field of adult analysis, the descriptive nature of many of the current diagnostic categories runs counter to the essence of psychoanalytic thinking, because it emphasizes the identity of or difference between manifest symptomology while neglecting those of the underlying pathogenic factors." (VI, 110).

The whole psychopathology of childhood has been fitted, more or less forcibly, into these existing patterns (VI, 110).

This third historical theme, which might be called "continually elaborating metapsychology," constituted a plea for a psychoanalysis in which nothing once achieved was ever neglected, or in which everything counted but no one thing counted more than others. It was a plea, in effect, not for giving any part of the evolving family of psychoanalytic notions special privileges—the kind of plea one might expect from a youngest child arguing against favoritism or prerogatives of seniority but also from a scientist well acquainted with the dangers (not to mention the dreary repetitiveness) of reductionist thinking.[10]

4

The history of psychoanalysis over the period that Anna Freud surveyed has generally been characterized by a great deal of reductionism, or a great deal of what might be called contests for a "most important" prize. Anna Freud's historical perspective, with its threefold stress on the widening scope of psychoanalysis, on the necessity of a developmental approach in theory, therapy, and diagnostics, and on metapsychological complexity, allowed her to assess *psychoanalytically* these various efforts at awarding the "most important" prize. It is to this contribution of hers as a historian that I would like to turn finally.

The field of "most important" reductions Anna Freud catalogued was as extensive as psychoanalysis. All analysts after Freud, for example, acknowledged the importance of sexuality and aggression—if not the dual instinct theory of Eros and Thanatos outlined in *Beyond the Pleasure Principle*—but in recent analysis many have asserted that aggression, less explored by Freud than sexuality, is most important in human development and in pathology. All analysts recited that dream interpretation is "the royal road to the unconscious," but many argued that transference interpretation is most important and asserted, in terms of technique, that transference should actively and purposefully be brought into the analytic process, not awaited as a spontaneous product of the process. Reconstruction of childhood events and experiences has been relegated by some to the category less important in comparison with analysis of present events and experiences, the here and now, especially the transference and countertransference here and

10. Among Anna Freud's contemporaries, the one who was most in accord with her approach to metapsychology and its intricacy was Robert Waelder, particularly in his classic paper on "The principle of multiple function," collected in *Psychoanalysis: Observation, Theory, Application* (New York: International Universities Press, 1976), pp. 68–83.

now. An object relations narrative is said to be most important, or certainly more important than an instinctual drive one. The analyst-analysand dyad is said to be a more important focus of the analyst's attention than the abstractions of metapsychology. And so forth.

Anna Freud considered these claims with two key assessment criteria. The first was that different developmental contexts, especially therapeutic contexts, produce different psychic phenomena, which, in turn, influence psychoanalytic concepts. For example, she noted that child and adult analyses, in their differences, will effect conceptualizations of sex and aggression:

> While free association seems to liberate in the first instance the sexual fantasies of the patient, free action—even if only comparatively free— acts in a parallel way on the aggressive trends. What children over- whelmingly act out in the transference are therefore their aggressions, or the aggressive side of their pregenitality which promotes them to attack, hit, kick, spit, and provoke the analyst. . . . Theoretically this linkage between acting out and aggression may produce a biased picture of the proportion between libido and aggression in the child. (VI: 30– 31)

Aggression is "most important" in the context of child analysis (and of analysis with adult patients who act out as much or more than they free associate), but this does not mean that aggression is most important generally (in all people or all pathologies) or theoretically.

Secondly, Anna Freud understood that interactions of phenomena and concepts are systemic: one change changes the whole system. For example, when the widening scope of psychoanalysis brought the pre-oedipal period, and thus preverbal communication to the fore, this, in turn, had an impact on the role of transference in analysis, thera-peutically and theoretically. In analyses emphasizing the preoedipal and preverbal, "remembering yields its place to repetition, verbal com-munication to re-enactment. This explains the heightened significance of communication via transference in many present-day analyses, when transference interpretations are considered the only thera-peutically effective ones and where transference phenomena are per-force given preference over memory, free association, and dreams, as the only real road to the unconscious" (VIII: 147).

In recent years, as psychoanalysis has been slowly acquiring a con-ventional textual historiography, diverse theoretical emphases or types of reduction have most frequently been explained as facets of insti-tutional and biographical competition. Competitions among theoreti-cal schools and individual personalities even get stereotyped: Anna Freud, thus, becomes the paternal, oedipal figure in child analysis and

Melanie Klein the maternal, preoedipal one; Freud is the father of analysis and Sandor Ferenczi the mother, and so forth.[11] Rather than creating this kind of psychobiographizing, Anna Freud was offering as a historian a look at the dynamics of analytic practice (including types of technique) and setting (including types of patients and pathologies).

5

In the two decades after Anna Freud wrote her historical papers, much has changed in psychoanalysis. Although the cultural hostility toward psychoanalysis that arose in the late 1960s has abated, a new challenge has arisen during the spectacular shift in psychiatry toward psychopharmacology: hostility to a treatment so long and expensive. The pace of internal institutional fissuring has slackened a great deal; once feuding contingents—such as the Anna Freudians and the Melanie Kleinians—address each other's meetings as all share the feeling of being beleaguered in a changing mental health climate. Certain institutional failings of psychoanalysis—crucially, on the question of lay analysis and the status of child analysis—have been somewhat addressed or redressed. The Freud biography industry is still flourishing, to the detriment of psychoanalysis, and the historical consciousness in the field is, if anything less sophisticated than it was twenty years ago and even more organized around the Freud literature.

But the most dramatic challenge facing child psychoanalysis is fundamentally socioeconomic. In many parts of the world, the past twenty years have been a period in which children are, generally speaking, more at risk than they have been at any time since the end of the Second World War. In the two eras when child analysis had its most important growth spurts—the decade after the First World War (1918–1928) and the decade around the Second World War (say, 1937–1947)—children were given great priority by progressive, socialist governments and societies, and elimination of poverty was a clearly articulated goal. Now, without much echo of this idealism, governmental policies and societal attitudes marked by thoughtlessness for the future are allowing children worldwide to sink into poverty in record numbers, and thus grow up in family and social circumstances that do not in any way favor normal development. Many children live in war zones, or under conditions of technical peace that are warlike; as a result they display the environmentally induced problems Anna Freud studied first in

11. For example, see Axel Hoffer, "Ferenczi's Relevance to Contemporary Psychoanalytic Technique," in *The Legacy of Sandor Ferenczi,* ed. Lewis Aron and Adrienne Harris (Hillsdale, NJ: Analytic Press, 1993), pp. 75–80.

Vienna and then as the director of the Hampstead War Nurseries. Ours is a time she would have recognized as in many ways familiar, and she would have argued for research into developmental disorders as of particularly pressing urgency. That is, she would have recognized the need for psychoanalysis to have another responsive growth spurt, to bring its history and tradition to bear on family and social planning agencies as well as on the legal settings she addressed in *In the Best Interests of the Child* and its companion volumes. Had she lived into our present moment, her sense of herself as a historian would have, I am sure, adapted and expanded to become a sense of herself as a social historian for psychoanalysis and its emerging social settings.

Meanwhile, to speak in the language of fact, not fantasy, Anna Freud's way of being a historian of psychoanalysis has had a very limited influence, and her conclusions—for example, about the need for a metapsychologically grounded diagnostic—have had their greatest significance for those trained in her manner or at her clinic. But, in my estimation, nothing in the past two decades has made her approach any less relevant or cogent or her historical example as a respondent to social conditions any less important.

PSYCHOANALYTIC THEORY

Offerings and Acceptances

Technique and Therapeutic Action

SAMUEL ABRAMS, M.D.

This paper presents several proposals about clinical psychoanalysis. One proposal suggests that an analyst's essential offering is a non-hierarchical partnership in discovering. Another implies that a valuable goal of psychoanalytic work is to acquire the adaptive tool of "insighting," an acquisition that is promoted by the structure of the partnership. The paper contains arguments that support the proposals, as well as an extended clinical anecdote that illustrates them.

IN THIS PAPER, I PROPOSE THAT AN ESSENTIAL OFFERING IN PSYCHO-analysis is a non-hierarchical partnership in discovering. I present the meaning and usefulness of this proposal in four interweaving sections. The first section describes some well-established conceptual perspectives about clinical work. The second defines "non-hierarchical partnership in discovering." The third section presents a clinical vignette of an adult treatment that illustrates my proposal. And, finally, there is a summary of abstract ideas, a concrete proposal, and a clinical vignette.

I anticipate, in response to my proposal, questions and objections

Clinical professor, The Psychoanalytic Institute at the New York University School of Medicine.

Presented at the Samuel Ritvo, M.D., and Albert J. Solnit, M.D., Annual Lectureship in Child Analysis, April 17, 1995, New Haven. Earlier versions were presented at the annual meeting of the American Psychoanalytic Association in San Francisco, May 1993; at the Washington-Baltimore Psychoanalytic Institute, September 1993; and the Psychoanalytic Association of New York, February 1994.

The Psychoanalytic Study of the Child 51, ed. Albert J. Solnit, Peter B. Neubauer, Samuel Abrams, and A. Scott Dowling (Yale University Press, copyright © 1996 by Albert J. Solnit, Peter B. Neubauer, Samuel Abrams, and A. Scott Dowling).

arising from abstractions, ambiguities, practical matters, and tactics; consequently, I have shaped my argument to address these concerns.

ABSTRACTIONS

Three of the potential problems in interpreting my proposals are implicit in the title of this paper. The first is a result of introducing abstract concepts. However necessary they may be, by their very nature, abstractions are difficult to explain and comprehend. To complicate matters, in our discipline these abstractions exist at various levels, some very close to empirical data, some very distant. One way to overcome this obstacle is to address the different levels promptly, before they cloud the subsequent narrative. The phrase "offerings and acceptances" in the title of this paper is on a descriptive plane while "technique and therapeutic action" implies a conceptual level. The title of the paper suggests a link in that the descriptive word "offerings" is related to the conceptual "technique," and "acceptances" to "therapeutic action." Or, put simply: what an analyst offers a patient empirically is linked to the theory of technique; how the patient accepts or actively processes the offering is linked to the theory of therapeutic action.

The title also raises the problem of differentiating interpersonal and intrapsychic features of clinical analysis. The analyst offers; that is, the analyst gives something more or less specific. The patient accepts; that is, the patient is in a position to accept or refuse what is offered. This adds an interpersonal as well as an intrapsychic component. The interpersonal—the give and take—reflects an operational feature of the treatment relationship; the intrapsychic defines how that operational feature is experienced within the minds of both participants. In other words, what is the analyst's intent in making offerings? What does the patient do with the offerings? Such moments in the transaction are often experienced differently by each participant. This is readily demonstrable during periods of silence. An analyst's offering of attentive listening evokes a wide assortment of responses. To some, the silence signals a warm, embracing caring; to others, a reproachful, disapproving action; still to others, a detached indifference. Offerings of silence and the variety of ways in which such offerings are psychologically processed illustrate how specific moments in the give-and-take of therapeutic transactions may not be experienced by the participants in the same way.

A third problem—and we're still in the title—follows from this. If technique conveys a plan, it follows logically that analysts have preconfigured goals, pre-existing designs for the treatment. However, technical precepts suggest that an analyst should be immersed in free-floating attention while assuring neutrality and maintaining anonymity. What place does a preconfigured agenda have in a free-floating, neutral, anonymous figure? In addition, the word "acceptances" suggests the patient's active acquisition of a pre-designed offering. What is acceptance doing in a treatment centered in free association? Can there be any room for passing on a pre-defined give-and-take in a setting purportedly suffused with such freedoms?

I will show that there are expectable outcomes in clinical psychoanalysis, and, furthermore, that it is the analyst's responsibility to structure the setting so that these outcomes are possible. I believe that delineating the anticipated goals more precisely will help to further differentiate analysis proper from other analytically informed treatments that promote alternate ways of getting better.

It will be easier to grasp these three abstract concepts if they are anchored to a familiar model. The one I have chosen is the first Freudian model of offerings and acceptances, of technique and therapeutic action. In 1893, Elizabeth von R. was referred to Sigmund Freud because of hysterical symptoms. Before she even stepped into his consultation room, Freud had a set of assumptions that accounted for her disease and the accompanying symptoms. Earlier, he had hypothesized that hysteria occurred when stimuli accumulated in the mind and remained trapped there because of inadequate pathways for discharge. Relying on this view of pathogenesis, Freud quickly concluded that Elizabeth was suffering from repressed memories that had left her with strangled affects, which had become translated into specific symptoms. Note his distinction between the empirical or descriptive symptoms and the underlying concept of strangled affects.

Freud had not only a pre-existing theory of pathogenesis but also a theory of therapeutic action. If he could join the here-and-now symptom with the there-and-then affect, he theorized, the "sluices of motility" would be opened, and the patient would become well. He had also designed a technique to bridge pathogenesis and therapeutic action, which thereby brought about the cure. He would let Elizabeth talk freely, deduce what her pathogenic memories were, and then offer them to her. Once she accepted his offering, the past would link with the present, and catharsis would follow. Note the interpersonal and the intrapsychic at work: she would talk, he would deduce, then he would offer a bridge, she would accept, and, consequently, electric-like currents would cause something to happen in her brain, and she would get well. His theory of technique entailed bridging repressed memories and feelings; therapeutic action was the yield of that link.

Freud listened to her talk freely, implemented his capacities for reason and inference, and, after a brief while, offered her the products of his deductive powers. He told her that she had a forbidden love for her employer. This was to be the curative link.

A surprise. Elizabeth declined his offering. Freud, undaunted, considered her recalcitrance. When he concluded that she was only resisting the recall he pressed her to try harder. In fact, he literally pressed his hand on her forehead, applying leverage to his inherent authority as her physician. You will remember! he asserted by this action. He was determined to make that potentially curative linkage even if a bit of medical coercion was required. Technically, such authority was fundamental to the therapeutic process in the 1890s. At length, she submitted. She remembered what he had inferred would be there, affect and memory were joined, and Elizabeth von R. became an instructive chapter in *Studies in Hysteria* (Breuer and Freud, 1893–1895).

We have learned much about mind and brain in the past hundred years. Psychoanalysis has come to be recognized as a far more complex enterprise than was initially thought. In fact, it is hardly justified to use the term "psychoanalysis" for what Freud did with Elizabeth in 1893. Nevertheless, the three conceptual issues flagged as problems in this paper's title are clearly delineated in this illustration: the empirical and the conceptual, the interpersonal and the intrapsychic, a structured as contrasted with an open-ended agenda. However naive Freud's thinking about Elizabeth seems to us today, the overarching framework he created for his work is far from naive. Schematically, Freud integrated the treatment relationship with the therapeutic process. He wove offerings and acceptances into his theories of technique, treatment process, and therapeutic action. He demonstrated that what transpired between the two of them had a recognizable yield within the mind of his patient and could be understood only by conceptualizing the intrapsychic consequences of interventions. The interpersonal actualized the struggle Elizabeth was having within herself. In one graceful stroke, Freud synchronized the operational component of the treatment relationship with his theories of clinical psychoanalysis. Much would change in the next century, but that fundamental framework bearing three overlapping conceptual perspectives would remain largely intact.

Some thoughtful scholar could probably use it to outline many of the developments in psychoanalysis over the ensuing years. For example, when a self psychologist offers empathic attunement, the patient's acceptance of the offering is expected to yield enhanced self-coherence and self-continuity. This statement contains all three conceptual perspectives: technique, process, and therapeutic action. Similarly, when a Jungian analyst connects current experiences with archetypes and myths, the healing effect is attributed to the patient's increased understanding and assimilation of pathogenic influences—even those originating from a remote past. Again: technique, process, therapeutic action.

THE CONCRETE PROPOSAL

In this section, I construct a contemporary proposal about offerings and acceptances based on that Freudian foundation. I cannot claim originality for the proposal, nor can I provide specific details about the influences that have led me to it. One possible source will be described later.

In my view, a contemporary analyst's essential offering is a non-hierarchical partnership in discovering. "Non-hierarchical" refers to an operational relationship characterized by regard and by the renunciation of power; "discovering" implies the capacity to engage and effectively act on unconscious meanings and unrecognized structures. In the 1890s, success was measured by a patient's capacity to accept an analyst's intellectually derived linking offerings. In the 1990s, success is measured by a patient's ability to acquire a more advanced relationship and a more adept adaptive tool.

Most patients have difficulty accepting such an offering. Obstacles and resistances are inevitable and generally plentiful because some patients expect something else from analysts, like authoritative reassurance; or prefer something else, like recognition or compensatory nurturing. Others hope for something else like the buttressing of established perspectives, or search for something like an opportunity for mourning. Others create something different, like transferences. Often, one or another of these expectations, hopes, preferences, searches, creations can be satisfactorily blended into the essential therapeutic transaction without compromising the goal of acquiring the more advanced relationship and liberating tool. On occasion, however, one of these interests may become compelling for a patient. As a consequence, the participants meet at a turbulent interface. Will the original contract be sustained? When equality and new ways of knowing prevail, the crisis has the effect of promoting the analytic work. When they do not prevail, the treatment can be torn apart or forced to become something else.

AMBIGUITIES

Having stated my somewhat novel proposal, I face the next obstacle to its being understood: ambiguity about the relationship itself and ambiguity in the way the relationship impacts upon ways of viewing analytic goals.

The term "non-hierarchical partnership in discovering" can readily be confused with other descriptive and conceptual analytic transactions. A considerable list of such transactions has been compiled since Freud first discovered transference with Dora (Freud, 1895). Adler (1980) focused on differentiating what he called the "traditional" transference from the concepts of the working and therapeutic alliances, the real relationship, and the self-object transferences, including mirroring and idealizing. The therapeutic interaction has also been studied as a setting for "new" objects, displaced objects, projective identifications, and externalizations of aspects of the self and a home for such descriptive terms as positive transference and transference-cure. In more recent years, much has been written about the therapeutic relationship as a rich, unique dyadic exchange, a product of empathic attunement, an expression of the transference/countertransference axis or matrix, and a repository for intersubjective experiences. A non-hierarchical partnership in discovering is different from all of these.

Some of those catalogued relationships draw impetus from the unrecognized past. This is true, for example, of the transference proper, projective identifications, the positive transference, the transference-cure, the transference/countertransference immersion, and, many believe, the working or therapeutic alliance as well. The non-hierarchical partnership has no such leverage. Others are intended to have a direct remedial effect. This is true, for example, of the self-object transferences, the dyadic exchange, the empathic attunement, and the intersubjective experience. The non-hierarchical partnership is strictly a vehicle, not in itself a remedy for anything. The "new" object feature of the therapeutic interaction, especially prominent in child and adolescent treatments, describes the relationship as useful in generating experiences necessary to facilitate the forward pull of an emerging developmental organization. While the non-hierarchical partnership is a novel feature, it is not a necessary ingredient for a new organization. Some of the others in the catalogued list are not truly transactional but are expressions of impaired self-organizations that are to be rectified within the transaction, as in the case of externalization and the self-object transferences. The non-hierarchical partnership, on the contrary, genuinely occurs between the two participants. Finally, some of the relationships imply something unique, a distinctive experience between the participants. This is implied in the real relationship and stipulated as an intrinsic value in some of the descriptions of the dyadic exchange. The non-hierarchical partnership, by contrast, transcends the concrete; it is a more generalizable capacity tapped for analytic work.

It may be more difficult to differentiate the therapeutic (or working) alliance from a non-hierarchical partnership in discovering. However, by distinguishing the therapeutic alliance from my proposal, it should also be possible to overcome confusions introduced about differences in the way goals are viewed.

The therapeutic alliance is conceptualized within a model of process that is principally used to generate interpretations and yield insights. In mobilizing that model, one that some view as "classical," the analyst begins with a pre-established conviction of pathogenesis. The most commonly recognized neurosogens are unresolved oedipal conflicts, rapprochement crises, fractured selves. These have become embedded in the unconscious as fantasies or transformed into pathological structures. The technique is designed to help the patient become aware of one or more of these underlying psychic intruders. Interpretations and genetic reconstruction serve to promote conviction and ultimately bring a coherent narrative home to the patient. With all of it, the patient acquires insight. This sometimes means that the patient accepts what the analyst believes was true all along; indeed, the working alliance is often predicated on the belief that the therapist is always at least slightly ahead of the patient in the "material" and acting as a skillful guide.

This model of psychoanalysis underscores a relationship of hierarchy producing a shared conviction. The non-hierarchical partnership is descriptively and conceptually not the same.

First, the so-called classical model contains a greater potential for analysts to authoritatively promote their perspectives of pathogenesis and for patients merely to comply. A relationship intended to generate interpretations and yield insights can too easily blur into an authoritative interaction.

Secondly, from the analyst's side, offering interpretations is not the same as establishing a setting where patients can make their own discoveries, ones that may surprise even the analyst.

And, thirdly, from the patient's side, acquiring insights is not the same as acquiring the independent capacity for discovering. Acquiring insights, as valuable as that may be, is very different from acquiring the capacity for discovering or, better, for "insighting"—a non-existent transitive verb meaning discovering, integrating, or knowing in a new way. Insights often rely on the analyst's convictions about pathogenesis; independent discoveries never do.

Freud (1913) once explained the so-called fundamental rule to a patient by suggesting that the two of them imagine they were traveling together on a train. The patient had the window seat. The implication about the alliance was clear: the patient was to describe what the terrain looked like and Freud would explain what it meant. I no longer see that analogy as useful in the overseeing analytic transaction because it cedes too much to authority and restricts the opportunity for joint experimentation, inquiry, and synthesis.

The Illustrative Vignette

I hope that I have reduced the obstacles derived from heady abstractions and helped separate my proposal from related descriptions of the analytic relationship. Essentially, it comes to this: hierarchy is different from equality, and insight is different from insighting. But how does all this work with people? It is time for a case.

The case I am about to describe shows, among other things, how readily a patient processes an analyst's offering into something else. This clarifies why the interpersonal yield is best tracked by focusing on what transpires within the mind of the patient rather than dwelling on the intent of the analyst. The vignette also illustrates the distinction between a hierarchical and a non-hierarchical relationship, i.e., between an alliance directed toward offering interpretations and acquiring insights and a partnership directed toward offering equality and the capacity to discover.

A woman in her mid-thirties was referred to me by her previous analyst. As far as he was concerned, the treatment had featured well-constructed and timely interpretations. The patient had a good clinical result: that is, she had insights, she felt better, and in terms of certain areas of functioning she lived a more satisfactory life.

I soon discovered that the getting better that followed those interpretations had little to do with her overcoming resistances to insight. On the contrary, if anything, the obstacles to discovering her self had been buttressed in the work. Neither of them had any idea that this had happened. For that matter, at the outset, nor had I.

Her first treatment had to be interrupted because the analyst moved to another city. The move was a bit precipitous, and the patient reacted with surprise, resentment, and eventually outrage. She felt her treatment was incomplete: there were still some serious problems in her marriage, her career was unsettled, and she wanted another child.

Her analyst offered her the names of replacements to continue the work. She turned down several for what seemed to be one reasonable excuse after another. I was the fourth name on her list. She found me more acceptable, partly because the departing analyst had come up with my name with a certain exasperation ("Enough is enough, already!") and partly because she had sufficiently expended some of her wrath and displeasure about the abandonment on the three initial prospects.

We agreed that a treatment committed to discovering unrecognized features of her mind was the way to go. She accepted the tasks that were to be divided between us and agreed on a contract that contained the goal of discovering more about herself.

Matters moved along smoothly between us for a while in spite of frequent emotional storms. Naturally, I was sensitive to the issue of her analyst's abrupt departure and helped her talk about it openly. She described how much she had admired him and valued his explanations. She especially recalled some key interpretations that occurred whenever she became furious. At those times, he would tell her that her anger was understandable in the face of provocations of her husband and co-workers. He also explained the intensity of her feelings as derivatives of equivalent concealed emotions that had originated in the early mother-daughter relationship.

She always experienced enormous relief from these interpretations and reconstructions. He linked her rage to specific here-and-now precipitants, and he accounted for its intensity by links to there-and-then episodes of being victimized by a tyrannical mother. The exchange between the two seemed analytically pure: the patient detailed events, the analyst interpreted their meaning, he rooted them in historical details, and the patient felt better.

I listened to the new explosive outbursts precipitated by her change of analysts. I suppose I could have said that her present anger was another reaction to the very real disappointment connected to the abrupt interruption; and I could have hypothesized that its intensity was rooted in early abandonments. But, I did neither. I waited, hoping that my attentive silence would promote the kind of climate that would facilitate her discovering. This was not to be a setting in which she talked and I explained but rather one in which she talked, she and I listened, and one or the other raised questions or hypotheses while both continuously jointly evaluated the proceedings.

As soon as she recognized that the interpretations she was accustomed to hear about her rage were not forthcoming, she complained bitterly. Had I nothing to say about her fury? Where were my linking skills? My intention in offering attentive silence was to promote the agreed-upon analytic transaction. However, she processed my offering in a surprising way. She did not conclude that my silence meant that I was incompetent or stupid, nor that I was provocative or uncaring. What she did say was that my silence was an indictment; it meant that I believed she had a very serious mental illness. I had not promptly interpreted her rage as a *reasonable* reaction to her analyst's departure nor had I accounted for its intensity by citing aspects of her infantile life. To her, this could mean only that I thought she was crazy or evil for feeling so angry.

I wondered how she got there. She explained. Whenever her previous analyst had interpreted her aggressive behavior as appropriate and reconstructed it in terms of antecedent mother-child confrontations, she had accepted his offering as a judgment of her sanity: a competent authority was conferring the diagnosis of rational-but-upset-person rather than crazy or evil person. As far as she was concerned, the diagnosis secreted within his explanations was a more important offering than all the links to antecedents and dynamics combined. She had been quieted by the implicit reassurance that she was a normal woman rather than by his explanations of meanings.

I asked about her concern about being evil or crazy. Over a period of months an extraordinary chronicle unfolded, one that featured her dread of death and psychosis and how she had managed it throughout her life. She explained that she had always harbored the view that she was some kind of witch. In addition, she secretly believed that she had lived many past lives and fully expected to live future ones. After a while, she described a long-standing conviction that much of the psychological distress that had brought her to treatment was justly inflicted on her present life because of some evil acts she had committed in past ones. The worst of these was the murder of a child named William in the twelfth century. Pain was necessary for her eventual redemption. She cited a rich literature authoritatively documenting such occurrences and urged me to become acquainted with that literature. She was aware of my interest but almost certainly sensed my skepticism.

She had been hesitant about discussing these ideas in her prior treatment because she was convinced that her first analyst would ridicule her. He was a down-to-earth, rational kind of person. More importantly, she held back because she preferred that her ideas not be challenged. She explained that she was even more afraid of dying than of going out-of-control crazy. Being a witch, as awful as that might be, was at least an implicit assurance that she would never die. It dawned upon me that by interpreting her rage dynamically and reconstructing its genetic roots, her analyst was unwittingly assuring that she was both normal and immortal. It was no wonder she always felt better.

His activities buttressed her established defensive positions while unwittingly enhancing obstacles to further self-inquiry and discovering. Her panic at the prospect of murder, on the one hand, and death, on the other, was held in check by unrecognized support masked as an alliance characterized by interpretations and insights. Her psychological equilibrium was stabilized as long as the implicit authoritative hierarchical relationship was kept in place. Her analyst was convinced that what he offered was true, and she built upon this conviction. When he left, the equilibrium was threatened.

Once she recognized the different tone of my offerings, the feared breakdown happened. She developed choking and gasping symptoms that reminded her of moments of near terror. As a child she had always felt helplessly vulnerable whenever she was alone; death felt close at hand, a death that was certain to follow once her breathing was fully compromised by panic. She also felt out of control when unattended. She had always harbored destructive feelings for her younger siblings and believed she was capable of acting on these feelings. She was forever suspended between personal annihilation and murderous intent.

Together, we studied how she had summoned her fertile imagination to provide a richly embellished adaptive fantasy to rescue her from the panic, rage, and suffering. We learned that if she were a witch, her dread of death was reduced because her life could never be extinguished. This also made it easier to account for her murderous feelings as the residue of some real event in a past life rather than a current wish. And it explained her abiding sense of guilt because it was attached to a genuine act, one in ancient history to be sure, but a real act nevertheless. However, if she were neither an immortal witch nor part of an expectable sequence of lives, then the dead were really dead, she was crazy, and murder was a likely prospect rather than merely an eight-hundred-year-old memory. Her remarkable system left her with the somewhat reduced fear of being an object of disapproval and the requirement to atone for ancient misdeeds, but there were ways to mute such pains and she was adept at those ways. A variety of dangers centered about death and sadism and psychoses had been concealed and held in a delicate balance through an elaborate reparative and adaptive unconscious fantasy.

Now about that word, "together."

Almost all analysts describe sections of clinical work as expressions of "togetherness." But the word "together" does not discriminate between a hierarchical together and a non-hierarchical one. The "we" in such reports may reflect a partnership characterized by domination and compliance just as easily as equality. In the "together" I described, I tried to renounce authority, even when the patient demanded that I assume it, and also tried to track the obstacles to what I viewed as truly essential: her acceptance of my offering of a non-hierarchical partnership in discovering. Sometimes such an effort is reflected more in the climate of the interaction than in the verbatim exchanges. For example, when my patient told me about being a witch, I expressed a grunt of surprise and urged her to elaborate. I do not believe that my response was experienced as either validating or ridiculing. She spoke of the idea for a while, then shifted to issues of death. It was more her idea than mine that being a witch was an assurance of immortality. I found myself saying something like, "Oh, yes, I see how that would work."

She moved on to recall a life long fear of mannequins. She said she always turned her head away when she passed store windows. She dreaded being near or touching a mannequin. They were like the dead, she explained. She was haunted by the idea that one might speak if she drew too near or, worse, that she could detect something animate in the texture of the figure if she touched it. She would never go to funerals; they were intolerable. This led her to her theories about sequential lives. She mentioned the many books she owned on the subject. I commented that one advantage of such a theory might be that it was another path to immortality. She agreed, shrewdly noting, however, that her use of theory to quiet her fears did not necessarily make that theory invalid.

She described a dream in which she gave birth to a dead baby boy. In the dream she showed him to her first analyst and to me and we both experienced a sudden "aha!" The dead baby finally persuaded us that she really had murdered a William some time in the past; giving birth to a dead child was an appropriate retaliation. In the year or so that all of this was engaged in her treatment, she had the second child she had been constrained to conceive. To her delight it was a boy, and it was not born dead.

I could follow her thoughts from her dread of retaliation and death to the protective retreat into visions of immortality. However, she seemed beyond viewing the sequence merely in defensive and adaptive terms. For her, immortality was a real possibility, even a necessary belief. What she now wanted from her treatment was the validation of her views by a respected authority.

At this point, a traditional psychoanalytic anecdote usually leads to a description of how the patient finally came to terms with her anxiety, accepted what had been discovered, grasped the adaptive value of her beliefs, disavowed them, and became another psychoanalytic treatment triumph. Regrettably, that is not what happened.

At first, she cooperated in the hesitant way I have briefly illustrated, but the feeling of panic prevailed. Looking back, I realize that her capacity to generate intense anxiety had not been adequately recognized in either of her two treatments. After a considerable struggle involving complex attitudes and feelings about me, she decided to repudiate my offering, a direction, I suppose, already heralded in her triumphant dream of the dead baby.

Rather than dwell upon what we might further discover in her head, she proposed a counteroffer. Her proposal had the advantage, she argued, of guaranteeing to quiet her anxious state more rapidly than psychoanalysis.

Insisting with renewed vigor that the defining site of her illness lay some eight hundred years in the past, she suggested that I hypnotize her, return her to that time, and bring back the memories of the murder of William that so haunted her. Re-uniting past events with her present affective turmoil would yield an old-fashioned cathartic discharge and cure. She assured me that there were many books documenting the effectiveness of such an approach as well as its scientific validity.

Notice the new contract she was proposing: the treatment relationship would be hierarchical and authoritative (I would control her through hypnosis and guide her back), and the site for exploration and discovery would be relocated from the intra-psychic in the present to England in the twelfth century. I would take her to the pathogens she knew had invaded her contemporary life. She assured me that if I agreed to this working alliance, she would have the courage to endure the journey and be liberated at last, her need to suffer finally overcome.

We met at a turbulent interface: she insisted on a cure by solving a dilemma in the distant past, while I offered a different adaptive implement: self-discovery and new ways of knowing. Her mode of coping would leave the illusion of immortality intact and assuage her abiding dread. Mine required her to know her feelings and the repository of memories and desires that informed her beliefs; and while she accepted the view that all of that might be useful, it offered her no reassurance against dying.

Because her approach held the promise of instantly quelling the erupting emotions, it became her main goal—one that I would not fulfill. She interrupted the treatment to find an expert who would take her to the place she knew existed. She had a list of reputable authorities on the subject. If her journey failed, she said on leaving, she would return.

She was disappointed that I would not accept her contract, and I was disappointed that she could not accept mine; I suspect that those reading this vignette also may be disappointed by such an outcome. Perhaps the heavy climate of disappointment expresses another essential, albeit inadequately, recognized feature of the patient that had not been properly fielded in either of her treatments.

However, having presented a clinical failure to illustrate my proposal, I face the last of the many problems I have encountered in offering my proposal, and perhaps the most difficult to overcome of all, a tactical one. The purpose of this paper is to demonstrate the value of concentrating on obstacles patients face in acquiring specific achievements in object relationships and adaptive capacities. This contrasts with the customary focus on resistances to uncovering past pathogens. I had promised to promote my proposal with a clinical vignette. It was reasonable to assume that the illustrative anecdote would demonstrate the benefit of such a way of proceeding by providing a *rewarding* outcome. Clinical cases customarily celebrate success, thereby implicitly confirming the inherent propositions of a paper. How can a vignette divested of such customary leverage still be persuasive?

One thing can be said about disagreeable outcomes: they stimulate critical thinking.

At that turbulent interface when she sought to radically change our contract, my patient renounced my offer of equality and self-inquiry; instead, she urged me to commandingly lead her to an etiologic time and place she had mapped out clearly in advance. She insisted that the newly transformed treatment become a setting for her to confirm what she already believed. By adopting such a pose, she precisely illustrated the pernicious approach to practicing analysis that I have denounced, an approach oriented toward confirming rather than discovering. Perhaps, by articulating her position in such a compelling way, she may have provided a more illuminating demonstration of the essence of my arguments about methods and goals by failing than she might have been able to do by getting well.

SUMMARY AND DISCUSSION

One simple way to describe clinical work is to say that therapists offer and patients accept. This statement, however, expresses several overlapping conceptual issues—technique and therapeutic action, interpersonal and intra-psychic, an unstructured as contrasted with a preconfigured agenda. Psychotherapies can be categorized by the kinds of offerings and the varieties of acceptances—that is, by the features of technique and therapeutic action.

A distinguishing feature of psychoanalysis is that an analyst principally offers how to discover, not what to discover, in a climate of non-hierarchical partnering. As a result those patients who successfully conclude analysis take with them a greater tolerance for ambiguities, a better way to continue to explore them, and the prospect of extending a newly won way of relating to others. This proposal orients an analyst toward a genuinely cooperative interaction, to the task of promoting discovering, and toward new future opportunities for relating and coping.

I have further suggested that analytic patients invariably resist such offerings. They transform the proposed climate of discovering into many other things. The psychoanalytic process unfolds as each of the inevitable resistances to the new capacities for relating and adapting is engaged and overcome. A patient has successfully terminated analysis once the more advanced object relationship has been established and the advantages of a continuing self-inquiry have been consolidated. I view such an outcome as the signature goal of analysis proper.

I offered a vignette to illustrate the proposal. My anecdote, an attempt to illustrate the usefulness of the proposal, was offered to emphasize the method of inquiry and the climate that best informs that method. Regrettably, the case failed. However, while a failed case may compromise theories of pathogenesis, it does not necessarily compromise instruction in method. In fact, some features of the failure underscore the argument, rather than undermine it.

I conclude with one application of this proposal that may be relevant for child analytic work.

When analysts relate to children they make every effort to differentiate their roles from those assigned by parents or expected by children. They extend a special form of partnership, something so different from what youngsters expect that sometimes it jars them. After a while, children generally come to recognize the uniqueness of the relationship. The interaction is principally applied toward tapping new ways of knowing through words, play, or behavior. Child analysts propose such a partnership and stimulate new ways of knowing because they are oriented more toward future possibilities than past pathogens.

These three features—the novel relationship, facilitating different ways of knowing, the orientation to new possibilities—are fundamental to child work. They appear to be very similar to the central components of the proposed non-hierarchical partnership in discovering.

Therefore, I believe that the proposal can be usefully extended to children and adolescents.

Some thoughtful person might offer the argument that one reason a non-hierarchical partnership in discovery seems so readily applicable to child work is that it is a derivative of experiences accrued with children in the first place. The evidence strongly supports such an argument. This paper may well be another illustration of how child psychoanalysis can provide the foundation for proposing some technical innovations useful in adult analytic work.

BIBLIOGRAPHY

ADLER, G. (1980). Transference, real relationships and alliance. *Int. J. Psycho-Anal.*, 61:547–558.
BREUER, J., and Freud, S., (1893–95). Studies in hysteria, *S.E.*, 2:135–169.
FREUD, S. (1905). Fragment of an analysis of a case of hysteria. *S.E.*, 7:3–122.
FREUD, S. (1913). On beginning the treatment. *S.E.*, 12:121–144.

Undoing the Lag in the Technique of Conflict and Defense Analysis

PAUL GRAY, M.D.

When the individual skills of a psychotherapist or psychoanalyst coincide with what serves as a sublimation for the practitioner, the gratification in the clinical work is especially enhanced. If those moments of applied skill also are a part of the specific therapeutic action of that form of treatment, a fortunate combination exists. As Freud expanded the potential of psychoanalytic treatment when he reformulated the theory of anxiety, he also provided access to improved therapeutic actions in the course of analyzing intrapsychic conflict. This meant that some of the sublimations in practicing the earlier techniques no longer coincided with what could be the therapeutic actions characteristic of the more effective analysis of conflict. The lag in adding new technical measures to psychoanalytic methodology is more fully accounted for by a reluctance on the part of some analysts to sacrifice certain traditional sources of sublimated projection in interpretations *and to seek other sublimations commensurate with Freud's more advanced view of analyzing defenses.*

GRATIFICATIONS AND SUBLIMATIONS IN THE ART OF INTERPRETATION

A tendency to conduct analyses in ways that are contradictory to our later developments in psychoanalytic theory is influenced, but not suf-

Training and supervising analyst emeritus at the Baltimore-Washington Institute for Psychoanalysis.

The Psychoanalytic Study of the Child 51, ed. Albert J. Solnit, Peter B. Neubauer, Samuel Abrams, and A. Scott Dowling (Yale University Press, copyright © 1996 by Albert J. Solnit, Peter B. Neubauer, Samuel Abrams, and A. Scott Dowling).

ficiently explained, by the fact that what we hold on to is familiar and traditional.

In this chapter I present my most recent hypotheses to explain the lag among analysts in applying to their methodology the full implications of Freud's structural theory as radically modified by his revision of the role of anxiety in the formation of neuroses. Included are, on the one hand, the tenacity of the opportunity for sublimation that the traditional methodology provides for the analyst and, on the other hand, the resistance analysts show to increasing their direct exposure to the patient's live drive derivatives and any concomitant expansion of their knowledge of the ego's defensive roles in response to conflict. Next I present an updated series of characteristics that differentiate between so-called traditional analytic technique and close process attention to the defensive activities in the field of the conscious ego. Finally, I make some observations about the potential gratifications the latter methodology offers to the individual analyst.

Waelder's (1954) metaphor that some of the mind's "jungle" had been "cleared" and that we should try to hold back its regrowth has become misconstrued so that the "jungle" is regarded as something growing from "outside" in rather than, as a better reading of the metaphor implies, that the defensive tangle would tend to grow on the very ground that had been "cleared." By maintaining the clearing Waelder meant reducing the analyst's resistance to having a clearer view of the mind in the first place. What has happened is that Freud, with his newer view of the nature of anxiety and a greater role for the ego, eventually provided us all with an even larger clearing in the mind. Many analysts accustomed to working within the original context are still defending that original clearing, but without including the larger cleared area to which Freud drew attention.

The characteristics of the wider clearing are represented by the concepts regarding the ego and consciousness itself. The neglect of consciousness, which Opitow (1989) aptly calls "the stepchild of psychoanalysis" (p. 645), is a prime example of analysts clinging to the original "clearing." Because the most charismatically influential force is associated with the most esteemed leader, Freud's own ambivalence (Gray, 1994) about making a greater use of his own wider clearing seems to have served as an example for many of his followers. The most telling evidence of this ambivalence is suggested by Freud's own characterization of where he wished to remain with his personal analytic technique. Freud declared to the others "follow your *own* style: but when you report on what I have done, remember that my watchword has always been: *more darkness*" (Waelder, 1960, p. 84; emphasis added.)[1] Considering that so many analysts shared this predilection for the "darkness," it appears as though Freud had espoused the contrary principle: "Do as I do, not as I say."

Although the earliest analysts very likely tried to do as Freud did because of their real and transferential esteem for him, admiration for Freud is not sufficient to explain the continued need to hold on to so many aspects of his early method. From my own experience with techniques of listening and interpreting, I have come to believe that, on the one hand, the specific sublimations that accompany the practice of analysis provide analysts with important satisfactions that are difficult to surrender or suspend. On the other hand, contemplation of a wider clearing, with the greater "light" that comes from a consistent emphasis on defense analysis, can evoke conflict in analysts over the possibility of having personally to face patients' sharply revealed instinctual derivatives, in particular those of aggression.

In support of this hypothesis, let us see what Freud and other analysts have said. I referred above to sublimations in the work not only to capture the degree of gratification that the various ways of being an analyst can provide but also to remind us that finding satisfaction in being an analyst is not a universal characteristic.

Gratification stemming from the aesthetic and creative components of traditional analysis silently confirms and enhances the analyst's sense that his hypothesized interpretations are correct. Freud (1936) recognized that the form of his attention to the patient's material was idiosyncratic and that he had gathered about him individuals who shared his characteristic of being able to "look at the material . . . in a *quite special way*." He felt that achieving success in the work required a skill that was part of the analyst's personality: as he put it, "A kind of sharpness of hearing for what is unconscious and repressed, *which is not possessed equally by everyone, has a part to play* (S.E. 20, p. 219 emphasis added). Therein lies a clue to our delay in taking methodological advantage of the most advanced Freudian theory.

In the beginning, it was the possession of that capacity for "hearing what is unconscious and repressed" that led, usually via self-selection, to entry into Freud's circle of analytic colleagues. Other personal characteristics were not unimportant, but as "training" became more formalized, it was for many years precisely that very capacity that counted most in the selection of candidates. As time went on candidates were

1. Here Freud, while using the metaphor of being a painter to characterize the work of analysis, was alluding to the alleged last words of Goethe: "More light" (Waelder, 1960, p. 84).

accepted whose skill of that kind was considerable but also some candidates in whom it was negligible. We now commonly recognize that this personality characteristic is something that one either has or does not have. It cannot be taught.

Arlow (1979) gives probably the most detailed attention to the working characteristics of someone with a traditional, "natural" analytic listening capacity when he discusses his own mental processes as they contribute to his initial, precognitive activity in making interpretations. When in the past, or selectively in the present, I have used the traditional interpretive method with certain types of patients, my own attention and intrapsychic work with a patient's productions are close to Arlow's description. Arlow divides his mental activities before he makes interpretations into "aesthetic and cognitive components"; the former, about which I write here, include introspection, intuition, and empathy, and are the "intriguing and dramatic phase." The various matters that the patient communicates are "elaborated and conceptualized [by the analyst] *unconsciously*, i.e., intuitively. *There is something intensely aesthetic and creative about this mode of functioning*" (JAPA, 1979, p. 201, emphasis added).

As Arlow says, this mode can occur with a rapidity that "suggests magical insight . . . especially when the patient's next productions correspond exactly to what the analyst had been thinking but had not yet said." In the material quoted and elsewhere (Arlow, 1993), he has conveyed an important, maybe the most important, source of gratification inherent in the traditional interpretive mode of analytic technique. Here, the analyst finds that aspect of the work "intriguing and dramatic" and "intensely" appealing.

This description does not yet explain the intensity of the appeal. We may understand this intensity by noting that the heightened and appealing affect on the part of the analyst *occurs at the very moment of sensing data that stimulates in the analyst the sudden conclusion (hypothesis) that there is present in someone else (the analysand) a constellation containing a drive derivative that only a moment before existed in an unconscious form within the analyst*. With that moment of conviction a sudden gratifying change in the analyst's equilibrium occurs. The analyst's experience, within a clinical setting that is superego-syntonic, can be intense and, I believe, involves a sublimation. Whether this process includes projective identification (Arlow feels "strongly" that it does not), the analyst has experienced some version of his own previously repressed unconscious material *now having an external context* in which he has coincidentally created an opportunity for *a sublimated version of projection*. Brenner (1976) has clarified the distinction between an ego capacity and its use as defense, with defense being the outcome. Obviously I regard projection as an ego capacity; its sublimated use in the act of interpretation is not necessarily a defense, but is a nonpathological opportunity for projection.

By just listening to an experienced analyst report such pre-interpretive insights a member of a conference audience or a supervisee can readily be caught up in the impressive magic of the moment. Noting the audible responses from many impressed members of clinical conferences or the chuckles of recognition, I suggest that the discharge-like process includes an aspect of Freud's observations on the dynamics in *Jokes and the Unconscious* (1905). We often generalize the cliché "fascination with the id" and obscure the fact that the "fascinating" material is always in *someone else's id*.

Creative experience can be a strong source of satisfaction. One either has or does not have creativity. It is not a question of whether sources of creation are of value; the therapeutic results of the interpretive approach, "using" the unconscious of the analyst in a significant way, are well known. Nevertheless, we should ask why Freud, after revising the heart of his theory of the neuroses with his newer discoveries regarding anxiety and the more detailed role of the ego, did not develop an ego-appropriate technique in addition to his capacity to "work in the darkness."

Let us consider one more way in which traditional analytic technique may include for the analyst avenues of sublimation that may inadvertently limit even more advantageous or effective therapeutic actions for the analysand. Freud (1915) familiarized us with the fact that if the analyst's comments have touched on, or near, a repressed element, the patient's equilibrium is suddenly disturbed. The various manifestations of this fact depend on the nature of a then newly formed compromise formation. There remains the relevant question to what extent having this power to disrupt a patient's defended equilibrium through interpretation is an avenue of the analyst's sublimated aggression. Certainly it is a procedure that depends on overcoming the analysand's defenses rather than analyzing them. A patient with a history of a helpful earlier analysis came for treatment to a new analyst who was more interested in defense analysis than his previous analyst. The patient responded to an opportunity provided by his analyst to reflect on the details of his ego's defensive activity with: "I don't want to look at that, just zap me with an interpretation."

Historically, authoritative power has always been a central aspect of analytic technique on which much of the therapeutic action depended. Freud's revision of the theory of anxiety made dependence on that particular source of therapeutic action obsolete, or at least unnecessary. Sterba (1941) identified the tendency of some analysts to seek gratification by making open "interpretations" of the behavior or manners of fellow guests in social settings. Although he underlined the inappropriateness of such ego disruptiveness and clinically illustrated some unconscious impulses motivating these "cocktail party analyses," he implied that the same sort of "interpretation" might be appropriate in clinical settings. Analysts still repeat an adage that captures the necessarily confrontational, aggressive aspects of early analytic methodology: "If you want to make an omelet, you have to break eggs."

I do not believe that only those of us who have what Reik feliciously called a "third ear" can enjoy the gratification that comes from making interpretations. There are analysts who do not experience much of a third-ear phenomenon but who acquire over time, on the basis of clinical experience and academic learning, an accumulation of a wide range of relevant templates or registrations of dynamic and genetic possibilities cognitively retrievable for interpretations. They also may experience intense satisfaction when they recognize that they have made a "good" interpretation. A traditional mode of teaching analytically oriented psychotherapy makes wide use of furthering the learned acquisition of "interpretive skills." I believe that the gratifications from these moments of interpretive "success" often equal or exceed those derived from therapeutic success itself.

COMPARING TRADITIONAL WITH DEFENSE ANALYSIS USING CLOSE PROCESS ATTENTION

TRADITIONAL ANALYSIS	DEFENSE ANALYSIS USING CLOSE PROCESS ATTENTION
1. In preparing for *interpretations*, traditional analysts turn their attention to awareness of their own "free associations" to the material. This may mean creative ways of resonating to their own unconscious (this is a listening capacity that cannot be taught) or drawing rapidly on their memory of acquired knowledge of hypothetically relevant dynamics or meanings.	1. In preparing for *interventions*, analysts practicing close process attention focus consistently on patients' verbal/vocal flow of material. Analysts' comprehension and memory of what they are observing in this manifest field is of central importance, but they do not use their own unconsciously influenced "free association." This is a form of analytic listening that can be taught.
2. Listening often includes attention to the probability of displacements as	2. The phenomenon of displacement is of importance only when it occurs

TRADITIONAL ANALYSIS

represented by what patients are verbalizing. Traditional analysts seek evidence of drive derivative across the repression barrier.

3. The traditional analyst may draw *connections* as part of the interpretive activity by pointing out to the patient those associations that on the basis of elements the analyst senses as familiar, have a demonstrable relationship to other material.

4. To a considerable extent the traditional analyst carries out dream analysis in the very early traditional form—i.e., asking the patient for "associations" to various elements of apparent importance. The assumption is that the associated elements coming to mind in that connection will be significantly closer to the material that is being repressed or warded off. The requests for associations take place in an atmosphere in which the analyst's authority, by virtue of transference, is present in an influential way and is assumed to help *overcome* resistance.

5. In making interpretations, traditional analysts convey their impression about something that they believe exists outside of consciousness (dynamically so, because it is being defended against). They may give such interpretations in authoritative ways or in ways that convey the idea as a tentatively held hypothesis. In either case they attempt to reach across a

DEFENSE ANALYSIS USING CLOSE PROCESS ATTENTION

clearly within the manifest sequence so that the analyst can demonstrate it to the patient as a defense against identifiable drive derivative.

3. In using close process attention, defense analysts do not need to draw "connections," because, if they carry out the central task of analyzing the defenses against emerging material containing conflicted drive derivatives, such an activity would be at least redundant and possibly distracting.

4. The defense analyst observes dream material and responds by noting its place in the sequence of vocalized material, as one would note anything else. The analyst assumes that the act of *telling the dream* will be at once stimulated by and subject to the ego's defense activity with the same alertness to conditions of *safety* to which the ego subjects all of the patient's productions once the analysis is undertaken. Defense analysts implicitly assume that, although asking for "associations" might indeed partially overcome the resistance, the ego, under the influence of defense, would have no problem in guiding these associations away from the immediate conflict instead of toward it.

5. The analyst using close process *intervenes* (rather than interprets) at any suitable opportunity to demonstrate to the patient some aspect of the ego's defensive activities against demonstrable elements of drive derivative and in that order, defense first, then drive. It is best to do this close to the moment the defense occurred. The defense analyst assumes that the drive

TRADITIONAL ANALYSIS	DEFENSE ANALYSIS USING CLOSE PROCESS ATTENTION
barrier of unconscious defense with the support of suggestion.	derivative that has been moved out of awareness by the defense is not repressed but is accessible if attention is directed to it.
6. Based on the material and appropriate timing, transference interpretations are made whenever traditional analysts conclude that they have become the object of ideas, impulses, and fantasies, which are or were also "cathected" to earlier figures of importance. In general, they are less likely regularly to interpret the authoritative images of transference than those where the analyst is the object of drive derivatives, because the former is the influential power that is needed to assist in conditionally overcoming resistance. This significantly limits the actual analysis of the superego elements within the ego.	6. In close process work, defense analysts make transference inquiries only in reference to the patient's ubiquitous, defense-motivated transference of an inhibiting authority or an affectionately permissive authority. Patients rapidly mobilize defense transferences of authority on an ad hoc basis. The analyst inquires about the nature of the ostensible risks or fantasied consequences whenever occasions arise that make it possible for the analyst to demonstrate successfully the occurrence of conflict and defense within what patients have been vocalizing. By "successfully" I mean that, as a result of the analyst's demonstration, the patient has clearly and *affectively reengaged the conflicted material.* The analyst assumes that the patient's perception of the presence of the listening analyst is distorted by defense-transference and that the patient senses the analyst at a conscious level, though not uncommonly at the periphery of awareness. Patients show differing degrees of reluctance to turn attention to the image of the listening analyst. The capacity to fully, consciously, look *in the mind* toward the analyst is usually inhibited. If necessary, the analyst may point to the patient's inhibition over attempting to observe and explore the details of that transference fantasy image, but the analyst does not attempt to hypothesize beyond a barrier of repression to achieve the patient's recognition and elaboration of it.

TRADITIONAL ANALYSIS

7. When traditional analysts give conceptual consideration to "overcoming the Oedipus complex," they not uncommonly stress the "giving up" of a "fixation" associated with certain *unconscious gratification*.

8. The *context* of the material to which the traditional analyst is listening and referring may vary. It may be in the past, the future, or the present.

DEFENSE ANALYSIS USING CLOSE PROCESS ATTENTION

7. Defense analysts regard a patient's being under the influence of the Oedipus complex as taking place under the ego's function of regression, serving a primary role in assuring "safety" via its *defensive activity*. That particular regression tries to reinstate triangular conditions so dangerously inherent in incestuous longings that the patient would have inhibited them. Therefore, it is not a matter of the patient's "giving up" certain emphasized "infantile" behavior but of analyzing the fears of more maturely gratifying states of ego function, so that defensive regression to such unconscious oedipal influence is unnecessary, and choice becomes possible. Ever since the revision of the theory of anxiety, "unconscious gratification" has been unnecessary theoretical baggage; it is not necessarily wrong, but for an analyst to draw attention to it is unanalytically manipulative, as it cannot help but stimulate the superego actively.

8. The *context* of the material to which the defense analyst is listening is optimally the *immediate one* (i.e., the content as it is being expressed). (Note: though this corresponds to the "here and now," it does *not* mean the same as "transference only.") Of course, the analyst is aware that patients' context of the experience, as they speak, may be the past, future, or immediate present. The intention of the analyst's intervening communications is appropriately to draw the patients' focus of attention to the awareness of the *process* taking place within the manifest sequence of the material task of ver-

TRADITIONAL ANALYSIS	DEFENSE ANALYSIS USING CLOSE PROCESS ATTENTION
	balized spontaneity—that is, the ego's immediate processing of what patients are manifestly *exposing* in the setting of the transference of authority.
9. In general, the traditional analyst ultimately regards drive derivatives associated with libido and aggression as of equal priority.	9. The focus of the defense analyst's attention to the sequence of what the patient manifestly reports typically reveals a predominance of various versions of the ego's superego defense of turning aggression on the self. Although this is often true (as in the case of obsessionals), because of the patient's tendency for regression to ambivalent issues and dynamics, the analyst's attention to the importance of defenses against aggressive derivatives is important. This is in keeping with Freud's late formulation (S.E. 21 p. 138) regarding the essential ingredient of aggression in the context of incestuous impulses. In no way does this diminish the importance of analyzing defenses against revealing libidinal derivatives, but when the emphasis in the analysis of defenses against aggression is missing, the result too often is failure to analyze fears of aggressive derivatives sufficiently.
10. Traditional technical attention to the patient's experiences of memory varies considerably and is difficult to generalize. Although ambiguities abound in the way traditional analysts use memory, one clear description comes from those who regard transference as "a way of remembering" (Freud) and who treat the patient's experiencing of the analyst as a defense against memories rather than against instinctual drive derivatives.	10. The defense analyst must be aware of how effectively the patient's capacity to experience in the past context, even as he speaks (memory or reference to the past), may serve as a distancing device to displace attention away from the immediate context. There, after all, is where the mind (and the neural system) is having to cope with the danger of anxiety. (see N. Reider, 1950).

GRATIFICATIONS AND SUBLIMATIONS IN CLOSE PROCESS ATTENTION
DURING DEFENSE ANALYSIS

Let us now consider work satisfactions in the practice of and emphasis on close process attention during defense analysis. The invitation and rationale for making use of phenomenological data were never more unequivocally stated than when Anna Freud wrote: "Id-derivatives— force their way into consciousness. . . . The ego bestirs itself again— and by means of one or other of its customary [defenses] intervenes in the flow of associations. . . . The analyst has an opportunity of *witnessing*) [and here I would add: *and demonstrating to the patient*] then and there the putting into operation by the [ego] of one of those defensive measures against the id . . . *and to make it the object of his investigation*" (1936, pp. 13–14 emphasis added). Unfortunately she did not candidly acknowledge that the necessary revision of the analytic focus of attention, like most new skills, takes time to acquire. Short of being a genius, a musician accomplished on one instrument does not usually pick up another instrument and play it adequately without significant practice. It is common for analysts to find that an intellectual understanding of Anna Freud's change of focus, with its emphasis on perceiving the ego's conscious activities relevant to defense analysis, does not lead at once to the ability to sustain that focus throughout the analytic hour.

As Anna Freud described, once the analyst has learned to change the focus of attention, the opportunities for observing conflict and solution *as they occur* become readily available. Though I know of a number of analysts who have put in the required time and successfully acquired that skill, nevertheless I do not believe that they were able to do so because they were patient. Rather, I believe that they were able to contend adequately with the drive derivatives that this method inexorably brought to the patient's full consciousness and also that they found a fresh and interesting factor, one that Anna Freud (1979) described so well: "As I see it, the reluctance of analysts to deal with the ego aspects comes from a *lack of fascination with the intertwining forces within the mind*, . . . I think . . . it is the constant intertwining battle, the never ending efforts from one side of the personality to come to terms with the other which is the real analytic pleasure."

There is less occasion for sublimation of projection when analysts observe the conscious surface of the patient's verbalizations for evidence of *manifest* drive derivatives in conflict. However, there is room for other forms of sublimated gratification when the analyst witnesses progress within the process and experiences a spectator's pleasure in a "constructive" context. Defense analysts who are not conflicted or instinctually excited by instinctualized material can confirm this. In a recent research seminar, an analyst described a private sense of pleasure at the clear evidence of the growing ego strength of a patient who could now set aside a traditional need to turn upon himself aggressive derivatives, intense, raw, and sadistic in form, and instead experience and verbalize them, undisplaced toward the analyst; the process brought with it, for the analyst, the bonus of a gratifying sense that this patient now was not apt to flee the analysis in fear.

To Anna Freud's description of sources of gratification I add the defense analyst's potential for sublimation of an *unconflicted capacity for an attitude of receptivity:* not in a passive-inactive sense, but in the analyst's readiness to provide the patient with conditions and insights for an analytic process that allows the patient to feel progressively safe to experience *and reveal* greater degrees of actual drive derivative *impulses toward the analyst.* These are conscious, conflicted instinctual affects or energies that patients are trying to accommodate rather than an "intellectualist" (Gill, 1982) interpreted reflection of something through which they may avoid anxiety by believing it existed in that form only in childhood. In the adult, the objects may vary from those in childhood, but not the primitive nature of the conflicted ungratified wishes and impulses. In guiding the patient's awareness of this, the analyst in a defense-oriented analytic situation is, rumors to the contrary, even more often verbal than the one in a traditional interpretive analytic situation.

In my supervisory work, when listening to evidence of patients' severe and chronic fear of their aggression, at times I find myself with a sense of satisfaction, telling supervisees that when patients dare to exercise gradually increasing amounts of oral aggression, the supervisees can well think of the nature of the therapeutic action as *also* providing patients, through the analyst's uncritical receptivity, with a reliable new "teething ring." Such examples of gratification in the process and goals of analysis point to the likelihood that they may provide the analyst with sublimations for formerly maternal or parental impulses.

Is there a future for Freud's prediction that we may some day move closer to the "hard" sciences? In spite of the efforts to assure psychoanalysis a place as a science (Waelder, Brenner, among others), I argue that traditional analysis, tied to art in its use of creative listening to and "interpreting" a patient's material, is *limited* in its potential for defining its therapeutic actions and results. Enduring skepticism about analysis as a natural science adds to the general resistance to the concept of psychologically reducing neurotic solutions to instinctual conflict. As long as this is so, psychoanalysis will remain outside the scientific community; on the one hand, neuropharmacology will enlarge its domination over treatment, and on the other hand, the competing "softer" social and humanistic approaches to human suffering will encroach further upon psychoanalysis.

A major appeal of the method involving close process analysis of the material available in the field of consciousness and confined to the vocalizations or verbalization of the patient is that it brings the data into the realm of phenomenology. It is there that more acceptable scientific evaluation and testing become available (Abend, 1989; Stoller, 1985). The gratifications of a more verifiable science are also a welcome sublimation.

In conclusion, I recognize that not all analysts are willing or able to increase their listening skills to include emphasis on observations of phenomenological data. For those who are willing to add to their skills in this way, I offer the following observations, which bear on some of the advantages offered by using the wider "clearing." Anna Freud (1969), in *Difficulties in the Path of Psychoanalysis*, observed: "The analyst's task is *not to create*, i.e., to invent anything, but to observe, to explore, to understand, and to explain" (p. 48 emphasis added). Robert Waelder, commenting on evaluating applicants for analytic training, said: "I would put less stock than many in what is often called empathy or *psychological intuition*. . . . Once this initial advantage of the highly intuitive analyst is gone, the odds may even favor the painstaking work with details over intuition, inasmuch as those heavily endowed with the latter are often impatient with the work on minutiae. Also, intuition, while always impressive, is not always correct, and those favored by the gods with this gift are sometimes slow in revising their early visions when necessary" (1962, pp. 276–277).

And finally, there is the issue of Freud's very late coming to terms with the importance of the aggressive drive. Because of its relevance for close process attention during defense analysis and because of the importance of the analyst's willingness to analyze the patient's fears of experiencing and verbalizing conscious aggression in the analytic situation is crucial to maturation of the ego, I quote Freud (1930):

> In the latest analytical literature a predilection has been shown for the view that any kind of privation, any thwarted instinctual gratification, results in a heightening of the sense of guilt, or may do so. I believe one obtains a great simplification of theory if one regards this as valid only for the *aggressive* instincts, and that little will be found to contradict this assumption. How then is this to be explained dynamically and economically that a heightening of the sense of guilt should appear in place of an

unfulfilled *erotic* desire? This can surely only happen in a roundabout way: The thwarting of the erotic gratification *provokes an excess of aggressiveness against the person who interfered with the gratification, and then this tendency to aggression in its turn has itself to be suppressed. So then it is, after all, only the aggression which is changed into guilt, by being suppressed and made over to the superego.* (Emphasis added) I am convinced that very many processes will admit of much simpler and clearer explanation if we restrict the findings of psychoanalysis in respect of the origin of the sense of guilt to the aggressive instinct. (1930, p. 138)

This is a neglected concept, reflecting Freud's most advanced judgment. It is also supportive of the principle that whenever external conditions and degree of internal conflict permit, analysis is most effectively carried out if analysis of the transferences of authority—*the major defensive "containers" of conflicted aggressive derivatives*—is consistently a priority.

BIBLIOGRAPHY

ABEND, S. (1989). Countertransference and psychoanalytic technique. *Psychoanalytic Quarterly*, 58:374–395.

ARLOW, J. A. (1979). The genesis of interpretation. *Journal of the American Psychoanalytic Association*, 27s:193–206.

——— (1993). Discussion: A clinician's comments on empirical studies of psychoanalysis. *Journal of the American Psychoanalytic Association 41s:143–152.*

BRENNER, C. (1968). Psychoanalysis and science. *Journal of the American Psychoanalytic Association, 16:675–696.*

——— (1976). Defense analysis. In *Psychoanalytic Technique and Psychic Conflict*, pp. 59–78. New York: International Universities Press.

FREUD, A. (1936). *The Ego and the Mechanisms of Defense.* New York: International Universities Press.

FREUD, A. (1969). *Difficulties in the Path of Psychoanalysis.* New York: International Universities Press.

——— (1979). Personal letter, 9 October, 1979.

FREUD, S. (1905). *Jokes and Their Relation to the Unconscious. S.E.* 8.

FREUD, S. (1915). The unconscious. *S.E.* 14. p. 175.

——— (1930). Civilization and its discontents. *S.E.* 21. p. 38.

GILL, M. M. (1982). *Analysis of Transference Vol. I*, Psychological Issues Monograph 53. New York: International Universities Press.

GRAY, P. (1994). *The Ego and Analysis of Defense.* New York: Jason Aronson Inc.

HARTMANN, H. (1958). *Ego Psychology and the Problem of Adaptation.* New York: International Universities Press, p. 25.

OPITOW, B. (1989). Drive theory and the metapsychology of experience. *International Journal of Psychoanalysis*, 70:645–660.

REIDER, N. (1950). The concept of normality. *Psychoanalytic Quarterly*, 19:43–51.

STERBA, R. (1941). The abuse of interpretation. *Psychiatry,* 4:9–12.

STOLLER, R. (1985). Psychiatry's mind-brain dialect, or the Mona Lisa has no eyebrows, in *Observing the Erotic Imagination.* New Haven: Yale University Press.

WAELDER, R. (1954). The function and the pitfalls of psychoanalytic studies, in *Psychoanalysis: Observation, Theory, Application.* Ed. Samuel A. Guttman, New York: International Universities Press, pp. 229–239.

―――― (1960). *Basic Theory of Psychoanalysis.* New York: International Universities Press, fn.84.

―――― (1962). Selection criteria for the training of psychoanalytic students. (p. 277), in *Psychoanalysis: Observation, Theory, Application. Selected Papers of Robert Waelder.* Ed. Samuel A. Guttman. New York: International Universities Press, pp. 275–282.

Dread of the Strength of the Instincts

A Psychoanalytic Contribution to the Understanding of Violence

JOHN HITCHCOCK, M.D.

Dread of the strength of the instincts develops as an affective state in which displacements generally available to an individual have been weakened, rendering that person more vulnerable to committing an act of violence.

Although the case presented here includes an act of violence, ways that this act could have been foreseen and thus possibly forestalled through analysis are explored.

Factors in this child's development are reviewed with regard to their possible predisposing contributions.

FREUD'S FORMULATIONS REGARDING HUMAN BEHAVIOR EMPHASIZE CON-flict between the instincts, as he defined them, and counterforces mediated by the ego (S. Freud, 1923). Anna Freud (1936) said that a person whose defense is prompted by dread of the strength of the instincts will not respond favorably to analysis. Subsequently, psycho-

Supervisor in child and adolescent analysis in the Pittsburgh Psychoanalytic Institute and a geographic rule supervisor in child and adolescent analysis in the Topeka Institute for Psychoanalysis. He is a former director of the Pittsburgh Psychoanalytic Institute.

This work is dedicated to Viola W. Bernard, M.D. An earlier version was presented to the Topeka Psychoanalytic Society on 19 November 1993. The author acknowledges with gratitude the contributions of Katherine Jean Hitchcock to both content and structure of this paper.

The Psychoanalytic Study of the Child 51, ed. Albert J. Solnit, Peter B. Neubauer, Samuel Abrams, and A. Scott Dowling (Yale University Press, copyright © 1996 by Albert J. Solnit, Peter B. Neubauer, Samuel Abrams, and A. Scott Dowling).

analysts' attention has been focused increasingly on ego development and on the factors promoting or interfering with the ego's capacities to perceive, defend, adapt, and otherwise exercise its functions in channeling, countering, and modulating instinctual derivatives, in addition to providing for the needs of the individual with respect to so-called external reality. Ultimately the ego mediates the functions of the superego as well. Since 1923, with the publication of *The Ego and the Id* (S. Freud), further definition of the ego has dominated psychoanalytic study. Instincts have been regarded as givens.

Yet it was Anna Freud, a pioneer and champion of the study of ego development, who not only recognized dread of the instincts in young children but saw it as a specific dynamic in adolescence and in climacterium. In her 1935 presentation to the Vienna Psychoanalytic Society, she pointed to the origins of anxiety and the sense of danger that lead to the development of defenses by the ego (1936). First she cites the defenses that result from the anxiety of conscience in adult neurotics— namely, dread of the superego. Second are the defenses generated by "objective anxiety" in infantile neuroses—that is, anxiety imposed on the child by caretakers' strictures and prohibitions, causing dread of the outside world. And the third source of anxiety in the child is dread of the strength of the instincts. If the powers of the superego and the outside world are insufficient, the ego may fear being overwhelmed or annihilated. Such dread can be more sharply identified in instances where, through analytic education or therapeutic analysis, the power of objective anxiety and the anxiety of conscience is diminished.

But dread of the instincts is a concept that has found neither theoretical currency nor clinical utility, with one exception (Frank, 1983) (see below). The aim of this paper is to propose not only that dread of the instincts can be dealt with psychoanalytically but that it has particular relevance for the understanding of violence.

Much has been written about the psychoanalytic view of the development of aggression and reactions to it (see especially Klein, 1932; Mahler et al., 1975; Kahn, 1964; Emde, 1989; Rubinfine, 1962; Green, 1987; Fraiberg, 1982; Parens, 1991, 1989). But again, with the exception of Anna Freud, no reference to dread of the instincts and little direct reference to violence are to be found. Although significant advances in exploring violence will probably be achieved, they are likely to be complementary to the understanding of intrapsychic experience— which calls for clinical psychoanalysis.

Violence has also been considered by writers from other vantage points, such as altered brain functioning (Mark and Ervin, 1970), societal pressure (Coser, 1968), and psychological and emotional factors in the individual and in groups (Biven, 1977; Galston, 1981; Parens, 1979). Menninger (1966) wrote convincingly of sociocultural contexts in which violence occurs but did not explicate the intrapsychic dynamics and experiences. Fromm's (1973) work centered on his view that aggression and its products and derivatives are entirely learned and on his formulations of a malignant oedipal configuration predisposing to a sadistic thrust and ultimately to death and destruction. He believed, along with the psychoanalytic developmental writers, that aggressive behavior ensues when there is a perceived threat to vital interests, but nowhere did he touch on dread of the instincts, even as a contribution to the dynamics of violent behavior.

The term "dread of the strength of the instincts" does not imply a change in the size of the id, which is part of the balanced triangle whose angles are id, ego/superego, and external reality. The vantage point is that of the ego, which perceives, judges, and assesses. We cannot say which element of the triangle is the cause of any imbalance. We can say only that the ego *perceives* its weakness relative to the id at this point. It is the ego that perceives an internal threat which it judges to originate in overwhelming inner forces and thus experiences dread. Psychoanalytic treatment offers the opportunity to explore these perceptions, especially in the evolution of those aspects that are out of awareness. We use "dread" in favor of "fear" because it connotes awe and aversion as well as anxiety (Random House, 1987). The term "awe," like "uncanny," conveys the sense of a powerful force that, with the added element of aversion, predisposes to avoidance and leads to displacement. This makes dread an apt descriptor of the experience of the instincts, especially by children in whom avoidance, externalization, and displacement result in nocturnal as well as diurnal phobias, with associated sleep disturbances.

The intense focus on separation anxiety, or anxieties, in the past several decades, emphasizing fear of loss of the object and of the object's love, has obscured an equally powerful childhood experience; namely, the loss of the object's assistance in countering the inner forces, resulting in dread of the strength of the instincts.

Portions of the analysis of a child's analysis are presented here. Although the analysis is considered to have been successful, it included a failure to explore the child's dread of her instincts.

G, the elder of two children, was five years old when she was brought for evaluation by her parents. Her parents' chief complaints were incessant autoerotic behaviors, present since she was eighteen months old, and night terrors centering on two popular puppet characters known for their outrageous behaviors.

Her parents were well educated, concerned people with a strong sense of propriety and a solid association with a formal religion. Despite their circumscribed standards, they were willing to consider their individual and collective contribution to their child's state of mind and had both been involved in their own therapeutic explorations.

Although the pregnancy with G was planned, from the time of the birth G's mother was uneasy about her competence as a parent. No early feeding problems or absorption with thumbsucking were noted. However, by eighteen months of age, shortly after the mother reported that she had experienced a significant depressive episode, G was positioning a pillow under her pelvis and was making pelvic thrusts to the point of orgasm. This behavior persisted with the progressive addition of oral activity until the autoerotic complex took the following form: G would hold the satin corner of her "blanky" to her mouth, with one finger along the side of her nose, and suck her lower lip, stroking her upper lip with the blanket, all the while in a state of reverie. She continues to display this sequence often.

Her mother described two incidents from G's infancy and early childhood. G, when she was just under a year old, had been standing in her crib screaming for some two hours. Her mother, exasperated, banged open the door and screamed "Shut up!" G appeared shocked and afraid, fell silent, and never again manifested screaming behavior. Her mother related this episode in a way that suggested that she felt herself to be emotionally volatile (although she did not appear to be so). Next, when G was about fifteen months of age, she poured milk from her cup onto the floor and her father slapped her hand sharply. Her mother felt he had overreacted.

Both parents and G denied problems with or concerns about G's impulse control. No breath-holding or tantrums were reported. From her early infancy, G had been emotionally contained. She did not hurt others or damage property, intentionally or otherwise. Her bowel and bladder training at two and a half was uneventful.

G was two when her mother became pregnant with her brother. G's responses seemed socially appropriate, with little expression of hurt, loss, or anger. She often participated appropriately in her brother's care. She was mostly dutiful. However, it was at this time that she first showed fear of cartoon characters. Other fears, such as of the dark or of being alone, were denied by G, and her parents reported no awareness of any other fears.

With peers, individually and in groups, G had always shown a readiness to participate and even leadership qualities, but always with a sense of being emotionally muted. She was rarely exuberant. She al-

ways denied any disappointment. She never acknowledged feeling
hurt if she was not included in group activities.

ANALYSIS AND INTERPRETATION

In the first analytic session, G lay on the couch, her face turned to the
wall, making animal growls; this was a far cry from her prim compo-
sure during the evaluation some weeks earlier. She acknowledged that
she felt scared and would feel better if her mother were present. After
two sessions, the mother's presence was no longer required. Throughout, G evinced a sense of being in control of herself.

G readily entered into imaginative play. The self-control her parents
described became clear at once: She engaged the analyst, but only as an
object to do her bidding—he the puppet, she the puppeteer. She easily
blocked his efforts to analyze or, in fact, to influence the proceedings in
any way that she felt diminished her control. Thus, she would routinely
"order" him to build something and then tear down his contribution,
rebuilding it in her own way. Interventions at any level—observations,
speculations, inquiries as to her thoughts or feelings, interpretations—
all were met with a grand dismissal. The presence of this highly evolved
and effective system of defense suggested that she had experienced an
absence of a sense of control, as yet undefined as to whether the threat
was primarily internal or external.

Several themes emerged in the first few months of analysis. Four will
be highlighted. First was autoerotism. Although it was slow to appear
openly in the analysis, it was clear that this mode of closing out the
world around her commanded a dominant position in G's life. It appeared suddenly one day in the third month of the analytic work. She
came in looking somewhat bleary-eyed, holding her "blanky" (I had
not seen "blanky" before), and behaved exactly as her parents had
described during the evaluation. She curled up in one corner of the
couch, the blanket draped over her, one satin corner stroking her
upper lip, a finger along her nose, a sucking action involving her
tongue and lower lip, and a dreamy look in her eyes. She maintained
this attitude for some two minutes, and then rapidly became her old
cheery self, going right into what I call her "containment" mode, the
second theme.

In the containment mode, she characteristically built houses out of
blocks—houses that enclosed her, and the building of which required
my help, although, as noted, she invariably knocked my contribution
aside and redid it. Remarkable here was the rapidity with which G
moved from one mode to the other: first from a pseudomature, com-

petent, independent person to an infantile, self-absorbed, exclusionary character, and then smoothly back to "normal," transitions I found disconcerting in their totality and in the ease with which they occurred.

My being cast in the role of "bad boy" was the third theme. I was commanded by G to be rowdy and disruptive and thus required punishment—no recess—from the teacher (herself), whereas she, the good girl, would receive approbation. This theme was an outgrowth of earlier nightmares and phobias involving the puppet characters—bad-acting children/men who commanded others. These fears, arising while G was both awake and dreaming, had been present for as long as she could remember. Although G reported that they had disappeared soon after the analytic work began, it was more probable that they evolved into the dreams she had of men who would kidnap and kill her and her brother. The puppet phobias clearly entailed projection and displacement, as did the fear of kidnappers, but the symbolic distortion, or symbolization, became more age-appropriate.

A control theme—exhibited through doctor games—developed and grew throughout this early phase of the analysis. G assigned herself the central role as the doctor who inflicts pain by giving injections and performing operations. She could assume full responsibility for her aggressive-sadistic impulses provided that she was acting as the male doctor/analyst. The transference enabled G to explore her feelings interpersonally in ways that the displacement and projection in the phobias precluded. Here again, as with the containment theme, my interventions emphasized the extent to which G needed to control me, transferentially reflecting the intensity of her feeling of having no control over her parents in ways that were essential to her in the past. In retrospect, her externalizing and projection were underrepresented in the interpretations. More attention to her need to control herself, and to recruit others to assist in controlling her, was called for (Rochlin, 1961).

An erotized transference was evident in G's activities even in this early phase of analysis. During one session, she pretended to hide in her house and I was told to reach in and take something. Next she said the mother doll was pregnant. G often attempted to be physical by climbing up behind the chair and sitting on my shoulders. The following session, about the seventieth, illustrated many of these points.

G arrived with her mother and brother, as usual, on a Monday. I had canceled her previous session. She had her "blanky" and obvious cold symptoms. She cuddled on the couch for a few minutes. I noted that it had been a long time since she'd brought the blanket and asked how she decided when and when not to. She said, "If my mother lets me or not." Next she folded some paper, drew an outline, and cut the paper to make a chain of paper dolls. Instead of making a chain, she got individual dolls and seemed disappointed. She persisted until she made ones that were connected. We talked about which dolls she pre-ferred. She had trouble with the scissors and asked for my help, and when I noted her left-handedness was causing some difficulty, she said her mother and brother are left-handed also, then that she and her mother are left-handed, and her brother and father are right-handed. I said that she and her mother are alike. She agreed heartily, and hummed "The Twelve Days of Christmas." Next she pretended to be a little girl. I was to be a father who divorces the mother but was to be very nice to G. I was told to bring her breakfast in bed, and she ordered a sumptuous meal. Then G said "Dr. H, I was angry with my father, *for real!*" I asked whether the missed session had troubled her, whether she felt she had missed out on something that all those gifts over the twelve days of Christmas and the wonderful breakfast might make up for. G stayed angry: "I punched my father. He was unconscious. He needed pills!" The session was over, and G said dramatically, "I have to get my shoes on! If not you'll have to *carry* me! You're too old! You don't know where I live. I'll have to stay all night!" Then she told me her address. I said, "So you'll get home after all." When we returned to the waiting room, G yelled at her brother for tearing her paper doll. The mother was protective of the brother.

This session is remarkable for its focus on G's conflicts about attach-ment. She presumably wants to construct a string of connected dolls. She initially produces separated ones, followed by a more successful effort. She then creates an exclusionary similarity between herself and her mother—their left-handedness. Meanwhile, in the waiting room, her brother, with their mother, has been playing with—tearing, ac-cording to G—G's paper doll. G chastises her brother, and mother comes to brother's defense. G had been producing her dolls with the father/analyst, but in so doing was deprived of the mother.

G's troubled relationships with mother, brother, and father are ex-pressed anew several sessions later, when G pretended to construct a tent and carried her baby in with her. I was asked to get into the tent, too, or, failing that, I was told to snatch the baby. She, the mother, promised to be perfectly quiet. I asked what to do when I snatched the baby. She replied, "Drink the blood and eat the body!" chantlike, sev-eral times. When I reached in and couldn't get the baby, my hand was supposedly cut off. Next I was told to ask the mayor how to get in. He suggested getting in the tent myself or, using my other hand, pushing down the tent, thereby killing the mother. I asked G about the snatching. She said, "It's a baby brother! If you can't have your whole body in here, there'll be trouble! I might have to get divorced from my husband!" In the next session, she reported a "real life" situation in which she is followed by a man who intends to kidnap and kill her and her brother. She agreed she was frightened by the previous play and her feelings.

Another issue was a change in schedule initiated by G's mother. Her mother had G call my office to announce to my answering machine that a change was being requested and that I might call G if I had any questions. She did so in a firm, competent voice. I called back, G answered, and, when she heard my voice, she immediately disguised hers to sound gruff and said, "She's not here" and hung up. I called again. This time her mother answered and was unable to induce G to come to the phone.

In the next session, G sat comfortably and quietly on the couch. When I asked her about the phone calls, she said, "I didn't make the call; it must have been the man who stole my mother's purse and found your phone number in it. It couldn't have been me!" She made up a different phone number that she claimed was her real one. When I asked if she was aware of being upset about the calls, she then realized I had heard her message on the tape. She brightened at once and asked if she could hear it. She then noticed a sketch of a face on a magazine and said, "Just like the puppet in my *dreams!*" Focussing on the mouth, she noted "she'll need braces" (a reference to the damage done by her oral autoerotism) and wanted to explore my mouth. To summarize, I said to her that sometimes I scared her as the puppets did and that she tried to be the scarer rather than the one scared (imitating a gruff voice), and that this results in her need to deny her responsibility for having made the call. I did not emphasize, however, the centrality of her fear of what she might do if her aggression were unleashed.

These themes—autoerotism, containment, analyst as bad boy, and control plus oedipal—played out by G in the analytic sessions converge in her dread of the strength of her instincts. Her masturbatory activity excluded the help she might get from others. At the same time, the containment theme reflected G's efforts to recruit the analyst's assistance in her defense against her instincts. The projection of her destructiveness on the bad boy analyst was a current version of the abandoned-puppet phobias and, like them, failed to reduce the intensity of her instincts sufficiently to permit the exercise of more constructive interpersonal experiences. The way she used control was also exclusionary. As the puppeteer, she resisted any influence emanating from the puppet (the analyst's interventions). Similarly, manifestations of oedipal interests were fragmenting and served to intensify tensions with her mother. At this point, the autonomy she achieved remained at a narcissistic level. The aim of her control was to exclude rather than to promote interaction. In general, I was insufficiently attentive to the magnitude of her autoerotic state of being, which allowed her to express aggression unencumbered by an age-appropriate sense of responsibility for her actions. Clues provided by her massive displacements and primitive denial and projection were obscured by her otherwise highly developed social skills and performance. Her realistic worries about her ability to control herself were downplayed in my view of her in favor of the formulation that she experienced separation as the intolerable loss of her source of nurturance.

In another session a few days after we had discussed her calling me, G attempted to dress the man doll, musing "Remember, they fell?" "Yeah," I say, "at the amusement park, and they had to get to the hospital." She nodded and took the family to the hospital she had built. I was told to pass surgical items to her. She sat behind my chair, filled syringes, and then made one with the sharp end of a pipe cleaner sticking out. She said that I was to get a test for mononucleosis (as she had once had), and after some preliminaries, made a rather sharp jab. She immediately said, "Oh, Dr. H! I think it went through your *skin!*" and when she scrutinized the area, she saw it hadn't. I commented on G's fear of being capable of inflicting pain and wondered whether she had experienced it before.

The next day, G's mother called to say that G's brother was having an asthma bout and that it would interfere with G's next session. Two days later, I overheard G and her father in the waiting room. G was whining in a baby voice, "You're making *fun* of me! I *hurt* myself!" Moments later, when I arrived, both were straight-faced. Father produced a handkerchief, into which G blew dramatically. In the office, she denied the exchange with her father and explained the handkerchief incident by saying she hadn't blown her nose all day. I said it sounded as if a lot was going on that she didn't want to talk about.

In this session, G had us play construction at a zoo with blocks, and characteristically she wanted me to do the work. I commented on this, highlighting the possibility that in having me do it, she felt it wasn't just her own initiative, and that perhaps she had concerns about her initiatives. She built arches on arches and acknowledged my observation that they looked like places you can get out of but you can't, continuing the containment theme. G made a ball-shaped mother and baby; I was told to make a square mother and baby. Then a mother and baby were to wait in the waiting room while the others went to the zoo. I said, "Like what happens here." Those at the zoo got hurt by the animals and had to go to the hospital. G, the doctor, checked my wrist—it was broken, so I needed a shot in the shoulder.

In the next session G asked me to build structures with specific blocks. I said that she wanted me to be her puppet but that she hid her role as director. At this point, there was some dull construction pounding somewhere in the building. G said, "M [her brother]! Stop that!" I said, "You can't get away from him, even here."

Before the next session G's mother called and told me in a frantic voice that G had dislocated her brother's elbow and immediately said to her mother, "You want to kill me!"

In the following session, G again set up games in which she ordered me to do things that she would then rearrange: In my interpretations, I emphasized her control of me and of herself in the process. She could not deal directly with her act of aggression toward her brother although indirect references were expressed in the play themes that included the pregnant mother doll. She heard impassively—that is without overtly accepting or rejecting—my comments about her anger toward her brother and how fearful she must be of her capacity to inflict harm.

Although she initially denied having said to her mother, "You want to kill me," she eventually was able to recognize that the statement was a reflection of how she felt at the time of her act of violence and to begin to reflect on earlier times when she was overwhelmed by her own rage. She lively and affectively described the ways that her brother received special treatment, her deep resentment of what she saw as gross inequity, and her fear of her own fury, necessitating the soothing retreat to the autoerotic reveries.

The interpretive focus up to the point at which G committed her act of violence against her brother had been on her displacements, her projection of her hostility and on the self soothing aspects of her autoerotism. Following the act of violence, her dread of the strength of her instincts was emphasized, and was associated with a steady reduction in her internal tension and in the intensity of her interpersonal conflicts. Thus, in Glover's terms, my interpretations had been inexact in that they were incomplete (Glover, 1931).

The analytic work with G continued for two more years. At termination G was essentially asymptomatic, much more cheerful, and with more solid evidence of latency psychological structures as well as latency-appropriate object relationships. The "blanky" had been retired.

She could openly disparage and berate her brother while she contin- ued to express affection for him as she always had.

DISCUSSION

Dread of the strength of the instincts arises from the fear that one could do violence and that this possibility is imminent. It occurs when there is a perceived external threat, which in turn is genetically linked to an earlier experience or experiences in which the individual felt overwhelmed. Any or all of the elements constituting these phenomena may be outside the individual's awareness.

The important element to interpret and analyze as to its origins is the dread. To circumvent this in any way is to reinforce defenses against recognition of the dread.

G's early experiences included at least one discrete "shock" trauma (Kris, 1956)—namely, her mother's scream at her to shut up—with the probability that this was not an isolated event but may even have characterized her mother's behavior when she felt threatened. Her father also was known to overreact at times. In addition, mother's withdrawal and absence because of her own depressive experience must have had an impact on G. Finally, mother's pregnancy with G's brother had a profound effect, judging from the coincident appearance of G's phobias, involving nightmares as well as waking fears. Her intense focus on genital masturbation, noted at one year of age, by eighteen months had reached an intensity which, according to her mother, included orgasm. Gradually, oral elements were added (re-added?) and other facets discontinued, but the overall frequency and duration remained at a high level into her seventh year.

In her experience of her mother screaming at the door and possibly of her father's sharp physical reactions, G may have sensed that she was more than her parents could handle, probably at times of her greatest need; this could readily predispose her to fear or dread her own instincts. "If I am too much for my mother, I indeed have something to fear." It is unknown if this set of dynamics is understood by the child. Nonetheless, the child reacts to it. It is the understanding that undergoes developmental evolution and may be facilitated by psychoanalysis.

The ability to attribute aggressive intention to others, as noted by Mayes and Cohen (1993, p. 158), underlies both projection and displacement, as in G's phobic symptoms and in her belief that her brother was harboring aggressive intent. By projecting her hostility and by displacement from her mother to the puppets and her brother, the good child-mother relationship is preserved. The displacement of aggression from the mother to brother was acutely reversed when, following G's dislocation of her brother's arm, she immediately accused her mother: "You want to kill me!" The case of Sophie, reported by Mayes and Cohen (p. 160), has some remarkable parallels with G. In fact, Sophie sounds like a younger G—perhaps, like Klein's Erna (1932)—with only an imagined younger sibling. Sophie, at 38 months, responded to separations with outbursts. Like G, she would retreat to autoerotism. The slave theme in Sophie's play resembled the orders given to the analyst by G, even down to the "vile threats to their [therapists'/mothers'] bodies" if they don't respond quickly enough. For Sophie, the mother of a badly behaving baby says, "Just throw him in the garbage"; for G, it's "Drink [the baby's] blood and eat the body." For Sophie as for G, separation exposed her to the dread of her own instincts, and, although this is never formulated as such in their paper, Mayes and Cohen give the correct interpretation to Sophie (p. 161) following her retreat from her angry outbursts: She feared that the power of her feeling could harm herself or the therapist. Upon hearing this, she could resume her play.

The faculty of intention and the sense of responsibility are of interest in considering G's development. She appeared to have erected strong defensive constellations against recognition of her intentions, and she often denied her responsibility for her wishes and behavior. What better object to perpetrate outrageous acts than a puppet, which can neither intend nor be held responsible? Yet, in investing her, and her mother's, aggression in the phobic object, she forfeited the opportunities to modulate her experience and expression of aggression that should have been afforded by expected maturation in both intrapsychic and interpersonal realms. In this sense, G's displacement failed her (Neubauer, 1994).

G probably was exposed to both "cumulative trauma" (Khan, 1964) and "shock trauma" (Kris, 1956), according to the parents' account of their tensions and outbursts during G's first two years; this can also be inferred from her behavior in analysis. In addition, she experienced the loss imposed by her mother's depressive withdrawal and absence while hospitalized. She then was faced with the direct and indirect impact of her mother's pregnancy with her brother. G's earliest recognized response seemed to be the development of intense autoerotic activity, entirely genital at its inception, at about fifteen months of age. Her withdrawal during her prolonged preoccupation with masturbation reflects an early avoidance of her interpersonal world, which must have been intolerable in some respects. The intensity of her aggression necessitated denial of her intentions and responsibility for her actions.

G's early and unsuccessful avoidance maneuvers predisposed her to the phobic solution she attempted at age three, when her brother was born. The phobias also failed to protect her from the dread of her instincts, especially at night.

G's superego development was profoundly disturbed. For example, unabashed prevarications flowed freely when she felt threatened with discovery of her sexual interests. The Pinocchio character served her remarkably well in this regard. Although her nose did not grow, she used the syringe repeatedly in her attempts to enact and to master her own and others' aggression. G's saying to her mother "You want to kill me" is a direct confirmation of Sandler's (1960) comments about the pre-autonomous superego schema. The child transfers the intolerable aggressive and sadistic part of herself from her "model" of her self to her "model" of her mother. Yet for G, such transfer, or projection, came too late, in reaction to an act of violence; thus it reflected a flawed projective mechanism, just as her effort to manage her instincts by means of autoerotism and her efforts at displacement by means of her phobic symptoms were flawed.

Sandler notes (p. 157) that the narcissistic support provided by an analyst may reduce the dependence of the patient's ego on its superego sufficiently to permit working through of inner conflicts. Such reduction in dependence by means of partial analysis can also lead to the direct expression of a drive, as happened with G. Her projections, displacements, and need for autoerotic retreat were analyzed, but not her dread of the strength of her instincts.

Sandler refers to the "superego transference" (p. 158) in which superego projection represents the ego's effort to restore the original superego objects.

In G's case, the inconsistencies of her parents' handling of aggression, and their evident guilt, left her feeling that her own inner control mechanisms were unreliable. The analytic work, by focusing initially on her defensive avoidance and her fears of abandonment by the nurturing object, failed to address her dread of her instincts and her need for containment by a reliable external authority; thus it may have contributed to the violence G enacted against her brother. In particular, G's need to recruit external sources to defend against her aggression was underrecognized and underestimated. When this perspective was brought into the analytic work, G showed considerable relief.

G's dread of the strength of her instincts, especially her fear that she would destroy her brother, arose in conjunction with both particular and generalized experiences of being overwhelmed. Her intense commitment to autoerotism and then to phobic symptoms characterized by the disavowal of intention and responsibility can be understood as her response to the dread of her instinctual demands and as predisposing to an act of violence.

To generalize the genetics and dynamics identified in G's case to others, including adults, we need only to explore and recognize deficiencies or distortions in the development of superego precursors before the oedipal stage, the experience of dread of the strength of the instincts, and the transferentially expressed need for external protection. Frank (1983), describing an epileptic analysand whose symptoms included fear of loss of control, a sense of being overwhelmed, and fear of the destruction of which she might be capable, emphasized the importance of recognizing the id resistance entailed in the repetition compulsion. Information about her early development was not included.

If dread of the strength of the instincts is experienced more generally, and if it is useful to identify and analyze this dread, forces impeding this recognition are probably operative in analysand and analyst alike. The threat underlying G's hypertrophied defensive constellations was perceived by the analyst in a way that enlisted his participation in protecting G from the narcissistic injury she expected if she were made fully aware of her dread. The analyst unconsciously colluded with G in keeping the dread out of awareness.

Dread of the strength of the instincts may be understood to be a powerful effort to recruit others to provide control. It is experienced with terror and shapes the phenomena underlying separation fears. It needs to be interpreted and explored as such, not only in terms of its manifold derivative manifestations, such as autoerotism, inhibitions, phobias, or hyperactivity.

Factors that appear to predispose one to violence include the child's experience that external control of his or her impulses is not present, or is present in unpredictable ways. It is important to recognize and explore inconsistency in the imposition of limits and in the provision of comforts in the earliest months and years for its contribution to a faulty sense of control and a failure to develop confidence in the ability to channel instinctual forces and their derivatives.

BIBLIOGRAPHY

BIVEN, B. (1977). A violent solution. *Psychoanal. Study Child* 32:327–352.

COSER, L. (1968). Violence and the social structure. In *Violence in the Streets*. Chicago: Quadrangle Books, pp. 71–84.

EMDE, R. (1989). *Relationship Disturbances in Early Childhood.* Ed. Sameroff and Emde. New York: Basic Books.

FRAIBERG, S. (1982). Pathological defenses in infancy. *Psychoanal. Quart.* 51: 612–635.

FRANK, A. (1983). Id resistance and the strength of the instincts: A clinical demonstration. *J. Amer. Psychoanal. Assn.* 34:47–67.

FREUD, A. (1936). *The Ego and the Mechanisms of Defense.* Revised edition (1966). New York: International University Press.

FREUD, S. (1923). The ego and the id. *S.E.,* 19:13–63.

FROMM, E. (1973). *The Anatomy of Human Destructiveness.* New York: Holt, Rinehart and Winston.

GALSTON, R. (1981). The domestic dimensions of violence: Child abuse. *Psychoanal. Study Child* 36:391–414.

GLOVER, E. (1931). On the therapeutic effect of the inexact interpretation. *Int. J. Psycho-anal.* 12:397–411.

GREEN, A. (1987). Instinct in the late works of Freud. In *On Freud's "Analysis Terminable and Interminable,"* Ed. Sandler. J. *Int. Psycho-anal Assn.* Educational Monograph.

KHAN, M. (1964). Ego distortion, cumulative traumata, and the role of reconstruction in the analytic situation. *Int. J. Psycho-anal.* 45:272–279.

KLEIN, M. (1932). *The psycho-analysis of children.* London: Hogarth Press.

KRIS, E. (1956). The recovery of childhood memories in psychoanalysis. *Psychoanal. Study Child* 11:54–88.

MAHLER, M., PINE, F., & BERGMAN, A. (1975). *The psychological birth of the human infant.* New York: Basic Books.

MARK, V., & ERVIN, F. (1970). *Violence and the brain.* New York: Harper and Row.

MAYES, L., & COHEN, D. (1993). The social matrix of aggression. *Psychoanal. Study Child* 48:145–169.

MENNINGER, K. (1966). *Man against Himself.* New York: Harcourt, Brace and World.

NEUBAUER, P. (1994). The role of displacement in psychoanalysis. *Psychoanal. Study Child* 49:107–119.

PARENS, H. (1979). *The Development of Aggression in Early Childhood.* New York: Jason Aronson.

PARENS, H. (1989). Toward an epigenesis of aggression in early childhood. In *The Course of Life: Vol. 2, Early childhood.* Ed. Greenspan and Pollack. 2nd edition. New York: International University Press, pp. 643–687.

PARENS, H. (1991). A view of the development of hostility in early life. *J. Amer. Psychoanal. Assn.* 39, supplement: 75–108.

THE RANDOM HOUSE DICTIONARY OF THE ENGLISH LANGUAGE. 2nd. ed. (1987). New York: Random House.

ROCHLIN, G. (1961). The dread of abandonment: A contribution to the etiology of the loss complex and to depression. *Psychoanal. Study Child* 16:451–470.

RUBINFINE, D. (1962). Maternal stimulation, psychic structure and early object relations. *Psychoanal. Study Child* 17:268–282.

SANDLER, J. (1960). On the concept of superego. *Psychoanal. Study Child* 15: 128–162.

Anna Freud and Developmental Psychoanalytic Psychology

LINDA C. MAYES, M.D.
DONALD J. COHEN, M.D.

When reviewed in its entirety, Anna Freud's legacy represents her efforts to address the deepest of metapsychological dilemmas: What moves development along, and is it inherently progressive and linear? She created a developmental psychoanalytic psychology that is remarkably current and draws upon principles of neurobiology, genetics, pediatrics, and social psychology. Her general developmental psychology builds upon three fundamental notions: (1) development proceeds not predominantly stage-based but more continuous and cumulative, with progressions and regressions; (2) progression along developmental lines involves the maturational push of innate or biologic givens as well as the interaction between biology and environmental conditions; and (3) understanding the complexities of normal development is a means of understanding the presence or absence of psychopathology in any given symptomatic presentation. These contributions and the notion of a developmental psychoanalytic psychology are reviewed through the contemporary lens of the field of developmental psychopathology. The enduring contributions of Anna Freud's developmental psychoanalytic psychology to child psychiatry and child development are in asking how mind and body are brought together, and in asserting that the interaction between the biologic and the mental remains the common ground of all disciplines concerned with children.

Linda C. Mayes is the Arnold Gesell Associate Professor of Child Psychiatry, Pediatrics, and Psychology in the Yale Child Study Center and a candidate in the Western New England Institute for Psychoanalysis. Donald J. Cohen is the Irving B. Harris Professor of Child Psychiatry, Pediatrics, and Psychology; director of the Yale Child Study; and a training and supervising analyst at the Western New England Institute for Psychoanalysis.
The Psychoanalytic Study of the Child 51, ed. Albert J. Solnit, Peter B. Neubauer, Samuel Abrams, and A. Scott Dowling (Yale University Press, copyright © 1996 by Albert J. Solnit, Peter B. Neubauer, Samuel Abrams, and A. Scott Dowling).

IN 1909, WHEN FREUD CAME TO CLARK UNIVERSITY, PSYCHOANALYSIS AND academic psychology, as represented by G. Stanley Hall, symbolically met. At that meeting, American audiences, relatively naive to psychoanalysis but familiar with the empirical tradition of the psychology of motivation and drive, heard Freud outline his discoveries of a dynamic unconscious, repression and resistance, conflict as psychogenic, and the psychoanalytic therapeutic and investigative technique (1910). Forty years later, Anna Freud came to Clark to commemorate explicitly the sixtieth anniversary of the university and implicitly her father's visit and the introduction of psychoanalysis to America. She reluctantly accepted the university's suggestion that she elaborate on the theme of the conceptual and practical interface between psychoanalysis and the academy of psychology (Young-Bruehl, 1988), although she insisted that she was neither conversant with nor experienced in the empirical tradition of academic psychology. She nonetheless summarized her views of the progress made when analysts applied empirical methods and statistical proofs to analytic hypotheses (A. Freud, 1951a). Building on the complementary strengths of the two disciplines as well as on her own convictions about the uniqueness of psychoanalytic data, she laid out the beginnings of what became an increasingly elaborate developmental model for the building up of the mind that allowed for interactions among constitutional, experiential, and maturational factors. In the thirty years following her Clark lecture, Anna Freud quietly explicated a developmental psychoanalytic psychology that remains remarkably current. An opportunity for retrospective appraisal invites us to take stock of the evolution of Anna Freud's particular brand of developmental empirical study, evaluate its place in contemporary developmental psychology, child psychiatry, and child psychoanalysis, and propose the challenges for a developmental psychoanalytic psychology in the years to come.

Anna Freud's Metapsychology of Development

Anna Freud concluded her comments on "The Contribution of Psychoanalysis to Genetic Psychology" (1950) with the proposal that the collaborative meeting ground for academic psychology and psychoanalytic inquiry would be based not on data from the psychoanalytic consulting room but on "analytically directed observational child study" (A. Freud, 1951a, p. 142). The distinction is worth pausing over for it contains important elements that would shape Anna Freud's clinical research at the Hampstead Clinic founded the year after her Clark lecture and presages her creative contributions regarding models of normal development.

Anna Freud was at her natural bent an observer of children, and her observational skills, colored by a psychoanalytic environment, were honed pragmatically. She had begun her work as a nursery-school teacher, spent the war years caring for children in nurseries, and based her earliest contributions to psychoanalytic theory on observations of young children gathered in nurseries, playgrounds, and classrooms. Her child-development education such as it was for her individually or as was available generally in the 1920's was experiential, not formal. When invited to speak at Clark, she quickly asked her friends to mail her current materials on academic psychology, a field she had known little about up to that point (Young-Bruehl, 1989), and she immersed herself in an intensive self-instructional course in both language and method. Her first professional language was not from the empirical tradition of measurement, of observational data that could be reliably gathered by properly trained individuals or of statistically based hypothesis testing. She had not endured either the influences of working toward a doctorate or other professional status. Indeed, the honorary degree conferred upon her by Clark in 1950 was her first university degree. She had learned by doing and, relatively uninfluenced by contemporary academic trends in infant studies and observational methods (e.g., Hetzer-Wolff, Gesell), had created through years of practice her own framework for gathering observational data.

Such experience gave her a paradoxical blend of ultimate confidence in her capacity to observe and organize her observations and at the same time, a sense of not belonging to the more proper and generally accepted scientific academic world. Reflecting on a dream on the eve of her American tour and Clark lecture, she insisted some elements of the dream suggested "the academic world for which I am in no way fitted, neither by my type of mind nor by my analytic upbringing" (Young-Bruehl, 1989, p. 343). Thus, while she was respectful of the empirical contributions many of her analytic colleagues had made to academic psychology (including Spitz, Bowlby, Fries, Rappaport, Hartmann, Kris, and Lowenstein), she maintained a diplomatic but cautious alliance with a tradition she felt had at times misunderstood and misused the psychoanalytic method. Her caution perhaps permitted her to nurture a clearer view of the points of similarity and difference between psychologists and psychoanalysts attempting to study children.

While both seek to "understand present-day behavior and present-day existence as an evolution of possibilities given at some past date" (1951a, p. 118), Anna Freud suggested that the analyst was involved in "action research" in which findings emerged in the context of the relationship between analyst and child. Standard tools of measurement to codify objectively specific behaviors or reactions to experimental situations did not adequately describe the child's response to more usual and complex life situations as separation and loss, nor did these techniques give sufficient weight to the unconscious background of conscious behaviors. At the heart of each of the distinctions was the nature of observational data—how they were gathered, categorized, coded, and interpreted, and what were the limits of behavioral observation. On the one hand, she argued for meticulous, carefully recorded observations of children's moment-to-moment activities and behaviors; on the other, she felt that one of the dangers of academic psychology ran the risk of deriving meaning solely from conscious behaviors with little to no understanding that one behavior might have multiple unconscious determinants: "the observation of manifest, overt behavior marks a step which is not undertaken without misgivings. We ask ourselves whether observational work outside of the analytic setting can ever lead to new discoveries about underlying trends and processes, and can thereby supplement the data gathered through the analyses of adults and children" (A. Freud, 1951b, p. 144). This was a persistent tension that had preceded her 1950 declaration about the promise of analytically informed child observations and continued through her creation of developmental lines and her emphasis on learning about normality through studies of pathology. Defining and refining her observational process was a central part of Anna Freud's methodology for understanding development.

DEFINING THE NATURE OF OBSERVATION

Early in her career, Anna Freud used her observations of normal children in nurseries and her own beginning analytic work with young children to examine from a different vantage point developmental propositions her father had discovered in his work with adults. Combining a clinical analytic practice in which she saw both children and adults with hands-on teaching and supervision in a nursery school, she began to gather observations of very young children in groups and individually. In the work of her contemporaries, psychoanalytic principles were being generously and eagerly applied to manuals for enlightened childrearing, and parents brought more direct observations of their children to both their analysts and their children's teachers. More teachers and childcare workers came into analysis and through the influence of their personal analyses, began the as yet unlabeled activities of psychoanalytically informed child observers. The establishment of the Jackson Nurseries in Vienna (and later the Hampstead Nurseries in London) for very young and disadvantaged children meant that similar observations of instinctual life, ego development, and defenses were applied to children at risk. In this work, Anna Freud was finding her way through the twin shoals of filial dedication to her father's work and understanding how her experiences with children supported but also challenged certain deeply held psychoanalytic principles.

Observations of children might be made in many contexts other than the analytic setting, including nursery schools, residential care centers, hospitals, and group homes. Anna Freud insisted that such observational work was not:

> governed by a pre-arranged plan. In emulation of the analyst's attitude when observing his patient during the analytic hour, attention was kept free-floating, and the material was followed up wherever it led. The fact that the effects of early separation from the mother, feeding habits, toilet training, sleep, anxiety, etc., were in the center of attention at different times was determined by the happenings among the children, not predetermined by the fixed interests of the observers. . . . The material which presents itself is seen and assessed neither by an instrument, nor by a blank and therefore unprejudiced mind, but on the basis of pre-existent knowledge, preformed ideas, and personal attitudes (although these should be conscious in the case of the analyzed observer) (A. Freud, 1951b, pp. 147–148).

Thus, the process involved less recording data using a pre-arranged schema and more "checking the children's behavior against the analytic assumptions about the hidden trends in the child's mind" (ibid.). This was a hybrid form of observation that was not purely analytic as defined by the adult method, nor was it empirical like an academic psychology experiment. The observer was a very active participant, both as someone caring for the child and as a selector of those behavioral moments and their surrounding context that seemed most indicative of the child's inner world. The standard empirical technique involves recording the quantitative (e.g., frequency or duration) and qualitative (e.g., intensity) aspects of specific behaviors (e.g., crying and fussing) at every instance of a specific situation (e.g., separation). Observers using this standard approach may be relatively uninformed about pre-existing theories or assumptions; they need know only how to recognize reliably the behavioral events and the triggering situations. The meaning and interpretation of the collected behaviors are supplied later in the analyses of the data, and conclusions take forms, such as the expected age periods for peaks in separation distress. In contrast, the analytically informed observer as defined even in Anna Freud's earlier works is both recorder and interpreter of the moment. Noting a child's intense distress upon separation, analytically informed observers may also note the child's fatigue or mild fever, or know about his mother's recent depression or illness; they may recognize that this particularly intense moment of distress with separation following a frustrating encounter with another two-year-old in which a toy was abruptly lost in an unsuccessful scuffle. Behind these notations of the context of both event and response is an understanding of the theories of drive and defense, displacement of wishes and affects, and the regulation of impulses. There is also the presumption that behaviors do not simply reflect singular aspects of mental life but that mental life also determines the quality and quantity of behavior.

Using this approach to observation, Anna Freud suggested a number of revisions to phenomena that had emerged from analytic reconstructions with adults. For example, on the basis of observations of children, she questioned the separation of ego and drive regression and suggested the now-familiar phenomenon of loss of recently acquired developmental skills under the impact of stressful or traumatic experiences. She raised the possibility of a similar phenomenon in adults involving the temporary breakdown under stress of ego achievements such as specific sublimations (1951b). Similarly, she suggested that children in institutions and those who have grown up with only one parent nonetheless demonstrate play usually presumed to imply primal-scene experiences and also assume some behaviors characteristic of the gender of the absent parent (1951b). Through observations such as these, she spoke about innate tendencies for "family life" or for seeking out relations with others that are not based solely in experiences but rather suggest a basic biology of relatedness. Her report on "An Experiment in Group Upbringing" contains some of her most detailed reporting of observational data and is a model of her insistence on a public record of the observations from which her conclusions were drawn. In these studies of six children who had survived the concentration camps and were a closely knit group unto themselves, she evolved her notions of the relation between aggression and libidinal drives or of the modification of aggression by the strength of object relations (1951c).

CREATING A GENERAL DEVELOPMENTAL PSYCHOANALYTIC PSYCHOLOGY—DEVELOPMENTAL LINES

By the early 1950s, with her observational technique well practiced and integrated, Anna Freud made a major synthetic shift in her approach to children and in her efforts to create a child analytic psychology. The founding of the Hampstead Clinic coincided within a few years with the centenary of her father's birth, and in her efforts to organize and consolidate both events, she began to reflect on the implications of her father's insistence on the creation of a *general* psychology (Young-Bruehl, 1989). The deepest implication of a general theory of mental functioning was the rejection of any single theoretical or practical element as primarily causal or explanatory. Such reductionism appeared in many forms—substituting or emphasizing one part instead of the whole (e.g., libidinal over aggressive, ego over drive), highlighting one focus of research at the expense of all others (e.g., the primacy of object relations at the expense of constitutional givens), or neglecting one side of a complementary series or interaction (e.g., ignoring the biological given in the fluctuation of drive expression). Freud constantly attempted to reintegrate and maintain a consistency within his entire model of mental functioning even as revisions and new components were added. Reductionism in its various guises, with its associative divisive and blinding possibilities, threatened the progress of psychoanalysis. Anna Freud began to comment on the similar dangers of emphasizing parts rather than the whole as she spoke about the activity of assessment and diagnosis in child analysis:

> "one element of the human mind after another moved into the center of attention and naturally received prominence in publications: infantile sexuality and the sequence of libidinal stages; repression and the unconscious mind; the division of the personality into various agencies and the conflicts between them; the Oedipus and castration complexes; the role of anxiety; aggression as an independent drive; the relationship between the mother and infant and the consequences of early interruptions of the mother-child relationship. Yet, no single one of these factors was ever meant to be considered the only or even the foremost pathogenic agent, as happens all too frequently in clinical evaluations (1962, pp. 360–361).

She emphasized a synthetic view in which a child's presentation at any given point in time was seen across multiple domains. There was to be no special emphasis on any one period or event as pathogenic; such causal thinking implied a static view that was increasingly antithetical to Anna Freud's commitment to a historical vision of S. Freud's primary mission and her increasingly dynamic view of children's development. While respectful of the work of her Viennese émigré colleagues, Mahler and Spitz (indeed, both provided examples of empirical developmental research that Anna Freud followed closely and built into her developmental lines), she refused to follow either of them in attributing primary pathogenicity to disturbances in mothering in the first years of life: "theory as to the causation of pathology . . . veered, rather wildly, from the oedipal period as the responsible constellation to the mother-infant relationship at the beginning of life; to the separation-individuation phase (Margaret Mahler); to the disturbances of narcissism (Kohut). . . ." (1978a, pp. 98–99).

Implicit in this more broadly synthetic view of children's development were three principles that moved increasingly to the center stage of her thinking and define today the fundamentals of a developmental psychoanalytic psychology: (1) While individual periods or stages in development are apparent (e.g., oral, phallic), these stages are not clearly demarcated in actuality and mark only the relative saliency of a particular developmental concern at a given point in a child's maturation. Moreover, so-called phase-specific issues reappear with new saliency throughout development. Development proceeds not in a predominantly stage-based manner but more continuously, with progressions and regressions; (2) while generally progressive and linear, development involves complex interactions among various lines or functions. At any given moment, progression along individual lines may be harmonious (e.g., synchronous) or imbalanced. Periods of imbalance not only mark potential developmental problems but also (under proper environmental conditions) may provide the impetus for further development and efforts toward self-righting. Progression along developmental lines involves the maturational push of innate or biologic givens as well as the interaction between biology and environmental conditions; and (3) understanding the complexities of normal development is a means of understanding the presence or absence of psychopathology in any given symptomatic presentation.

If defining psychoanalytically oriented observation characterized Anna Freud's early work and outlined her research methodology, the concept of developmental lines marked her next efforts toward synthesis and the creation of a new developmental metapsychology. The metaphor of developmental lines or sequences provides a comprehensive approach to understanding the interactions among innate, maturational, and environmental contributions in developmental progression. For example, the child's relationship to important others involves movement along multiple lines including "dependency to emotional self-reliance to adult object relationships," "from wetting and soiling to bladder and bowel control," "from sucking to rational eating," and "from irresponsibility to responsibility in body management." At their face value, the developmental lines are clinically useful descriptors. They provide an analytic metric for measuring a child's level of mental maturity and integration. In a sense, developmental lines are to inner worlds what neurodevelopmental assessments are to directly observable social and language behaviors and responses to cognitive/perceptual tasks—a method of measuring a child's development and mental-age equivalency. Developmental lines are theoretically grounded in both the psychoanalytic structure model and notions of drive and defense; standard assessments of developmental competency, by contrast, are grounded in theories of neuromaturation and cognitive development. Both, however, are fundamentally observational methods of assessing the linear progression of a child's mental development, and both constitute a metric of a child's developmental maturation:

> What these lines represent are ladders leading up to every one of the expected achievements of the child's personality, each step on them being the result of interaction between id, ego, and environment, the way leading upward in the course of normal, progressive growth, or downward whenever regression occurs. (1974, p. 63).

Thus, one value of Anna Freud's developmental lines is their provision of a semi-scaled method for assessing children's relative normality or deviancy from expected patterns of psychological development. Large discrepancies in positions on the various lines and/or notable delays in progression along one or more lines are indications of potential disturbance or increased risk for psychiatric disturbance. It is important to note, too, that developmental lines describe children's maturity or immaturity apart from specific psychiatric symptoms. By using the framework of developmental lines, clinicians focus on phase-appropriate developmental issues (e.g., dependency to self-reliance) and the meaning of a given behavior in the context of that phase (e.g., when does "falsification of truth begin to deserve the name of lying" [A. Freud, 1965, p. 114]). Moreover, inherent in the interactions among developmental lines is the notion of adaptation across developmental lines. A child who is functioning at a lower level across all developmental lines compared to his age-matched companions may nonetheless be functioning adaptively in the face of his maturational retardation or cognitive delays.

However, to view lines of development as simply descriptive maps of developmental normalcy or deviation is to be lulled by the deceptive simplicity in Anna Freud's presentation. Contained in the notion of progression along different lines of development is a radical rethinking of the basic questions of developmental psychology: what moves development along, and how does maturation occur? The notion of developmental lines contains within it a heuristic framework for understanding (and investigating) mechanisms of development. Anna Freud inherited a multilayered psychoanalytic theory of development in which the question of how maturation takes place was only implicitly addressed. Freud offered drives and instinctual stages as the first model of a developmental theory. Shifting erotogenic zones defined a child's libidinal maturation to full genitality and a mature instinctual life. Drives expressed in instincts were the implicit force in maturation; development was a maturational given that was interfered with if environmental conditions blocked expression of the drives in age-appropriate ways. As instincts acquired objects in the evolution of the theory, development involved the shifting valence of instincts directed toward self and others.

With the advent of the structural model and Anna Freud's contributions regarding the defensive functions of the ego, the psychoanalytic theory of development became a model of ego versus id, with later modulation by superego. Ego functions including neuromotor competence, language, and cognition permitted children the increasing ability to contain, shape, and express instinctual life. Still a biological given, development in this frame of reference reflected a balance between the relative strength of instinctual needs and the maturational functions of the ego. For example, impaired ego functions (e.g., delayed language) might negatively influence a two-year-old's ability to deal with aggressive impulses, or increased sexual drives in puberty might overwhelm the adolescent's ability to think rationally about the consequences of his behavior. Defenses represented the ego's response to instinctual needs and became more sophisticated as other ego functions matured. Distortions or imbalances between the maturation of ego functions and instinctual life contributed to developmental deviations including regressions, fixations, and apparently precocious maturation; and imbalances had their roots in both constitutional deficiencies in essential ego functions and environmental conditions that impeded and constrained the expression of and response to children's basic needs.

Each of these closely related models of development suggested that the process of development reflected the maturational taming and shaping of basic instincts. Drives were the fuel, and the biological developmental imperative was to deal with the drives. How this happened was not clear. But that it would happen in some form or another was a biological given. Experience might constrain, slow, or accelerate the maturational necessity, but maturation was the presumed constitutional black-box. Also, implicit in the model of development Anna Freud inherited was a notion of layering and stages—orality followed by anality with the phallic or genital stages necessarily built on previous layers. "Failure" at one level impeded or prevented progression to subsequent stages. Up to this point, developmental theory was not "experience-near" because it was not based as directly on observations of children. Developmental lines, rooted in direct observations of infants and young children, afforded a rethinking of a stage theory based on the unfolding of instinctual life.

Anna Freud offered a model for a linear, progressive, regulated process of development in which the expression of individual biological capacities influenced the later expression and integration of other biologically based functions. But in her model, there was no singular stage and no singular or all-explanatory function. A maturational imperative was still contained in the theory—she remained true to the psychoanalytic tradition of an emphasis on constitution and endowment and built upon the psychoanalytic thinking about genetics that had preceded her. Her enduring interest in the developmental progression of biology to psychology is reflected in her frequent returning to physical illnesses as perturbations for understanding the psychological expression of body/biological processes. But in a subtle, synthetic shift she presented developmental lines not just as descriptive evidence that maturation was occurring but as metapsychological structures involved in the actual regulation of development: "it becomes possible to describe all progressive development as an intricate pattern which owes its unfolding to the integration of the most diverse influences with each other" (1978b, p. 342).

In the deepest phase of her work, developmental lines are superordinate, integrative functions contained within the child. In contemporary terms, developmental lines might be thought of as regulatory genes—that is, as genetic factors that control the emergence and unfolding of a given, genetically influenced capacity (e.g., motor control for walking or cognitive ability for symbolic thinking). The activation of a given regulatory genetic system will in turn activate other genetic substrate. Progressive, linear development occurs as individual regulatory genes are expressed at different points in time. Well-known examples of regulatory genetic processes include the timing of puberty through which many other processes of growth, cognition, anxiety regulation, and full sexuality begin. Similarly, between 3 and 5 years of age, a marked reorganization of psychological life occurs, formally demarcated in psychoanalysis as the oedipal period. The process of "oedipalization" involves dramatic shifts in neural activity, cognitive capacities, symbolic thinking, and social-affective life.

As regulatory structures, developmental lines are models of biologic-environment interaction, the most current paradigm of development. Once a set of capacities is activated, the range of expression of those capacities is sensitive to environmental influences. To state this in the terms of developmental genetics, a given genotype has a phenotypic range of reaction; that is, a gene may be fully or only partially expressed depending both on the timing of the expression of other genes and on environmental conditions. The most basic example is the phenotypic expression of height. While a child may have the genetic endowment to be tall, environmental conditions including nutrition and early illnesses may limit the range of expression of that genotype. Further, the timing of these external events may alter the expression of other regulatory processes involved in the full expression of height including the timing of puberty. The model of biologic-environment interaction is equally appropriate when applied to psychological structures. For example, complete expression of the capacity for full and intimate relationships with others may be limited by early deprivation that affects the development of the capacity for empathy and for an integrated sense of self and other. In terms of developmental lines, it is the regulatory process of moving from "dependency to emotional self-reliance to adult object relationships" that is altered by early deprivation. Changes in this regulatory process also change the regulation of progress along other lines (or, in the genetic metaphor, the expression of other genetic substrate and the subsequent activation of other regulatory genetic systems). For example, a child's failure to progress toward emotional self-reliance is paralleled by disturbances in his care of his body.

As a child moves at different rates along different lines, a disharmony results, with attendant possibilities of developmental delays and arrests. Anna Freud insisted that "progress along the lines is interfered with constantly by conflict, repression, and consequent regression" (1974, p. 70). Minor degrees of disharmony across the developmental lines are ubiquitous—harmonious, even development is only a metaphor (Yorke et al., 1981)—but major disharmony across lines may be indicative of current pathology as well as a potential nidus for later neurotic disorders. However, how notions of "harmony" and "disharmony" differ from earlier ideas of developmental fixations and regressions is the last and perhaps most radical aspect of Anna Freud's developmental metapsychology. That biology becomes psychology is implicit in developmental lines. For example, a child's first independent steps, a neurologically timed event, are part of the psychology of self-reliance and beginning independence. A parent's reaction of surprise and joy versus fear and anxiety to the toddler's first steps further contains that neuromaturational event in the varying psychological palette of the meanings of separation. But even more radical for her time, Anna Freud allowed in her notion of developmental lines and disharmony that experience becomes biology—psychology becomes "hard-wired," or experience shapes the function of basic neural processes. Changes in one line of function changes the timing of various other events, and that initial alteration may reflect any number of environmental conditions, including traumatic events as well as parental neglect and serious illnesses. Classic and simple examples include changes in visual cortex development if there is no visual input during a critical period. Other more complex events include alterations in synaptogenesis and synaptic pruning based on levels of environmental stimulation. Or in conditions of profound environmental neglect in the first months, the development of capacities for state and arousal regulation is slowed, which in turn alters the expression of basic capacities for anxiety regulation. In each of these examples, environmental conditions alter biologic expression, which in turn influences the expression of other biologic functions.

How developmental lines are related to studies of psychopathology is also contained in the notion of harmony or disharmony in progression along the lines. In her last papers, Anna Freud continued to struggle with the metapsychology of harmony and disharmony along the developmental lines. While disharmony reflected in part the classic analytic emphasis on conflict between id and ego, "harmony" and "balance" were part of her deeper efforts to understand the interplay between biological and psychological processes and to understand development as an integrative, progressive process. Harmonies and disharmonies of developmental lines integrated the normal and the psychopathological points of view. Developmental lines emphasized a "study of the norm": "We have broken with the tradition according to which every mental difficulty is seen and explained by comparison with severe pathological patterns, and instead, try to see it against the background of the norm, expectable for the particular child's age, and to measure its distance from that" (1974, p. 61). In this manner, she presaged the study of developmental psychopathology, an academic discipline that Anna Freud would probably have found quite harmonious and reflective of the metapsychology contained in the notion of lines of development.

ANNA FREUD'S LEGACY: DEVELOPMENTAL PSYCHOPATHOLOGY

In recent years, a course of inquiry outside psychoanalysis has gradually come to focus on the interplay between normal and atypical development in the expression of childhood psychiatric and psychological disorders. The central tenets of a developmental psychopathology approach (Cicchetti and Cohen, 1995; Zigler & Glick, 1986; see also Cicchetti, 1993; Sroufe and Rutter, 1984) sound remarkably similar to Anna Freud's emphasis on a general developmental psychology for children. These tenets include: (1) examining transactions between biological or genetic factors and external environmental conditions as related to patterns of disordered behavior; (2) focusing on individual patterns of adaptation and maladaptation; (3) allowing that individuals may shift between normal and abnormal modes of functioning as a consequence of differing developmental stressors and environmental conditions; (4) utilizing naturally occurring events or "experiments of nature" to understand the expected developmental ontogeny of specific functions; and (5) employing the conceptual frames and methods of multiple disciplines to study any one mode of function, adaptation, or behavior. In the lens of developmental psychopathology, the study of normality is one route to understanding the origins of psychopathology, and vice versa: psychopathology may magnify normally expected paths of development that are less evident when development is going well. One example (see also Marans, this volume) will serve to illustrate the contemporary developmental psychopathology approach and its notable harmony with the later phases of Anna Freud's work and with a developmental psychoanalytic psychology.

TRAUMA IN CHILDHOOD

For all those working with children in this epoch of wars and violence, no area is of greater contemporary concern and reflective of Anna Freud's developmental psychology than the understanding of what is traumatic for children in different developmental phases, living in different families and communities (Marans and Cohen, 1993; see also Marans, this volume; Schwab-Stone et al., 1995). Child analysts have long been sensitive to the many types of stress and trauma in response to external and psychological experiences that overwhelm the child's ability to adapt and sometimes lead to long-term changes in children's mode of experiencing and paths of development (e.g., Greenacre, 1952; Provence, 1983). Analysts have been particularly interested in the relations among persistent trauma, personality, and the effects of acute trauma that may lead to symptoms, character, or new patterns of adaption (Arlow, 1987; Pruett, 1984; Terr, 1984). They have constantly worked to find the balance, for individual children, between the real and the imagined and between biological predispositions and overwhelming events shaping biology. Often the analytic understanding of a child's positive and negative response to trauma can be traced to early vulnerabilities and sensitivities which predispose children to anxiety and anxious attachments and ultimately alter how the child responds to trauma and stress (Escalona, 1963; Bergman and Escalona, 1949; Anna Marie Weil, 1956, 1978; Phyllis Greenacre, 1941a,b). How children perceive, react to, and change in response to stressful life circumstances represents one of the most interesting areas of confluence between psychoanalysis, neurobiology, and developmental psychopathology.

The psychoanalytic view of trauma and stress has focused on the individual's internal experience of any given event; the developmental approach to studying stress and trauma has more often categorized the stress first externally, by considering the characteristics of the events and observing changes in the child's behavior and adaptation to the external world. In the past two decades, multiple studies have addressed the related issues of how stressful events are perceived, metabolized, and reworked in children across development (see Cicchetti, Toth, and Lynch, 1993; Pynoos, 1993, 1995; Pynoos, Nader, and March, 1991). Defining the range of effects of traumatic events has involved creating typologies of traumatic circumstances that take into account such dimensions as whether the event involves a single individual, a family, or a whole community; whether it is an act of random or group-related violence; and how proximal the child and family were to the life-threatening event (Pynoos, 1993). A parallel and equally essential effort has been the creation of descriptive schemas to help in understanding children's behavioral responses to stressful events (Nader and Pynoos, 1991; Pynoos, Steinberg, and Wraith, 1995) and to make use of data from multiple sources, including parents, teachers, and other family members (Yule and Williams, 1990). Disturbances in memory, information processing, relatedness to others, and arousal regulation (e.g., sleep-wake disturbance, increased vigilance and startle, and impaired attention) are psychobiological manifestations of stress reactions (McNally, 1991; Ornitz, 1991). There is also increased awareness that variations in the traumatic intensity of an event relate to the child's developmental level—that is, the developmental saliency of the stressful or traumatic event (Pynoos, Steinberg and Wraith, 1995). For example, for young children, most salient may be the loss of protection and safety, whereas for an older child, the traumatic valence is carried in the feeling of helplessness (e.g., Laor et al., 1995).

Inherent in studies of the responses of children (and adults) to trauma is the notion of anxiety and arousal regulation. Within developmental variations in the experience of a stressful event is the individual variation in a child's ability to deal with markedly increased states of arousal and nearly overwhelming affects. Studies of arousal and anxiety regulation bring developmentalists closest to the biological roots of development. Children's capacity to tolerate increased arousal varies individually as well as maturationally, and those children with a predisposition to become excessively aroused in novel situations are at increased risk for being acutely, and perhaps chronically, overwhelmed in any number of traumatic circumstances. The neurophysiological core of self-regulatory capacities in children involves the regulation of arousal states in response to stimulation through the interaction of inhibitory and excitatory mechanisms in the central nervous system (Fox and Fitzgerald, 1990; Thompson, 1994). Arousal level is increased in the context of novelty, and the regulation of arousal serves as a gating mechanism to optimize orientation and attention and thus information processing, learning, and memory (Posner and Petersen, 1988, 1990; Rothbart and Posner, 1985).

In the first year of life, at least two neurophysiological shifts in arousal regulation take place (Thompson, 1994). First, there is a general decline in the lability of diffuse excitation with stimulation, which is attributable in part to the maturation of the hypothalamic-pituitary-adrenocortical system, which modulates reactions to stress (Stansbury and Gunnar, 1994), and in part to maturational changes in parasympathetic regulation (Porges, Doussard-Roosevelt, and Maiti, 1994). Second, cortical inhibitory controls over arousal gradually emerge (Dawson, 1994; Fox, 1994; Papoušek and Papoušek, 1984; Prechtl, 1984). Through the early preschool years, brain-stem and midbrain functions subserving arousal regulation, selective and sustained attention, and memory continue to mature. These maturational patterns may be altered by environmental conditions, such as parental neglect, by perinatal complications, such as prenatal drug exposure (Mayes, 1995), and by postnatal events, such as severe illness and acute, overwhelming trauma (True et al., 1993; Ornitz, 1991; Ornitz and Pynoos, 1989; Pitman, 1989).

Arousal regulation and the experience of stress and trauma converge at the level of central processes. When a given threshold of arousal is exceeded, the central nervous system registers a particular experience as so far out of the ordinary that it responds with different modes of functioning (Pittman, 1988). These highly emotionally charged experiences lead to a complex state of heightened arousal and sensory sensitivity; overpowering affects of surprise, terror, uncertainty, fear, and rage; the outpouring of hormones and neuromodulators related to acute stress; and varied defenses, including actual flight, arrested flight, and dissociations. These states are registered in the central nervous system differently from the average, expectable experiences with which a child may cope, and they may lead to enduring alterations (Pynoos and Nader, 1989; van der Kolk, Greenberg, Boyd, and Krystal, 1985; Watson, Hoffman, and Wilson, 1988). When the protective barriers give away, both psychological structures and biological structures are overwhelmed.

Maturational differences in arousal regulation or in the threshold for the activation of stress-related neuromodulators account for some variation in what is experienced as traumatic. Because of their less mature arousal-regulatory capacities, younger children are more likely to experience as overwhelming the body-based effects of anxiety and other affects associated with stressful events and the mental experience of trauma. The more capacities for arousal regulation have matured, the more differentiated and less global are children's responses to traumatic events, and the nature of what is traumatic—that is, over-arousing—also changes. Level of maturation and individual variations in the biology of arousal regulation also interact with the level of acute and chronic environmental stress and chaos. The more children's environments are also disrupted or overwhelmed, the more likely it is that they will experience any given event as stressful and traumatic. Moreover, children living amid pervasive environmental neglect have less reserve in their ability to tolerate acutely stressful events at any maturational level and any level of arousal regulation; and there is an interaction between arousal-regulatory capacities and level of environmental chaos. Children who have especially labile arousal-regulatory capacities and who live in chaotic environments are more susceptible to the developmentally debilitating effects of stress than children in less chaotic environments or those with more integrated arousal-regulatory capacities.

Short-term distress, as in brief separations, may lead to adaptive coping, structure formation, and healthy defenses—Anna Freud's notion of inherent self-righting tendencies. These prime the child's psychological immune system, allowing him to accommodate to the experiential viruses of the real world. Persistent distress, as in repeated moves from one foster home to another, predispose the child to failure in developing the ability to feel safe and secure with others or when alone, to enjoy reciprocity, or to tolerate normal frustrations and regulate shifts in states of arousal. What constitutes a normal, immunizing dose and what overwhelms the mental adaptive immune system remain crucial questions for those studying children with combinations of biological and psychosocial risks (see also Marans, this volume).

In a sense, traumatic or stressful events are experiments of nature that permit a closer appraisal of the interaction between often psychologically and biologically overwhelming events and developmental adaptation—an actualization of Anna Freud's harmony and disharmony along developmental lines. They also serve as a magnifying lens through which we can view the developmental ontogeny of arousal and anxiety regulation—an example of how studies of dysfunction can further the understanding of normality. Accounting for the long-term negative (or positive) impact of trauma and overwhelming stress represents an important convergence among the psychoanalytic understanding of individual differences in the processing and meaning of events, biological theories of brain functioning, and developmental theories about critical stages in development—an inherently multidisciplinary enterprise and one that is compatible with a developmental psychoanalytic psychology.

Conclusions: The Place of a Developmental Psychoanalytic Psychology

Anna Freud had a remarkable capacity for fantasy and for being what she called a "quick sketcher" (Young-Bruehl, 1989, p. 382). She felt that in her work she painted pictures rather than methodically building structures, and she took great pleasure in being able to play in thought. Against the background of that self-perception stands a body of work that is remarkably detailed and methodical, the work of an investigator who professed no knowledge of or aptitude for the academy of empirical research. Through the creative energy of her imagination, she created a general psychology of development built not on discontinuous phases but on seamless continuity. It allows for innate endowment and for complex interactions among areas of development and between biology and experience. Despite her relative isolation from the formal academy, Anna Freud created a remarkably current model of development that implicitly draws upon principles of neurobiology, genetics, pediatrics, and social psychology.

Of all the child analysts who were her contemporaries, the body of data from which she created her psychology is the most public and available for discussion. Her model of development presents testable hypotheses about, for example, the saliency of a given symptom profile for psychopathology or impaired adaptation. In her notion of the harmony/disharmony of development along the different lines is an implicit undertone of her father's central emphasis on conflict but with a less dichromatic coloring. Disharmony comes in many forms and intensities and may be transient or permanent; it is not inevitable but, unlike conflict, may not be present. At the most profound level of synthesis, disharmony and harmony are the metapsychological by-products of the regulatory process that move development along.

And yet, the notion of disharmony and harmony also contains an outline of unfinished work. Recognizing what Anna Freud left for others to finish is as much a part of her intellectual legacy as understanding what she left fully articulated. Up to the time of her death, Anna Freud struggled to clarify not just how developmental lines were metapsychologically the regulators of development but also how a fully integrated self emerged from those multiple regulatory processes. For psychoanalysis, how self differentiates is the internal-world subtext of the question what moves development along. Anna Freud's disharmony and harmony, balance and imbalance, were metapsychologically subtly different from the relation between drive and defense and contained suggestions of a beginning self-psychology. In her emphasis on harmony, she implicitly moved away from the primacy of drives in developmental processes toward increasing emphasis on development in the context of the social/parenting environment. She was close to an organization of self-differentiation that was outside traditional phase/stage theory. In this nascent organization, instinct emerges out of interaction with the environment, a model Loewald would later explicate more fully (1962). However, she was not able to articulate explicitly the concept of drives as regulated or shaped by self and other or to step outside the most fundamental early psychoanalytic notion of conflict and defense as defining of self and character. Such an adherence was perhaps the fate of her synthetic mind: like her father, she was constantly concerned with how to integrate new ideas with the old and maintain both in her metapsychology. In her efforts toward synthesis, she could not completely foreclose on the old to turn traditional drive-driven notions of self-development on their head; and she left developmental psychoanalysts with the challenge of more fully articulating a developmental self-psychology.

Nonetheless, Anna Freud's completed work is quietly elegant, so much so that it often appears understated. Precisely because she wanted to create a general developmental psychology, she did not create a canon around which followers could congregate. Late in her life, she expressed the wish that "a more or less comprehensive developmental psychology could be added to the existing body of psychoanalytic metapsychology" (1978b, p. 343). This is the wish of a true investigator, never certain that she has completely articulated the necessary synthesis of ideas or the full integration she thought others might achieve. While such a non-personalized legacy may represent a danger to the enduring reputation of its creator, it does free child analysts to follow ideas rather than a person. Indeed, perhaps Anna Freud's greatest legacy is her encouragement of child analysts working to understand the most central developmental question—what moves development along—to gather conceptual approaches from multiple disciplines while maintaining a respect for the analytic observational tool (A. Freud, 1958; Lustman, 1967).

How to move closer to Anna Freud's vision of a general developmental psychoanalytic psychology is the crucial task for child analysis in the next decades. The task requires understanding what distinguishes child psychoanalysis from other disciplines working with children and simultaneously opening up increasing dialogue with those disciplines. Child psychoanalysis is a method of understanding and of asking questions. It is defined by its primary emphasis on the emergence of the child's inner experiences and internal world. In particular, the child psychoanalyst is interested in the ways in which the child takes in the social world and transmutes experience into psychic structures and into a mental life. At the very start of life, the social world plays a major role in shaping the child's internal, biologically given regulatory capacities into the psychological forces that present themselves as having the driving or motivational role of instincts. In the first years, the child creates his sense of being a valued person within the intimate family. The inner world of the child is constructed in relation to the dynamic biological and experiential influences that are operative at the moment, as well as in relation to the underlying biological and experiential continuities that provide development with a sense of historical coherence. Developmental currents or lines course through changes in surface, or behavioral, manifestations. The child analyst sees children's growth in terms of the building up of complex internal mental structures and fantasies that integrate desire, constraint, action, and defense and continuously influence response, action, and thought.

These same types of interactive models, albeit stated in a different operationalized terminology, constitute the central biologic-environment interaction paradigms guiding contemporary child psychiatry, child development, and studies of developmental psychopathology. Child psychiatrists are actively concerned with how the expression of, for example, anxiety disorder is modified by the child's experience and vice versa, how the child's anxiety-regulation difficulties modify his or her response to the environment. Thus, in the next years, an essential part of refining a developmental psychoanalytic psychology is the juxtaposition of child psychoanalysis with other ways of studying and caring for children, including the process of therapy. Interest in child psychoanalysis will persist; however, it evolves in the next decades but that interest is more likely to be sustained if the field becomes more accessible to non-analysts and is brought into an integrated place that allows critical debate, teaching, and research. This openness to change, this catholicity of concern, is hard to sustain, especially as related investigative approaches become more technical and specialized, and there is always a tendency for defensive orthodoxy and thus for heresies to develop as in all fields. But what is most remarkable is the fertility of the child psychoanalytic enterprise, the range and depth of the ideas that emerge from spending time with, observing, and trying to help children through focusing on the force and nuances of their inner experience. The information gained from prolonged work with children enriches the more structured empirical disciplines of child psychiatry and child development.

Through the observational method, the psychoanalytic enterprise generates hypotheses for research in the areas of common interest to all fields dealing with child development—for example, the range of expression of psychiatric disorders across development, the effects of early and persistent trauma, the interaction between experience and biology. Conversely, active contact with non-analytic colleagues will enable child psychoanalysts to better integrate their work into the current models of genetic-environment interaction and understanding about the neurobiological underpinnings of a number of mental processes and early disorders. Thus, child psychoanalysis will be more likely to remain a viable and productive academic discipline shaping the mainstream of child research. The past and enduring contributions of Anna Freud's developmental psychoanalytic psychology to child psychiatry and child development are in asking how mind and body are brought together, and the interaction between the biologic and the mental remains the common ground of all disciplines concerned with children.

BIBLIOGRAPHY

Arlow, J. A. (1987). Trauma, play, and perversion. *Psychoanal. Study Child,* 42:31–44.

Bergman, P., & Escalona, S. K. (1949). Unusual sensitivities in very young children. *Psychoanal. Study Child, 3/4:* 333–352.

Cicchetti, D. (1993). Developmental psychopathology: Reactions, reflections, projections. *Developmental Review, 13:* 471–502.

Cicchetti, D., & Cohen, D. J. (1995). *Developmental psychopathology.* New York: John Wiley and Sons.

Cicchetti, D., Toth, S. L., & Lynch, M. (1993). The developmental sequelae of child maltreatment: Implications for war-related trauma. In L. Leavitt and N. Fox, eds., *Psychological effects of war and violence on children* (pp. 47–71) Hillsdale, NJ: Erlbaum.

Dawson, G. (1994). Frontal electroencephalographic correlates of individual differences in emotion expression in infants: A brain systems perspective on emotion. In N. Fox, ed. *The development of emotion regulation*, pp. 135–151 *Monographs of the Society for Research in Child Development*, 59(2–3, Serial No 240).

Escalona, S. K. (1963). Patterns of infantile experience and the developmental process. *Psychoanal. Study Child*, 18:197–244.

Fox, N. A. (1994). Dynamic cerebral processes underlying emotion regulation In N. Fox, ed. *The development of emotion regulation*, pp. 152–166. *Monograph of the Society for Research in Child Development*, 59(2–3, Serial No. 240).

Fox, N. A., & Fitzgerald, H. E. (1990). Autonomic function in infancy. *Merrill-Palmer Quarterly*, 36: 27–51.

Freud, A. (1951a). The contribution of psychoanalysis to genetic psychology *The Writings of Anna Freud*, vol. 4, pp. 107–142.

Freud, A. (1951b). Observations on child development. *The Writings of Anne Freud*, vol. 4, pp. 143–162.

Freud, A. (1951c). An experiment in group upbringing. *The Writings of Anne Freud*, vol. 4, pp. 163–229.

Freud, A. (1958). Clinical observation and prediction of development: A memorial lecture in honor of Ernst Kris. *Psychoanal. Study of the Child*, 13: 92–116.

Freud, A. (1974). A psychoanalytic view of developmental psychopathology *The Writings of Anna Freud*, vol. 8, pp. 57–74.

Freud, A. (1962). Clinical problems of young children. *The Writings of Anna Freud*, vol. 5, pp. 352–368.

Freud, A. (1965). Normality and pathology in childhood. *The Writings of Anna Freud*, vol. 7.

Freud, A. (1978a). The principal task of child analysis. *The Writings of Anna Freud*, vol. 8, pp. 96–109.

Freud, A. (1978b). Inaugural lecture for the Sigmund Freud Chair at the Hebrew University, Jerusalem. *The Writings of Anna Freud*, vol. 8, p. 343.

Freud, S. (1910). Five lectures on psychoanalysis. S.E. 11.

Greenacre, P. (1952). Trauma, Growth, and Personality. New York: W. W. Norton.

Greenacre, P. (1941a). The predisposition of anxiety. I. *Psychoanal. Q.*, 10: 66–94.

Greenacre, P. (1941b). The predisposition of anxiety. II. *Psychoanal. Q.*, 10:610–638.

Laor, N., Wolmer, L., Mayes, L. C., Golomb, A., et al. (1995). Israeli preschoolers under SCUD missile attacks: Developmental perspectives on risk-modifying factors. Unpublished manuscript, Tel Aviv-Brull Community Mental Health Center.

Loewald, H. (1962). Instinct theory, object relations, and psychic structure formation. In *Papers on Psychoanalysis*, pp. 207–218. New Haven: Yale University Press.

LUSTMAN, S. L. (1967). The scientific leadership of Anna Freud. *Journal of the American Psychoanalytic Association, 15:*810–827.

MARANS, S., & COHEN, D. (1993). Children and inner city violence. In *Psychological Effects of War and Violence on Children*, L. Leavitt and N. Fox, ed. In press.

MAYES, L. C. (1995). Substance abuse and parenting. In M. H. Bornstein, ed., *The Handbook of Parenting*, (pp. 101–125). Mahwah, NJ: Erlbaum.

McNALLY, R. J. (1991). Assessment of posttraumatic stress disorder in children. *Psychological Assessment, 3,* 1–7.

NADER, K., & PYNOOS, R. (1992). Drawing and play in the diagnosis and assessment of childhood post-traumatic stress syndromes. In C. Schaefer, K. Gitlan, and A. Sandgrun, eds., *Play, Diagnosis, and Assessment*, (pp. 375–389). New York: Wiley.

ORNITZ, E., & PYNOOS, R. (1989). Startle modulation in children with post-traumatic stress disorder. *American Journal of Psychiatry, 147:* 866–870.

ORNITZ, E. J. (1991). Developmental aspects of neurophysiology. In M. Lewis, ed., *Child and adolescent psychiatry: A comprehensive textbook* (pp. 38–51). Baltimore: Williams and Wilkins.

PAPOUSEK, H., & PAPOUSEK, M. (1984). Qualitative transitions in integrative processes during the first trimester of human postpartum life. In H. F. R. Prechtl, ed., *Community of Mental Functions from Prenatal to Postnatal Life*, (pp. 230–244). Clinics in Developmental Medicine, 94. Philadelphia: Blackwell Scientific Publications.

PITTMAN, R. K. (1988). Post-traumatic stress disorder, conditioning, and network theory. *Psychiatric Annals, 18:*182–189.

PORGES, S. W., DOUSSARD-ROOSEVELT, J. A., & MAITI, A. K. (1994). Vagal tone and the physiological regulation of emotion. In N. Fox, ed. *The Development of Emotion Regulation*, pp. 167–188. *Monographs of the Society for Research in Child Development, 59* (2–3, Serial No. 240).

POSNER, M. I., & PETERSEN, S. E. (1988). Structures and functions of selected attention. In T. Boll and B. Bryant, eds., *Master Lectures of Clinical Neuropsychology* (pp. 173–202). Washington, DC: American Psychological Association.

POSNER, M. I., & PETERSEN, S. E. (1990). The attention system of the human brain. *Annual Review of Neuroscience, 13,* 25–42.

PRECHTL, H. F. R. (1984). Continuity and change in early neural development. In H. F. R. Prechtl, ed., *Community of Mental Functions from Prenatal to Postnatal Life* (pp. 1–15). *Clinics in Developmental Medicine, 94.* Philadelphia: Blackwell Scientific Publications.

PROVENCE, S. (1983). Struggling against deprivation and trauma: A longitudinal study. *Psychoanal. Study Child, 38:*233–256.

PRUETT, K. D. (1984). Chronology defensive adaptations in severe psychological trauma. *Psychoanal. Study Child, 39:*591–612.

PYNOOS, R., STEINBERG, A. M., & WRAIT, R. (1995). A developmental model of childhood traumatic stress. In D. Cicchetti, and D. J. Cohen, eds. *Developmental Psychopathology*, pp. 72–95. New York: John Wiley and Sons.

PYNOOS, R. (1993). Traumatic stress and developmental psychopathology in children and adolescents. In J. M. Oldham, M. B. Ribs, and A. Tasman, eds., *American Psychiatric Press Review of Psychiatry*, vol. 12, p. 208. Washington, DC: American Psychiatric Press.

PYNOOS, R. S., & NADER, K. (1989). Children's memory and proximity to violence. *Journal of the American Academy of Child and Adolescent Psychiatry*, 28, 236–241.

PYNOOS, R., NADER, K., & MARCH, J. (1991). Childhood post-traumatic stress disorder. In J. Weiner, ed., *The Textbook of Child and Adolescent Psychiatry*, (pp. 955–984). Washington, DC: American Psychiatric Press.

ROTHBART, M. K., & POSNER, M. I. (1985). Temperament and the development of self-regulation. In H. Hartlage and C. E. Telzrow, eds., *Neuropsychology of Individual Differences: A Developmental Perspective*, (pp. 93–123). New York: Plenum.

SCHWAB-STONE, M. E., AYERS, T. S., KASPROW, W., VOYCE, C., ET AL. (1995). No safe haven: A study of violence exposure in an urban community. *Journal of the American Academy of Child and Adolescent Psychiatry*, 34:1343–1352.

SROUFE, L. A., & RUTTER, M. (1984). The domain of developmental psychopathology. *Child Development*, 55: 17–29.

STANSBURY, K., & GUNNAR, M. R. (1994). Adrenocortical activity and emotion regulation. In N. Fox, ed. *The Development of Emotion Regulation*, pp. 108–134. *Monographs of the Society for Research in Child Development*, 59(2–3, Serial No. 240).

TERR, L. C. (1984). Time and trauma. *Psychoanal. Study Child*, 39:633–665.

THOMPSON, R. A. (1994). Emotion regulation: A theme in search of definition. In N. Fox, ed. *The development of emotion regulation*, pp. 25–52. *Monographs of the Society for Research in Child Development*, 59(2–3, Serial No. 240).

TRUE, W. R., RICE, J., EISEN, S. A., HEATH, A., GOLDBERG, J., LYONS, M., & NOWAK, J. (1993). A twin study of genetic and environmental contributions to liability for posttraumatic stress symptoms. *Archives of General Psychiatry*, 50: 257–264.

VAN DER KOLK, GREENBERG, M., BOYD, H., & KRYSTAL, J. (1985). Inescapable shock, neurotransmitters, and addiction to trauma: Toward a psychobiology of post-traumatic stress. *Biological Psychiatry*, 20: 314–325.

WATSON, I. P. B., HOFFMAN, L., & WILSON, G. V. (1988). The neuropsychiatry of post-traumatic stress disorder. *British Journal of Psychiatry*, 152: 164–173.

WEIL, A. (1978). Maturational variations and genetic-dynamic issues. *J. Amer. Psychoanal. Assn.*, 26:461–492.

WEIL, A. (1956). Deviational development in infancy and early childhood. *Psychoanal. Study Child*, 11:292–299.

YORKE, C., KENNEDY, H., & WISEBERG, S. (1981). Some clinical and theoretical aspects of two developmental lines. In *The Course of Life* (pp. 619–673). Adelphi, MD: US Department of Health.

YOUNG-BRUEHL, E. (1988). *Anna Freud: A Biography.* New York: Summit Books.

YULE, W., & WILLIAMS, R. (1990). Post-traumatic stress reactions in children. *Journal of Traumatic Stress, 3:* 279–295.

ZIGLER, E., & GLICK, M. (1986). *A Developmental Approach to Adult Psychopathology.* New York: Wiley.

Anna Freud

A Historical Look at Her Theory and Technique of Child Psychoanalysis

JILL M. MILLER, PH.D.

This paper traces historically the development of Anna Freud's thinking about the theory and technique of child psychoanalysis. Representing more than fifty years of work, her ideas were refined and many were altered, influenced by naturalistic and clinical observations and her developmental viewpoint. The paper begins with her 1926 Introductory Lectures, which contain both her early views about the technique used with children as compared to adults and the origins of many of her later ideas. It follows her theories up through her final papers, published in the late 1970s.

BACKGROUND

ANNA FREUD BEGAN HER CAREER AS A TEACHER, APPLYING PSYCHOANALY-
tic principles to education. She created a network of people devoted to work with children and in 1937 opened the Jackson Nursery in Vienna, providing day care for children aged one and a half through three years. It was here that she began her studies on separation and substitute caregivers, libidinal development, the impact of the internal and external world on a child, child development, and the systematic use of

Faculty, Denver Institute for Psychoanalysis and Colorado Center for Psychoanalytic Studies; clinical instructor, Department of Psychiatry, University of Colorado, Health Sciences Center.

The Psychoanalytic Study of the Child 51, ed. Albert J. Solnit, Peter B. Neubauer, Samuel Abrams, and A. Scott Dowling (Yale University Press, copyright © 1996 by Albert J. Solnit, Peter B. Neubauer, Samuel Abrams, and A. Scott Dowling).

observations of children. A year later when Anna Freud and her family were forced to flee to London, the Jackson Nursery was closed. Two years later, along with Dorothy Burlingham, Anna Freud opened the Hampstead War Nurseries, where she was able to continue her work.

The War Nurseries began as a Children's Rest Centre with the aim of serving the needs of London children who had been made homeless by air raids and had not yet been evacuated. In 1941 the funding for this project was taken over by the American Foster Parents' Plan, which gave Freud and Burlingham the opportunity to improve and stabilize the original center and to open two new residential houses, the Babies' Rest Centre in London for children too young to be sent to the country without their mothers, and a country house in Essex for those who had been evacuated. These nurseries provided wartime homes for children whose family life had been disrupted temporarily or permanently. While it was impossible to replace their families, Freud and Burlingham thought it important to try to establish the security of a stable home with its opportunities for individual development. This idea broke from the traditional thinking by which institutions had previously been run.

Volume III of Anna Freud's writings (1939–45) includes fifty-six monthly reports on the activities of the Hampstead War Nurseries and lays down the major scientific conclusions drawn from this work. These reports were the first studies of children who had to go through their early years deprived of family care. Others soon came to share this interest in the effects of early loss and separation on families, particularly John Bowlby and Donald Winnicott in London and later René Spitz in the United States. The war was the precipitating and aggravating agent for these studies, but their importance lay in their findings on the effects of the dissolution of families and the impact of residential care on children. Reviewing her work three decades later, Anna Freud was "glad to note that . . . many of the findings presented here as new have become familiar tenets on which a much more critical view of residential upbringing and its consequences for personality development [is] based" (1939–45: xx).

In 1945 the War Nurseries closed, but Anna Freud's concerns about and interest in child development and the impact of loss and separation persisted as she turned her attention to children who were concentration-camp survivors. This work provided an unrivaled opportunity to observe the development of these young victims after their liberation, especially in terms of children's social relationships.

Anna Freud's activities also focused on the training of child psychoanalysts. The aftermath of the war saw an increased interest in children and the need for child training and guidance centers. It also brought renewed interest worldwide in psychoanalysis. In 1947, the Hampstead Child Therapy Training officially began training candidates who had previously been workers in the War Nurseries. Five years later Anna Freud opened the Hampstead Clinic. (The name was changed to the Anna Freud Centre after her death in 1982.) In 1958 the Hampstead Nursery admitted its first group of preschool-aged children.

It is difficult to assess Anna Freud's work without also seeing the teacher in her. Her interest was first in normality and only subsequently in the deviations that constitute pathology, an approach that was both normative and prospective. Anna Freud maintained a strong tie between clinical material and theory throughout her life, integrating findings of clinical psychoanalysis and observational studies. She pioneered naturalistic observations of the child as a research tool in an attempt to extrapolate developmental theory as opposed to basing it on the reconstructed child. These studies included infants and toddlers in residential care, her experiments in group upbringings with child survivors, and later work with children from deprived homes who were in daycare at the Hampstead Nursery. This work, along with that of others who followed her tradition, has successfully verified, extended, or re-examined aspects of developmental and psychoanalytic theory and in some cases has resulted in new theories. Through observations and the careful examination and classification of data from direct analytic work, Anna Freud's theories were constantly developing. This paper is an attempt to trace this development historically.

THE EARLY YEARS

Introductory Lectures on Child Analysis, published in 1926, outlined Anna Freud's early thinking. As no model existed for child psychoanalysis other than the applied work of Siegfried Bernfeld (1925) and August Aichhorn (1925), Anna Freud formed a group of interested analysts composed of Marianne Kris, Hedwig and Willi Hoffer, Editha and Richard Sterba, and Jenny Waelder-Hall. The *Introductory Lectures* were based on seminars Anna Freud gave to this small group of pioneers and were a response to Melanie Klein's first paper, which had been published a year earlier.

The origins of Anna Freud's thinking about development, technique, and the task of child analysis can be seen in these early papers. Basing her findings on the analysis of ten latency-age children, Anna Freud introduced child analysis and compared it to adult analysis. The child, she said, was different from the adult in many respects, necessitating modifications in the technique used for neurotic adults. She had no qualms about modifying this technique saying, "In my opinion, it is no reflection on the analytic method, designed as it is for a single particular object, the adult neurotic, if one seeks to apply it with modifications to other types of objects. There is no harm in contriving to use it for other purposes. Only one should be at pains to know what one is doing" (1927a: 69). However, Anna Freud also thought that there were some similarities between child and adult analysis. She said: "I maintain that in order to suit a new situation I merely extended certain elements of an attitude that you all show to your patients, though without especially stressing it" (1927b: 20). The elements she thought were irrespective of the age of the patient and included: arousing the patient's interest in analytic work, indicating that the analyst was there to help and support the patient, accepting the patient's version of his conflicts with his family and the external world, and making oneself interesting and useful to the patient. Anna Freud's interest in what became known as the widening scope of psychoanalysis, the application of psychoanalysis to other than neurotic disorders, began with this development of a technique particular to children.

Anna Freud suggested a preparatory period prior to analysis, an idea that she later abandoned but that contained the roots of many commonly known techniques today.[1] The task of the preparatory period was to make the patient analyzable—that is, to induce insight into his disturbance, impart confidence in the analyst, and turn the decision for analysis into the child's own. This phase, she thought, did not involve "real analytic work" in the sense of making unconscious processes conscious or analyzing transference and resistance, nor did it mean establishing a positive transference. The aim of the preparatory phase was "to create a tie strong enough to sustain the later analysis" (1927c: 14). Implied is the establishment of a treatment alliance that could be maintained in the face of resistance, a concept introduced by Elizabeth Zetzel (1956) thirty years later.

As it was thought that children were often not as troubled by their symptoms as were parents and other adults, another aim of the preparatory phase was to make egosyntonic symptoms dystonic. Here the roots of the present-day term "creating conflict" can be seen.

The development of a transference neurosis, a concept introduced by Freud in 1914, was conceived of as the aim of analysis with adults and the primary vehicle for change. At this time Anna Freud strongly

1. Anna Freud always maintained that her ideas about a preparatory phase were misunderstood. What she had in mind was forming a relationship with a child prior to doing analysis. (Hansi Kennedy, 1990: personal communication)

believed that children did not develop a transference neurosis. She defined the concept as follows: "He [the patient] gives up the old objects on which his fantasies where hitherto fixed, and centers his neurosis anew upon the person of the analyst . . . he replaces his previous symptoms with transference symptoms, transposing his existing neurosis, or whatever kind, into a transference neurosis, and displays all his abnormal reactions in relation to the new transference person, the analyst" (1927d: 44). In the case of a child, she thought the original objects remained real and important figures. Unlike the adult, the child was dependent on them in the present. Consequently, the original objects were never fully replaced by the analyst in the transference. Transference was still a feature in child analysis, although at this point she believed it involved only single episodes of friendly and hostile impulses and did not readily lend itself to interpretation. The negative impulses directed toward the analyst could foster dangerous feelings and tempt the child to act upon them; therefore they should be dealt with immediately. It was in the positive transference that the fruitful work of the analysis was thought to take place as an affectionate attachment was a prerequisite for all later analytic work. These views were to undergo many changes in years to come.

In 1926 analysts thought their task was to raise conflicts between the instinctual unconscious, ego, and superego to a higher level, making what was unconscious conscious. Instinctual impulses would then be freed from repression and made accessible to the influence of the superego which would determine their fate. This applied to both children and adults. However, with children the outer world affected the mechanisms of the infantile neurosis more deeply as their investment and dependence on parental objects were greater and more necessary. This factor created two differences in the analysis of children. First, the child's superego was still in the process of developing, requiring help from the environment. Secondly, as the child's superego and ego were not yet sufficiently mature to reject some impulses, sublimate others, and allow gratification to still others, the responsibility for the fate of these impulses remained with the parents. This created problems, for "the parents who are now called upon to help in the child's recovery are still the same people who let the child get ill in the first place" (1927a: 59). Consequently, "there remains but one solution to this difficult situation. The analyst must claim for himself the liberty to guide the child at this important point, in order to secure, to some extent, the achievements of analysis" (1927a: 60). Anna Freud called this process educational, using the term in its widest sense. The need to both analyze and educate made the analyst's task a difficult one. "The analyst accordingly combines in his own person two difficult and diametrically opposed functions: he has to analyze and educate, that is to say, in the same breath he must allow and forbid, loosen and bind again" (1927a: 65). Here were the roots of what was to be defined as the task of child analysis—restoring the child to the path of normal development—as well as the origins of Anna Freud's thinking about the multidimensional aspects of the analytic relationship and the mixture of technical approaches.

In order to accomplish the dual task of analyzing and educating, the analyst needed to assess not only the internal state of the child but also the external forces that contributed to the disturbance. Parents had to be able to support the child's treatment and aid in his further development once analysis was completed. Here Anna Freud was alluding to the idea that the analyst should work with parents as well as the child. In addition, because of the child's continuing development and the ongoing influence of his environment, Anna Freud thought analysis was no guarantee that the child would have no difficulties in the future. She always believed that analysis could restore the child to a path of normal development, thus improving his chances in the future, but not necessarily protecting him from later problems.

ANNA FREUD'S DEVELOPMENTAL POINT OF VIEW

Throughout her life Anna Freud maintained that the task of child psychoanalysis was to both analyze and educate. The implied meaning of "educate"—to intervene in a child's development—became explicit in later writings as she formulated what was to become the central focus of her theory of child analysis—a child's development.

THE SEARCH FOR CRITERIA FOR CHILD ANALYSIS

Anna Freud struggled to identify the proper criteria for analysis with children. Obviously, the criteria used for adults did not suffice. To begin with, the degree of suffering was not adequate as an indicator, for it could be the environment that suffered rather than the child; or a child's defenses could be strong enough to prevent suffering although at a cost. Secondly, a disturbance in a child's capacity to love and to work was hard to gauge. The equivalent to the adult's capacity to work was the capacity to play. In children a disturbance could manifest itself in an inability to play or in excessive imaginative play at the cost of constructive play; however this was not a sufficient criterion. Anna Freud concluded that the criteria for child analysis were disturbances in a child's development. The indications for treatment were not the neurotic manifestations themselves but the bearing these had on the developmental process: "there is only one factor of such central importance that its impairment through a neurosis calls for immediate action; namely, the child's ability to develop, not to remain fixated at some stage of development before the maturation process has been concluded" (1945: 17).

Anna Freud incorporated her developmental viewpoint into her theory and technique as well as her thinking about assessment. This viewpoint ushered in her Diagnostic Profile and the idea of developmental lines. It was "the essence of this approach," she said, "that developmental considerations take precedence over consideration of symptomatology and manifest behavior" (1962: 26).

SYMPTOMS

The child's overt symptomatology, said Anna Freud, could be deceiving. In some instances symptoms could be transitory and appear at a time in development when high demands were made on the child's personality. When that time passed, the symptoms could disappear. This was not a sign of pathology but a reaction to a stressor. In other instances symptoms could be lasting, the first sign of permanent pathology. They could also shift, as when an anxiety moved from one important object to another or one compulsion was substituted for another. Furthermore, the same symptom or behavior exhibited by two children could have different roots and internal meanings. Thus, symptoms were not the key to understanding. Instead, Anna Freud believed the analyst needed to look to the nature of the child's internal world, the level of development he had reached, and the organization of his intrapsychic structures. Her focus was on the whole child, with all elements of his functioning and internal organization, both healthy and disturbed, emphasizing the deviation from, and interferences with, normal personality development.

THE DIAGNOSTIC PROFILE

Anna Freud thought that through a diagnostic assessment the analyst could pinpoint the relevance of a symptom to a particular child at a particular time. This involved assessment of the child's developmental level psychic structure and the dynamic significance of the symptom. Anna Freud's Diagnostic Profile was an attempt at such an assessment, a way to hypothesize the underlying metapsychological pathogens in order to ascertain the appropriate therapeutic intervention. Its basis was a developmental viewpoint and dynamic considerations rather than descriptive ones. It was basic to Anna Freud's thinking that "the value of no single item should be judged independently, i.e., not without the item seen within its setting" (1965: 138). The Profile presented both an external picture of the child and an internal picture containing "information about the structure of his personality; the dynamic interplay within the structure; some economic factors concerning drive activity and the relative strength of id and ego forces; his adaptation to reality; and some genetic assumptions" (1965: 140). The primary questions the Profile attempted to answer from a metapsychological perspective were: what level of development has the child attained, is he where he needs to be, and what is holding him up? The diagnostician would then recommend the best way to help the child move forward.

THE CONCEPT OF DEVELOPMENTAL LINES

By means of the Diagnostic Profile, the state of a child's inner agencies, functions, conflicts, attitudes, and achievements is seen against a background of developmental norms. Development had long been thought of as passing through phases. But psychosexual phases had their origins in the reconstruction of adults not children. In addition, all theories about phases were tied to particular areas of interest—for example, Freud and neurosis, Margaret Mahler and psychosis, Erik Erikson and social-psychological development. Anna Freud found the notion of phases inadequate and supplemented it with imbalances in development when she introduced the concept of developmental lines in 1963. Longitudinal lines of development distinguished a mature individual from an immature one, irrespective of health or illness. They were both descriptive, pointing to surface manifestations which are the observable steps, and metapsychological constructs. From these surface indicators conclusions could be drawn about the state of a child's mental organization and capacities. Lines of development, thought Anna Freud, were valid for almost every area of the child's personality. The lines delineated first included: from dependency to emotional self-reliance and adult object relationships; from suckling to rational eating; from wetting and soiling to bladder and bowel control; from irresponsibility to responsibility in body management; from egocentricity to companionship; and, from the body to the toy and from play to work. Over the years Anna Freud was to formulate others (1965, 1974b, 1979a).

THE WIDENING PARAMETERS OF CHILD ANALYSIS

Anna Freud came to the conclusion that the area that belonged to child analysis was development and that a child's development was the aim of analysis. With expanding research into this field, child analysts were learning more about developmental processes, which in turn had an impact on theory and technique. As with adult analysis, neurosis had been the focal point for child analysis, but in the 1960s Anna Freud's thinking led her to the idea of applying psychoanalysis to disturbances other than the neuroses. She thought that the more knowledge analysts gained, the wider the parameters of analysis would become. However, she warned that any extension of the parameters needed to have the aim of "bringing about the ultimate purposes and processes of the analytic end requirements" (1954b: 358).

Anna Freud and her colleagues at the Hampstead Clinic began to assess and treat analytically a variety of pathologies other than the infantile neuroses[2] such as excessive delays in acquiring ego functions, primary disturbances of narcissism or object relatedness, and disorders due to a lack of ego control, faulty superego development, or both. In 1966 Anna Freud introduced the concept of developmental disturbances, defined as "disorders which arise owing to the particular external and internal strains and stresses, dangers and anxieties connected with particular developmental phases, and which are transitory in the sense that they fade away with the passing of the developmental level on which they have emerged" (1966: 216). However, between the infantile neuroses and the developmental disturbances were a whole range of disturbances that needed to be considered.

In 1958 Michael Balint introduced the concept "basic fault" to describe certain disorders which did not originate in the three person relationship of the oedipal phase, an idea he elaborated in 1968. A fault was not a situation, complex, or a conflict. Instead it arose from the early mother-child relationship.

Anna Freud was interested in Balint's theories and struggled with the question of early deficits. She wondered if it was possible to treat them and whether they were reversible. Was analysis the method by which this could be done? In 1957 she was skeptical, saying: "While the effects of such early deprivation can be mitigated by later favorable influences, they cannot be undone or reversed or solved in a more age-adequate way, as conflicts can: this means that they are not in the true sense of the word a legitimate object of analytic effort" (1970c: 19). But by 1968 she had further examined interferences with development

---

2. Some of this work was carried out by a research group on the study and treatment of children diagnosed as borderline. See Sara Kut Rosenfeld, 1972a and 1972b, and with Marjorie Sprince, 1963 and 1965. As part of this research, Ruth Thomas in collaboration with Rose Edgcumbe, Hansi Kennedy, Maria Kawenoka and Lilian Weitzner, adapted the Diagnostic Profile to borderline and psychotic children (1966).

that were the result not of internal strife but of ongoing influences from the environment. Anna Freud thought analysts knew little about treating disorders of this type, and she continued to wonder whether and how far the neglect of developmental needs could be undone in treatment. Yet she did believe the child's response to the aftereffects could be alleviated. The neurotic superstructure that overlaid the basic damage could be dealt with analytically. With regard to the underlying deficit, the analyst could work within a framework of an improved version of the child's initial environment, aiming at a belated fulfillment of neglected developmental needs. Anna Freud did not think this approach was analytic. The "corrective emotional (i.e., developmental) experience" (1968b: 119) could be successful when the original frustration of needs and later fulfillment were not too far apart in time. In addition, the analyst could work with the parents with the idea that those who did the harm are the best ones to undo it. Success was dependent on the health and receptivity of the parents and the extent to which the child had internalized environmental influences. Franz Alexander (1948) introduced the term "corrective emotional experience," meaning that the analyst should actively behave in a different way than the patient expected. In this way, he thought, faulty development was corrected. Anna Freud's meaning was different. She thought when a disturbance was created by the environment the child had a chance in the analysis of having a different experience which could, perhaps, be correcting. This meant not starting development over but returning to the path of normal development.

Developmental disturbances now included not only those transitory disturbances defined in 1966 but also the broad category of nonneurotic disorders that resulted from the impact of the neglect of developmental needs on structure formation. Anna Freud concluded that treating these patients did fall under the auspices of child analysts. In treating these children it was important to recognize that the technique employed differed from that used in the treatment of neurotic children. The original psychoanalytic technique had been devised for the resolution of internal conflict, helped by interpretation of unconscious elements. In 1970 the analytic approach "now embraces the basic faults, failures, defects, and deprivations, i.e., the whole range of adverse external and internal factors, and it aims at the correction of their consequences" (1970b: 203). Nevertheless, Anna Freud thought there was no undoing of the past; rather, analysts helped the patient's ego come to terms with the residue, to face and cope with the consequences. This distinguished her approach to developmental defects from a more "corrective" approach.

152   *Jill M. Miller*

DEVELOPMENTAL DISHARMONY AND DEVELOPMENTAL LINES

In 1978 Anna Freud introduced the concept of developmental disharmonies, which encompassed early disturbances belonging to the basic fault. Disharmonies were tied to developmental lines and could be intrasystemic or intersystemic. Development, she said, is multiply determined. Forward moves along any one line are neither simple nor uncomplicated as "they owe their impetus not to a single determinant but to a variety of them, all of them different from each other" (1978a: 102). Each step along a line depends on interactions between various influences—for example, drive development, the maturation of ego functions, affect development, object relations and modes of attachment, and superego development, in addition to environmental contributions. In order for the personality to be harmonious, growth on one developmental line needs to correspond with growth on another. Moderate disharmonies produce the many variations of normality. If the disharmonies are more severe, pathology results. The analytic task is to trace the interaction between lines and to determine what components are causing the child's difficulties.

In 1979 Anna Freud proposed additional developmental lines that she thought would contribute to the understanding of childhood disturbance and child analytic technique. Under the rubric of ego functions or mechanisms she included secondary process functioning; distinguishing between the inner world and outer world; discharging mental excitation via mental, as opposed to somatic, pathways; impulse control; and the development of a time sense and insight. She concluded that the normality or pathology of development was dependent on four factors: (1) constitutional and experiential elements within an average and expectable range; (2) the maturation of internal agencies at approximately the same rate of speed, i.e., neither delayed nor precocious; (3) the timing of external interventions; and (4) age-adequate ego mechanisms, neither too primitive nor too sophisticated.

Development entails not only growth along numerous lines and harmony between lines, but synthesis, the integration of influences from internal and external sources into a whole. "Integration," Anna Freud said, "serves healthy growth provided the elements synthesized by it— namely, the constitutional givens, the rate of structuralization, and parental influence—remain within the limits of an expectable norm" (1979a: 128). However, this is not always the case: constitutional handicaps can exist; structure building can be uneven resulting in defects; environmental factors can influence integration. As Anna Freud explained: "It is the hallmark of the synthetic function that, while doing its work, it does not distinguish between what is suitable and unsuitable, helpful or harmful for the resulting picture. Thus, every step on the developmental line, besides being a compromise between conflicting forces, also represents an amalgamate of beneficial with malignant ingredients. The various mixtures which thereby are produced can be held responsible for the numerous variations, deviations, quirks, and eccentricities displayed in the final personality" (1979a: 129).

It was now thought that developmental disharmonies underlay infantile neuroses and that the two were inextricably bound together. "Developmental disharmonies," said Anna Freud, "are a fertile breeding ground for almost every type of infantile neurosis" (1978a: 108–9). Insight into developmental disharmonies and a variety of developmental disturbances influenced her view of infantile neuroses. An infantile neurosis was no longer seen only as the outcome of the child's inability to resolve the Oedipus complex; now it involved the whole personality and the convergence of difficulties throughout the child's preoedipal and oedipal development.

Anna Freud's developmental viewpoint continued to be refined and expanded throughout her life. A child's development was the focus of child analytic work and the basis of her Diagnostic Profile. As she struggled to understand the origins and metapsychology of other than neurotic disturbances and the appropriate treatment methods, she reformulated the way in which development was viewed, away from the notion of phases into a series of developmental lines. She suggested that each and every achievement the child was expected to make had its own line, and that lines interacted and affected one another's progress. This freed her to look at the intricacies of personality formation as influenced by constitution, the external environment, and the internal world of the child, and subjected to the ego's synthetic function. Over the years she expanded her ideas about developmental lines, introduced the concepts of developmental disharmonies and disturbances, and re-evaluated the notion of the infantile neurosis. While Anna Freud concluded that developmental disturbances were best treated analytically, she remained pessimistic about the results (Kennedy, 1990: personal communication). She believed that the effects of deprivation could not be undone or corrected, as Alexander and others thought, but that perhaps new adaptations could be found.

THE PROCESS AND TECHNIQUE OF CHILD PSYCHOANALYSIS

In 1923 Freud published 'The ego and the id,' followed in 1926 by 'Inhibitions, symptoms and anxiety.' They marked the beginning of a shift in psychoanalysis from content analysis to the analysis of structures, mechanisms and ways of functioning. They became the basis of Freudian and Anna Freudian thinking.

In 1936 Anna Freud wrote *The Ego and the Mechanisms of Defence,* which she presented to her father on the occasion of his eightieth birthday. In this important contribution to the field she developed Freud's 1923 and 1926 ideas of the centrality of the ego and its defenses against anxiety and other affects. She emphasized the ego's mediating position between the impulses of the id and the demands of the outside world and expanded Freud's revised 1923 concept of the superego. Although psychoanalysis had as its aim the discovery of repressed instinctual impulses, affects, and fantasies—i.e., the analysis of the id or the unconscious—Anna Freud thought it also needed to be concerned with the ego. She said: "From the beginning analysis, as a therapeutic method, was concerned with the ego and its aberrations: the investigation of the id and of its mode of operation was always only a means to an end. And the end was invariably the same: the correction of these abnormalities and the restoration of the ego to its integrity" (1936: 4). As a process, psychoanalysis was aimed at psychic structures and the interaction between them. Anna Freud thought that only when the examination was extended to all aspects of the personality "can we speak of psycho-analysis" (1936: 15); otherwise the picture was incomplete and distorted.

In 1954 Anna Freud outlined the "classical definition of psychoanalysis" as it was understood at that time. A therapeutic procedure was psychoanalytic if it recognized and worked with transference and resistance. Unconscious instinctual strivings attempt to manifest themselves in the present, using objects in the external world. The analyst offers herself as the object on whom these past unconscious experiences can be made conscious and relived. This is the transference. Resisting counterforces from the ego aim to keep id strivings down and prevent them from becoming manifest. To deal with this resistance, the analyst helps the patient become aware of his defensive devices, making them inefficient. By dealing with both the transference and the resistance, the analyst and patient bring about a revival of earlier times when the id and the ego clashed. Conflicts are then reactivated and new solutions formed. This, Anna Freud said, is the analytic process. How the analyst goes about doing this is the technique, which changes according to the disturbance. In order to understand how and why the technique changed Anna Freud said the analyst must examine the intrapsychic structure of the patient. Variations in technique were based on the nature of these.

In 1965 Anna Freud published *Normality and Pathology in Childhood,* which was the watershed of her work to date. In refining her definition and outlining analytic techniques with children, she again looked at the question of child analysis versus adult analysis. Child analysis, she thought, proceeded along the same therapeutic principles as adult analysis and implied not making use of authority, eliminating suggestion as far as possible, discarding abreaction as a therapeutic tool, and keeping manipulation and management of the patient to the minimum. Anna Freud conceptualized the legitimate tools of this method much as she did in 1954: the analysis of resistance and transference, and the interpretation of unconscious material. The definition of the analytic process with children and adults was therefore similar "to analyze ego resistance before id content and to allow the work of interpretation to move freely between id and ego, following the emergence of material; to proceed from the surface to the depth; to offer the person of the analyst as a transference object for the revival and interpretation of unconscious fantasies and attitudes; to analyze impulses so far as possible in the state of frustration and to avoid their being acted out and gratified; to expect relief of tension not from catharsis, but from the material being lifted from the level of primary process functioning to secondary thought processes; in short: to turn id into ego content" (1965: 26).

Anna Freud disagreed with Melanie Klein that a child's play was equivalent to free association because it was not used by the child with the aim of being cured, as free association was with adults. Furthermore, by interpreting a child's play symbolically one avoided the process of going from the surface to the depth and systematically working through conscious and preconscious resistances, defenses, and distortions. Another technical difference Anna Freud elucidated was that by nature children act out instead of verbalizing. Therefore, the distinctions between remembering, repeating, reliving, and acting out are blurred. Rather than attempting to contain expressions within the psychic sphere, the child had free motility within the session allowing him to use his natural mode of expression through action. Thus, the analyst was required to attempt to reduce reality actions to play actions in the transference with fantasy elaboration, and move toward verbalization and secondary process thinking.

By the 1970s child psychoanalysis had achieved the status of a treatment modality in its own right. No longer was it continually compared to adult analysis. In 1978 Anna Freud outlined the process of child analysis in treating the infantile neurosis. "The uncovering of unconscious motivation, reconstruction of past events (traumatic and otherwise), interpretation of transference feelings and behavior serve well for combating wrong conflict solutions and inadequately primitive defense, and above all for undoing the regressions which have initiated the whole neurotic process" (1978a: 109). She thought that the analytic method could clarify the clinical picture and reveal the cause of developmental disturbances. Although "by itself it is unable to undo the damage," analysis could "identify developmental defects wherever they are located [and] help the child patient at least cope with their consequences" (1978a: 109). The expected aims of child psychoanalysis were generally in line with those established for adults. An aim exclusive to child analysis was to free developmental forces from inhibitions and restrictions, and enable them once more to play their part in the child's further growth.

DEFENSE

Any discussion of Anna Freud's theories must include defense as it was always at the core of her thinking. Defense mechanisms are now considered basic to analytic thinking. Anna Freud's classic book *The Ego and the Mechanisms of Defence* was the first extensive study of this concept, revisited nearly fifty years later at the Hampstead Clinic (J. Sandler with A. Freud 1985). In these writings she began to investigate the specific defenses, their modes of operation, their role in normal and pathological development, their relation to specific forms of illness, their hierarchical organization, and their relation to developmental phases along with their influence on development. Ten defense mechanisms were outlined: regression, repression, reaction formation, isolation, undoing, projection, introjection, turning against the self, reversal, and sublimation. She also discussed denial (in fantasy, work, play, and action), identification with the aggressor, and altruistic surrender. Among the defense mechanisms repression was assigned a unique function as it was seen to be central, with the other defenses allied, subordinate, or supplementary.

Defenses, Anna Freud thought, are a special group of ego functions that operate automatically outside of awareness—in other words unconsciously, and are mobilized by anxiety and other affects. They can be adaptive as well as pathological, as they serve a protective function against an inner or outer danger situation. The analysis of defense is inextricably linked to the analysis of conflict, thus holding a central place in psychoanalytic technique.

Following the introduction of the structural theory in 1923, Freud began to elaborate the idea of resistance. Over a decade later, in *The Ego and the Mechanisms of Defence*, Anna Freud expanded the concept. Resistances, she said, provided useful information as to the patient's mental functioning. "Analysis of resistance could be seen as essentially the analysis of those aspects of the patient's defences which entered into and contributed to the pathological outcome of conflicts" (Sandler et al., 1973: 77).

Resistance develops during the course of every analysis and is related to transference and defenses against anxiety-evoking material. The inability to carry out the conscious intent of working in analysis showed the resistance due to defenses. Where there was no intent, resistance could not be seen. Anna Freud distinguished resistance from conscious withholding, which was opting out of the therapeutic contract. Resistance also differed from a basic unwillingness to participate in the analytic process. This was an indication that the child had no real wish for treatment.

Anna Freud thought that children and adults experienced similar resistances. The ego resists analysis so as to safeguard the defenses; the superego resists analysis because of forbidden thoughts and fantasies which are perceived to threaten existence; drive derivatives released by analysis act as a resistance if they press for fulfillment in action; and the id resists change because of its tie to the principle of repetition.

At the same time there were differences arising from the immaturity of a child's personality and the developmental process itself which caused complications, intensifications, and variations. Children do not take a long-term view of situations. Consequently, the discomfort and anxiety that analysis can create in the present often outweigh the idea that one may feel better in the future. The child's first choice may be to end treatment and get away from this difficult situation. Second, the child's ego is immature and insecurely balanced between internal and external pressures, so that he feels more threatened by analysis, holding on to defenses more rigidly than the adult. Third, immature and primitive defenses tend to operate alongside more sophisticated ones, thus doubling the resistance. Fourth, children tend to externalize their conflicts, which results in battles with the environment, rather than experiencing them internally. Fifth, children look for external solutions and act in preference to talking. The treatment alliance with the child, as well as with the parents, is a crucial element to counteract these difficulties. Finally, the analytic process, with its aim of dissecting the personality and bringing conflicts into consciousness, is opposed to the developmental process, whose aim is to resolve conflicts and establish character attitudes. Therefore, the developmental process itself can contribute to resistance. These factors make for an especially difficult situation when trying to treat children in analysis. As Anna Freud said, "the forces opposing analysis are, if anything, stronger with children than with adult patients" (1965: 33).

CONFLICT

Conflict and the adaptation of conflict were central to Anna Freud's thinking about analysis and development. She conceptualized conflicts as developmentally determined inner disharmonies which were normal byproducts of structural development. They were usually dealt with by the child's ego in conjunction with parental support. When conflicts were resolved inadequately or in a way that disrupted internal harmony, they became the subject of analysis. Thus, conflict could be seen not only in a variety of disturbances but in normal development.

Anna Freud thought the type of conflict experienced by the child was important in determining the appropriate intervention. External conflicts, those between the child and the outside world, were best handled by guidance or other educational means. Internal conflict was conceptualized as conflicting forces within the id. Anna Freud was referring to constitutional and organic factors that were important contributors to a child's development, a far-sighted outlook. While it was crucial to take these into consideration when considering technique, they are not true conflicts as they cannot be resolved. In contrast, internalized conflicts, by definition, were intersystemic, between the agencies of the mind. Analysis was best suited for children suffering from internalized conflicts, which were the source of the infantile neurosis.

But what about the role of conflict in other disturbances? When conflicts were ongoing and acute, caused by the strains of the developmental phase the child was currently going through as opposed to the past, analysis was indicated if it appeared too difficult for the child's ego to handle the crisis, come to a resolution, and move on. The child's chance for normal development was then enhanced. When conflicts were not resolved by means of an infantile neurosis but were removed altogether through the lowering of ego standards, as in delinquency, the analyst was faced with the task of creating conflict. Anna Freud said: "intrapsychic conflict has to be reintroduced within the structure and experienced by the child before its analytic interpretation can be accepted and become effective" (1965: 225). It is clear that Anna Freud thought conflict featured in all kinds of disturbances. In 1966 she referred to the neurotic superstructure that overlaid developmental disturbances. Analyzing this superstructure could alleviate the after-effects, but it did not address the underlying deficit.

Anna Freud continued to ponder the question of conflict versus deficit. In the last decade of her life she obtained clarity, resulting in her theory of a twofold causation of childhood psychopathology. One cause, she said, was rooted in conflict. The other was rooted in developmental defects—in other words, defects in the personality structure itself caused by irregularities and failures along and between developmental lines. The former was responsible for the infantile neurosis, the latter for "psychosomatic symptomatology, the backwardness, the atypical and borderline states" (1974b: 70). Although different in origin, the two types of psychopathology were intertwined owing to the way in which development and structure formation proceeded.

Beginning early in the child's life, when the groundwork for personality building is laid—"i.e., the more or less successful starting off of a number of developmental lines" (1974b: 71)—clashes or external conflicts occur, resulting in developmental setbacks. Two simultaneous processes then occur: growth along developmental lines and the resultant structure formation, and conflicts, defense, and compromise formations, which require some degree of structuralization. "Progress on the [developmental] lines is interfered with constantly by conflict, repression, and consequent regression, while the conflicts themselves and quite especially the methods available for their solution are wholly dependent on the shape and level of personal development which has been reached" (1974b: 70). Over the course of development, as differentiation and structuralization occur, "the resultant deviations from normal growth become involved in the phase-adequate internal conflicts as they are known to us" (1974b: 71). So while not all disturbances originate in conflict, conflict is involved in all disturbances as deficits gather conflicts around them, and the two become intertwined.

AFFECT

Anna Freud thought the role of affects was crucial to child analysis. Defenses were against drives but also against anxiety and affect. Because a child's play was not equivalent to free association, the analyst examined the way a child's affects were transformed within the session. This gave clues to the patient's attitudes not only toward his drives, the nature of his symptom formation, his self and object representations, and the nature of the ego's activities, but toward all aspects of his inner and outer worlds. By bringing resistances and defenses against affects into consciousness, the analyst also brought an understanding of the unconscious.

THE TRANSFERENCE, THE TREATMENT ALLIANCE, AND THE REAL RELATIONSHIP

In the 1930s and 1940s, the infancy years of child psychoanalysis, there were two contrasting views about the role of transference in the analysis of children. Melanie Klein believed that transference was evident from the beginning of an analysis and that all of the child's feelings directed toward the analyst arose out of the transference. Anna Freud disagreed. In 1945 she said that even if part of a child's neurosis was governed by a transference neurosis (which she doubted), another part remained with the child's original and ongoing objects. Over the years Anna Freud's views about transference in child analysis changed. In 1954, responding to a symposium on the widening scope of psychoanalysis, she spoke of modifications forced on the analyst by the individual features of the patient's personality and the nature of his transference. Focusing on patients of all ages, she discussed variations of the classical transference of neurotics as outlined by Freud, including narcissistic transferences based on need satisfaction or early deprivation and loss, ego distortions, idealized transferences, and the patient's need for a real object. The different types of transferences raised a number of technical issues. The implication was that as analysts broaden their parameters, variations resulted which changed technique and improved theory.

By 1957 Anna Freud had gone beyond her early conviction that a negative transference was detrimental to therapy and threatened its continuation. Now she thought the analyst could work through these phases of negative transference and that they could add valuable material. However, she maintained that negative transferences should be interpreted promptly "to prevent their increasing to quantities which might defy interpretation and carry the patient away from the possibility of any alliance with the analyst" (1970c: 5).

By 1965 Anna Freud no longer thought that transference in children was restricted to a single transference reaction, or that it did not develop into a complete transference neurosis. She remained unconvinced, however, that what was called transference neurosis in children was the same as in adults. She now considered the idea that there were various forms of transference that did not fit the classical mode, and that transference formations could be seen from the beginning of treatment. However, initially the analyst was not only an object for transference but also a new object; consequently, the analyst needed to learn to move between the two relationships, a complicated task. "If he accepts the status of new object, different from the parents, he un- doubtedly interferes with the transference reactions. If he ignores or rejects this side of the relationship, he disappoints the child patient in expectations which the latter feels to be legitimate. He is then also apt to interpret items of behavior as transferred which, in fact, are nothing of the kind" (1965: 38). Transference should be taken up at the begin- ning of treatment, but Anna Freud cautioned: "don't interpret trans- ference before it is transference" (1965: 66). She thought not all re- sponses to the analyst were transference; rather, some were linked to the child's anxieties about strangers and new situations.

Anna Freud now thought that children *did* form a transference proper during analysis in which they used the object of the analyst to transfer their object relations from all levels of development. With regard to interpretation of the various levels of transference, she re- mained strong in her belief that the analyst should move from the surface to the depths, which also encouraged the development of a treatment alliance.[3] Going to the deepest layer first would contribute to the negative transference and resistance. It would also require sym- bolic interpretations of behavior and activities, ignoring "the ego de- fenses which are built up against the unconscious content, and this means increasing the patient's anxieties, heightening his resistances, in short, committing the technical error of bypassing analytic interpreta- tion proper" (1965: 21).

A subspecies of transference proper was externalization, a notion Anna Freud introduced in 1936 and expanded on in 1965. In present- day psychoanalysis externalization would be seen as a part of the transference. Anna Freud explained that the child has a tendency to externalize, using the analyst to represent an aspect of the patient's personality structure rather than an object representation. Thus, ex- ternalization is not only a repetition of the past resulting from the child's distortions, if one thinks of externalization of internal object representations as many do today, but reflects the child's intrapsychic structure. These externalizations of internal and intersystemic con- flicts, which cause the child to battle with the analyst rather than con- taining his conflicts within himself, were important for "they reveal

---

3. Liselotte Frankl and Ilse Hellman (1962) demonstrated clearly in a clinical paper arising from their work at the Hampstead Clinic that a child had the capacity to form a therapeutic alliance and was capable of entering a therapeutic contract. This constituted a radical change. Previously some analysts had been convinced that a child had to be wooed into treatment as the decision to enter analysis was not his; nor did he, by nature, wish to cooperate.

what happens in the child's inner world, in relations between his internal agencies, as contrasted with the emotional relationships to objects in the external world" (1965: 42).

Anna Freud also thought there were other aspects of the transference that involved not only instinctual impulses. Ego defenses could be transferred (as she first outlined in 1936) and equally needed to be interpreted. In this type of transference she included "the repetition of the measures which the patient had taken, early in his life, to protect himself against the painful consequence of childhood and sexual wishes" (Sandler et al., 1973: 42). A related type of transference, delineated by Sandler et al. in 1969 and elaborated still further by Anna Freud in 1980, was the transference of habitual modes of relating. These are modes of relating often seen in the first few sessions that involve feelings of great intensity. They are not specific to the analyst per se but are in the nature of character traits. They link to transference of defense if the origin of character traits is understood as defenses that are incorporated into a character style and attain a degree of autonomy. A habitual mode of relating is a form of transference in the broadest sense of the word, but not on the same level as a full-fledged transference manifestation or transference neurosis.

Anna Freud also distinguished the transference of current relationships and of past relationships as children bring their current life concerns, as well as the transference of internalized relationships based on past experiences, into the relationship with the analyst. In the case of the transference of current relationships, the analyst needed to differentiate the transference from the spillover of ongoing pathological relationships. With regard to the formation of a true transference neurosis in children Anna Freud said: "The question then is: How far does the child transfer past relationships and fantasies from the present-day objects to the analyst? This is the distinction" (Sandler et al., 1980: 92).

As the child's primary objects remain important to him, he rarely transfers everything in the analysis. Anna Freud went on to say: "it is largely a matter of quantity, that is, of how much is transferred . . . The appearance of transference material in a young child's analysis does not diminish . . . the living out of the neurosis at home, quantitatively speaking. The qualitative differences are the differences between real objects and fantasy objects in the child and the adult" (Sandler et al., 1980: 93). Always holding to her developmental viewpoint, Anna Freud said that in order to work within the transference with children, the analyst must understand what stage of development the child's object relationships were in and how he normally used his objects to support his development.

ANNA FREUD'S THEORY OF TECHNIQUE

The psychoanalytic theory of technique was originally based on Freud's model of the neurotic adult. One of the questions confronting Anna Freud when she began analyzing children was whether this same model applied. In 1926 she demonstrated that it did, but already influenced by a developmental viewpoint, she also thought that some adaptations were indicated. These were necessary because the child was in the midst of a developmental process and did not yet have established psychic structures at his disposal. In order to address these structures in the making the child analyst needed "to analyze and educate" (1927a: 65). While rudimentary in their conceptualization, these two functions became the cornerstones of Anna Freud's theory of technique.

Development was the orienting premise for Anna Freud and the foundation of her approach. Not only was personality formation viewed through a developmental lens, but all components and threads of child psychoanalysis. Interferences with the child's ability to develop were the bases of her criteria for therapeutic intervention. The aim of child analysis was to intervene in the developmental process, helping the child return to the path of normal development, something which she had earlier called educational. The orienting premise behind the way in which the analyst intervened was this developmental viewpoint.

Anna Freud came a long way from her original ideas about transference manifestations and their role in child analysis. Not only transference but also the multiple dimensions of the child-analyst relationship occupied her thinking throughout her lifetime and held a central place within her theory of technique. To understand the complexities of this relationship, Anna Freud was once again influenced by her developmental viewpoint. The age of the child, the degree of his reliance on parents in everyday life, the child's ego capacities and his level of object relationship, both actual and age expected, were all factors to consider when assessing the relationship and the analyst's technical approach.

Over the years, as Anna Freud's views about development were crystallizing and she was refining her ideas about the child-analyst relationship and her theory of technique, input from another direction was having considerable impact on her thinking. The scope of child analysis was continually widening as analysts were treating children with a variety of disturbances. Were these children best treated by analysis, and if so, how? Anna Freud was clear that in the area of permanent regressions and fixed neurotic symptomatology nothing but analysis could change the child. However, few patients present with one pure form or another; rather, most disturbances consist of mixtures and combinations of many elements. To this she said in 1965: "It is this mixed psychopathology of childhood for which the comprehensive method of child analysis is needed. Only in child analysis proper is the whole range of therapeutic possibilities kept available for the patient, and all parts of him are given the chance on the one hand to reveal and on the other to cure themselves" (1965: 232).

By 1972 Anna Freud had redefined the concept of an infantile neurosis to mean the "massive and complex upheaval" which occurs during the oedipal phase. "Although the precipitating events belong to the area of the oedipus and castration complexes," she said, "the whole neurotic involvement is contributed to by the residues of past stages from infancy onward" (1972: 30). By 1974 her conceptualization of developmental disturbances had moved beyond the original definition of a transitory disorder. Now the causation of a developmental disturbance was placed within the developmental process itself. Both structures were affected, "deficits in the personality structure itself" (1974b: 70), and the developmental lines where "the developmental progress itself is defective or unbalanced" (1974b: 72).

All of these theoretical advances led Anna Freud to formulate her theory of a twofold causation of childhood psychopathology, which in 1965 she had referred to as the mixed psychopathology of childhood. Although different in origin, conflict and developmental disturbances were intertwined. While the degree, severity, or balance may vary, each patient had some mixture of these. What then must be considered was the technical approach, to which Anna Freud said, "I cannot help feeling that there are significant differences between the two therapeutic tasks and that every discussion of technique will need to take account of these" (1970b: 203). Psychoanalysis was in familiar territory with the conflict-neurotic disturbances where interpretation of defense and resistance, conflict, and transference were central to the technique and aims of child analysis, as was using the child's affect and anxiety as a guide. In the analytic process with these patients "interpretation lifts repressed or otherwise defended material into consciousness and helps the child's ego to find solutions for his internal struggles, which are no longer based on anxiety, panic, and infantile misapprehensions of reality" (1974b: 72).

Over the years Anna Freud tried to delineate the therapeutic tasks and technique for developmental disturbances. In 1965 in *Normality and Pathology in Childhood,* she discussed the interpretation of transference and resistance; the widening of consciousness at the expense of the unconscious parts of the id, ego, and superego; and the increase of ego dominance. She said there were other elements as well, such as the verbalization and clarification of preconscious material, which lessened anxiety and prepared the way for interpretation proper. With regards to borderline pathologies she said: "therapy is served for the patient by verbalization and clarification of internal and external dangers and frightening affects which are perceived preconsciously but which his weak and helpless ego, left to itself, cannot integrate and bring under secondary process dominance" (1965: 230). With regard to early deprivations and defects in object relationships, interpretation could not restart development; rather, it was the intimacy of the patient analyst relationship which was important. In other instances where the child had a weak ego and suffered from archaic fears, it was possible to interrupt the process so the child could proceed developmentally. Here the therapeutic element responsible for the improvement "is the analyst's reassuring role, not his analytic one" (1965: 232). Reassurance meant the explanation of reality aimed at dispelling anxieties. In another example Anna Freud discussed patients in which the ego exerted too much pressure on an impoverished drive constellation. This sort of child needed help with the stimulation of fantasy and the opening of outlets for id derivatives. Here the analyst acted as an auxiliary ego when drive activity was insufficiently controlled by an undeveloped ego. Additional techniques such as verbalization, clarification, and confrontation paved the way for or supplemented interpretation.

With the twofold causation concept, Anna Freud refined her theory of technique and addressed developmental disturbances in more detail. With regard to the areas in which the two types of pathology intertwined, the analytic work could "undo regressions and lift crippling conflicts off the developmental lines." But when it came to the developmental disturbance, the effective techniques were different. Interpretation could not "undo the damage," as in conflict pathology. It could clarify the past and "help the child toward better ways of facing and coping with its consequences"; however, that was not enough. Rather, success was due to the "admixture to the technique," or what was known in the child analytic literature as the byproducts of analysis. Byproducts were the other so called nonanalytic things analysts did, perhaps without thinking about them or because it was agreed that one couldn't behave toward children as toward adults or have the same expectations of them. Byproducts were mentioned in the literature, but for decades they were never openly discussed. While Anna Freud agreed they were not "the truly analytic work," in 1974 she elevated these other measures to the level of technique, implied an aim and intent by the analyst, and placed their importance within the context of psychopathology. In her comments about technique she once again emphasized the child-analyst relationship as central to the work, giving the examples of "a new positive object attachment, new superego iden-tification, suggestive influence, or even corrective emotional experi-ence" (1974b: 72). She remained firm in her belief that a corrective emotional experience could set arrested developmental lines going again only with the very young. These admixtures to the technique were for many years the focus of a study group at the Anna Freud Centre under the direction of Hansi Kennedy, and are now commonly known within that culture as developmental help.

Even though Anna Freud thought developmental disturbances were best treated analytically, she remained ambivalent about the degree to which the effects of early damage could be altered. Rose Edgcumbe, in recalling her experiences with Anna Freud, said: "I remember that I would feel rather indignant on behalf of our patients when Anna Freud implied that they were not suitable for analysis, or were incapa-ble of using it. Surely one's patient could use treatment in some way? Anna Freud made us feel that somehow it was not right. Yet she un-doubtedly encouraged us to carry on experimenting" (1995: 22). Thus, Anna Freud thought it important to continue to work with these pa-tients and to study the technique and results. In 1978 she said, "to the extent to which developmental harm can be undone belatedly child analysis may accept it as its next duty to devise methods for the task" (1978a: 109).

Anna Freud died before she could fully engage herself in this task; however, in her later writings it is apparent that she had ideas about what needed to be done. While the infantile neurosis could be con-ceived of, in part, as the result of what the child did with the internal structures he had, developmental disturbances arose from imbalances between developmental lines and from deficits in the structures them-selves. For Anna Freud, rooted as she was in drives and Freud's struc-tural theory, this meant disturbances in the ego and its functions. She proposed as the "next rewarding trend for child analytic work" (1979a: 136) the study of various ego mechanisms and how they developed; disharmonies between lines of development, as well as between and within internal agencies; the impact of constitutional factors; the rate of structuralization; environmental influences; and a more detailed examination of developmental lines themselves.

Anna Freud also had ideas about what in the analytic situation could provide relevant research data. Following the tradition she adhered to throughout her life, the clinical material itself was an important vehicle for study. She believed that children took what they needed from an analysis, and understanding what they took and why would refine technique. As she said in 1965: "the choice of therapeutic process does not seem to lie with (the analyst) but with their patients . . . The nature of the child's disturbance reveals itself via the specific therapeutic elements which he selects for therapeutic use when he is offered the full range of possibilities that are contained in child analysis" (1965: 228–29). Anna Freud also proposed that, as no two analysts are alike and thus would not treat a given patient in the same way, technical variations were also based on the nuances of the individual analyst's personality. These nuances, she thought, should be treated as important findings rather than chance occurrences, as they could lead to new theoretical understanding, an idea expanded and refined by Joseph Sandler in 1983. She said: "In the variations of the analyst's 'acting out' in technical behavior we may, therefore, find new clues for the systematic study of character structures and personalities" (1954b: 369).

In 1980 Joseph Sandler, Hansi Kennedy, and Robert Tyson published a comprehensive book on technique in child psychoanalysis based on discussions with Anna Freud. Here they elucidated the question of what is child psychoanalysis. They described how a technique was fashioned that complied with the main demands of classical psychoanalysis: to interpret resistance and transference phenomena; to undo repressions and regressions, and to substitute sophisticated, adaptive measures for primitive, pathogenic mechanisms of defense; and to strengthen ego functions and widen the area in the mind over which the ego could exert control. With children there were adaptations to the analysis of resistance as this was originally defined as the resistance to free association.

The authors went on to say that there was no absolute psychoanalytic technique for use with children; rather, there was an adaptation of a set of analytic principles. What was important was that the aims of treatment were conceived of psychoanalytically. They endorsed Anna Freud's contention, spelled out in 1965, that analysis is a mixture of techniques based on psychoanalytic understanding of the child and the child's development, and that analysis proper is the whole range of therapeutic possibilities kept available for the patient; thus elaborating the contemporary meaning of "to analyze and educate." They said: "The therapist departs from child analysis and enters the realm of psychoanalytic psychotherapy when he intentionally limits himself to specific procedures and avoids following the material into certain areas or avoids making use of any of the wide range of child psychoanalytic techniques available when such techniques are indicated" (1980: 254). The analyst's approach required a mixture of techniques that addressed the intertwining of conflict and developmental disturbances. In addition, as the child-analyst relationship was multidimensional, necessitated by the child's developmental level and needs and by the aims of the analysis; the analyst needed to be comfortable moving between her roles when appropriate and to understand these shifts within her analytic framework and based on analytic principles. This framework and principles included not only the establishment of an analytic process but, in parallel, a developmental process as well.

Anna Freud's theory of child psychoanalysis was constantly developing and her techniques were ever evolving. Many of her ideas changed considerably over the years, some remained consistent, and others grew out of her early ones. She was aware how far child analysis had come from its inception, but she also knew the work that was left to her followers. In the last decade of her life she said: "We should gradually evolve a technique which fits the child perfectly, whether it is similar to the adult technique or not. . . . We haven't done so yet. We are nearer than we were twenty years ago, or even ten years ago, but we are still quite a long way off" (Holder, 1983: 115).

BIBLIOGRAPHY

AICHHORN, A. (1925) *Wayward Youth*. London: Putnam, 1936.

ALEXANDER, F. (1948) *Fundamentals of Psychoanalysis*. New York: W. W. Norton.

BALINT, M. (1958) The three areas of the mind: Theoretical considerations. *Int. J. Psycho-Anal.*, 39:328–40.

BALINT, M. (1968) *The Basic Fault*. London and New York: Tavistock Publications.

BERNFELD, S. (1925) *Psychology of the Infant*. London: Kegan Paul, 1929.

EDGCUMBE, R. (1985) Anna Freud's contribution to the technique and clinical understanding in child psychoanalysis. *Bull. Anna Freud Centre*, 8:155–68.

EDGCUMBE, R. (1995) The history of Anna Freud's thinking on developmental disturbances. *Bull. Anna Freud Centre*, 18:21–34.

FRANKL, L., & HELLMAN, I. (1962) Symposium on child analysis. *Int. J. Psycho-Anal.*, 43:333–37.

Freud, A. (1927a) Child analysis and the upbringing of children. In *Introduction to Psychoanalysis: Lectures for Child Analysts and Teachers 1922–1935*. London: Hogarth Press, 1974: 50–69.

Freud, A. (1927b) The methods of child analysis. In *Introduction to Psychoanalysis: Lectures for Child Analysts and Teachers 1922–1935*. London: Hogarth Press, 1974: 19–35.

Freud, A. (1927c) Preparation for child analysis. In *Introduction to Psychoanalysis: Lectures for Child Analysts and Teachers 1922–1935*. London: Hogarth Press, 1974: 3–18.

Freud, A. (1927d) The role of transference in the analysis of children. In *Introduction to Psychoanalysis: Lectures for Child Analysts and Teachers 1922–1935*. London: Hogarth Press, 1974: 36–49.

Freud, A. (1928) The theory of child analysis. In *Introduction to Psychoanalysis: Lectures for Child Analysts and Teachers 1922–1935*. London: Hogarth Press, 1974: 162–75.

Freud, A. (1936) *The Ego and the Mechanisms of Defence*. New York: Int. Univ. Press, 1946.

Freud, A. (1945) Indications for child analysis. In *The Writings of Anna Freud*, 4: 3–38. New York: Int. Univ. Press, 1968.

Freud, A. (1950) The significance of the evolution of psychoanalytic child psychology. In *The Writings of Anna Freud*, 4:614–24. New York: Int. Univ. Press, 1968.

Freud, A. (1954a) Problems of technique in adult analysis. In *The Writings of Anna Freud*, 4:377–406. New York: Int. Univ. Press, 1968.

Freud, A. (1954b) The widening scope of indications for psychoanalysis: Discussion. In *The Writings of Anna Freud*, 4:356–376. New York: Int. Univ. Press, 1968.

Freud, A. (1956) The assessment of borderline cases. In *The Writings of Anna Freud*, 5:301–14. New York: Int. Univ. Press, 1969.

Freud, A. (1958a) Adolescence. In *The Writings of Anna Freud*, 5:136–66. New York: Int. Univ. Press, 1969.

Freud, A. (1958b) Child observation and prediction of development: A memorial lecture in honor of Ernst Kris. In *The Writings of Anna Freud*, 5:102–35. New York: Int. Univ. Press, 1969.

Freud, A. (1960) The child guidance clinic as the center of prophylaxis and enlightenment. In *The Writings of Anna Freud*, 5:281–300. New York: Int. Univ. Press, 1969.

Freud, A. (1962) Assessment of pathology in childhood: Part I. In *The Writings of Anna Freud*, 5:26–37. New York: Int. Univ. Press, 1969.

Freud, A. (1963) The concept of developmental lines. *Psychoanal. Study Child*, 18:245–65.

Freud, A. (1964) Assessment of pathology in childhood: Part II. In *The Writings of Anna Freud*, 5:38–52. New York: Int. Univ. Press, 1969.

Freud, A. (1965) *Normality and Pathology in Childhood*. London: Hogarth Press, 1980.

FREUD, A. (1966) Links between Hartmann's ego psychology and the child analyst's thinking. In *The Writings of Anna Freud*, 5:204–20. New York: Int. Univ. Press, 1969.

FREUD, A. (1968a) Acting out. In *The Writings of Anna Freud*, 7:94–109. New York: Int. Univ. Press, 1971.

FREUD, A. (1968b) Indications and contraindications for child analysis. In *The Writings of Anna Freud*, 7:110–23. New York: Int. Univ. Press, 1971.

FREUD, A. (1970a) Child analysis as a subspecialty of psychoanalysis. In *The Writings of Anna Freud*, 7:204–19. New York: Int. Univ. Press, 1971.

FREUD, A. (1970b) The infantile neurosis: Genetic and dynamic considerations. In *The Writings of Anna Freud*, 7:189–203. New York: Int. Univ. Press, 1971.

FREUD, A. (1970c [1957]) Problems of termination in child analysis. In *The Writings of Anna Freud*, 7:3–31. New York: Int. Univ. Press, 1971.

FREUD, A. (1970d) The symptomatology of childhood: A preliminary attempt at classification. In *The Writings of Anna Freud*, 7:157–88. New York: Int. Univ. Press, 1971.

FREUD, A. (1972) The widening scope of psychoanalytic child psychology, normal and abnormal. In *The Writings of Anna Freud*, 8:8–33. New York: Int. Univ. Press, 1981.

FREUD, A. (1974a) Beyond the infantile neurosis. In *The Writings of Anna Freud*, 8:75–81. New York: Int. Univ. Press, 1981.

FREUD, A. (1974b) A psychoanalytic view of developmental psychopathology. In *The Writings of Anna Freud*, 8:57–74. New York: Int. Univ. Press, 1981.

FREUD, A. (1976) Changes in psychoanalytic practice and experience. In *The Writings of Anna Freud*, 8:176–85. New York: Int. Univ. Press, 1981.

FREUD, A. (1978a) The principal task of child analysis. In *The Writings of Anna Freud*, 8:96–109. New York: Int. Univ. Press, 1981.

FREUD, A. (1978b) Psychopathology seen against the background of normal development. In *The Writings of Anna Freud*, 8:82–95. New York: Int. Univ. Press, 1981.

FREUD, A. (1979a) Child analysis as the study of mental growth, normal and abnormal. In *The Writings of Anna Freud*, 8:119–36. New York: Int. Univ. Press, 1981.

FREUD, A. (1979b) Mental health and illness in terms of internal harmony and disharmony. In *The Writings of Anna Freud*, 8:110–18. New York: Int. Univ. Press, 1981.

FREUD, A., IN COLLABORATION WITH BURLINGHAM, D. (1939–1945) *The Writings of Anna Freud Volume III*. New York: Int. Univ. Press, 1973.

FREUD, S. (1914) Remembering, repeating and working through. *S.E.* 12:145–56.

FREUD, S. (1923) The ego and the id. *S.E.* 19:3–66.

FREUD, S. (1926 [1925]) Inhibitions, symptoms and anxiety. *S.E.* 20:77–174.

HOLDER, A. (ED.) (1983) Anna Freud Memorial Issue. *Bull. Hampstead Clin.*, 6.

KENNEDY, H. (1978) The Hampstead Centre for the psychoanalytic study and treatment of children. *Bull. Hampstead Clin.*, 1:1–4.

KENNEDY, H. (1990) Personal communication.

ROSENFELD, S. KUT (1972a) Notes on self and object differentiation and communication in borderline children. In *Beyond the Infantile Neurosis*. London: Hampstead Clinic, 85–90.

ROSENFELD, S. KUT (1972b) Some reflections arising from the treatment of a traumatised 'borderline child'. In *Beyond the Infantile Neurosis*. London: Hampstead Clinic, 76–84.

ROSENFELD, S. KUT, & SPRINCE, M. (1963) An attempt to formulate the meaning of the concept of borderline. In *Beyond the Infantile Neurosis*. London: Hampstead Clinic, 20–37.

ROSENFELD, S. KUT, & SPRINCE, M. (1965) Some thoughts on the technical handling of borderline children. In *Beyond the Infantile Neurosis*. London: Hampstead Clinic, 28–50.

SANDLER, J. (1983) Reflections of some relations between psychoanalytic concepts and psychoanalytic practice. *Int. J. Psycho-Anal.*, 64:35–45.

SANDLER, J., DARE, C., & HOLDER, A. (1973) *The Patient and the Analyst*. London: Maresfield Reprints.

SANDLER, J., WITH FREUD, A. (1985) *The Analysis of Defense: The Ego and the Mechanisms of Defense Revisited*. New York: Int. Univ. Press.

SANDLER, J., HOLDER, A., KAWENOKA, M., KENNEDY, H., & NEURATH, L. (1969) Notes on some theoretical and clinical aspects of transference. *Int. J. Psycho-Anal.*, 50:633–45.

SANDLER, J., KENNEDY, H., & TYSON, R. (1980) *The Technique of Child Psychoanalysis: Discussions with Anna Freud*. Cambridge: Harvard Univ. Press.

THOMAS, R., IN COLLABORATION WITH EDGCUMBE, R., KENNEDY, H., KAWENOKA, M., & WEITZNER, L. (1966) Comments on some aspects of self and object representations in a group of psychotic children: The application of Anna Freud's Diagnostic Profile. *Psychoanal. Study Child*, 21:527–80.

ZETZEL, E. (1956) Current concepts of transference. *Int. J. Psycho-Anal.*, 37:369–76.

Object Relations, Affect Management, and Psychic Structure Formation

The Concept of Object Constancy

PHYLLIS TYSON, PH.D.

Object relations are central to contemporary structural theory. This paper first reviews the various ways in which the key concept object constancy has been used. To reconcile the apparent contradictions in definitions, the concept is viewed along a developmental continuum in which each step is defined by its functions. It is proposed that at its most mature stage, a capacity for affective self-regulation is achieved, a capacity that is central to characterological structure formation and optimal adaptation. Possible interferences with the achievement of mature object constancy are briefly explored.

MUCH CURRENT DISCUSSION OF OBJECT RELATIONS THEORY CASTS STRUCtural psychology as outmoded and inadequate; in fact the two theories are often seen as contradictory. It is my contention that the significance of perceived interactions with others and how these interactions affect psychic functioning are central to contemporary structural psychoanalytic theory. Although Freud's first two models of the mind viewed the object primarily in terms of the sexual drive, the object shifted into

Associate clinical professor of Psychiatry at the University of California at San Diego; an adult and child supervising and training analyst at the San Diego Psychoanalytic Society and Institute.

The Psychoanalytic Study of the Child 51, ed. Albert J. Solnit, Peter B. Neubauer, Samuel Abrams, and A. Scott Dowling (Yale University Press, copyright © 1996 by Albert J. Solnit, Peter B. Neubauer, Samuel Abrams, and A. Scott Dowling).

central theoretical focus seventy years ago, following the introduction of the structural model and the reformulation of the theory of anxiety (1926). The work of Anna Freud, Spitz, Hartmann, Mahler, Loewald, and many others was largely directed toward better understanding of the role that interaction with the environment (i.e., objects) plays in personality development and functioning.

Contributing to the impression that structural psychology and object relations theories are contradictory is the fact that, instead of using terms like "self" and "self structure," analysts adhering to contemporary structural theory use concepts like "psychic apparatus" and "psychic structures," or ego, id, and superego; these concepts seem to be easily confused with drive psychology. In addition, structural psychologists concentrate on the formation, development, functioning, and continued integrity of these hypothetical mental organizations instead of focusing primarily on the experiential self.

The division in theories probably goes back to translation problems and the work of Hartmann (Spruiell, 1981), who pointed out that in his early work, Freud used the term *das Ich* (translated "ego") to refer to an experiential sense of one's self. When he proposed the structural hypothesis, he implied that a stable experiential sense of self was based on an underlying "coherent organization of mental processes" that functions to regulate drives and adapt to reality (1923, p. 17). Two levels of abstraction were now implied—an experiential sense of self and a hypothetical, nonexperiential, organizing, and regulating set of processes. The coherence and stability of the experiential self were insured by the smooth functioning of the underlying hypothetical psychic apparatus. I see this as a major conceptual difference between contemporary structural psychology on the one hand, and self psychology or object relational theories on the other. These latter theories are not explicit in defining the assumptions that underlie the notions of self, or self structure, whereas structural psychology focuses on both levels of abstraction. In this paper when I refer to ego development, or the development of a psychic apparatus, I intend to imply both the development of a stable experiential sense of self *and* the development of the underlying hypothetical nonexperiential mental structures, as these are what insure the continued integrity of the stable experiential sense of self (see Tyson and Tyson, 1990, for further discussion).

Probably of central concern to both contemporary structural psychologists and object relational theorists is the question of the relation between early development and optimal adaptation. The question is not a new one. Recognizing that the infant-caregiver relationship provides the envelope from which the child's psychic functioning emerges,

Hartmann (1952) asked what it was in this relationship that contributed to the formation of a secure, independently functioning individual. Critical of oversimplified views of a "bad" or "good" mother, he noticed that what appeared on the surface to be "good" object relations may nevertheless be a developmental handicap if the child does not learn to function independently but instead clings to and remains dependent on the mother (1952, p. 15). He observed that it was "a long way from the object that exists only as long as it is need-satisfying to that form of satisfactory object relations that includes object constancy" (p. 15) and concluded that ego development and object relations were correlated in complex ways and that satisfactory object relations could be assessed only by considering what it meant in terms of ego functioning. He thought that by assessing the extent to which *object constancy* is achieved, some judgment could be made about the child's ego development and capacity to function independently.

Hartmann's idea had immediate appeal, and the concept of object constancy quickly found a place in the psychoanalytic lexicon. Unfortunately, Hartmann did little to define or elaborate what he meant by object constancy other than to note that it implied a stable psychic representation and probably presupposed a degree of neutralization of aggressive and libidinal energy (p. 163). This lack of definitional precision has resulted in the use of the same term by several theorists to refer to different phenomena. Spitz (1959), for example, referred to the mother's becoming the *constant libidinal object;* that is, once a firm attachment is made to the mother, she becomes irreplaceable. Substitutes are not easily accepted as the infant searches for the safety of the mother.[1] Anna Freud (1963, 1965) referred to *libidinal investment* as the child's capacity to maintain the attachment to the mother, whether she frustrates or satisfies drive wishes. Piaget and other cognitive psychologists focused on the cognitive image and on the steps leading from perception of an object, recognition memory, and eventually to evocative memory and the formation of an integrated *mental representation* of the object. Fraiberg (1969), quoting Werner (1957, p. 108), clarified that the "constancy" of Piaget and other cognitive psychologists referred to a mental representation of the object that "preserves its essential character despite variations introduced into the situation surrounding it." Mahler, in contrast, did not stress the irreplaceability of the mother, her safety-keeping function (as did Spitz), the drive-determined nature of the attachment (as did Anna Freud), or simply the

---

1. Throughout this paper I shall use the term *mother* to refer to the primary caregiver, recognizing that this could be mother, father, other, or a composite of all.

stability of and ability to recall the mental representation (as did Piaget). Rather, she concentrated on the *way in which the representation functions*. She said (Mahler and Furer, 1968), "By object constancy we mean that the maternal image has become intrapsychically available to the child in the same way that the actual mother had been libidinally available—for sustenance, comfort, and love" (p. 222). McDevitt added that some resolution of rapprochement ambivalence is required so that "good" and "bad" aspects of the mother can be unified in one representation (1979, pp. 333–334).

Definitional discrepancies lead to confusion. Yet if Hartmann was right in thinking that by assessing object constancy one can determine a person's level of psychic functioning, perhaps the concept has not realized its full potential and needs to be revisited. Instead of arguing about which of these definitions is more correct, however, I follow a suggestion made by Solnit (1982, p. 212) and examine the psychic *functions* of object constancy. In so doing, I will show that object constancy is not a fixed phenomenon. Rather, object constancy has its own developmental trajectory, and each of the several definitions refers to a different step along this developmental path.

A capacity for self-regulation, particularly the regulation of affect, is central to competent adaptation. In an earlier paper (1988), I suggested that this capacity, which relies on the capacity to use the signal function of affect, develops alongside and in conjunction with a relatively advanced level of object constancy. I elaborate that proposal here, as a great merit of the object-constancy concept lies in its ability to help us understand the development of a self-regulatory capacity. In so doing, I compare the child's progress in acquiring the capacity for affect regulation with the degree to which the child has attained a useful level of object constancy. I choose affect regulation because of the central role affects play in psychic life. Affects appear to be related to cognition, to drives, to the sense of the object, and to the sense of self. Furthermore, affect regulation plays a central role with regard to conflict and adaptation (P. Tyson, 1988).

Affects are chiefly associated with danger or with pleasure. Danger can be perceived as real, in the external world, or it can be intrapsychic, related to conflict and fears of consequences should forbidden impulses be gratified. Affects associated with danger can function in two ways in psychic life. When they are especially intense, or when self-regulatory functions are weak or immature, affects assume a peremptory quality and can disrupt self-regulation. Stated in the terms of structural concepts, intense affects disrupt organizing and regulating ego functions. If instead, before it reaches this intensity, the child (or adult) can perceive the affect, identify the danger (external or internal), and adjust behavior accordingly, with the help of defense and compromise, we can say that the affect has served a signal function (Freud, 1926). The child's capacity to use affect as a signal is not an automatic characteristic of affect but rather a developmental achievement.

Throughout life there remains the possibility that affects, particularly the ones associated with danger, can reach proportions that would overwhelm or disorganize self-regulation. This may be because of real, unexpected, traumatic experiences, or because of an intensification of inner conflict such that previous defenses and compromises no longer function effectively. However, under average expectable circumstances, affect regulation depends on the extent to which the individual can develop the capacity to use the signal function of affect effectively.

Usually pleasurable affects are originally associated with gratifying interactions with the mother, often in relation to feeding and other drive experiences. But pleasure, interest, surprise, excitement, enthusiasm, delight, joy, etc., can quickly come to be experienced in relation to exploration, discovery, and mastery. These positive emotions lead to a pleasurable sense of well-being and competence. Eventually, if all goes well, these affects function to insure that a sense of competence and well-being remains relatively stable. Pleasurable affects such as those associated with anticipation of and participation in enjoyable and exciting fantasy or play activities can also disorganize self-regulation. That is, experiences such as exciting play with siblings, peers, or a parent, parental overinvolvement with the child's body, exposure to adult nudity, sexual molestation, or even overexposure to television, movies, and video games can be destructive to the young child in certain circumstances if the effects on immature self-regulation are not considered. Therefore even the regulation of pleasurable affects depends on the capacity to develop the signal function of affect.

Is there something in the child's early interactive experiences with parents or other important people that fosters the development of the capacity to regulate affects by use of the signal function? And if so, what is it? These questions are intriguing because, as clinicians are well aware, there are individuals who are incapable of self-regulation despite a constant attachment and despite an enduring mental representation of the mother.

DEVELOPMENT OF OBJECT CONSTANCY AND AFFECT REGULATION

When Spitz (1962, 1963) introduced the idea of mother-infant reciprocity, he wanted to emphasize the importance of a basic, two-way, meaningful communication process, an affective dialogue between mother and infant. He thought that this dialogue provided the basis for object relations and for self-regulatory ego functioning. In the decades following his work, we have learned much about the details of this dialogue. For the most part, the mother regulates interaction in the beginning. Although the neonate has a complex organization of endogenously determined behaviors that function to regulate the system and maintain physiological homeostasis, this is not a psychologically determined regulation, and it is easily overwhelmed. However, this endogenous integrative synchronization is facilitated by the affective ambience of mother-infant reciprocity, as the "attuned" (Stern, 1984) mother responds to the intact infant's affective expressions and makes timely interventions that assist the infant in making the transition from a state of distress to a more comfortable, distress-free state. Once this affective dialogue becomes well established, the infant begins to participate in regulating interactions and to develop some self-regulatory skills. Varieties of these can be observed as early as four months (Stern, 1974, 1985).

At times the mother fails in this role, and the infant's tensions escalate. This may be because of a deficiency of the infant, or because mother herself is emotionally unavailable, overanxious, unpredictable, or otherwise inadequate in her response to the infant's needs, or because of a child-care situation in which the infant does not get timely and adequate care. The infant may then experience persistent and diffuse tension states. Instead of fostering self-regulation, the persistent distress predisposes the infant to self-regulatory disorders (Greenacre, 1941; Bergman & Escalona, 1949; A. Freud, 1967; Weil, 1970, 1978; Settlage, 1977; Settlage et al., 1990, 1991; Solnit, 1982; Call, 1983). Although Greenacre suggested the notion as early as 1941, there is growing neurobiological research evidence to support the hypothesis that many of the self-regulatory psychiatric disorders seen so frequently in contemporary child psychiatric clinics have roots in the failure of early mother-child reciprocity to regulate affects (Schore, 1994).

Although in the first several months the infant easily accepts substitutes for mother, by seven or eight months the infant appears to regularly look for and respond in a special way to mother and to behave as if mother is preferred above all others. This behavior suggests that mother has become the *constant libidinal object* Spitz spoke of. The infant's attachment to the mother, furthermore, appears to persist regardless of whether or not she satisfies all wishes, so the kind of object constancy Anna Freud was looking for has also been reached. I think of this as the level of *investment object constancy*.

Spitz believed that a constant libidinal attachment to the mother

reflected a significant advance in ego development. We now understand that the distress he used to signal this development represents a
mingling of object relations, cognitive maturation, and affect management. That is, fear, surprise, and anger begin to appear alongside
recognition memory and means-ends connections at seven to nine
months. Spitz, and later Emde, demonstrated that the infant copes
with this extended repertoire of affects by using perception of the
mother's affective signals as a means of self-regulation. In what Emde
(Sorce et al., 1981; Emde and Sorce, 1983) called "social referencing,"
the infant looks to the mother for an affective signal of reassurance or
caution to cope with the surprise or fear generated by the unfamiliar.
An encouraging smile he links with safety; with such a signal he explores the unfamiliar with delight and seems to experience a sense of
competence. Because the infant's self-regulation and sense of safety
are so dependent on approving nods from his mother, he quickly dis-
solves in tears in response to a frown or a look of distress. He then turns
to mother to relieve his distress and to help him make the transition to a
calmer state, thereby insuring that the distress does not totally disorganize self-regulation.

In terms of our task of comparing progress in self-regulatory skills
with stages in object constancy, we can conclude that by the time the
infant is able to maintain a consistent attachment to the object irrespective of the consistency of drive gratification—the first level of object
constancy—he takes an important step toward self-regulation. That is,
he begins to use the mother's affective signals as a means of regulating
his affect and maintaining his sense of safety. Thus he is not overwhelmed, and anxiety and distress remain within a manageable level.

In elaborating the notion of object constancy, Solnit and Neubauer
(1986) emphasize the strength and enduring nature of the mother-
child bond that develops with what I have called the first level of object
constancy. Once achieved, this attachment remains constant even when
the relationship is not a healthy one. Indeed, it can endure despite
abusive, destructive, even life-threatening pathological situations, and
despite long separations. Children who have suffered extreme deprivation and abuse and who as a result have been separated from a
mother judged as unfit, nevertheless cling to their memory of her,
maintaining the hope that one day she will return. I believe that this
early attachment is so tenacious because, even though the constant
object may be unreliable, unpredictable, even destructive and abusive,
she symbolizes the only source of safety and affective regulation the
infant knows. When mother as the constant object disappears, so does
the source of affective regulation. Spitz (1946) also observed that at-

tachment to the mother, once formed, may interfere with a child's making further attachments. A child unable to form a lasting attachment to a suitable caregiver who can provide safety and affective regulation may never learn self-regulation. The experience of such a child is then one of affective disregulation, in which he may experience repetitive rejections, because the disregulation often leads to apparently aggressive behavior, masking enormous anxiety. If we are to intervene meaningfully in situations of neglect and abuse, it is imperative to keep in mind the tenacity of the bond with the original object and the important anxiety-regulating function this object serves.

By eighteen months or so, speech develops. Psychologists (Piaget, 1946; Flavell, 1963) have used this as evidence that the toddler is in possession of the symbolic function and that he is able to evoke at will a mental representation of the object. At this early stage in preoperational thinking, representations are characterized by sensorimotor thinking. The representation is concrete in comparison to the form it might later assume, and its characteristics tend to be highly influenced by emotionally charged events (mother "is" what she seems to be at a moment of high emotional intensity). Nevertheless, this representation remains stable and available despite variations in emotional or physical surroundings. This marks the level of object constancy Piaget and cognitive psychologists described. I think of this as the second level of object constancy and label it *representational object constancy*. Representational object constancy functions to bring a certain sense of continuity and stability to the child's inner and outer world. Now wishes and demands of the object can be differentiated from self-interest, and differences can be communicated. The inner and outer worlds can be ordered and categorized. To compare levels of object constancy with progress in self-regulation, we might say that the capacity to organize, categorize, and label the inner and outer worlds carries the potential for eventual mastery.

Labeling, ordering, and categorizing brings the toddler face to face with the differences between his wishes and his mother's expectations. Object relating moves to a new level of organization, as conflict emerges (P. Tyson, 1988; Tyson and Tyson, 1990; R. L. Tyson, 1991), and the young child begins to fantasize about consequences should mother's demands not be met. More and more he recognizes ways to insure mother's love. The way in which the young child resolves conflict and finds ways to regulate the sometimes intense dysphoric affect and associated sense of helplessness and loss of libidinal connection to mother depends on a number of variables and has far-reaching consequences. If the child is to reach the level of object constancy Mahler proposed—i.e., the representation of the love object functioning as an inner source of "sustenance, comfort, and love" (Mahler and Furer, 1968, p. 222)[2]—some mastery of these conflicts and the development of some capacity to regulate affect are crucial.

Focusing now on psychic organization and functioning at each level of object constancy, we come to the question of what it is that is necessary for the young child to master emotional storms with some kind of self-regulatory balance. To answer this, we must return to the mother-child relationship and consider again the ways in which the mother responds to and regulates the young child's affects.

The issues that begin to emerge with the anal/rapprochement phase can be difficult ones for mothers. Can a mother share with her child a pride in his growing independence? Can she be supportive and encouraging of the child's independent strivings while at the same time setting appropriate limits? Can she be tolerant of her child's moodiness as the young child constantly changes his mind about what he wants and seems unhappy with whatever he gets? Or does the mother's need to be in control cause her to feel angry when her child struggles for control and challenges her authority? Does the child's anger arouse mother's anger? How does mother handle her own aggression?

If the mother herself is not overly distressed by the young child's anger, demands, or distress, she can respond to emotional storms with a regulating balance, providing soothing and comforting responses that help the young child make the transition from a state of high distress to one of relative calm, tolerating some drive expression yet expecting certain compliance. A balance of responsiveness insures that the child's affective storms do not reach proportions that undermine self-regulation, yet mother's timely confrontation also makes these emotions seem much less frightening and more manageable for the young child. Appropriate experiences of delay (e.g., not being given what he wants when he wants it, or not being allowed to do what he wants whenever he likes) also encourage the building of frustration tolerance and self-coping skills. If the mother is successful in helping the child negotiate these characteristic issues of the anal-rapproche-

2. I believe that Mahler's emphasis on the object representation in her definition of object constancy has led to some confusion. Students sometimes confuse cognitive and libidinal aspects and assume that during emotional storms it is the integrated representation that becomes lost, disrupted, and split apart. This does not fit with clinical experience. The child may feel the loss of the loving connection at times of heightened hostility, but under most circumstances, by eighteen to twenty months a child is able to maintain an integrated mental representation of the mother that preserves its essential character despite variations in the physical or affective surrounding situation. It may be that, by emphasizing representational concepts, we have brought about a blurring of cognitive and structural concepts.

ment phase, a loving, secure, attachment balances the sometimes hateful feelings. Ambivalence comes to be tolerated, and optimally the child comes to feel an inner sense of security and experiencing the mother as an enduring, loving, and supporting inner presence.

The mother's regulating responses in the context of her constant love also encourage the formation of what Emde (1988, 1990) has called an executive "we" or "we-go"—that is, a representation of shared pleasurable experiences of safety and togetherness between mother and child, which has motivational aspects. The pleasure gained from this shared "we" begins to outweigh the push for immediate gratification. As he struggles with conflicting motivations, the child experiences mother's support, and this pleasurable sense of togetherness functions to encourage identification with the wishes of the mother (Ritvo and Solnit, 1960). Conflict gradually becomes internalized, representing an early step in superego development. The sense of safety and pleasure derived from pleasing mother helps balance the seeming loss of gratification, and increasingly the enduring nature of the mother's libidinal availability feels like a more stable inner presence.

If the mother is successful in her role as an auxiliary ego (some might call it a self-object), identification with her will include identification with her demands for drive restraint but also identification with her recognition of and regulatory response to affective signals. In other words, the child internalizes mother's use of his affects as signals for intervention and begins to identify affects as they arise and take self-defensive measures. Rather than seeming to be all powerful, affects come to be experienced as manageable, and delay instead of immediate expression becomes possible. In this way the signal function of affects becomes an ego function.

With regard to determining the functions of object constancy, I suggest that affect regulation is the function of the third level of object constancy. If one compares levels of object constancy with progress in self-regulation, I think that object constancy as Mahler described— that is, the representation of the love object functioning as an inner source of comfort and love—is not possible without affect regulation and the use of the signal function. We can therefore label this level of object constancy *self-regulating object constancy*. The extent to which the child can engage in the more complex object relations that we associate with the Oedipus complex and can master the associated conflicts may depend significantly on the extent to which the child feels supported by an internal sense of a constant loving object and can consistently utilize the signal function of affect to insure self-regulation.

Although we usually associate object constancy with preoedipal object relations, it may be important to remind ourselves that achieving this level of object constancy is a process that takes place over developmental time. Conflict is ubiquitous, and although what begins as mother-child conflict becomes internalized, the issues nevertheless repeatedly emerge and challenge the young mind for resolution. Abstract thinking also becomes available, and the child moves from thought bound to the world of sensation and action to thought organized progressively more around abstractions. This means that the concrete, situation-bound, emotionally laden representation of the mother changes to one of greater flexibility as the child becomes capable of appreciating multiple perspectives (see Frosch, 1995). Greater capacity for abstract thinking becomes coupled with the capacity to utilize the signal function of affect, and the child is better able to recognize and label certain associated inner sensations as feelings. Affects can then have a less peremptory quality and can be more easily controlled once they can be regarded and labeled. The child comes to be more in control of his emotions instead of his emotions being in control of him. This, Anna Freud thought, was the major task of early childhood.

OBJECT CONSTANCY AND CHARACTER FORMATION

It is my contention that the means by which we assess normality and pathology needs updating. In another context (1996) I have proposed that we revise our view of neurosis. Typically we equate neurosis with the Oedipus complex. I think, however, that neurosis is more usefully viewed as a particular form of psychic structural organization that the mind may assume. This structural form is characterized first by internalized conflict, and second by a capacity for affective self-regulation. Internal compromises and self-defensive maneuvers, as opposed to peremptory affective expressions and manipulating attempts to control the environment, can then be found as solutions to conflict. Finally, a neurotic character structure implies a capacity for self-responsibility (Loewald, 1979, 1985). Although such a neurotic structural form may lead to inner pain and suffering, with or without manifest symptoms, this intrapsychic organization also provides the structural basis for optimal adaptation.

I have suggested this revision in the way we view neurosis, or neurotic character structure, because, first, years of child-analytic experience have taught us that although oedipal wishes challenge the young mind, they do not automatically lead to inner conflict, internal modification, and compromise. Instead, a wide variety of alternative solutions can also be sought. A second reason for eliminating the obligatory link between the Oedipus complex and a neurotic psychic organization is that a neurotic structural organization is built over developmental time; it is also the product of a variety of developmental influences, not simply the Oedipus complex. Internalization of conflict and superego formation begins long before the Oedipus complex (Mahler, 1975; Gillman, 1982; Tyson and Tyson, 1984; Tyson, R. L., 1991) and in response to a number of motivational influences, not just castration anxiety (see Freud, 1926; Emde and Buchsbaum, 1990; Tyson and Tyson, 1990). Self-regulation of affects—i.e., the capacity to use the signal function—also central to a neurotic structural organization, is related to object constancy, not the Oedipus complex. This means that the third level of object constancy, what I have called self-regulatory constancy, is central to adaptive neurotic structure. With the capacity to use the signal function, the affect associated particularly with sometimes very painful conflictual oedipal wishes can be regarded and responded to with compromise and self-defensive measures so that it does not disrupt self-regulation.

A capacity for self-responsibility, Loewald (1979) suggests, is also a necessary characteristic of neurosis. Guilt, self-punishment, repression, and *mastery*, or "owning up to one's needs and impulses as one's own," are needed to cope with the Oedipus complex and its vicissitudes in childhood, adolescence, and at various stages throughout the life cycle. In Loewald's view, this kind of oedipal mastery can be achieved only by developing a superego capable of self-responsibility (p. 392). Self-responsibility means the existence not simply of a guilt-producing, punishing superego, a superego that acts after the fact, but also of a superego that insures compliance with internalized rules. Such internal compliance means internal compromise in response to conflict. And such self-responsibility is achieved only gradually over developmental time. However, if the child or adult is ever to be capable of "owning up to [his] wishes and impulses as [his] own," he must be reassured that such impulses can be mastered. This brings us back to self-regulation.

Two brief clinical descriptions will illustrate what I am trying to clarify.

Tom is terrified of his emotions. He easily loses control of his feelings, especially his aggression, but he always blames someone else—"It's his fault, he made me angry!" Tom controls his family. That is, they make special allowances for him and give in to whatever he wants so that he doesn't get angry. They make few attempts to set limits and in general become passive in the face of his anger, until ultimately they are provoked and become furious and then harshly punitive. Their passivity, followed by their own seeming lack of control, is understood by Tom to mean that they, too, are frightened of his aggression. The only way Tom has found to control his affect, however, is to engage in provocative sado-masochistic interactions. This keeps him hopelessly dependent on his family; panic attacks during brief separations are what brought him to treatment. In treatment Tom has found that his analyst is not intimidated but instead confronts Tom's anger. Such confrontation conveys the message that the analyst is not afraid of Tom's affective storms. This gives him hope that perhaps he, too, will eventually be able to control his affects.

Sally is a good, nice, sweet, friendly, likable sixteen-year-old who is depressed. She admits she doesn't know much about her feelings, and any time she comes close to an affect, she changes the subject. She imagines screaming profanities at the top of her lungs during school assembly and wishes she could find a place to be alone where nobody would hear her, so she could scream her head off. She doesn't think anyone would like her if they really knew her. Sally is able to regulate her affects and so can take responsibility for her own impulses, but at a cost—she is severely inhibited. She fears that if she came close to expressing her rage she would lose all self-control. She wonders if anyone else would be able to control her. As it is, she does not take the chance and, fearing loss of self-regulation, turns away from all her feelings.

DEVELOPMENTAL FAILURE OF THE SIGNAL FUNCTION

Why is it that some individuals never develop the capacity to use affects in a signal manner? Instead, as children and as adults, affects retain a peremptory, omnipotent, overwhelming quality, continually disorganizing self-regulation. Self-esteem maintenance is a major difficulty.

The answers to such questions are never simple, for there is always a complex interaction between genetic, predispositional influences and environmental forces. As I have mentioned, we know that some infants are particularly vulnerable; they are easily stressed but not easily comforted. The diffuse tension states of early infancy evolve into diffuse anxiety and/or primitive rage states that may interfere with the infant's being able to experience the mother's libidinal investment. This quickly leads to a distortion of the maternal introject, and ordinary developmental, phase-specific conflicts become intensified and distorted (see Weil, 1978). The conflicts of the anal-rapprochement phase, for example, easily become exaggerated and intensified. Aggression leads to marked ambivalence, and object relations become distorted and organized around sado-masochistic fantasies. Projected aggression, as well as the child's ability to provoke aggression in the object, has a double impact. As a feature of the child's experience, it may produce over-whelming anxiety. However, internalization of and identification with the perceived frightening parent provide a continuing internal source of anxiety (Ritvo, 1981). When the child is unable to experience the mother as a comforter and organizer, anxiety, rather than coming to serve a signal function, is readily generated. Instead of internal com-promise in response to conflict, the child maintains a sense of entitle-ment and anxiously attempts to control and manipulate the environ-ment.

Winnicott (1969) discusses certain pathology often found in the mother-child interaction that may also interfere with the optimal de-velopment of the signal function. Winnicott describes the "use" of the object, or mother functioning as an auxiliary ego. Winnicott observes that at times, especially during early childhood, there is not a clear differentiation between object and subject, and it is not unusual that the child's perception of the object is colored by his own libidinal or aggressive impulses, his own affects, his own projections. When the child is able to distinguish between his own inner world and the reality of the object, he is more able to "use" the object. That is, he must perceive the nature and behavior of the object as free of his projec-tions, different from his expectations. If the object is to be "used," Winnicott explains, it must "be real in the sense of being part of shared reality, not a bundle of projections" (p. 88). That is, the object must survive the child's projections. Said another way, the object must not feel threatened and frightened of the child's emotions and not be stimulated or manipulated to respond in kind to the child; hence the child must experience that his mother's behavior is not altered by his affective storms.

Frequently mothers become distressed or are provoked into rage by a child's behavior. If a mother cannot tolerate the affective outbursts, presumably because she cannot tolerate these affects in herself, she may either abandon the child (become passive and do nothing, give in, or isolate him) or retaliate in some way, identifying with the child's projections. The object then ceases to function as an auxiliary ego that supports a feeling of safety, and the child's anxiety increases.

A better situation is for the object to feel and be able to convey that a sense of continuing safety prevails in spite of the child's affective storm. For example, the child may have murderous fantasies and erupt in rage. Mother's role is to be in charge, to intervene in a timely way, and not be manipulated to retaliate or to give in for fear of the child's aggression or because of the guilt she feels about her own (uncon-scious) murderous rage. By remaining steady and strong in the face of the child's intense affective storms, mother reassures the child that his angry murderous thoughts do not frighten, hurt, or kill her, nor do they provoke her to attack in response. Furthermore, her timely intervention prevents the child from being overwhelmed by these feelings, and he will be able to discover that the mother is different from his projections. If the object can "survive" the child's attacks (which in this context, Winnicott explains, means "not retaliate"), the child can begin to recognize the object as an entity in its own right. The child will then have the opportunity to "use" the object, to learn from the object that these feelings can be managed, and that there are adaptive ways of doing so. If he can manage his behavior, be in control of his emotions, the child can eventually also take responsibility for his actions and feelings.

The superego is heir to the object-related conflicts of early childhood. There are as yet many unanswered questions about superego development, and we can observe that often the superego seems rigid and harsh, yet functions inconsistently in early childhood. As I mentioned earlier, however, optimal adaptation depends on a superego able to assume self-responsibility. A child able to use the signal function of affect who comes to regard and have some control over his feelings and actions will have the potential for this adaptive step. Such a child will eventually be able to distinguish inner and outer worlds, the world of the superego, and the world of outer reality. This affords mastery over harsh, critical introjects, as well as mastery over peremptory, seemingly omnipotent emotions, and eventually self-esteem is more manageable.

When young children are not able to "use" their parents in the manner Winnicott described, superego development is delayed and impaired. Such children frequently become preoccupied with narcissistic issues related to omnipotent demands for control and/or domination. They easily erupt in anger when they cannot control the outside world. They blame others for their problems and feel cheated and victimized. These children, instead of a consistently loving inner presence and the capacity to self-regulate, suggesting the third level of object constancy, appear to have a consistently negative relationship with a critical, easily projected, primitively constructed, emotionally laden inner object representation (Blum, 1981). The persistent tendency to split object representations into idealized and devalued, good and bad, persecutory and protective, make affect regulation almost impossible. Such a clinical picture suggests that these children fail to tolerate ambivalence or to find some balance between the libidinal and aggressive forces within their personalities. They may have reached the first two levels of object constancy but not the third, judging by self-regulatory failure.

SUMMARY

I have suggested that we revisit the concept of object constancy. The development of object constancy is essential to understanding the linkages between psychic structure formation and object relations and a key concept in understanding psychic adaptation. I have suggested three levels of object constancy, or three stages along a developmental continuum. The first is a constant investment. Self-regulation depends on the child's receiving and using the affective signals of the object. The second is representational constancy, which functions to organize the inner and outer world. The third level I call self-regulatory constancy, in which the individual, through identification with the object, has become able to use the signal function of affects and self-regulation is now possible.

I have also described a revised view of neurosis that exemplifies the linkages between object relations and psychic structure formation. Central to this view of neurotic character formation is the concept of object constancy and the development of the signal function of affect. Finally I have briefly considered certain situations that might foster or interfere with the development of the signal function.

BIBLIOGRAPHY

BERGMAN, D. & ESCALONA, S. K. (1949). Unusual sensitivities in very young children. *Psychoanal. Study Child, 3/4:333–352.*

BLUM, H. P. (1981). Object constancy and paranoid conspiracy. *J. Amer. Psychoanal. Assn., 29:789–813.*

CALL, J. D. (1983). Toward a nosology of psychiatric disorders in infancy. In *Frontiers in Infant Psychiatry,* ed. J. D. Call, E. Galenson, and R. L. Tyson. New York: Basic Books, pp. 117–128.

EMDE, R. N. (1988). Development terminable and interminable II: Recent psychoanalytic theory and therapeutic considerations. *Int. J. Psychoanal., 69:283–296.*

——— (1990). Mobilizing fundamental modes of development: Empathic availability and therapeutic action. *J. Amer. Psychoanal. Assn., 38:881–910.*

EMDE, R. N. & BUCHSBAUM, H. K. (1990). Play narratives in 36-month-old children: Early moral development and family relationships. *Psychoanal. Study Child, 45:129–155.*

EMDE, R. N. & SORCE, J. F. (1983). The rewards of infancy: Emotional availability and maternal referencing. In *Frontiers of Infant Psychiatry,* ed. J. D. Call, E. Galenson, and R. L. Tyson. New York: Basic Books, pp. 17–30.

FLAVELL, J. H. (1963). *The Development of Jean Piaget.* Princeton: Van Nostrand.

FRAIBERG, S. (1969). Object constancy and mental representation. *Psychoanal. Study Child, 24:9–47.*

FREUD, A. Personal communication, 1971.

———— (1963). The concept of developmental lines. *Psychoanal. Study Child* 18:245–265.

———— (1965). *Normality and pathology in childhood: Assessments of development* Vol. 6 of *The Writings of Anna Freud*. New York: Int. Univ. Press.

———— (1967). Comments on psychic trauma. In *The Writings of Anna Freud*, vol 5. New York: Int. Univ. Press, 1969, pp. 221–241.

FREUD, S. (1923). The ego and the id. *S.E.*, 19:3–66.

———— (1926). Inhibitions, symptoms and anxiety. *S.E.*, 20:77–175.

FROSCH, A. (1995). The preconceptual origin of emotion. *J. Amer. Psychoanal* *Assn.*, 43:423–447.

GILLMAN, R. D. (1982). Preoedipal and early oedipal components of the super ego. *Psychoanal. Study Child*, 37:273–284.

GREENACRE, P. (1941). The predisposition to anxiety. In *Trauma, Growth and Personality*. New York: Norton, 1952, pp. 27–82.

HARTMANN, H. (1950). *Comments on the Psychoanalytic Theory of Ego: Essays on Ego Psychology*. New York: Int. Univ. Press, 1964, pp. 113–144.

———— (1952). The mutual influences in the development of ego and id. In *Essays on Ego Psychology*. New York: Int. Univ. Press, 1964, pp. 155–182.

LOEWALD, H. W. (1979). The waning of the Oedipus complex. In *Papers on Psychoanalysis*. New Haven: Yale University Press, 1980, pp. 384–404.

———— (1985). Oedipus complex and the development of self. *Psychoanal. Q.*, 54:435–443.

MAHLER, M. S. (1975). On human symbiosis and the vicissitudes of individuation. *J. Amer. Psychoanal. Assn.*, 23:740–763.

MAHLER, M. S., & FURER, E. (1968). *Infantile Psychosis*. Vol. 1, *On Human Symbiosis and the Vicissitudes of Individuation*. New York: Int. Univ. Press.

McDEVITT, J. B. (1979). The role of internalization in the development of object relations during the separation-individuation phase. *J. Amer. Psychoanal. Assn.*, 27:327–343.

PIAGET, J. (1946). *Play, Dreams and Imitation in Childhood*. New York: Norton, 1962.

RITVO, S. (1981). Anxiety, symptom formation and ego autonomy. *Psychoanal. Study Child*, 36:339–364.

SCHORE, A. (1994). *Affect Regulation and the Origin of the Self: The Neurobiology of Emotional Development*. Hillsdale, NJ: Erlbaum.

SETTLAGE, C. F., ROSENTHAL, J., SPIELMAN, P. M., GASSNER, S., AFTERMAN, J., BEMESDERFER, S., & KOLODNY, S. (1990). An exploratory study of mother-child interaction during the second year of life. *J. Amer. Psychoanal. Assn.*, 38:705–731.

SETTLAGE, C. F., BEMESDERFER, S., ROSENTHAL, J., AFTERMAN, J., & SPIELMAN, P. M. (1991). The appeal cycle in early mother-child interaction: Nature and implications of a finding from developmental research. *J. Amer. Psychoanal. Assn.*, 39:987–1014.

SOLNIT, A. J. (1982). Developmental perspectives on self and object constancy. *Psychoanal. Study Child*, 37:201–220.

SOLNIT, A. J., & NEUBAUER, P. B. (1986). Object constancy and early triadic relationships. *J. Amer. Psychoanal. Assn.*, 25:23–29.

SOLNIT, A. J., & RITVO, S. (1960). The relationship of early ego identification to superego formation. *Int. J. Psycho-anal.*, 41:295–300.

SORCE, J. F., EMDE, R. N., & KLINNERT, M. (1981). Maternal emotional signalling: Its effect on the visual-cliff behavior of one-year-olds. Paper presented at the meeting of the Society for Research in Child Development, Boston.

SPITZ, R. A. (1946). Anaclitic depression: An inquiry into the genesis of psychiatric conditions of early childhood. *Psychoanal. Study Child*, 2:313–342.

—— (1959). *A Genetic Field Theory of Ego Formation*. New York: Int. Univ. Press.

—— (1962). Autoerotism reexamined. *Psychoanal. Study Child*, 17:283–315.

—— (1963). Life and the dialogue. In *Counterpoint: Libidinal Object and Subject*, ed. H. S. Gaskill. New York: Int. Univ. Press, pp. 154–176.

SPRUIELL, V. (1981). Self and the ego. *Psychoanal. Q.*, 44:577–595.

STERN, D. N. (1974). The goal and structure of mother-infant play. *J. Amer. Acad. Child Psychiat.*, 13:402–421.

—— (1984). Affect attunement. In *Frontiers of Infant Psychiatry*, vol. 2, ed. J. D. Call, E. Galenson, and R. L. Tyson. New York: Basic Books.

—— (1985). *The Interpersonal World of the Infant*. New York: Basic Books.

TYSON, P. (1988). Psychic structure formation: The complementary roles of affects, drives, object relations, and conflict. *J. Amer. Psychoanal. Assn.*, 36(Suppl.):73–98.

—— (1996). Neurosis in childhood and in psychoanalysis: A developmental reformulation. *J. Amer. Psychoanal. Assn.*, In press.

TYSON, P. & TYSON, R. L. (1984). Narcissism and superego development. *J. Amer. Psychoanal. Assn.*, 32:75–98.

TYSON, P. & TYSON, R. L. (1990). *Psychoanalytic Theories of Development: An Integration*. New Haven, Yale University Press.

TYSON, R. L. (1991). Psychological conflict in childhood. In *Conflict and Compromise*, ed. S. Dowling. Madison, Conn.: Int. Univ. Press, pp. 31–48.

WEIL, A. P. (1970). The basic core. *Psychoanal. Study Child*, 25:442–460.

—— (1978). Maturational variations and genetic-dynamic issues. *J. Amer. Psychoanal. Assn.*, 26:461–491.

WERNER, H. (1957). *Comparative Psychology of Mental Development*. New York: Int. Univ. Press.

WINNICOTT, D. W. (1969). The use of an object. *Int. J. Psycho-anal.*, 50:711–716.

Diagnosis in Clinical Practice

Its Relationship to Psychoanalytic Theory

CLIFFORD YORKE, FRC PSYCH., DPM

The rapidly growing diversity of psychoanalytic clinical practice calls for a reexamination of its relationship to psychoanalytic theory. This is as strikingly evident in the field of diagnosis as it is elsewhere. Many analysts bring together their clinical observations in a clinical theory that may appear to fit their clinical findings well. But a clinical theory is not to be identified with a theory of the way the mind works (metapsychology), and an attempt is made, in what follows, to clarify the relationship between the two. It is argued that an uncritical attachment to clinical theories unsupported by metapsychological understanding has been furthered by two main longstanding developments: "object relations" theory and the extension of the clinical concept of transference. A misapplication of Freud's structural model may, in part, have contributed to these developments. This argument, and matters related to it, is pursued in some detail in respect to problems of psychoanalytic diagnosis, with special reference to some of Anna Freud's contributions to the field that seem to be somewhat neglected. Finally, in pointing to metapsychology as a check to clinical speculation, some of the illustrations are drawn from psychoanalytic treatment material, on the grounds that psychoanalytic work with the patient can be viewed in terms of continuing diagnosis.

Honorary consultant psychiatrist to The Anna Freud Centre, London; formerly psychiatrist-in-charge.

The stimulus for writing this paper came from re-reading two papers by Thomas Freeman (1992 and 1995) and reading a third that I had not hitherto come across (1994) and which Dr. Freeman kindly sent me.

190

PRELIMINARY COMMENTS

THE RELATIONSHIP BETWEEN CLINICAL PRACTICE AND PSYCHOANALYTIC theory calls for urgent reexamination in a world where theoretical assumptions are increasingly challenged and clinical practice has an ever widening diversity. Nowhere is this more evident than in the field of diagnosis. The assessment of psychological disturbance, whether of adult or child, is based above all on clinical procedure. One human being faces another in a clinical interchange, and the diagnostician hopes to make enough sense of what takes place to get some idea of what (if anything) is amiss with the patient and what (if anything) may be needed to put it right. An adult patient who has sought the assessment of his own free will tries to help the diagnostician and hopes for some success. And although a child rarely seeks treatment of his own accord, the diagnostician will normally begin his clinical encounter supplied with a social history, obtained in a clinical setting, and with school reports based in part on academic performance but also on the personal impressions of teachers. Psychological testing (by a *clinical* psychologist) may play a significant part in the assessment. In most clinics and institutions, a case conference follows and, if possible, a *clinical* diagnosis, however tentative, is made.

If the diagnostician is a psychoanalyst working with psychoanalytic colleagues, the diagnostic discussion will probably take place against a theoretical background that acknowledges the importance of unconscious mental processes, aggressive and sexual fantasies, oedipal and preoedipal organizations, and other concepts closely in tune with clinical practice and clinical findings.[1] The theory itself may be tacit, but its influence will be felt everywhere. Case conferences at the Anna Freud Centre were conducted on these lines until about 1961, when one of her younger colleagues asked Anna Freud if a more ordered and structured way of presenting case material could be found and, if so, whether this might facilitate the formulation of a psychoanalytic diagnosis. Anna Freud suggested that they try to work something out together and the metapsychological profile schema began to evolve.

Not everyone viewed the innovation with enthusiasm. Even at a center where metapsychology was an accepted part of teaching and training, its disciplined application to the diagnostic task was seen by some as an irksome chore, a demanding and profligate use of time and

---

1. These comments apply to a *Freudian* analytic clinic. At other clinics with, say, a Kleinian orientation the underlying theoretical assumptions either would be different or would be seen differently.

effort.[2] But Anna Freud's enthusiasm was infectious and led her to establish a Profile Study Group (chaired by Humberto Nagera), in addition to the regular diagnostic meetings. The deliberations of that group did much to refine the profile, establish its advantages, and explore the further possibilities of metapsychological assessment. Its use was extended to adolescents (Laufer, 1965) and to adults (A. Freud et al., 1965), while Thomas Freeman (1973) devised a schema for adult psychoses that he used extensively before and after its publication. Freeman drew up some twenty profiles on his mental hospital patients and brought them to the clinic for discussion. Ruth Thomas and her colleagues (1966) made profiles on child borderline cases, compared their findings with those of Freeman, and discussed them with other staff members experienced in psychosis. Lastly, the profile has been applied to diagnostic studies of seemingly specific clinical syndromes (e.g., Radford et al., 1972).

It was in 1962, at Anna Freud's insistence (she would not have called it *insistence*), that I wrote my first profile and presented it to the Profile Study Group. It was on an adult patient whom I had taken into analysis on the clinic's behalf six months before, but the group had already

2. It is of interest that some trained psychoanalysts are unfamiliar with Freud's use of the term. It first appears in a letter to Fliess dated February 19, 1896, where Freud says: "I am continually occupied with psychology, really *meta*psychology" but adds nothing more, presumably taking his meaning to be self-evident (Masson, 1985, p. 172). And on April 2, 1896: "I hope you will lend me your ear for a few *metapsychological* questions as well" (ibid., p. 180). On December 17, in a letter discussing periodicity and its possible significance for neuroses, melancholia, and mania, he observes, "Hidden deep within this is my ideal and woebegone child—metapsychology," but again there is no definition (ibid., p. 216). On September 21, 1897, he writes to Fliess: "The dream [book] stands entirely secure, and my beginnings of the metapsychological work have only grown in my estimation." (ibid., p. 266). In a letter dated March 10, 1898, he says his dream book has come to a halt again, adding: "it seems to me that the theory of wish fulfillment has brought only the psychological solution and not the biological—or, rather, metapsychological—one. (I am going to ask you seriously, by the way, whether I may use the name metapsychology for my psychology that leads beyond consciousness)." (Freud, 1954, p. 246). Lastly, on August 26, 1898, he says that he has set himself the task "of making a bridge between my germinating metapsychology and what is in the books, and I have therefore plunged into the study of Lipps whom I suspect of being the best mind of present-day philosophical writers." (Freud, 1954, p. 260). Finally, in a letter on the progress of the dream book (July 22, 1899) the term is listed among a number of important matters to be discussed in clarifying the theory of repression. (p. 287). (The last two references appear in Masson, op. cit., p. 324 and 362, respectively but are not mentioned in the index.) The roots of metapsychology are to be found in the *Project* (Freud, 1895) but in the language of neuroscience; the full psychological foundation is set out in the dream book (Freud, 1900); the first published use of the term appears in the book on jokes (Freud, 1905); and the clearest definition is to be found in the paper on "The Unconscious" (Freud, 1915c).

decided that profiles could—and in many cases should—be done at varying stages of analytic treatment, as a way of assessing progress or the lack of it. I was not at that time familiar with the clinic's methods or its mode of operation (I joined the staff a little later), but I was impressed and even a little daunted by the active and knowledgeable participation of the Group, though I was no stranger to metapsychology. But what convinced me more than anything else of the value of the profile was the increased understanding of my patient that followed from my efforts to form an articulate view of the nature of his disturbance *and its status at that time.* The analysis itself, at that point flagging, began to move again.

That was the year that Anna Freud first published her profile schema.[3] But, elsewhere, not everyone was convinced that metapsychological inferences drawn from available clinical data could be of real value in reaching a diagnosis, pointing to appropriate treatment, and giving some idea of prognosis. The analytically coherent and comprehensive schema, though put to work in a few centers and a source of interest to many who made no practical use of it, did not in general find wider favor among psychoanalysts of adults or children. This was partly because many of them had the erroneous impression that they were being invited to divide the patient into bits and address each bit separately, and they did not relish the idea of a procedure that seemed to mean the dissection of a clinical whole. This point and others call for consideration. But in this essay, I want to address the question of why so many analysts are reluctant to make use of metapsychology at all, let alone to employ it in a diagnostic procedure, and I hope perhaps to draw the attention of the skeptical to the benefits that may result from its use.[4] I shall not, however, review the profile schema itself; that has been done elsewhere (e.g., Yorke, 1980) and many provisional profiles based on cases seen at the Anna Freud Centre have been published in the *Bulletin of the Anna Freud Centre* and in some of the papers cited (e.g., Thomas et al., 1966; Radford et al., 1972).

CLINICAL PRACTICE AND ITS RELATIONSHIP TO THEORY

In 1954, Anna Freud read a contribution to a symposium on problems of technique in the psychoanalysis of adults. "In the history of psycho-

---

3. The version in *The Writings of Anna Freud* is less fully elaborated but is part of a more extended account of diagnostic assessment. It formed part of a grant application to the National Institute of Mental Health in Washington.

4. The widespread criticism of metapsychology based on the belief that advances in the biobehavioral sciences have rendered it out of date have been considered at length elsewhere (Yorke, 1995), and the arguments are not repeated here.

analysis," she said: "every advance in insight has been followed closely by an advance in technique; conversely, every technical rule has only been considered valid when rooted in a specific piece of analytic theory. Any doubt concerning the justification of a particular technique, therefore, had to be dealt with by inquiry into the assumptions which had given rise to it." (pp. 377–78).

Perhaps that is still broadly true, if what we mean by theory is *clinical* theory. For although most psychoanalysts want to be good clinicians, a comprehensive knowledge of the psychoanalytic theory that addresses the questions of the nature and functioning of the mind may, for many, play but a minor part in their professional interests. Such a theory (metapsychology) goes beyond a clinical theory or a theory of therapy. It takes account, as far as psychoanalytic knowledge permits, of normal and abnormal development. Many see its relevance in that regard but fail to see its advantages for conceptualizing the treatment process itself.[5]

Many clinicians who keep their eye firmly on the patient are inclined, when reading a psychoanalytic paper or listening to a presentation, to have one question uppermost in their minds: will they learn anything that will help them with their therapeutic tasks? And when they read or hear about assessment, their interest is less in diagnosis than in treatability. Metapsychology may not seem relevant for these endeavors.

Not that most clinicians are averse to new theoretical thinking, provided that it is closely attuned to observable human behavior, whether in the consulting room or not. To take a familiar example: when Winnicott (1953) introduced the concept of the "transitional object," he took as his starting point the everyday observation that a bit of cloth, a pillow, a rag doll, or similar object could become an indispensable companion to the child. But Winnicott's notion of a transitional object acquired the status of a *clinical concept* because he showed that these inanimate companions afforded intermediate object *stages,* by way of the thumb as a surrogate nipple, between the mother's breast and the outside world—sources capable of providing the comfort and pleasure initially afforded only by the mother's body. Furthermore, the intermediate object to which Winnicott pointed was not an object of love alone. If it could be stroked and cuddled, so too could it be bitten, torn, and dirtied without complaint or reciprocity. The success of the concept, its universal acceptance, lay in its high level of accordance, not simply with clinical but with *everyday* observation, and to that extent it was a discovery closely akin to that observation, making use of the

5. See Yorke, 1965a.

concepts of aggressive and libidinal forces in the clinical forms of love and hate.[6]

The practical value of Winnicott's contribution is at once evident. It is not only an essential concept in understanding child development, but may be helpful in clinical practice with adults as well, especially in states of regression. A woman patient of mine, whose levels of regression in her illness were sometimes profound, would prevail on her general practitioner, consultant physician, and especially her husband, to ring me up in the evenings and on weekends with repeated enquiries about her welfare, her progress in the analysis, or about some psychological "crisis," to a point that I found increasingly harrassing and, because I could not break analytic confidentiality, very difficult to deal with. One day during a session the trend of her associations suggested an explanation. I said I thought that in many ways her relationship to me, ostensibly through her husband or physician, was essentially like that to her favorite bedtime bit of towel as a child: I could be loved, psychologically stroked, spat on, and subjected to all kinds of abuse, without any protest and without betraying any feelings of my own. The point was well taken; ground was regained from enactment for analysis, and the extra-analytic intrusions came to an end.[7]

There are two major clinical concepts that many believe are the hallmarks of psychoanalytic practice proper, are put to use in it, and distinguish it from other kinds of psychotherapy: *resistance* and *transference*. Both of these play a major part in clinical theories but are manifest only clinically: the behavior of the patient I have just described strikingly exemplifies both a regressive transference and the special kind of resistance called "acting out." We know that both resistance and transference can take many forms and that often the two combine to hold up analytic work. Resistance can range from prolonged and even total silence, to lateness, to not turning up for sessions at all. But we are particularly struck when, after a treatment alliance has been won, and the patient is not only willingly present but actively

6. It is a metapsychological concept, too. Winnicott's theoretical discussion of the concept is of great interest, though perhaps Anna Freud (1967) puts the nub of the matter more succinctly when she says that the transitional object is "cathected doubly, narcissistically and with object love, and this enables the child to transfer his attachments gradually from the cathected figure of the mother to the external world in general" (p. 305). This is a clear metapsychological statement, involving structural, dynamic, economic, developmental, and adaptive points of view; but the statement is especially interesting because one can see it shift from the metapsychological to the clinical in the course of its exposition.

7. I do not believe that the patient felt "told off" or that she desisted through fear. I think she was able to make use of a genuine piece of insight.

engaged in reporting his associations with all the candor he can muster, he finds them suddenly and unexpectedly interrupted from sources unknown to him. The analyst may suspect that the interruption is occasioned by an unacceptable transference thought and may say for example, "Sometimes when nothing at all comes to mind there may be some thought about *me* that you're afraid to recognize." And if that is indeed the case, the offending thought may then surface. In such an event we might once again say that we have been dealing with a *transference resistance.*

We all recognize that transference is manifest in innumerable clinical situations. It is strikingly obvious when the patient behaves towards the analyst in ways uncharacteristic of any relationship other than that between a child and parent, and we would regard this as regressive, meaning regressive in time. But we also recognize far more subtle ways in which transference is expressed, and this affords the analyst a powerful therapeutic tool. The *clinical concepts* of resistance and transference do not in themselves have great explanatory power but, because they are lived out in the clinical interplay of the consulting room, they readily lend themselves to the explanations provided by clinical theories. In any given instance such an explanation may be ready to hand. If, in the example I have just given of transference resistance, the analyst's intervention had been effective, he might ask himself why. And he might well say that, in pointing to the patient's *fear* of the thought, he had shown that *he,* the analyst, was not afraid of it, thus freeing the patient to recognize and divulge its content. And, depending on his knowledge of the patient's clinical state at the time, he might have other explanations close to the clinical truth.

Clinical concepts are not as a rule self-contained. Close behind each lies a *theoretical concept* linked, at least loosely, with others in a network of *clinical theory.* For example, behind the transference resistance described one might postulate the theoretical operation of *repression* or some unconscious defensive device. A theoretical concept such as repression or other defense mechanism cannot be directly observed; it can only be *inferred* from observational data. It is not, however, a concept with which many people have any difficulty: it is readily and convincingly related to clinical phenomena. But a further theoretical question posed by my example would be this: did the defensive measure operate at the border between the systems *Pcpt.Cs.* and *Pcs.* or between the systems *Pcs.* and *Ucs.*?[8] A question involving considerations of psy-

8. In this instance, brief consideration will suggest that it takes place at the border between the system *Pcs.* and the system *Pcpt.Cs.*

chic topography and cathectic systems would not interest those who are entirely happy with clinical explanations of the kind suggested. A *clinical theory* need not concern itself with a *theory of the mind*.

Let me give an example from my own analysis of a sudden block in a chain of associations. At the time I was working at the Cassel Hospital. On the day in question the then-director, Tom Main, had called his staff together and raised with them the problem of the theft of library books. He had given them a severe verbal lashing, saying, among other things, that when it came to books analysts seemed to have no control over their thieving instincts. And he said much else besides.

That evening, in the course of an analytic session, my flow of associations came to a sudden stop, though my mind did not become a complete blank. I said to my analyst, "I can't think any more. In my mind I've just got a visual image—an image of a tin, the top of an old tin can." Reflecting on this curious experience, I went on: "It reminds me of a time I was home on holiday, and my mother said to me, 'There's a large tin of tongue we've had for many years. I don't know if it would be safe to eat now. Perhaps you should take it down to the Inspector of Health and ask his opinion.'"

I continued. "My grandmother was always wary of tinned foods that had been kept a long time. She thought there was always a risk of ptomaine poisoning."

My analyst, who was not a medical doctor, intervened to ask: "*What* kind of poisoning?" "Ptomaine poisoning," I said. I spelt it out. "Tommain poisoning."

Well, it would certainly be possible to explain *that* clinical experience in terms of a clinical theory: an intervention from the unconscious interrupts a train of thought, condensing and replacing a whole series of thoughts within a single visual image: the verbal lashing replaces a dangerous tongue, and so forth. And one might well regard that as sufficient explanation, follow the further ramifications of the material in the analysis, look at the transference implications, and so on. Yet it would be hard to find a better example of the intrusion of the primary process into what, until that moment, is secondary process thinking: only the underlying theme of such a session is influenced from the system *Ucs.*, due to the element of regression fostered by the analytic process. The sudden, fleeting appearance of a thing-presentation (Freud, 1915c)—an irruption from the id—displays its degree of condensation, displacement, and symbolization and reveals (some of its) meaning only when word-presentations are put back in touch with it, clearly distinguishes this interference in thinking from that of my first example. But to give a full explanation of the difference in terms of the way the mind works would, for some, go beyond the general bounds of either clinical theory or clinical necessity.

THE DREAM, CLINICAL THEORIES, AND METAPSYCHOLOGY

To have a wider conceptual value a clinical theory has to be integrated into a more comprehensive model, a model of the mind itself of what Freud called the mental apparatus; and since no one knows the nature of mind that model will be at a higher level of abstraction—more remote, that is, from the clinical phenomena for which it may have to account. That model can be no more than a map (Noy, 1977), at best a very rough one, that may help one find one's way in unknown territory. So although regression is a theoretical concept invoked to indicate some of the mental events underlying certain transference phenomena, it is above all the *past in the present* (temporal regression) that strikes the clinician most forcibly. The issues of formal and topographical regression may not be concepts that concern him, though you cannot begin to explain *why* the analytic process works without the concept of *formal* regression, or explain dream experience without the concept of *topographical* regression.

This last point is worth a brief discussion. Clinically, analysts feel quite at home with their patients' dreams; they note the associations brought to them and, depending on the patient's readiness for understanding and capacity to tolerate any anxiety that may be aroused, generally interpret the underlying content of which the patient was hitherto unaware. All they need in order to undertake this task successfully, or, for that matter, to analyze their own dreams, is to be found in the first six chapters of *The Interpretation of Dreams* (Freud, 1900). With few exceptions, to be noted shortly, they need not, for clinical purposes, set eyes on Chapter VII—the chapter Freud entitled "The Psychology of the Dream-Processes." So it may be well worth recalling that Freud begins that chapter with an account of the famous dream in which the boy stands by his father's bed and says, reproachfully: "Father, don't you see I'm burning?" and of which, given the circumstances and the context, the interpretation is obvious. Freud continues:

> Hitherto we have been principally concerned with the secret meaning of dreams and the method of discovering it and with the means employed by the dream-work for concealing it. The problems of dream interpretation have hitherto occupied the centre of the picture. And now we come upon a dream which raises no problem of interpretation and the meaning of which is obvious, but which, as we see, nevertheless retains the essential characteristics that differentiate dreams so strikingly from waking life and consequently call for explanation. It is only after we have

disposed of everything that has to do with the work of interpretation we can begin to realize the incompleteness of our psychology of dreams.

But. . . *it must be clearly understood that the easy and agreeable portion of our journey lies behind us.* Hitherto, unless I am greatly mistaken, all the paths along which we have travelled have led us towards the light—towards elucidation and fuller understanding. But as soon as we endeavour to penetrate more deeply into the mental process involved in dreaming, every path will end in darkness. There is no possibility of *explaining* dreams as a psychical process, since to explain a thing means to trace it back to something already known, and there is at the present time no established psychological knowledge under which we could subsume what the psychological examination of dreams enables us to infer as a basis for their explanation. On the contrary, *we shall be obliged to set up a number of fresh hypotheses which touch tentatively upon the structure of the apparatus of the mind and upon the play of forces operating in it* (Freud, 510–511, my emphasis).

In this way, as we know, the hypotheses were set down on which Freud's theory of the mind, or metapsychology, was founded. The father's dream of the boy at his bedside pointed to two characteristics of the dream that no amount of interpretation could elucidate: its immediacy and its hallucinatory quality. The events depicted were experienced as if they were happening there and then, and the dream had all the vividness of reality. The discussion of this remarkable fact was the starting point of what was the most exciting chapter on psychology I had ever read.

At this point it may be helpful to outline the notions around which the overall argument of this paper is structured. Clinical *observations* lead to clinical *explanations* from which clinical *concepts* derive; clinical concepts lead to *explanatory theoretical concepts* that tend to be brought together, however loosely, into *clinical theories*, which vary from the plausible to the convincing but appear in tune with clinical facts; these theoretical systems ought to be compatible with a theory of the mind or *metapsychology*.[9] And, to anticipate the argument to come, metapsychology can—indeed should—be used as a check on (1) clinical theories that appear to meet the facts but which may seem dubious on closer inspection (cf. Glover, 1947, 1961) and (2) the reconstruction of the mental organization in conditions where clinical (analytic) scrutiny is impossible—such as earliest infancy or disorders not normally analyzable (e.g., the severe drug-addictive syndromes [Radford et al., 1972] or intense monosymptomatic hypochondriasis).

9. I am grateful to Mrs. Barbara Sullivan for helping me to clarify this schematic summary.

Freud's metapsychology was well known to and accepted by the early psychoanalysts and many of the following generations. Certainly it was familiar to the people whom Anna Freud addressed when, so many years later, she spoke the lines with which I opened this paper.[10] But that was in 1954, and even then it could be said that Freud's pre-structural papers on metapsychology (notably, in addition to the chapter just discussed, 1911a, 1911b [section III], 1914, 1915a, 1915b, 1915c, 1917a) were widely neglected—a neglect repeatedly emphasized by Glover (e.g., 1947, 1961) and called by Rapaport (1960) "one of the most puzzling problems in the history of psychoanalysis."

Yet I am not altogether sure that the puzzle is as great as that. Perhaps we should put the question another way: how has it come about that some immensely popular clinical theories are so rarely subjected to the disciplined check of metapsychology? For it may even be that a major development in Freud's theory of mind—the structural model—unknowingly and unwillingly played a part in this unfortunate neglect. At first sight this would seem highly improbable, but the suggestion does bear examination.

An uncritical overattachment to clinical theories unsupported by metapsychology has been furthered over the years by two main developments, now of long standing: "object relations" theory and the extension of the clinical concept of transference. Object relations theory is often contrasted with what is referred to as Freud's "drive theory." Drive theory, in this sense, is held to reduce the complexities of human relationships to a search for instinctual satisfaction. But that use of the term is a caricature of Freud's views. And the concept of transference, too, was greatly widened, in a way that served some object relations theorists very well, from its initial and comparatively restricted concept until it came to refer to *"the whole actual life of the patient* during the analysis" (Klein, 1943). And the concept of countertransference was also widened by Paula Heimann (1950), to include the use of the analyst's feelings as a source of information about the patient. Years later, Betty Joseph (1985), stating a view she had held for some time, declared that transference was not only the total analytic situation but included the analyst's experience of countertransference as well. I have discussed these issues elsewhere in relation to child analysis and need not repeat the arguments here (Yorke, 1994).

Now, the structural model (Freud, 1923) was an immense advance, and it cannot be blamed for these developments. So it is worth recalling

10. They included, among others, K. R. Eissler, Dora Hartmann, Maurits Katan, Marianne Kris, Rudolph Loewenstein, Margaret Mahler, Eli Marcovitz, Annie Reich, and Jennie Waelder-Hall, with Robert Waelder as chairman.

how and why it came into existence and how it involved a radically new approach to the theory of mental structure. It came into being on account of two conceptual difficulties: the first clinical, the second theoretical. The clinical problem was posed by the negative therapeutic reaction: why, in spite of careful analytic work in which both patient and analyst came to fresh insights, did the patient's condition not just *fail to improve* but actually *get worse?* The theoretical problem was posed by the difficulty in pointing to a psychic location for repressing or defensive agencies. A defense of which the patient was aware would be no defense at all. Yet to locate defense in the system *Ucs.* would be an absurdity, because it would be part of the very system it was defending against.

The concept of the ego as the executive apparatus of the mind, striving to hold the balance between the conflicting claims of the superego, the id, and external reality, opened up new possibilities for understanding the nature of mental development and mental disorder. It also opened the way for the study of this executive apparatus that had in many respects been previously neglected; understanding of the nature of the system *Ucs.* had certainly taken the lion's share of psychoanalytic attention. Freud's extension of the theory of instincts (in the psychoanalytic sense) in 1920, by affording aggression the status of a drive, had also contributed to a better understanding of unconscious guilt and the superego as an agency through which its derivatives were mediated and directed toward the self. But the advantages conferred by the structural model were not always appreciated in the context of the development of Freud's theory; the new formulations lent themselves to misapplication. The fact that the superego was founded on parental internalizations in the course of the resolution of the Oedipus complex gave added impetus to the notion of internal objects. (It is of some interest that the one metapsychological paper that almost everyone reads is "Mourning and Melancholia" Freud, 1917b). If the ego were still understood (erroneously) to be identical with the self,[11] then a basis was laid for a theory of the mind in which the major part was played by endopsychic object relations. This was for many a welcome development because it was now possible to transfer a clinical situation—the relationship between the patient and the analyst (*in its totality*)—into a theoretical concept that appeared to be fully in line with it.

The loss of interest in the prestructural metapsychological formulations may also be explained, at least in part, by the erroneous notion

11. This was always the case with Klein. Fairbairn took the matter a step further with his concept of a libidinal ego and an antilibidinal ego, meaning a libidinal *self* and an antilibidinal *self*, respectively.

that the structural model made the concept of psychic topography entirely out of date. But if it can be argued that the topographical *model* of the mind is superseded by the structural model, it cannot be denied that the concept of *qualities* of mental content to which the designations *Pcpt. Cs., Pcs.,* and *Ucs.* can be assigned cannot be dispensed with. For that reason, in spite of attendant difficulties, there is a very strong case for speaking of a topographical *point of view* to stand alongside the structural viewpoint. The points of view of metapsychology could then be listed as the dynamic, economic, structural and topographical, seen as operating within the structural *model*. This was a view to which Anna Freud[12] was wholly sympathetic.[13] This issue is more fully discussed elsewhere (Yorke, 1996).

In any case, metapsychology hardly came to a stop with the structural model. And it is surely clear that, while they were given further impetus by the structural model, Freud's poststructural metapsychological formulations repeatedly rely on prestructural ones, while modifying, developing, and expanding them. But these further contributions to the field (in particular, 1924a, 1924b, 1924c, 1925a, 1925b, 1926 [addendum A], 1940) more often than not, tend to be quoted selectively, if at all, by object relations theorists. For, in general terms, the structural model appealed to the new theorists because it made great *clinical* sense to misunderstand it in terms of internal agencies seen as "objects" in conflict with each other and the outside world. To preserve Freud's new insight it was necessary to bear in mind that the ego could no longer be equated with the self.[14]

Following this misguided line of thinking, it was also easy to view transference as the totality of self/other relationships and to refer to object relations theory as a "*two-person psychology.*" This replaced metapsychology, because metapsychology was a "*one-person psychology*"—a psychology concerned only with what went on inside the mind of a single individual. "Drive theory," as a pejorative term was equated with a one-person psychology, which failed to take into account the fact that relationships took place *between* people. It had long seemed evident to

12. Personal communication.

13. This is a view to which the "ego psychologists" adhered, sometimes adding, as, for example, Rapaport (1960) did, adaptive and developmental points of view. These two viewpoints still require explanation in terms of the others, though psychoanalysis is, above all, a developmental psychology.

14. Freud's use of the term thereafter was not always consistent, but this general meaning was clear. Self and objects could now be understood as organized representations within the ego, in active relations to each other, and all other aspects of the mental apparatus including the representations of the outside world (see, for example, Jacobson, 1965).

me that if relationships between people were simply reduced to a search for gratification of an "instinctual drive,"[15] whether successful or frustrated, that the individual would be relegated to something akin to a narcissistic psychopath. That was not, I believe, the intention, but perhaps the exaggeration will make the point.

Any attempt to conceptualize the way the mind works must involve a "one-person psychology." As Gertrude Stein might have said, a mind is a mind is a mind. It is certainly not *two* minds. But it is a mind peopled with representations of the self and others, of relationships with and attitudes toward them, in all the complexities of their interactions (conscious and unconscious), in all forms and stages of activity or quiescence, of conflict, internal harmony or disharmony—and so on through all the myriad forms of psychic experience. A mind does not exist in a relationship between two or more people but it makes it possible for an individual to relate to others, to spurn or embrace them, to love them, hate them, make friends with them, make common cause with them, betray them, defer to them, and foster or hinder all the complexities of social interchange—and to do all this consciously and unconsciously. It is the fact that metapsychology seems remote from these human realities that makes people doubt its value. So a theory of endopsychic object relations seems to offer a much more viable alternative, and to give the transference totality flesh and blood. Paradoxically, the danger is that the true richness of analytic work is replaced by what has aptly been called "relationship therapy" (e.g., by Kennedy and King in personal communications). But understanding the mind is the key to understanding what it is that makes people human.

Let us now turn to a diagnostic difficulty and examine it in the light of metapsychology, enriched by the structural model. Some years ago I discussed the case of an unhappy four-year-old boy, who was uncommonly prone to injuries (Yorke, 1983). He hurt himself when he jumped recklessly into a bath. He looked up and watched without moving as a cricket ball hit him in his eye. He would trip and lose his balance as he scrambled over furniture. He fell off swings. In a preliminary discussion—before a formal diagnostic assessment had been made—some participants observed that the boy *turned aggression against himself*. But that was simply a clinical observation; a great deal more had to be known before one could say how this might have come about. Did he attack himself rather than an object he needed to preserve? Did he attack himself through guilt? through masochism? Did

15. Adherents of this kind of theorizing fail to see that a *drive as such* can never be known. All that can be apprehended are representatives or derivatives of a drive, as Freud repeatedly pointed out.

he attack his body through a conviction that it was the source of all evil, of sexuality and murderousness? The structural model made it possible to approach these problems in a more systematic way, and though it was still feasible to try to answer them in purely clinical terms, the contending nature of the forces, the dynamic interplay between them, and their relative strengths and distribution needed careful consideration before the nature of the presenting clinical phenomena could be more clearly understood.

TRANSFERENCE, RESISTANCE, AND THE STRUCTURAL MODEL

A theoretical model based on the notion of endopsychic object relations loses the metapsychological advantages of the structural model and some of its usefulness for clinical understanding. Let us take a further look, in the light of the new model, at transference and resistance. In an addendum to his revision of the theory of anxiety, Freud (1926) drew attention to the different types of resistance as they could now be understood in terms of the structural model. Resistance could come from the side of the id, the ego, and the superego. If the patient (often unconsciously) tried to use the analysis for purposes of gratification—whether sexual or aggressive—it could be said that this was an *id resistance*. If the normal unconscious defensive operations stood in the way of progress, one could speak of an *ego resistance*. If the patient was in danger of losing the unconscious advantage he gained from his illness, of losing a secondary or epinosic gain, then a second type of resistance might stem from the ego. And there is a third type of resistance that also stems from the ego—the transference resistance itself, of which clinical examples have been given above. Finally, resistance may come from the side of the superego: the patient feels he does not deserve to get well, and a *superego resistance* in the form of the negative therapeutic reaction may result.

Of these resistances, the one students most frequently overlook, in my experience, is the id resistance. This can, of course, take many forms, though sado-masochistic gratification experienced in the transference comes more readily to their attention than most.

Transference also calls for explanatory concepts that were usefully extended by the new theoretical model. Clinically, we might be content to say that the use of the couch fosters regression, meaning regression in time, and use a clinical theory. And to that end we are accustomed to say that, under the conditions of psychoanalytic treatment—the basic rule, the recumbent posture with its restriction of physical discharge, the analyst's absence of view—the patient regresses, so that his verbal material begins to take on an infantile quality—an element, perhaps, no more—that accounts for the character of his utterances, the way in which the sequence of his thoughts departs from the normal conventions, and a departure not to be understood simply by the fact that the patient does his best to avoid conscious censorship.

All this could have been said before the advent of the structural model. But a great deal could now be added, and similarities with the revised concepts of resistance will be evident. Transference can take different forms at different times. The analyst may certainly be seen as a whole person, a personification of an important figure from childhood. But very often he becomes, by projection, the patient's id—the tempter, seducer, aggressive attacker—or some aspect of the patient's superego: aim-giving, helpful, corrupt, or persecutory. He may be treated like an auxiliary ego and his supposed or assumed behavior taken as a model to be emulated or dealt with in all kinds of ways. Of course, splitting of the transference was as easy to recognize in the prestructural model as it was thereafter, but the complexities of transference to which the structural model points, its diversities and subtleties, can be vitiated if the analyst is seen only in terms of object relations, of (bodily) part or whole. The *widening* of the concept of transference that I have described has, I believe, done no service to subtlety. The idea that everything the patient says, thinks, or infers about the analyst is transference reduces the value of the transference concept: it is also an object relations concept of a wholesale kind that, paradoxically, reduces the value of all the patient's other relationships and exalts the "you mean me" and the "here and now" at the expense of personal history.

CLINICAL THEORIES AND THE PSYCHOSES

These developments do not vitiate the value of the structural theory from the standpoint of metapsychology. Its value is enhanced if it is not regarded simply as a point of view that diminishes the importance of topography, dynamics, and economics. If it is merely seen as an organization of representations that do not need these points of view, then the bottom would fall out of psychoanalytic theory. There was always a danger, even with what came to be known as "ego psychology," that psychoanalytic psychology would become excessively structuralized (Yorke, 1965b), but this outcome was largely averted. It would be a pity if Edith Jacobson's valuable concept of the representational world (1965) were to give way to a notion of representations that excluded metapsychological concepts, but there are signs that this may happen.

Freeman (1992) has argued that critics of metapsychology generally find dynamics and topography more acceptable than economics. "They observe daily in their psychoanalytic practice the phenomena on which these explanatory concepts [dynamics, topography] are based. . . . [They are troubled by the economic concept because] this introduces the controversial concept of instinct and the idea of quantities of mental energy, instinctual (mobile) and ego (bound) cathexes, their distribution and redistribution within a hypothetical mental apparatus. [But] the critics of metapsychology are silent about the psychoses. The only exception in this regard are Arlow and Brenner (1969), who state that mental economics can be dispensed with in a theory of the psychoses," [arguing that] "the phenomena of the psychoses can be understood in the same way as neurotic symptoms—that they are the result of conflict, regression and defense" (p. 497). Freeman shows, through an examination of the metapsychology of chronic brain syndrome and schizophrenic psychoses, that the economic point of view is indispensable for the theoretical understanding of these conditions. But Freeman also concludes, correctly, that the economic factor is also essential for the full understanding of non-psychotic disorders, and he illustrates this view from Anna Freud's (1967) account of children who are as forgetful and neglectful of their personal possessions as are schizophrenic patients—a paper for which, interestingly enough, Winnicott's concept of the transitional object is a point of departure. Elsewhere Freeman (1995) has argued that clinical theories of psychosis (e.g., Arlow and Brenner, 1969; Klein, 1946; Pao, 1979; Rosenfeld, 1954; Bion, 1959) overextend "the use of the dynamic concept as explanatory for the entire symptomatology and courses of psychotic illnesses" (p. 19). Furthermore, "they tend to neglect the economic factor in mental life despite its explanatory potential" (p. 20).[16]

I am in full agreement with these statements but would add a further point. If dynamics and topography/structure are unsupported by the economic viewpoint, they too lose a great deal of their theoretical force, however much they may otherwise lend plausibility to clinical theories. For dynamics are not simply a matter of conflict between different parts of the personality: the strength and disposition of contending forces (economics) is of first importance in deciding the outcome of dynamic contentions. Equally, a topographical viewpoint is essential in conceptualizing the *qualities* of the mental contents concerned in terms

16. Unfortunately, the circulation of *The British Psych-Analytical Society Bulletin*, in which this paper appeared, is restricted to members.

of their characteristics and relationship to consciousness. All these points of view are necessary to understand the nature of any mental event (Freud, 1915c., p. 181); a formulation lacking any one of them is not metapsychological.

CONCLUSIONS

CLINICAL THEORY VERSUS METAPSYCHOLOGY: SOME IMPLICATIONS FOR DIAGNOSIS

It may seem strange to begin these concluding remarks with a brief discussion of symptoms, but that may prove a convenient way to bring together the various strands of the argument. Psychoanalysts have not generally set great store by symptoms as such, whether in adults or in children. The early interest in unconscious mental processes meant that surface presentations could be largely neglected in favor of the depths that had to be explored. But Freud took symptoms seriously, as did Anna Freud; for if they arise from deep within the mind there are still very good reasons why they take the form they do. Consider the following:

Elizabeth was nine years old when she complained that her writing and reading skills had fallen behind those of her classmates because voices were interfering with them. The voice of a girl told her to be good and do whatever she was doing—in particular, reading and writing—well; a boy's voice told her to be bad and to read or write poorly. She would tell the bad voice to "buzz off," sometimes successfully. Sometimes she felt "confused," wondering if the good voice were really the bad one, the bad voice the good.

She heard the voices very distinctly but did not attribute them to people in the outside world: they had no delusional quality. Although the speakers were unknown to her, the *content* of the girl's voice was essentially the same as her mother's exhortations. The content of the boy's voice evoked the sayings of a boy who lived nearby, of whom she strongly disapproved, and who was wayward and delinquent in his schoolwork.

It is possible, even on the basis of this scanty information, to make at least a rough guess at the meaning of these phenomena. The girl's voice represented the maternal superego, or rather the ego ideal, because, though exhortatory, it was aim-giving and helpful, acting as a spur to higher standards. The other was a malign tempter, urging her to ignore her mother's advice and play havoc with what authority told her to do. It derived from the id, apparently acting through a corruption of the superego, and made counterclaims on the ego to those of the maternal ego ideal. A form of compromise was represented in a symptom that alternated claim and counterclaim, and seriously interfered with the ego's ability to initiate and sustain effective action. But the distinctive perceptual identities represented by the voices were not consistently maintained: when Elizabeth became "confused," good and bad appeared to be changing places. For all that, the compromise formation remained. But if there is a clear clinical indication of the symptom's *content*, this does not explain its *form*. Perceptions, rather than thoughts, are in conflict and present as the source of psychic discomfort. Nevertheless, the memories on which they are based are not completely replaced because Elizabeth could still make links with the mother and wayward boy, though the voices were not theirs. At the times the voices were heard there was a topographical regression. But there was not a breakdown of reality testing as there would be in a psychotic hallucination.[17] But there is clearly a limit to what we can deduce from the examination of a symptom alone. To extend the diagnosis of this little girl beyond these limits requires much more information.

There is an important paper by Anna Freud relevant to diagnosis that seems to me somewhat neglected: her remarkably comprehensive account of "The symptomatology of childhood" (1970). There she acknowledges, as others do, the "deceiving nature of overt symptomatology" in childhood. But, "on the other hand, symptoms are negligible in the analyst's view only for the purposes of the technique of therapy; in their eyes, too, symptoms have retained full significance so far as diagnostic classification is concerned. Whether a patient is assessed as a hysteric or phobic subject, as suffering from an obsessional neurosis or a paranoid state, is decided wholly on the basis of his manifest symptomatology, i.e., on the overt evidence of bodily conversions, anxiety attacks, avoidance mechanisms, compulsive acts, ruminations, projections, etc." (p. 20).

It is in the next passage that Anna Freud begins to provide a key to the whole dilemma—if, that is, we are inclined to put it in (false) opposition to metapsychology on the one hand and clinical observation on the other:

17. Freeman (1994) has drawn attention to a view put forward by Ey (1969) to explain the perceptual nature of dreams and hallucinations, namely, that there is a dissolution or "unstructuring" of the field of consciousness (in Freudian terms the system *Pcs.*) that impairs selective attention, conceptual thinking, and memory schemata without which adaptive and realistic relationships to the outer world cannot be sustained.

There is an incongruity here between the analyst's therapeutic thinking, which is *metapsychological,*[18] i.e., directed towards the dynamic economic, genetic, and structural aspects of psychic functioning, and his thinking as a diagnostician, which proceeds on the basis of concepts and categories which are descriptive.[19] The difference between these viewpoints is so fundamental that it has caused many analysts to withdraw their interest altogether from diagnostic assessment as from an area which is neither essential nor very significant for their field of work, and has caused some others to regard all their patients' abnormalities as mere variations of many vagaries and complexities of human behaviour.

But before subscribing to a diagnostic nihilism of this extreme kind, the attempt seems worthwhile to bridge the gap between the two contrasting approaches and to use the vast array of overt symptoms themselves for the purpose of forging links between them. There is no reason, after all, why the very classification of symptomatology should not go beyond enumeration and description and why probing into dynamic clashes and genetic antecedents should be excluded from it, to be reserved for scrutiny within the analytic procedure. It is inevitable, of course, that such a different mode of classification will sacrifice the neatness and order of any system based on phenomenology. It is only to be expected that in many instances there will be no one-to-one correlation between underlying unconscious constellation and manifest symptom. (pp. 20–21).

She then demonstrates, in her two-part classification, that the unconscious constellations can give rise to a variety of manifestations, while similar symptoms can result from a variety of causes. But: "Far from being confusing for the analyst, it can only help to sharpen his diagnostic acumen."

It is tempting, but unnecessary, to summarize this preliminary classification. It must suffice to indicate its scope. And so, under the heading of "symptomatology proper," the reader is taken on a survey of symptoms resulting from initial non-differentiation between somatic and psychological processes (psychosomatics); from compromise formations between id and ego (neurotic symptoms); from irruption of id derivatives into the ego; from changes in the quality and direction of aggression; from undefended regressions; and from organic causes. In the second part of the paper, the tour takes in fears and anxieties (surveyed chronologically, in terms of manifest and latent content, and

18. My emphasis. The *thinking* is metapsychological, but the *listening* is through free-floating attention.

19. Footnote by Anna Freud: "Or, at best, on the basis of unconscious content converted into conscious symbols."

in terms of defense and absence of defense); delays or failures in development; school failures; and aches and pains. If the survey is compact, it is remarkably comprehensive.

Anna Freud opens her concluding remarks with a very significant assertion:

> The diagnostic profile, as it is in use in the Hampstead Child-Therapy Clinic at present, is intended to draw the diagnostician's attention away from the child's pathology and to return it instead to an assessment of his developmental status and the picture of his total personality. The present attempt at classifying the symptomatology of childhood may serve to amend and amplify this procedure by returning to the symptoms themselves a measure of diagnostic significance. If symptoms are viewed merely as manifest phenomena, dealing with them remains arid so far as analytic interest is concerned. If the clinician is alerted to see opening up behind these the whole range of possible deviations, causations, and developmental affiliations, the field becomes fascinating, and scrutinizing a child's symptomatology becomes a truly analytic task (p. 184).

There is a good deal to be said for starting any case scrutiny with a close consideration of the symptoms or presenting disturbance, difficulties or sources of complaint by teachers or parents. The diagnostician can combine this scrutiny with a question drawn from the examination of all the available data, perhaps even *before* he sees the child at diagnostic interview: what is it that strikes me most about all this? It may be a disparity between the I.Q. assessment and school performance, or something quite dramatic and even unexpected: a child who is otherwise scrupulously clean and excessively careful about his appearance but who conceals packets of feces about the house, or a child who has a real physical disability, who is hypochondriacal about illnesses for which there is no objective evidence but who takes risks that jeopardize the improvement of the disability from which he suffers. These, together with other striking features that may be presented by the same child, suggest possibilities to be explored by closer metapsychological assessment. The good clinician observes the clinical findings but brings a metapsychologically practiced eye to bear on its elucidation. But having, as it were, started with a diagnostic fulcrum—the symptoms and signs—he explores the whole personality as far as his available knowledge allows, before attempting his diagnostic formulation. He need not use the profile schema except as a check to see whether he has missed anything. Above all, he does not try to answer profile "questions" if he does not have the necessary information at his disposal. If he begins his task by using the profile as a checklist, without first doing the necessary work in *profile thinking,* his exercise is likely to be self-defeating by pointing to unreliable and unsupported diagnostic guesses or, worse, mere assertions.

I have suggested elsewhere (Yorke, 1980) that the profile alone may not be enough to support a true *developmental* understanding of the case. A full consideration of the developmental lines (A. Freud, 1963) is helpful in pointing to the way in which the patient has arrived at his current state of mental functioning and levels of adaptation in both successes and failures. In that way the horizontal cross-section, provided by the profile, of the metapsychology of the mental organization at a particular moment in time is provided with the vertical, developmental dimension it may otherwise lack. It is customary, in any event, to include the developmental and the adaptive points of view to metapsychological understanding: after all, psychoanalysis is first and foremost a developmental psychology.

Lastly, we need to stress the meeting point of clinical observation and metapsychology. Metapsychology *is* psychoanalytic theory, and a metapsychological assessment is simply the psychoanalytic understanding of the patient's mental state. If its ideas seem abstract, the formulation itself can readily come back to clinical life. Once the metapsychology is understood, a formulation can, as a rule, be presented in clinically comprehensible terms in a final, though provisional, diagnostic statement. That has for many years been standard practice at the Anna Freud Centre, even though, inevitably, the best of formulations will be incomplete at this initial stage and will point to many unanswered questions. But without metapsychology, formulations may be arrived at that have more plausibility than substance. They may seem to meet the clinical facts but be full of hidden holes, lacunae, and serious errors no less detrimental for being unseen. In the end, metapsychology is the only instrument that enables us to arrive at a picture of the whole person: with his physical and psychological strengths and weaknesses, endowment, disabilities, and capacities to relate to self and others. Above all, it is a guide to treatment—to what is the most appropriate way of helping the child—in Anna Freud's terms, to restore him to the path of normal development. That may not, of course, be feasible, but at least it may make it possible to avoid some serious errors that might otherwise perpetuate or intensify maladaptation.

Finally, I have long held the view that although one does not consciously *think* in theoretical terms behind the couch, or in the room with a child one is treating, it is possible to look at treatment in terms of continuing diagnosis if changes are taking place in the course of analysis. That is why, in this essay on diagnosis, I have not hesitated to draw for illustration on the work of analysis itself.

BIBLIOGRAPHY

ARLOW, J. W., & BRENNER, C. (1969). The psychopathology of the psychoses. *Int. J. Psychoanal.*, 50:5–14.

BION, W. R. (1959). Attacks on linking. *Int. J. Psycho-Anal.*, 40:308–315.

EY, H. (1969). Outline of an organo-dynamic conception of the structure, nosography and pathogenesis of mental diseases. In: *Psychiatry and Philosophy*, ed. Strauss, E. W.

FREEMAN, T. (1973). The metapsychological profile schema. In: *A Psychoanalytic Study of Psychoses.* New York: Int. Univ. Press.

—— (1992). Psychiatric perspectives on Freud's metapsychology. *Int. Rev. Psycho-Anal.*, 19:497–502.

—— (1994). On some types of hallucinatory experience. *Psychoanal. Psychotherapy*, 8:273–281.

—— (1995). On the formal aspects of psychotic phenomena. *Brit. Psycho-Anal. Soc. Bull.*, 31:3,17–21.

FREUD, A. (1954). Problems of technique in adult analysis. *The Writings of Anna Freud.* 4:377–406.

—— (1962). Assessment of childhood disturbances. *Psychoanal. Study Child.*, 17:149–158.

—— (1963). The concept of developmental lines. *Psychoanal. Study Child.*, 18:245–265.

—— (1967). About losing and being lost. In: *The Writings of Anna Freud.* 4:302–316.

—— (1970). The symptomatology of childhood: A preliminary classification. In: *The Writings of Anna Freud.* 7:157–188.

FREUD, A., NAGERA, H., & FREUD, W. E. (1965). Metapsychological assessment of the adult personality: The adult profile. *Psychoanal. Study Child.*, 20:9–41.

FREUD, S. (1895). *Project for a scientific psychology.* S.E. I.

—— (1900). *The interpretation of dreams.* S.E. IV and V.

—— (1905). *Jokes and their relation to the unconscious.* S.E. VIII.

—— (1911a). Formulations on the two principles of mental functioning. S.E. XII.

—— (1911b). Psycho-analytic notes on an autobiographical account of a case of paranoia (dementia paranoides). S.E. XII.

—— (1914). On narcissism: An introduction. *S.E.* XIV.

—— (1915a). Instincts and their vicissitudes. *S.E.* XIV.

—— (1915b). Repression. *S.E.* XIV.

—— (1915c). The unconscious. *S.E.* XIV.

—— (1917a). A metapsychological supplement to the theory of dreams. *S.E.* XIV.

—— (1917b). Mourning and melancholia. *S.E.* XIV.

—— (1920). Beyond the pleasure principle. *S.E.* XVIII.

—— (1923). The ego and the id. *S.E.* XIX.

—— (1924a). Neurosis and psychosis. *S.E.* XIX.

——— (1924b). The economic problem of masochism. *S.E.* XIX.

——— (1924c). The loss of reality in neurosis and psychosis. *S.E.* XIX.

——— (1925a). A note upon the "Mystic Writing-Pad." *S.E.* XIX.

——— (1925b). Negation. *S.E.* XIX.

——— (1926). Inhibition, symptoms and anxiety. *S.E.* XX.

——— (1940). An Outline of Psycho-Analysis. *S.E.* XXIII.

——— (1954). *The Origins of Psycho-Analysis: Letters to Wilhelm Fliess, Drafts and Notes.* Ed. Bonaparte, M., Freud, A., & Kris, E. London: Imago.

GLOVER, E. (1947). *Basic Mental Concepts.* London: Imago.

——— (1961). Some recent trends in psychoanalytic theory. *Psychoanal. Quart.*, 30:86–107.

HEIMANN, P. (1950). On counter-transference. *Int. J. Psycho-Anal.*, 31:81–84.

JACOBSON, E. (1965). *The Self and the Object World.* London: Hogarth.

JOSEPH, B. (1985). Transference: The total situation. *Int. J. Psycho-Anal.*, 66:447–454.

KLEIN, M. (1943). Memorandum to the Training Committee of the British Psycho-Analytic Society, 25 October. In: King, P., & Steiner, R. (Eds.): *The Freud-Klein Controversies, 1941–45.* London/New York: Routledge, 1991.

——— (1946). Notes on some schizoid mechanisms. In: *The Writings of Melanie Klein,* 3.

LAUFER, M. (1965). Assessment of adolescent disturbances: The application of Anna Freud's diagnostic profile. *Psychoanal. Study Child.*, 20:99–123.

MASSON, J. M. (1985). *The Complete Letters of Sigmund Freud to Wilhelm Fliess: 1887–1904.* Cambridge, Mass: Belknap/Harvard Univ. Press.

NOY, P. (1977). Metapsychology as a multimodel system. *Int. Rev. Psycho-Anal.*, 4:1–12.

PAO, P. N. (1979). *Schizophrenic Disorders.* New York: Int. Univ. Press.

RADFORD, P., WISEBERG, S., & YORKE, C. (1972). A study of main line heroin addiction: A preliminary report. *Psychoanal. Study Child.*, 27:156–180.

RAPAPORT, D. (1960). *The Structure of Psychoanalytic Theory: A Systematizing Attempt.* New York: Int. Univ. Press.

ROSENFELD, H. (1954). Regarding the psycho-analytic approach to acute and chronic schizophrenia. *Int. J. Psycho-Anal.* 35:135–140.

THOMAS, R., IN COLLABORATION WITH EDGCUMBE, R., KENNEDY, H., KAWENOKA, M., & WEITZNER, L. (1966). Comments on some aspects of self and object representation in a group of psychotic children: An application of Anna Freud's developmental profile. *Psychoanal. Study Child.* 26:527–580.

WINNICOTT, D. W. (1953). Transitional objects and transitional phenomena: A study of the first not-me possession. *Int. J. Psycho-Anal.* 34:89–97.

YORKE, C. (1965a). Some metapsychological aspects of interpretation. *Brit. J. Med. Psychol.* 38:27–42.

——— (1965b). Review: *Essays on Ego Psychology: Selected Problems in Psychoanalytic Theory.* By Heinz Hartmann. [1964]. *Brit. J. Med. Psychol.* 38:185–186.

——— (1980). The contributions of the diagnostic profile and developmental lines to child psychiatry. *Psychiatric Clinics of North America.* 3:593–603.

—— (1983). Clinical notes on developmental pathology. *Psychoanal. Study Child.* 38:389–402.

—— (1994). Freud or Klein: Conflict or compromise. *Int. J. Psycho-Anal.* 75:375–385.

—— (1995). Freudian psychology: Can it survive? *Psychoanal. Study Child.* 50:3–31.

—— (1996). Childhood and the Unconscious. *American Imago.* (In press.)

DEVELOPMENT

Anna Freud: Observation and Development

ALICE B. COLONNA, M.A.

Anna Freud taught the importance of observation, suggesting that students jot down their observations in a systematic manner. She urged observers to amplify their notes, which were later discussed in meetings. Observations made in the nursery school, for example, were discussed afterwards and classified in a file under appropriate headings somewhat similar to the technique used at the Anna Freud Centre. In this paper I describe my observations of a subject as an infant and a toddler with special reference to the way she looked intensely at the world around her. To some degree, the way she herself looked—i.e., her appearance—was also interesting. The relationship between the child's looking in infancy and the oedipal child's sexual curiosity, exhibitionism, and scoptophilia is suggested by these observations.

INTRODUCTION

IT HAS BEEN SAID THAT ANNA FREUD DID NOT GIVE SUFFICIENT ATTENTION to development that took place in infancy. Anna Freud's interest in infants first was demonstrated in the daycare center in Vienna that she, Dorothy Burlingham, and Josephine Stross began, with support from Edith B. Jackson. This served the most deprived families with infants from one year of age. Anna Freud further observed infants and toddlers who were evacuated from London during World War II. Child care workers made daily observations of the children, recording brief

---

Lecturer at the Yale Child Study Center; child analysis faculty at the Western New England Institute for Psychoanalysis; graduate, Anna Freud Centre.

The Psychoanalytic Study of the Child 51, ed. Albert J. Solnit, Peter B. Neubauer, Samuel Abrams, and A. Scott Dowling (Yale University Press, copyright © 1996 by Albert J. Solnit, Peter B. Neubauer, Samuel Abrams, and A. Scott Dowling).

notes from memory at the end of the day for discussion in evening meetings. Important findings about early development resulted.

Anna Freud's nurseries became an important part in the immense program of evacuating children from London during the war. At the same time she relied on and taught observational skills to the workers responsible for childcare. After the war Anna Freud undertook an important project described in a paper she wrote with Sophie Dann (1951). This paper demonstrated how observational data served as the basis for new insights that in turn served as a model of the way psychoanalytic theory could be used for clarification of children's often bewildering and difficult behavior. This group of children presented many problems for their caregivers. Anna Freud was able to classify many of these behaviors, link them to the deprivations the children had experienced, and make valuable inferences about normal infant and toddler development. It was characteristic of Anna Freud's style that new knowledge arose from what she called the "accidents of fate" rather than from a previous plan.

Her close rapport with those who worked directly with children and her respect for and empathy with the mothers of young children were important aspects of her skill. Her awareness of the immense developments that took place in the first three years of life is evident in Anna Freud's subsequent elucidation of the developmental lines and in the various profiles she and her colleagues produced (e.g., Ernst Freud's infant profile [1967], Moses Laufer's adolescent profile [1965], the adult profile described by Anna Freud, H. Nagera, and E. Freud [1965], and Burlingham's important study of fathers and infants [1972]).

According to observations by Anna Freud and others, infants react positively to their caregivers when their discomfort is alleviated. Thus, positive relationships develop through bodily care. Anna Freud did not ascribe fantasies to the infant until there was sufficient verbalization for confirmation. She appreciated Klein's interest in infant development and acknowledged it in her description of the first stages of the developmental lines. Her work predated other important infancy studies that elaborate on the infant's sense of self, awareness of the other person, and mode of differentiating among caregiving figures. (Emde and Sorce, 1983).

Anna Freud observed that the infant interacts with the two parents in different ways and that this interplay is enjoyed by both caregiver and infant. The developmental lines convey that the normal infant is actively engaged in eliciting what he needs from a caregiver who can read these signals and respond to them. As the child becomes progressively more aware of his own boundaries and those of the caregiver, he learns that his needs will be responded to. In this way trust gradually develops.

In her dual interest in observation and meeting communal needs, Anna Freud began a mother-toddler group that also led to insights into normal development and opportunities for trainees to learn about them. The developmental lines she formulated were based in part on her interest in the characteristics and achievements the teacher looked for in the child before his or her entry into nursery school at about three years of age. Anna Freud helped colleagues and students to understand how the ways in which the child had moved through earlier phases contributed to subsequent oedipal and post-oedipal character formation. This clarified the reasons that many children showed problems in adjustment to nursery school and later. For example, in the prototypical line from dependency to self-reliance, the toddler moves from the first stage "of biological unity between the mother-infant couple, to the second one of the need-fulfilling relationship based on the urgency of the child's bodily needs and drive derivatives, which is intermittent and fluctuating, reaching out when in need and withdrawn with satisfaction of need, to the third stage of object constancy, which enables the child to maintain a positive inner image irrespective of dissatisfaction and frustration." The fourth move is to "the ambivalent relationship of the anal-sadistic stage characterized by the ego attitudes of clinging, torturing, dominating, and controlling" (pp. 64–65). Remnants of these phases of life could be observed in preoedipal and preverbal infants and toddlers.

The Hampstead Clinic nursery school, which Miss Freud opened in 1957, served the needs of a group of normal children and provided an opportunity for trainees in child psychoanalysis to examine the play and verbalizations of the children. Again, their observations were recorded and classified according to a psychoanalytic framework. For some years the nursery school was viewed as an additional experience for mostly middle-class children who came for three or four hours a day five days a week. Later it became an all-day program for children mostly of immigrant families struggling to adapt to a new country and language, experiencing difficulty in finding jobs and opportunities.

A nursery school for blind children was started in 1958 by Dorothy Burlingham. In this setting, as the school's first teacher, I noticed that blindness itself imposed many restrictions on the child's capacity to explore and enjoy new experiences. I therefore suggested that each child have an hour a day alone with an adult who could thereby observe, support, and assist him or her so that the group experience would be more pleasurable and more positive. This became a part of the program. Attempts were made to provide as many nonvisual experiences for the children as possible through the use of tactile, auditory, and sensory materials. Important findings concerning the early role of object relationships were elucidated (Burlingham, 1972; Colonna, 1968; Nagera, 1965; Sandler, 1963; Wills, 1965). Later I worked closely for some years with a family whose infant daughter had become blind shortly after birth. The mother, after dealing with her depressive reaction to the infant's blindness, gradually, with my help, found ways to share in her child's way of interacting with and learning about her world through nonvisual means.

When the opportunity presented itself to observe a normal infant who demonstrated unusual visual alertness, I became involved in extended observation (Provence and Naylor 1983) at the Yale Child Study Center. The data I recorded followed Anna Freud's suggested method of noting what seemed to me to be intriguing or of particular interest. Thus these observations, which use my subjective impressions as an initial guide, are not as systematic as those of an academic psychologist. They consist primarily of notes concerned with the way this infant looked out at her environment as well as the way she looked to the environment—that is, her own appearance. In many interesting ways her appearance seemed linked to her sense of her gender identity. This feature has often been noted in preoedipal girls, who combine some aspects of oral greed with what they see and wish to take into themselves. Later, in the phallic-oedipal phase, this may be understood as envy of the boy or of the mother, particularly when the mother is pregnant (Balsam, 1986).

OBSERVATION

Paulette was a pretty and unusually expressive infant who was in daycare from the age of eleven weeks. From very early on she had the capacity to show differentiation in the expression of positive and negative affect. Her demands seemed more compelling and intense than those of other children of the same age. Observers thought that she seemed to resent the presence of other children as well as the attention they received, even when her needs had been attended to. In her second year of life Paulette was not only unpredictably aggressive toward other children but also frightened of them (probably an early development of projection and externalization of her own hostility). She seemed to demand constant admiration and attention and showed great capacity to elicit it, but this was generally regarded as a negative quality by the adults. From her earliest entry to the nursery she made an exclusive contact with her special caretaker, who was able to supply some of the needs her mother had not responded to.

When interviewed before her baby's birth, Paulette's mother, who was very young, showed signs of conflict about her new role. She and her husband were determined to improve their educational and financial circumstances and had not planned for the pregnancy. The mother worked full time in addition to studying and was glad to join the daycare project, although at first she was concerned about the potential effects of multiple caregivers. She herself had had a difficult childhood with two alcoholic parents and had been in foster care. She was particularly attached to her grandmother. This mother experienced talks with her social workers in the daycare intervention program as a threat and was guarded and suspicious. She was never able to talk about problem areas in her or her family's life.

Despite concern for their financial situation and the father's stated preference for a boy, after the baby's uneventful birth both parents appeared to be thrilled with her. They seemed ecstatic about her attractive appearance and delighted in dressing her up and showing her off. This conveyed to observers how much her gender contributed to the parents' pleasure in her (a girl can be dressed in frilly clothes and exhibited—sometimes at the expense of the child's comfort). It also conveyed the high value the parents placed on appearance, which may have had something to do with Paulette's own intense interest in the visual mode, in the sense that she too came to overvalue the way things looked. This interest suggested a superficial or shallow quality.

On an early home visit, the observer felt that the mother experienced discomfort in holding the infant for breastfeeding and that the baby seemed to adapt more comfortably than the mother. (The hospital nurse said she had never seen an infant who took to the breast so well.) The mother was initially reluctant to breastfeed, but her husband insisted she do so. She soon gave up the attempt. There were many other early signs of the mother's ambivalence in responding to her infant's needs. For instance, she was afraid of "spoiling" the child by picking her up; she criticized the baby in the pediatric examination (at age one month) for wetting and soiling, and she made references to aggressiveness when the baby swung a rattle and hit the pediatrician. By the time the mother returned to work, when Paulette was ten weeks old, she had a marked feeding disturbance, which disappeared rapidly under more skillful handling in the daycare situation.

Paulette's intense watchfulness and enjoyment of gazing at people and moving objects was remarked on in daycare. Jacobson's references to the "first image of the gratifying mother" (1961, pp. 35, 61) and memory traces related to the orally gratified or deprived self, as well as fantasies of reunion with the mother, may be relevant in this context. In daycare, after crying with hunger, Paulette stopped when she saw her caretaker open the cupboard door. This indicated the normal ability to wait, based on the expectation of satisfaction and relief of tension from hunger. Anna Freud (1953[1952]), in describing the very early mental process of the young infant, maintained:

> that the inner world of the infant . . . consists essentially of the two contrasting feelings of the pleasure-pain series, the sequence being that pain arises under the impact of body need, pleasure when the need is satisfied. . . . Repeated experience of pleasure teaches what it is that brings pleasure. For instance, after the hungry child has been fed several times, the impact of these experiences will create something in him which did not exist before, namely, the image of the satisfying food. From then onward, whenever hunger arises, the image of the desired food will be evoked simultaneously. . . . Imagery of this nature is regarded as the first step in mental functioning.

This may lead to the ability to distinguish between this inner image and "the perception of a person in the outside world" (p. 575).

In the group situation Paulette showed how these aspects of mental functioning were taking place. At the same time, while being fed she always watched intently as other adults moved about the room. Many observations showed how the wish to look seemed to motivate the child to motor activity and early achievements such as raising her head, turning her head to look, keeping her head erect, looking at pictures painted on her crib, and trying to reach them by turning her torso from side to side. Perhaps the active stance promoted a certain disposition toward involvement and participation in the outside world.

Three weeks after starting daycare Paulette (at thirteen weeks) was noted as turning away from two adults, avoiding visual contact, and seeming to be "angry." No amount of talking or cajoling would make her look at the adult who was feeding her. Avoidance of looking at strangers was also noted at an unusually early age. Watchfulness of other children with a puzzled expression was noted when another child received an injection. She seemed to be dissatisfied with and disconnected from others and uninvolved with what other infants were experiencing. One might speculate that even at this early age she was developing this perceptual mode in an attempt to read and adapt to her mother's confused messages. The mother appeared awkward and clumsy, sometimes very slow, often somewhat depressed, and this may have been conveyed in the way she held the child. (In good daycare, teachers will always ask the mother at the initial period of group care how she prefers to hold the child so that the child is not subjected to more changes than are necessary. If a mother holds the baby in a manner uncomfortable or inappropriate for the child the attempt will be made to gradually help the mother "tune in" to her infant more accurately. At the same time the caregiver will introduce changes gradually as there are usually many correct ways that are comfortable for both.)

Paulette was noted as being able to entertain herself for longer periods than most children of her age. This may suggest a capacity to cope with frustration and at the same time lack of a sense that others will respond to her needs. Might this be related to her own apparent lack of empathy for other children? Another example shows how watching led her to reach out, touch, and bring objects to her mouth at about sixteen weeks:

> Paulette was held in a sitting position on the counter. She looked in the mirror and smiled at her reflection. She observed the picture of the red fish on the counter, leaned forward, reached for the picture of the fish, touched it but couldn't grasp it. Mrs. C. picked the picture up and held it close to Paulette's hand. Paulette's arms activated in jerky movements. She opened her mouth and protruded her tongue as though trying to lift the fish, then put both fists into her mouth. As she continued to observe the fish she became excited, moved in jerky movements, and vocalized a little by making squeaky, squealing sounds. She got the hiccups, tried again to grasp the fish; but when she couldn't, she put both fists into her mouth again. She continued to observe the fish and worked to grasp it. She made a distressed little squeal and started to fuss. Her father picked her up and carried her into the adjoining room, trying to comfort her. Her caregiver picked up the fish from the counter, rattled it, and called, "Hey, Paulette." Paulette responded by turning her head to observe her caregiver and the rattling fish and smiled a big smile.
>
> The staff noted that her active visual interest seemed to be useful to her in diverting her from an "inner discomfort." It "seemed to organize her." At seventeen weeks, during a pediatric examination, she seemed to "search the room as if exploring an unfamiliar place, using looking away to shut out unwanted stimuli such as a stranger." Her mother was at this time holding her either facing her "as if at a distance" or increasingly in an upright position with her arms around the baby's stomach

facing away from her. Escalona (1968) has commented on the meaning of this seemingly unrelated positioning between the mother and the child. At the same time it does give the child immediate visual contact and interest in the outside world.

This period coincided with the mother's more active social life, which allowed her little time for interaction with the baby. It was also noted that the mother was eager to present herself as a good mother and was often critical of the child for her appearance, etc. Later the mother shared her feeling that people on the bus would always judge a mother as neglectful, as she evidently did, if her child was not perfectly dressed for going out. The mother would come for the child at the end of the day and prepare her for the bus ride home by vigorous washing, brushing, and dressing, reproachful of staff while ignoring the baby's fatigue, insistent on her tidy appearance, despite the neglected state in which she brought Paulette in the mornings. (She was usually rushed at that time and not very worried about the child's appearance then.)

That the child's sense of time is very different from the adult's often has been pointed out (Goldstein, Freud, and Solnit, 1973, pp. 32–35). It is often not taken into account that the working day, suited for adult needs, is long indeed for the child. At home the toddler becomes a part of the mother's or other caregiver's workday, which includes other tasks and provides for variation in degree of stimulation, times alone, quiet, etc., within the context of the life of the mother. In daycare such variations need to be planned for. This mother, tired from her workday, appeared unaware of the child's fatigue. Her busy attitude and overvaluation of appearance at the price of the child's comfort may have conveyed to the infant a sense of uncertainty about her world and stimulated a certain lack of trust. Observers began to comment that Paulette looked solemn, puzzled, and serious. She sometimes remained silent and looked intently at her mother when she came for her. She showed more interest in moving objects such as trees, leaves, the ceiling, etc., than in interaction with people. The feeling of anger was ascribed to her—for instance, when she watched another child being fed or bathed. She was described as "imperious." At six months she looked "sober and wary, rather inactive, and unwilling to change her position to obtain a toy" and "easily distractible." An observer noted her intensive watchfulness of adults:

> Some people she tolerates but does not warm up to. Other people Paulette ignores. She has a way of looking past, through, or around people as though they are not there. This has to be deliberate. She is too keenly aware of her environment not to notice someone who is trying to get a

response from her. Paulette now pays rapt attention to conversation between two adults as though she understands what they are saying. One day while listening to Mrs. B. talk to Mrs. M. she intently looked at the face of first one and then the other. As each spoke her head turned back and forth from one to the other.

At her eighth monthly physical examination she shrieked after being given the intradermal tuberculin injection but seemed able to restore herself to a state of equilibrium by being placed to face the mirror. It seemed to the observer that this visual reflection helped to organize her sense of her body following the sudden localized pain. Her visual activity was frequently commented on as her development proceeded. At thirty-five weeks, two days, she was noted watching absorbedly and trying to pick up a tiny ant on the sidewalk or to catch a small piece of leaf. Often she enjoyed watching the children outdoors or in the playroom. At thirty-six weeks she warily and suspiciously studied a new teacher and after a lengthy stare responded in a friendlier fashion. Frequently she looked very angry when her exclusive time with an adult was interrupted by the entrance of another adult. An interesting observation was made at thirty-six weeks, one day:

Sitting on the floor with K., who was playing with an hourglass, she observed the hourglass intently, then reached over and took it away from K., who did not protest. The observer handed K. another hourglass. P. again observed K.'s hourglass, dropped the one she was holding, and reached out and took the second hourglass from K. This she did with four hourglasses. Even though there was one in her hand and two on the floor in front of her she wanted the one K. had.

These examples highlight the very early emergence of the desire to reach out and obtain everything she saw. No examples of the usual delight and enjoyment of give and take were noted. Manifestations of displeasure, anger, and distress were markedly more numerous for Paulette than those noted with other children of the same age. Her precocity in many directions was also striking as was its relationship to the active striving to obtain objects. It is difficult to assess the meaning of this because the desire to reach out actively is often more important at this age than the object being reached for. However, the frequency of observations of this sort suggest that for some reason this behavior was notable. There were subsequent observations highlighting Paulette's intense interest in people at this time. At forty-six weeks she recognized an adult she had not seen for two months. She then studied this person, went to her, smiled, and talked to her. On one occasion her sober look

changed on her arrival at the familiar playroom, when she suddenly
appeared to remember the visual scene.

From the age of about eight months there were observations noting
her careful scrutiny of faces, and sometimes these seemed directly
related to her mother's prohibitions about touching the television set,
going upstairs by herself, etc., and Paulette's attempt to read from the
adults' expression whether her behavior would be acceptable. It was
noted that the mother was immediately engaged when Paulette did
something she disapproved of but that generally the mother appeared
somewhat absent-minded or withdrawn. During a feeding, for instance, the mother was very slow, resting the spoon on the plate and
staring out the window. Paulette had to stare intensely and make a little
noise to attract her attention.

One may speculate about the meaning for a child when the most
important person in her life so often interprets her behavior negatively. At twelve months Paulette did not appear to care whether she
pleased the adult in the developmental test, was distractible, and
showed off to her father instead of carefully looking at the test item
(pegboard) presented to her. Increasingly she used her looking as a
part of her teasing relationship to adults. A "teasing" situation between
child and parent may be a play enjoyable to the adult but confusing for
the child, who usually feels left out or tricked. However, Paulette consistently enjoyed looking at books, and this seemed to help her to cope
when she arrived in the morning. The child's learning to read and
otherwise perform like a schoolgirl was already much supported by her
mother, who was employed as a teacher at this time. She was never able
to understand how inappropriate her expectations were.

At about eighteen months the mother seemed to enjoy her child
more. At nineteen months, Paulette often watched the interaction between other children and adults, particularly when a child was mis-
behaving; she seemed ready to interfere and take on the adult role.
Once, seeing that breakfast was in preparation, she interrupted another child at his play and said sternly to him, "come on, baby." He
obediently complied. Perhaps this represents a somewhat moralizing
attitude rather than an empathic or playful one. Was this the way she
experienced her mother's care of her? Observers were struck by an
occasion at around fifteen months when she was angry and distressed,
realizing that the meat (which she always ate, ignoring vegetables) had
been removed from her plate in the hope that she would eat the vegetables first. Her reaction was said to be of shock and surprise in addition to disappointment, as though something was not right. The sense

of something missing in herself or in the outside world seemed characteristic. Was this an early emergence of envy of the boy?

Paulette's early comparison of self with others has a special application to the daycare situation, when most of the child's waking life is spent in the presence of her peers. It certainly demonstrates how different the toilet-training experience is when done in the presence of peers rather than within the mother-child dyad alone.

The intense searching, increasing watchfulness, and lack of absorption in her own activity appeared to have a number of possible meanings for Paulette. On one level they seemed to reflect an attempt to cope with changes (in persons and places, as from home to daycare, etc.) by visual means. On another level, there were indications that they related to her acute powers of observation and early awareness of sexual differences. She watched boys often, and if one went into the bathroom for a drink of water she followed and imitated him. At twenty-four months Paulette would often rush to grab the pencil away from the observer and would walk around for long periods holding a piece of chalk or a crayon. It seems reasonable to consider the relation of her intense use of the visual mode to her overvaluation of her appearance.

At the time when Paulette's restlessness and interference in other children's activities were intense, interviews with the mother confirmed that the parents often walked about in the nude and that Paulette often touched or pinched her mother's buttocks, pulled at her pubic hair, etc. The early exposure to parental nudity and the teasing that went on at home resulted in a precocious excitability of a phallic quality. Perhaps she saw her mother's dissatisfaction as related to her gender. At twenty-six months she took a boy into the bathroom, helped him pull down his pants, told him to go "pee pee," helped him pull up his pants, clapped and cheered that he had performed successfully, and returned to the playroom. She tried to urinate standing, like a boy. Her overdevelopment of the visual mode and increasingly restless activity, such as grabbing, snatching, and teasing other children in the group, became more characteristic as Paulette approached her second birthday.

The general overemphasis on the attention-seeking side of her affective development is characteristic of all the observations of Paulette, in striking contrast to those of most of the other children in the group. Her smiles, flirtatiousness, and exhibitionistic qualities gained her attention and sometimes admiration, but for the most part they appeared to observers as indications of a shallow way of relating. From the beginning her mother's pleasure seemed in anticipation of a later time. For instance, when Paulette was four weeks old her mother looked forward to the time when she would be toilet-trained. Later she tried to teach the child to read long before this would be appropriate. She took some pleasure in their interaction after the first year, when Paulette responded to her mother's playfulness, though at times this seemed to be on the mother's terms—for her pleasure rather than the child's need. She had never appeared to derive much enjoyment from nurturing or protecting her daughter. And Paulette did not seem to develop a sense of real trust. Paulette's increasing exhibitionism and negativism appeared to entertain and amuse her parents. Her role as a performer seemed important to their active social life at this time.

The behavior of a child in this preverbal period demonstrates to the observer and caregiver how the child is progressing in the capacity to socialize and empathize with other children. The observers felt that Paulette was unable to fully enjoy the other children's pleasures because she was so watchful and concerned that they might receive something she wished for. The experience of sharing did not seem one she enjoyed. Paulette did not at this time act in an overtly aggressive manner toward other children and was able to relate closely to her caregiver, although she demanded her full attention. It is interesting to speculate about how much this had to do with Paulette's endowment and how much with her complicated relationship with a mother who also was very concerned about the acquisition of possessions.

The link to her mother's ambitions and concentration on improving the family's material status has to play a part that the child was aware of. Anna Freud, in discussing the then-popular notion of the rejecting mother, cited a remark by Waelder on the impact of the mother's preferences on the development of the child:

> Waelder offers the helpful formulation "that the mother, as the earliest and foremost representative of the environment, has a selective influence upon the constitutional endowment by stimulating and encouraging some things and discouraging others." This is what I had in mind when I expressed the conviction that the mother is not responsible for the child's neurosis, even if she causes "chaotic" development in some instances. By rejecting and seducing she can influence, distort and determine development but she cannot produce either neurosis or psychosis (1954, p. 348).

Many children gain a great deal at three to four years of age from the group experience, at a point in development when there is a special need for socialization with peers and with an adult outside the family. Paulette might have blossomed had this been possible at this time.

Unfortunately, the daycare project had to close owing to lack of funds, and it was not possible to continue observations of Paulette into the next phase of her development. Christina, a child discussed in meetings at the Yale Child Study Center (Senn, 1953), showed some features similar to those of Paulette, particularly in the visual sensitivity in her earliest years, and was able to enjoy the experiences available in the nursery school. Her pleasure in looking was expressed in an absorption in painting. This demonstrates the important developmental move to the fifth stage described by Anna Freud in the developmental lines, at age three to four. This is "the completely object-centered phallic-oedipal phase, characterized by possessiveness of the parent of the opposite sex, jealousy and rivalry with the parent of the same sex, protectiveness, generosity, curiosity, bids for admiration and exhibitionistic attitudes; with girls a phallic-oedipal (masculine) relationship to the mother precedes the oedipal relationship to the father" (1966, p. 65).

The observer of a child of this age will come to realize how much has gone before in the child's experience. One is always impressed with the way many children make use of their new opportunities and with the variations in style of skilled and talented teachers. At the same time it is worrying to note how many programs lack skilled teachers and how many children, often because of past deprivations in their lives, need special preparation to be ready for this experience. Many cannot become deeply engaged. This attitude was described by Anna Freud (1953[1948], pp. 515–16) when she referred to the difficult wartime conditions when children were strictly disciplined. Today we still note many situations in which discipline is less rigid but the children seem relatively lifeless and compliant. Often these children are from backgrounds of deprivation, and the attitudes of parents and teachers show this low-keyed depressive affect and a sense of hopelessness.

In good nursery school programs, when the child is ready for the group experience, the trained psychoanalytic observer gains many glimpses into his or her inner life through the child's play, verbalizations, and drawings. At the same time, as Anna Freud pointed out (1974, pp. 63–65), ease of access does not make problems easier or quicker to resolve even though the child at the age has an openness that can be useful to the observer in terms of learning and understanding to make less intrusive interventions. The normal child of this age demonstrates passionate loves, hates, and rivalries. At the same time she will be able to enjoy group life to the fullest; play and other sublimated activities provide many experiences of satisfaction and a gradual sense of mastery and enjoyment, as was noted with Christina. The deep engagement of three- or four-year-olds in the group circumstances is evident.

In their play children may be enacting totally different fantasies while being very much engaged with each other. The degree of the child's involvement has much to do with his subsequent capacity to enter into more formal school life. The oedipal phase brings the capacity to tolerate ambiguity and inner contradiction in a new triadic way. Rivalry with and jealousy of the needed parent becomes a difficult dilemma that the child needs to resolve.

Without the ability to observe Paulette's play and verbalizations during the three- to six-year-old period, predictions about her future development were necessarily limited, particularly because the mother was so uncommunicative. Paulette was seen a few years later at eight years of age. One would look for data relating to her social relationships and her capacity for learning at this time. In the latency period, as Anna Freud noted (1965) in her developmental lines, there is the "postoedipal lessening of drive urgency and the transfer of libido from the parental figures to contemporaries, community groups, teachers, leaders, impersonal ideals, and aim-inhibited, sublimated interests, with fantasy manifestations giving evidence of disillusionment with and denigration of the parents ('family romance,' twin fantasies, etc.)."

At the follow-up interview by her pediatrician when Paulette was eight years old, her mother was pregnant and seemed tired. She said she was "still easily manipulated" by Paulette. Interestingly, this had not been raised as a significant problem during the time the child was in the daycare project. Both parents had continued their education, and the mother had improved her work status. The mother presented a totally positive picture of her child's development. Previously she had avoided problem areas. Paulette herself had begun pubertal development very early and already had a little pubic hair and beginning breast development. She was also a little overweight and had dental problems that had resulted in the extraction of three lower teeth and a bridge. She seemed to enjoy the experience of being tested and was cooperative. At eight years, five months, she tested at the equivalent of six years, seven months. The psychologist commented that what was "most salient about Paulette is her lack of persistence in the face of frustration and the degree to which this interferes with her performance. . . . One senses that she at times is not thinking carefully and trying but is giving the examiner 'any old answer' without putting much effort into it . . . there was a lack in the degree of social judgment appropriate for her age. . . . She had seemed tired and hungry in the test, yawning frequently. . . . Her polite and friendly approach, at times inappropriate, is also noteworthy."

She was indiscriminate in her social interactions, partly demonstrated by her effusive greeting of all the secretaries in the unit. Also, at the end of the exam she kissed the examiner as well as the pediatrician as they walked down the hall. On this occasion there was no indication of a wish for guidance or treatment on the part of the child or the mother, who in fact resisted sharing information about problems with Paulette. One might speculate that Paulette, in her effusively affectionate greetings, reflected her mother's need to please and a lack of interest in performing a task (as had been demonstrated at twelve months) or learning a new skill and achievement. The evident hope of getting something for herself by pleasing may reflect the earlier emphasis on superficial ways of coping and relating. The behavior suggested an attempt to show herself as positively inclined toward all adults. Because she did not come into psychoanalytic treatment, we had no access at this time to her inner life. However, there was a certain lack of sublimation potential and frustration tolerance and a somewhat passive attitude with respect to school performance.

In the next phase, that of the "preadolescent prelude to the 'adolescent revolt,' there is frequently . . . a return to early attitudes and behavior, especially of the part-object, need-fulfilling, and ambivalent type." Paulette's family was followed up again when Paulette was twelve years of age, by an interview with the mother. At this time the parents had given up on further education for themselves. The mother felt that she no longer had the energy or motivation to continue study. She had a full-time job and worked a second job as well three nights a week and some weekends. She reported disagreements with Paulette over control and social difficulties.

SUMMARY

In the case described, Paulette's visual sensitivity was first noted as a positive factor that furthered her active stance, helped her to reach out, and served to stabilize her and strengthen her sense of equilibrium. That is, as the hand follows the eye and a child reaches for objects, the movement in itself as it is repeated and the exercise of the needed muscles has a positive effect on physical and mental development. Looking at herself in the mirror, as Paulette enjoyed doing, was helpful for bodily balance and confidence. It was later noted that the visual activity appeared to be related to envy of other children. As Paulette became mobile and acquired some verbal skills, she was described as looking suspicious or angry. At the same time she seemed disinterested in engaging adults other than her caregiver, toward whom she remained possessive. She was distractible and not interested in task completion. The parents confirmed that they included her in much of their own social and sexual lives, walking about in the nude and permitting her to touch their bodies. Follow-up interviews indicated that in school her learning capacities were restricted and that she had difficulties in concentrating and learning, indications of unfulfilled potential and some vulnerabilities. Recent hearsay reports emphasize, however, that she is presently "doing well and will soon be married."

Unfortunately it was not possible to treat Paulette through psychoanalysis. This might have helped to verify or not some of the earlier inferences made with respect to Paulette's behavior. This would have provided the model that particularly interested Anna Freud. That is, observational data can point the way to psychoanalytic issues and questions about development. Usually psychoanalytic data or its equivalent regarding the inner life of the child is necessary to corroborate, revise, or elaborate the issues and questions raised by the psychoanalytic theory of development.

BIBLIOGRAPHY

ARIES, PHILIPPE. (1962). *Centuries of Childhood*. New York: Vintage Books.

BALSAM, R. (1996). The body of the pregnant mother. Unpublished.

BETTELHEIM, BRUNO. (1950). *Love Is Not Enough*. Glencoe, Ill.: Free Press.

BOLLAND, J. & SANDLER, J. ET AL. (1965). The Hampstead psychoanalytic index. *Psychoanal. Study Child.* Monograph no. 1. New York: Int. Univ. Press.

BURLINGHAM, D. (1961). Some notes on the development of the blind. *Psychoanal. Study Child.* Vol. 16, p. 121–145.

BURLINGHAM, D. (1973). The preoedipal infant-father relationship. *Psychoanal. Study Child.* Vol. 28. pp. 23–49.

COLONNA, A. (1968). A blind child goes to the hospital. *Psychoanal. Study Child.* Vol. 23. pp. 391–423.

EISSLER, R. S. ET AL. EDS. (1977). *Psychoanalytic Assessment: The Diagnostic Profile: An Anthology of the Psychoanalytic Study of the Child*. New Haven: Yale Univ. Press.

EMDE, D. & SORCE, J. E. (1983). The rewards of infancy: Emotional availability and maternal referencing. In J. D. Call, E. Galenson, & R. Tyson. (Eds.). *Frontiers of Infant Psychiatry*. Vol. 2. New York: Basic Books.

ESCALONA, S. K. (1968). *The Roots of Individuality*. Chicago: Aldine Press.

ESCALONA, S. K., & HEIDER, G. (1959). *Prediction and Outcome*. New York: Basic Books.

FRAIBERG, S. (1968). Parallel and divergent patterns in blind and sighted infants. *Psychoanal. Study Child.* Vol. 23:264–300.

FREUD, A. (1968). *The Writings of Anna Freud, Vol. 4: Indications for Child Analysis and Other Papers 1945–1956*. New York: Int. Univ. Press.

———— (1947). Emotional and instinctual development. In A. Freud, 1945–1956. Vol. 4: pp. 535–539.

———— (1953[1948]). Instinctual drives and their bearing on human behavior. In A. Freud, 1945–1956, Vol. 4: pp. 515–522.

———— (1949). Expert knowledge for the average mother. In A. Freud, 1945–1956, Vol. 4: pp. 529–535.

———— (1949). Nursery school education: Its uses and dangers. In A. Freud, 1945–1956, Vol. 4: p. 558.

———— (1951[1950]). Observations on child development. In A. Freud, 1945–1956, Vol. 4: pp. 158, 522.

———— (1951). An experiment in group upbringing. In A. Freud, 1945–1956, Vol. 4: pp. 163–230.

———— (1951). August Aichorn. In A. Freud, 1945–1956, Vol. 4: pp. 629–630.

———— (1952). Answering teachers' questions. In A. Freud, 1945–1956, Vol. 4: p. 567.

———— (1953[1952]). Some remarks on infant observation. In A. Freud, 1945–1956, Vol. 4: p. 575.

———— (1954). Problems of infantile neurosis. In A. Freud, 1945–1956, Vol. 4: p. 349.

———— (1954). Problems of technique in adult analysis. In A. Freud, 1945–1956, Vol. 4: pp. 391, 394.

———— (1955[1954]). The concept of the rejecting mother. In A. Freud, 1945–1956, Vol. 4: p. 602.

———— (1965). The concept of the developmental lines. *Normality and Pathology in Childhood: Assessments of Development.* In *The Writings of Anna Freud*, Vol. 6. New York: Int. Univ. Press.

———— (1974). Diagnosis and assessment of childhood disturbances. *Journal of the Philadelphia Association for Psychoanalysis.* Vol. 1, p. 54–63, No. 1.

FREUD, A., NAGERA, H., & FREUD, E. (1965). Metapsychological assessments of the adult profile. *Psychoanal. Study Child*, Vol. 20, p. 9–41.

FREUD, E. (1967). Assessment of early infancy: Problems and considerations. *Psychoanal. Study Child.* Vol. 22, p. 216–238.

GOLDSTEIN, J., FREUD, A., & SOLNIT, A. (1973). *Beyond the Best Interests of the Child.* New York: Free Press. p. 32–40.

GREVEN, P. J. (1973). *Child-Rearing Concepts, 1628–1861.* Itasca, Ill.: F. E. Peacock.

HUNT, D. (1970). *Parents and Children in History.* New York: Basic Books.

JACOBSON, E. (1964). *The Self and the Object World.* New York: Int. Univ. Press.

LAUFER, M. (1965). Assessment of adolescent disturbances: The application of Anna Freud's diagnostic profile. *Psychoanal. Study Child*, Vol. 20.

MAHLER, M. (1975). *The Psychological Birth of the Human Infant.* New York: Basic Books.

NAGERA, H. & COLONNA, A. (1965). Aspects of the contribution of sight to ego and drive development: A comparison of the development of some blind and sighted children. *Psychoanal. Study Child.* Vol. 20. p. 267–287.

NEUBAUER, P. (1985). Preoedipal objects and object primacy. *Psychoanal. Study Child*, 40. 163–182.

———— (1984). Anna Freud's concept of developmental lines. *Psychoanal. Study Child*. Vol. 39, 15–29.

PROVENCE, S. & NAYLOR, A. (1983). *Working with Disadvantaged Parents and Their Children*. New Haven: Yale Univ. Press.

PROVENCE, S., NAYLOR, A., & PATTERSON, J. (1977). *The Challenge of Daycare*. New Haven: Yale Univ. Press.

ROSEN, R. (1995). Anna Freud in her own words. *Bulletin of the Anna Freud Centre*, V. 18, part 4.

SANDLER, A. M. (1963). Aspects of passivity and ego development in the blind infant. *Psychoanal. Study Child.*, Vol. 18, 343–361.

SEITZ, V., ROSENBAUM, L., & APFEL, N. (1985). Effects of family support intervention: A ten-year follow-up. *Child Development*. (pp. 376–391.)

SENN, M. J. E., ED. (1953). *Problems of Infancy and Childhood*. New York: Josiah Macy, Jr., Foundation, p. 121–140.

STEIN, J., & URDANG, L., ED. (1966). *The Random House Dictionary of the English Language* (unabridged) New York: Random House.

SOLNIT, A. J., COHEN, D., NEUBAUER, P., ED. (1993). Playing, technical implications. In *The Many Meanings of Play*. New Haven: Yale Univ. Press.

WEISBERGER, S. (1987). *When Your Child Needs You*. Bethesda: Adler & Adler.

WILLS, D. M. (1965). Some observations on blind nursery school children's understanding of their world. *Psychoanal. Study Child*, Vol. 20:344–364.

WINNICOTT, D. (1987). *Babies and Their Mothers*. Reading, Mass.: Addison-Wesley Publishing Co.

The Analytic Resolution of a Developmental Imbalance

CARLA ELLIOTT-NEELY, PH.D.

This paper explores the treatment of developmental imbalance in the young child. Examples from the treatment of a prelatency girl are examined for the usefulness of analysis in redressing early conflicts, which Anna Freud termed "a fertile breeding ground for the later infantile neurosis." In this case the child, whose history included significant prematurity, also sustained environmental stresses to which she reacted by constructing a developmentally precocious independence designed to protect her from overwhelming affect states. This defensive stance could not be maintained over time, and its breakdown brought her to treatment.

IN THE LAST DECADES OF HER LIFE, ANNA FREUD WAS OCCUPIED SUBSTANtially with developmental considerations as they affect the methods and goals of child psychoanalysis. To that end she and her colleagues at the Anna Freud Centre sought to examine the course of normal development and the variety of ways in which development can go awry (e.g., A. Freud, 1974, 1976, 1978, 1979a, 1979b). Their long-term goal—he "distal" aim of child analysis, as Moran and Kennedy (1990) put it—was to establish the potential for further development. If one conceptualizes change in structural terms, then the possibility of change is based on the individual's capacity to develop new patterns of organization, new ways of constructing experience. Moran and Kennedy write: "The distal aim of child analysis is reached when previous pathogenic organi-

Graduate of the Hampstead Clinic (currently the Anna Freud Centre), London. In private practice in Washington, D.C. and guest lecturer at the Washington Psychoanalytic Institute.

The Psychoanalytic Study of the Child 51, ed. Albert J. Solnit, Peter B. Neubauer, Samuel Abrams, and A. Scott Dowling (Yale University Press, copyright © 1996 by Albert J. Solnit, Peter B. Neubauer, Samuel Abrams, and A. Scott Dowling).

zations and solutions cease to be applied automatically to deal with conflict" (p. 112).

Analysis of the prelatency child can provide an opportunity to address developmental imbalances before they have been overlaid and obscured by the conflicts of later periods. In describing the prelatency child, Anna Freud (1979b) noted, "Irregularity and interruption of advance in this . . . period are normal, provided the relapses are temporary. If prolonged or even permanent, they cause pathological manifestations which resemble neurotic symptoms but which, according to their structure, are not identical with them. They are pre-neurotic insofar as the conflicts which they are trying to solve are not yet truly internal but due in equal parts to disharmonies within the personality and with the external world. However, they represent a fertile breeding ground for the later infantile neuroses" (pp. 134–35).

Greta, the child whose analysis I am going to describe, developed just such a developmental imbalance in response to significant environmental insult and an endowment that was compromised by premature birth. She attempted to manage conflict through a defensive precocity that resulted in a constriction of further development. Analysis eventually enabled her to experience in a more manageable way the infantile wishes and affects that were formerly unacceptable to her. It also helped her to understand experience in new ways. As a result she was able to move more comfortably forward in her development, utilizing her general precocity in a more adaptive manner.

THE INITIAL CONTACT

I first saw Greta when she was age three years, two months. This contact was not with a view to psychoanalysis; her parents brought her on the referral of her mother's therapist. They were concerned about her chronic demands of mother during the day and night terrors in her sleep. Despite her demanding neediness, Greta also displayed a precocious independence, a determination to do things herself, without the help from others that would have been appropriate to her age and developmental capacities. Her symptoms were relatively new. The family had been stressed by the sudden illness of a younger sister when Greta was almost 29 months. The parents had been very much involved with this child's recovery, and Greta's symptoms appeared to be related to their emotional absence. I saw the family over a two-month period, during which the strained relationship between Greta and her parents was much improved.

At that time I viewed the parents as reasonably healthy, very invested in both their children, and on the verge of recovering their own equilibriums after a frightening year, which had sorely taxed their emotional resources. In our work together Greta seemed to relinquish her defenses against her longings toward her mother relatively easily, and Mrs. C. was quite receptive to Greta's rekindled wishes for warmth and holding. The night terrors disappeared, and Greta's demandingness was much diminished. She was doing well in her nursery school, and her parents felt that they had their daughter back. It was not yet clear whether this family could help Greta sufficiently on their own or might require further intervention, but we agreed that they would contact me should any concerns arise.

RECOMMENDATION FOR ANALYSIS

Greta returned to see me six months later. During the intervening period she had done well until a nanny had been discharged. Now she was verbalizing concerns about abandonment; the upsets at night and the daytime demands of her mother had returned in full force. It was clear that Greta's conflicts would be best addressed by an analytic treatment and that her parents had recovered sufficiently from their own distress to support an analysis.

HISTORY

The Cs met and married a few years after college. They waited several years to have a baby. Once the decision was made, it took a year for Mrs. C. to become pregnant. She felt like "the happiest person in the world." Early in the first trimester she began to bleed heavily and was confined to bed until an ultrasound could be used to determine whether the pregnancy was viable. It was, but the bleeding and severe restrictions on her activity continued, so that the initial joy she had experienced turned to anxiety and dread. At 29 weeks she went into labor that could not be stopped. Her physician at first considered her labor to be false and did not realize the severity of her condition. A long labor ensued, during which no medication could be given because of concern over the baby's welfare. The Cs knew nothing about such prematurity and assumed that the baby would be born dead.

Greta was born in distress, thus neither parent was allowed to hold her. They continued to assume that she would die. Mrs. C. spent the night recounting to herself all the reasons she was to blame. Greta remained critically ill for seven days. Her birth weight of three pounds six ounces declined to two pounds twelve ounces. Mrs. C. finally had to go home without knowing if Greta would join her family and, if so, in what condition.

After a week Greta improved suddenly and, although various surgeries were considered, none became necessary. She gained weight steadily and thrived, although she found it difficult to discontinue her reliance on oxygen. By six weeks she was able to come home with a heart monitor, which she wore at night until nine months, primarily to relieve her parents' anxiety. Once home, Greta developed severe colic, keeping her parents awake for several weeks. When the colic abated, her mother found her delightful.

Greta's regulatory capacities were tenuous. She had rages as an infant that continued throughout her early childhood, but her mother was confident in her own ability to manage them. She noticed that, unlike other babies, Greta could not tolerate delay when hungry. If she missed a nap it took her two difficult days to recover her equilibrium. Despite these high tension states, Greta developed well and was a happy baby.

The Cs decided to begin to try to have a second child when Greta was eighteen months of age, thinking that it would again take at least a year for Mrs. C. to become pregnant. She was pregnant within a month. The second pregnancy began with difficulty. A threatened miscarriage kept her in bed for ten days and then unable to lift Greta throughout the pregnancy. The pregnancy did stabilize in the first trimester and Mrs. C. felt well, happy with Greta, and optimistic about a normal birth. A nanny, Vanessa, joined the family, and Greta became attached to her.

Late in the second pregnancy, Mr. C. changed his place of employment; however, he and his former partners were sued for millions of dollars. Confronting possible bankruptcy placed tremendous stress on both parents. Mr. C. became preoccupied by these troubles and less available to his family. Mrs. C. began premature labor at 34 weeks and was kept in bed on medication for four weeks. Greta must have reacted to the stress and preoccupation of her parents, but they were so overwhelmed that they later remembered little of that time. Vanessa helped Greta to manage.

Anna was born after a short labor. She was a healthy baby, and all seemed well. Greta seemed pleased to have a baby sister and was proud of being "big." Two weeks later Anna had a stroke, which took another week to diagnose. She was in the hospital for several weeks and Mrs. C., who was nursing, spent most of her time there. Greta was left in the care of Vanessa. The nanny was unable to understand the seriousness of Anna's condition and was not comfortable with infants; she and Mrs. C. began to have difficulties with each other, and Vanessa departed abruptly. A new nanny was found, but Greta's attachment to her was tentative. Her response to Vanessa's departure was to throw herself out of her crib and cry inconsolably. Regrettably, Mrs. C. was at that moment with Anna at the hospital.

Anna's condition was unstable for two months. She underwent brain surgery and then began to improve. In the meantime, Mr. C's firm was suffering, and he was not paid for several months. The family was near default on their mortgage and still liable on old debts. After Anna's surgery, the immediate relief was shattered by the physician's announcement that cerebral palsy and retardation were strong possibilities. Both parents were again overwhelmed with grief.

Greta's life was disrupted not only by Anna's illness but also by her rehabilitation. There was a prolonged stay for the family in Philadelphia while Anna learned to crawl at the Brain Injury Institute. This meant that Greta had her third birthday far from home. When the family returned, Mrs. C. took Anna to physical therapy daily, leaving Greta in the care of one of a succession of nannies, whom she ignored. Anna's progress was excellent, however, and the Cs began to feel optimistic about her.

The parents' relationship with Greta had been seriously disrupted. Mrs. C. was thoroughly absorbed in her second daughter's recovery. As she put it, "Until Anna's illness I was in love with my husband and Greta. Now I have begun to turn away from them." When I first saw this family, Mrs. C. was worried about abusing Greta. Greta's tempers, her constant demands, and her poor tolerance for frustration were wearing on her mother. This usually sensitive and able woman found herself screaming at and shaking her older child. In reporting this history Mrs. C. said, "The day Greta was born was the saddest day of my life. The day of Anna's birth was the happiest." Compare this with Greta's statement at three: "Anna makes everyone happy. I make everyone sad."

Greta was petite and pretty and looked about six months younger than her age. Her early developmental milestones were two to three months delayed, but her parents were not concerned, perhaps because of their acquired knowledge of prematurity but also because they had observed a pattern of plateaus and then sudden leaps ahead. The most troubling part of her personality was her low frustration tolerance, to which her parents reacted with structure and soothing. They were rewarded by a good response as she grew older, and they were also proud of her sociability and warmth toward others. Her intellectual development appeared always to be excellent. She began preschool at three, separated easily, and until the second referral at three years, ten months, was viewed as a healthy child by her teachers. Mrs. C. insisted that Greta's skills and capacities had followed the same general developmental path before and after the birth of her sister.

I found Greta's parents likable, extraordinarily concerned and loving parents, committed to providing well for their children's needs. Mr. C. thought of his wife as an excellent mother who was much too hard on herself. He found Greta difficult at times, but until well into the analysis her mother was the main target for her difficult behavior. When I first saw the C's, financial pressures were still occupying much of Mr. C's attention. He had clearly been affected by the difficulties of his children, but his own tendency to deny and isolate affect was bolstered by the need to concentrate on his career. At the time of the first referral Mrs. C. was suffering from guilt over her anger with Greta, but also from the hurt she experienced in not being able to comfort and feel close to her child.

Anna was a tiny, persistent child but without the lability of her sister. She had a much greater ability to tolerate frustration. By the time she was two years and in preschool, she was viewed by all as completely recovered. She and Greta had a loving relationship. It was striking that Greta remained protective of and kind toward Anna for the most part, despite the tremendous sibling rivalry evident in her relationship to her mother.

When I saw Greta at three, soon after her sister's illness, she was like a waif-like and very stressed two-year-old, with limited and unclear language and an inability to engage in sustained play. She constantly asked "Why?" about everything to try to make sense of her situation. I thought then that she was reacting to fears of further abandonment and a feeling of danger regarding her own impulses. Prior to Anna's birth, her mother had always been able to help Greta to feel safe despite her frustration and intense emotion. Now Greta was feeling endangered by her affects and by the idea that she was a naughty child.

Weider (1966) described the analysis of a precocious boy in which the acquisition of knowledge served to ward off the perception of object loss; lack of knowledge symbolized the absence of the object. With Greta's "why" questions, I was aware of her active effort to use knowledge to allay anxiety. This would have seemed natural enough, except that the acquisition of knowledge did not help her to tolerate painful affects but only to defend against them. It was as if she were saying, "If I can make sense of it, I won't have to feel it." However, in the brief work we did she became visibly more relaxed and happy, once again in touch with her mother.

In the intervening summer, Greta's nanny was discovered to be involved with drugs and was discharged. Greta, though not strongly attached to this nanny, began to verbalize her anxieties over being left and to have night terrors once again. The first nanny, Vanessa, asked the C's if she could return. Their differences were resolved, and she joined the family permanently. Greta denied her pleasure at Vanessa's return but quickly grew attached again.

At three and a half years, Greta began preschool in September. At first she did extremely well but then began to have difficulties. Unfortunately, she had a teacher who had little patience for regression and emotional distress. Her teacher recognized Greta's initial precocity but then complained that she had become distractible and socially immature, displayed a persecution complex, seemed unable to protect her rights, and often resorted to tears as if torn up inside.

WORK WITH GRETA'S PARENTS

Several months into Greta's analysis Mr. C. accepted a position in another state and began to be away four to five days each week. He was therefore not often available for meetings.

Mrs. C's own psychotherapy, three times weekly, helped her to cope with Greta's difficulties. I saw her every two to three weeks to discuss Greta's progress and to help her gain greater understanding of Greta's conflicts. She was a very bright and insightful woman who readily made connections between Greta's and her own childhood experiences. When she understood what Greta needed, she was often able to respond positively. It seemed to me that without her sister's illness and despite her tenuous beginning, it is unlikely that Greta would have required treatment. Both she and her parents were overloaded by that event, but until then her development was proceeding quite well.

ASPECTS OF THE ANALYTIC WORK

The C's agreed to psychoanalysis as Greta's distress grew. At first, Greta took great pleasure in coming to see me every day although she might complain with a smile, "Oh, not Dr. Carla's again!" If we had to miss a session, she was distressed and provocative at home. She conveyed her happiness at finally having her own doctor, as Anna had had so many.

Greta's play initially focused on the hospital, where the emphasis was on keeping the mother doll close to the sick baby so that the baby would not be lonely. Eventually the big sister, named Greta, was put in diapers and allowed to sleep in the baby sister's bed. But the big sister decided she did not want to go to bed and instead had a temper tantrum. The mother doll did her best to help the big sister calm down and return to bed, but the mother fell out of the house and I was enlisted to catch her. This play sequence was repeated with pleasure throughout many sessions while I spoke first of the mother's absence at the hospital with the baby, then of the big sister's conflicting wishes about the special feelings of babyhood and the big-girl privileges of staying up late, the nighttime distress the big sister wanted to avoid, the mother's efforts to help her with her upset, and their need for Dr. Carla to help them solve their dilemma.

For many weeks Greta elaborated the theme of her conflict over infantile wishes and a precocious defense against the pain attached to those wishes. She repeatedly portrayed the loss of mother to a baby sister, the big sister's wishes to control and dominate the household, and the parents' somewhat successful attempts to punish the big sister's naughty provocations. There were many timeouts for the Greta-doll, and some seemed to help. At the end of each session Greta returned to the table to draw a happy picture, and she went daily to the waiting room to greet her mother or nanny, showing more mature behavior.

Increasingly the "naughtiness" of the Greta-doll came directly into the analysis as Greta became demanding of me, dissatisfied with anything I did for her, and oppositional. Over many sessions these behaviors and the underlying conflicts were elaborated in the transference without genetic interpretation until it seemed clear that Greta was enacting responses to the consequences of Anna's illness. One day she threw paper scraps all over the room because I had not put the correct amount of glue on her project, and she then refused to clean up the mess. She withdrew for about twenty minutes, holding her ground longer than most children her age, while angrily hiding under the table. I spoke of her painful feeling that if I did not do things just as she wanted, then I must not care about her—and that she was very angry with me, just like with Mommy, for not knowing what would help her to feel good. I also said I thought that when things did not go perfectly she was reminded that lots of things had indeed gone badly in her family, and she had been left alone to be a big girl when her baby-feelings were not yet finished. Her angry scowl disappeared, and she crawled into my lap and began to suck her thumb.

Greta asked me to tell her the story of baby Greta and baby Anna. I talked about how hard it had been for baby Greta to lose her mommy and her daddy—even her nanny—when baby Anna got sick; how baby Greta had tried to be a big girl before she was ready, and how very sad and angry it had made her. Greta added "and lonely." She directed me to take her to the waiting room to be deposited like a baby into her mother's lap.

After numerous sessions working on these issues Greta's night terrors disappeared, only to be replaced by nightmares with some reported content. This was also the time when her oedipal development first appeared in the analysis. At home she had begun to take greater interest in her father. He was reporting big, romantic kisses and a preference for his company. In analysis Greta alternated between the wish to have her father's love and the wish to be the father in the dollhouse play. The nightmares were eventually taken up as a reflection of her anxieties over her oedipal rivalry with her mother. The quality of her excitement and anxieties can be seen in the following session, at age four years, three months—five months into her analysis.

Greta left her mother in the waiting room with an extra hug and kiss. In the previous day's session, she had brought in a book about a cat and its ambivalence about babies. She had also cut up bits of Play Doh and taped them tightly inside the can, saying that they were the naughty monsters from her bad dreams. In this session, she immediately retrieved the can from the storage room, placed it in the playroom, and proceeded for the first time to go into the adult office to "read" the grown-up books. After a short period she returned to the playroom, where she cut the Play Doh into tinier pieces. Upon my inquiry she told me that the monsters were lady shark monsters who were naughty. First she cut off their mouths, saying that they said naughty things. She quickly retracted, saying the words weren't naughty but that she did not want them to talk. She then cut off their "bottoms," as they were "too big." Safely taped inside the can, the lady monsters were left in the playroom while Greta went to the adult office to make presents for them. With increasing excitement she began to chase the monsters because they had stolen something from her. She then ran out to tell her mother about the monsters. When she returned she took her box (i.e., the storage place for things she made in analysis and wanted to keep there), which contained wild animals, and put them in a cage. She asked the monsters (who had become ghosts by now) if she could come in to get the tape in order to secure her wild animals. She complained that the monster-ghosts would not let her in to get the tape that she so much wanted to make a present for her mother. She then quickly got the tape, saying, "You naughty ghosts!" She took a paperweight out to her mother as a present, returned, and sat on the wild-animal cage. She said at first that they couldn't get out but then she fell off, saying that they had pushed her. She pulled the curtain closed on the windows, saying that now nobody could see her. She continued to take presents to her mother. Then, excited, she wet her pants.

Until this point I had not said much to her. The enactment of oedipal excitement and anxiety was very fast, and its speed rather took my breath away. This day I commented only on how hard it was to manage the wild, excited animal feelings inside, especially when she thought the lady monster-ghosts would not approve. She told me that the lady monster-ghosts were angry because she had cut off their bottoms, but she did not like their bottoms to be bigger than her own. As we left this session she told me that her daddy was home ill, watching baseball, and that he looked quite handsome in his pajamas.

During this time her father brought her to a session. She did not demonstrate much excitement, but she was preoccupied throughout the session with making Play Doh presents for him, returning from the waiting room glowing from his praises. In her doll play she tended to hand the mother-doll over to me, playing the father-doll herself "because he's so cute." She had me cover my ears while she sang songs about babies, poop and pee, vaginas and penises. At other times she made these things from Play Doh and let me talk with her about her mixed feelings for her mother—her wish to be a baby with mother and her wish to get her mother out of the way so that she could be the mommy with her daddy. She agreed, saying she liked her daddy best but she did not want her mommy to know. At this time the material was not elaborated greatly in the transference but was expressed directly and in the displacement of the doll play.

The spring holiday arrived, and Greta's family planned a one-week trip. As it happened, I was called out of town unexpectedly, and Greta missed almost two weeks of analysis. We had had a ten-day break at Christmas that she found difficult. On this holiday she managed well, but on her return she began a new play sequence with a game of magnets. She talked about how the magnets did not stay where she put them and this frustrated her. I took up the subject of my absence in this context. She agreed and said I had been gone too long; she had been lonely. She devised a game in which her puppet ran from my puppet and then, as mine chased her, she could run back and land in my lap with giggling pleasure. She was quite physical with me until she was certain that I was not leaving her again soon. During this time she included the hospital in her play once again and talked about her mother's disappearances to take care of Anna. She took a lion to the hospital and had the doctors say it did not belong there. The lion growled at having been excluded. I linked her feeling of being left behind in regard to my trip to the feelings she had had when her mommy went to the hospital and her nanny disappeared.

Greta's anxieties over abandonment were now intertwined with oedipal issues. It was particularly hard to have me go away unexpectedly at a time when her oedipal rivalry was so great; however, the internal pressure toward reliving her anxiety over object loss was also apparent, as she made an effort to integrate old patterns of experience with newer conflicts of the oedipal phase. She began to cling to her mother and to have difficulties with transitions whenever her mother was present. At first the upset occurred at any event over which Greta had no control. Eventually the focus became that of leaving her nursery school to come to her analytic sessions if her mother happened to transport her. Mrs. C. could not tolerate remaining with Greta after a few sessions in which Greta would not let her leave without tears. Those sessions involved Greta's clinging to and physical aggression toward her mother, which Mrs. C. found hard to manage in my presence. I talked with Greta about the worries she was having about her mommy, saying that my recent absence right in the middle of Greta's angry feelings about Mommy had made her frightened that her mommy might go away forever. She was able to be comforted and to distract herself with play so that when Vanessa arrived to get her, she was again her sunny self.

The despair gave way to provocativeness with her mother and at times with me, but also to sexual interests again—lots of talk, while I was to cover my ears, of poop and pee, vaginas and penises. Her mother reported that Greta repeatedly asked, "Mommy, are you mad at me? Do I have good manners?" We talked about her "naughtiness" with her mother, how hard it was to be a good girl all the time, and her great wish to be the biggest. Her mother stopped trying to hide her anger at Greta's behavior, and this allowed Greta and me to talk more openly of the anger both she and her mother were feeling. Thereafter she seemed less worried about the anger between them and better able to engage in oedipal fantasies in the transference.

At times in this period Greta found herself in a loyalty conflict, clearly preferring to come into the treatment room with me but guilty about leaving her mother. I began to represent her father in the transference as she had me play the games with her that her father normally did—games of ball, climbing, building, and exploring. Soon her father began to travel weekly. She missed him, and I took up her play both in its oedipal context and as a response to her father's absence. She spelled out her father's name, saying "T.C., I love you." One day we had a condensed play sequence that contained much of her current conflict. She made a snake of Play Doh, then said "No"; she called it a penis and said "No"; then she called it a baby cradle and a vagina but covered it over, saying "ginas are yucky-looking." At the end of this session she walked out to give the Play Doh to her mother as a present, saying cheerily to me, "This means she's dead."

Greta was working both in the transference and directly in relation to her parents, as oedipal conflicts unfolded. A shift out of the transference occurred then as a consequence of Greta's need to deal with a new trauma that was stimulating distress over old ones. Her grandparents arrived for a visit, and her grandfather had to have emergency cardiac surgery. Once again her parents spent a great deal of time at the hospital. This time Greta and Anna had Vanessa to continue their care, but Mrs. C. later said that Greta's behavior during her grandparents' visit was the "worst ever."

In the analysis we saw the same patterns of precocious advance that her parents had described during Anna's illness. Greta became interested in the latency board games. She tried to do them the "big kid" way but eventually gained some comfort from constructing "Greta's rules." She frequently spoke of "when I am five" as representative of a time when she would no longer be humiliated and otherwise endangered by her sense of helplessness.

Daily she made presents for her grandfather. In one session she became extremely bossy toward me as well as giving me contradictory orders—"Don't talk! I'm busy! I can do it myself! Help me!" When I commented on how hard it was to know what she wanted from me, she extended her lower lip and was angrily silent for a long time. As she worked on her present for her grandfather with jerky movements, I said I thought the bossy feelings came because she worried that I had forgotten what a big girl she was—that it seemed especially important for me not to forget now, when she was having to be so big for everyone at home because of her grandpa's illness. I spoke of how hard it was to have her mommy and daddy so busy with someone else that she felt left out and unimportant. Greta replied that Anna had gone to the hospital with a hurt brain a long time ago, and Greta had been left behind. I agreed and said since that time she had tried so hard to manage her upset feelings by being extra big, but that inside she felt awfully sad and naughty as well.

When her grandparents returned to their home Greta's upset diminished and she returned to a more manageable working-through, within the transference, of oedipal conflicts, with the particular slant they took for her, given her history. At this time she began to focus on her feelings about my summer vacation. She returned to the magnet game and was much less frustrated. As she played Greta talked about the magnets cooperating, then of my cooperating and not being gone too long; she occasionally reassured herself that I would be coming back. One day we left the magnet game to go outside, and she commented how pleased she was to be able to do the magnet game even though she was not good at it, because it had an age minimum of six years. She also wondered why I wasn't very good at it because I'm a grown-up. Then we talked about how clever she was to notice that even grown-ups could not do everything. This exchange was elaborated over time as Greta came to understand that trying to be unduly grown-up and independent could neither protect her from painful feelings nor help her to tolerate them.

Once outside we spent some time dropping a tissue from the top of the building atrium down to the ground and then taking the elevator to retrieve it. Greta talked about letting the tissue float off alone and was delighted to find it each time. I said I thought she wanted just to make certain that when something went away it could be found again.

Mrs. C's work in her own treatment and with me began to give her a greater understanding of Greta's concerns about abandonment and about her naughtiness. Earlier in the analysis, when Greta cried over leaving her mother to come to her sessions, Mrs. C. was embarrassed at having me observe her management of Greta. Her solution was to have the nanny bring Greta. After working on this issue, Mrs. C. began to bring Greta on occasion and to engage with us in the analytic work around the separation. Greta, who had earlier gotten the idea that she could not cry or be provocative if she wished her mother to transport her, was able to relax the prohibition on her feelings. We then had an opportunity to begin to deal with these feelings. On one occasion, Greta was tearfully sad about letting her mother go but was able to do so. I commented that I thought she sometimes wished her mommy would never have to go away because it reminded her how sad, angry, and lonely she had felt before. Greta took the Play Doh and taped up the monsters, a game she had not played for weeks. She said she did not want the monsters to be allowed to talk to their mothers. I said that it certainly made sense that if she could not talk to her mother, it would not be fair to let the monsters talk to theirs. She then taped the monsters even more firmly, saying that if the monsters got free, they would keep the other Play Doh pieces from being with *their* mommies. This particular play then receded, but as her mother was more able to deal with this aspect of their relationship, Greta could tell me more about this longing.

This play occurred again in the second year of the analysis, when it became apparent that Anna was the monster who kept Greta from her mommy. This material arose in the working through of struggles over reciprocity and empathy regarding Greta's sister. The greatest insult possible was imagined as Greta contemplated her fury at a fantasy that Anna might someday be bigger than she. The recurring phrase epitomizing her experience during this time was "It's not fair."

A game developed that involved a further elaboration of oedipal conflict with Greta's own particular concern for object loss built in. Each day we built from blocks a house in which Daddy Bear, Mommy Bear, Baby Bear, and Greta would sleep together. Greta and I then made numerous signs (she often suggested we make a hundred) to tape on the wall, saying "Go away, Mommy." Then Greta had me hide the Mommy Bear while she and Daddy Bear cuddled together in the house. They were very glad that Mommy Bear had gone and were not interested in her return. However, after sufficient cuddling, Greta and Daddy Bear decided to look for Mommy Bear, not because they missed her but because they wanted to speak with her. Without my questioning, Greta told me that this story was about Mommy Bear, not about Greta's mommy.

I want to mention some aspects of Greta's functioning that were not caught in conflict and which gave evidence of her appropriate moves ahead. Just prior to age five she was pleased about moving into an older preschool class and demonstrated a sustained interest in letters, numbers, and rules. Her mother said that Greta's once-remarkable memory was no longer so remarkable, suggesting to me the first signs of repression as her oedipal conflicts were being worked through. As noted above, there began to be a greater displacement in her play; she was no longer consciously aware that her play-characters were representative of her own family.

DISCUSSION

When Greta came to analysis, she was making a great effort to fend off her infantile wishes for closeness and nurturing as well as for the auxiliary regulatory functions her mother had provided so well prior to Anna's illness. Greta's mother had been remarkably attuned to the particular needs of her prematurely born infant. She understood that, whether by temperament or as a result of her precarious beginning, Greta was a highly sensitive child who needed routine and calmness in her caretakers to aid in the management of her intense affect states. Mrs. C. felt confidence in her mothering, and Greta had thrived in her care. Greta was able to manage the loss of her parents to Anna's needs, Vanessa's departure, and her helplessness and anger in the face of those losses only barely, by the development of a precocious independence. She was left to struggle alone and unsuccessfully with those affects. She alternated between denial of her need for help, with subsequent frustration at not being able to manage on her own, and demanding, clinging, dissatisfied behavior toward her mother. Both stances left her unable to move beyond an ambivalent, uncomfortable attachment. She was not free to enjoy relationships with peers, to play with abandon, or to master new tasks. Greta's parents, whose own resources were overtaxed, could not respond adequately to her distress. Greta was preoccupied with the traumatic events of the previous year and their sequelae, so that the first year of her analysis tended to focus on the elaboration and integration of those experiences, just as a child with, for example, a chronic illness will use the illness to represent a variety of conflicts. Once the traumas had been sufficiently worked through, later phases gave fewer signs of the old content, although Greta's modes of handling current conflict continued to be influenced by wishes for independence to ward off painful feelings.

With regard to Greta's precocity, which seemed most noticeable in the months following our first contact, Mrs. C's contribution bears examining. I learned over the months of work that Mrs. C. had held a previously unconscious view that her own lot was more difficult than Greta's. That is, given a choice whether to be the sibling of a dying or seriously impaired infant or the mother, Mrs. C. would have chosen Greta's position. Through her own treatment Mrs. C. was able to uncover and to relinquish this attitude and its consequences in her relationship with Greta. We were then able to look more closely at her expectation that Greta would deny her distress. Mrs. C. was also aided by a dream at a time when I was absent in which her therapist announced he would be moving away. The conscious affects were of helplessness and despair. Her work on this dream allowed her to better understand Greta's experience at the time of Anna's stroke.

Another factor in Mrs. C's personality adds to a picture of Greta's precocity in terms of the nature and timing of her superego development. Mrs. C's own childhood with an alcoholic mother had left her angry and guilty. Her expectations for perfection in herself were partially carried over to her expectations of Greta. Greta's intensity and her independent strivings were characteristics that Mrs. C. described in herself as a young child. There is a question, I believe, as to the balance between two factors—i.e., how much Mrs. C's expectation of Greta would have been out of line with her daughter's development in any case as Greta began to negotiate anality and autonomy issues, as well as moral dilemmas, and how much it was the current extraordinary stress Mrs. C. was having to manage that made her particularly needful of high functioning in her first child.

We are accustomed to thinking of precocity in young children as the outcome of an effort to adapt to quite disturbed mothers who are limited in the ability to nurture. In Greta's case the noticeable use of precocity as a defense against painful affects arose not out of a fundamentally deficient environment but certainly out of extraordinary environmental circumstances. Alongside these unusually severe stresses were many experiences of pleasure and of being soothed and comforted by loving and competent parents. This factor may relate to some of Greta's strengths in the face of such a difficult history.

The quality and nature of Greta's superego development is intricately bound up with the general precocity in her approach to life. The "naughty" Greta-doll for a long time continued to qualify for more than a child's usual share of time-outs, and when Greta took the parental role she could be harsh and unrelenting. At the same time a broken toy or an unexpected mess in the playroom was met with a more tolerant, benign response. Toys can be played with a long time, Greta told me, but eventually they do get broken.

I do not have much clinical evidence of the role of identification in her superego development; however, there is a striking similarity in Greta's and her mother's attitudes toward their own aggressive impulses. Mrs. C's treatment focused a great deal on the motives and consequences of her harshness toward herself. Both mother and child could at times spoil their opportunities for pleasure because of a preoccupation with devalued views of themselves. One positive development in the analysis was Greta's increased ability to recover from the anger that arose in sessions.

The analysis aided Greta's tolerance for the painful affects associated with the losses she had sustained. Her precocity continued but in a more adaptive vein, I think in part because she was able to have the experience of regression in tolerable doses. The infantile wishes no longer threatened her in the way they once did, and she became more free to move ahead.

Greta's self-esteem was no longer so impaired, first because she gained an increased understanding of her own angry behavior, and secondly because she experienced less anger and helplessness as the analysis took hold. Life became better, too, and her capacity for tolerance of frustration increased.

Our work was finished after two years. Greta had become a much happier child, able to share and to negotiate with confidence in her peer relationships, proud of her accomplishments, and still full of progressive wishes. As she settled into kindergarten at almost six, there was no sign of overwhelming anxiety—only the age-appropriate concerns of a child beginning a new school experience. She was ambivalent about terminating her analysis. As she put it to her mother, "It is hard to say goodbye to someone when you have felt so special." But Greta knew that she was ready to finish, and increasingly she valued her free time for playing with peers.

Typically, the interpretation of trauma to children when the events have been forgotten or otherwise covered over is not particularly helpful; only what was immediate relevance is of interest to them. The cognitive sense of a past and a present is not yet meaningful to the prelatency child. Greta's ability to use interventions around the trauma resulting from Anna's stroke and the losses of nannies was based on the fact that the events were close in time to the analysis and had been kept alive in her mind by the ongoing nature of the trauma.

Greta's primary defensive maneuver, the use of precocious independence to avoid painful feelings of anger and helplessness, was one that required considerable tact in confronting. It was very important to Greta that I acknowledge the health, usefulness, and pleasure she felt in being able to manage for herself. It was only by doing so that I was also allowed to point out the disadvantages in this way of solving her problems.

Defenses are not given up easily, no matter what the age or developmental capacities of the patient. But this particular defense was one that held great potential for progressive development if it could be used more appropriately. Thus it was important to help Greta retain its more adaptive aspects while relinquishing its wholesale quality. Support for her progressive wishes was vital. Greta was able to learn that painful affects could be managed through loving relationships, and the infantile feelings that were evoked at such times did not have to interfere with her basically "big girl" stance. This allowed her greater flexibility in her response to psychic pain.

Lastly, in the second year of her analysis, which I have discussed briefly here, Greta's move into latency became increasingly clear. At the end she liked to come to analysis but no longer needed my help to solve conflicts. Repression had produced much more distance from oedipal concerns, and her interests were those of the typical early-latency child. The developmental phase itself mitigated against further work, although had she expressed crippling conflict we would have persevered.

Termination brought with it the potential for a rekindling of Greta's troubles over feelings of abandonment, but she did not apply her earlier interpretations of loss to this new experience. When she began preschool at three and a half, despite a valiant effort to use her precocity to manage painful feelings, Greta was constructing experience in terms of her past—in terms of loss, feeling unloved and naughty, feeling helpless in the face of expectation. The analysis of these constructs and their working through, along with the new responses given to her feelings as they emerged in treatment, allowed her to develop new ways of constructing experience, even in the face of difficult events such as termination. Kennedy and Moran (1990) focused on the alteration of the automatic quality of pathogenic solutions as they are applied to conflict. Despite Greta's potential for applying old solutions to new conflicts, her capacity for progressive development had been activated by the analytic work. It seems unlikely that Greta could have faced and found adaptive solutions to oedipal conflicts without the work she and her parents did to redress the imbalance in her development. When Greta was seen again, at age ten, because of a mild learning disorder, she was found to be a healthy latency child, despite several more years of massive stress related to her sister's further medical problems.

With regard to development, normal or abnormal, Anna Freud repeatedly emphasized the synthesis of constitutional givens, the rate and timing of structuralization, and parental influence. It is from these perspectives that developmental imbalance can be viewed.

One could observe environmental expectations for Greta's behavior mature beyond her normative development—that is, expectations that Greta would function independently and without recourse to the emotional attunement and support of her parents, on which she had relied prior to her sister's illness. On the side of constitution, Greta brought a great sensitivity to any change in routine and an easily stimulated distress potential. On the side of the ego and its defenses, Greta's adaptation remained primitive; that is, she persisted in the effort to ward off painful affects and impulses through denial and a precocious independence that disregarded reality. In addition, her defensive stance was unsuccessful, collapsing intermittently as rage and helplessness overwhelmed her.

The pathology resulting from the synthesis of these factors was developmental, inherent in the interaction of these factors in the early structuralization of the personality. Neurosis, as we know, has a different genesis, beginning specifically with frustration in the confrontation of oedipal conflict with subsequent regression, danger from ego/superego, anxiety, and compromise typically in the form of neurotic symptoms.

Anna Freud believed that the two forms of conflict were intertwined and often indistinguishable on the surface, but their different constructions necessitated differentiation in treatment. The question remains as to how the analytic resolution of a developmental imbalance differs from or is similar to the analysis of the later-developing neurotic conflict. Anna Freud left this to a future generation of psychoanalysts, expressing her view that although the analytic method is necessary for elucidating the cause and nature of the disturbance, it is not sufficient for its resolution (A. Freud, 1978).

Clearly, the idea that neurotic conflict is underpinned by developmental imbalance implies an intimate relation between the two types of conflict. The question of the adequacy of a traditional psychoanalytic intervention applied to developmental imbalance may vary, depending on a number of factors (e.g., the particular elements of imbalance in the various agencies of the mind, constitutional givens, and the environment; the timing of the disharmony in the developmental process; the duration of pathogenic stimuli. I believe that the analytic method is particularly beneficial with the prelatency child when imbalances and neurotic conflicts are newly forming and have created relatively few distortions in the personality.

Greta's environment was alterable though not enough in and of itself to restore her potential for normal developmental progress. But surely this factor counted a great deal toward therapeutic effectiveness. Her own difficulty in later taking from her environment what she had been denied in the year her parents were so preoccupied with Anna was the result of a pathological adaptation that she could not relinquish without analytic intervention. Had she not had analysis until her latency years, when the family again had to deal with serious illness in her sister, the question arises: would the underlying developmental imbalance have yielded to analytic interpretation, which makes conscious elements from all parts of the psychic structure, thus enabling the patient to construct more adaptive solutions? Or would the effects of her continuing developmental imbalance on subsequent developmental tasks not only obscure the imbalance but limit her solutions?

The efforts of Anna Freud and her colleagues at the Anna Freud Centre to understand developmental psychopathology as distinct from neurotic conflict have stimulated a more refined clarification of both types of conflict as they are interrelated through the developmental process. Analytic work with the very young child provides a lens for viewing that process in regard to normal pathways as well as deviations along the way.

BIBLIOGRAPHY

FREUD, A. (1974). A psychoanalytic view of developmental psychopathology. *The Writings of Anna Freud,* New York: International Universities Press, Vol. 8:57–74.
FREUD, A. (1976). Psychopathology seen against the background of normal development. *British Journal of Psychiatry,* 129:401–06.

FREUD, A. (1978). The principal task of child analysis. *Bulletin of the Hampstead Clinic*, 1:11–16.

FREUD, A. (1979a). Mental health and illness in terms of internal harmony and disharmony. *The Writings of Anna Freud*, New York: International Universities Press, Vol. 8:110–18.

FREUD, A. (1979b). Child analysis as the study of mental growth, normal and abnormal. *The Writings of Anna Freud*, New York: International Universities Press, Vol. 8:119–36.

KENNEDY, H. & MORAN, G. (1990). Distal and proximal aims of child analysis. *The Bulletin of the Anna Freud Centre*, 13:103–12.

WEIDER, H. (1966). Intellectuality: Aspects of its development from the analysis of a precocious four-and-a-half year old boy, *Psychoan. Study Child*, 21:294–323.

Developing Developmental Lines

ALAN J. FLASHMAN, M.D.

Anna Freud's concept of developmental lines itself followed a complex path of development. Ms. Freud came to psychoanalytic maturity during a time when Sigmund Freud was rethinking many of his theories. He was engaged in adding to his analytic understanding of his patients' past, a new approach to the intrapsychic synthesis that takes place in the present and potential future. Anna Freud extended this view in her work with children whose treatment and process of development overlapped in the continuous present and in the clinically foreseeable future. She provided a general system of thinking while respecting Freud's distrust of general systems and preserving his commitment to detailed observation and to poetic perception. This approach required the ability to distinguish clearly among different levels of generalization. Her complex experience as both daughter and analysand of her father contributed to her intuitive talent in making such distinctions. It was her mourning for her father after his death that pulled these trends together into her own unique contribution. Her mourning and her contribution took the form of continuing alone along the path she and her father had once traveled together. In the concept of developmental lines she gave most cogent expression to this continued journey.

Analyzing the Past, Synthesizing the Future

SIGMUND FREUD WAS KEENLY AWARE OF THE NATURE AND LIMITATIONS OF his method of study. He knew full well that he was able to wrest the most

---

Adjunct faculty, Paul Baerwald School of Social Work, Hebrew University of Jerusalem.

I gratefully acknowledge the helpful comments of Susan Baur, Alan Zaitchik, Gerda Elata-Alster, and Hannah Avnet. Albert J. Solnit was, as always, both generous in encouragement and constructive in critique, for which I am doubly indebted.

The Psychoanalytic Study of the Child 51, ed. Albert J. Solnit, Peter B. Neubauer, Samuel Abrams, and A. Scott Dowling (Yale University Press, copyright © 1996 by Albert J. Solnit, Peter B. Neubauer, Samuel Abrams, and A. Scott Dowling).

closely guarded secrets from human nature—but at the cost of possibly rending the whole cloth to shreds. He took things apart—*analyzed* them—and microscopically viewed and focused on the newly distinguished pieces he had bravely and proudly discovered. Freud felt that this method was consistent with his loyalty to natural science and materialism, that it tamed his troublesome but brilliant propensity for making the most general speculations (Gay, 1988), and that it was his destiny as a male (see Appignanesi and Forrester, 1992).

Freud could also appreciate others—especially women—who did not share his limitations. A striking example is his relationship and prolonged correspondence with Lou Andreas-Salomé. He continuously admired "Frau Lou's" womanly capacity to put back together what he had taken apart. He felt that she surpassed him in speculative power and that she used it precisely in reassembling the puzzle that he had so vigorously dissected. There could be no question of her understanding of his science—and himself—for she understood better than he the meaning of his discoveries: "I am amazed at your talent for going beyond what has been said, for completing it and making it converge at some distant point. Naturally I do not always agree with you. I so rarely feel the need for synthesis. The unity of this world seems to me so self-evident as to not need emphasis. What interests me is the separation and breaking up into its component parts of what would otherwise revert to an inchoate mass. . . . In short, I am of course an analyst." (Freud and Andreas-Salomé, 1985).

Freud began to address explicitly the tension between taking apart and putting together during the initial period of this relationship. Starting with "On Narcissism" (1914), he tentatively reformulated the previously singular "ego-instinct" as a complex putting together of libido and investment in oneself. In "Beyond the Pleasure Principle" (1920) he proposed a revised theory of instincts, in which libido was connected to the tendency to put things together and the death instinct to the tendency of things to fall apart or to be taken apart. This ultimately led him to formulate the ego as a psychic agency capable of synthesizing (1923,1926).

For Freud, this new logic of synthesis arrived concurrently with a new approach to analyzing time. Psychoanalysis had heretofore been primarily the science of the past (witness Freud's famous affinity for archaeological analogies). Now, for the first time, a logic of the future appeared in Freud's work (see 1927, 1930; Andreas-Salomé, 1995, p. 99). Only the past can be analyzed; the future is a matter for speculation of how things may be put together. I think it no accident that it is in his first paper addressing the future (1919) that he openly discussed the matter of synthesis: "In actual fact . . . the neurotic patient presents us with a torn mind, divided by resistances. As we analyze it and remove the resistances, it grows together, the great unity which we call his ego fits into itself all the instinctual impulses which before had been split off and held apart from it. The *psycho-synthesis* is thus achieved during analytic treatment without our intervention, automatically and inevitably" (p. 161).

Anna Freud came of age as a woman as well as a companion and colleague to her father during these same years (1912–1922). Frau Lou became a psychoanalytic second mother for Anna, a sometime consultant to Freud's analysis of his daughter, and an informal supplementary analyst for Anna (Young-Bruehl, 1988; Appignanesi and Forrester, 1992). Anna Freud's first steps along the path of psychoanalysis were steadily guided by these two new markers, Freud's concern for putting the pieces back together, and his new views regarding the future. These twin themes set her course over the next half-century.

CHILDREN: THE CONTINUOUS PRESENT

Anna Freud's work with children exposed her to a new aspect of time, the continuous present, in addition to the past and the future. Any experience—even several months—with a young child exposes the analyst to a relatively large portion of the child's life span. In addition, important life events often happen to the child while in analysis, challenging the analyst to understand not only how past events have affected the child, but also how events are currently affecting her or him. Anna Freud's concept of child analysis involved long-term contact with her patients; in the case of Dorothy Burlingham's children, she saw them throughout a lifetime (Young-Bruehl, 1988). At the same time, adult analyses were becoming lengthier, challenging Freud and his disciples with the similar experience of a continuous present in adult treatments (Freud, 1937).

The continuous present poses theoretical difficulties qualitatively different from those of analyzing the past or of synthesizing the future. Because the activities related to both past and future are speculative, the analyst has the freedom to see them as performed by the analysand alone, with only prompting and facilitation by the analyst. The analyst can imagine, by analogy, that the patient is getting to where he or she belongs. By contrast, in the continuous present the analyst becomes a part of the process of synthesizing, a partner in establishing the vector of the analysand's life. For the analyst to be clear about the nature of his or her role and contribution to the patient's life, he or she needs a detailed understanding of the mechanisms by which the analysand puts things together. Developmental lines provide precisely the framework necessary for distinguishing as clearly as possible between the activity of the analysand and that of the analyst in the ongoing development that is taking place simultaneously in the continuous present and in the analysis.

POETIC SCIENCE, POETIC SYSTEM

In his last major work, the eminent scholar and translator of German philosophy, Walter Kaufmann (1980) traced two paths in the "discovery of the mind" within the Germanic philosophic tradition of the past two centuries. According to Kaufmann, Goethe approached psychological life according to the emotional realities encountered within the human world *as it is*. His approach was rooted in a deep understanding and acceptance of his own inner world. Kant, by contrast, approached the mind according to principles of how the human world *should be*. This direction was based on a deep limitation of his self-knowledge (1980, vol. 1). Hegel (1980, vol. 1) to some extent, Buber, and especially Heidegger (1980, vol. 2) are among those who followed Kantian principles of prescribing before describing. Following the thinking of Goethe are Nietzsche (1980, vol. 2) and Sigmund Freud (1980, vol. 3). Kaufmann points to the many quotations of Goethe in Freud's work as well as to Freud's unquestionable literary talent. He adds that Freud's "poetic science" shared a basic outlook with Goethe and Nietzsche. Freud took life—and himself—as they came. He preferred a deep encounter with singular aspects of mental life to the claim of a complete system of explanation. He constantly struggled with his capacity and desire for the most general abstractions, at times limiting himself very strictly to the details under his analytic and scientific nose (see Gay, 1988). This struggle was central to Freud ever since his adolescent flirtation with, and ultimately his forceful rejection of, philosophy in general and theism in particular (Freud and Silberstein, 1990; see Flashman, 1993).

Freud's correspondence with Lou Andreas-Salomé (1985) is full of references to his struggle with the concept and his wish for a more general system of psychology. He was particularly dismayed at the tendencies of Adler and Jung (Kaufmann, 1980, vol. 3, groups both Adler and Jung with Kant!) to systematize prematurely and prescribe how things should turn out (pp. 8f, 18f, 24, 42f, 54f). Freud ultimately defined his approach in the last of the *New Introductory Lectures* (1933):

> A *Weltanschauung* is an intellectual construction which solves all the problems of our existence uniformly on the basis of one overriding

hypothesis, which, accordingly, leaves no question unanswered and in which everything that interests us finds its fixed place . . . psycho-analysis . . . as a specialist science, a branch of psychology—a depth psychology or psychology of the unconscious is quite unfit to construct a *Weltanschauung* of its own: it must accept the scientific one. But the *Weltanschauung* of science already departs noticeably from our definition. It is true that it too assumes the *uniformity* of the explanation of the universe; but it does so only as a programme, the fulfillment of which is relegated to the future. Apart from this it is marked by negative characteristics, by its limitation to what is at the moment knowable . . . there are no sources of knowledge of the universe other than the intellectual working-over of carefully scrutinized observations—in other words, what we call research (pp. 158–159).

Seen within the context of this tension between the specific and the general, the concept of developmental lines provides a solution. It offers a broad general psychology of normality as well as pathology. This general psychology, however, does not close the gaps in our knowledge. It does not presume to explain anything that cannot be observed. It does not rely on any source of information other than careful observation and intellectual reworking of the facts. On the contrary, the concept of developmental lines expresses the results of extremely exacting observation and reflection over many years. It constitutes, rather precisely, Freud's scientific program for further observation and reflection.

Anna Freud succeeded in coordinating the details of life as it is lived with a broad conceptual framework that leaves room for the facts. The facts find their place in the specific developmental lines she outlines, and in others that could be added. Only careful observation—both developmental observation of children and psychoanalytic observation of adults—could convincingly connect various behaviors along a particular line. Anna Freud's examples are all taken from the field, in which she slowly and carefully collected data of both kinds. Perhaps for this reason she did not include linguistic development, which at the time was dominated more by theory than by observation (see Holland, 1992).

The precision and simplicity of her writing (Greenson, 1972) belie a profoundly poetic outlook on life. Anna Freud was a great reader and a lover of poetry, which she wrote as a young adult (Young-Bruehl, 1988, pp. 81ff). Poetry in Kaufmann's sense flows deeply and broadly through the seemingly dry developmental lines. Her poetic approach is often missed because of Anna Freud's singular ability to allow the poetry of life to speak—and to develop—through the words and deeds of the children she treated. Anna Freud was gifted with poetic ears and eyes that enabled her to appreciate the poetry of life as it presented itself to her. She developed a framework of responding and thinking that allowed poetic listening *and* analytic thinking at the same time. In the concept of developmental lines she sketched her own method of appreciating the poetry of child development. Rather than make her own poetry, she presented her students and colleagues with a way that could help them to appreciate the poetry before them. It was a way of appreciating, as Kaufmann says of Goethe, "the way things become the way they are." This is not a *Weltanschauung* but an *Anschauung,* a way of seeing, precisely the goal Goethe sought in poetry (Kaufmann, 1980, vol. 1, p. 47; cf. Andreas-Salomé, 1995, p. 99).

Both system and poetry play roles in the thinking of Goethe and Anna Freud, but each writer places the two in a distinct relationship one to the other. An analogy borrowed from the Soviet developmental psychologist L. S. Vygotsky (1978, p. 95) will help express these relationships. Vygotsky criticized the "Western" absolute distinction between "free play" and board games. He demonstrated a fact that has tantalized many a child therapist. According to Vygotsky, even symbolic play has many rules in the child's mind. The existence of these rules had often been overlooked because these rules are covert, while the fantasy content of the play is overt. In board games this relation is inverted: the rules are overt, the fantasy content covert. Goethe applied his poetry to his less well-known scientific investigations of color and visual perception (Kaufmann, 1980, vol. 1, pp. 35ff.). For him, fantasy was the overt stuff of poetry, while his systematic way of thinking about the mind remained covert. In Anna Freud's developmental lines, the direct continuation of her father's "poetic science," the systematic approach to the mind is quite overt. I emphasize the very present—if covert—poetic aspect of this theory.

Combining poetry and science can be tricky. Historically, many shifts in psychoanalytic theory can be attributed to the balance between the two. Different writers and perhaps different schools or even continents have given more weight to either one. Some of the past excesses of ego psychology could be conceptualized as "science" at the expense of poetry; some recent trends in European psychoanalysis emphasize poetry at the expense of science.

An instructive example of the latter is Christopher Bollas (1987, 1989, 1992, and 1995). Bollas, identified with the British "Independent School," is concerned with how an individual comes about (1989) and how things are put together in the unconscious (1992,1995). In a recent book (1992) he devotes much attention to synthesis, cohesion, and integration (pp. 42, 82, 86, 87, 88, 92, 102). Despite what seems to be a great deal in common with Anna Freud's concerns, he never mentions her work explicitly, but makes oblique and critical reference to it: "However are we to describe the character of the internal world, given its dense complexity? We do not have separate or overlapping lines of development, we have mazes of evolving devolutions" (1992, p. 52). Bollas's straw man (woman) would see us as "having" developmental lines. Nothing could be further from the poetic science of Anna Freud, who sought to make useful conceptualizations about the dense complexity that analysts have long recognized. "Mazes of evolving devolutions" no doubt has a poetic advantage over "developmental lines." I question, however, whether such a term fosters clarity of communication and scientific inquiry in Freud's sense of questioning and testing assumptions. Bollas himself makes frequent note of a caveat lest his terminology become too mysterious (e.g., 1992, p. 58). Current poetically inclined writers could find a kindred spirit and an unusually wise guide to restraint in Anna Freud.

Frau Lou first met Anna Freud through the eyes of the girl's father. In expressing her regret over failing to meet the seventeen-year-old woman, she wrote, "I am sorry I did not get to know your youngest daughter in 1912/13—I was about to do so on one occasion, but, alas, she escaped me. Perhaps she has become a poet-translator from foreign tongues? Or perhaps a poetess on her own account? That would be the finest translation of her father's psychoanalysis into a feminine medium (Freud and Andreas-Salomé, 1985, p. 62). Robert Coles (1992, p. 78) wrote, "Anna Freud was a theorist, as a poet can be."

SCIENTIFIC DISCOURSE: CONTENT, PROCESS,
AND LEVELS OF ABSTRACTION

The poetic aspects of Anna Freud's thought in no way contradict the scientific precision of her work. To the contrary, in the concept of developmental lines, she was able to use her poetic gifts to enhance the simultaneous play of several viewpoints at different levels of abstraction, while preserving a clear distinction among these levels. The beguilingly simple concept of developmental lines enlists three clearly distinguished levels of abstraction. First is the level of psychic *contents*. Second is the level of the *lines of continuity over time*, within which the psychic contents can be conceptualized. The developmental lines are of a higher level of abstraction than any of their contents: the contents are included within the lines. Third is the level of *the process of integration of the lines*. This is the most abstract level as it involves a process performed on the various lines. A process is generally more abstract than a particular object of the process (see Bateson, 1979). A supervening structure of even higher abstraction would be the *ego,* the author of the process of integrating of lines. The ego is more abstract because it performs many functions and includes all of the other functions it performs.

Anna Freud makes sharp and consistent distinctions among the various logical levels. She clearly distinguishes a psychic content—say, *biting,* with its meaning at a given developmental stage—from the role it plays in creating the developmental line from dependent to autonomous eating. The present meaning of biting will become part of the longitudinal meaning of biting to be developed over time. The line of development of eating will need to be coordinated with many other lines of development. The next level of abstraction involves the degree to which the various lines develop at the same rate and how they can or cannot be coordinated. This coordination of lines is more abstract than any given line. A certain line may stand out in its own developmental fixation, on its own level, but this fixation may also produce a failure to integrate all the lines at a more general level. The overall relative success or failure at integration would then serve as a more general diagnostic category than the fixation of any given line. To this extent one can specify the level of abstraction at which a given diagnostic statement is being made (cf. Greenson, 1972).

DAUGHTER OF THE ANALYST

The concept of developmental lines makes such clear distinctions among these levels of generalization that one could think all this is obvious. Still, is it possible to explain this rare precision within complexity by examining Anna Freud's life—that is, her most unconventional personal psychoanalysis? Ernest Jones, in defense of Melanie Klein, suggested to Freud that the father-daughter analytic team perhaps left important territory untouched. Freud's irate response is well known and should have sufficed to silence Jones's misuse of analytic interpretation in the service of political infighting (Young-Bruehl, 1988; Gay, 1988).

I consider here a different perspective. An analysand will gradually internalize and identify with the analyst's view of his or her psychic functioning. To a certain extent, an analysand will identify with the analyst's view of the analysand's emotional development as well. The analyst becomes a sort of auxiliary parent as the analysand imagines how the analyst would have regarded the analysand when he or she was a small child. Often an analysand will also identify with what he or she thinks is the analyst's view of the analysand's parents during childrearing.

In this context, analysis by her own father created a situation that encouraged Anna Freud's unusual facility in juggling a variety of viewpoints simultaneously. For her, the analytic auxiliary father was the same person as her real father. As a result, she would have identified a *real* analytic father of her real childhood. Both the present analyst and the past parent serve a twofold function, as each is present in its own right and each also elicits the other. The result would be the image of an analytic parent performing a sort of analytic parenting. This parenting would involve an attitude much like that of developmental lines, at least in Anna Freud's imagination. It would consist of understanding the nature of psychic contents as they appear, imagining the future of these contents in a vector directed toward later developments, and perceiving the whole of the child through the analyst's efforts to pull all these contents and lines into an increasingly coherent person. In this context Anna Freud's lifelong feeling of kinship with children of psychoanalysts assumes additional significance (Young-Bruehl, 1988). Developmental lines would constitute an empathic viewing of her own development through the eyes of her analyst father.

On Losing, Finding, and Creating

Thirty years separate Anna Freud's analysis with her father from her conceptualizing some aspects of this analysis as developmental lines. Certainly many experiences and conversations with Freud contributed to her thinking. Ultimately, it was the *loss* of her father that made this conceptualization possible. Here, in detail, are some special aspects of Anna Freud's grieving process.

In her beautiful biography of Anna Freud, Elisabeth Young-Bruehl (1988) describes this process. Anna Freud considered her father's comments on grieving, presented in a more metapsychological than clinical form in "Mourning and Melancholia" (1917), to be a preliminary communication. Over many years and through deep and repeated self-analysis, she examined her own responses to her father's death. Anna Freud stated her conclusions in "On Losing and Being Lost" (1967), a work that operates on levels of content and process simultaneously. On the level of content, she offered an extension of Freud's provisional proposal in "Mourning and Melancholia." Her father had taken his understanding of the early stages of mourning up to the point of a slow and repeated *severance of attachment* from memory after memory. Anna

Freud attempted to extend this view toward the final stages of mourning. She suggested that mourning is not so much completed as transcended, often with the expectation of some future shared eternal life, psychologically explained as a form of perpetual oneness or assimilation of the lost one into the loser's psychic structure. On the level of process, she was creating precisely such oneness with her father by extending his theory in a way she felt was loyal to the principles they had worked on in common.

Beyond these theoretical formulations, Anna Freud expressed an additional element of grieving that she did not fully formulate. It seems reasonable to view the mourning process as involving a tension between a relatively complete renunciation of an actual relationship with the departed and an experience of a life that continues within the context of that previous relationship. In the latter, grieving would involve a significant alteration in the form of the relationship but not its complete disavowal. This change would involve primarily the placing of the actual relationship into the past but would include a sense of continuity with the relationship as previously lived. This continuity could be formulated by analogy as continuing along a path once walked together. The common path of the past sets a vector of mutual understanding and relating. However, in order to set the part of the path that was once conjoint into the past, the mourner is called upon to progress further along this path, only now entirely on her own. Connectedness would be experienced in continuing along where the mourner feels she would have walked together with the deceased. Relinquishment is accomplished by the very act of walking alone what would have been a common path (cf. Andreas-Salomé, 1995, p. 135).

Anna Freud's grief over the loss of her father speaks for itself in her 1942 dreams:

> About Losing and Being Lost / Concerning last night's dream: I dream, as I have often done, that he is here again. All of these recent dreams have the same character: the main role is played not by my longing for him but rather by his longing for me. . . . In the first dream of this kind he openly said: "I have always longed for you so."
> The main feeling in yesterday's dream is that he is wandering about (on the top of mountains, hills) while I am doing other things. At the same time, I have an inner restlessness, a feeling that I should stop whatever I am doing and go walking with him. Eventually he calls me to him and demands this himself. I am very relieved and lean myself against him, crying in a way that is very familiar to both of us. Tenderness. My thoughts are troubled: he should not have called me, it is as if a renunciation or a form of progress has been undone because he called. I

am puzzled. In the dream the feeling is very strong that he is wandering around all alone and "lost." Sympathy and bad conscience.

Associations: The poem by Albrecht Schaeffer, "You strong and dear wayfarer":

> *I was with you at each step of the way—*
> *there was no victory I did not also win—*
> *no sorrow I did not suffer beside you,*
> *you strong and dear wanderer. . . .*

The reproach is: he is unfaithful to me in his travels, in spite of my faithfulness; like Odysseus toward Penelope.

The self-reproach which is projected in this reproach: I am unfaithful to him. (Young-Bruehl, 1988, pp. 286–287)

The themes of loyalty and faithfulness bespeak a wish to continue along what could have been the next steps along a common path. Anna Freud analyzed this dream in a disguised and generalized form (1967):

> The painful accusations, regrets, etc., in the manifest content correspond to the dreamer's realization that he is on the point of becoming disloyal to the dead and his guilt about this. The anxiety which interrupts the dream corresponds to the defense against the opposite wish: to yield to the dream image's invitation, turn away from life altogether, and follow the lost object into death. (1967, p. 18)

While preparing herself for the annual May 6 celebration of her father's birthday in 1948, Anna Freud again dreamed about roads:

> I dreamed: "there was a big road, going up in a serpentine fashion . . . but people were rebuilding it or changing it. I saw the very wide road and felt activity going on. Instead of going on the road, people (I too) were going straight up, cutting out the curves. But it was like going in through one house after another, in and out of windows, not doors. I thought, all the walls will be spoilt by doing that. At last I arrived at the highest point, and there in a room, very quietly and peacefully sitting were Mama and Tante Minna. Tante Minna was sewing and Mama was mending something (a doormat?). There was a feeling that my father was present all through. That ending was a curious anticlimax. I felt, in the dream, after all that commotion and activity, this peaceful household scene."
>
> I was puzzled at first and then I had two associations which put me on track. (1) the first line of the poem which I like: "Does the road wind uphill all the way?" It is the road to heaven, death, on which I take destructive shortcuts (Dorothy had reproached me the day before that I was self-destructive [for working too hard]). (2) I could not reach my father in death because Tante Minna was there before me. This time Mama and Tante Minna were there as they had been in life. That is the anticlimax: after all my efforts I find exactly the same situation which

aroused my jealousy in life. So death is not much good either. (Young-Bruehl, 1988, p. 293)

Anna Freud tried to be loyal to her father by interpreting her dream much as he would have. It is even possible to suggest that dreaming a "Freudian" dream was in itself an act of loyalty to her father-analyst.

Another meaning to this dream may be one that was not yet apparent to Anna Freud at the time but which guided her directly to developmental lines. "After all my efforts," meaning "after all that commotion and activity," refers as well to her analytic efforts to continue to expand and perhaps straighten the path set by her father. There was danger of being disloyal. She was relieved, at the cost of some letdown, that she was a loyal member of a peaceful household, the one her father loved. In other words, her capacity for innovation was carried out with a "feeling that my father was present all along."

Parenthetically, Anna Freud's process of mourning may shed light on an alternative, normative path of bereavement among women. I tentatively propose that women achieve mourning more in connectedness than in relinquishment. Parkes documented his findings in widows, and Bowlby speculated on a possible gender-based difference in mourning outcomes (Bowlby, 1980; Volkan, 1981). Gilligan (1982) and others (Gilligan, Lyons and Hanmer, 1990; Brown and Gilligan, 1992) have described the central role of embeddedness in the development of adolescent girls. I, too, suggest that the notion of continuing alone along the path once walked jointly deserves further consideration and research.

PUTTING IT ALL TOGETHER

The centenary of Freud's birth, on May 6, 1956, occupied Anna Freud both as daughter and as scientist. On the scientific level, she prepared a new series of lectures (compare the 1952 lectures [1992]) that later constituted the first draft for *Normality and Pathology in Childhood* (1965; Sayers, 1991, p. 182). As Young-Bruehl (1988) has pointed out, "the Centenary had given her occasion for historical reflection" (p. 359). The results were threefold. On the level of *recapitulation,* she defined basic principles of her father's path. She especially distinguished his opposition to reductionism—to giving overriding priority to one system of explanation at the expense of all others. On the level of *their common path,* she formulated the *process* of Freud's scientific method. He had been committed to explanation of many levels. He had sought to add new discoveries without abandoning the old. He had repeatedly reorganized the puzzle as new pieces were added. He had sought to create a general psychology. This formulation of the path she had shared with her father allowed her to set out *the extended path* she was now ready to begin to traverse. To her mind, it was a route Freud would have continued to travel with her. This provided her with a comforting and necessary sense of his continued presence.

At the center of this extended path was "constant intellectual mobility" (Young-Bruehl, 1988, p. 360). She was now ready to attempt to add to her father's work a qualitatively more general psychology. He had moved "beyond the pleasure principle," and she was now ready to move "beyond the infantile neurosis." She placed the symptomatic profile of the child in an entirely new light, because the child lives in a developmentally continuous present and is actively engaged in synthesizing his or her intrapsychic structures (see Greenson, 1972). Developmental lines constitute the most direct expression of this intellectual mobility.

Here follows one more biographical speculation to the importance of the centenary. In 1955 Anna Freud turned sixty. It was Freud as a man of sixty that Anna Freud came to know and accompany on his psychoanalytic path. In 1916 Anna Freud attended her father's "Introductory Lectures" (Appignanesi and Forrester, 1992, p. 279), and in 1918 she commenced her four-year analysis with him. This was precisely the period in his life when Freud was displaying extraordinary intellectual mobility, first by reformulating and summarizing his initial theories and then by rethinking and revising them entirely. His new formulations attempted to approach a much more general psychology. It seems plausible that at the age of sixty Anna Freud, with her bold new formulations, saw that she was doing precisely what her father had done, in her presence and later with her help, at the same age (see Flashman, in Baur, 1994, ch. 12). To this extent, developmental lines is a concept reflexive of its author's process: Anna Freud was able to "put it all together" within herself as she formulated the process of "putting it all together." What she said to Robert Coles (1992) could well be applied to herself: "We have learned to hold our breaths rather often, and let the children show us how they are going to 'put it all together'—I like that phrase" (p. 75).

BIBLIOGRAPHY

Appignanesi, L., & Forrester, J. (1992). *Freud's Women.* New York: Basic Books.

Andreas-Salomé, L. (1995). *Looking Back.* Trans. E. Pfeiffer. New York: Marlowe.

BATESON, G. (1979). *Mind and Nature*. New York: Dutton.

BAUR, S. (1994). *Confiding*. New York: HarperCollins.

BOLLAS, C. (1987). *The Shadow of the Object*. New York: Columbia University Press.

—— (1989). *Forces of Destiny*. London: Free Association Books.

—— (1992). *Being a Character*. New York: Hill and Wang.

—— (1995). *Cracking Up*. New York: Hill & Wang.

BOWLBY, J. (1980). *Loss*. New York: Basic Books.

BROWN, L. M., & GILLIGAN, C. (1992). *Meeting at the Crossroads*. Cambridge: Harvard University Press.

COLES, R. (1992). *Anna Freud*. Reading, Mass.: Addison-Wesley.

FLASHMAN, A. (1994). "Death do us part": Personal and family risk in the adolescent family (Hebrew). In *Risk-Taking in Adolescence*. Ed. H. Deutsch & S. Schneider. Jerusalem: Summit Institute.

—— (1993). God of a godless Jew. Paper presented at George Shrut Conference on Letterality and Literality: The Biblical Text and Its Readers. Ben-Gurion University of the Negev and University of Glasgow, Sdeh Boker, Israel, March, 1993.

FREUD, A. (1965). *Normality and Pathology in Childhood*. New York: International Universities Press.

—— (1967). On losing and being lost. *Psychoanal. Study Child* 22:9–19.

—— (1992). *The Harvard Lectures*. Ed. J. Sandler. Madison, Conn.: International Universities Press.

FREUD, S. (1914). On narcissism: An introduction. *S.E.*, 14:69–102.

—— (1917). Mourning and melancholia. *S.E.*, 14:237–258.

—— (1919). Lines of advance in psycho-analytic therapy. *S.E.*, 17:157–168.

—— (1920). Beyond the pleasure principle. *S.E.*, 18:3–64.

—— (1923). The ego and the id. *S.E.*, 19:3–66.

—— (1926). Inhibitions, symptoms and anxiety. *S.E.*, 20:87–178.

—— (1927). The future of an illusion. *S.E.*, 21:5–56.

—— (1930). Civilization and its discontents. *S.E.*, 21:64–145.

—— (1933[1932]). New introductory lectures on psycho-analysis. *S.E.*, 22:1–182.

—— (1937). Analysis terminable and interminable. *S.E.*, 23:216–253.

FREUD, S., & ANDREAS-SALOMÉ, L. (1985). *Letters*. New York: Norton.

FREUD, S., & SILBERSTEIN, E. (1990). *The Letters of Sigmund Freud to Eduard Silberstein, 1871–1881*. Ed. W. Boehlich, trans. A. J. Pomerans. Cambridge: Harvard University Press.

GAY, P. (1988). *Freud: A Life for Our Time*. New York: Norton.

GILLIGAN, C. (1982). *In a Different Voice*. Cambridge: Harvard University Press.

GILLIGAN, C., LYONS, N. P., & HANMER, T. J., eds. (1990). *Making Connections*. Cambridge: Harvard University Press.

GREENSON, R. (1972). "The voice of the intellect is a soft one." In *Explorations in Psychoanalysis* (1978). New York: International Universities Press.

HOLLAND, H. (1992). *The Critical I*. New York: Columbia University Press.

KAUFMANN, W. (1992 [1980]). *Discovering the Mind*. New Brunswick, N.J.: Transaction.

SAYERS, J. (1991). *Mothers of Psychoanalysis*. New York: Norton.

VOLKAN, V. (1981) *Linking Objects and Linking Phenomena*. New York: International Universities Press.

VYGOTSKY, L. S. (1978). *Mind in Society*. Cambridge: Harvard University Press.

YOUNG-BRUEHL, E. (1988). *Anna Freud: A Biography*. New York: Norton.

The Psychoanalytic Legacy of Anna Freud

ANNE-MARIE SANDLER

This paper presents some aspects of Anna Freud's work in a way that is rather different from the conventional accounts of her contributions. It focuses on some of the factors that I believe have led to her particular contribution to psychoanalytic theory and practice—inevitably, with special emphasis on her work with children. In looking back at Anna Freud's work from today's vantage point, it is clear that she was, as Robert Wallerstein put it (1984), a radical innovator as well as a staunch conservative.

IN ORDER TO UNDERSTAND ANNA FREUD'S LEGACY FULLY, WE MUST TAKE into account a number of dominant aspects of her professional life. We are all aware of her very strong identification with her father and with his metapsychology. This identification was consistent and unwavering. Yet she nevertheless managed to make substantial and original contributions of her own. She was able to do this by virtue of her skill and capacity to maintain her adherence to classical theory while taking fundamental steps forward in theory and technique.

A good example of this is the innovative way in which she explored and described the activities of the ego in its dealings with the id, the superego, and the outside world in *The Ego and the Mechanisms of Defence*

Director, Anna Freud Centre, London; supervising and training analyst, British Psycho-analytic Society.

Paper presented to the British Psychoanalytic Society on 6 December 1995. Many colleagues at the Anna Freud Centre have contributed suggestions and ideas for this paper. I have drawn on their work and should like to express my gratitude to them for their help.

The Psychoanalytic Study of the Child 51, ed. Albert J. Solnit, Peter B. Neubauer, Samuel Abrams, and A. Scott Dowling (Yale University Press, copyright © 1996 by Albert J. Solnit, Peter B. Neubauer, Samuel Abrams, and A. Scott Dowling).

(1936). There Anna Freud discusses the many variations and diverse maneuvers the ego can use to protect itself from danger arising both from inside the individual and outside. She described how the excessive use of certain mechanisms of defense can distort reality and impoverish the ego, and she introduced a number of defenses on the basis of acute and perceptive clinical experience. In this she continued and extended the emphasis her father had come to place on the role of the ego and on the need to analyze the patient's resistances to the analytic process, particularly to the transference. In her book Anna Freud elaborated the link between resistances and the mechanisms of defense. Her ideas were not immediately acceptable to all her analytic colleagues. Thirty-six years later, discussing her book, Anna Freud commented:

> It is perhaps not quite easy for those who read the book today to grasp the atmosphere in which it was written. . . . These were the years when the introduction of the ego as such into psychoanalytic discussion or into the literature was suspect to most analysts. . . . There was quite a big body of opinion very much hostile to any attempt to deal with the ego or with ego activity as such. This was never the case in my father's writings, but it was very much so in the minds of the other analysts. I remember Helene Deutsch . . . saying that I will finish myself with analysts forever with that book because I dealt with the ego and not with the id. Of course, this is not true because I dealt with the relations between the two (Sandler and Freud, 1985, pp. 6–7).

In addition to its profound clinical implications, we can detect in Anna Freud's book on defenses her increasing interest in constructing a systematic developmental view of pathology. Thus she found it important to distinguish so-called primitive defenses from more sophisticated ones, which require more mature levels of ego functioning. One of the striking features of her work was her description and elaboration of a group of mechanisms that involved an interaction between the individual and others in his world. For instance, after commenting that identification was "one of the ego's most potent weapons in its dealings with external objects which arouse its anxiety," she described the specific mechanism of identification with the aggressor, in which the child copes with the fear of an external figure by transforming himself "from the person threatened into the person who makes the threat." And in her description of what she called "a form of altruism," Anna Freud showed how one can surrender one's own impulses and wishes in favor of those of another. This mechanism, she said, represented a combination of identification and projection, and she viewed it as a way of consolidating one's relationship with others. She saw this mechanism as typically showing itself in the form of "living through another person," exemplified by the self-sacrificing governess who satisfied her own desires by helping and encouraging members of the family she worked for to gratify these same wishes in themselves; she attained satisfaction by proxy, so to say. Today both of these mechanisms could be subsumed under the heading of projective identification.

Clearly, the interpretation of such mechanisms as identification with the aggressor and so-called altruistic surrender had great importance in the analysis of children as well as adults and influenced analytic technique considerably, particularly in increasing the emphasis on the analysis of resistances as an essential part of the analytic process. In this connection, Anna Freud spoke of the "transference of defense" and pointed out that in this form of transference analytic attention must be focused on the ego rather than on the instinctual drives and the wishes associated with them. This represented a clinically important extension of the concept of transference, which could no longer be seen as simply the repetition of instinctual cathexis from an infantile object to the person of the analyst. Years later, Anna Freud remarked, "What I point out in the book is the use of the analysis of defence to discover the ingrained defensive methods of the ego . . . the idea of the trans-ference of defence was *not* common knowledge at the time. . . . It was really a new aspect" (Sandler and Freud, pp. 41–42).

Quite apart from Anna Freud's delineation of the mechanisms of defense, a major aspect of her work from the beginning, was her insistence on the importance of direct child observation with a psychoanalytic eye. She was not content to develop psychoanalysis in the consulting room or to approach development through the reconstruction of childhood experiences on the basis of the patient's analytic material: she insisted on the importance of the interaction between child observation and psychoanalytic theory. Her observations were, of course, colored by her psychoanalytic point of view, but at the same time they influenced her psychoanalytic understanding of both developmental pathology and technique. Throughout she was concerned not only with the hypothetical psychoanalytic child within the patient in the consulting room but also with what she could learn from the observation of children.

It is well known that Anna Freud trained and practiced as a teacher before she started to see child and adult patients in analysis, and her interest in education persisted throughout her life. In 1937, when still in Vienna, Anna Freud and some colleagues were given the chance, through the generosity of an American friend, Edith Jackson, to open an experimental nursery for underprivileged children under the age of two. She saw this as a unique opportunity to learn and to test psycho-analytical ideas in an active program of day care. In January 1937 she wrote to Jackson, "They laugh at me at home, because I think and talk of babies continually and because I lead a sort of double life at the moment." A month later, in another letter to Jackson, she commented, "After a week the children seem to have made themselves much at home, there is very little crying, much activity, they eat much better, and they now have stools—the first week not a child had a stool. I am sure that it is a sign that they now feel at home. However, they do not look well, probably a result of strain the adaptation meant for them" (Young-Bruehl, 1988, p. 221).

During the war, having moved with her father to England, Anna Freud, with Dorothy Burlingham, took on the responsibility for caring for at times more than one hundred children, from newborns to five-year-olds, in residence at what was known as the Hampstead War Nurseries. As she once said, "It provided an opportunity to maintain a close connection between theory and practice, to check constantly our theoretical ideas by practical application and to widen practical handling and practical measures with the growth of theoretical knowledge" (A. Freud, 1966, p. 227).

All staff working in the War Nurseries took notes about the children's behavior. These notes were copied and filed thematically at the end of the day and were then used as source material for discussion. This method is still employed today at the Anna Freud Centre Nursery and the toddler groups.

Anna Freud's approach to child observation was deeply rooted in the developmental point of view. When she observed a child she thought not only of the child in the present but also of the history of the child's development and of the significance of what she saw for the child's later development, normal or pathological. This preoccupation was reflected in her statement in 1965:

> It is one thing for the child analyst to reconstruct a patient's past or trace back symptoms to their origins in earliest years, and quite a different one to spot pathogenic agents before they have done their work; to assess the degree of a young child's normal progress; to predict developments; to interfere with the child's management; to guide his parents; or, in general to work for the prevention of neurosis, psychosis and dissociality. While the recognised training for psychoanalytic therapy will prepare the child analyst for the former tasks, no official curriculum has been devised so far to equip him for the latter.
>
> Concern with problems such as prediction or prevention leads inevitably to a study of the normal, as opposed to the study of the patholog-

ical mental processes, or the . . . transitions between the two states with
which the analyst of adults is concerned" (pp. 54–55).

When the Hampstead War Nurseries closed after the Second World
War, Anna Freud set up the Hampstead Child Therapy Course and
Clinic (now The Anna Freud Centre) in order to provide formal and
comprehensive training in psychoanalytic work with children. Here
again, from the inception of the clinic, she saw both the clinical services
and the training as having to be rooted in the careful observation of
children of all ages who showed normal and pathological behavior. She
insisted that observation of the child's behavior, the careful study of
surface phenomena, would allow the analytically trained professional
to make inferences about the child's psychic life.

Anna Freud always claimed that she was not essentially a theoreti-
cian, and, with the benefit of hindsight, we can see that this position
gave her a degree of freedom and independence while allowing her at
the same time to retain her identification with her father's metapsychology. She was prepared—and said so specifically—to move from
one frame of reference to another as she found it convenient to do so.
Thus she moved easily between the topographical and structural theories when it seemed appropriate, resisting the pressure of her American ego-psychological colleagues to encompass all psychoanalytic
propositions within structural theory. At the same time she found no
contradiction between using the framework of psychosexual phases
and simultaneously using other developmental frameworks that took
account of different aspects of mental growth as observed in the child.

For decades Freud's schema of psychosexual phases, as spelled out in
his "Three Essays on the Theory of Sexuality" (1905), had provided the
essential and fundamental framework for the psychoanalytic theory of
development. Freud's approach had been from the side of the libido,
and he had taken the view that neurosis in adults was the negative of
the perversion—that is, the outcome of the revival of so-called perverse
sexual wishes that originated in childhood and represented impulses
from early psychosexual phases. During the course of the individual's
development, these wishes had become unacceptable and a source of
the inner conflict that led to neurosis. Psychoanalysts tended to see the
libidinal stages—oral, anal, phallic-oedipal, and so on—as the appropriate phases relevant to the normal and pathological processes in all
areas of child development. For many, the psychosexual phases represented *the* psychoanalytic theory of development. Anna Freud became
increasingly aware of the inadequacy of the libidinal phases as a frame-

work for viewing all aspects of development and pathology in child-hood. It was clear to her, for example, that the classical libidinal phases did not adequately fit the development of aggression in the child, nor were they entirely suitable for a developmental categorization of the child's object relationships; they were certainly an insufficient basis for understanding the complexity of ego and superego development. From the point of view of pathology, it was increasingly evident that not all disturbed children suffered from neurotic pathology—that is to say, from the consequence of a drive resulting from unresolvable oedipal conflict, with the subsequent emergence of symptoms as compromise formations between revived pre-oedipal instinctual wishes and unregressed ego and superego constraints.

Anna Freud's awareness of the limitations of the classical psychosexual theory of development led her to offer a brilliant solution to the problem, by introducing the concept of lines of development (see A. Freud, 1965). This solution, while not contradicting the idea of libidinal-phase development, allowed it to be supplemented in a way that avoided the restrictions inherent in the classical view.

The developmental lines were based on the central idea that detailed observations of the child's behavior, the careful study of surface phenomena, were to allow the analytically trained professional to make inferences about the functioning of the child's inner life. Anna Freud constantly reiterated that one had to move from what could be observed to the intrapsychic, and this approach was exemplified in her idea of steps in development that could be used as surface markers of normality or pathology in the growing child. In this connection, Anna Freud commented, "Whatever level has been reached by any given child in any of these respects the developmental [lines] represents the results of interaction between drive and ego-superego development and their reaction to environmental influences, i.e., between maturation, adaptation and structuralisation. Far from being theoretical abstractions, developmental lines, in the sense here used are historical realities, which, when assembled, convey a convincing picture of an individual child's personal achievement or, on the other hand, of his failures in personality development" (1965, p. 64).

As a prototype of a developmental line, Anna Freud described a sequence leading from the newborn's utter dependence on maternal care to the young adult's emotional and material self-reliance. Other lines described by Anna Freud concerned bodily independence and delineated the progression from suckling to rational eating, characterized by the following steps: being nursed at the breast or bottle;

being able to tolerate weaning; the transition from being fed to self-feeding; the use of the spoon and fork; and so on. Further developmental lines ranged from dependency to emotional self-reliance, from body to toy and from play to work, from egocentricity to companionship, from wetting and soiling to bladder and bowel control, and from irresponsibility to responsibility in body management. Although she described the steps in each of these developmental lines much more fully than I can do here, their relation to discrete observational phenomena is clear. The developmental lines were not limited in number; other lines can be added as our experience in linking significant surface phenomena to the depths increases.

Anna Freud showed how the use of the developmental lines enables us to see the interactions between and interdependence of maturational (internal) and environmental (external) determinants and how each interference will leave its mark on the individual's personality. The developmental lines provide a series of predictable, interlocking, overlapping, unfolding pathways that are characteristic of each child's development.

The developmental lines enable the psychoanalytic diagnostician to look at a specific child and—with the *Diagnostic Profile,* another instrument devised by Anna Freud—to try to assess the normal and the pathological components in that child's mental and physical life. Briefly, the Profile is an organized set of headings that is essentially a set of metapsychologically framed assessments. As Anna Freud put it: "In the analyst's mind, the whole bulk of material collected during the diagnostic procedure organizes itself into what may be called a comprehensive metapsychological profile of the child, i.e., a picture which contains dynamic, genetic, economic, structural and adaptive data. This can be seen as the analyst's synthetic effort when dealing with disparate findings, or, conversely, as showing his diagnostic thinking broken up analytically into its component parts" (1965, pp. 139–140).

Once a systematic profile of a child had been constructed, a developmental diagnosis could be made. Anna Freud differentiated very clearly between childhood neurosis and developmental disturbances and believed that the same technical approach was not always entirely suitable for both groups of disturbance. In her 1974 paper on "A psychoanalytic view of developmental psychopathology" she clearly said:

> If we accept the view that childhood psychopathology has a twofold causation, one rooted in the conflicts, defence and compromise formations, the other in the developmental processes, we have no reason to believe that the same therapeutic measures will be equally effective for

both. We are on familiar analytic ground with the conflictual-neurotic pathology where interpretation lifts repressed or otherwise defended material into consciousness and helps the child's ego to find solutions for his internal struggles, which are no longer based on anxiety, panic and infantile misapprehensions of reality. . . . But so far as the developmental process itself is defective or unbalanced due either to innate or to environmental conditions, we cannot expect interpretation to undo the damage, even if it clarifies the past and may help the child towards better ways of facing and coping with its consequences. If, in spite of that, children also profit from analysis in this respect, such success may be due not to the truly analytic work but to admixtures to the technique such as new positive object attachment, new superego identification, suggestive influence, or even corrective emotional experience which with the very young can set arrested developmental lines going again (1974, p. 72).

Anna Freud always underlined the view that the diagnostic heading "developmental disturbance" relates to a wide spectrum of pathology, from the normal to the most disturbed.[1] We are all aware that young children go through transitory developmental upsets, particularly in the areas of feeding and sleeping. Many young children present delays in motor development, speech, the achievement of cleanliness, the appropriate control of aggression, and reaching age-appropriate readiness for formal learning. In most cases these problems disappear in the course of development, especially if the environment handles them in a "good enough" manner. They can be regarded as a temporary response to conflict between the child and the external world, well within the limits of normality; and thus, in Anna Freud's view, they would not require treatment for the child—mother guidance could be envisaged in certain cases.

The diagnostic picture in cases of persisting developmental disturbance is different from what can be observed in "normal" transitory upsets. Anna Freud was particularly aware of the consequences of unevenness in development and frequently stated that developmental disharmonies provided fertile ground for enduring psychological disturbances.

Anna Freud placed children with developmental arrest—that is, borderline children, children with psychotic or autistic features, and children presenting atypical symptoms—at the pathological end of the

1. For a number of years a group of colleagues at the Anna Freud Centre, led by Peter Fonagy (and, before his death, by George Moran) has been preparing a manual of child psychoanalytic technique for purposes of outcome research. Particular emphasis has been placed on the presenting symptoms, psychopathology, and variations in technique appropriate to the treatment of developmental disturbances.

spectrum of developmental disturbances. Children who have been the victims of exceptional environmental conditions, such as abuse and other traumatic experiences, also frequently show signs of developmental disturbance. All these children seem to suffer from deficient structuralization of their egos, poorly defined mental representations, and difficulty in distinguishing fantasy from reality. They are often overwhelmed by affects, lack internal sources of safety and suffer from poor frustration tolerance and impulse control. It should be emphasized, however, that for the most part they show a combination of developmental disturbance and neurotic pathology.

Many children with developmental disharmonies tend not to have age-appropriate object relationships and have difficulty acquiring object constancy and a stable sense of self. Their peer relationships are frequently disturbed and their capacity for awareness of other people and their needs is deficient—for example, a child may see others as there only to fulfill his wishes. Self-esteem is a particular problem. Their self-representations may be damaged, often having been distorted by defensive grandiosity; further, their capacity for self-object separateness may be flawed and inadequate. They may show problems in cognitive functioning, such as magical thinking, limited attention span, memory problems, and distorted perception of causality. Verbal understanding and the experiencing as well as the communication of emotions often seem to be faulty; moreover, awareness of an emotional capacity in others may be impaired.

On the surface, the symptoms of these children sometimes resemble those we see in severely neurotic children with phobias and other forms of heightened anxiety, obsessional manifestations, specific avoidances and inhibitions, and regressive behavior. But while the neurotic child tends to respond positively to a classical analytic approach, we have found that the children with developmental disturbances do not; consequently we have to modify our technical procedures with these youngsters. As Anna Freud (1965) put it, "As we move away from the conflict-based neurotic disorders to the arrests, defects, and deficiencies of development, the therapeutic process changes its nature." (p. 227). And as late as 1978, Anna Freud made it clear that she did not yet feel confident that appropriate methods had been devised for the analytic treatment of children with developmental disorders. She wrote, "The study of purely developmental aspects has not been taken up very seriously in child analysis so far. At least, it is still waiting to advance from the realm of mere observation and description of facts to their application to the technique of treatment. . . . To the extent to which developmental harm can be undone belatedly, child analysis may accept it as its next duty to devise methods for the task" (pp. 108–109).

Throughout her writings Anna Freud made it clear that certain technical procedures that were not strictly analytic had their place in child analysis, especially for children with non-neurotic disorders. She did not hesitate to advocate the use of educational methods with children whose egos are easily overwhelmed and who would often misunderstand interpretation as an invitation to act out. Anna Freud very early spoke of the special difficulties such cases posed to the child analyst: "the analyst accordingly combines in his own person two different and diametrically opposed functions: he has to analyse and educate, that is to say in the same breath he must allow and forbid, loosen and bind again" (1926, p. 49). She also acknowledged that developmental help at times involved praise, suggestion, and reassurance.

Let me present a vignette to give some flavor of the approach taken by those working with Anna Freud. There was much concern about the acute anxiety that many of the children with developmental disturbance displayed, particularly at the beginning of treatment. Their impulsive, aggressive, and often dangerous and provocative behavior did not respond to interpretation. What was needed, it seemed, was an adult who could be seen and felt as willing and able to protect the child from external dangers and from the blind acting out of impulses. The thought was that only when the child had a sense of safety could interpretative work begin. There were, however, always questions regarding the interpretation of aggression and aggressive fantasies as opposed to ego-supportive handling, and it seemed clear that the real question was one of balance and timing.

Carlo, aged six-and-a-half, initially enacted his feelings of helplessness by identifying with a train engine, which he saw as the most powerful vehicle in existence, immune to all danger. The engine was never to be allowed to run dry, so Carlo drank large quantities of water throughout the hour and urinated freely in the session. To prove that the engine remained powerful he climbed onto the window sill while whistling shrilly like an engine. He pulled down the curtains and said he was going to jump through the window. The therapist thought that Carlo might carry out this threat, because he appeared not to acknowledge danger and insisted that his powerful train could never be damaged. The therapist introduced the idea that really powerful engines have brakes and that strength meant being able to use these brakes to stop and start whenever the engine wanted to. Gradually Carlo's game changed to one in which he would turn his brakes on and off and stop at stations to let people in and out. This provided welcome intervals during which the therapist could start giving explanations and interpretations. The engine game was elaborated by the introduction of a mechanic who wanted to understand how the train worked so that he could prevent breakdowns and damage.

Because many children with developmental disturbances have problems in communicating with others and do so on a primitive or chaotic level, the analyst will need much ingenuity in trying to establish contact with them. Sometimes simple games of the sort that mothers use with infants and toddlers will open the way to more viable forms of communication. Sessions five times weekly are appropriate for these children as the analyst needs to become a predictable, safe, and reliable figure. The frequency of sessions is intended to help the child develop an intimate relationship with the analyst, a new object of particular importance to the child. The analyst aims to function as the child's auxiliary ego, helping him to control his impulsive behavior, and to give meaning to events and actions. Clarifications and interpretations will encourage discrimination between reality and fantasy, and the introduction of appropriate language to describe states of mind is aimed at controlling affect, facilitating reasoning and the understanding of causality. The disentangling of fantasy and reality is particularly important in work with children who have experienced actual abuse. Abuse may serve to exacerbate frightening fantasies, which heighten the child's anxiety to a point that his capacity to regulate affect is diminished or overwhelmed.

The aim of analytic work with such patients may be not the provision of insight but rather to establish a situation in which it gradually becomes safe for the child to begin to understand himself and others and to experience affects without being overwhelmed or forced to carry them over into action. However, if negative transferences are not interpreted early, hostile affects may quickly become overwhelming, threatening the new relationship. The interpretation of the transference is essential because of the excessive projection characteristic of these patients. The combination of the containment of projections through transference interpretations and the relative safety of the alternative relationship to the analyst creates the opportunity for the child to benefit from the analyst's understanding through identification and internalization. Furthermore, the analyst's understanding and verbalization of the child's non-verbal communications are important in helping the child to comprehend his own mental states. The analyst acts as a model for the thinking capacity the child lacks, by verbalizing it as well as by relating to it.

In recent years, we at The Anna Freud Centre have come to think that in a number of children with developmental disturbances, the development of specific mental processes has been defensively inhibited in an attempt to cope with unmanageable environmental pressures or unbearable inner states (Fonagy and Moran, 1991; Fonagy et al., 1993). The therapeutic approach will thus need to be aimed at freeing the inhibition of the relevant mental processes. The main thrust of the work is to give content and meaning to the children's feelings and fantasies by creating a coherent narrative and by labeling their mental states, emotions, and thoughts whenever possible. To achieve this the analyst will also at times spell out her own thought processes and feeling states concerning events in and around sessions, and the child himself. Thus children who have difficulty acquiring the notion of mutuality may be helped by hearing the analyst verbalize her own thoughts and feelings of, for example, being excluded, ignored, or teased in a game. This material is later presented to the child as relating to his own feelings as well. All such measures represent attempts to provide the child with a structure to put certain derailed thought processes back on the rails, so as to increase the chances of further, more normal development.

Anna Freud was strongly opposed to the blind application of a technique for work with children that simply mirrored adult psychoanalytic technique. For her, what was most appropriate was that which offered the greatest hope for restoring the child to the path of normal development. She stimulated us to examine more closely the specific elements of psychoanalytic technique necessary for the treatment of an individual child, and inevitably this has prompted us to look more closely at the technical implications of analytic work—not only with children but also with adults. One of the conclusions we can draw is that there is no hard and fast dividing line, in the analysis of children or of adults, between pure interpretation and developmental help.

It is worth singling out an aspect of development that may or may not be regarded as pathological but that is clearly relevant to the evaluation and treatment of adults and children. This relates to what Anna Freud referred to as "ego restriction." In her view, this mechanism, which superficially resembles a neurotic inhibition or phobic avoidance, is in fact something quite different, representing what is in many ways a normal developmental process that may or may not lead to pathology. Restriction of the ego is a consequence of the child's giving up interest or participation in certain areas of activity because they are not pleasurable and turning instead to areas that are more gratifying. As Anna Freud said, "Restriction of the ego deals with unpleasurable affect that is aroused by external experience. The idea is that after the child has once had the experience that such an affect can be aroused, the easiest thing for him is not to enter into the same situation again . . . this is by no means a neurotic mechanism, but really one of the mechanisms which help us to build up our different personalities. From the earliest time there is more or less automatic avoidance of the disagreeable, and after all why *should* we have disagreeable experiences? The ego feels that there are other things that one can do instead" (Sandler and Freud, 1985, pp. 359–360).

The notion of ego restriction is exemplified by remarks that Anna Freud made in a seminar. She recalled from her own experience a boy whose aggressive and competitive tendencies, especially in games with other boys and a little later on the football field, were inhibited by enormous fear of injury. So he turned toward intellectual activities, which became highly developed and through which he felt able to be competitive without having to face the anxiety he felt on the football field. Anna Freud added that she did not think he ever, in spite of analysis, restarted the physical activities he had given up; the capacities involved were not actively inhibited but became merely unused.

This experience from child analysis has implications for analytic work with adult patients, as it underlines the importance of differentiating among neurotic inhibition, phobic avoidance, and ego restriction. There are parts of the personality that even the best conducted analysis cannot reach.

In this paper I have been able to touch on only a few of Anna Freud's contributions to psychoanalysis. However, there is one significant area of her work that has to be emphasized. I refer here to her role both as a teacher—in this regard she was quite outstanding—and as a promoter and facilitator of psychoanalytic clinical and conceptual research. From the inception of the Hampstead Clinic, Anna Freud set up and encouraged research groups that met weekly to consider special topics. These groups continued for years and produced a remarkable number of contributions to the psychoanalytic literature, advancing our knowledge both clinically and theoretically. One such group was formed for the study of adopted children and their parents. Another studied clinical and theoretical concepts. There were groups for the study of pre- and early adolescence, of congenitally blind children, of borderline and atypical children, of psychoanalytic psychiatry, of the Diagnostic Profile. A special group was concerned with emotional problems in children with chronic diabetes. There was also a substantial project known as the Hampstead Index, which had a variety of specific subgroups attached to it. The techniques evolved in these research groups have been applied elsewhere, as, for example, in a study of trauma conducted at the Sigmund-Freud Institut in Frankfurt (Sandler et al., 1991). Current projects at the Anna Freud Centre include research on the efficacy and outcome of child psychoanalysis, on the study of attachment in parents and children during the first eighteen months of the child's life, on children's theories of emotion, and on mental representations in young children who have an abusive or disrupted background. An extensive project is under way on the analysis of a number of young adults with severe difficulties in achieving the transition from adolescence to adulthood.

I conclude by saying that I belong to a generation of analysts who have been profoundly influenced in their psychoanalytic understanding and clinical practice by the work of Anna Freud and who have been able to build on the foundation she established. The practical humanity with which she approached each patient was always impressive and shone through in the way she approached the problems presented in the analyses of children at the Clinic.

BIBLIOGRAPHY

Fonagy, P., Edgecumbe R., Moran, G., Kennedy, H., & Target, M. (1993). The roles of mental representation and mental processes in therapeutic action. *The Psychoanalytic Study of the Child*, 48:9–48.

Fonagy, P., & Moran, G. S. (1991). Understanding psychic change in child analysis. *Int. J. Psycho-Anal.*, 78:15–22.

Freud, A. (1926). *The Psycho-Analytical Treatment of Children*. London: Imago, 1946.

Freud, A. (1936). *The Ego and the Mechanisms of Defense*. London: Hogarth.

Freud, A. (1965). *Normality and Pathology in Childhood*. New York: International Universities Press.

Freud, A. (1966). Residential versus foster care. In *Problems of Psychoanalytic Training, Diagnosis, and the Technique of Therapy*. London: Hogarth. pp. 223–239.

Freud, A. (1974). A psychoanalytic view of developmental pathology. In *The Writings of Anna Freud, Vol. VIII*. New York: International Universities Press, 1981.

Freud, A. (1978). The principal task of child analysis. In *The Writings of Anna Freud Vol. VIII*. New York: International Universities Press, 1981.

Freud, S. (1905). *Three Essays on the Theory of Sexuality*. Standard Edition, 7.

Rosenfeld, S. K., & Sprince, M. P. (1965). Some thoughts on the technical handling of borderline children. *The Psychoanalytic Study of the Child*, 20:495–517.

SANDLER, J., DREHER, A. U., & DREWS, S. (1991). An approach to conceptual research in psychoanalysis illustrated by a consideration of psychic trauma. *Int. J. Psycho-Anal.*, 18:133–141.

SANDLER, J., & FREUD, A. (1985). *The Analysis of Defense: The Ego and the Mechanisms of Defense Revisited.* New York: International Universities Press.

WALLERSTEIN, R. S. (1984). Anna Freud: Radical innovator and staunch conservative. *The Psychoanalytic Study of the Child*, 39:65–80.

YOUNG-BRUEHL, E. (1988). *Anna Freud: A Biography.* New York: Summit Books.

CLINICAL CONTRIBUTIONS

Trauma and the Developmental Process

Excerpts from an Analysis of an Adopted Child

SHLOMITH COHEN, PH.D.

The adopted child faces a complex developmental task. Having a vital need for a parent, he has to deal with the traumatic loss of one set of parents and at the same time has to allow new, alien adults to become his parents. Some implications of this life situation on the developing representations of self and other and on self-other relations are explored in the three-year course of psychoanalysis of a five-and-a-half-year-old boy.

THE FACTORS THAT MAKE ADOPTION A MENTAL HEALTH RISK (BRINICH, 1980) are numerous. The adopted baby is typically born to maladjustive parents who cannot provide for him and have to give him away. Pregnancy might be unwanted, or the baby may not be cared for in other ways. The baby might have a poor attachment with parental figures that cannot take care of him. Neglect or abuse might be the cause for adoption, which in turn brings about a traumatic separation and loss. And being adopted, the child is raised by adoptive parents with their own histories of frustration and loss that bring them to actualize their parenthood through adoption. From a psychoanalytic perspective, these factors also serve as sources of anxiety for both the

Member, Israel Psychoanalytic Society; faculty, Israel Institute of Psychoanalysis.

This paper is based on a presentation to the Israel Psychoanalytic Society in spring 1994.

The Psychoanalytic Study of the Child 51, ed. Albert J. Solnit, Peter B. Neubauer, Samuel Abrams, and A. Scott Dowling (Yale University Press, copyright © 1996 by Albert J. Solnit, Peter B. Neubauer, Samuel Abrams, and A. Scott Dowling).

adopted child and the adoptive parents, and may become themes in the fantasy life of the persons involved and in the development of their relationships within the family. The exploration of adoption in psycho-analysis enables us to see the interrelationships of these factors as they come together to shape the development of a particular child.⁾

Adoption may be particularly illuminating with regard to the highly complex function of parenting in the development of a child (Col-arusso, 1987). It is evident that a child has a vital need for a parent. Theories differ in the ways in which the child conceptualizes this basic need, ranging from the need for satisfaction of drives to the need for the object's love to the need for the parent to enhance the cohesiveness of the self. Nevertheless, all agree on the child's need for an adult who focuses on her needs.

Goldstein et al. (1986) stress that the parents' uniqueness lies in their total involvement with their child. The child knows that the parent is *her* parent. This may be called a sense of belonging, of merging with a parent who should provide appropriate holding and containing. Dif-ferent terms are used in different theoretical frameworks to capture the very basic sense of being born to a caring parent, not to an environ-ment that is alien and indifferent to one's existence.

Our psychological investigations and therapeutic endeavors often oblige us to deal with pathology concerning the process of individua-tion. This process involves needing the parent less and less in dealing with frustration and anxiety. The adoption of older children provides an opportunity to follow development that proceeds in the opposite direction—the process of becoming somebody's child and hence of transforming an alien adult into a parent. This process occurs naturally at the beginning of life, when the baby has the need and capacity to form a relationship with the parent, and the parent is ready to enter into the relationship. When we meet a child who is adopted later in life, we find him attempting to form a relationship with a parent after having experienced a complex of feelings toward parental figures who have disappeared from his life. The case of late adoption allows us to investigate the child-parent relationship from two viewpoints at the same time: that of trauma, when parenting has been disrupted, and that of development, the processes involved in building a parent-child relationship. To what extent may we consider the later process as analo-gous to the earlier one, and the new relationships as equivalent to the primary parent-child relationships?[1]

From a theoretical perspective, we are dealing with the relationship between the experience of an actual relation with actual external ob-

---

1. From the Kleinian point of view it is a question of reparation vs. development.

jects and the construction of an internal object that is part of the child's internal representational system (Solnit, 1982). In the case of adoption the actual relations change at least once while the internal representation of the parents is being formed. In exploring the internal experience of an adopted person, we may, then, look at the self and the objects from a different angle that may help us differentiate internal from external reality. A better differentiation may also help us learn more about the constructive processes of the self and the object—two key configurations in inner reality (Green, 1972; Loewald, 1973).

A Clinical Case

Danny, age five and a half, was referred to therapy by the psychologist of the special education nursery he attended. Danny could not participate in the school's activities. He was tense and restless and developed no relationship with his teachers. He was considered intellectually normal but was difficult to evaluate more specifically because he resisted contact with his teachers.

History. Danny had been adopted at age three by a couple who could not have children of their own. Little information was available to his adoptive parents or to me about Danny's life prior to the adoption. He lived with his biological parents for the first year and was taken to a sheltered home apparently because of physical abuse and neglect. His mother had lost interest in him. His father kept in touch with him while he was in the home, but when he was given to his adoptive parents the biological father was considered dangerous and the child had to be sneaked away from him. Danny seemed to have some memories of his father's visits at the children's home.

At three years old, Danny did not talk. In the beginning he played a lot at being a dog who hides in the house and asks to be allowed in. He was not fully toilet trained but easily yielded to toilet training during the day. Yet, to his mother's distress, he was not successful during the night. No eating or sleeping problems were noted by the parents, and no fears, except some fear of strangers.

The parents were warm, gentle, and intelligent. Their inability to bear children could not be solved medically, and they were united in the decision to adopt. Both came from loving families who were basically supportive of the adoption and helpful with Danny. Wishing to have a child soon, the parents agreed to adopt an older child. When they came to therapy, both parents were denying the effect of lacking the parent-baby experiences in their bond with Danny. This was especially true of the mother. They needed a few months in treatment to become aware of this emotional fact, an awareness that encouraged them to adopt a second child, a baby.

First Contact—Evaluation. Danny came to his first session alone. He had convinced his mother that he did not need an escort, so she went with him to the gate and then left.

Danny ran in, looked around for a second, went to the toys on the other side of the room, and picked up a gun. I said something about his being in a new place with a strange woman, but there was no reaction: no smile or sign of relief. Danny then shot me with the toy gun. After a few more attempts to talk about fear in the new situation, while Danny repeatedly shot me, I entered the game and played being hurt and then fell dead. This response brought laughter, which sounded like a dog barking. The game was repeated a few more times, and soon Danny was throwing things all over the place, almost at the point of breaking things and hurting me and himself. I then introduced other toys that seemed less harmful and fragile and pushed aside the riskier ones, but the pattern did not change—a few seconds of manipulation of toys ended with his throwing and breaking them. No relating to his fear of a new person and a new situation could create a bridge between me and the wild child. He was like an untamed little savage. Before our time was up Danny became eager to see his mother and ran downstairs to wait for her. I accompanied him.

Upon meeting his mother Danny gave no sign of stress or complaint. All the anxiety seemed to have been only my experience. Another meeting was needed before I could further evaluate Danny and thus make recommendations.

The next meeting started a bit more calmly. Danny ran in again, telling his mother that she could leave. Again he picked up the guns and touched a few other toys with some sense of recognition. But soon his restlessness took over. He was upset that the ball he had seen at the previous session had disappeared. He was not relieved by my explanation, and he would not stay in the room with me. No reflection of anxiety had any relieving effect. As Danny wanted to go downstairs to play, I agreed. Once there, he started running away and into the street and did not allow me to come close to him, making me tense and afraid of losing control over the situation. After a while he came back and started to play with the door of the building—me outside and him inside, opening the door for me and closing it. Something about the interaction reminded me of the first few minutes of our meeting—of my coming down and greeting Danny and his mother. It was the only moment of joy Danny had had in our time together—when he shot the gun at me and I played dead. I felt he had put me in a position in which

I had to see things from his standpoint, with him in control. So I decided to take up his role.

I said: "I am Danny now. I want to go in but the door is locked. Let me in. I am scared to be alone here. I have to come in. You are so strong and I am so afraid. Let me in." In that moment Danny changed as if by magic. He said: "I am Shlomith." I was amazed that he knew my name. He came to me, told me not to be afraid, and gave me his hand. Until that moment no physical contact with him was possible. I said I wanted to go and see her (Shlomith's) room but I was afraid of the many new and unknown things there. He gave me his hand, reassured me that there was no need to be afraid, and led me in. After a few minutes he became restless again and wanted to go outside for a stroll. I said I was afraid of the cars and of getting lost and hurt. Again he gave me his hand gently and reassured me, and we went out together.[2]

To my great surprise, when his mother came to pick him up she looked around at the room and said. "I see you had a very nice time," and Danny agreed.

I have paid detailed attention to the beginning of my contact with Danny, because it contained most of the motifs that occupied us in our efforts to communicate therapeutically:

1. Danny may be a wild, frightening child who has no mercy on humans or objects and may hurt them with or without intention.
2. Danny has an extraordinary capacity for imagination and pretense and can use it anywhere, at any time, and seemingly with anyone.
3. Danny may be remarkably gentle in relating to a weak person who is not himself.
4. Danny may have astonishing trust for a caring adult, alongside a great fear of her.
5. The content that was introduced (by me, following cues from Danny) was of wanting to be accepted, the urge and the fear in wishing to be let into the home of a strange woman.
6. Meeting with Danny involves a high level of emotional intensity that is difficult to contain in a regular therapeutic setting. The first dilemma for the therapist, then, had to do with the need to ensure her containing capacity so that she could meet Danny's excessive needs and emotions, which were so immediately directed toward her.

Considering Danny's capacity for play, on the one hand, and his disturbance in emotional expression and in relating to others, on the other hand, psychoanalysis was recommended.

2. Abrams (1991) describes a similar experience in the first contact with a girl who had suffered a history of abandonments and losses. Being deaf, Abrams's patient raised other problems of communication.

Danny demonstrated that his preferred communication would be with someone who was ready to see through his aggressive shield and reach out to his scared and longing core. He also seemed to relate only to someone who was ready to respect and share his fantasy world. This could be accomplished best in intensive treatment. From a diagnostic point of view, Danny's immediate response to an intervention that contained a playful element served as a testimony to ego strength with the potential for internalization and sublimation, on which the psychoanalytic process can rely. Another consideration was related to Danny's parents, who could be trusted to provide the necessary support for analytic treatment.[3]

Danny started four-times-a-week analysis. From the start he presented a blend of a high-intensity wish for contact with the therapist and with the room and its contents, along with a total disregard of what could happen to them as a result of his behavior. The close contact was physical and contained reliance on the therapist and at the same time fear of her. For example, in the first session, after throwing things all over the place Danny asked me to hold him while he jumped from a high spot onto a pile of pillows. Then he continued to throw things, and when I hugged him to stop his destructive behavior he started to cry because he had hurt his finger.

A few sessions later Danny climbed to a dangerous spot in the hallway, ignoring my warnings. Then he asked for my hand and immediately started to cry: "You are knocking me down. You are knocking me down." I was taken by surprise by his confusion of protection and threat. But soon afterward a stranger came by and Danny resorted to the behavior of an interested and curious child. By this move he showed that he was pretending within a situation of play—that he was recounting a hurtful experience while actually feeling safe. At the same time he was demonstrating how blurred the boundary was for him between the experience of safety and of danger *with the same object.*

For a long time, physical contact was the only way to restrain and protect Danny when he was agitated. It seemed as if he was protesting furiously against being in charge of his own restraint. For example, using the dollhouse, he pushed all the dolls into a corner and tried forcibly to find a way to get himself into the house or at least on its roof. The fact that the house was too flimsy to bear his weight only added to his fury. I had to limit Danny's efforts in order to prevent him from breaking the house. Thus, he experienced the therapist as providing and forbidding at the same time.

There were many ways in which Danny felt the therapeutic situation

3. On the importance of parents' cooperation see Weider, 1978, and Colarusso, 1987.

as both enabling and frustrating. He increasingly expressed his wish to be a baby to a mother who does not abandon him; yet, he often confronted realistic limits to the fulfillment of his wish. Coming to the session and leaving the room at the end of the session were experienced as abandonment, reasons for distrust, and arousal of great rage. There was no consolation for abandonment. For instance, he could not leave the play materials I had prepared for him behind in his box, knowing that he would meet them again in the next session. Rather, he put them into his bag and destroyed the box.

Danny did not allow me any way of avoiding a fully direct contact with him. The attack was on the abandoning mother. He could not use any symbolic representation of mother as a consolation in her absence. Any substitution of the real relationship of baby and mother was felt as a cheat, to be destroyed. The new good object was experienced as seductive and dangerous. In the playroom I offered Danny a large doll, with which, I assumed, he could feel safe playing and being aggressive. But within a few minutes he stabbed it murderously. He and I were often left alone with no mediation. There was no transitional space that contained us and protected us from the unbearable reality of destruction and pain.

In this chaotic period I participated mainly by protecting Danny and the room from his violence and, secondly, by increasingly taking on the role of the confused, helpless, lost child who is eager to get to the therapist but is stopped in many ways. In the role of the adult, Danny was frustrating but also considerate, as he was in our first encounter.

FORMING THE EXPERIENCE OF THE MOTHER-BABY BOND

From the beginning Danny made it clear that he could not afford to experience himself as a needy baby who expects a mother. The prohibition of this anticipation left him with unbearable chaos. In the therapy the infantile wish for mother came to life through a complex process.

After about two months in therapy the parents reported that Danny was not eating at home or at school. Gradually it became clear that this was his way of expressing his wish to stop growing, or, rather, to become a baby again. At this point Danny's mother remembered how when he arrived as a three-year-old child, she did not comply with his wish to have a baby bottle and insisted that he eat as a grown child. This was an opportunity in the therapeutic contact with the parents to touch on some of their feelings of loss over not having received Danny as an infant and not being able to conceive an infant of their own. The parents acknowledged their feelings of loss and frustration as they increased their tolerance of Danny's longings to be a baby for his adoptive parents.

Regression took place mainly through body sensations. Danny wanted to be carried, touched, and caressed. He created situations where he had to be carried, letting me feel his full weight. Yet, Danny was only a baby waiting to be soothed. Touching was also loaded with sexual feelings, thus being at the same time exciting and dangerous. As a consequence, in setting limits to the actualization of sensual engagement, the therapist was again experienced as both frustrating and rejecting.

To express the complexity of his emotions concerning his wish to be a baby to a caring mother, Danny started to urinate and defecate on the floor of the playroom. This behavior introduced a new challenge to the therapeutic situation and raised questions of management. It was clear that Danny had found a way to bypass the control of the therapist, demonstrating his control over his excretions. The dilemma of the therapist came down to the question of whether to stop the session when this behavior occurred or take it as an expression of an inner state that had to be worked through like any other expression in the therapeutic situation. The urgency of this behavior and Danny's limited options of expression both within and outside the analysis persuaded me to find ways of dealing with the excretions in the room without breaking the session. (The therapist's own tolerance played a role in this decision.)

From the start this behavior conveyed the meaning of retaliation and punishment of a bad mother, but other elements entered the scene. Danny resented my insistence on cleaning the floor and accepted the interpretation that he wanted his products to be accepted and enjoyed, not thrown into the toilet. This point is illustrated by a vignette from the last part of a session, ten months into the analysis: In the play I was a bad mother who could not protect her baby from being hurt by a dangerous driver. This led to interruption, and I actually became "bad" by forbidding Danny to play with a ball in a destructive way. Danny snatches the ball and runs to the toilet.

D. calls me into the bathroom to show me how he can throw things through the window.

> S. You want to see what happens to things that fall out? Maybe you also want to know what happens to the peepee and kaka that disappear in the hole of the toilet. Maybe you think that this also happened to the baby Danny who fell out of mother's tummy and got lost.

D. I am a kaka boy. I came out from the behind.

S. If you came out from the behind like kaka, then you are afraid that it can happen to you like to the kaka, that Mommy and Daddy and Shlomith will not want you.

For Danny to become the baby means reviving an abandoning mother who treated him like excrement—something that came out of the body and was doomed to be thrown away.

Now the task of the therapy is to help Danny develop confidence in his worth, in not being disposable, but in having inherent value. At this stage in Danny's experience being accepted as a urinating baby stands for acceptance of him.

One year and one month into the analysis:

D., at the door, is very upset, reluctant to come in. Has a pink elephant doll that he calls "Shira," which is alternatively his baby and his baby sister. In the room he immediately starts a war with me, pees and defecates.

S. There is a war today between us. You are very angry with me.

D. runs to his mother and demands some food that she has in her bag. He wants her to be with us in the playroom and I support him, feeling that he cannot stay alone with me. In the playroom he lies on the table like a baby and wants Mom to feed him.

S. Danny wants so much to feel like Mom's baby. But when he comes to Shlomith and feels like a baby with me he is not so sure any more that he is Mom's baby.

D. wants to cover Mom's eyes and make a surprise. Gets under the table, and pieces of clothing are thrown into the room. Danny actually succeeds in surprising us when he comes out fully naked.

S. Surprise! A new baby was born now. You want to really be the new baby from the beginning, naked as it comes out of Mom's belly. But there is a rule that we do not play naked here, and you will have to get dressed.

D. becomes very upset, runs away from his mother so she won't make him get dressed. He plays with a chain he had in his hand, tightening it around his penis. He pees, wants to pee on Mom and on the pillows, runs into the toilet with me and invites me to touch his kaka.

S. I am not playing with the kaka, but I see how much you want me to play with you.

D. is very wild, runs back to the room and hurts his Mom; he kicks, bites, hits with his fists. She leaves the room and I stay with Danny, as we had agreed before.

S. It is so confusing to be Mom's baby and Shlomith's baby at the same time.

D. cries furiously while I am sitting beside him. He screams: "You are a liar! You are a liar!"

S. You feel that I lie when I let you feel like a baby, like my baby, that I protect you and love you, and then I set all these limits and say that you cannot pee everywhere, you cannot be naked, you have to leave me at the end of the hour. You feel that I lie to you and you cannot really be the baby that you want so much to be.

D.'s cries become deep and has changed from rage to despair. After a few minutes he asks for the time, which is about the end of the session, and tells me to call Mom. He has difficulty getting ready to go.

Coming to terms with what he cannot experience in reality is painful for Danny and a source of countertransference reactions for me. Some reconciliation with the reality of loss and absence had to occur before the process of symbolization and formation of an internal mother-child bond could continue. Now bonding was represented in a rope, in a thread of yarn, in adhesive tape, or in toilet paper. All these materials were used alternately to tie me and Danny together, to bridge the distance between us, but mainly to make him mine—my puppy, my baby.

As therapy developed, Danny continued to want to be my baby, to be born from me, to feel inside me. On one occasion he lay on my lap and covered himself with a blanket. He pretended I was pregnant with a goat's kid, telling how I feel my baby inside my womb. Birth created a dangerous situation. Now the kid also felt threatened by the one who had him inside her.

Danny played many variations on the theme of the dangers of pregnancy and birth and of the longings for a gentle, caring mother. Yet, the theme of the beginning of life brought us back into the story of mother-baby bond.

Another vignette, a few months later.

Danny creates a scene where he is a baby and I am a woman who wants to slaughter and eat it. I found this a difficult role to play, feeling like the witch in Hansel and Gretel. Yet to my surprise the baby-Danny is not frightened. He comes willingly to the woman and waits eagerly to be eaten. This unexpected emotional response mobilizes me to see the eating experience in a new light, hence my interpretation: "The baby wants the woman to eat him, and he wants to be tasty to her. He wants me to want him inside my body, for then he will know that I love him."

Danny says: "Now we shall start again. I am a baby in an institution, and you take me and eat me." Now, following Danny's clear exposition of his fantasy, it is possible to connect the feeling of abandonment with the wish to have a mom whose body he is so much a part of that he will be hers forever.

The play changes gradually to another kind of appropriation, stemming from the Jewish tradition of circumcision. Now the baby is taken over by the mother, giving himself to her while protesting at the same time. The therapist as mother is now requested to do the painful act of appropriation through circumcision while at the same time feeding, holding, and soothing the crying, frightened baby.

The important experience for Danny at this point in his development was that of being loved as a part of Mommy—that is, the experience of belonging to a mother.[4] As part of the object he could become himself and acquire his own unique existence. Now we can have a better understanding of the mental state Danny was in before reaching that stage, when he could not enjoy having his own things or use them constructively for the purpose of symbolization. Prior to the experience of merging with a loving mother, he could only experience himself, his body and drives, as dangerous. In that position he could not use objects, for they were parts of a dangerous world. Toys and other objects had to be thrown away or turned into weapons, means of projection in the battle for survival. Merging and belonging were essential in creating the potential space that allowed for a new meeting with the world outside and with his own internal tensions. The last part of the session suggests that the trauma of abandonment and adoption also had an impact on the development of gender, sexuality, and guilt.

With his new achievement, Danny entered another stage in the treatment. He became more interested in sharing things with me and in mutual play, such as our joint training in basketball, and in competitive games. He would lend me his own things so that I could play with him, as long as he got his property back at the end of the session. His tension diminished considerably, and he could tolerate being with broken things, such as a broken window, without experiencing a collapse of his world. He became more interested in his box in the room. He enjoyed

---

4. The relationship between the experience of merging and that of belonging merits discussion beyond the scope of this chapter. While merging is a well-used psychoanalytic concept, the sense of belonging has scarcely been discussed. See Kohut (1984) for a preliminary exposition of the issue. The material presented here points to an important experience that has to do with the loss of sense of an individual self—that is, a sense of "I"—but rather with an experience that is best expressed in the Hebrew word *shel*, which expresses belonging: *the son of*. . . .

leaving his own things there and looking to see what was inside and finding old things he had forgotten about. He showed in several ways that he saw me as a special person with whom he shared special secrets the secrets of the baby with his primary object, with whom he experienced passionate love, hate, abandonment, and destruction. His sense of self became more cohesive, while the object became more reliable

EXCRETA—A ROUTE IN FORMING THE MOTHER-BABY BOND

I have already mentioned that early in the analysis Danny initiated many of the contacts with the therapist through urinating and defecating in the consulting room and that I decided to include these disturbing moments in the analytic situation. This decision allowed us to explore their meanings and functions more deeply. Here I look at the tensions of drives and needs expressed in this mode.

Soon after Danny introduced urination as a way of protest and revenge, it became evident that for him peeing and defecating in the playroom were a main route of regression to a baby-mother relationship. Generally, descriptions of early mother-infant relationships emphasize the baby's hunger and the mother's provision of nurture; hence the good breast. On the other side is the absence of the mother, leaving a needy infant to its pain; hence the bad breast. However, there is another facet of the mother-infant relationship that hardly draws attention in these descriptions: that which deals with the infant's excrement and the mother's task of cleaning and thus mending the infant's state of discomfort. The experiences of the body as a source of excrement have been discussed mainly as expressions of infantile aggression or sadism (Freud, 1905) aimed as a revenge against the bad breast (Klein, Riviere, Isaacs, 1952). Considering their dirt and smell, it is no surprise that excrements are easily perceived as carrying all that is repulsive and hostile in the early relations. Yet, Klein and her followers recognized another side of the excrements: they are also a gift, the infant's expression of love to the mother. Winnicott was not satisfied with the perception of the infant as totally passive, and he added some observations of the baby as an active participant in infant-mother relationship (1969). Interestingly, Winnicott looked again at the situation of feeding and ignored Klein's suggestion about excrements. The material from Danny's analysis offers an opportunity to investigate excrements as a vehicle for the infant's initiation and self-expression within the early mother-infant relationship.

Object relations concerning excrements differ from that of feeding. In feeding the tension is experienced when the infant is alone and needs the mother to end the stress by satisfying his hunger. In urination and defecation, by contrast, the tension starts and is relieved within the infant; the mother can help only as an outsider who mends the results of the process and restores the position of well-being by changing a dirty diaper and cleaning the baby. This repetitive experience within the mother-infant dyad can serve as a prototype of the object's acceptance of inner pressure that the self is unable to contain. Conversely, we commonly see that a parent who rejects the infant will typically feel repulsed by its excrements. (It is also typical that parents are more repulsed by the excrements of other infants than by those of their own.)

This analysis adds another dimension to the place of the phallus and the excrements in the development of the self. Generated from inside, the excreta can be an everlasting source of fullness and a reliable sign of existence. The object typically responds to what comes out of the infant's body with recognition and care. But through this care the infant comes to a new awareness—that his body creates products that are thrown away. The infant is now in a position to differentiate the valuable self from its discarded excrements (Winnicott, 1964). In Danny's case we could see that either he did not develop this differentiation or that it was erased by his experience of total rejection. So disposing of his excreta equaled disposing of his whole self, and he became "a kaka boy," fighting against a rejecting mother for his right to exist.

From another perspective we can say that at a period prior to sphincter control, a relationship of mother and infant is created that is mediated by the excrements. Being in the intermediate space between inside and outside, and between infant and mother, the excrements may easily acquire the status of transitional objects. The baby's blanket contains the smells of mother's milk and also traces of the baby's own bodily functions. But when such a reliable object is not available for the baby to become attached to, the excrements themselves may serve this function. This may have been the case with Danny.[5]

PROJECTIVE IDENTIFICATION—FORMING THE MOTHER-BABY BOND

In the analysis of Danny we saw time and again that projective identification was a main channel for the communication of inner experiences. The nature of this mechanism has been discussed extensively (Klein, 1955; Ogden, 1979; Rosenfeld, 1987; Sandler, 1987; Kernberg, 1992). It is widely accepted that projective identification is a mecha-

5. Interestingly, Brinich (1980) has described a case of an adopted child where the issue of messiness was at the focus of the mother's complaint and of the child's feelings of rejection.

nism of defense and a mode of communication rooted in early development, at the phase of emerging awareness of subjective self and the existence of the other, yet when boundaries between self and other are not fully established. This very primitive mode of relations is typically looked at from the point of view of pathology, as a testimony to the patient's incapacity to develop a higher-level object relation that better distinguishes between self and other.

The case of Danny allows us to look at the mechanism of projective identification from another angle, that of development. For Danny, having an adult who was ready to experience Danny's own experience became the cornerstone of the therapeutic relationship. At the initial stage, meeting someone who was ready to experience in herself the frightened and longing child created the license for coming close to him. Later, as in the play of the devouring mother, the experiencing adult was the channel through which he expressed his uncompromising wish for a mother of his own—a mother who loves him so much that she wants him inside her. Having been traumatized by abandonment, Danny points to a disruption of the early unique mother-infant relationship. In this special relationship, which Winnicott called *primary maternal preoccupation,* the mother is not only a feeding object but also an object who allows herself to be affected by the infant's internal emotional state. This is the function of the mother as mirror. From the mother's perspective we are talking about her experience of the infant inside her, yet distinct from her own self. From the infant's perspective we are talking about his sense of existence inside the mother, as a separate yet actual part of her being. For the baby, motherhood starts in the womb, in the sense of being contained by someone. Feeding and serving as a protective barrier are important elements in mothering but are not sufficient without the essential element of containment. The idea is not new, but the case of Danny provides a dramatic illustration of this theoretical conception.

Traumatized by abandonment and by the experience of being adopted, Danny was facing two developmental issues at the same time: First, he had to transform an alien adult into a parent; second, he had to resume the line of development of object relations toward differentiation between self and object. The two tasks were interdependent, for the continuously developing internal object had to include a new external object. It seems that Danny put to use the mechanism that was designed for such tasks, namely, projective identification. Differentiation could not have meaning before a sense of belonging was established. The premature experience of separateness meant estrangement and danger and mobilized a fight for survival. The experience of containment by a caring adult opened a new relationship with external reality, where it could become a field for exploration and be used for further growth.

CONCLUSION

"There is no such thing as a baby separated from a mother"—this statement of Winnicott's (1964) has become a cornerstone of our understanding of the parents' vital function in child development. It stands out against a diversity of opinions as to the specific contributions of parents to the development of their child. Adoption is a situation where the process of developing a relationship with parents is intertwined with loss and restitution. The case of the adopted child, and particularly that of the child adopted at an older age, may teach us about the internal processes involved in having a parent. A caring adult may replace an abandoning parent. But it is the child's issue to construct an internal representation out of the actual experiences with the new adults who are introduced to him. When development proceeds on its natural course, a child constructs his internal objects through intensive negotiation with the actual objects who take care of him. In the normal course of development the person eventually comes to differentiate between the internal object and the external one: with this achievement he can reach a higher level of relationship between internal and external reality. But for the adopted child the natural process of negotiation with an actual person is disrupted, and the child is invited to start again with another adult. The case of Danny shows that "starting again" means for the child being represented in somebody's mind, feeling part of the existence of that person. One can rephrase Mahler's notion of psychological birth and call this "psychological pregnancy" within the representational world of a caring adult. Child care consists of nurturing and satisfying the child's hunger, and also of caring for his body and its excretions. These are two ways of meeting the child's tensions. Beyond the actual care, both serve as building blocks for the child's experience of a secure existence within the mind of a new and alien person, who thus becomes his parent. The experience of having a parent is essential for the child, not least in enabling him to develop a sense of security in his own existence.

BIBLIOGRAPHY

ABRAMS, D. M. (1991). Looking and looking away. *Psychoanalytic Study of the Child* 46:277–304.

BRINICH, P. M. (1980). Some potential effects of adoption on self and object representations. *Psychoanalytic Study of the Child* 32:107–133.

COLARUSSO, C. A. (1987). Mother, is that you? *Psychoanalytic Study of the Child* 42:223–237.

FREUD, S. (1905). Infantile sexuality: Three essays on the theory of sexuality. *S.E.*, 7:185–187.

GOLDSTEIN, J., FREUD, A., SOLNIT, A. J., & GOLDSTEIN, S. (1986). *In the Best Interest of the Child.* New York: Free Press, 123.

GREEN, A. (1972). The analyst, symbolization and absence. In Green, *On Private Madness.* Madison, Conn.: Int. Univ. Press, 30–59.

ISAACS, S. (1952). The nature and function of phantasy. In M. Klein, P. Heimann, S. Isaacs, & J. Riviere. *Developments in Psycho-Analysis.* London: Hogarth, 67–121.

KERNBERG, O. F. (1992). Projection and projective identification: Developmental and clinical aspects. In Kernberg, *Aggression in Personality Disorders and Perversions,* New Haven: Yale Univ. Press, 159–174.

KLEIN, M. (1952). Some theoretical conclusions regarding the emotional life of the infant. In: M. Klein, P. Heimann, S. Isaacs, & J. Riviere. *Developments in Psycho-Analysis.* London: Hogarth, 206, 227.

—————— (1955). On Identification. In: (1957). *Envy and Gratitude.* New York: Basic Books, 48–56.

KOHUT, H. (1984). The selfobject transferences and interpretation. In *How Does Analysis Cure?* Chicago: University of Chicago Press, 192–210.

LOEWALD, H. W. (1973). On internalization. In *Papers on Psychoanalysis.* New Haven: Yale University Press, 1980, 69–86.

OGDEN, T. H. (1979). On projective identification, *Int. J. of Psychoanalysis,* 60:357–373.

RIVIERE, J. (1952). On the genesis of psychical conflict in earliest infancy. In M. Klein, P. Heimann, S. Isaacs, & J. Riviere. *Developments in Psycho-Analysis.* London: Hogarth Press, 37–66.

ROSENFELD, H. (1987). Projective identification in clinical practice. In *Impasse and Interpretation.* New York: Tavistock, 157–190.

SANDLER, J. (1987). The concept of projective identification. In J. Sandler, ed., *Projection, Identification, Projective Identification.* Madison, Conn.: Int. Univ. Press.

SOLNIT, A. J. (1982). Developmental perspectives on self and object constancy. *Psychoanalytic Study of the Child* 37:201–218.

WIEDER, W. (1978). Special problems in the psychoanalysis of adopted children. In Glenn, J., ed., *Child Analysis and Therapy.* N.Y. Jason Aronson 557–577.

WINNICOTT, D. W. (1964). Further Thoughts on Babies as Persons. In *The Child, the Family, and the Outside World,* Pelican Books, 88.

WINNICOTT, D. W. (1964). Psycho-somatic illness in its positive and negative aspects. In *Psychoanalytic Explorations.* Cambridge: Harvard Univ. Press, 1980, 103–114.

—————— (1969). The mother-infant experience of mutuality. *Psychoanalytic Explorations.* Cambridge: Harvard Univ. Press, 251–260.

The Concept of Penis
Envy Revisited

A Child Analyst Listens to Adult Women

E. KIRSTEN DAHL, PH.D.

Current psychoanalytic scholarship concerning gender development rejects recognition of the genital difference, or "penis envy," as central to the construction of "femininity," substituting the concept of "primary femininity." This shift in the paradigm of gender construction has occurred in part because of contributions from child-observational research showing that "gender identity" is acquired by age three. It has also been stimulated by the observations of adult analysts that interpretations organized around the concept of penis envy appear to have little mutative value in contrast to the communications in play and action from the analyses of preschool girls, which seem to reflect intense intrapsychic conflict stimulated by the girls' recognition of the genital difference. Using clinical material, this paper contrasts fantasies of gender found in oedipal girls with those presented in the analyses of adult women. The differences reflect not only the vicissitudes of gender construction and developmental changes in the mind's capacity to adapt to the demands of reality but also the fate of aggressive and narcissistic derivatives as they become entangled in conflict created by recognition of the inherent limitations of the body. The fantasies referred to by the concept "penis envy"

Associate clinical professor, Yale University Child Study Center, New Haven.

I wish to express my appreciation for the help given me by Drs. Elizabeth Brett, Jonathan Lear, Sidney Phillips, and Lynn Reiser. Their thoughtful comments on earlier drafts of this paper at critical junctures in its development contributed substantively to the clarification of my own thinking.

The Psychoanalytic Study of the Child 51, ed. Albert J. Solnit, Peter B. Neubauer, Samuel Abrams, and A. Scott Dowling (Yale University Press, copyright © 1996 by Albert J. Solnit, Peter B. Neubauer, Samuel Abrams, and A. Scott Dowling).

are not constitutive *of femininity; however, they reflect one approach to*
a defensive solution to intrapsychic dilemmas stemming from awareness
of bodily and generational limits.

DURING THE 1920S AND 1930S, WHEN THE PSYCHOANALYTIC THEORY OF
gender construction was developed, Freud (1925, 1931, 1933) and his
followers (Abraham, 1922; Lampl-de Groot, 1927; Deutsch, 1930,
1932; Brunswick, 1940) argued that the girl's discovery of the anatomical difference between the sexes was a critically motivating factor in her
entry into the Oedipus complex and her subsequent construction of
femininity. Although Horney (1924, 1926), Klein (1932), and Jones
(1927, 1935) disagreed with Freud's formulation concerning the centrality of the discovery of anatomical differences to the construction of
gender, they did not reject the clinical usefulness of some aspects of the
concept of penis envy. When female analysts of this period, notably
Lampl-de Groot (1927) and Deutsch (1930, 1932), discovered the importance of the girl's preoedipal tie to her mother in the development
of the Oedipus complex and femininity, it led to a richer and more
complex understanding of the vicissitudes of female development,
with an appreciation of the multiplicity of contributory factors. The
concept of penis envy lost its status as a necessary and sufficient cause in
the construction of femininity and became one of several dilemmas
facing the little girl.[1]

With the linked concepts of penis envy and castration anxiety, Freud
argued that at its core the construction of femininity and masculinity
involve an attempt to repair the narcissistic damage inflicted by the
recognition of genital difference and bodily vulnerability. In his view,
the paired domains of femininity and masculinity connote fantasies
that function to represent, defend against, and contain the anxiety
stemming from awareness of the inherent limits and immutability of
the body.

In the past twenty years, psychoanalytic theory has again become
interested in the construction of gender and feminine development.
Current psychoanalytic scholarship rejects recognition of the genital
difference as central to the construction of femininity, substituting the
concept of "primary femininity." The formation of gender identity is
now placed at an earlier developmental period during which the child's
identifications with the parents, self-object differentiation, and body
ego schematization are central. In this view (Tyson, 1994), the concept

1. For an excellent reconstruction of this historical debate, see Fliegel (1973).

of "core gender identity" is privileged over the earlier concepts of femininity and masculinity. The girl's identification with her mother (Kleeman, 1976; Stoller, 1985) and of the mother's response to her daughter's body (Lerner, 1976) are seen as important contributors to the small girl's intrapsychic reaction to discovery of the anatomical difference. Although some psychoanalytic observers of young children (Tyson, 1989; Galenson and Roiphe, 1980, 1976) use the concept of penis envy in reporting their data, many writers ignore the concept or suggest that it is best understood as a metaphor for something else (Kaplan, 1991; Mitchell, 1984; Lerner, 1976). In this view, the girl's sense of vulnerability concerning femininity is linked to the contribution of hostile aggression to difficulties in separating from the mother during the pre-oedipal period (Tyson, 1994).

The shift in the paradigm of gender construction has occurred in part because of contributions from child observational research showing that children acquire gender identity by age three. Starting in infancy, the girl develops a sense of her body as anatomically intact and female (Kleeman, 1976); she does not view herself as a "disappointed little boy" (Mayer, 1995). Most modern analysts would agree that both boys and girls develop at an early age a sense of being anatomically intact and gendered. To the degree that the concept penis envy is seen as useful at all (Mayer, 1995), it is taken to refer to a complex web of *fantasies* created by the little girl as she struggles to understand what meaning to give to the genital difference, rather than to a perception on her part that she suffers from some actual anatomical defect. The waning of the usefulness of the concept has also been stimulated by the observations of adult analysts that interpretations organized around it appear to have little mutative value (Grossman and Stewart, 1976; Tyson, 1994; Mayer, 1995), especially in contrast to the communications in play and action from the analyses of preschool girls, which seem to reflect intense intrapsychic conflict stimulated by the girl's recognition of the genital difference. I have been struck by the clarity with which material concerning reactions to the genital difference between the sexes is presented in the analyses of young girls in contrast to the lack of clarity, even obscurity, of such clinical material in the analyses of adult women. In this paper, I present, explore and contrast fantasies of gender in four- to six-year-old girls and those presented in the analyses of adult women. I argue that the marked differences between the clinical phenomena reflect not only the vicissitudes of gender construction and developmental changes in the mind's capacity to adapt to the demands of reality but also the fate of aggressive and narcissistic derivatives as they become entangled in conflict created by recognition of the inherent limitations of the body. In the course of development, fantasies having to do with the meaning of the genital difference, which may be expressed so directly in the play of the young girl, are transformed by the demands of the ego and superego (A. Freud, 1936, 1965). These fantasies are not *constitutive* of femininity. Under the developmental transformations of puberty and young adulthood, however, such fantasies may serve as a defensive solution to intrapsychic dilemmas stemming from awareness of bodily and generational limits.

CLINICAL MATERIAL FROM CHILDREN

VIGNETTE ONE

One warm spring day a nursery-school teacher set up a water table outside for the children with a variety of objects—squeeze bottles, funnels, basters, egg beaters, measuring cups and spoons—that could be used in the water. As the morning progressed most of the children in the class spent some time playing at the table. Toward the end of the morning a group of boys was playing a loud, exciting, socio-dramatic game while riding around on trikes. Several girls were at the water table. Suddenly, one of the girls picked up a squeeze bottle and laughingly called to the other girls, "Look, we can make water too!" The other girls also grabbed squeeze bottles and immediately began to parade around holding the bottles between their legs and excitedly squirting water into the air. With much giggling, they shouted, "We're making peepee. We can do it too! Look at us!" Although the boys appeared oblivious to this play, the girls' hilarity brought them to the attention of the boys, who watched briefly and laughed but then returned to their own tricycle play. Laughing teasingly, the girls dashed ever closer to the boys, who were apparently ignoring them. Finally one girl rushed at the boys, squirted them, and shouted, "You *can't* do it! We *can* do it!" At this point, fearing an outbreak of hostilities between the boys and girls, the teacher intervened.

VIGNETTE TWO

Four-and-a-half-year-old Clarissa entered analysis because of her symptoms of elective mutism, general inhibition, and her fear that there was something wrong with her toes.[2] She was the only daughter

2. Clarissa's analysis is described in detail in Dahl, 1983.

of a professional couple and had an adored brother two years younger. A bright, engaging child who revealed a talent for imaginative play, Clarissa began to speak to her analyst in the fifth week of analysis. Although her mutism persisted outside the sessions for the first year of treatment, Clarissa proved to be quite articulate within her sessions. During the third month of her analysis, she depicted in play as well as speaking directly about her fantasies concerning the anatomical differences between boys and girls. She had a girl doll that she had named "First Class" and identified as being like herself become angry at some boy dolls. Clarissa said angrily about one of the boy dolls, "He's a show off, 'peepee' boy, and First Class doesn't like that. He makes her mad!" Later in this session Clarissa made the boy doll dance about, gaily calling attention to himself. Then she announced that First Class felt very jealous of "the peepee boy." I wondered whether First Class was mad because she wanted to be able to show off as the boy did. Clarissa responded gravely, "Yes, she does—she wishes she could be fancy on the outside like a boy and she's not and she gets so *mad* about that!" Noticing a pretty star in the playroom closet, Clarissa had First Class clamor for it, saying, "I want that star to wear! Then I can be fancy on the outside too!" I commented that sometimes girls thought boys were special because they were fancy on the outside. Clarissa said solemnly, "Yes, girls do get mad—they don't like those fancy boys." Then, leaning against me, she said, "You know, a long time ago First Class *was* fancy on the outside and you know what happened? A bad witch-monster came along and this witch cursed First Class and made her be a girl and be cursed and be not fancy—and First Class feels so sad all the time and she worries and worries about this. She needs help."

Although Clarissa's envy of fancy boys was by no means her only worry, she continued to grapple with this issue during the first year of her three-year analysis. In Clarissa's mind, maleness, anatomical "fanciness," activity, and exhibitionism were linked. She directly expressed her envy of boys and their capacity to be and do what she felt had been denied her. The mother depicted in these fantasies curtailed the little girl's activity and exhibitionism. It was only later in Clarissa's analysis that material emerged to suggest that she now viewed the mother as envious of and potentially damaging to her daughter's feminine desires to be beautiful, to be loved by a man, and to have children.

VIGNETTE THREE

Six-year-old Katie was referred for analysis because of temper tantrums and provocative behavior, both directed primarily toward her mother. The younger of two daughters, Katie was often cranky and bossy toward her very bright and bossy older sister. Her parents wondered whether Katie felt overshadowed by her. Katie was reported to be performing well in school academically and socially. Her parents worried, however, that their daughter was too hard on herself, failing to appreciate how well she was doing and pressuring herself to do better.

In her fifth session, Katie told a story about a complicated, but somewhat obscure, contest between a group of boys and a group of girls. At first it seemed that the contest involved running up and down a long ladder trying to be the first to get a mysterious present with a big bow. Gradually this contest evolved into one in which running up and down was to determine who had the real pencil and who had the rubber pencil. With great fierceness, Katie announced, "The boys always win because they have the real pencil, and that's the only way you can ever get the rubber pencil." She seemed at a loss to explain why either type of pencil was so desirable, answering, "They just are. That's what the kids want!"

Following this session, there was a blossoming during her analytic sessions of play focussing directly on competitive themes. Katie announced, grinning, that the basic rule in any game was that she should win and I lose; rules would suddenly be altered to insure that this fundamental rule was upheld. At first, Katie was a smiling, timid player whose anxiety about competition was revealed only by the quickness with which she would announce a change in the rules if she appeared to be losing. However, when I drew attention to her discomfort with her wish to win, Katie began to be openly competitive and to develop more age-appropriate rule-based strategies. Often, after a winning at checkers, Katie would turn to an imaginative story in which a little girl named Christy had a stallion named Speedy, the fastest horse in the world. Christy was the only one who could ride Speedy, and she was forever challenging "the boy who lived next door" to a race to demonstrate her prowess. Sometimes Christy would generously offer to slow down so the boy would not be left behind. When he appeared to be almost catching up, however, Katie would make Christy speed ahead, laughingly calling to the boy, "I'm winning! You're losing! I have the fastest horse in the world!"

In conversation, Katie referred contemptuously to the boys in her first-grade class as "dumb" and "yucky"; "I would *never* want to play with a boy!" In fact, her mother reported, at home Katie had a friend who was a little boy. Although there was certainly nothing markedly "boyish" about Katie's style of dressing, the analyst gradually became aware that she rarely wore a dress. Toward the end of her first year of analysis, Katie asked to have her hair cut quite short. The haircut gave Katie a kind of gamin appearance. Katie herself came in angrily to one session announcing that a classmate had asked if she were a boy! When the analyst attempted to explore with her why the classmate might have wondered, Katie responded adamantly that she *didn't* look like a boy and she *didn't want* to look like a boy. She then began to play out a story in which Christy, surrounded by neighbor children and siblings, "raced like the wind on Speedy" while the other children expressed envious admiration. Katie said, "They'll never be as fast as Christy because they'll never have a horse like Speedy. Speedy is just Christy's. And she can ride him so well it's like Speedy is a part of Christy." When the analyst commented that Christy seemed to feel she was better and faster than any boy, Katie laughed approvingly.

As Katie and her analyst continued to explore Katie's conflicts around her wishes to win, to be the best, and to be admired, Katie began to talk more about her father and all the special things she did with him. She drew a picture of a bride and groom getting married. Off to the side of the picture was a cross looking figure of indeterminate sex whom Katie described as "an angry lady. She's watching and she wishes she could be in that wedding, but she can't. All she can do is watch."

All three of these vignettes suggest the young girl's preoccupation with the meaning of the anatomical difference. As I have argued elsewhere (Dahl, 1993, 1983), both boys and girls during the oedipal period struggle to make sense of the anatomical distinction between the sexes as an aspect of their intrapsychic dialogue concerning what it means to be either masculine or feminine. The oedipal-age girl is often preoccupied with complicated thoughts and attendant fantasies about her body and its intactness, about her relationships to and with her father and mother, and about sexual excitement. These thoughts are associated with complicated affects of envy, jealousy, rage, love, affection, anxiety, and transient depression. Girls of this age frequently represent in play fantasies such as Clarissa's suggesting envy of male "fanciness" and a concern that they have been deprived of some important body part. Like Clarissa and Katie, many oedipal-age girls wonder whether possession of a penis is a necessary condition for being active and admirable. And as with Clarissa and Katie, such fantasies find direct representation in their imaginative play; often such play material appears relatively early in the analysis of the oedipal-age girl. For this reason child analysts may disagree about the role envious fantasies about the penis play in the construction of gender and the Oedipus complex,[3] but there is little disagreement that such fantasies, wishes, and fears are part of the mental life of young girls.

I have never heard material from an adult analysand presented as directly as that reported in Clarissa's session. It has been my experience that far along in an analysis, material may appear that can be understood as referring to fantasies of bodily lack, damage, or, more usually, dissatisfaction with the attractiveness of the body. Such fantasies are often represented indirectly by notions of gender stereotypy (men have privilege, they can have adventures, they can be active, they rule the world; whereas women are supposed to be passive, can't do anything, should be neat and tidy) or thoughts about having a defective mind, not being able to keep it all together (Kalinich, 1993). In general these archaic fantasies are highly defended against. However much we may hypothesize their motive force, in the absence of more direct expressions, the analyst is likely to become aware of their presence only through elusive derivatives, obscure references—thoughts hinted at through dreams and their associations, particular choices of words or defensive patterns. In marked contrast to analytic work with little girls like Clarissa or Katie, in analytic work with adult women, such fantasies may be inferred from more complex, even obscure, material but are not seen or heard directly.

The following brief vignettes from the analyses of three women illustrate the ways in which themes having to do with the body and its femininity or masculinity typically present.

CLINICAL MATERIAL FROM ADULTS

VIGNETTE ONE

An attractive, spirited woman whose self-presentation was reminiscent of a young Katherine Hepburn, Inge sought analysis because she felt confused about the directions she should pursue in both her professional and personal life. She felt intensely self-critical of what she

3. This argument began during the 1920s with the debate concerning the construction of femininity (Fliegel, 1973). Freud (1925, 1931, 1933) argued that the development of penis envy was a critical motivating factor for the girl's entry into the Oedipus complex. Karen Horney (1924, 1926, 1931) countered that there were two forms of penis envy, a primary, transitory form rooted in exhibitionistic and scoptophilic desires and a secondary defensive form employed in efforts to resolve the Oedipal complex through regression. Klein (1932) and Jones (1927, 1935) argued in favor of the notion of primary femininity as "bedrock" with penis envy seen as a transitory dilemma.

regarded as her professional underachievement. Inge was engaged to be married to a longtime beau but said she was uncertain about whether she would consider marriage to him or anyone. Although she had lived independently for several years, she said she still felt like her mother's baby. She viewed her older brothers, much admired by her mother, as accomplished "men of the world" and worried that she would never become as successful or worldly as they were. Inge thought she was postponing growing up and she said she was stuck— she could neither turn the clock backward and be a child again nor could she seem to bring herself to take those steps she regarded as quintessentially adult.

In the middle of her third year of analysis, Inge recalled a vivid daydream she had during latency; in this conscious fantasy she was a boy who could best her brothers in all sorts of athletic competitions. She remembered that she had in reality been a tomboy, hanging out with a gang of boys who got into mischief throughout the neighborhood. It was at this time as well that she had begun to play tennis, a sport in which she continued to excel. Although as an adult she had a number of close female friends, she recalled that as a child she had hated girls, thinking they were dumb and ugly. She had gone through a period during latency when she had refused to wear dresses and for a time had even worn underwear handed down from her brothers. Although Inge consciously looked forward to marriage and children, as she explored this childhood daydream during her analysis, she became aware that "to some extent I still think of myself as being a boy—or at least as not being female." To Inge this meant trying not to pay attention to her female body and its demands, instead emphasizing her athletic prowess and training. She liked her body best when it was in top athletic condition, "lean and mean." She began to realize that the very qualities she consciously prized in her fiancé—his gentleness, his uncompetitiveness, and his somewhat plump body—she secretly, and somewhat contemptuously, viewed as passive, even effeminate. Inge wondered whether her scrupulous insistence on following the cultural, gender-stereotyped conventions in her relationship with her boyfriend might not mask a pleasurable fantasy, that in their relationship it was really *she* who "had what it takes," "had the get up and go," "had the right stuff." She found herself feeling very uncomfortable with the competitive aspects of these thoughts. Suddenly she became aware of how furious she was with her boyfriend for what she insisted was his inability to be more assertive and self-promoting at work. She began to recognize that rage was a common feature in all her significant relationships in which she inevitably felt unappreciated.

VIGNETTE TWO

Eleanor, a successful professional in her mid-thirties, sought analysis because of a chronic depressive mood. Her malaise did not appear to interfere seriously with her work or her friendships, but it cast everything she did in a somewhat gray, sad light. She felt inadequate at work and unappreciated by her female friends, even at times unloved and unlovable. In the fourth year of her analysis, some time after her depression had lifted, Eleanor began to observe that she frequently felt in a "one-down position" in her relationships with men. For a person with a keenly analytic mind, Eleanor was remarkably uncritical of her deeply held conviction that men were inherently assertive and active while it was women's "nature" to be passive and dependently connected to others. Eleanor insisted that there was a biological basis to these gender differences; because she could not change them, she would just have to learn to live with them. She judged herself to be an unfeminine woman because she experienced herself as "messy and smelly" and because she so valued her independence. "A real woman should be neat, tidy, and compliant," Eleanor said forcefully, recalling that when she was a child, her mother had always worn white gloves when she went shopping. Although Eleanor presented as a carefully groomed, attractively dressed woman, she was irritated by her mother's occasional criticism of her appearance. Exploration of the gender stereotypes Eleanor cherished revealed that she viewed men and women as polar opposites, virtually "different species," with men embodying all positive attributes and women representing everything Eleanor held to be negative. Although she was an active and accomplished woman, in her inner world Eleanor experienced herself as a dependent, helpless female continually in danger of being exposed as inadequate and held in contempt by powerful, competitive, competent men. She realized that she was very much attracted to men like this, even though the price of a relationship with such a man seemed to be that she feel humiliated and dumb. Often Eleanor felt during an affair with a man that she wanted more than he would ever give her; sometimes the "more" had to do with sexual desire, but it referred to other desires as well. Eleanor believed it was important to conceal the extent of her desire because it would frighten the man. She then resented what she experienced as masculine insensitivity. At those moments during an analytic hour when she was puzzling over whether she had sufficiently concealed her desires and whether she could trust that the man would nevertheless satisfy her desire, her thoughts often became confusingly circular. "Well, you know how it is with me—I'm always having trouble keeping my thoughts straight just at the critical point. Just like a woman, I guess," she said sadly.

VIGNETTE THREE

Alice began analysis because she viewed herself as having a tendency toward damaging inhibition in her work life. She hated her job, which she felt was beneath her level of professional training, but she couldn't imagine holding a more responsible position. She described herself as "creeping along," trying to do a good job without ever feeling that her skills were recognized. During the first four years of her analysis, Alice's conflicts around aggression were prominent. Much of the time she felt that she struggled against a depressive mood by making conscious attempts to engage in many activities and make new friends. However, she continually found herself in situations in which she felt both unrecognized and pushed aside by very "narcissistic, competitive" women; Alice would feel furious but would "bite back" her anger and give way politely.

Alice recalled her mother's emphasis on appearances; as a small child she was expected to be neat, tidy, pleasant, and silent. In contrast, her older brother, Sam, had been an unruly and impulsive child, demanding and, Alice felt, consuming all his parents' attention. She remembered watching silently, frightened, during Sam's temper tantrums. Alice expressed fury that Sam had not failed in life as an adult, as she had once expected him to do. Sam's professional success was astonishing to her, and she felt rageful envy that he seemed to be the apple of her mother's eye.

As the analysis proceeded, we began to appreciate the intensity of Alice's wish to be desired and admired, besting all rivals, like Sam. At times she experienced the analyst as a "briefcase woman," by which she meant a woman successful (like a man) in a man's world. She became aware that she often felt very angry at her husband for his success in the world. As she explored this theme, her relationship with her husband became quite stormy. She spoke of what she felt was a dangerous wish to be "swept away by desire" and of her anger that her husband worked so late that Alice was often exhausted by the time they went to bed. She reported that sometimes she felt frightened by the fury she felt toward her husband during intercourse; she contained her anger by "detaching from him." And added, "but then I don't come." I commented that she surrendered her orgasm in the service of containing her rage and desire; she kept herself from being "swept away," but then she felt frozen.

In the months following this hour, Alice's conflict between suppressing or surrendering deepened. She felt increasingly angry at her husband, whom she condemned as exhibitionistic and impulsive. She remembered her love of pocket treasures as a child. With bitterness she recalled how once her mother had cleaned out her pockets, throwing away some of Alice's treasures. This recollection led directly to her recall of a movie scene in which a little boy, afraid of the rage of his terminally ill and bedridden mother, hides under her bed. Alice thought the boy longed for closeness with his mother but was driven away; how terrified he was of her anger! I realized, having also seen the film, that what was striking in Alice's recall of the movie scene was her failure to notice that as the little boy hides under the bed he is angrily mocking his mother, who is yelling at him for having made a mess. When I drew Alice's attention to her omission, she wondered whether the little boy felt he had made his mother sick. In a way, thought Alice, he had made his mother sick, because he was too much for her. We began to understand Alice's confusion surrounding who was angry—she, her mother, or both together—and how scary for a child to feel such "killing" fury.

Although a theme of envy toward men, especially her brother, flickered through the clinical material during the first five years of analysis, Alice's conflicts around aggression were most salient in our work together. These conflicts and her habitual defenses against aggression—"biting it back," "surrendering" her desires, being a "good soldier," and feeling "frozen"—were the dominant issues. The transference became organized around negative maternal themes in which Alice experienced herself as longing for my help and for greater intimacy with me, but experienced me as withholding, icily distant, and silently critical of her. Our work led us to appreciate the malignant identifications Alice had made with her mother that were employed in the service of her harsh, punitive superego. This seemed, at times, to prohibit any expression of desire, need, or aggression. During this period, Alice's envy was directed primarily toward women whom she thought were more expressive of their desires, and more successful in achieving them, than Alice felt able to be. From Alice's point of view, the most difficult aspect of her envious feelings was the associated aggression, which she felt was unacceptable and to which she responded with an intensification of her defensive maneuvers.

Gradually we were able to understand that as a little girl Alice had taken great pride in her competence; she wasn't naughty, messy, or out of control like her brother Sam. We recognized that being a "good soldier" not only was about suffering silently but had originated in the pride of being a "big girl." But no one seemed to appreciate what a big girl she was being; it was always Sam who was "center stage." I commented that being a good soldier did not lessen her hateful, envious feelings, and, as a result, she feared that she would be swept away by them, as had seemed to happen to Sam in his rages. As Alice began to rely less on being a good soldier in the service of disavowing and regulating her aggression, she began to acknowledge the intensity of her professional ambition.

In the sixth year of her analysis Alice reported a dream:

> I'm walking with Sam and I feel sort of wet, like I'm aroused. Then I'm sitting at a word processor typing but the master processor is on my right. Then my husband and I are in the examining room with a nurse. She says to him, "You are in fine shape." He is ahead of me. The nurse wants me to walk toward her. I don't have any clothes on, and I feel juicy and I'm afraid she can hear that juicy sound as I walk. She makes a gesture like an X over my torso and I have the feeling something is wrong with me.

Alice's associations led first to a report of brother-sister incest that she had read, then to her small daughter's excited pleasure in a tickling game. Alice said she didn't like the Freudian view that her daughter's excitement had "something sexual in it." She was quite sure she and Sam had never played any tickling games like that. She noted that in the dream she felt she was not allowed to touch the "master computer—I'm just at the little one." She reported that in reality she had never been able to master the computer and still typed on a standard typewriter, even though her husband used a computer at home. I wondered about the nurse making an X over her torso; Alice said it made her think of healing, the laying on of hands—"a way of curing the body in a deep way." She commented that somehow in the dream there was something wrong with her body in contrast to her husband's. "Juicy?" Alice laughed, "Well, that has to do with being a woman—all those ways your body betrays you, all that leaking, dripping, *juiciness*—no *man* can really understand that—this is what I have to contend with—my body, my sexual body." When I wondered about her walking toward the nurse, Alice suddenly recalled that when she was thirteen, because there was concern about the possibility of a physical anomaly, she had been examined by a senior orthopedist at a teaching hospital. "I had to take off all my clothes, and he and his residents were looking at me standing there all naked. I knew my body was defective. I wanted to hide. I felt I must look grotesque to them." This memory led to her recall that she had felt ashamed when first attempting to nurse her newborn daughter because of an inverted nipple. Alice remembered that she had wondered briefly whether her breast was deformed.

In Alice's dream and her associations we can see a complex inter-weaving of thoughts and feelings about her body. Her sexual excite-ment, while pleasurable, arouses anxiety that she will be swept away, embarrassed by and ashamed of her loss of control. Her thoughts suggest an unconscious linkage between being swept away by desire, being female, and feeling defective contrasted with being in control, having mastery, and having a body that is "fine" (and probably mas-culine). What was most useful to Alice in our analytic work together was her becoming more aware of how she employed "hiding away" and "being a good soldier" as ways of containing the anxiety generated by her own desires.

A month later Alice reported another dream: I am sitting in the living room quietly. There are a lot of people in the room, but no one seems to notice me. Suddenly everyone is looking up—there's a stage with a rock musician—he's really strutting his stuff. Alice's associations had to do with her husband's occasionally exhibitionistic behavior at parties and her own admiration of certain male rock stars. She said, "Boy, those guys really know how to strut their stuff—and everybody loves watching them!" She said enviously, "Guys just get away with that kind of thing—it's a male thing, I guess." Naming a female rock star famous for "strutting her stuff," I commented that I hadn't realized she was a *man*. Alice laughed, "I wonder why I forgot all about *her*." Following this session, Alice began to explore her own professional ambitions more directly. During one hour she exclaimed, "You know, it's not just that I'm sort of competitive. I am incredibly competitive. I don't want to be one of the best—I want to be the best."

In these sessions, Alice's associative links connected being admired and being successfully competitive with being a man, as if competitive, even exhibitionistic, activity is a *masculine* prerogative. However, in the context of the earlier clinical material, we can see that this fantasy has been shaped by defensive activity aimed at containing or warding off Alice's recognition of her own aggression. In her effort to avoid being "swept away" Alice tries to "hide," to make herself unnoticed and un-noticeable, which she links to being a "good *girl*." Her shame, her sense of *defect*, is linked to the shame she anticipates she would feel if she were to be overwhelmed by her desires, both erotic and aggressive. The fantasy of "being a man" is employed to represent the wish to be active and competitive. The fantasy also functions as a defense in denial: *only* men can be active and competitive. Alice, a "good *girl*," doesn't have these wishes and so does not need to fear being swept away.

The clinical material presented by Inge, Eleanor, and Alice suggests some shared thematic ground. For all three, their thoughts during these hours seem to be shaped by fantasies having to do with the differences between men and women, ideas about what it means to be masculine or feminine, the nature of the female body, the relationship to the mother, and perceptions of the mother's views regarding masculinity and femininity. For all three women, representations of the tie to both the preoedipal and oedipal mother remain a salient part of their mental life. There are also notable differences.

Inge's material is suggestive of an unconscious fantasy structure in which being active, assertive, and athletic is equated with being masculine; to a large extent, femininity, which she sees as entailing an intolerable degree of passivity and inadequacy, is rejected. One could speculate that her notion of having a "lean and mean" body may derive from an archaic belief in the entire body as phallus.

Similar issues, although organized quite differently, are represented in Eleanor's material. Eleanor's view of femininity also involves a fantasy of the feminine as signifying defect or relative inadequacy. There is an anal cast to her perception of the female body as smelly and messy as well as in her conviction that a truly feminine woman would conceal this. Her masochistically tinged relationships with men suggest the centrality of aggressive conflicts to her construction of femininity.

Alice also appears to make an unconscious equation between being masculine and being competitive; in addition, she links masculinity with an exhibitionistic presentation of sexuality. Like Eleanor, Alice associates the female body with a messiness that should be tidied up or a defect that must be hidden. However, we can see that Alice employs these fantasies in the service of warding off her perception of her *own* aggressive and competitive strivings, which she experiences as dangerously intense, possibly overwhelming, and certainly destructive of her relations to others.

DISCUSSION

A hallmark of the oedipal period is the appearance of the capacity to represent complex fantasies, desires, fears, and defensive maneuvers in imaginative play (A. Freud, 1965; Cohen et al., 1987). This play appears to give the analyst a direct window on the child's inner world and its wishes, fears, and characteristic defenses. What is presented in play, however, represents a compromise between the demands of the ego, defenses, and the desires of the id; it does not represent direct transcription of unconscious fantasy (A. Freud, 1965). Imaginative play allows the child to engage in conversations with different aspects of herself; play permits the child to hold in mind many different possibilities simultaneously, as well as to try out various combinations of and balances between fantasies (Cohen et al., 1987; Dahl, 1993). Through play the child is able to represent thoughts, wishes, and fears in a far more complex fashion than would be possible if she had to rely solely on her verbal abilities. Although linguistically competent, the oedipal-age girl still organizes her most complex thoughts through action and imaginative play. Nevertheless, the analyst, guided by theory, often can feel reasonably certain that the derivatives of unconscious fantasy structures are given dramatic representation in play. Not only is play for the oedipal-age child stimulated by the central desires, fears, associated conflicts and characteristic modes of defense of the period; play gives visible representation to these complex fantasy structures. This capacity to represent the mind in play serves the child's developmental needs as she struggles to reach some agreement within herself concerning the resolution of the central dilemmas of the oedipal period: What does it mean to be little? Does it necessarily mean weak, broken, or vulnerable? Am I too little to have such big, exciting feelings? What does it mean to be big? Does it necessarily mean powerful, intact, destructive? What if I am big and my parents are little? What would it be like if my parents and I were big together? How can I hate and want to destroy those I love most in the world? Am I bad because I want to be big? What if I am good and they are bad? (Cohen et al., 1987) As the child analyst watches and listens to the play, the child's inner world appears to come to life on the play stage.

The situation is inherently very different with adults who have left the world of the imaginative play stage far behind; consciously, adults rely on their verbal abilities to give shape to their inner world. In contrast to the young child, who frequently represents her defenses in action, the defensive activity of adults is usually silent and often not easily observed (A. Freud, 1936). The ego, too, has become more complex and its activities are no longer so clearly observable. These developmental changes in the ego brought about by the transformations entailed in puberty and adolescence mean that by adulthood the ego is firmly consolidated. As Anna Freud points out (1936) the ego of the young child is quite capable of sudden revolts against the outside world in favor of the gratification of infantile desires. For the adult, such a rebellion brings the ego in conflict with the superego. By adulthood there is a firmly established relationship between the id and the superego embodied in character structure that the ego is committed to preserving. For this reason the fantasies of early childhood become densely layered by adulthood, having been substantially transformed by being reworked and reorganized many times in light of later experience and cognitive development. This retroactive transformation of childhood fantasies involves the recasting of old issues in a new light, influenced by experiences in reality, advances in ego structuralization, superego development, and defensive activity (Freud, 1913; Grossman and Kaplan, 1989). Adult thinking is dominated by the capacity for representing itself linguistically. The permission the young child analysand grants the analyst to view the play as a communication is not available to be granted by the adult analysand. Even if the analyst is able to "read" the unconscious fantasy being alluded to in the words of the adult, an interpretation that simply spoke to the unconscious, bypassing the ego and its defenses, could not be heard; to the degree that it is actually heard it is experienced as an assault or a seduction.

These developmental differences between child and adult analysands and their developmentally characteristic modes of representing the inner world account only partially for the differences between the clarity with which the oedipal-age girl represents fantasies stimulated by the awareness of the anatomical difference and the relative paucity of such clear material in adult women analysands.

Many of the questions that so preoccupy the oedipal girl seem to concern what the early psychoanalytic theorists intended to connote by the concept of penis envy. Under the pressure of a biologically driven upsurge in genital arousal, increased cognitive capacities and greater ego structuralization, earlier fantasies and experiences become recast in a new light. The puzzle of what it means to have *this* body and not some other body takes on a new urgency in light of the intensification and increased organization of genital sensation. At its core, one strand of the oedipal story for the young child involves the wish to experience genital pleasure with another body. In this segment of the oedipal narrative, the body and its desires and the bodies of others and their desires hold center stage. In this narrative, the young girl must grapple with such dilemmas as: How is it that my body is little and the other's is big? Why is my body different from his? What is the meaning of these differences? Are they significant differences? Does "different" have some kind of explanatory power for all my grievances? Is it best understood in terms of presence/absence, intact/defective, plus/minus? Should this difference be viewed in pejorative terms?

This dilemma is given dramatic representation in the play of the nursery school girls reported by their teacher. Squeeze bottles in hand, the girls are experimenting with what it might be like to have a penis. What seems to be revealed to the observer appears to be a fantasy of how much fun it would be to have a penis. By their hilarity and provocative insistence that the boys watch, the girls suggest that they imagine they would feel powerful and excited (A. Freud, 1992).

For the oedipal-age child, more is almost always better. The clinical material from Clarissa and Katie suggests that some girls construct a fantasy in which the presence of the penis signifies permission to be exhibitionistic and powerful. Cognitively, the oedipal-age child's mind is drawn to the construction of binary oppositions—good/bad; more/less; big/little; male/female, etc. It is along this line that the meaning of bodily, especially genital, differences becomes an intriguing, potentially disturbing puzzle for the oedipal girl. She plays with the question of whether to give the genital difference meaning through the principle of binary opposition. As she struggles with the anxiety-generating questions this cognitive approach raises, earlier experiences and fantasies are reworked. It is here, I think, that a theory of gender construction based on the concept of primary femininity fails to address the complexity of the psychological tasks facing the little girl. It is not that she doesn't know she is anatomically female or that the schematization of her intact female body has not been imbued with psychological meaning derived in part from her identification with her mother. It is that in light of this newly charged information—that there are differences between bodies having to do with the highly pleasurable genitals—the question of what it means to have one genitally configured body and not the other becomes salient. The central dilemma of the oedipal narrative is driven by the child's developing psychological capacity to recognize the limits imposed by the *generational* difference. The strand of the narrative that involves the body and its desires also entails the dilemma posed by limitations—in this case the body's limits and its inherent immutability. For the girl, this dilemma is stimulated by awareness that intact though her body may be, other bodies may have "more" or be visibly "fancy." It is this fantasy that possession of the penis signifies "more" or "fancier" that stimulates envy in the small girl. For both the boy and the girl, the recognition that the body is inherently limited and immutable functions as a narcissistic threat and excites envy. As Clarissa imagines that having a penis would make her feel "fancy" and give her permission to be exhibitionistic, she says she feels "cursed" that her fanciness is not "outside."

By locating the construction of femininity and masculinity in the need to ward off narcissistic danger to the desiring body, Freud and his followers made a crucial psychological link between gender construction and desire. This theoretical approach also recognizes that gender may become entwined with those defensive strategies intended to ward off narcissistic threats stemming from a perception of the body's inherent limitations and vulnerabilities.

We now know that during the preoedipal period both the boy and the girl achieve a schematization of a genitally intact body (Galenson and Roiphe, 1976, 1980; Kleeman, 1976; Fast, 1978). This body schematization is given psychological meaning in part from identifications with the parents and their bodies (Tyson, 1994; Mayer, 1995). However, recognition of the anatomical difference in the light of the oedipal narrative ushers in a new dilemma stimulated by the question of what meaning, if any, to assign to bodily, especially genital, differences. It is this developmental dilemma that retroactively transforms earlier fantasies, creating new meanings for previously acquired libidinal and aggressive aims (Grossman and Kaplan, 1989). Recognition of the genital difference is a significant psychic organizer (Grossman, 1976). At their core, the fantasies created in response to the dilemma of what meaning to give the genital difference are concerned with the limits of the body and its immutability and are associated with feelings of envy. The fantasy is structured along the lines of "If I had that body (in addition to my own) I would have more and then I could really be the best. I would be first. I'd be loved the most." Katie's play suggests she imagines that if she had her own "stallion" or "real pencil" she would win all competitions (oedipal or otherwise). She has imbued the possession of a penis with a state in which all wishes are realizable and no superego retaliation occurs.

The waning of the oedipal period is associated with new cognitive and social-emotional capacities that permit the child's move into the wider world of school and peer groups. This developmental progression is spurred, in part, by the waning of the intensity of the oedipal conflicts as the child achieves some resolution of its central dilemmas. For a young latency child like Katie, internal conflict stimulated by newly enhanced cognitive capacities involving competitive strivings and the superego may, via regression, be given an oedipal valence. Katie alludes in her drawing to the earlier oedipal competition, which she "lost." Her play makes clear, however, that newer competitions have greater salience for her; she not only fears the shame of losing, she fears that winning will put her in conflict with superego injunctions to control her aggression, to be likable and "good." Her play employs body imagery in order to give representation to this dilemma: If I had a speedy stallion or a real pencil I would not only be able to win the race but I would not feel bad about winning.

The developmental transformations brought by puberty, adolescence, and young adulthood, especially menstruation, sexual intercourse, and pregnancy, spur further consolidation of the body/genital schema as functional and intact. Throughout the lifespan, the centrality of the body, its needs and demands, must be balanced against the demands of reality; this is a potential source of conflict. Because the body is close to the drives it also functions well as a medium for representation of internal conflict. In adulthood, fantasies constructed around the notion of the feminine body as limited and the masculine body as unlimited may be employed in the service of representing the dilemma inherent in body immutability. The adult ego recognizes the limitations imposed by the demands of reality, but for some women wishes for limitless possibility may continue to be salient as an imagined solution to inner conflict. Inge's perception of herself as developmentally "stuck" was a clue to the competing demands imposed by her psychologically intact ego, refusing her relief via regression, by her superego's insistence that she "grow up," and by her *wish* that all libidinal and aggressive possibilities remain open to her. Moving forward developmentally, whether by marriage and children or by taking her professional life more seriously, was linked in Inge's mind to accepting her body as feminine—that is, limited in its capacity to be active and invulnerable. This dilemma and Inge's attempted solution of postponement was given representation in Inge's inner world through her fantasy that it was she, not her boyfriend, who was the "real man."

Other women may use the fantasy of the male body as limitless in the service of attempting to placate superego criticism through defensive disavowal via externalization of conflicted aggressive or libidinal desires. "If I had that body I wouldn't feel limited and therefore vulnerable to aggressive or libidinal urges." Eleanor's fantasy of a dichotomous world in which women are contained, tidy, and passive and men are powerfully competitive and competent gives representation to her defensive attempts to deny her own competitive strivings and to conceal her "messy, smelly" sexual desires, which she fears will sweep her away. Her insistence on the biology of gender difference and her envy of male prerogative functions to permit her to disavow her own competitive wishes just as her fantasy of a messy, smelly, desiring, female body which must be tidied up embodies and defends against anticipated shame.

As the experiences of puberty and adolescence help to consolidate the girl's schematization of her female body as intact and functional, so traumatic experiences centering on the body may reawaken the fantasy that in its vulnerability, the body is defective. We can speculate that for Alice, the experience in early adolescence of the repeated medical examinations in which she felt her developing body exposed to the eyes of men contributed to the development of her fantasy of masculine privilege containing permission to "strut your stuff." For Alice, the fantasy of "being a man" has been shaped by defensive activity aimed at containing or warding off recognition of her own aggression. In her effort to avoid being overwhelmed by her aggression, as perhaps she once felt as a child, Alice tries to hide by making herself unnoticeable, which she links to being a "good girl." The fantasy of the rock-and-roll star strutting about on stage represents her disavowed wish to be active and competitive: if only men can be actively competitive, then Alice doesn't have to fear being swept away by her aggressive and libidinal urges.

For all three women, the complex fantasy structures described include notions of what it is to be masculine or feminine, aggressive and libidinal wishes, fears of being overwhelmed by the drives, superego prohibitions, and efforts to adapt to the demands imposed by reality; these fantasy structures employ representations of the male and female bodies. In the fantasy, men are envied as having the capacity to be active or having permission to exhibit themselves, attributes that the subject disavows in herself but presents herself as wishing for and feeling denied. Because these fantasies are organized around what it means to the subject to be feminine or masculine and contain envious feelings directed toward men, the concept penis envy is a useful and appropriate designator. Penis envy should be understood, however, not as the bedrock of what it is to be feminine, but rather as a compromise formation involving both drive and defense created by the dilemma of the inherent immutability and limitations of the body. This dilemma is most salient for the young girl during the oedipal period as she struggles to accept the implications for her of generational and anatomical difference. For each girl there are costs and gains, specific to her, in becoming a gendered subject. The fantasies encompassed by the term penis envy represent one aspect of these childhood explorations of what it means to become gendered. Analogous fantasies may emerge in the course of an adult woman's analysis that contain pejorative notions of masculinity and femininity and associated feelings of envy. Although such fantasies bear a relationship to those of the oedipal period, they have been transformed through many reworkings and reorganizations in the service of new libidinal and aggressive aims. The thread common to the transformations is the recognition of the body's inherent limitations and vulnerabilities. These fantasies appear with such regularity in the mental life of women because they are closely associated with the body, the drives, and the demands of reality and are, therefore, extremely useful in representing core psychological

324   *E. Kirsten Dahl*

dilemmas. The fantasies referred to as penis envy may be employed in
a number of ways: in the avoidance of superego conflict, in the service
of defense against drives, or in the representation of the drives. Like
any other product of the mind, these fantasies should not be accepted
at the level of manifest content; rather, the questions to be asked are:
To what purpose are they being put in this woman's mental economy
and why? What dilemma is being solved by their construction? What
does this particular woman gain in employing such a fantasy, and at
what cost? To answer these questions with a particular female analysand is to understand what are the costs and benefits for her of becoming one gender and not the other.

BIBLIOGRAPHY

ABRAHAM, K. 1922. Manifestations of the female castration complex. In: *Selected Papers*. New York: Brunner/Mazel. 1979. pp. 338–369.
BRUNSWICK, R. N. 1940. The preoedipal phase of the libido in development.
In: Fleiss, R. (ed.) 1948. *The Psychoanalytic Reader*. New York: Int. Univ. Press.
pp. 261–284.
COHEN, D. J., MARANS, S., DAHL, E. K., MARANS, W., & LEWIS, M. 1987. Analytic
discussions with oedipal children. In: *The Psychoanalytic Study of the Child*. v.
42. New Haven: Yale Univ. Press. pp. 59–83.
DAHL, E. K. 1983. First class or nothing at all? Aspects of early feminine
development. In: *Psychoanalytic Study of the Child*, 38. New Haven: Yale Univ.
Press. pp. 405–428.
——— 1993. Play and the construction of gender in the oedipal child. In:
Solnit, A. J., Cohen, D. J., & Neubauer, P. B. 1993. *The Many Meanings of Play:
A Psychoanalytic Perspective*. New Haven: Yale Univ. Press. pp. 117–135.
DEUTSCH, H. 1930. The significance of masochism in the mental life of women.
In: Fleiss, R. (ed.) 1948. pp. 223–236.
——— 1932. On female homosexuality. In: Fleiss, R. 1948. pp. 237–260.
FAST, I. 1978. Developments in gender identity: The original matrix. In: *Int.
Rev. Psycho-anal.*, 5:265–278.
FLIEGEL, Z. O. 1973. Feminine psychosexual development in Freudian theory.
In: *Psychoanal. Q.*, 42:385–408.
FREUD, A. 1936. *The Ego and the Mechanisms of Defense*. In: *The Writings of Anna
Freud, v. II*. 1973. New York: Int. Univ. Press.
——— 1965. *Normality and Pathology in Childhood: Assessments of Development*. In:
The Writings of Anna Freud, V, VI. 1965. New York: Int. Univ Press.
——— 1992. *The Harvard Lectures*. Sandler, Joseph (ed.) Madison, CT: Int.
Univ. Press.
FREUD, S. 1920. The psychogenesis of a case of homosexuality. In: *S.E. XVIII*.
pp. 147–172.
——— 1925. Some psychical consequences of the anatomical distinction between the sexes. In: *S.E. XIX*. pp. 243–258.

—— 1931. Female sexuality. In: *S.E. XXI.* pp. 223–243.

—— 1933. Femininity. In: *S.E. XXII.* pp. 112–135.

GALENSON, E., & ROIPHE, H. 1976. Some suggested revisions concerning early female development. *J. Am. Psychoanal. Assoc.* 24(5):29–57.

—— 1980. The preoedipal development of the boy. *J. Am. Psychoanal Assoc.* 28(4):805–828.

GROSSMAN, W. 1976. Discussion of "Freud and Female Sexuality." In: *Int. J. Psychoanal.,* 57:301–305.

GROSSMAN, W. & KAPLAN, D. 1989. Three commentaries on gender in Freud's thought: A prologue on the psychoanalytic theory of gender. In: Blum, H. et al. 1989. *Fantasy, Myth and Reality: Essays in Honor of Jacob A. Arlow.* Madison, Conn.: Int. Univ. Press. pp. 339–370.

GROSSMAN, W., & STEWART, W. A. 1976. Penis envy: From childhood wish to developmental metaphor. In: *J. Amer. Psychoanal. Assoc.,* 24 (suppl.):193–212.

HORNEY, K. 1924. On the genesis of the castration complex in women. In: Horney, K., 1967. *Feminine Psychology.* New York: W. W. Norton. pp. 37–54.

—— 1926. The flight from womanhood. In: *Feminine Psychology.* pp. 54–71.

JONES, E. 1927. The early development of female sexuality. In: *Int. J. Psa.* 8(4):459–472.

—— 1935. Early female sexuality. In: *Int. J. Psa.* 16(3):263–273.

KALINICH, L. 1993. On the sense of absence: A perspective on womanly issues. In: *Psychoanal. Q.* 62(2):206–229.

KARME, L. 1981. A clinical report of penis envy: Its multiple meanings and defensive functions. In: *J. Amer. Psycho-Anal. Assn.* 29(2):427–447.

KLEEMAN, J. 1976. Freud's views on early female sexuality in the light of direct child observation. *J. Am. Psychoanal. Assn. (Suppl.)* 243–47.

KLEIN, M. 1932. (1975) The Psychoanalysis of Children. New York: Delacorte Press/Seymour Lawrence.

LAMPL-DE GROOT, J. 1927. The evolution of the oedipus complex in women. In: Fleiss, R. 1948. pp. 207–222.

LERNER, H. 1976. Parental mishandling of female genitals as determinant of penis envy and learning inhibitions in women. *J. Am. Psychoanal. Assn. (Suppl.)* 24:269–283.

MAYER, E. L. 1995. The phallic castration complex and primary femininity: Paired developmental lines toward female gender identity. In: *J. Amer. Psycho-anal. Assn.* 43(1):17–38.

MITCHELL, J. 1984. The question of femininity and the theory of psycho-analysis. In: Kohon, G. (ed.) 1984. *The British School of Psychoanalysis: The Independent Tradition.* New Haven: Yale Univ. Press. pp. 381–398.

STOLLER, R. 1985. *Presentations of Gender.* New Haven: Yale Univ. Press.

TYSON, P. 1989. Infantile sexuality, gender identity, and obstacles to oedipal progression. *J. Am. Psychoanal. Assn.* 37(2):1051–1069.

—— 1994. Bedrock and beyond: An examination of the clinical utility of contemporary theories of female psychology. In: *J. Amer. Psycho-Anal. Assn.* 42(2):447–467.

Oedipal and Preoedipal Transference Transformations

Comments on the Analysis of a Latency-Age Boy

RHODA S. FRENKEL, M.D.

The critical importance of both oedipal and preoedipal unconscious conflicts in child and adult analysis as these conflicts unfold through the transference is documented using analytic process data. Evidence is provided that demonstrates the equal relevance of these psychic conflicts and their continuous interactions. The concept of transference transformations is proposed to explain these and later psychic conflicts that are resolved through the mutative interpretations unique to psychoanalysis. Extensive clinical data from the analysis of a latency-age boy are presented in support of this thesis. Thus, transference neurosis that arises from the infantile neurosis, the structural residue of the Oedipus complex, would be subsumed within the group of transference transformations. This concept eliminates the obligation to emphasize one developmental phase over another.

MY PURPOSE IN THIS CHAPTER IS TO EMPHASIZE THE IMPORTANCE OF BOTH oedipal and preoedipal themes in child and adult analyses. As the themes emerge in both the patient's material and the transference manifestations, they often overlap or interact. Therefore, they should be treated with equal respect. To this end the term "transference trans-

Training and supervising analyst, Dallas Psychoanalytic Institute; clinical professor of psychiatry, University of Texas Southwestern Medical Center at Dallas.

The Psychoanalytic Study of the Child 51, ed. Albert J. Solnit, Peter B. Neubauer, Samuel Abrams, and A. Scott Dowling (Yale University Press, copyright © 1996 by Albert J. Solnit, Peter B. Neubauer, Samuel Abrams, and A. Scott Dowling).

formations" is proposed to clarify and redefine transference manifestations throughout development. This broader concept not only would allow us as psychoanalysts to describe our work more accurately but would widen our theoretical definition of analysis.

In the analysis of a latency-age boy, infantile-phase-specific unconscious conflicts were reactivated sequentially through the transference and *transformed*, as Freud (1917) stated, into "new editions of the old conflicts" (p. 454). Transformation does not describe the movement from preoedipal to oedipal; rather, as Weinshel (1971) emphasized, Freud used the element of transformation to characterize a fresh expression of the original symptoms, so that "in place of the patient's true illness there appeared the artificially constructed transference illness" (p. 454). The transference neurosis has been defined as the revival in analysis of the infantile neurosis, an internal structure and organization resulting from intrapsychic conflicts during the Oedipus complex (Moore and Fine, 1990). My patient, however, was fixated at the earlier phallic-narcissistic phase (Edgcumbe and Burgner, 1975). Analysis was recommended to resolve the preoedipal issues so that the patient could engage in and resolve oedipal conflicts, which he did in the final months of analysis. Analysis of the transference led to conflict resolution and intrapsychic restructuring, but most of the analysis dealt with preoedipal conflicts; thus the conundrum of what terminology to use. The transference manifestations met the criterion of new editions of old conflicts, but how can they be called transference neuroses arising from infantile neuroses if they, by definition, develop only after some sustained engagement and resolution of oedipal conflicts? This type of inconsistency has created the confusion and prompted the call to discard these classic concepts (Brenner, 1982).

Instead of eliminating these historically important and clinically valid concepts, I suggest a reformulation, incorporating Anna Freud's concept of developmental lines (1963, 1965), to restructure and resolve the ambiguities surrounding them. The term "transference transformations" would encompass all those qualitatively and quantitatively different transference manifestations in adult and child analysis that unfold and re-form in a gripping redramatization which brings to the surface the deepest conflicts in the patient's mind and allows for the mutative interpretations that are unique to the psychoanalytic process. Subsumed under the group of transference transformations would be the transference neurosis as we have known it, arising from the infantile neurosis, the structural residue of the Oedipus complex. This would provide the freedom to describe pre-oedipal and post-oedipal transference transformations portraying earlier and later developmental conflicts. We would be relieved of the obligation to emphasize one phase over another; rather, we could focus on the relation between them as they evolve in the analysis. Furthermore, following Anna Freud's intent in assessing progressive development (1963, 1965), the various phases from the oral phase through adulthood would no longer be constricted to id derivatives but would refer to time periods reflecting the maturation of the ego and superego as well as the instinctual drives.

The following case summary focuses on how early infantile conflicts restricted the patient's normal development. It provides an opportunity to see how a patient's perception of historical events, as related by parents and teachers, first were metaphorically translated in the analytic situation and later were transformed into a transference illness that occupied most of the analytic work. The preoedipal transference transformation describes this critical aspect of the analysis, as it telescoped the diadic conflicts of the oral, anal, and phallic-narcissistic phases. When the patient was able to face the triadic conflicts of the oedipal phase, the analysis of the oedipal transformation was accomplished with greater rapidity and ease. The case material delineates the relation between preoedipal and oedipal conflicts; data on the oedipal phase are abbreviated because they are consistent with classical theory and nomenclature.

CASE MATERIAL

Mrs. B. sought analysis for her son Cal, age 8; she claimed that he had a "brain bound down by fear. . . . He has always been withdrawn. . . . He shrinks from life . . . prefers to be secluded and watch television and refuses to play at anyone else's house, join Cub Scouts or a soccer team, and complains that the other boys laugh at him." At age 5 Cal was treated with behavioral modification for enuresis and with supportive psychotherapy for severe separation anxiety. These symptoms persisted in a muted form. Although no longer refusing to leave his mother, he generally refused to leave his house except to go to school. And occasionally after school his pants were damp. Also, despite his very high I.Q., he had little interest in school, where his grades were B.'s and C.'s.

FAMILY HISTORY

Mrs. B. was distressed by the family's recent move from the East for a temporary business opportunity for Mr. B. Having benefited from analytically oriented psychotherapy, she missed her therapy and therapist. As a child Mrs. B. had a hostile-dependent relationship with her mother, who abused her physically and emotionally, blaming her for her father's death when she was a toddler. She had murderous impulses toward Cal, and she rarely spoke his name but stated, "I have horrible thoughts about the little guy. I imagine him walking to school and being hit by a car. If the poor little guy got killed, he wouldn't have to go through treatment and I wouldn't have to go through the next twelve years wishing he were happy. . . . How can I say anything like that?" Occasionally she wore a T-shirt labeled "Out to lunch," conveying her confusion.

Mrs. B. had been angry at her husband since her first pregnancy, when he abandoned her affectively and actually. Mr. B., whose mother died in childbirth when he was about Cal's age, was in fact intolerant of pregnant women and infants. Before and after the birth of each of their three children he left town for several weeks. Although Mrs. B. genuinely loved her children, she was often overwhelmed by the responsibility of caring for them and ashamed of her inability to prevent occasional vocal and physical outbursts with them. At times her mood shifted for no observable reason; one minute she appeared warm, reasonable, and eager to help, and the next she flew into icy rage or was emotionally inaccessible. It was easy to understand how unpredictable and frightening she must have appeared to Cal.

Mr. B., a successful entrepreneur, was pleasant but controlled. He acknowledged that his childhood was difficult. He complained that his wife's constant criticism reminded him of the relatives who reared him after his father's death. I observed that Mr. B. often passively provoked his wife to be bossy, giving him an excuse to escape his family. Cal's siblings—a sister age 15 and a brother age 11—were protective toward and fond of Cal, often acting as parental surrogates.

DEVELOPMENTAL HIGHLIGHTS

Mrs. B. focused on the pathological and failed to see or be comforted by more positive aspects of herself or others. Cal's birth was unplanned. She stated, "The night I conceived him, I woke up nauseated and threw up." When her husband commented that she sounded pregnant, she said, "If I am, I'll kill you." Nauseated throughout the pregnancy, she resented her husband's lack of support. Although birth and delivery were normal, Mrs. B. felt frustrated by her inability to nurture or pacify her son and bitter at her husband's absence.

Mrs. B. described difficulties at every stage of Cal's development—severe colic, inability to sleep, milk allergy, food refusal, enuresis and encopresis, among other complaints—but Cal smiled, sat up, and had stranger anxiety at the appropriate times, and he walked by age 1. He didn't speak until he was 3, which she blamed on his siblings' catering to him. She claimed that a baby sitter bowel-trained him at age 3-$\frac{1}{2}$, but he remained enuretic until treated with behavior-modification therapy at age 6. When placed in preschool at age 3-$\frac{1}{2}$, he initially had severe separation anxiety, screaming for an hour after Mrs. B. left. Later he became actively oppositional, frequently destroying class projects, overturning furniture, and hurting other children or throwing away their lunches. Once, after he had been forcibly removed from the class, Mrs. B. had to pick him up early. That was the one occasion when she beat him. Subsequently, Cal refused to go to school, feigning illness. When Mr. B. took him to school despite his complaints and occasional vomiting, Cal played alone but stopped being defiant and destructive.

At age 7-$\frac{1}{2}$ psychological testing indicated that Cal was a compliant child with a very high I.Q. Tests revealed that he was depressed by his father's neglect but hopeful of finding a way to meet his standards so that his father, whom he admired, would spend time with him. By contrast, he felt severely deprived of emotional support from his mother and convinced that he was doomed to be unacceptable and unloved by her.

EVALUATION AND INITIAL FORMULATION

Cal entered the office cautiously, easily separating from his mother. A small boy wearing worn-out clothes and a serious, sad expression, he was nevertheless an attractive child with an infrequent but appealing smile. Entering the play area, he said he was unhappy, especially at school. After examining the toys, he complained that there were no rockets and said he wanted to build rockets at home. Then his speech and behavior became inhibited. Silently and deliberately he set up a war between cowboys, "the good guys," and Indians, "the bad guys." I commented that he seemed to be carefully placing each man according to some plan. When he nodded in agreement, I asked him to explain his plan. Looking surprised, he pointed to the men. When I asked whether he thought I could understand without his speaking, he nodded yes. I said I could only guess, not really understand, unless he explained, to which he shook his head in disbelief, continuing to play silently. After setting up the men, he stopped and looked around the room. I asked what he was looking for and why he hadn't played out the war. He replied that he had pillow fights with his brother for fun. When asked if this war was for fun, he lowered and shook his head.

Then, speaking with some urgency, he talked of a stray cat that his sister had brought home before they moved. He agreed when I said that the cat seemed important to him but gave no further associations. The meaning of the cat was partially clarified when Mrs. B. explained later in a consultation that Cal had tried to tie up their cat with a rope, but the cat ran off and accidentally hanged itself on their fence. Mrs. B. related the episode as though it were an important current event, though later in the hour she placed the episode in Cal's fifth year. She added that they now had another cat with the same name which Cal believed was the old cat reborn. The theme of the cat's death and rebirth became a critical one in the analysis.

Asked at the end of the first session what he liked to do besides build rockets, he did not reply. He complained of hating homework, soccer, being teased, and most of all waiting, however, almost in tears, he explained that he was waiting for "some army ships and planes and things" and that if only these toys would come he'd feel better.

This session indicated that Cal unconsciously longed to deal with phallic and oedipal concerns, as manifested in his wish to build rockets and the desperate quality of his wish for army toys, which actually were present in the playroom. However, earlier unresolved conflicts made him too fearful to proceed. He couldn't play out the cowboy-Indian conflict. Then he became preoccupied with preoedipal concerns; he thought I could read his mind, his inhibited behavior and speech were both fearful and controlling, and the as-yet vague story of the cat seemed to encapsulate a significant early problem.

At the next session he found the army men and imaginatively set up a war, speaking only to identify the good and bad guys. Asked what they were fighting about, he related that his father, a very smart man, said that men always fight for land. When the bad guys demolished the good guys, he said he felt bad that the enemy had won, but they had more men. Then he sat in a chair, barely moving, and remained silent and motionless when I asked whether the enemy's winning had upset him. Later, when I encouraged him to draw a person, he drew a round face with a frightened expression and a large open mouth with a black center. He said that the center was a bottomless black hole and that the picture was a surprise, because it would scare anyone who looked at it. Next he drew a large black bat with the same wide-open mouth, but with a red center. Describing the bat as angry and preparing to attack someone who had stolen its nest, he noted that whoever stole the nest didn't even care about the eggs in it and was interested only in watching how babies were born. He then explained that the angry bat was a smart father bat and was sure to get his nest back. Asked how, he said only that he wouldn't want to be the thief and again became silent and still. When, after some time, he tried to sneak some candy from his pocket, I asked whether his story had upset him and whether that was why he wanted the candy. He didn't reply, but at the session's end said that he wanted to come back soon because there were so many interesting things to do.

This session elaborated his preoedipal and oedipal problems. His associations to the war in which the bad guys won indicated oedipal conflicts with men fighting over possession of mother earth. Momentarily immobilized by fears of his destructiveness, he retreated to the chair. His drawings illustrated more specifically the nature of his conflicts, primarily oral and oedipal. In the first picture he seems frightened by his oral-dependent needs, while his thoughts about the next picture related his fear of his father's retaliation for Cal's scopophilic and oedipal impulses: his wish to steal his father's nest and watch how babies are born.

The evaluation indicated that despite his earlier conflicts, Cal had reached the oedipal phase but was unable to remain there. His parents' apparent inability to resolve their own conflicts over their impulses may have amplified Cal's panic at the multiple dangers of triadic relationships; thus his regression to phallic narcissistic and oral concerns. He had evoked some good mothering and fathering from his siblings, and with his high intellect developed some ego strengths but only primitive superego functions; that is, his behavior seemed controlled more by fear of external punishment than by guilt. Analysis was recommended because his intrapsychic conflicts left him with insufficient ego and superego strengths to actively enter the oedipal phase or progress to latency. With a weak ego and superego he was unable to adequately sublimate his drives, had diminished academic achievements, avoided sports, and had infantile interactions with his family and peers.

OPENING PHASE

Cal's initial eagerness to come to his sessions, his ability to identify with the analytic task—that is, his awareness of his inner turmoil and the facile way in which he accurately symbolized his conflicts—seemed to indicate that a therapeutic alliance might be easily established. But as his mother had said and he had shown, his mind was frozen with fear. He needed to test the analytic situation, my reliability, tolerance, and understanding, and his parents' sincerity and their capacity to allow him to use the analytic process to work through his problems. The following vignettes illustrate how his play and actions portrayed his defensive regression from phallic-oedipal fantasies to oral and anal wishes and fears.

At the first session after the evaluation, he immediately began setting up a war. As he silently planned the battle, I told him about the analytic arrangements: that he would be coming four times a week; that he couldn't hurt himself, me, or the major office furnishings; that our communication was private and that he could freely express his thoughts and feelings whether they were happy, sad, friendly, or angry. With the word *angry*, he abruptly put away the toys, whispered, "I'm never angry," and denied that angry feelings had anything to do with his stopping.

He then began to draw a series of pictures. First was a large, simple face he called a happy pumpkin. Next was a more intricate picture of a medieval castle with tall towers, protected by armored guards and a night on horseback, all carrying lances. In the center he drew a taller tower (a phallus), with a large triangular roof filled with small, oblong green dots (semen), coyly noting to me, "You know what *those* are!" I replied that I could only guess, commenting that they seemed to be moving. Mockingly, he said that they were tiles and then immobilized them in black grout. When asked about the castle, he said it was on an island and was inhabited by a hungry king with a big stomach. The king lived with a nice queen, but she also had a big stomach and was hungry, as there was never enough food. The king was powerful and had made a lot of enemies by scaring them, which was why his castle was so heavily guarded.

Then he drew a playful but hungry dinosaur with an open mouth, noting that he didn't believe in dinosaurs now but was sure they had existed in the past. Last he drew a picture of a spaceship landing on Mars with a figure about to descend a ladder to explore. My comments were limited to identifying or amplifying the apparent affect of the drawings. I thought the first picture conveyed his happiness at beginning analysis, but he drew himself as a pumpkin head, a comic. Behind the comedy was the tragedy of the second picture, which was replete with oedipal and preoedipal wishes and fears. His third picture, a benign but hungry dinosaur, hid the hungry monster he perceived in himself from his earliest years. The figure emerging from the spaceship seemed to be Cal about to explore the unknown territory of analysis.

Despite this propitious beginning, the new territory was rocky and led to a regression. He was hesitant entering the office, had difficulty beginning, and often wanted to leave early, complaining of boredom. Using clay to craft ammunition for a civil war, he often made a mess. He blatantly cheated at the board game Candyland. Eventually he grew too fearful even to enter the office, and for over a month he refused to leave the waiting room. At times he stayed limp in his chair, refusing to move or speak. At other times he sat hyperalert, rigidly grasping the chair. Occasionally he wrote, "I hate this place. . . . I'm BORED!" Once or twice he broke down sobbing, "My only problem is coming here. . . . I wish I were dead." For weeks he resisted all attempts to help him overcome his distress and withdrawal. He seemed impervious to a wide range of toys and activities, as well as to any questions, clarifications, comments, or interpretations. Often I just quietly sat with him.

One day while we sat silently in the waiting room, Cal appeared less fearful and more provocative. Suspecting that now he was defending himself in the sessions by identifying with his father's passivity to annoy his mother, I used a puppet play to interpret this transference reaction. He was fascinated when, after a clever prince passively provoked a mean queen into a rage, the prince went fishing. He continued the play with a mean alligator puppet fighting and biting other puppets, but when he tried to make up a detective story about the murder of a man—in fact, a father puppet—he got "bored." In subsequent sessions, he appeared depressed, refused to speak, tried to sneak out the door, and one day hid in the stairwell for the entire session. Importantly, his parents related improved behavior at home, school, and in the neighborhood, which he now visited freely. For the first time, they saw him as cheerful and lovable.

In spite of Cal's complaints, they regularly brought him to his sessions. One day he vomited in the hall just outside my office. His father carried him into the office and laid him on the couch, commenting that Cal's behavior was identical to his behavior on first going to nursery school. After his father left, Cal remained calm but silent, and I commented that perhaps he, without knowing it, was trying to show me just how bad he had felt when he began nursery school. As he left he said that he was feeling much better. After several sessions of playing freely in the waiting room, he easily moved into the office to sail paper airplanes. Following this he made a series of paper missiles but, unable to overcome his fears of launching them, he retreated to the playroom to find the mean alligator puppet. When I asked the alligator if it was mean because it was hungry, it nodded yes. Becoming absorbed in figuring out how to feed the alligator enough food, Cal now complained that the sessions were too short. This began a long theme about alligators. Thus my reliability, nonintrusiveness, understanding, and occasional humor, reinforced by his parents' support of the analysis, allowed Cal to form a working alliance in which he felt sufficiently safe to allow his most feared impulses to emerge in conjunction with beginning to work through his nuclear conflicts.

MIDPHASE

With the alligator theme the analysis became the central issue of Cal's life. Each day he eagerly awaited his visit, rushing into the office to set up the puppets. His impatience to begin his session, annoyance if I was even a minute late, disappointment when the sessions ended, slight depression over weekends, jealousy of a little girl whose sessions preceded several of his, and outright anger at my leaving for vacation gave evidence of a qualitative and quantitative transformation in the transference. This occurrence signaled to me that we had entered the midphase.

Cal, using the mean-alligator puppet, bit or destroyed all the animal puppets I brought to befriend it. Following my suggestion that the alligator was mean because he was hungry, we spent weeks feeding the alligator. At first all the food had to be brought by my puppets. Later Cal joined in the initiative. In time Cal understood that his fear that the alligator was dangerously insatiable was like his pictures of the dinosaur and the scary head. When the alligator had more than enough food, Cal left him in a well-supplied swamp, commenting that with plenty to eat, the alligator wasn't dangerous any more.

Next he introduced a lion puppet as king of the jungle. I noted that the lion looked more like a cub, to which he retorted that the lion wasn't afraid of anything. I replied that the lion was very brave. First the lion became busy fighting off hunters trying to capture the jungle animals for a zoo or circus. When the lion seemed fatigued, I complimented the lion's skill but asked whether he needed some help, as it seemed he had too much to do all alone. Cal then added a prince and princess to provide a kingdom to protect and to supply food for all the animals and a place where they could learn to take better care of themselves. Living apart from the others, the lion was the main defense against the ever-present hunters but was rewarded by the princess, who taught him to speak. He did dazzling tricks to gain the admiration of the princess but refused to join the group. I asked whether there was something about the group that frightened the lion. Cal then added a king who was really in charge, because he had all the gold to buy the supplies. Shortly afterward Cal dispersed the kingdom to avoid a flood and allowed the lion to be killed by a hunter. When Cal refused to explain this sequence of events, I said that the trouble began after the lion made some attempts to attack the king. Cal didn't respond, so I asked him why the lion rescued the king when earlier the lion had tried to hurt the king. Cal remained silent while he built a grave and headstone for the lion. I commented that the lion seemed to both fear and need the king but that killing the lion was an unhappy solution, and there must be better ways to solve the problem.

This began a series of dramas in which Cal moved from animal puppets to people puppets and toys to portray his conflicts. The imaginative plots and actions increased in complexity while multiple variations of his oedipal wishes and fears became less disguised. Nevertheless, his scenarios inevitably ended with his demolishing the setting and usually killing whoever represented him. Afterward he might retreat to the waiting room or revive his play with the lion puppet. Then several reality events escalated his anxiety. Twice, after a summer and December break, the puppets were stolen. In time they were replaced. Some, like the lion, were old so their replacements were visibly different. Cal was convinced that because he had been angry at my leaving, I had taken the puppets away to punish him.

At about this time I had an operation that briefly left me limping and with a bandaged foot. After my recovery Cal made a Frankenstein monster puppet attack, tie down, and blindfold an eye, ear, and nose doctor, who, at my suggestion, he agreed was a "head doctor." When I said children are often afraid that their feelings make bad things happen, he had Frankenstein bind and blind the doctor more securely, saying this was necessary to prevent the doctor from recognizing and later attacking Frankenstein. I asked whether he was afraid that he had hurt my foot and that I would hurt him back. When he yelled, "You bore me," I said his scary feelings often bored him. At the next session he remained mute and motionless in the waiting room.

After a year and a half we reached a turning point in the analysis. With his head lowered, Cal somberly returned to the office, but refused to look at me. Finding the new puppets, present for several weeks, he picked a lion for himself and, keeping his eyes lowered, handed a black cat to me. He nodded in agreement when I asked whether the cat had something to do with his fear of looking at me. He then grabbed back the cat, tied it up, knocked it unconscious, and buried it, explaining that the cat was mean and dangerous, and had to die. I said that if he had similar feelings about the cat and me, I could see why he didn't want to look at me. Then, raising his eyes, he said, "It's not you, it's her; see, she's back again; all cats have nine lives; you can't kill them." Thus emerged the saga of how to kill the cat. Although this was a new puppet, there had been previous cats, which he had ignored. For the next three months without interruption, the lion tortured and ultimately killed the cat in a most impressive and varied series of vicious, sadistic, and remorseless attacks. No comments on affect, clarification of content, or interpretation at any level modified or abated his intense fear and rage at the mere sight of the cat. Justified by the lion's accusations that the cat hated him, that the lion could do nothing to make the cat like him, that she attacked without warning or reason, and that she wished the lion were dead, Cal insisted that the lion had to find a way to kill her. Once I commented that the lion treated the cat the way the lion felt the cat treated him. Afterward Cal had the lion die of "cat fever," as he believed there was no cure for hating cats. Another time, remarking on the lion's intense hatred, I asked if the lion feared becoming a cat. As Cal remained silent, I noted that a lion is in fact a big cat. Cal then made the cat shoot the lion. But the lion was soon resurrected and resumed killing the cat. I commented that the lion couldn't live with the cat, but he couldn't live without her. Although Cal's play was imaginative, its repetitiveness and lack of resolution or movement clearly indicated an obsessional defense. By contrast, outside the analysis, Mrs. B. reported that Cal was making friends, that his grades were almost all A's, and that he had joined a soccer team but still played fearfully. Nevertheless, he had elicited hugs from her normally undemonstrative husband, which made her happy but jealous.

After discovering that the puppets were gone a second time, Cal withdrew for several sessions, complaining that there was nothing to do. At the end of one session he began throwing darts with considerable strength and accuracy. Apparently frightened by his effectiveness, he again refused to leave the waiting room for three sessions. Efforts to reach him were ignored or blocked by "Shut up. You bore me." After a canceled session Mr. B. reported that Cal had lost control at home, requiring physical restraint and a spanking. Mr. B. felt bad about the spanking but pleased with the results, as Cal was again relaxed and cheerful. Returning to the playroom, he won two games of Sorry. Exploring some of the reasons he had chosen this game, he explained that he was sorry he needed to change the rules to win, but also that he enjoyed knocking off the players and was sorry that sometimes he felt mean. Then he hesitantly revealed his fantasy that it was his fault the puppets were gone, that I had removed them because I was angry and scared by the lion killing the cat. I explained that I wasn't frightened or angry but that I was concerned we had been unable to understand why the lion couldn't stop killing the cat. However, I commented that because Cal had enacted the lion's killing the cat over and over, perhaps it had been an important way for him to avoid other, more frightening feelings, which returned when the puppets disappeared. Thus, while playing darts, he became frightened by his strength and accuracy and, fearing that I couldn't help him or that he might hurt me, refused to come to his hour. After Mr. B. spanked him, he knew his father wasn't afraid of him and cared enough to control him if necessary.

Cal spent a few sessions flying paper airplanes, throwing darts, and playing detective. With renewed confidence in the stability of the analytic situation and in his relationship with his father and with himself, he one day allowed himself to find the newest puppets, returning once more to the lion-cat conflict, but with some significant changes. He pursued his theme with less rigidity and forcefulness, and his affect was more freely available. Often he switched briefly to playing with darts or airplanes, but he was unable to avoid a more definitive working through of his (the lion's) conflict with the cat. The new lion beat, starved, and tortured the cat into abject submission and helplessness, but did not kill her. At one session, while being tormented by the lion, the cat feebly attempted to paw him off. In a sudden outburst of despair Cal cried, "She bit me; she hates me; she doesn't even like me at all; she's crazy!" Returning to the waiting room for several sessions, he refused to speak. Reminding Cal that he felt responsible when the puppets disappeared, I asked him whether he wished his cat problem was his fault because then he wouldn't feel so helpless when bad things happened that he couldn't control. I thought that the recent lion-cat episode activated a memory of similar feelings when he was very small. He dropped his head and tried not to cry. I said that having a mother who in the past had sometimes acted crazy was a good reason to cry. When he again returned to the waiting room I brought out some puppets, but he angrily smashed them against the wall. I said that maybe he wanted to throw away his problems, but throwing away the puppets wouldn't help, because the problem was in his head.

Returning to the playroom, Cal complained that there were no new games. Asked what game he'd like, he answered Stratego. I replied that perhaps he wanted a new strategy, a new way to solve the old problem. Cal then returned to the puppets, the lion and a dog, whom he assigned to be a detective, and declared that they were in a ship headed toward the Bermuda Triangle. But triadic relationships were still too dangerous, for when they reached the triangle they disappeared to a new continent, where it was very safe. However, after several sessions, monsters appeared, and Cal formed a search party that included the cat to find the missing ship and to help get rid of the monsters. Returning to Earth, the lion once again attacked the cat; strangling her with a rope, he hung her from the wall. This time I recalled to him how once a real cat had run away when he tried to tie her up and accidentally hanged herself. He said it was his fault she died, as he had put the rope on her.

But I pointed out that he had put on the rope to stop her from running away from him, to control her, not kill her; that maybe he had *thought* about killing her, mixing up his feelings with his actions, and then felt helpless when the accident occurred. Pretending to kill the cat purposefully might be Cal's way of proving he wasn't helpless. Near the end of the hour Cal took the cat down and skillfully threw darts. As he left, he said, "That hit the bull's-eye. It was a grand slam." And it was.

Although the interpretation was correct and needed some elaboration, it also was a slam at Cal's fantasied omnipotence. It took several weeks for him to work out his anger at me and to rework his sorrow and fears about his mother, the cat's death, and his now diminished needs for "super" control. The relationship with his father improved as Cal was able to respond to Mr. B's encouragement to be more active in sports and become the star player of a winning soccer team. Less anxious and more confident, Cal was freer, less desperate in his play, so our sessions felt much lighter. Constructing a series of paper airplanes, he proudly showed me that he could not only sail them across the office but make them do single and double loops and land safely. When I admired his skill, he was pleased, not frightened.

For several weeks he worked on concerns of tumescence. First constructing a series of missiles, he now allowed himself to launch them and by remote control managed their flight and safe landing. Then he took some time making a fail-safe parachute that would always open in time and never crash. Finally he made some whirlybirds, paper planes which, if tossed straight up, would make rapid spins as they slowly descended in an elegant and appealing dance. These were most exciting to him, and he decorated them with bright colors and designs. Beginning with his concern about safe landings, our conversation moved from children's concerns about their bodies to little boys' fears about controlling *all* their arms and legs, and finally to Cal's specific worries about his penis. Although somewhat concerned about its size, he was more concerned that detumescence meant losing his penis. Asked if he had the same fear at other times, he became silent. Noting his thrill with the whirlybirds, I asked if flying them gave him exciting feelings and thoughts that also scared him. He replied, "I'm bored!" For a while his play had no consistent focus; then he began playing chess. Sometime before the summer break, I commented that he seemed intent on knocking off my queen. He corrected me, saying that he was capturing the queen and all the king's men so that all the land would be his. He showed me how carefully he was protecting his prisoners, adding, with an impish grin, that prisoners can't leave. We were then able to talk about his missing me and his sessions. Although he was looking forward to a vacation with his family, he wanted me to stay put in the office or, if I went away, to go away with him.

Cal demonstrated considerable growth in his ego functions: he made friends, was less fearful of and more proficient at sports, improved his grades, and spent more time with his father. There was evidence of an early superego in his improved self-esteem and an interest in, rather than a fear of, following rules in sports, at school, at home, and in the office. Nearing the end of the midphase of his analysis, Cal had achieved a major resolution of his preoedipal conflicts and no longer regressed from his oedipal concerns. With the triadic conflicts activated, when the analysis resumed in the fall an oedipal transformation emerged around earlier themes. For instance, at first there was a brief revival of the jungle theme with the lion and the king as lethal rivals for the affection of the prince and princess. Ultimately the king and lion became partners, with the lion showing the king around the jungle and the king, sharing his resources, showing the lion how to better defend against hunters. Together, the king and the lion provided for their kingdom but also enjoyed going fishing. Similarly, other themes that Cal had avoided, as the detective story and his army battles reemerged, however phallic competition, rather than narcissism, predominated. Although there were victors and vanquished, no one was destroyed or unalterably injured. With clear understanding of the difference between his fantasies and reality, Cal gradually lost interest in his dramas and became more involved in board games and rules. After six months he had sufficiently resolved his oedipal conflicts and entered a termination phase. His analysis was brought to a close two years and eight months after it had begun.

DISCUSSION

Cal's analysis reveals the importance of preoedipal material in transference reactions during the evaluation and early analysis, and in transference transformations during the midphase and termination. Importantly, the presence of oedipal content does not necessarily mean that an oedipal phase has been traversed, or that its accompanying conflicts have been actively engaged. Oedipal themes appeared fleetingly throughout Cal's analysis, but it was only in the final six to eight months that they were predominant. In his first interview he indicated that he desperately wanted to enter the oedipal phase but was unable to do so. That is, although he wanted rockets, army ships, and planes, and even meticulously arranged a cowboy versus Indian war, he was unable to play war because it was too dangerous and associated with the as-yet vague conflict about a cat. The next session he found the army toys, and played out a war, but was upset that the bad guys with superior forces beat the good guys. This indicated the presence of superego precursors, in that he knew right from wrong. However, he had not internalized a sufficiently firm and less primitive superego structure to help him with his internal war between what he felt to be his overpowering bad side, his impulses, and his weaker good side, his ego. This lack of development impaired his reality testing, his cognitive development, and his social interactions. Later, in his drawings he identified with a thief who stole a smart father bat's nest. Convinced that the smart father would retrieve and punish the thief, Cal didn't want to be the thief—but because he feared external punishment, not because he would feel guilty. Even his fantasies of stealing the nest, of wanting to see how babies are born, and his envy of his father's phallic power, as in the picture of the medieval castle, are not completely oedipal because they are more diadic than triadic. He really wanted to spend time with his father. One of the first changes his mother reported was Cal's ability to get his father to hug him. Although envious of the king, his nice queen was hungry, not sufficiently appealing for Cal to risk an oedipal battle with an equally hungry king. As we began, Cal regressed, not from the oedipal, but from the phallic-narcissistic phase to earlier phases, evident first in his making a mess with clay (anal) and cheating with Candyland (oral). Subsequently he was unable to tolerate his aggressive or libidinal drives at any level, and his frozen behavior and muteness in the waiting room spoke loudly of his fear that his drives and fantasies were actually hazardous. Additionally, he was afraid that I could read his mind and wouldn't tolerate his dependency needs or anger, an early maternal transference reaction, illustrated by his mouth as a scary, bottomless black hole, the hungry dinosaur, the wars that were not fun, and his mentioning of a cat which later was transformed into the pivotal drama of "cat fever."

The waiting room war gradually subsided as Cal felt sufficiently safe to be passively provocative, like his father, trying to avoid his conflicts by provoking me to give up on him. When, instead of being exasperated, I interpreted his behavior with the humorous puppet play, he became secure enough to begin to explore his problems. But, frightened by moving too fast to oedipal conflicts in his puppet play (murdering a father puppet), he refused to come into the office. This culminated with his throwing up outside my office door. As he didn't vomit inside the office, I thought we had a treatment alliance and he was acting out a new edition of his conflicts when he began to attend nursery school. Rather than neurotic conflicts based on guilt, Cal's behavior reflected his attempts to alter the environment to void persecutory fears (Renik, 1993). When he came to believe that we would be working to understand his behavior, not punish it, he finally relaxed, consistently playing out rather than acting out his conflicts.

In the preceding sessions, while we learned how to work together and Cal portrayed his difficulties, he had many transference reactions that I interpreted. Aside from the frequency of the sessions, much of our work would be hard to distinguish from good analytically oriented psychotherapy. Significantly, entering the midphase, the qualitative and quantitative changes in Cal's behavior in the sessions were palpable and unique to psychoanalysis. His eagerness to come to his sessions and intense involvement in developing and sustaining the alligator theme with me became the primary motivation in his daily life. This was not transient like the earlier themes but over many weeks became an all-encompassing, continually evolving focus for working through his conflicts over his oral rage and dependency needs. Through the puppets, Cal had transferred and transformed his old internalized oral conflicts with his mother to the new alligator drama with me. His rapacious, insatiable alligator portrayed the colicky, sleepless infant who Mrs. B. complained made her feel helpless and inadequate. Speaking through the puppets, my comments and interpretations were accepted and understood by Cal, enabling him to resolve his oral transference transformation.

The emergence of the lion puppet signaled the beginning of increasingly complex scenarios depicting multiple dramatic metaphors of infantile conflicts. Although Cal's creative, expressive, and cognitive ego skills had progressed, his persecutory worries persisted, so his attempts to work on oedipal themes failed. In a reaction formation to reinforce his newly won control over his oral concerns, Cal became the brave, independent little lion who helped supply food and protect the other animals—the opposite of the alligator. However, Cal was still worried about his other impulses projected onto the ever-present hunters. The hunters weren't killers; they wanted to cage the animals and watch them, like the thief who wanted to steal the father bat's nest to watch how babies are born. With the introduction of the prince and princess he acknowledged a need for help and relationships. They represented his brother and sister, who were parental surrogates for him. Later, recalling his earlier muteness, the lion became affectionately involved with the princess (his sister, a mother surrogate and me, his analyst), who taught him the language of his feelings. Contrary to his mother's view that Cal simply didn't need to speak, Cal's lion didn't speak because of fear and anger. When the lion agreed to learn to speak, it was for love. Furthermore, the lion tried to gain more admiration from the princess with a charming series of phallic exhibitionist feats. When the king/father, with the real power and gold, appeared, the lion's aggression became too dangerous. Cal's only solution was to kill the lion. The subsequent more intricate themes with people puppets and toys followed the same progression to oedipal struggles, at which point Cal's character was killed.

The real events of the stolen puppets and my bandaged foot escalated Cal's anxiety, reactivating traumatic memories of his early relationship with his mother, which he had acted out at nursery school and with the cat. His fantasies about these events were transformed into a new illness, "cat fever." This was a diadic struggle between his fears of hating and killing and his fears of being hated and killed. Again, this was not neurosis. There was never a trace of guilt, shame, or sympathy for the agonizing tortures and deaths of the cat. The hostile-dependent relationship with his mother spanned all the preoedipal years, and this was truly a preoedipal transference transformation, in which I was assigned the role of the cat, the preoedipal mother. The cat also was an externalization of what he feared he was, because a lion is a big cat. His mother was the primary source for identification, as his father was unavailable and his siblings were in school. Additionally, despite his mother's inconsistencies, her episodic hostile outbursts and withdrawals, she was his primary nurturer. Beneath her illness, she wanted to be able to love Cal and occasionally she did. Cal's conviction that his pervasive neediness and rage, throughout all phases of his preoedipal development, had caused all his conflicts made any further growth too perilous. Thus, the critical turning point in the analysis came when Cal understood that he had not caused his mother's illness and that, despite his fantasies, the cat's death was an accident. Relinquishing his need for omnipotence, which had compensated for his feelings of helplessness, he was able to mourn the chaos of his early life. The resolution of the preoedipal conflicts freed him to develop an oedipal transformation, through which he rapidly resolved his oedipal struggles. His increased ego strengths and improved relationship with his father helped him to identify with his father and to incorporate a less primitive, more stable superego. With a more mature intrapsychic structure, he entered latency, becoming an outstanding athlete and student, as well as developing a few close friends and maintaining good relationships with his family.

Do transference neuroses fully develop in child and adolescent analysis, as in adult treatment (Kut, 1953; Fraiberg, 1966; Tyson, 1978; Chused, 1988)? In my experience they do (Frenkel, 1991a, 1991b,

1993). However, Cal did not develop a transference neurosis as he had not traversed the oedipal terrain until the end of the analysis, when an infantile neurosis, the residue of his oedipal struggles, was formed as part of his new inner psychic structure (Tolpin, 1970; Loewald, 1974). Whereas the infantile neurosis has the potential to cause symptoms manifested in the transference neuroses of children, adolescents, and adults, it had not done so in Cal's case. Recently, during an accidental meeting, Cal told me he had been free of symptoms since his analysis. Currently, he was enjoying his postgraduate studies at a prestigious university and was about to be married.

Cal's case clearly demonstrates analytic process with preoedipal conflicts. Although it is tempting to call these conflicts neurotic, this would be inaccurate, as Cal's immature ego and superego anlage prevented him from dealing with oedipal concerns. Similar observations have been commented on previously. Dealing with an adult patient comparable to Cal, Loewald (1971), by including oedipal and preoedipal concerns, broadened both the clinical and the theoretical meaning of the transference neurosis so that it remained the *sine qua non* of psychoanalysis. Miller (1987) suggested that the term "transference formation" be used to replace "transference neurosis," to relieve the concept of its restriction to the Oedipus complex. Tyson (1993) also suggested that we drop the obligatory linkage of neurosis to the oedipal constellation. Although these concerns are understandable, there is much to be lost by changing the meaning of neurosis or by deleting or replacing the concept of the transference neurosis. The concept persists because of its well established bond to a specific developmental phase. In addition, its tangible presence, unique to psychoanalysis, becomes the force field for conflict resolution and intrapsychic restructuring. By contrast, restricting the defining characteristics of psychoanalysis to the Oedipus complex, the infantile neurosis, and the transference neurosis limits the growth, viability, and credibility of analysis.

It is well documented that internalized psychic conflicts can produce symptoms prior to the oedipal phase. Calling all these symptoms neurotic loses the significant difference between preoedipal and post-oedipal development with its immense expansion of ego functions and the pivotal establishment of the superego. This is relevant not only developmentally and theoretically but clinically. The analysis of a neurotic patient of any age is an entirely different experience from the analysis of a patient with preoedipal conflicts who lacks a stable superego. Not understanding this difference can lead to analytic stalemates and to the rejection of some patients as unanalyzable. It has also resulted in major schisms in our field, some of which disagreements may be more apparent than real. As infants and toddlers are more helpless and dependent on primary caregivers than older children and adults, object relations are more important in their sense of well-being and the formation of their inner world. By contrast, even partial resolution of the oedipal drama makes an individual more independent and concerned with conflicts in his own mind than with fears of the external world. Moore and Fine (1990) stress the importance of the Oedipus complex in integrating superego functions so that the child develops self-expectations and self-criticism with the potential for loss of self-esteem and guilt. The presence of guilt has been called "hallmark" of the superego (Beres, 1958) and the basis of neurotic symptoms. The distinction between pre- and post-oedipal development is extremely relevant. The move to the oedipal phase signals the shift to triadic relations and the beginning of the capacity to care for another. Progression beyond the oedipal phase ensures ego expansion and superego formation, an indispensable psychic organizer in the life of the individual and the development of civilization.

Cal's analysis provides in-depth developmental and clinical process data supporting the need for the formulation "transference transformations." Brenner (1982) described the transference neurosis as merely an increase in transference. Calling it anachronistic and repetitive as transference and neurosis are compromise formations, he proposed the term "analyzable transference." However, as compromise formations exist throughout psychic life, they are ubiquitous and thus lose the explanatory power inherent in the specificity of developmental lines. Furthermore, as Cal's process data detailed, the distinction between transference reactions and transference transformations critically distinguishes psychoanalysis from other psychotherapies. Accordingly, transference transformations, which include the transference neurosis, are the most powerful propellant of the analytic process, and their evolution and resolution are discernible by both analyst and analysand (Bird, 1972).

The advantage of the concept of transference transformations is that it expands our capacity to understand and more accurately interpret and describe a wider range of transference manifestations specific to psychoanalysis. It eliminates the debate over whether oedipal or pre-oedipal conflicts are more critical in the development of the individual and in the formation of mental conflicts. Because both are crucial, but distinctly different, we must pay more attention to the ways in which they overlap and interact with each other. Moreover, the relative prominence of one phase over the other can be determined individually. In most analysands they probably vary not only over the course of the analysis but also over a series of sessions or even within a particular session. Thus, the concept encompasses the current findings of both infant research and clinical studies, which have enhanced and expanded our understanding of the complexities and diversity of human growth and development from early infancy through adolescence, adulthood, and late adult life. Additionally, it allows for equally significant mental conflicts to occur at all phases of post-oedipal development. This does not mean that conflicts of infancy and childhood disappear but, rather, that the derivatives of these conflicts and their concomitant internalized object representations are recast by working through the developmental tasks of latency, adolescence, and adult life. Accordingly, in the analytic situation unconscious conflicts from specific developmental phases throughout life are first reactivated by the transference as transference reactions and later are redramatized in transference transformations through which they are analyzed and resolved. The concept of transference transformations is more than a nosological addition; it is a conceptual expansion enabling us to retain clinically convincing and descriptively useful formulations while eliminating much that has been and still is potentially divisive and/or reductionistic. At the same time it provides a base for further expansion of our theory and technique.

BIBLIOGRAPHY

BERES, D. (1958). Superego functions and superego precursors in childhood. *Psychoanal. Study Child* 13:324–351.

BIRD, D. (1972). Notes on transference: Universal phenomenon and hardest part of analysis. *J. Amer. Psychoanal. Assn.* 20:267–301.

BRENNER, C. (1982). *The Mind in Conflict.* New York: Int. Univ. Press.

CHUSED, J. F. (1988). The transference neurosis in child analysis. *Psychoanal. Study Child* 43:51–81.

COOPER, A. M. (1987). The transference neurosis: A concept ready for retirement. *Psychoanal. Inq.* 7:569–585.

EDGCUMBE, R., & BURGNER, M. (1975). The phallic narcissistic phase. *Psychoanal. Study Child* 30:161–180.

FRAIBERG, S. (1966). Further consideration of the role of transference in latency. *Psychoanal. Study Child* 21:213–236.

FRENKEL, R. S. (1991a). The early abortion of a pseudocyesis: Some observations from the analysis of an adolescent girl. *Psychoanal. Study Child* 46:237–254.

——— (1991b). Termination in the analysis of an adolescent girl: "I grew to the point I should be." In *Saying Goodbye,* ed. A. Schmukler. Hillsdale, N.J.: Analytic Press, pp. 211–229.

———— (1993). Problems in female development: Comments on the analysis of an early latency-age girl. *Psychoanal. Study Child* 48:171–192.

FREUD, A. (1963). The concept of developmental lines. *Psychoanal. Study Child* 18:245–265.

———— (1965). *Normality and Pathology in Childhood.* New York: Int. Univ. Press.

FREUD, S. (1917). Introductory lectures on psychoanalysis. *S.E.,* 16.

KUT, S. (1953). The changing patterns of transference in an eleven-year-old girl. *Psychoanal. Study Child* 8:355–378.

LOEWALD, H. (1971). The transference neurosis: Comments on the concept and the phenomenon. In *Papers on Psychoanalysis.* New Haven: Yale Univ. Press, 1980.

———— (1974). Current status of the concept of infantile neurosis. *Psychoanal. Study Child* 29:183–188.

MILLER, J. P. (1987). The transference neurosis from the viewpoint of self psychology. *Psychoanal. Inq.* 7:535–550.

MOORE, B. E., & FINE, B. D. (1990). *Psychoanalytic Terms and Concepts.* New Haven: Yale Univ. Press and American Psychoanal. Assn.

RENIK, O. (1993). Clinical presentation: Transference neurosis. Panel on Current Controversies about Transference. Presented at the fall meeting of the Amer. Psychoanal. Assn.

TOLPIN, M. (1970). The infantile neurosis. *Psychoanal. Study Child* 25:273–305.

TYSON, P. (1978). Transference and developmental issues in prelatency analysis. *Psychoanal. Study Child* 33:213–236.

———— (1993). Neurosis in childhood and psychoanalysis: A developmental reformulation. Presented at the May meeting of the Amer. Psychoanal. Assn.

WEINSHEL, E. M. (1971). The transference neurosis: A survey of the literature. *J. Amer. Psychoanal. Assn.* 19:67–88.

The Role of Passivity in the Relationship to the Body during Adolescence

M. EGLÉ LAUFER

For some adolescents the bodily changes occurring at puberty and during adolescence are a source of intense anxiety. Rather than integrate the new sexual body within the existing body image, these adolescents respond to the physical changes with behavior that attempts to maintain the omnipotent fantasy that they are in control of their bodies. Unconsciously they experience the changes as if they are able to prevent physical change from taking place and therefore can remain passively dependent on their parents. They feel as if the sexual body has the power to make them helpless by forcing them to submit passively to its demands. The case of an adolescent seen in analysis is presented to illustrate the defensive function of such symptomatic behavior and its repetitive, compulsive quality.

FROM MANY YEARS OF WORKING WITH SERIOUSLY DISTURBED ADOLES-cents who have been assessed as having suffered a developmental breakdown, it has become increasingly clear to me that the symptomatology of these adolescents is typified by some form of self-destructive behavior. Whatever its form, this behavior always has a driven quality and unconsciously represents an attack on the adolescent's body. Although at first we thought that this concept applied only to adolescents who had actually attempted to kill themselves or were mutilating their bodies, it now appears that it can be extended to other

Member and training analyst at the British Psychoanalytical Society and staff member at the Brent Adolescent Centre/Centre for Research into Adolescent Breakdown.

The Psychoanalytic Study of the Child 51, ed. Albert J. Solnit, Peter B. Neubauer, Samuel Abrams, and A. Scott Dowling (Yale University Press, copyright © 1996 by Albert J. Solnit, Peter B. Neubauer, Samuel Abrams, and A. Scott Dowling).

symptomatic behaviors such as anorexia, bulimia, substance abuse, and violence, as well as to such sexual behaviors as promiscuity and compulsive masturbation. Attacks on the body can be understood as symbolizing the adolescent's relationship to his body in that it is being treated as an object of the adolescent's hatred. In even more disturbed adolescents, the relationship to the body has broken down completely. Instead of feeling compelled to attack the body, which we regard as evidence that they have a relationship to the body, they have compelling thoughts or persecutory hypochondriacal ideas of a more delusional nature, indicating that the relationship to the body is taking place only in fantasy. This paper discusses how such compulsive, self-destructive behavior in adolescents results from a developmental breakdown following puberty and represents a defense against the anxiety created by the experience of the changes in their body.

Adolescents have always been regarded as prone to action or "acting out." The psychoanalytic literature suggests that this is caused by an increase in the strength of the sexual and aggressive drives that occurs with the physical changes of puberty or to poor impulse control owing to an inadequately functioning superego. However, in the clinical treatment situation, I have been more impressed by the sense that the behavior of such adolescents was impelled by intense anxiety rather than expressive of an instinctual need demanding to be gratified. The compelling need for action reveals the extent to which these adolescents feel threatened by the experience of passivity in the relationship to their body. Although I regard this fear of passivity as omnipresent in all adolescents, including those developing normally, in the seriously disturbed adolescent it derives from the experience of the body as forcing them into a passive relationship to it. These adolescents relate to the body as an object that has the power to force them to relinquish childhood and submit to their adulthood and adult sexuality. When this experience presents the adolescent with unbearable anxiety, his sexual body becomes the object of his attacks and driven behavior. Carrying out an action in relation to the body allows the adolescent to feel in active control of it once more and in possession of some defense against being forced to feel helpless or passive in relation to it. The adolescent is not aware that his action is driven by anxiety and is out of his control but instead believes that it is something he has chosen to do. In severe cases, where it is necessary to constrain this behavior in order to protect the adolescent from his destructive attack on himself, the intervention makes the adolescent aware of the compelling nature of his behavior and confronts him with the terror of madness—that is, the awareness of having lost control over his mind—which lies behind the omnipotent fantasy of being in control. The adolescent then fears being totally dependent on such compelling behavior for his psychic survival, even if it threatens his physical survival.

The fantasy of having omnipotent control of his body allows the adolescent to believe that he can maintain the relationship to his pre-pubertal body, as though he can prevent the physical changes from obliging him to deal with having a sexual body, with all its psychological significance. Furthermore, the behavior—for instance, starving him-self—expresses the hatred he feels for the actual sexual body.

To illustrate this situation I will describe Jean, a girl of 18, who was seen at our walk-in treatment center. At times she would feel driven to stuff herself with food, making herself so ill that she had to make herself vomit. This behavior was not her original reason for seeking help, but it gradually became central in her treatment as it became clear how compelling it was in certain situations. For instance, she was afraid of going out to eat with friends lest she reveal her greedy, needy self. Or when she had given in and eaten some food her mother had prepared for her instead of rejecting it, she would hate herself for having given in to her passive wish to be cared for by her mother, feeling that in so doing she had lost control of her body. She was then compelled to stuff herself with food before she could once more feel autonomous and in control. Making herself vomit subsequently was a way of punishing herself for her passive longings, forcing her to experience herself as disgusting as well as representing an attack on her body. Masturbation similarly can be seen as permitting a sense of autonomy over the grati-fication of sexual desire and a defense against passive dependence on an object. However, to regard bulimic behavior simply as a displace-ment from a genital to an oral impulse would not sufficiently empha-size the use of the action as an expression of conscious hatred of the body. In fact, it can be argued that it is the inability to masturbate, for fear of losing control of the hatred of the sexual body, that necessitates the displacement from the genital to the oral domain.

For Jean the main motivating force seemed to be the anxiety she experienced when she felt as if her body was giving in to her hunger for a caring object. The compelling self-destructive behavior acted both as a defense against this anxiety and an expression of her hatred for her body. I have called such forms of defensive pathological behavior re-petitive compelling behavior. Paradoxically, although this repetitive compulsive behavior is used unconsciously by the disturbed adolescent to feel in control of her body, it leaves her vulnerable to experiencing herself as being out of control because of its compelling nature. Clini-cally it can be identified by its repetitive, addictive quality, that is, it is a behavior that, however self-destructive, cannot be given up because of its function as a means of dealing with intense anxiety.

In *Analysis Terminable and Interminable,* Freud (1937) describes the "repudiation of femininity" as a "remarkable feature in the psychical life of human beings," affecting the attitude of both male and female children when faced with the reality of the oedipal situation and the need to identify their body as being like that of the parent of the same gender. But Freud (1931) also emphasized that before the polarity of masculinity and femininity is finally established, after puberty, the opposition is between that of an active and a passive mode of being. The repudiation of femininity can therefore be understood on a more primitive level to be the repudiation of passivity. We can observe this repeatedly, acting as a resistance in the clinical situation.

The changes of puberty revive the demands made on the child's psychic structure at the time of the classical Oedipus complex, impelling the adolescent to identify his or her body as that of a sexual male or female identified with that of the oedipal parent's. This renewed demand on the psychic structure is the basis for the anxiety the adolescent experiences and motivates his need to repudiate passivity by turning the passive experience into an active one. Having a sexual body makes it possible for him or her to identify with the active role of the oedipal parent. To attack the body is to reject this identification with the parent of the same gender. The process of identification itself takes on an active or a passive meaning. If this development is desired by the adolescent, it can be described as an active identification. The adolescent who dreads becoming like the oedipal parent yet the possibility becomes compelled to undertake actions that deny the identification; this can be described as a passive identification. Instead of being able to allow for a gradual integration of the new sexual body to become part of his new psychic reality, the adolescent is compelled to control, attack, or repudiate the body while struggling to achieve an acceptable masculine or feminine identity.

Freud's statement regarding the repudiation of femininity by both genders has important bearing on postpubertal development. If we also ask how such a repudiation affected the earlier identification the infant made in the preoedipal period with the active (phallic) mother, we can then see how this earlier identification can be regarded as a defense against the wish for the passive relationship to the mother's breast, by replacing it with an active one in order to repudiate passivity and ward off feelings of helpless dependence on the mother. The outcome of this early phase of development is crucial in determining the relationship the child has to his body in the prepubertal period.

This is of special significance in the case of the girl where the conflict may become that of wishing to remain a child and not have to become identified with the mother's sexual body, on the one hand; while at the same time she still needs to maintain the identification with the active phallic mother in order to defend against early passive longings to remain the mother's helpless infant. For some adolescent girls becoming a sexual woman herself and feeling forced, by the identification of their body with the sexual mother, as if it forces them into a passive sexual role in relation to the new male sexual object. The repudiated passive longings can then remain projected onto the male. While for the boy, identification with the active phallic mother may be the only way he can feel able to defend against his early infantile passive wishes when the identification with the active sexual father is too conflictual. The danger for the boy is that with the arrival of puberty his body has to remain identified with that of a woman, and he may be unable to integrate his new active penis-possessing role. For these male adolescents possession of an active penis can unconsciously be experienced as a threat to their dependence on the female identification of their early childhood, which they need in order to repudiate their passivity. Identifying their body with their father's makes them feel as if they must destroy their penis in order not to give in to surrendering to their passive longing for the early nurturing mother.

The meaning of the fantasy being enacted by the adolescent in his self-destructive behavior in relation to the body can be better understood as it becomes repeated and used as a resistance in the transference. As described by Freud in *Analysis Terminable and Interminable* (1937), it constitutes a severe resistance to psychic change within the analysis and is the most frequent reason for a breakdown in the analysis of adolescents. It is as if the adolescent unconsciously projects his sexual body onto the analyst and in the transference relationship enacts the fantasy of being in omnipotent control by controlling the analyst. It is for this reason that any holiday break or other changes in the setting initiated by the analyst become a period of increased risk of the adolescent patient's attacking his own body. When he feels abandoned by the analyst and confronted by the reality of not being able to control him the adolescent is put in touch with his feelings of dependence and helplessness in relation to the analyst, compelling him to attack his own body as the source of his neediness.

The fantasy compelling the adolescent to action is that his body is responsible for making him feel vulnerable and out of his control and in the helpless situation of being left by the analyst. Self-inflicted pain, as long as it can be denied, takes on the unconscious meaning of having a "dead body"—that is, one that is safe because it has no feelings and thus acts as a defense against the compulsion to attack or kill oneself. The painful experience is taken as proof that the body has lost its power to threaten the adolescent's ego with being made helpless. For some adolescents, the fantasy of needing to have a dead body becomes projected onto the external objects as well as the analyst, who in turn must be experienced as "dead"—that is, having no power to evoke an affective response. Any awareness of feelings is feared as something that would threaten psychic survival. These adolescents may also be compelled into violence against the object as a means of defending against the anxiety they experience when the denial of affective response breaks down—for instance, the male adolescent who walks around with a knife in his pocket because he needs to feel that he can control and, if necessary, destroy the object who could evoke the feared anxiety in relation to his body if he experienced any sexual arousal. The adolescent may also use the idea of suicide as such a weapon, as, for instance, expressed by an anorexic girl telling her analyst, "If I were to put on one more pound, I would kill myself."

For other disturbed adolescents, as mentioned earlier, the need to deny any feelings coming from their bodies may have already led to a complete rupture with external reality when they were unable to maintain the fantasy of having omnipotent control of their body. But they re-experience the anxiety of their passive wishes in their inner psychic experience when they hear voices or have compelling delusional thoughts about the body, which makes them feel out of control of their mind and, as if in fantasy, being forced to submit passively to an alien unknown object that has taken over their mind and thinking.

Such a psychotic mental state can itself become addictive for the adolescent in that it temporarily protects him from the need to destroy his body because he no longer feels the threat of the experience of passivity as coming from his body. The conflict is with his thoughts or voices. This may also help to explain the adolescent's vulnerability to becoming addicted to drugs, if it can be used as a means of deadening the body and controlling the mind through chemically induced states of depersonalization.

For the adolescents I describe here, the reality of the pubertal changes in the body and the need to change their relationship to it do not result in the ambivalent and confusing relationship to the new sexual body characteristic of the normal adolescent—that is, one that can allow for a mixture of pain and pleasure, passive waiting for experience and excited, active anticipation. Instead, the physical changes have brought intense anxiety leading to a fear of being overwhelmed and made helpless, and therefore leaving them dependent on compulsive activity or thoughts in order to maintain the fantasy of being in omnipotent control through their activity.

In analytic treatment the terror of losing control if they are obliged to give up the symptomatic behavior, which maintains the omnipotent fantasy, leads such adolescents to look to the relationship to the analyst as a means of feeling controlled. At times of greater anxiety, the intensity of the resulting dependence can make the adolescent blame the analyst as causing his anxiety. This can make the adolescent need to avoid the analyst and be unable to come to the session, especially, for instance the last session before a holiday break. In the more disturbed adolescent, such staying away is not just a turning of "passive into active," leaving instead of being left, but is evidence of an increase in the paranoid anxiety the adolescent feels when his positive or negative feelings toward the analyst, related to his dependence on him, are experienced as sexual or violent fantasies about the analyst. The fantasy can then be of the analyst as responsible for making the adolescent lose control of his body sexually or of his violence. These paranoid anxieties may also be experienced in relation to the mind, making the adolescent feel that the analyst has power to control his thoughts and make him mad. It is through these experiences in the transference that the analyst, together with the adolescent, can explore the fantasies regarding the original object, the threatening preoedipal mother, underlying the intense anxieties that necessitated the adolescent's defensive use of the compelling repetitive behavior.

When these paranoid anxieties lead to a crisis in the transference situation, with the risk that the analysis will break down, it can be a relief for the adolescent to be admitted temporarily to a psychiatric unit, where he can feel protected from his fear of madness and his self-destructiveness and where the hospital acts as a protective barrier between him and the analyst. At the same time it is of course important for the analyst to maintain contact with the adolescent in some way, offering reassurance that he has not abandoned the patient but is ready to continue with the analysis when the adolescent is in a less vulnerable and unstable state.

To illustrate the issues I have emphasized so far, I will describe the case of Ann, a 21-year-old woman who came for help complaining of being depressed.

In fact, Ann was not only depressed but had become unable to get on with her life; it seemed as if she had broken down in her day-to-day functioning. She appeared to have cut herself off from all her former friends and was remaining at home, feeling completely dependent on her mother for protection from the external world. It emerged that she was compelled at times to scratch or pluck at her breast, causing sufficient damage to require medical attention in the past. This had begun when she was 14, at a time when her mother developed breast cancer. Ann saw her own behavior as irrational and was afraid that there was something mad about her that needed to remain concealed. She consciously hated her body and had had to avoid physical contact with men while at college. She saw the feminine state as despicable and weak. Plucking at her breast expressed her unconscious wish to destroy this sign of her own femininity and also represented the object on which she feared feeling so dependent, her mother's breast.

According to Ann, her mother had been the dominating influence throughout her childhood, and when her mother developed cancer, Ann was faced with the anxious dread of losing her mother at a time when she still felt completely dependent on her. Uncommonly, becoming a sexual woman herself meant that she now had the power to destroy her mother through seeing her as the weak one. This resulted in hating herself for being weak and passively attached to her mother instead of being able to turn away from her and relate to men. These powerful conflicting feelings had become directed at her breast as representing both her own vulnerability and her mother's. The anxiety she experienced had not allowed for the integration of her sexual body, and by the end of adolescence, when she was faced with having to enter the adult world, she felt totally helpless and frightened. She had always seen her high academic achievement as something that would make her powerful, as did her mother, and therefore independent of her. Nevertheless, she felt she had no sexual identity based on a body she could rely on. Continuing to damage herself while denying any fear about what she was doing allowed her to feel as if she was free of anxiety by making her own breast and unconsciously her mother's dead and meaningless.

The adolescent also feels acquiring a sexual body at puberty as a loss of the childhood body that allows him or her to continue to feel a sense of closeness to the mother's body. It is part of the adolescent process that involves a process of mourning, as described by Anna Freud (1958). But for Ann, there was not only the normal sense of loss heightened by the threat of loss of the mother in reality but also the threat posed by the new sexual body that could make her vulnerable to becoming identified with her mother's body and, in fantasy, responsible for destroying the mother.

Although statistically there appear to be more female adolescents who are driven to attack their bodies than males, it seems in the males the anxiety tends to be related to the activity of the penis instead of involving the whole body or the breast, as in the female. The struggle against allowing the integration of the sexual body to proceed normally will continue to dominate the adolescent period for the seriously disturbed adolescent and, if unresolved, will prevent the final integration of the sexual body, which can allow them to feel sexually normal in adulthood (Laufer M. E.). During adolescence, while the conflict is ongoing between the forces that press for integration of the body and those that need to reject it, the extent to which development is threatened can be assessed by the extent to which the adolescent remains dependent on repetitive compulsive behavior involving the body. In such cases, as with Ann, the risk of suicide if the defense fails to contain the anxiety must always be kept in mind. For the adolescent killing themselves can become the ultimate means of repudiating the body while restoring the fantasy of omnipotent control without which they feel they cannot survive.

SARAH

In some cases, what can be observed is a swing between periods of manic activity, which maintain the fantasy of omnipotent control, and periods of despair and total helplessness. Such extreme swings characterized Sarah when I first saw her, at age 18. Such adolescents may be diagnosed as manic depressive, but what I want to show is how in the case of Sarah, the characteristic mood swings form part of the struggle against the integration of the sexual body and how this becomes expressed in the transference as a struggle against the experience of passive surrender to the analyst while at the same time having to experience total dependence.

Sarah first came to our Walk-In Centre at the suggestion of a psychiatrist who had treated her after a suicide attempt. While Sarah was being seen in regular interviewing—that is, before she had been recommended for and begun her analytic treatment—she became suicidal once more during a holiday break, but her friends helped her to get herself hospitalized. She remained in the hospital for six months, until she was thought well enough for discharge. During her stay in hospital, medication was prescribed to help control periods of extreme violent behavior toward herself. But initially she had remained totally inert on her bed in a darkened room. As it became clear after her discharge that these two states could alternate in extreme mood swings she was diagnosed as manic-depressive, and her medication was changed accordingly.

Sarah used any medication as part of her need to confuse herself as well as everyone else about her state of mind. She was aware of needing help, of the feelings of total helplessness which left her completely dependent on those caring for her, and at the same time of her compelling need to reject all help consciously because it meant that she was ill and unconsciously because it threatened her omnipotent state of mind. From her behavior in relation to her environment it was clear that she was involved in a frightening conflict between allowing herself to be helped to live and acting totally self-neglectful and self-destructive because of her feeling that she had no right to live. Her anxiety about being out of control of her body had become displaced to her mind; she was confused about whether her thinking was under her control and she knew all the answers to her behavior, or out of her control and therefore mad. I now think that it was when she felt invaded by her mother's thoughts and no longer in control of her mind and overwhelmed by violent feelings that she needed to deaden her body and had made the first determined attempt to kill herself. Sarah's deepest fear was of being like her violent mother, whom she regarded as mad. Thus becoming a sexual woman for Sarah carried the threat of becoming mad and violent like her mother.

The interviewer who first saw Sarah when she came to the Centre had found it very difficult to make contact with her. Sarah laughed inappropriately at any comment indicating that her state was being taken seriously, while talking in an intense and manic way about her view of herself. Her confusion was shown in the way she related to her physical state. During the hot weather she arrived in heavy, long-sleeved clothes and wondered why she was feeling so hot; later, during the winter, she arrived in thin cotton shorts. She said that after her suicide attempt she had begun to cut her arms and was afraid she might cut her face—or, as she put it, "cutting didn't bother her as long as she did not cut her face." The baggy clothes had concealed her shape, and the interviewer suspected that she was quite slight and possibly so thin that she might be anorexic. Sarah denied any awareness of being thin and instead complained of being forced to eat in the hospital and that she was getting too fat. However, Sarah continued to attend her interviewing session and agreed to start five-times-weekly analysis with me as soon as she was well enough to leave hospital and suitable living arrangements could be made.

Within the first weeks of beginning the analysis, Sarah made three further, though not so serious, suicide attempts, as though needing to be reassured that I and the hostel staff who had to look after her wanted her to live. At the same time, her lack of affect left me feeling numb, as if I could not experience any anxiety myself about her possible death. It was as if I had been made into a "dead," feelingless object unable to feel any anxiety. It was as if we both knew that this was a risk we were taking in treating her disturbance as serious and it was not safe to experience hope or hopelessness in the struggle for her survival. At the same time, it was only by feeling that she was still in control through being able to kill herself that she was able to risk beginning to have a relationship to me and the analysis and eventually to give up her dependence on medication to control her violence.

Sarah had run away from home at the age of 16. But she had nowhere to run to and had ended up sleeping on a park bench until she was housed by social services. Life at home had become unbearable when she could no longer feel in control of her own violence in response to her mother's violent behavior toward her. Her mother, from all accounts, not just Sarah's description, was an extremely disturbed woman who avoided all social and professional contacts because of her paranoid anxieties. According to Sarah, she had wanted to have an abortion when she became pregnant with Sarah and had had to be prevented from killing herself by Sarah's father. She blamed Sarah for all her unhappiness. Shortly before Sarah left home, her mother had developed breast cancer and had had to have a breast removed. This she also blamed on Sarah.

Teachers had told Sarah that she should not take her mother's accusations seriously, but this did not help her to feel less frightened of her mother and of becoming like her. She told me that she knew she was not mad like her mother because she could tell the difference between reality and her own thoughts. At the same time, I often could not tell which of her statements about herself were her own thoughts and which were her mother's. For instance, she would tell me that there was nothing wrong with her, that she was just bad and lazy, implying that I should not be treating her but should be punishing her, as her mother had done. At the same time this also meant that she could not bear for me to take her illness seriously because then she really had become like her mother. Sarah had begun to cut her arms during this period, and if she felt she had succeeded in making me flinch or show any anxiety about her self-destructive acts, she would taunt me with gruesome accounts of much worse things she had thought of doing to herself. It felt as if she wanted to show me how strong and unshockable she was as compared to me while forcing me to experience all the feelings she was having to deny.

She was quite overtly paranoid in her relation to me, refusing to lie on the couch because she said she could not trust me not to attack her when she could not see me. She explained these fears as based on her memories of when she was little and her mother had come into her room while she was asleep and had beaten her for some misbehavior during the day. But what Sarah had found particularly unbearable as a child was her mother's expectation that she would be able to forget the beating the next morning and be the cuddly and affectionate child the mother wanted. Being beaten was part of Sarah's childhood. She remembered being beaten so severely by her father at mother's behest that she thought she would die. Later this had become not just a feared fantasy but a sexualized wish that she had enacted in her suicide attempts at the beginning of her analysis. This became clear when she told me of a fantasy she had had as a child that one day she would do everything her mother told her she must do (as she was doing then by coming to her sessions), but that inasmuch as her mother's demands were totally unrealistic and unrealizable, she would die of exhaustion at her mother's feet, making her mother feel guilty and at last aware of how mad her expectations had been. Unconsciously this fantasy contained her wish to die rather than having to be identified with her mother through submitting to her mother's madness and become mad herself. The fantasy when beginning analysis had been that she could see me as if I was making mad demands on her, expecting her to come, talk, and show that she had total understanding of herself.

Sarah did not have one organized compelling behavior around which her pathological development was organized, as might be true of an anorexic adolescent. As well as cutting herself, she had many other ways of maintaining the omnipotent fantasy of being in control of her body and her mind and keeping out the persecuting mother/analyst, who she felt was trying to take her over. She insisted on being in charge of her food intake in order to undertake extreme diets; she also undertook physically demanding activities, forcing herself to the point of exhaustion. These periods of activity would alternate with periods where she would give up completely and just stay in her room, finding that even getting washed or dressed was too much of an effort. She talked with a manic-like intensity during her sessions, using her considerable intelligence to produce insights into the meaning of what she was doing but also using it to control me and my thoughts, for fear of what I might otherwise do to her mind. She used her friends and other professional helping agencies in the same way—telling them what was wrong with her while at the same time pushing away any help that challenged her belief that only she could understand or care for herself; no one could be trusted because of her fear of her wish for total passive submission. When she felt as if she had failed to control her mind and thus as if she had submitted to the "invasive attacks" of others, as for instance in the class room if having to listen to the teacher, she went back to using compulsive self-destructive behavior like cutting herself to restore the belief of having omnipotent control of her body. Neglecting her body at times when she felt unable to care for herself was also a way of attacking her body for making her aware of needs or desires that could make her feel helpless in relation to an object on which she felt dependent, as on me when she experienced me as some-one whom she needed. Despite this, she was able to come to her sessions most days after the first few weeks when the sessions had been inter-rupted by her hospitalization following the suicide attempts.

Sarah's breakdown in relation to her body apparently occurred soon after she reached puberty. She remembered in a confused way that she had become addicted to chocolate at this time and had felt that her mother was driving her mad by locking her in the house to prevent her from going out to buy chocolate. As evidence that her mother was the one who was disturbed, she said that her mother was trying to control her eating because she regarded Sarah as fat, while the doctor at school had been concerned by how thin she was. Her statements about her own mental state, however, contained as many contradictions as those she attributed to her mother and others. The role, which unconsciously she expected me to perform, was to bring together these contradictory and fragmented parts of herself into a harmonious whole that could be allowed to live. I think this also represented the relationship between her parents, who had tried to use her to reconcile their differences. Sarah had felt very oppressed by this role but also showed constantly how she was in fact trying to bring together the opposing views of her parents into her own relation to herself. In the first year of her analysis, when Sarah talked of her mother, it often was difficult to tell whether she was expressing her own ideas or her mother's—a confusion I felt sure Sarah shared. But at the same time she would refer to statements of her father as if trying to use them to keep herself from being taken over by the mother's thoughts, only to have to reject them because she felt they were an attack on her mother. If I tried to discuss her depres-sion at times when she was unable to do anything such as get up and get dressed, she would say she was bad and lazy and wonder whether she should be having analysis at all because there was nothing wrong with her—at the same time telling me that this was what her mother said when Sarah had tried to tell her she was depressed. She would then tell me her father believed that a certain diet could cure her depression instead of having to rely on medication or analysis.

The need to leave home had occurred when Sarah no longer felt safe in the mother's presence because it made her feel as if she could no longer keep her mind or her actions under her own control and that her father was not there to come between them. Sarah's mother at that time was telling her that her cancer had been caused by having such a bad daughter and also behaving as if she was afraid that Sarah would attack her. When Sarah did lose control, her violence against her mother not only confirmed the mother's view of her as dangerous but made Sarah feel as if she was being taken over by her mother's "mad" ideas. Sarah's mother had been violent toward her since she was little, but Sarah had always tried to keep herself from responding with violence or anger and to ignore her mother's outbursts, as her father did. But this time, when her mother threw something at Sarah, she had thrown it back at her mother and hurt her. Sarah could no longer deny that her body was now strong enough to retaliate against her mother's attacks. I think the conjunction of her mother's accusations and her actual harming of the mother is what made Sarah feel compelled to leave. She described herself as having been totally happy during the first months after leaving home. She felt in control of her life and could work or spend her time with friends as she liked instead of feeling controlled by her mother. She told me she could not understand why she would have wanted to kill herself, some months later when she had taken a large overdose. She was also aware that her happy state had been destroyed by feeling that she was unable to prevent her mother from invading her mind with guilt feelings through letters and phone calls complaining that Sarah had deserted her at a time when she needed help to cope with the younger children because of her recent operation. Having thought she could survive separation from her mother and feel herself to be normal, Sarah felt hopeless once more. In feeling guilty the fantasy was that she was once more being invaded by her mother's thoughts, which to Sarah meant her body being taken over by her mother.

In fact there were signs that Sarah was breaking down for some time before she left home. From having been a star pupil at school, she had become increasingly unable to function despite her attempts to remain in control of her mind. And from her subsequent desperate attempts to convince herself that she was sexually normal, I assume that she had also begun to worry about her ability to feel normal in a physical relationship. When I first saw Sarah, she was still a patient at the hospital and had formed a relationship with a male patient with whom she wanted to live. Although she blamed me at times for having insisted that she move into the protected environment of a hostel, she also acknowledged that she had been afraid to permit any sexual intimacy.

She complained of having no sexual feelings and wished she could feel something, regardless of whether it meant she was heterosexual or homosexual. At the same time it was clear in the transference how important it was to her to maintain the belief that she felt nothing, no pain or desire, and to put me in the position of the persecutor who was trying to invade her mind with my feelings and whom she had to keep at a distance. This suggests that her relationship to her sexual body was already impaired to the extent that she could feel no longer threatened by it; rather, she felt the threat as coming from the object.

In order to maintain a relationship to someone she felt dependent on, such as a doctor or hostel staff, Sarah needed to be able to hold the person's hand or use hugging to reassure herself of the person's presence and of her own and the other's lack of sexual desire. In the analytic relationship, where this was not possible, she was extremely anxious, and there were times when she was unable to look at me or would attack her body in some way, as by pulling out her hair in the session. In the transference Sarah enacted her belief that if she could not continue to be the weak and helpless child who had to submit to the powerful, controlling mother/analyst, she could only become the sexual woman, powerful enough to destroy a damaged and weak "mad" me. She often reassured me that I was not like the other helpers she had talked to, that I was not stupid like them and taken in by her and her apparently "brilliant" self-analysis—thus reassuring herself and me that she had not been able to destroy me and that we could continue with the analysis. But I think that danger was always present in her mind and when finally, after some years, she had overcome enough of her anxieties not to need to force herself to fail or to attack herself, she found it increasingly difficult to come to the sessions. This led to her finally deciding to terminate the analysis in order to feel safe in taking over her life once more, freed from the danger of destroying me through her newly acquired strength. She was by then no longer dependent on the compulsive repetitive behavior to defend against the fear of passively having to give in to her sexual body and the identification with her mother.

So far I have not tried to link Sarah's pathology to her earlier experiences and development although she gave me sufficient information to confirm that she had been a very disturbed child suffering from many overwhelming anxieties. This is not because I do not give the earlier experiences full weight in the subsequent developmental breakdown. In fact, as I noted earlier, I see the early infantile experiences with the mother as central in determining how Sarah was able to respond to the pubertal changes and other events during adolescence.

But clinically there is an important reason for not giving explanations based on early events and relationships priority in the treatment of the kind of adolescents I describe here. Because they are constantly at risk of having to give in to either passive surrender, with the hopelessness this implies, or hatred and rejection of themselves, we have to be able to focus, as does the adolescent, on his present experience of himself. We cannot be out of touch with the present reality of the new sexual body lest we collude with the adolescent's own compelling need to deaden it psychically or to destroy it. To interpret Sarah's problems in terms of her early experiences with her mother would seem to her to confirm her fear that she was now becoming mad, like her mother, rather than that she had been damaged by her early experiences in a way that could be understood and overcome. So although I was very much aware that Sarah's disturbed relationship to her body was the result of the early relationship of her mother to her body, it was important to stay with what Sarah was now compelled to do to herself in order to help her tolerate the anxiety she felt in relation to having a sexually alive body. Only in this way could I enable her to use the relationship with a man to give her some feeling of safety from being taken over by the mother. This was enacted in her terminating the analysis with me but retaining contact with the male psychiatrist who had been responsible for prescribing her medication and for admitting her to the psychiatric hospital at times when she could not feel safe in coming to her sessions with me.

In conclusion I come back now to the theme of this paper. What I have wanted to highlight is the role of passivity, or rather the conflicting modes of active and passive, in the adolescent's experience of his relationship to his body. By looking at the pathological behavior of the seriously disturbed adolescent where the unconscious meaning can be understood as representing an attack on the relationship to the sexual body, I examined the nature of the relationship these adolescents have to their body as an internal object. The repetitive and compelling nature of their behavior and the defensive function it plays unconsciously shows, I believe, the fantasy of the body as a persecuting object that has to be either controlled, or destroyed if the control breaks down. The nature of the relationship to the body is dominated by the fear of passive surrender to the object, represented by the changing body, which is experienced by the adolescent as having the power to abandon him and leave him feeling totally helpless and starved of vital supplies. What is sought after defensively is a relationship in which the adolescent can feel omnipotent through being united with an omnipotent object, represented by the indestructible body, in order to feel safe from the threat of breakdown or annihilation. Winnicott (1974) talks of this fear as the feared repetition of something that has already been experienced in infancy. From the transference and the history of the patients whom I have treated, I feel that this could be true in their case. It seems that at a time of potential helplessness during infancy there must have been a failure of the caring matrix within which they could develop a relationship to their body that would have enabled them to feel less vulnerable to the impact of the changes at puberty. The conflict between passive and active fantasies of sexual gratification through the experience of their sexual body, as normally experienced in masturbation for instance, becomes dominated in these adolescents by the need to maintain control over the passive wishes while at the same time not allowing for the integration of the new sexual body into the existing relationship to the body. Thus, what I have described as the repetitive compelling behavior that characterizes these adolescents can be viewed as the only defense they have against allowing any change to occur.

BIBLIOGRAPHY

FREUD A. 1958. Adolescence. *Psychoanal. Study Child,* 13, pp. 255–78.
FREUD, S. 1931. Female sexuality, *S.E.* 21, pp. 223–43.
———— 1937. Analysis terminable and interminable, *S.E.* 23, pp. 216–55.
LAUFER, M., & LAUFER, M. E. 1984. Adolescence and Developmental Breakdown. New Haven: Yale University Press.
LAUFER, M. E. Body image, sexuality and the psychotic core. *I.J.P.A.* Vol. 72 Part 1 pp. 63–73.
WINNICOTT, D. Fear of breakdown. 1974. *I. Review PSA.* Vol. 1, pp. 103–07.

Observations on the Long-term Effects of Child Analysis

Implications for Technique

SAMUEL RITVO, M.D.

This paper examines the issue of the lasting influence of child analysis on subsequent development, focusing particularly on the normative developmental crisis of the transition from adolescence to adulthood. The cases presented here are of two children from a longitudinal study analyzed in childhood with follow-up to age 35 and the analysis of a young adult whose childhood analysis had been reported in the literature. The author considers the significance of changes in the theory of technique in child analysis for improving its long-term effectiveness.

INTRODUCTION

CHILD ANALYSTS TEND TO SAY THAT THE AIM OF ANALYSIS IN CHILDHOOD is to restore the child to the path of normal development. They also say that the indications for analysis are that the child is functioning on a regressive ego, instinctual and object relations level. In this paper, I examine our concerns about the lasting influence of child analysis on subsequent development, particularly on the normative developmental crises encountered in the transition from adolescence to adulthood.

Clinical Professor of Psychiatry Yale University Child Study Center; Training and Supervising Analyst, New York Psychoanalytic Institute and The Western New England Institute for Psychoanalysis.

A version of this paper was presented at the Robert J. Kabcenell Memorial Lecture in Child Analysis to the New York Psychoanalytic Society, May 9, 1995.

The Psychoanalytic Study of the Child 51, ed. Albert J. Solnit, Peter B. Neubauer, Samuel Abrams, and A. Scott Dowling (Yale University Press, copyright © 1996 by Albert J. Solnit, Peter B. Neubauer, Samuel Abrams, and A. Scott Dowling).

To illustrate, I have rich material from my own clinical experience and research.

Two of my cases were children in the longitudinal study of child development at the Yale Child Study Center who were analyzed as children and followed up to ages thirty-five and forty; third is the case of Frankie, who was analyzed by Berta Bornstein (1949) as a child and had a period of analysis with me as a young adult.

Adding to the difficulty of assessing the lasting influence of analysis are the changes in analytic technique over time, thus, even if the same analyst treated the patient as child and adult, the psychoanalytic process would be different. This would certainly be true for me. I shall, therefore, use this occasion to raise some questions about technique and the psychoanalytic process in childhood.

CASE STUDY: JERRY

After a predelinquent childhood and a roaming, adventurous adolescence, Jerry's father, a shrewdly intelligent compulsive gambler, enlisted in the military, where he continued his gambling. Upon his discharge, a routine X ray disclosed a chronic, recurrent pulmonary infection that required several long hospitalizations and left him a semi-invalid capable of only sporadic employment.

Jerry's mother was a physically active, emotionally labile woman with shifting, tempestuous moods and poor impulse control.

As a newborn, Jerry was hyperactive and vigorous. He reacted to external stimuli and physical discomfort with massive discharge movements. Breast-feeding was distressing for mother and infant. The mother's frustration at the evidence that he was not satisfied, combined with her disgust at the messiness of dripping breasts, reduced her to exhaustion and tears. She was relieved when the pediatrician recommended bottle-feeding.

Both parents handled Jerry in exciting, stimulating, seductive, and punitive ways. His first words were "bad boy," and a wooden spoon was the signal for an imminent spanking. The mother's furious outbursts were immediately followed by reconciliations in which she cuddled him quietly and affectionately. Rapid alternation between violent activity and quiescence later became a feature of Jerry's behavior in nursery school and in his treatment.

Neither parent was ever observed to play with Jerry. Although the objects forbidden to him were in full view in the home, his own toys were kept out of sight in a toy chest and offered to him only in his playpen or outdoors.

Disturbances in Jerry's capacity to play began to appear in the developmental tests in the first year. Although earlier tests had been satisfactory, he showed increasing signs of developmental difficulties between nine and twelve months. He did not do well on the adaptive items that reflect the infant's integrative functioning, an early indicator of ego functioning. From nine months on, his failure to use toys and test materials adaptively was striking. The deficit in his play with toys foreshadowed his later disturbance in play and learning.

Because of the serious portent of Jerry's inability to play, his pediatrician recommended that he start nursery school at twenty months, where he might be taught to play and would be in an environment that would mitigate the adverse effects on play and learning of the fighting and overstimulation by both parents. From the first school session, Jerry was hyperactive, impulsive, poorly controlled, reckless, and aggressive. He was so poorly organized in both play and behavior that it was difficult to discern his thought processes. By the end of the second year in school, with the aid of a gifted and devoted teacher, he began to make friends and to show an interest in manipulating materials and in quieter play. Dramatic play of an active nature became a source of pleasure and an avenue for expression of ideas, as well as for discharge of energy and tension.

In the next year his brother was born. At school Jerry was very disruptive, moody, and generally ill-humored. The organization and control he had shown the previous year were lost in wild, aggressive behavior. It was clear that anxiety played an important part in his unrest and that he was attacking head-on any object or situation that frightened him. He once bit a rabbit as if to keep it from biting him. Analytic treatment was begun at this time, when he was three and a half.

In the treatment room, the hyperactivity and the sexualized, exhibitionistic mode of relating to the adult were immediately in evidence. The play was a literal and direct repetition in action of scenes and sequences from his home life without much disguise or elaboration in fantasy. The most sustained play in the beginning was cooking and feeding, giving a nursing bottle to the doll, then drinking from it himself, and ending either by smashing the bottle against the wall or throwing both the bottle and the doll out the window, enacting his wishes to be in his brother's place and to be rid of him. He vividly portrayed primal-scene experiences that were abundantly stimulated at home, as Jerry's crib was next to his parents' bed in the tiny bedroom.

Jerry's mode of coping with increasing anxiety over attacking and being attacked was to develop a phobic symptom in the treatment room. He feared there was a monster in the next room who would bite, scratch, and yell. The monster incorporated aspects of the paranoid grandfather on the other side of the wall in the next apartment. With the creation of the symptom and the illusion of the monster on whom he concentrated his aggression, his attitude toward the analyst became friendlier and less aggressive. In response to my interpretation that he liked to be noisy and act big and strong (identifying with the aggressor) because then he did not have to be afraid of the monster, he acquiesced and shouted that he was Superman.

In the analysis, he enacted the strongly instinctualized object relations with the parents, both the active aggressive side and the passive, defensive side. He rapidly alternated between excited, aggressive behavior and passively lying on his back, imitating both the mother's position in the primal scene to which he was a regular witness and the father's position in the resting periods required by his illness. Jerry commented as he did so that he "sweats like hell" and must rest. In keeping with his hyperactive, impulsive nature, his most relied-on defense was identification with the aggressor. Although there was evidence that his teacher and the analysis had an ameliorating effect, it was not enough to shield him from the pathogenic effects of the external family life.

Throughout the study the staff was concerned for Jerry's future. They predicted delinquency stemming from impulsivity and conflict over defensive passive homosexual strivings.

On a follow-up visit to his home when he was fifteen, the family situation appeared more stable than at any previous time. They had moved to the suburbs, and both parents were working. Jerry was limping along academically in high school but getting much recognition from the community for his athletic skills. He had a close, supportive relationship with a teacher who was also his athletic coach, reminiscent of the devoted nursery school teacher who coached him carefully. We learned much later, however, that, under the influence of an older boy, he was already involved with drugs and in difficulty with the police, true to the earlier prediction.

At twenty-three he initiated a visit, expressing nostalgia for the Child Study Center. In dress and manner he conveyed a self-conscious image of a relaxed, confident man of the world, but he told of the hurt of being rejected by a sixteen-year-old girl with whom he was in love. We learned only later that he had come to us because of trouble with the law over activities in which he engaged under the influence of an older man, just the kind of outcome the study had feared.

After extricating himself at the age of thirty-two from his dangerous illicit activities and recovering from a life-threatening illness, which he was convinced was caused by an attempt by his older associate to poison him, he was left without a vocation, only a marginal position in the community, and feeling trapped in a hopeless, troubled marriage. His capacity for self-reflection was very limited. He seemed unable to take an imaginative or creative approach to planning the next steps in his life. His viewed the world as cynical and concrete. What he idealized most was power. He had retained some of his early appealing qualities but seemed colorless and lacked depth.

At forty he had a semiskilled trade but was temporarily laid off, living amicably with a divorcee and her children; he was engaged in a bitter custody battle with his former wife over their two children. Indicative of his limitations in imagination and empathy was the difficulty he was having in understanding that the court was not interested in meeting his wish to have the children but was guided by their best interests. For him the two were identical.

Jerry's initiation of a visit at twenty-three, seemingly looking nostalgically for his analyst and his pediatrician, indicates that he had a lasting internal image of the doctors and the institution as a source of help in understanding his difficulties. At that point, the opportunity for further analysis at a time of developmental crisis in the transition from late adolescence to adulthood was not recognized, partly because in this brief encounter his expansive air of self-assurance effectively hid his suffering from himself and others.

Throughout his life, his difficulty in adaptively controlling his impulses, aggravated rather than mitigated by the parenting in infancy and childhood, interfered with his ability to establish and maintain stable and gratifying object relationships. The relatively brief period of analysis in prelatency before the development and internalization of a reliable superego was not enough to prevent such an outcome.

CASE STUDY: EVELYNE

Evelyne had a vastly different beginning in life. Her father was a steady, responsible, obsessional man, constrained in the expression of his feelings. A major issue in his life was his deep resentment of his own father's preference for his sister, who was two years older than he. The resentment he bore toward his sister was transferred to Evelyne at the birth of his second child, when in his mind Evelyne increasingly became the older sister. Evelyne's mother had lived in an all-female household after age ten, when her father died. Shortly after her older sister married and moved away, she avoided being left with her mother and spinster aunt by marrying, replacing her sister with her husband

and then with her first child. An introspective, imaginative woman with artistic talents and a strong interest in teaching her children, she suffered from depressive moods sometimes accompanied by obsessional symptoms and at times had difficulty controlling impulsive, angry outbursts.

From birth, Evelyne and her mother seemed well suited to each other. The parents had hoped for a boy but were very happy and pleased with the baby. The mother, a sensitive, introspective young woman, was paired with an infant who was receptive to her care, easily satisfied and pacified. The mother had a strong empathic tie to Evelyne and constantly tried to be aware of the infant's feelings, carefully gauging and responding to her needs. The sensitive interactions between mother and child were observable in the early feeding and toilet training. Throughout the early feeding, the mother carefully exerted varying degrees of pressure on Evelyne to mold the child in the form the mother preferred. Evelyne seemed to adjust quite well to the mother's pressures, aided in this by her receptive temperament, which left her relaxed and relatively easily pacified.

Evelyne's interest in dolls and toys with faces, encouraged and shared by her mother, led to very early fantasy play with imaginary companions in which Evelyne assumed many roles. The fantasy play went quite beyond the domestic mimicry usually seen in the second year, and Evelyne used it as an effective means of coping with the arrival of a new sibling and the concomitant brief separation from the mother at age two. By pretending and role-playing she was able to bridge physical separations, an impressive early demonstration of the adaptive sublimatory function of play (Kris, 1956).

But Evelyne's world was severely shaken with the birth of her sister, Wendy. Both parents had wished for a boy, and the father's shame and disappointment were so great that he did not announce this baby's arrival. However, fostered by Wendy's active and assertive temperament, he soon identified her with himself and saw her as a symbol of the masculinity he wished for, often calling her by a boy's name.

Within months, the father shifted his affection from Evelyne—now identified with his own disliked older sister—to Wendy. The changes in the family had a disturbing effect on Evelyne, and she developed a number of symptoms. At two and a half, she was severely frightened when, on Halloween, her great aunt appeared as a ghost with a face cut from a white sheet. The fear spread to pictures of clowns and people in masks on television and in books. She was afraid of the dark and of her bedroom at night. All toys with faces and paintings on the wall had to be removed before she would go to bed. She was also distressed by loud noises like the doorbell, by the aggression of neighborhood children, and by her parents' arguments. It was unmistakable that the fears were related to her conflict over her own aggression and the aggression of others, primarily her parents. Her mother stressed that Evelyne had a mind of her own, was slow to anger, but could be fierce when she became angry. Often aware of the shift in her father's affections to Wendy, Evelyne was reluctant to go out alone with him or remain in the house with him.

The same fantasy play with special interest in the face now became the preferred means of representing the conflict and anxiety arising from her own aggression and determined the features of her symptoms. What had been free creative play and fantasy was now fixed in coping with neurotic conflict.

Psychoanalytic treatment three times a week was started at three years, four months, when Evelyne was in nursery school. Her aversion to being alone with her father was transferred to the analyst, and she was quite explicit that it was because the analyst was a man. At first she was unable to use her capacity for fantasy play to establish herself comfortably with the analyst. For the first six months she refused to come to the treatment room alone with him, insisting that her teacher accompany her and remain in the room with her. In her play, her drawing, and her relationship to the analyst, she made it clear that she preferred the woman and had no room for the man. Yet there were times when she was coquettish and teasingly contrary. After six months, in recognition of the analyst's steadfastness, Evelyne, though still declaring to the nursery school teacher that she did not want to stay with him, began to be close and cuddly, reading a book with her head in his lap and letting him know she thought about him at home. She was able to tell the teacher that she loved her analyst.

When she returned in the fall (four years, seven months) after a second sister, Tammy, was born, she interfered with the analyst's looking at the baby in mother's arms and told him proudly that she was not afraid of clowns any more, that she was even going to be a clown on Halloween. She added that she had not liked him last year but did not feel that way any more. This declaration ushered in an oedipal transference that became more intense as time went on. She revealed her secret that the analyst was her best friend and played marriage games in which a new doll became her new baby that she mothered contentedly while the analyst was sent out to work.

After the mother had given her permission to like the analyst, explaining that he was a doctor interested in what children were thinking and in helping them with their worries and fears, Evelyne directly expressed her affection toward the analyst and her sadness at the thought of leaving him one day. She followed this by playing doctor with the analyst. She was the mommy, excited and giggling, then she shifted to playing with messy stuff and ended by washing her hands, an indication of how anal messing at this time served as a regressive avenue of discharge for the oedipal excitement. Furthermore, the guilty feelings toward the mother could be dissipated easily with the hand washing, predictive of a lenient, permissive superego. The mother subsequently reported that Evelyne was very attached to the analyst. The mother was very pleased about it.

In the transference Evelyne became jealous and competitive with Jerry. Her wish to win her father over was expressed in the fantasy that girls can change into boys while they are very small. It was taking place in Tammy, still an infant, who had short hair but no penis yet. This was one of the rare instances when Evelyne admitted that there were times when she would like to be a boy, apparently in the interest of winning her father back. Through identification and fantasy gratification, she was able to have a secret closeness with her father. About the birth of Tammy, the favorite of both parents, she said, "That is when I had *my* baby." The fantasy gratification of her wish to have a child from the father and be the mother to the child both parents loved came in the oedipal period, and Tammy remained her child in some real senses, as well. Today as adults they have houses across the street from one another, Evelyne taking a mothering role with Tammy that is satisfying to both of them. This degree of gratification of the wish to have a child in the oedipal period may have influenced the striking absence of penis envy.

She was curious about the analyst's steadfast interest in helping her and wanted to know why he never got mad at her the way her parents did. Did he want to know all about her because she was pretty? Evelyne's observation implies that, with her excellent capacity for gratification of her desires in fantasy play and in the transference, she had achieved a degree of security in the feeling of being valued as a girl, despite her father's critical and aversive response to her, an essential experience for a girl in the oedipal period if she is to feel confident in her femininity.

Later in latency, with the greater ego resources available to her from the developmental thrust of latency and her analysis, Evelyne achieved a more secure position in the family. She earned the respect and approval of both parents, had become a mother substitute for Tammy, and was able to use her own endowments for sublimated activities. Her artistic creativity in school was commended glowingly. Although often awkward there, spilling and dropping things, she had developed as a defense the ability to laugh at herself. Her characteristic ability to tolerate disappointment and gain the ultimate reward of mastery through persistence served her well.

The analysis continued with some interruptions until she was eleven. In her twelfth year, on the threshold of puberty, she appeared considerably less imaginative and creative than she had been and derived little satisfaction from feminine interests. This generalized inhibition of libidinal impulses continued through adolescence. At fifteen, she gave the impression of docility, compliance, and inhibition with no hint of rebellion. There were no outward signs of imaginative or creative ability, and her fantasy life was not accessible in the interview setting. This massive inhibition persisted until she left for college. In part it was a defense and protection against aggressive encounters with her mother. Since childhood she had responded to her mother's outbursts with a quiet, stricken look that had a guilt-manipulating, restraining effect on the mother. In contrast, Wendy's response was angry, provoking an every angrier reaction in the mother. Thus the inhibition of her aggression had an adaptive function as well in the relationship with her mother, whereas Wendy reacted to her aggressive rebelliousness by turning the aggression against herself in depression, eventually running away from home, ending in a tragic death.

At eighteen, after her freshman year in college, Evelyne actively tried to overcome her inhibitions. In a meeting she requested with the analyst, she spoke of having a "strict superego" and of feeling guilty if she failed to please others. She wanted to feel less opposed to her desires. In this meeting she spontaneously expressed the realization that her father could never be close and loving toward her because he identified her with his own older sister. The ability to observe and examine her mental activities and personality traits as determinants of her behavior is a further sign of the long-term effects of the analytic experience in childhood.

Over the next several years she made the transition to adulthood with the aid of illusion and fantasy, this time in the form of religion. She joined an evangelical group led by a charismatic male teacher. In this setting, she found her future husband, an evangelical churchgoer. From this point on, she felt secure that, through her actions and feelings, she was carrying out God's will. By finding God, loving God, and being loved by him, she replaced her rejecting father with a loving father, as she had replaced him with the analyst in her oedipal fantasies. The sublimated oedipal gratification via religion enabled her to be more independent of both parents without feeling guilty.

At thirty-four, Evelyne, putting her professional career on hold, appears to be leading a satisfactory and fulfilling life. Despite serious financial limitations, she counts her blessings. She has achieved a good marriage and has established an apparently happy family. Her friends are a source of deep satisfaction. She attributes her capacity for friendship in part to her mother, whom she experienced as a sensitive, attentive listener throughout her childhood. She volunteers that she learned the art of good listening and communicating from her former analyst, another significant long-term effect.

The combination of her nurturing role in human relationships, her professional success at the level to which she limited herself and her religious conviction suggests that Evelyne, an integrated, compassionate individual, has attained an adult balance and maturity. At the same time, we have to question at what cost. There are indications that her adaptations have a major defensive function—to ward off conflict in relation to instinctual strivings whose derivatives might surface as ambition, lust, or hostility. When her husband was considering retraining for a more interesting and better paying job, she acquiesced readily in his decision to settle for a lesser, rather than a higher, skilled occupation. She confided to the analyst that she was thinking of a career change when she was able to return to work. Although she likes the personal contact with people in her work as a health professional, she would like to do something more creative, like hair styling. She also gave some indication of awareness that her religious interest and involvement in the church community and activities were not only a sublimation and source of gratification but served to buttress her inhibitions as well. She told of a friend, a fellow choir member, who was tempted to have an affair. Evelyne counseled her not to and indicated that she had been in that situation and knew how difficult it is. It appeared that while analysis had enabled her to be more aware of her internal processes, it had not enabled her to tolerate awareness of her impulses without resorting to stringent inhibitions. These observations suggest that upward mobility may threaten to precipitate conflict over aggression, resulting in anxiety and guilt, and that Evelyne uses her well-established capacities for adaptation and sublimation and her defense of avoiding anything disagreeable to maintain a viable contentment with the status quo.

Very gratifying to Evelyne was the birth after two sons of the daughter much wished for by both Evelyne and her husband. With pleasure and pride, she repeated her husband's statement that he must cherish his daughter now because some day he would have to give her up to another man. What more fitting reward for a woman who long ago had resigned herself to the realization that she could never regain her father's love.

Evelyne, like Jerry, had maintained an internal representation of the analyst and the analytic experience in childhood as a source of self-awareness and self-understanding to which they turned at times of internal crisis.

CASE STUDY: FRANKIE

Frankie, the subject of Berta Bornstein's (1949) classic case report, came into analysis at the age of 5½ because of a severe school phobia which had existed for over two years. Like Jerry, he had had a difficult start in life. Though he was a healthy child and his delivery normal, his mother felt estranged from him from the start. His constant screaming and crying as an infant, the difficulties in feeding, and his mother's difficulty in comforting him showed a poor attunement between mother and child. The result was intense and prolonged frustration which prepared the ground for aggressive reactions, creating what Bornstein referred to as the "primal trauma." At three years, three months, he experienced the birth of his sister as an abandonment by the mother. The separation and loss evoked aggressive reactions that not only served a discharge function but also, in Bornstein's view, as defenses against the suppressed feelings of sadness. On rereading the case of Frankie, one realizes that throughout the complex and rich analysis of the preoedipal, oedipal, and latency conflicts and symptoms, the problem of the regulation and control of aggressive impulses is central to Frankie's difficulties.

One impression on rereading this case is how much the technique and the underlying concepts of child analysis have changed over the past fifty years. The introductory phase in which the analyst might manipulate the situation, even enlisting the aid of the child's school so that the child would experience the analyst as indispensable to the satisfaction of some need, was considered essential to engage the child in the treatment. (p. 184) Attention to the development and analysis of transference had a much lesser role as it was thought that children did not make significant transferences because of their strong attachment to the primary objects. Reconstructions and deep unconscious interpretations, or "unconscious thrusts", as Bornstein (1949) called them, were offered with less attention than now to the cognitive capacities of the child or to the preliminary careful analysis of defenses.

Although the analysis was presented with emphasis on the defenses, one gains the impression from the case that in resorting to "unconscious thrusts," defenses were bypassed. Also, the analyst seemed to have less concern about the possible disruptive effect on the analytic situation of too-free contact with the parents. Most striking to present-day readers is the major modification of analytic technique in the analyst's threat that Frankie would be sent away to a hospital if he did not control his troublesome behavior.

When Frankie returned to analysis in his mid-twenties, the immediate situation was the conflict between the brilliant conclusion of the college phase of preparation for a career and beginning the next, more definitive phase, which would end in his being on an equal professional footing with his father. He had postponed this step once and taken a brief moratorium to obtain relief from the unpleasant, burdensome strain he felt in the effort to keep up his performance. The prospect of continuing this effort from one hurdle to the next was frightening and depressing. The intense competitiveness of the school situation, the pending irrevocable commitment to a career with its measurement of achievement that might be less than he considered ideal and might tarnish his hitherto bright record, all contributed to the outbreak of anxiety and the feeling of being trapped and wanting to escape. In this state, he had an urgent longing for a safe, peaceful, carefree existence that he often associated with a longing for mother. It was the same anxious feeling of being trapped that had made it difficult for him to remain in school at age five and had led to his entering analysis then.

Equally disturbing was his full-blown obsessional neurosis, with obsessional doubts about the functioning of his mind. These doubts had an unmistakable similarity to his earlier concern about masturbation and the intactness of his genital. He wondered whether his mind would continue to function as it had in the past. If he did something well once, would he be able to do it again? Was his mind working the way it should? In two exacerbations during adolescence, the anxiety and doubts about his mind had become so severe that he could not read or listen to the radio because he had to keep going back over a word to test his retention. He now feared the symptoms would return with the intensity they had in adolescence. At the time of his return to analysis, the older man who had made advances to him in his late adolescence was again on the scene. Thus, at the time of his return to analysis, when he was faced with taking the step to adult status, Frankie was mired in a regressive oedipal conflict in which his aggressive, competitive strivings with authoritative, paternal figures evoked anxiety. The fantasied defeat and collapse that would follow represented the prohibiting superego defense against aggressive strivings.

In striking contrast with the phobic neurosis of the oedipal period and the emerging obsessional neurosis in latency was the firm establishment of the mind, mental functioning, and mental prowess as the transcendent representation of masculinity and the main pathway to achievement, success, and power. He had honed his mind to razor-edged sharpness, a positive adaptive asset in the world he was entering.

The shift from phobic to obsessional neurosis, so regularly an accompaniment of development, interested Frankie. His interest surfaced when he won a coveted position in a competition but turned it down because he was assailed by obsessive thoughts that his ability to do what was expected of him was only a façade. He thought his father respected and accepted him as an equal only because of his façade and not because of any underlying worth. In his self-deprecatory response to success, we can hear the superego defense against the danger of the aggressive impulses that the ego, still engaged in the regressive oedipal conflict, could not tolerate in consciousness. His doubts about his success again made him curious about how they had arisen. He recalled his childhood and current fears that he would not be able to control himself and that he would have a wild or destructive outburst, underscoring the conflict over the control of aggression. He recalled his superstitious, supernatural mode of thinking as a child that made the world full of danger—his fear of wolves, of being trapped on the school bus, of death—and his way of trying to cope with these dangers, earlier by avoidance and later by obsessive-compulsive rituals. The fears had once made it necessary for him to avoid large parts of the outside world that contained real dangers as well as the danger created by projection of his impulses. If he had been so afraid of what could be done to him, he must have had very little power himself, making it necessary for him to avoid most of the outside world.

The idea of the outside world being too much for him he referred to as the "womb-type notion." He frequently felt he needed more protection from danger than others. At such times he tried to find that protection by thinking of his mother. Whether the "womb-type notion" had originated in the womb or whether his fear had given him a "womb-type view of the world," he wanted to retain it to feel safe and protected. With the advancing capacity for abstract, logical thinking and reality testing, the phobic symptoms could not pass the ego's scrutiny except in periods of intense conflict and anxiety and accompanied by ego regression which compromised the ego's reality-testing function. He turned instead to obsessive thoughts about losing his mental powers as a way of self-punitively turning his competitive, aggressive, oedipal strivings against himself.

He felt that by taking him into analysis because of his neurosis I was indicating that I felt sorry for him and was treating him delicately—as I would treat someone who had lost a hand. His associations then shifted to his penis, and he recollected that as a child he had noticed how large his father's penis was and how small his own. The difference was so marked that he felt his was not just smaller but was a different kind of organ. When he thought I would regard him as defective and castrated because of his neurosis, he expressed the concern that the "removal" of the conflict by analysis might remove the anxious insistence that he use his mind rigorously and would result in the loss of something very precious—namely, his ability to think things through, which he regarded as his masculine style of thinking.

The mind had a preeminent place in his image of himself. As he described it, "The mind is me and the body is attached to it." Thus, in the transference, the analysis was conceived and experienced as a struggle and contest with me. He enjoyed what he called his "mental jousting" with me. He thought it was like comparing himself to his father. He enjoyed using his mind as a probing, attacking instrument. He rarely took a position in an argument but devoted himself to probing the positions of others. In his relations with his colleagues, he had what he called his "big man complex." To be recognized socially by someone with high academic standing and a powerful mind made him feel secure and important. A slight by such a person—real or imagined—made him feel lonely, rejected, and abandoned. Seeking intellectual solutions to psychic conflicts was also doing something he thought his father had done.

As he came to understand more of his father's accomplishments, his respect for his father's intellect and ability grew. He thought his father presented him with a comfortable figure for emulation and identification—someone to be proud of but not overwhelmed by. One of the determining factors in his decision to stay in school and analysis was his father's amicable but firm statement that school was Frankie's primary task and obligation and he should remain there. This not only had an encouraging and reassuring effect but seemed to give him permission to be competitive with peers and his father. A more direct oedipal significance of the obsessive symptom was contained in the notion that he must keep up his good mental hygiene so that his mind would be ready when he had to take father's place after his death. At that time he would no longer have to maintain his good habits because he would have achieved and obtained what he had been preparing himself for. They would no longer be needed as a defense against the danger of his aggressive oedipal strivings.

His object relations had a similar obsessional quality. For years he had trained himself to remove all feeling from his relationships with the important persons in his life. He practiced this isolation of affect so he would be protected against the consequences of emotional dependence. He would be insulated against the rage that separation, disappointment, and hurt at the hands of parents, wife, friends, and analyst threatened. Partly to protect himself from the risk of dependence on the analyst, he married during the analysis. He welcomed his wife's dependence on him because of her anxieties. It gave him the opportunity to be the reassuring, protective, parental figure and lessened his fear of dependence on the analyst. In the transference, I had to be "depersonified" to guard against his having feelings toward me. I had to be, in his words, merely the "presumed bundle of skills."

The intellect and its achievement were a highly valued part of his ego ideal. The power of the intellect had replaced the magic omnipotence of the immortal King Boo-Boo (p. 214ff) of childhood. Products of the intellect, like writings, were especially important because they were considered the way to immortality. Children as a way to immortality were scorned because of the intense, conscious repugnance of pregnancy, a subject of anxious, obsessive preoccupation for him that retained numerous unconscious connections with the birth of his sister and with phobic symptoms related to that event.

The childhood analysis itself was a further determinant in the selection of the mind and intellect to play a large role in his neurosis. He had remained in intermittent contact with his first analyst and had consulted her about returning to treatment. Thus the analyst was not simply a memory but remained an authoritative transference figure. He remembered the physical setting of the analysis and the problems for which he had come to child analysis, although he felt frustrated that he could not remember specific hours in detail. Among the prominent recollections he reviewed at the start of the adult analysis were his anger with and jealousy of his younger sister, refusal to stay in school at age five, fear of riding the bus where he was once injured, and inability to sleep in a room without a light on or the door open. When content important in the earlier analysis came up in the hours, he recalled interpretations made by the analyst, some of them recorded in her report—for example, his fear that mother would become pregnant and bring home another child, his concern about women not having a penis, etc. Thus he had a history of trying to understand and know the meaning of his anxieties and symptoms. His investment in thinking carried over to a strong interest in his own thought processes, so that throughout the analysis he was a perceptive observer of his own associations and liked to make his own interpretations, particularly when the analytic material touched on areas that had been prominent in the childhood analysis. For instance, he offered the interpretation that his dread of making long-term commitments as in school, marriage, or analysis and his need to provide himself with a way out were connected with his abhorrence of death and pregnant women, which involved fears of entrapment and irreversibility that persisted from his similar childhood terrors.

Despite the absence of subsequent external trauma, the childhood analysis of Frankie did not prevent the outbreak of neurotic illness in the critical transition from adolescent to adult. But the analytic experience in childhood did leave him with the knowledge and conviction that the way to a healthier mental state was through better understanding of how his mind worked and was to be gained by greater self-observation and self-awareness in the psychoanalytic process. This raises the question whether the changes in our conceptualization of the psychoanalytic process in childhood and the concomitant changes in technique of the past five decades offer the possibility of increasing the effectiveness of child analysis in preventing or ameliorating adult neurosis.

Discussion

One important area of progress has been in our attention to analyzing conflict in the ego, starting with anxiety and defense as it appears in or close to consciousness (Frankl and Hellman, 1962) and to do so, not by modifying the analytic method, but by adapting it to the child's level of ego development, including cognitive development and the capacity for communication. In this way the ego's capacity for self-observation and self-awareness can be strengthened and increased rather than remaining inhibited.

Modifying the analytic method—for example, intervening to change the patient's environment, counseling and advising the parents, introducing educational measures to correct sexual or other misconceptions before the conflicts and the fantasies underlying them are analyzed—may interfere with or disrupt the analytic process (Harley, 1986). Such modifications tend to establish the analyst as another authority figure in the child's mind, like parent or teacher, and interfere with the possibility of analyzing the transference of authority as a defense against the conflict over aggressive drive derivatives. The modifications are more in the service of overcoming resistances than analyzing them.

In child analysis, technique needs to be adapted to the level of the child's mental development. Reviewing current research on children's emerging understanding of mental life, Mayes (1995) points out that, in therapeutic work with young children, both child and therapist implicitly assume that the child's imaginary play activity conveys his desires, beliefs, and feelings. But not until the age of five or six does the child have a firmly established awareness that play actions and illusions are connected to mental activity and that the actions of others are connected to their separate mental activity. Only then is the child able to make use of interventions that invite him to reflect on the operation of his own mind. Before that, the child uses action, play, and illusion as an intermediate space for the enactment of thought (Ritvo, 1993), and the analyst's interventions are best kept to commenting on the child's fears, desires, and beliefs and the interactions between them within the action of the play.

When the idea of ongoing mental activity that is not associated with action is firmly established (by age seven or eight), the child is able to create an inner psychic reality that encompasses his own thoughts and an internal representation of the thoughts of the other. These capabilities underlie the superego functions of the ego because the child can then oppose and contain drive derivatives without the external pressure of the prohibiting authority. It also means that in the analytic situation the child is capable of transferring this authority onto the analyst. With these advances in mental development, the child is able to make use of therapeutic interventions that invite him to use the capability to reflect on the operations of his own mind with respect to anxiety, conflict, and defense (Friedman, 1976).

The role of transference in child analysis was slow to be recognized. Until the late 1940s, non-Kleinian child analysts thought that transference played little or no role because the child was so strongly linked emotionally to his primary objects. As in the case of Frankie, child analysts thought they had to demonstrate their benevolence toward the child and their ability to satisfy a need in order to motivate the child to cooperate in the analytic endeavor. The observations of Anna Freud (1965) and her colleagues at the Hampstead Clinic showed that transference did play a role in child analysis. Marianne Kris had a leading role in introducing these new findings in this country.

With the recognition that transferences and the analysis of them are essential features of the analytic process in childhood, attention has focused on the nature, extent, and intensity of their manifestation and the technique of analyzing them. Anna Freud (1936) distinguished three types of transference—the transference of libidinal impulses, the transference of defense, and acting in the transference. If we bear in mind that the child makes a basic transference to the analyst as a helping adult (a "talking doctor") (Ritvo, 1978), that he comes to the analyst on the urging and authority of the parents, and that all communication (direct verbal and enactive fantasy play) takes place under the influence of the analyst's presence, attention, and participation, then we can appreciate the potential for all these types of transference in the analytic process of childhood. Of these, the transference of defense is probably the most important to appreciate because the child is developmentally in the process of building internalized psychic structures for the control of impulses and still relies heavily on the externalization of psychic structures to the authoritative adult—parents, teachers, analyst. This transference of defense presents analytic surfaces that the analyst can use to acquaint the child with how he or she defends against the dangers of drive derivatives. The child's play offers opportunities for doing this in displacement and eventually more directly in the transference, which has the advantage of affective immediacy.

Much of the debate about transference is concerned with whether the child develops a transference neurosis. Brenner (1982) has made the convincing argument that transference neurosis is an anachronistic and tautologous concept and "means no more than that the patient has intense transference manifestations that can be successfully analyzed."

Whether the child shows intense transference manifestations that lend themselves to analysis depends to a large extent on the analyst's management of the analytic situation. In examining what is required of the analytic situation in childhood to foster intense transference manifestations, Chused (1988), who prefers the concept transference neurosis, identified the specific limiting factor as the analyst's and the child patient's tendency to respond to each other automatically as the adult who educates and directs and the child who learns, complies, or rebels. She emphasizes that a thoughtful analytic procedure—with strict attention to the analysis of resistance and to countertransference interferences and taking into account the level of the child's ego functions—can lead to a "full-blown transference neurosis." In her view, the precedent among child analysts to behave primarily as a benevolent object, to strive to maintain a positive transference at the expense of maintaining analytic abstinence and neutrality (as with adults) can interfere with the development of more intense transference manifestations that provide opportunities for experience-based interpretations, enabling the analyst to keep to the minimum hypothetical genetic reconstructions and the deep unconscious thrusts referred to earlier.

With increasing recognition of the importance of transference in child analysis have come changes in how reconstruction is conceptualized and employed in the analytic process. In his paper on the recollection of childhood memories, Kris (1956) emphasized that childhood experience cannot be recovered in its original form in analysis. Rather, we are dealing with a period in which a traumatic event may have occurred and the distortions of later developmental conflicts may be superimposed on the earlier situation. Kennedy (1971) states that Anna Freud, like Kris, observed that experiences are molded into patterns, so that the analyst is dealing with complex ego states rather than specific contents. Using these concepts, Kennedy proposed that reconstruction in child analysis functions primarily as a way to provide the child with a conceptual framework whereby he can better understand his present experiences and conflicts. The emphasis is not specifically on connections with the past but on enlarging the child's insight and self-awareness by drawing attention to previously unconscious feelings and fantasies that can be made available to the conscious ego by analyzing the defenses against them. Although the transference represents some reliving of the past, the analysis of the transference, particularly the transference of defense, is aimed at increasing the child's awareness and understanding of why he feels and behaves as he does at the moment in the analytic situation and not at reconstructing the past.

In examining the cognitive factors in reconstruction with children, Rees (1978) observed that the prelatency child reacted to attempts to reconstruct the past as interesting stories rather than as the child's own history. Rees observed that what was most effective in helping the child to undo distortions and progress to more reality-oriented perceptions was for the analyst to verbalize the *here and now* interactions of the analysand with the analyst or with the mother. She noted that the latency child's increasing capacity to grasp causal connections enables him to understand the workings of defense. He does so best with immediate, concrete examples within the session.

Presumably concerned that analysts would feel her views about reconstruction threatened to deprive them of a cherished activity, Kennedy (1971) expressed the hope that "in spite of all that was said, we will all continue to get that feeling of satisfaction that usually follows a 'good' reconstructive interpretation."

Viewing the analytic process in childhood from the side of the ego, we realize that it is difficult for the child to maintain control over instinctual drives and mental functioning at the highest level of maturity in the face of conflict and stress (A. Freud, 1952). The immature ego, unable to maintain its developmental position, often regresses and complies with the regressed instinctual demands. While the ego's compliance may reduce the intensity of the child's internal conflict, it may result in arrests in development marked by regressive behavior and maladaptive solutions to conflict. Verbalizing the defensive or maladaptive response as well as the drive derivative and gearing the verbal interventions to the child's level of cognitive development (Katan, 1961) help the ego to tolerate the instinctual impulse without losing control or regressing, enabling the child to maintain or regain the path of normal development.

From such considerations, it follows that the best possibilities for long-term positive effects would lie in focusing on the analysis of the ego's immature and maladaptive defenses as a way to strengthen the ego in its control of the pressure from the instinctual drives. However, the ego remains at risk from two dangers: an increase in the intensity of the drives—particularly aggression—as a consequence of trauma, frustration, or entering a new developmental phase, as in puberty or adolescence or in the transition from adolescence to adult; a second risk stems from the vulnerability of the ego to regress to immature, anachronistic defenses. In "Analysis Terminable and Interminable," Freud (1937) identified early alterations of the ego, caused by trauma and the quantitative factor in the instinctual drives, as a main factor responsible for the length of analyses. These alterations, which are the primary modes of defense erected early to cope with trauma, stress, and frustration, are difficult if not impossible to render totally inoperative or unavailable. Therefore, they play a large role in the individual's falling ill again.

With her favorable start in life, Evelyne had fewer of these ego alterations or deformations to contend with than the other two. Jerry and Frankie, with the early, intense frustrations and concomitant stimulation of aggression, remained more vulnerable to characterological distortion or neurotic illness. But in each of them, a lasting effect of the child analysis was some degree of realization that the way out of their difficulties was through a better understanding of the working of their minds.

BIBLIOGRAPHY

BORNSTEIN, B. (1949). The analysis of a phobic child: Some problems of theory and technique in child analysis. *Psychoanal. Study Child,* 3/4:181–226.

BRENNER, C. (1982). *The Mind in Conflict.* New York: International Universities Press.

CHUSED, J. (1988). The transference neurosis in child analysis. *Psychoanal. Study Child,* 43:51–82.

FRANKL, L., & HELLMAN, I. (1962). The ego's participation in the therapeutic alliance. *Int. J. Psa.,* 43:333–37.

FREUD, A. (1936). *The Ego and the Mechanisms of Defense, The Writings of Anna Freud*, Vol. 2. New York: International Universities Press, rev. ed., 1966.

―――― (1952). The mutual influences in the development of ego and id: Introduction to the discussion. *Psychoanal. Study Child*, 7:42–50.

―――― (1965). *Normality and Pathology in Childhood*. New York: International Universities Press.

FREUD, S. (1937). Analysis Terminable and Interminable. *Standard Edition*, 23:209–53. London: Hogarth Press, 1964.

FRIEDMAN, L. (1976). Cognitive and therapeutic tasks of a theory of the mind. *Int. Rev. Psa.*, 3:259–75.

HARLEY, M. (1986). Child analysis, 1947–1984: A retrospective. *Psychoanal. Study Child*, 41:129–54.

KATAN, A. (1961). Some thoughts about the role of verbalization in early childhood. *Psychoanal. Study Child*, 16:184–88.

KENNEDY, H. (1971). Problems in reconstruction in child analysis. *Psychoanal. Study Child*, 26:386–402.

KRIS, E. (1956). The recovery of childhood memories in psychoanalysis. *Psychoanal. Study Child*, 11:54–88.

MAYES, L. C. (1995). Children's emerging understanding of mental life. *J. Amer. Psa. Assn.*, in press.

REES, K. (1978). The child's understanding of his past. *Psychoanal. Study Child*, 33:237–59.

RITVO, S. (1978). The psychoanalytic process in childhood. *Psychoanal. Study Child*, 33:295–305.

―――― (1993). Plan and Illusion. In: *The Many Meanings of Play: A Psychoanalytic Perspective*, eds. A. J. Solnit et al. New Haven: Yale University Press, pp. 234–51.

The Good Boy Syndrome and Malignant Academic Failure in Early Adolescence

ROBERT L. TYSON, M.D.

The shift into adolescence coincides with an increase in academic demands that reveals a large diagnostic range of difficulties underlying academic underachievement or failure at this developmental stage. A group of compliant boys of high intelligence and proved abilities, previously apparently well-adjusted and well-liked, unexpectedly come to attention because of sudden academic failure. Their puzzling difficulties indicate a serious underlying disorder, including depression, which requires intensive treatment. Intrasystemic superego conflicts of ideals form an intrinsic part of the psychic picture.

IT IS A CLINICAL TRUISM THAT ADOLESCENTS AS A GROUP ARE SUSCEPTIBLE to many disturbances, including disruptions in their academic performance during these sometimes turbulent years. I will describe a not infrequent clinical picture of sudden academic failure in young adolescent boys, which is often unrecognized. These compliant boys have a history of good behavior and high academic performance but unexpectedly run into apparently benign school difficulties; only later does the more malignant character of the problem become manifest. As parts of this picture, their good-natured cooperativeness and the high esteem in which they are held obscure the underlying depression, which progresses relentlessly. In my experience, conflicts over hostility

Clinical professor of Psychiatry, University of California, San Diego; Training and Supervising Analyst, San Diego Psychoanalytic Institute.

The Psychoanalytic Study of the Child 51, ed. Albert J. Solnit, Peter B. Neubauer, Samuel Abrams, and A. Scott Dowling (Yale University Press, copyright © 1996 by Albert J. Solnit, Peter B. Neubauer, Samuel Abrams, and A. Scott Dowling).

and efforts to avoid narcissistic injury play a central role in their lives. The clinician may underestimate the severity of the situation, including the underlying depression, because of the same factors that mislead families and teachers—that is, the patient's history of good performance and his compliance and good nature. For these reasons, I designate the clinical picture "The Good Boy Syndrome."

THE SOCIAL AND CLINICAL CONTEXT

The boys I describe are part of a significant segment of the adolescent population that wins the approval of parents, teachers, and even some of their peers by being successfully compliant and doing what they are told. They do not come to the attention of disciplinarians or the authorities except to be held up as positive examples for others less "good." They achieve the personal, social, and academic goals others set out for them; many even believe that these goals are their own. When presented with questionnaires, they dutifully fill in the blanks to indicate that no, they have never suffered from *stürm und drang*, rebellion has never been, is not now, and never will be an important or upsetting ingredient in their lives, and yes, they feel fortunate in having understanding parents and siblings with whom they have close and warm relationships. They are often obviously well endowed intellectually and physically, and they have never suffered from any disruption of their apparently smooth functioning. The developmental history from infancy typically is free of any sign of disorder in eating, sleeping, and elimination. If anything, their intellectual development has been precocious, much to the pride of their parents, many of whose marriages are stable.

The underlying psychopathology is concealed by a collusive denial that is part of the family structure. Many of these individuals who do not come to attention during adolescence remain in balance, their academic difficulties glossed over. They mature into productive adults who do what they are told, achieving the goals that are set out for them. Near midlife, some gradually feel a sense of inner emptiness, resulting in a puzzling contrast with their often impressive achievements; a small number of these good citizens eventually come to treatment.

Theirs is not a crisis that originates in midlife but one of which they gradually become aware after decades of good behavior. As treatment begins, one often hears that the adolescence of these midlife malcontents was unremarkable except that it appeared unruffled, benign, and filled with various achievements, recognition, and honors. However, as treatment progresses, one begins to hear of some so-called adolescent adjustment problems attributed to a change in school, the death of a grandparent, a family move—in any event, to some external circumstance that bears the burden of having caused their apparent temporary deflection from the path of normalcy. To the observer, this path begins to appear more like a narrow and confining track than the happy trajectory everyone, including the patient, has always believed it to be. Often the patient recalls an episode of academic difficulties understood to be the result of some external factor—an illness, for example, a severe case of flu, as it is commonly believed that depression is a frequent complication of influenza. Or it will be rationalized as a consequence of the great change inherent in going away to college, where the patient faces an entirely new atmosphere with different standards and misses home, family, and friends, perhaps even complicated by feelings of homesickness recognized as such. Typically, the history goes, within a few months these more obvious signs disappear and are forgotten. Calm is restored, together with the usual smooth functioning, or perhaps there is now a short period of some questioning of goals—do they really want to go into the family business, or become a lawyer, doctor, teacher, etc. In psychoanalytic treatment as an adult, the patient recalls these experiences only hazily at first, but the underlying dynamics and symptom constellation that emerge are the same as those among adolescents in this group who are seen at the earlier age. Therefore I will focus on the more unusual circumstance, at least in comparison to the total numbers involved: when the clinician is asked to help the adolescent who is obviously intelligent but is now having unexpected and persisting academic troubles, underachieving in comparison to his previously demonstrated excellent capacities and talents. While on occasion the student may have been aware of some disturbances such as increasing difficulty concentrating or getting things done, the rapid unfolding of the problem over a period of a few weeks gives the impression of a threshold being exceeded or a wall breaking down.

I have said "he," because the adolescents I have seen with this syndrome are male, though adolescent girls presumably can demonstrate it. As Dalsimer (1975) has pointed out, fear of success is significantly more prevalent in adolescent girls than in boys of comparable age. If such fear is a general constraint on female academic work from early on, it might help to explain the absence of this syndrome in girls. Freud (1920) described a relevant defense, "retiring in favor of someone else," a renunciation in order to avoid the painful circumstances and consequences of a competition, including feared retaliation and other "very complicated conditions in the mind" (p. 159, fn). The issue is still very much alive; for example, a recent questionnaire study by Jones (1993), who studied 113 female and 160 male students between the ages of 13 and 17 years, found that the females showed significantly more interest on items relevant to concern about performance and anticipated critical interactions with parents, teachers, and peers. It may be that the "good girl" handles the conflicts described in this syndrome differently from the "good boy" and so attracts attention in other ways. As Gilligan (1982) pointed out, women respond to situations on the basis of what is best for a relationship, while men more often respond on the basis of abstract principles. The reasons for this difference in response are based on gender differences in superego development (Tyson & Tyson, 1990).

DIAGNOSTIC CONSIDERATIONS

One must differentiate descriptively between the syndrome of the good boy with sudden academic failure, on the one hand, and academic difficulties that appear as a part of a whole host of disturbances, on the other. Among these latter disturbances are overt depression, bipolar mental illness, delinquency, various learning disorders, drug dependencies, alcoholism, borderline manifestations, minimal brain dysfunction, epilepsy, brain tumor, multiple sclerosis, and so on. Many articles in the psychiatric and psychological literature consider the differential diagnosis of academic underachievement in adolescents (e.g., Hinshaw, 1992; Sugar, 1987), but even in Sugar's excellent and concise review, external factors are primary. He makes only a brief reference to oppositionalism (p. 432) but does not consider any dynamic factors.

Anna Freud (1936) made a useful distinction between an inhibition and an ego restriction. Thus one could contrast restrictions resulting from an impairment of function as a consequence of the symbolic meaning an activity has come to have with those resulting from the avoidance of painful disappointment, such as narcissistic mortification, anticipated, for example, when the young adolescent comes to compare his previously lauded accomplishments and abilities with those of peers, who are at least equal if not superior in their abilities. In such a defense against a fear of failure a previously competent student may now procrastinate and refuse to study until the last minute, convinced that he really didn't need to study, but that if he had worked as hard as the others, he would have gotten the highest grade instead of a lesser one.

It is easy to see that the educational shift to more difficult work and greater competition is simultaneous with the onset of early adolescence. Often enough in boys, the two inhibitions based on symbolic significance, involving fears of success, guilt, castration anxiety and fears of failure leading to narcissistic mortification, occur together, linked to struggles over masturbation. Those external events, typically seen as causative, resonate with intrapsychic tensions in such a way as to require a shift in the defensive equilibrium, resulting in the academic failure. Klein (1949) accounts for depression in adolescents, at least in those whose parents take good achievement for granted, by the students' turning against themselves the hostility their attitudes generated in them. He also points out that the narcissistic adolescent's withdrawal is often accompanied by a denigration of that which is being withdrawn from. The opposite occurs in those for whom a fear of success, a sexualization of the activity, or other symbolically based dynamics underlie the withdrawal, accompanied by feelings of inferiority and self-reproaches. Klein also mentioned that if the mother is the more intelligent parent, the boy's ambitions to learn may be drawn into gender-identity conflicts and conflicts over homosexuality.

Newman et al. (1973) examined academic failure in fifteen gifted underachieving boys (they found no girls) between the ages of seven to thirteen; most were between 9 and 11. The authors considered the possibility that at least some of these boys could perform well on intelligence tests but encountered difficulties based on an unrecognized disability when obliged to perform "tasks requiring planning, effort, the integration of a large body of material, and sustained activity toward a goal" (p. 84; see also Sandler, Hooper, and Scarborough, 1993, who describe this behavior as associated with learning disabilities in adolescents). In order to hide this defect such a boy would then defensively seem to be in control to the extent that he appeared oppositional, leading adults to say, "He can but he won't." Newman et al. thought a source of such a defect might be early and persistent negativism, though this history was not characteristic of many in the group, and they did not view negativism developmentally (cf. R. L. Tyson, 1994).[1] They did find glib, intellectualizing speech that covered up a lack of age-appropriate knowledge, an appearance characterized by physical apathy and lethargy, and loquacious mothers in love with their sons' precocious speech from early on, reflecting the mother's investment and consequent enhancement of the child's verbal development. They compared this relationship to Mahler's (1952) finding of the mother's overinvestment in a particular body part of the child with a symbiotic

---

1. At the college level a good performer in high school with a high IQ who flunks out of college has been called "the student who refuses to succeed" (Baker, 1975).

psychosis and to Greenacre's (1959) concept of focal symbiosis in which an intense interdependence between mother and child was limited to a particular aspect of their relationship rather than being the more usual comprehensive, total one of mother and child.

Berman (1971) reports boys with a symptom picture somewhat similar to the "good boy syndrome" but with several differences. The boys he studied suffered from a passive-aggressive character disorder that defended against a neurotic depression. In his experience, these boys had a high verbal score but low performance on the Wechsler-Bellevue psychological test, which he believes reflects their intense passive-dependent longings. They do poorly if they move away from home, contrary to their own expectations and those of their parents. The early history of his patients is marked by much promise that they never live up to. Berman sees the problem as beginning with defective parental identifications during the oedipal phase. Like Newman et al., he finds a pathological relationship with the boy's mother and her ambivalently overprotective response in contrast to her expectations of her son's performance.

The good boy with academic failure, as I speak of him here, suffers from none of these afflictions though to some degree he may partake in a disturbed maternal relationship. While he may be unhappy at this turn of events, he does not appear to be suffering from an overt depressive illness. As Masterson (1970) has pointed out, adolescents generally defend vigorously against painful depressive affect. Typically the good boy has made so little trouble for anyone in his whole life that when his difficulty first appears, he and everyone else are truly surprised. The initial response from family and teachers is sympathetic, supportive, and understanding. When these responses do not work and his academic difficulties persist, the understanding diminishes, and as time goes on, so do the sympathy and the support. When his depression becomes manifest, he is likely to worry that it is a burden to others.

The clinician's usual way of proceeding is to rule out all the so-called major illnesses. Then the diagnosis by exclusion is a "minor illness," something "just psychological." The hunt begins for an explanation, typically assigned to some external factor like the flu, and a treatment is often based on that rationalization. However, this "minor illness" has sufficient power to ruin the adolescent's life, to foreclose the avenues of education and training, to interfere with his family relationships, and to disrupt his friendships by isolating him as a consequence of making him "different." In the clinician's office he is appealingly pleasant, intelligent, polite, articulate, and suffering. This is not the challenge to the therapist's capacity to tolerate those horrendous counter-transference reactions to adolescents the literature so often warns about, those intense feelings of discomfort if not rage stimulated by nasty, attacking, contemptuous "borderlines." With the boys I am de-scribing, the therapist has no fears that the patient will imminently make a suicide attempt or become drug addicted, sexually promis-cuous, or a thief, or will demonstrate some other piece of dangerous activity or enactment. There is a pleasant countertransference feeling and atmosphere of wanting to help a pleasant, apparently intelligent, verbally fluent, but slightly benighted youngster who probably just needs someone to talk to a bit, to help him over this hurdle. And, so the therapist often thinks, perhaps it would also be helpful to have some sessions with the parents, or all of them together, to restore the family to its previous level of harmony and understanding. Thus the more subtle and perhaps therefore more dangerous countertransference patterns exert their influence, and the would-be helper repeats the pattern the patient's family has lived through before. It may be that such an ambience facilitates underdiagnosis with many adolescents as remarked on by several observers (e.g., Looney and Gunderson, 1978; Weiner and Del Gaudio, 1976).

CLINICAL EXAMPLES

A few clinical examples will illustrate these points. I will describe the psychoanalytic work with Johnny, Don, and Ted relatively briefly; then I will give more details about Andy and his treatment. Following the clinical material, I will outline the common elements that comprise this syndrome and discuss some of the underlying factors.

Case 1. Johnny was 13 when he was referred for evaluation by his pediatrician, incidentally an unusual source of referral. Johnny was known to be intellectually gifted and was put into an appropriate class. Testing done independent of the school revealed an IQ of 155. For about a year he had done poorly in one or another subject—it did not seem to matter which subject; there was always one trouble spot. His parents gradually became exasperated, especially because Johnny was in all ways such a good boy and had always done what he was supposed to. They had helped him with his work, they had talked with the teachers and the counselors at school, they had obtained tutors with whom their son got along famously, and at times it even appeared that his work was better. Eventually, however, the original pattern reap-peared each time. On the last occasion, Johnny was so mortified that he had received two Cs on his report card that he ran away from home for three days. After realizing that they had exhausted all avenues of assistance, his parents finally felt there was nothing else to do but ask for help. The father, a highly intelligent, hardworking, and successful professional, was concerned about his son and wanted to do anything that might help. He felt closer to the patient than he was to his two younger daughters, even though the demands of his work kept him away from home more than either he or his devoted wife liked. The mother was a sensitive, articulate, insightful, well-organized college graduate who feared that she had done something wrong in raising Johnny to account for his present difficulties. Both parents described him as a delightful boy with a good sense of humor, cheerful and willing, and with a happy relationship with his younger sisters, an impression confirmed when Johnny appeared in person.

In the course of the evaluation, it appeared that Johnny had a pattern of procrastinating on work in one or another course; then just before the last examination he would attempt to complete all the assignments and study all the material to "pull a rabbit out of the hat," to get a good grade. This feat had been accomplished a number of times, though no one knew it. Only when he had not been able to accomplish it had it come to anyone's attention. It gradually became clear that Johnny himself was surprised he was doing this, totally unaware that it was a pattern. In fact, it was just this point that got him interested in treatment, as it offered him a way to learn and to be in control of himself. Over a period of two years of analysis Johnny's marks gradually returned to where they should have been, and it became abundantly clear that the central focus of his problem had to do with his need to control his hostile aggression. For Johnny, to succeed meant to do someone else in. With treatment, Johnny gradually became better able to put into words more of his angry feelings than ever before, and incidentally, he no longer appeared always to be such a very pleasant person all of the time.

Case 2. Don was 15 years old when his mother asked for him to be seen. She had some psychotherapy a few years before, when Don's brother, who was six years older, dropped out of high school and left home following several years of drug abuse and earning poor grades; she asked her previous therapist for the referral. She was concerned because Don had always been a straight A-student, but now he was getting several Bs, which upset him considerably. In addition, she worried he was becoming progressively more withdrawn, and she was frightened by his excessively angry responses to rare visits by family members and neighbors. This came to a head after the maternal grandmother refused to visit because she did not want to have any contact with her grandson. On her last visit she was most distraught by his attitude to her, and she complained that he didn't listen to what she said, often failed to respond to her remarks and questions, and looked furiously at her if she said anything.

Don's father was a highly competent, articulate, and intelligent professional whose work required long periods away from home, similar to Johnny's father. He had been bitterly disappointed in his older son and all his hopes were on Don. He was more open with Don than was the mother about their hopes for him and the wish that he not be like his brother. The mother strove to be closer to Don, feeling that if she had given more to the brother, he would not have fallen into bad company, consequently disappointing them so. When the times for treatment were proposed, there was a conflict with Don's sports activities in which he had been active and successful for several years. The father openly said he thought sports were more important, the mother just as openly said she thought that treatment was more important; they left the decision up to Don, who, to my surprise, decided to drop sports this year or until treatment was over, in favor of starting.

Don's entire life and thoughts centered around school and homework. If there were no assignments, he either read science fiction books or watched television. He had gone out for sports because his father wanted him to, and because his brother had not done so. In fact, everything about his life was dedicated to being different from his brother, that is, to being as good a boy as his brother had been bad. A concrete example of this was the parents' decision after fifth grade to move him from public school to a strict fundamentalist institution. They felt he would be less likely to be influenced there by drug abusing delinquents, an association that they were convinced had ruined their older son. Don had embraced the fundamentalist teachings and a glimmer of rebellion could be seen in his report of how his mother tried to convince him of the scientific validity of Darwinian evolution, while he easily demolished her arguments and demonstrated what he called her scientific bigotry using what he had been taught in school. To her fears that he had been brainwashed, he replied that he had a similar concern about her.

The details of this way of life only gradually emerged over the first year of treatment, as Don was an extremely cautious and slow conversationalist. He had decided on treatment after due deliberation because it would be less "hassle" and also because he agreed he had some problems that could be helped. He was chiefly concerned about the fact that his mind would often wander while studying, and that this had caused his grades to drop. He became concerned because he feared his difficulties in studying were getting out of control, and he saw treatment as a way of regaining it. In fact, over the first year of treatment his ability to focus on his studies did improve and he returned to his sought-for straight-A status. Thus treatment enabled Don to extricate himself from what was, for him, academic failure, getting less than straight As. It is interesting to speculate on the possibility that without treatment the interference with his concentration might have progressed to the point that others would have been alarmed about his academic performance.

While at this juncture many adolescents drop out of treatment, or get their parents to interfere; Don continued, perhaps because he was more influenced by treatment compliance, because of his passivity, than by treatment alliance.

As he slowly talked more about himself in addition to the details of his subjects, tests, quizzes, grades, projects, grading methods, teachers, etc., a more complete picture of his complex personality emerged. In structure and function, Don had an obsessional personality with a few symptomatic compulsions—for example, he repeatedly checked whether he had turned off the lights. His feelings of anger and resentment at his mother, and then at his brother, came up and were covered over and then worked through repeatedly. This initial ventilation lessened the pressure contributing to Don's "mind wandering." Often enough such a complaint from an adolescent is related to sexual preoccupations, but Don made it clear in several ways that he was not ready to talk about anything in that area. The fundamentalist school's teachings about sex coincided with his needs to control his sexual feelings and thoughts. Only later was he able to talk about his first love, a girl with anorexia nervosa who was about to move away. He talked with her for hours on the telephone until she left the city, after which Don became quite overtly depressed. Eventually he worked through to find the sources of his anger and to resolve the associated conflicts over the next year.

Case 3. Ted was a 15-year-old all-American looking soccer player and gifted student who came to sessions in shorts and T-shirt. His mother said Ted was a good boy who had never gotten into any trouble, though she was concerned that he might be affected by peer pressure to indulge in drinking or drug abuse. She often questioned him about it, which insulted him and led to arguments. Ted asked his mother if he could see a therapist because he didn't feel right. He was really down after a girlfriend had rejected him, and by the way, he was having trouble finishing his homework assignments. Even though he did not do his homework, he usually studied the night before a test to get a top grade, thus keeping his semester grades up. Recently he was less successful and his semester grades were somewhat lower, but he was optimistic that he could bring them all back up next time and that he would just concentrate more on doing the work.

Ted's parents divorced when he was 8, seven years before. He had a brother three years younger. Their mother had always worked as a secretary, and they continued in the same school and lived in the same neighborhood after the divorce. The father, a successful entrepreneurial scientist, remarried shortly following the divorce and lived a few minutes away by car. There was weekly or more frequent contact with the father, even though disagreements between the parents continued, chiefly about financial issues. The mother had difficulties in finding a suitable man and had been in treatment for two years before Ted asked for help. She was glad to provide this for him, with the father's financial assistance though less enthusiastic concurrence. This was also a religious family in which church activities played a significant social role, so it was not surprising that Ted was careful at the beginning about his language and about what he revealed of his sexual thoughts. What emerged as treatment progressed was Ted's intense ambivalence about his mother with whom he had a very close relationship, one in which they were mutual confidants at one moment, and in the next embattled enemies shouting obscenities at each other—at least he contended that she shouted obscenities. Much more than Johnny or Don, Ted talked about his wish to be independent, looked forward to when that time would come, and at moments of crisis even had thoughts of taking his sleeping bag and living in the car or in the woods.

Treatment gave Ted an opportunity to spill out his overwhelming preoccupation: an absorbing and growing fantasy life devoted to the endless details of combat—attack and defense, weapons and armor, awarding points for experience and impregnability, subtracting points for wounds and vulnerability—all encompassed in games like Dungeons and Dragons, Car Wars, and Champions, including some games of his own design. He spent his spare time thinking, daydreaming, and reading about these games and their plots and accoutrements. He strove to stimulate his classmates with similar interests to meet with him to engage in the games, but no one could match his enthusiasm. In addition, he was aware that in his school, the social status of a person wholly devoted to these games was not the highest, and he was appropriately sensitive to how his friends and classmates regarded him.

Whatever else these fantasies of weapons and war did for Ted, they captured the essence of the ongoing battle with his mother, an insight that was of only little interest to him. What Ted wanted was not insight, but someone to encourage him to do better, to admire his clever fantasy life, to reassure him that he was worthwhile in spite of his mother's stinging criticisms and the low grades his teachers gave him, and to help him unobtrusively to deal with his fears about talking with girls.

Consistent with his somewhat grandiose view of himself, Ted felt that homework assignments and the need to study for assigned projects and exams were intrusions on his pleasurable fantasy life. He was efficient in maximizing the latter and minimizing the former, though the consequences were evident, especially in those areas that required sustained effort and combined skills, such as writing a critical report comparing two books. A report on one book was easy because it could be skimmed and summarized, for example, but to compare two required an effort he could rarely bring himself to expend. In contrast, he could with amazing facility compare and contrast complex weapons systems with many variables such as cost, weight, firepower, and vulnerabilities; he could initiate design changes that would give him the edge to beat his opponents if only he could convince them to play with him.

As treatment progressed, Ted's battles with his mother gradually subsided somewhat, though neither of them seemed eager to give up their habitual ways of relating to one another. He hinted at having been academically, socially, and athletically competitive with classmates, though he attempted to neutralize any impression of his aggressive intent. As his greatly repressed and only slightly sublimated hostile impulses began to become more apparent, Ted suddenly decided to go out for track, which required he be at school for several hours every afternoon. He was indifferent to any interpretation of this resistance, but said maybe he would come back when he had more time, but that never happened.

Case 4. Andy's story is more complex and has several elements that distinguish it from the others. I will give some details from his two years of analysis. He sought help shortly before his 16th birthday, but he had already dropped out of school by the time our sessions began. When I met with his mother prior to treatment, she reported that he was seriously considering dropping out but felt there was nothing she could do to prevent it. She described his development as normal, if not precocious as he walked, talked, and learned to read early. In addition, Andy, in contrast to the others described here, actually had dropped out of school, and he was overtly depressed and realized it. Andy may be an example of what can happen with the advance of an untreated underlying disturbance when feelings of depression become more manifest. School dropouts may have been more common among my patients if their treatment had not begun relatively early.

Andy's intelligence, good behavior, and eagerness to learn were appreciated by the school authorities who quickly referred him for treatment when he asked for help. He complained of depression; he felt sad, goalless, and had difficulty doing his schoolwork. He dropped out just before starting the last two years of pre-university schooling, after about a year of underachieving, that is, his grades began to drop progressively below what his capacities led him, and everyone else, to expect. His intention was to drop out for a year during which he would be in treatment and sort out the problem and perhaps then return to school. He found a job within walking distance of the treatment setting.

Andy was lean and frail with thin, long, blond hair to his shoulders; he wore glasses and casual clothes but was not unkempt. He was anxious at the outset, with a tremor noticeable as he chain-smoked. He was never interested in taking any so-called recreational drugs. His sensitive, intelligent, sad, and forlorn demeanor was paralleled by his articulate description of his feelings of depression and keen sense of loneliness. While never seriously ill, Andy suffered bouts of bronchitis during which he appeared even more like a pathetic waif. He lived with his mother and a sister, who was one and a half years older, in a small, two bedroom apartment.

His parents had separated five years earlier when he was 11, and overt marital discord preceded the separation by at least two years. His mother was from a middle-class family with intellectual aspirations, and she had taught Andy to read before he went to school. She always earned more money as a secretary than her husband, who had no education and was barely literate and now worked as a school janitor. Andy's sister dropped out of school at the same age Andy did. He perceived her as being depressed like himself, and he urged her to look for treatment. While they were often bitter rivals for their parents' affections, and Andy often served as the target for his sister's aggressive teasing, they had many interests in common including art and literature. In fact, Andy was talented as an artist though his urge to draw disappeared as his troubles mounted.

When treatment began, Andy continued our initial discussions about treatment and of the explanations I had given him. He said they made sense, but he feared being torn apart and found to be really bad inside; that I would dismiss him when I discovered that. He now confided that he had many thoughts of suicide; in fact, six months previously he had taken a handful of his mother's sleeping pills fantasizing about being found dead by her, but he had told no one, and no one found out. Also at that time he had imagined shooting himself in the head to prove to his mother he needed help, though he mentioned nothing about his wish at the time. He had always thought she was cold, uncaring, and distant, and he was pleasantly surprised when she proved to be warm, empathetic, and supportive when he brought up his need for treatment. Not surprisingly, this attitude toward his mother evolved into a transference in which his expectations of my uncaring responses were similarly pleasantly disappointed whenever he felt me to be the opposite. A complication emerged in the transference since his warm, positive and friendly feelings toward me eventually resulted in fears that I would attack him homosexually. Andy also voiced fears of being thought effeminate because of his long blond hair and fingernails; he worried that I might be tape recording the sessions and he was too vulnerable with me. In addition he complained that his self-esteem seemed always to be undermined by his mother who he felt consistently belittled his abilities.

Shortly after Andy's fears of being thought effeminate first came up for discussion, he reported having a series of what he called "peculiar ideas," which he later called "paranoid ideas." They were as follows: On the train home from the preceding session he saw a blind man with a girl, both of whom were carrying canes. However, he didn't realize the girl was also blind until they got up to leave. Then he felt he was being followed from the station by someone who wanted to do him in. Next, he saw a beautiful woman, and the setting seemed as if it were from the movie *Doctor Zhivago*, but it was near his house. Then, on the way to one session he saw a big black car in a garage occupied by two big men in black raincoats. It appeared that they were stealing the car, so he stepped up on the curb because he said he preferred to be shot in the back to being run over. He laughed about these ideas, and so I asked first about his defensive use of laughter, was it, for example, whistling in the dark to make himself feel less frightened? He agreed that, in general, he laughed first in case I might laugh at him. I then took up Andy's intense wish that someone like me would be interested in him but that he feared what my motivations might be. As our work progressed, I learned that at age 12 he had been seduced by a bisexual boyfriend of his mother's, but before he felt able to tell me about it in any detail, he spent a number of sessions working through his concerns about being controlled, "ripped open," and brainwashed by me in the course of treatment.

One aspect of his concern that I might do something to him against his will was linked to his resentment of his mother, who he felt used him as a weapon against his father. Andy felt his mother had planned the separation from his father like a military campaign in the course of which she reversed the earlier, pre-divorce alignment of father-son and mother-daughter. His mother treated him, instead of his sister, as a confidant, drawing him into opposition to his father whom she "painted black." At this point in treatment, Andy felt up to taking the initiative and he began to visit his father weekly and found him "not so bad." Andy was curious about how his father felt about his being in treatment and was disappointed to hear him say that he was against it— a position he assumed was based on his father's declaration that *he* didn't need any help to get over *his* nervous breakdown suffered during World War II. It became apparent that Andy was afraid his father would be angry at him, based on his alignment with the mother during the divorce, and this fear of his father's anger made Andy hesitant to visit him. I was able to link this fear to the attacks in the "paranoid" fantasies, and subsequently to his guilty feelings based on his positive oedipal wishes. These wishes to be his mother's favorite and to win out over his father and sister had come very close to being fulfilled in reality because of the mother's liaison with Andy against the father, and because of their subsequent triumphant departure from the father to live together away from him.

Andy now talked about his interest in some of the girls at work, but he wondered how much he would have to tell me about it. He felt it was dangerous to trust someone, namely me, for fear he "would be overwhelmed by some cheap emotion," and he began to make hypochondriacal references to his body, feeling he might have abused it by smoking. He tested my interest in him by emphasizing his deteriorating physical state and increased feelings of depression, while at the same time making plans to move out of his mother's house to share an apartment with another boy. This aroused my concern, and my advice to Andy to postpone his move was motivated more from a protective countertransference than derived from any technical considerations. However, it did lead him to confess how much he wished his mother would say she wanted him to stay at home with her.

As Andy always had shared his plans with his mother, he told her when an apartment might become available; on that day he came home to find all his belongings neatly packed up and waiting at the front door. Without his knowing, she had cleaned out his room, apparently unable to wait until he did it himself. Not surprisingly, Andy took his mother's action as a rejection of him and as an indication that she must prefer someone else to him. He cried and for several days suffered painful feelings of hopelessness, sadness, and confusion. He wondered if this was the same sort of thing that had interfered with his school work. He turned his anger at his mother against himself, with renewed suicidal fantasies that very slowly dissipated as his rage toward her decreased. Only now did he recall that over a year before, he had been briefly aware of intense anger at her when she had insisted on their moving, putting financial considerations ahead of any awareness of his feelings about it, as he felt it then. It was following that incident of the move that his difficulties with school work began, followed by feelings of goallessness and depression.

During the Christmas holiday, Andy met a girl who lived next to him at his new apartment. Christine invited him to bed with her, and he found great pleasure and relief in his first heterosexual encounter. In the first session of the new year, he blurted out the details of the homosexual seduction he had briefly mentioned earlier, in which he had allowed himself to be masturbated by his mother's boyfriend. In the following sessions he began to worry that I cared too much about him, then that I might be homosexual, and finally that the treatment might turn him into a homosexual. Like an antidote to me, he planned to move into an apartment with Christine and her three-month-old illegitimate son and talked about taking a "rest" from treatment. I interpreted his fears of "giving in" to talking with me, which might make him feel as if he was allowing himself to be masturbated by me. He agreed with a smile, and he was then able to talk about the guilty pleasure he had felt at the time of the seduction. In a subsequent session he fell asleep and had a dream he reported on waking. He was lying on a beach, a hand came down from nowhere and picked up a rock and bashed in his head with it. He thought the session was the beach and that the hand with the rock was mine. At the time, Christine was getting drunk every night, fighting with everybody, taking drugs, threatening to kill the baby, etc. He felt trapped between his feelings of responsibility to Christine and to me and the treatment. At the same time he feared that failing any of these responsibilities might result in harm to him. This scene reproduced and reenacted his conflict of loyalties as his parents' discord had mounted when he was 9 years old. Also, he feared the increasing positive attachment to me as the idealized father for whose approval he yearned, and earlier, as the mother whose love he craved.

At this point Andy recalled several episodes of what he called "school phobia" between the ages of 9 and 13, when he couldn't bring himself to go to school and cried inconsolably for his mother to come home from work. The growing dependence on me in treatment had become a threat to his attachment to his mother; his many thoughts about

avoiding sessions or ending treatment, I interpreted as efforts to preserve that now-threatened attachment. The attachment to me was defended against in other ways—by missing sessions and by fearing my
anticipated "livid, screaming rage" allegedly caused by his truancy
from treatment. Parallel with this was what I understood to be the
pattern of rapprochement disappointment and subsequent rage, in
which the mother is felt to be indifferent to the child's autonomous
strivings, thus abruptly deflating to his self-esteem. In Andy's case, it
was his mother who was intensely ambitious for him to achieve what she
could not, and to do so for the sake of her own motives without much
recognition and support of her son's autonomy. Thus, he had to test
her repeatedly, and me in the transference, in regard to what was for
him, and what was for someone else. Therefore he feared that I had
ambitions for him in the treatment, and for him to improve was to yield
to me. Consequently, there were a number of episodes of moderate
negative therapeutic reactions that only gradually diminished with
repeated interpretations of this theme.

The recognition, verbalization, and connecting of these impulses,
fantasies, fears and defenses gradually freed Andy to the extent that he
was, for the first time, able overtly to lose his temper with his mother,
and then with his friends, then with me, and to discover that none of us
were destroyed, nor was he. By the time the second year of treatment
ended, he had decided to return to school, but this time in a different
setting and with a different goal, one he had worked out for himself rather than one compliantly adopted from his mother. He went
through a series of girlfriends who appeared progressively less unsuit-

able and disturbed. These girls also served to progressively dilute the transference, and interpretations not withstanding, Andy seemed to titrate me into the gradual termination arranged by him. Although he felt there were still some problems (he would not tell me what they were), he felt able to cope with them. He said he was more content now than ever before and that treatment had helped him to come a long way. He sincerely thanked me in his last session.

DISCUSSION

The debate as to whether the usual path of adolescent development is beset by turmoil continues. Earlier studies found disruption, the appearance of symptomatology suggesting serious psychological illness, and crises central to the formation of the adult personality (Blos, 1962; Erikson, 1956; A. Freud, 1958; Hall, 1904; Josselyn, 1952; Spiegel, 1961). More recent findings, based on work with nonclinical samples, have thrown doubt on the universality of adolescent upheaval, at least in its visible forms (Looney and Gunderson, 1978; Masterson, 1967, 1970; Masterson and Washburne, 1966; Offer, 1969; Oldham, 1978; Weiner and Del Gaudio, 1976). Those data were obtained chiefly from questionnaires and other "short-term sources," which provide a different view of developmental events than that evolved by the clinician from long-term work with patients who ask for help or whose parents ask for them. The Scylla and Charybdis of diagnostic work with adolescents is between underdiagnosing because of the attribution of problems to "normal adolescent turmoil" and overdiagnosing because of a lack of appreciation of the wide range of acceptable disturbance in adolescence.

Looney and Lewis (1983) have found attributes of smooth developmental progress among well-functioning adolescents in a study of two socioeconomic and ethnic groups, those from Caucasian middle- and upper-class families, and those from black, working-class families. These families were chosen on the basis of their "competence," defined as "the capacity to produce autonomous children and provide emotional support for the parents" (p. 73). However, there is a problem of circular reasoning if the competence of a family is defined in terms of its ability to demonstrate a competent, that is, a descriptively asymptomatic and apparently well-adapted adolescent. Clinically one may see many well-knit and well-adapted families whose children—perhaps one or sometimes more—do not have such a smooth path to adulthood. The converse is also true: in disrupted and disturbed families, well-integrated, well-adapted, and apparently asymptomatic adolescents may emerge. Sometimes high performers from fragmented backgrounds do so well that they earn the designation of "super-phrenics." Not surprisingly, exceptional achievement is usually associated with high intelligence, and identifications with parental values are clearly relevant (Berman and Eisenberg, 1971).

There are some apparent paradoxes in the relevant psychological literature. For example, among white, middle-class, intact families, Williams and Radin (1993) found that as a group, adolescents whose mothers who worked part-time, especially during the pre-school years, did better academically than those whose mothers worked full time or who did not work at all. Gender differences did not appear to be important, nor did the degree to which the fathers were involved as caregivers during the early years. Other studies show that boys with high father availability do better academically than those with low father availability (e.g., Blanchard and Biller, 1971), so that paternal involvement in terms of availability may be a different variable from paternal involvement as caregiver. Reports of the impact of separation and divorce vary, with most finding deterioration in school behavior and performance. Interestingly, in non-intact families those children who spent significantly more time with both parents did notably better than those who did not (Bisnaire et al., 1990).

I emphasize here that while the nature of the adolescent's family is certainly important, the adolescent himself makes a contribution from his inner life to his own development and adaptation, a contribution that questionnaires are not able to gauge. I believe that a fuller understanding of this contribution and its sources will improve our ability to help the apparently healthy adolescent who appears to run suddenly into difficulties. These examples of the good boy syndrome with academic failure prove the point.

In all four cases, the boys were thought to have had optimal development and to be competent and well-adapted prior to the unexpected onset of academic failure. Also, their parents, teachers, peers, and last but not least, they saw themselves as good boys who were intelligent and doing well. Even Don, who was the most withdrawn, had various interests and social contacts and had been active in sports. Only Andy had not participated in extracurricular team sports, but up until the time of his troubles, he had been involved in a number of other activities.

In addition to various preoedipal and oedipal issues, several developmental factors stand out in the cases described. First, a strikingly close relationship with the mother was maintained well into adolescence, and while some ambivalence does appear, the close tie to the mother is not disrupted. Although a mother's pride in her son's development and achievements is considered a *sine qua non* for optimal personality growth, in these patients the mother's investment seems to have had the quality of being more for her own gratification and narcissistic needs than for the sake of the son's separation and individuation. Both mother and son may find this attachment to the mother threatened by the early adolescent's psychological and social progression and by the emergence of their different views of the child's future as an independent adult. All four boys had difficulties with object removal (Katan, 1951) and with the second individuation of adolescence (Blos, 1967). However, none of the mother-son relationships were disturbed to the extent described by Mahler (1952), Greenacre (1959), or any of the other authors referred to.

Second, a hungry attachment to a rather distant father was evident in all, but with deeply unsatisfied yearnings for paternal contact and interest. Homosexual conflicts were apparent especially in Andy, but none of the boys was able to develop a close "buddy" relationship with another boy, something they each said they wanted. The adolescent resolution of negative oedipal conflicts, an issue Blos (1967) believes to be crucial to the successful negotiation of the adolescent process, appears to have been deadlocked in these boys.

Third, the importance of learning and school work had a dual meaning to these patients in addition to its significance in the age-appropriate concerns of the adolescent: one meaning in terms of their relationship with the mother, another in terms of their relationship with the father. I have mentioned the mother's pride in her son's accomplishments. In each case the mother encouraged the son's precocious learning. But also in each case the father's position regarding education was crucial. In three instances the fathers were highly educated and successful far beyond the mother's apparent abilities; and in Andy's case, because of the opposite, that is, the father was almost illiterate while the mother was highly verbal and well read. It may be that with the first three, entry into high school confronted them with the reality that now they were being asked to take that last and important step that would propel them into college, careers, separation from the family, and last but not least, to challenge and perhaps to equal or surpass their fathers' achievements. In Andy's situation, simply to stay in school was to surpass his father and provide justification for his mother's divorce. Thus because of their wishes to fulfill what they perceived as their parents' sometimes incompatible ambitions for them and to attain expected independence and yet remain close to one parent, they all suffered from intrasystemic superego conflicts, a conflict of ideals (Tyson, P., and Tyson, R. L., 1990, pp. 215–216).

Last, intense depressive feelings in these boys emerged as a consequence of a developmental impasse, based on a failure to resolve conflicts over aggression, rather than the depression being simply a cause of the academic failure. The masking of the depression served their efforts to be "good" in meeting their ideals that coincided with their parents' expectations for them to be good boys and to achieve their incompatible aspirations. These efforts were part of the complex set of reaction formations that made up a significant portion of their character and that lent a "pseudo-narcissistic" cast to their personalities, based on the increasing need for approval as they felt themselves progressively failing to meet their inner standards (Tyson, R. L. and Tyson, P., 1982). Their difficulties in self-esteem regulation also were related to their guilt over the frightening presence of intense and murderous hostile impulses and fantasies that also interfered with the ability to employ cognitive abilities in a neutral and productive way. Certainly the question of aggression and its handling is central in all of these patients who had worked so hard to be compliant and to be good boys.

BIBLIOGRAPHY

BAKER, H. S. (1975). The treatment of academic underachievement. *J. Am. Coll. Health Assoc.*, 24:4–7.
BERMAN, G., AND EISENBERG, M. (1971). Psycho-social aspects of academic achievement. *Amer. J. Orthopsychiat.*, 41:406–415.
BERMAN, S. (1971). *J. Am. Acad. Child Psychiatry*, 10:418–443.
BISNAIRE, L. M. C., FIRESTONE, P., RYNARD, D. (1990). Factors associated with academic achievement in children following parental separation. *Amer. J. Orthopsychiat.*, 60:67–76.
BLOS, P. (1962). *On Adolescence: A Psychoanalytic Interpretation.* New York: Free Press.
BLOS, P.(1967). The second individuation process of adolescence. *Psychoanal. Study Child*, 22:162–186.
DALSIMER, K. (1975). Fear of academic success in adolescent girls. *J. Am. Acad. Child Psychiatry*, 14:719–730.
ERIKSON, E. H. (1956). The concept of ego identity. *J. Amer. Psychoanal. Assoc.*, 4:56–121.
FREUD, A. (1936). *The Ego and the Mechanisms of Defense.* In *The Writings of Anna Freud.* Vol. 2. Rev. ed. New York: International Universities Press, 1966.
FREUD, A. (1958). Adolescence. In *The Writings of Anna Freud.* Vol. 4. New York: International Universities Press, 1968, pp. 136–166.
FREUD, S. (1920). The psychogenesis of a case of homosexuality in a woman. *S.E. 18*:146–172.
GILLIGAN, C. (1982). *In a Different Voice: Psychological Theory and Women's Development.* Cambridge: Harvard University Press.

GREENACRE, P. (1959). On focal symbiosis. In: *Dynamic Psychopathology in Childhood.* Ed. L. Jessner & E. Pavenstedt. New York: Grune and Stratton, pp. 243–256.

HALL, G. S. (1904). *Adolescence: Its psychology and its relations to physiology, anthropology, sociology, sex, crime, religion and education.* New York: Appleton, 1916.

HINSHAW, S. P. (1992). Externalizing behavior problems and academic underachievement in childhood and adolescence: Causal relationships and underlying mechanisms. *Psychological Bull., 111:*127–155.

JONES, R. W. (1993). Gender-specific differences in the perceived antecedents of academic stress. *Psychological Reports, 72:*739–743.

JOSSELYN, I. (1952). *The Adolescent and His World.* New York: Family Service Assoc. America.

KATAN, A. (1951). The role of "displacement" in agoraphobia. *Int. J. Psychoanal., 32:*41–50.

KLEIN, E. (1949). Psychoanalytic aspects of school problems. *Psychoan. Study Child, 3/4:*369–390.

LOONEY, J. D., AND GUNDERSON, E. K. E. (1978). Transient situational disturbances: Course and outcome. *Am. J. Psychiatry, 135:*660–663.

LOONEY, J. D., AND LEWIS, J. M. (1983). Competent adolescents from different socioeconomic and ethnic contexts. *Adolesc. Psychiatry, 11:*64–74.

MAHLER, M. S. (1952). On child psychosis and schizophrenia. *Psychoan. Study Child, 7:*286–305.

MASTERSON, J. F. (1967). *The Psychiatric Dilemma of Adolescence.* Boston: Little, Brown.

MASTERSON, J. F. (1970). Depression in the adolescent character disorder. *Proc. Ann. Meeting Amer. Psychopath. Assoc., 59:*242–257.

MASTERSON, J. F., & WASHBURNE, A. (1966). The symptomatic adolescent: Psychiatric illness or adolescent turmoil? *Am. J. Psychiatry, 122:*1240–1248.

NEWMAN, C. J., DEMBER, C. F., & KRUG, O. (1973). "He can but he won't": A psychodynamic study of so-called "gifted underachievers." *Psychoan. Study Child, 28:*83–129.

OFFER, D. (1969). *The Psychological World of the Teen-Ager: A Study of Normal Adolescent Boys.* New York: Basic Books.

OLDHAM, D. G. (1978). Adolescent turmoil: A myth revisited. *J. Cont. Ed. Psychiatry, 39:*23–33.

SANDLER, A. D., HOOPER, S. R., & SCARBOROUGH, A. A. (1993). Academic confessions of high school students: An analysis of adolescents' developmental concerns. *Perceptual and Motor Skills, 77:*1052–1054.

SPIEGEL, L. (1961). Disorder and consolidation in adolescence. *J. Amer. Psychoanal. Assoc., 9:*406–416.

SUGAR, M. (1987). Diagnostic aspects of underachievement in adolescents. *Adolescent Psychiatry, 14:*427–440.

TYSON, R. L. (1994). Neurotic negativism and negation in the psychoanalytic situation. Psychoanal. Study Child, 49:293–312.

TYSON, R. L., & TYSON, P. (1982). A case of "pseudo-narcissistic" psychopathology: A re-examination of the developmental role of the superego. *Int. J. Psychoanal., 63*:283–293.

TYSON, P., & TYSON, R. L. (1990). *Psychoanalytic Theories of Development: An Integration.* New Haven and London: Yale University Press.

WEINER, I. B., & DEL GAUDIO, A. C. (1976). Psychopathology in adolescence. *Arch. Gen. Psychiatry, 33*:187–193.

WILLIAMS, E., & RADIN, N. (1993). Paternal involvement, maternal employment, and adolescents' academic achievement: An 11-year follow-up. *Amer. J. Orthopsychiat. 63*:306–312.

APPLIED PSYCHOANALYSIS

Complicating the Theory

The Application of Psychoanalytic Concepts and Understanding to Family Preservation

JEAN ADNOPOZ, M.P.H.

Anna Freud's recognition of the complex interactions between endowment and maturation, innate structuralization and environmental influences, have had a profound influence on the development of policies and programs in the United States that attempt to improve the adverse conditions, strengthen the tenuous maternal ties, and reduce the potential for behavioral problems and intrapsychic distress in certain high-risk families. This paper describes and provides a case illustration of the application of Ms. Freud's psychoanalytic theories to the Yale Family Preservation and Support Programs. It reviews and comments on national policies regarding the risks and benefits of family preservation and child placement, identifies a paradigmatic shift in the provision of mental health care, and cautions against overconfidence in our ability to intervene effectively.

It has already been generally recognized . . . that the lack of essential foods, vitamins, etc., in early childhood will cause lasting bodily malformations in later years, even if harmful consequences are not immediately apparent. It is not generally recognized that the same is true for the mental development of the child. Whenever certain essential needs are not fulfilled,

Associate clinical professor at the Yale Child Study Center.

The Psychoanalytic Study of the Child 51, ed. Albert J. Solnit, Peter B. Neubauer, Samuel Abrams, and A. Scott Dowling (Yale University Press, copyright © 1996 by Albert J. Solnit, Peter B. Neubauer, Samuel Abrams, and A. Scott Dowling).

lasting psychological malformations will be the consequence. These essential elements are: the need for
personal attachment, for emotional stability, and for
permanency of educational influence

(FREUD, 1944).

SINCE 1985 THE YALE CHILD STUDY CENTER HAS BEEN ACTIVELY ENGAGED
in developing home- and community-based interventions. These programs, which exist at the boundary between child mental health care
and child welfare, are informed by the psychoanalytic concepts and
theories that Anna Freud postulated, taught, and practiced. Described
generically as family-preservation programs, these services have as
their proximal goal the provision of in-home services to families in
which children are vulnerable to out-of-home placement, in order to
prevent the trauma of separation and loss and to increase the level of
safety and appropriate care giving. Their more distal goal is to prevent
long-lasting individual disturbances in behavioral, psychological, or
cognitive functioning and symptom formation that may result from
disruption of the mother-infant bond, the influence of a noxious environment, and/or the anxious attachments engendered by the instability of multiple placements.

Anna Freud's recognition of the complex interaction between endowment and maturation, innate structuralization, and "accidental environmental influences" (1965), has had a profound influence on the
development of a generation of policies and programs in the United
States that attempt to improve the adverse conditions and strengthen
the tenuous or distressed maternal ties often found in high-risk families. The children and families whose needs are targeted by these programs and policies are those on whom the environment exerts a powerful, potentially disorganizing influence. These are the children who
are reported as abused, neglected, abandoned, or at risk of maltreatment; they live in urban families affected by parental mental illness,
serious drug addiction, homelessness, and chronic illness, such as HIV
infection and AIDS. Such families are likely to be poor, underedu-
cated, unemployed, and black or Hispanic. Stable, loving marital relationships are less in evidence among the adults than are violent and
disrespectful short-term domestic alliances.

Anna Freud (1965) postulated that the behavior and pathology of
children are determined by the interaction between their psychic structures and their intrafamilial environments. For some children, there
are mediating internal factors that are protective and health-promot-

ing; for others, internal and external pathogens combine to create disturbances that require individual therapeutic intervention. Although altering the environment is not in itself an antidote for pathology, working to bring about changes in the family setting may help to create a more stable external environment for the child, thereby enabling him to attend to his individual treatment issues. The child whose basic needs are not met, who experiences multiple separations from his mother, who worries about her safety when he is not present, who is responsible for his own care and that of his siblings, and who must prepare himself for school is not likely to be able to make good use of treatment. Family preservation and support initiatives are vehicles that prepare both children and parents for entry into treatment by working to reduce the levels of dysfunction, uncertainty, and pathology in the familial environment, thus creating sufficient stability for treatment to take place.

The majority of families referred for family preservation and support service present with problems in multiple areas of functioning, both within the family and at the points of intersection between the family, the community environment, and the systems that serve them. The Yale experience with these families is consistent with the research on children at high risk for poor developmental, psychological, and educational outcomes. Bowlby (1953) and Caplan (1978) have found no evidence that a single pathogenic agent is responsible for the development of dysfunctional families. Rather, as Anna Freud (1965) suggests, it is the complex interrelationship among such factors as disease, poverty, social isolation, lack of education, exposure to violence, developmental susceptibility, constitutional inadequacy, and poor social and community support that contributes to the development of pathology and symptom formation. Rutter and Quinton (1984) have found that such conditions as parental psychiatric history, substance abuse, and chronic illness can be predictive of poor developmental outcomes for children, and when these conditions are joined with such environmental stressors as poverty, homelessness, and discrimination, the risk of family disintegration, dysfunction, and despair increases significantly.

Recognizing that there are no distinct pathways to differentiated poor outcomes for children, the Yale program has chosen to address universal developmental needs in the interest of promoting parental adaptation and coping skills in order to mitigate conflict, dysfunction, and disability across both functional and intrapsychic domains. The relation between regulation of aggression and failures of attachment reveals itself in diverse behavioral forms that are determined, at least in part, by what the individual child brings to his or her experience.

Diverse problematic behaviors such as delinquency, early pregnancy, school dropout, gang membership, and substance abuse may result from similar early experiences of parenting failures that intensify with chronicity and repetition. We can speculate but do not know with any degree of precision what combination of internal and external factors predispose or lead to these varied expressions of disturbed development. However, we believe that the inability to meet the child's basic psychological need for affectionate care, continuity of the primary caregiving relationship, safety, protection, and a sense of being uniquely valued sets in motion the potential for lifelong difficulties.

For some children the negative effects of multiple environmental and intrafamilial stressors are mediated by internal and environmental factors that lead to resilience. Garmezy (1993) has identified family cohesion, individual temperament, relatedness, and external support as protective factors enabling children to overcome stressful experiences and environments. In some cases, such as those cited by Anna Freud (1965), in which the internal disharmony is moderate, perhaps resulting from eroticized tendencies, inclinations, and predilections stimulated through emotional links between the child and his first object, the result may be some variation of normality. Thus, mediators of poor outcome can be said to exist at three distinct yet overlapping levels: the individual child, the family, and the extrafamilial system, each of which may engender and reinforce competence and improved functioning.

The Policies and Politics of Family Preservation

At this moment in history, we are witnessing a bifurcation of attitudes and approaches to child welfare policy. Economic, scientific, environmental, and political factors are affecting national policies regarding vulnerable children and families and reshaping both interventive and preventive mental health practice strategies for children and families. For some policy makers and child advocates, family preservation and family support interventions are believed to be effective. Indeed, they are being implemented with expectations that may stretch beyond our knowledge and understanding and that have not yet been rigorously tested. For others, punitive approaches that increase the likelihood for coercive intervention by the state and threaten the termination of parental rights for behaviors—such as parental substance use during pregnancy—are seen as appropriate strategies for protecting children.

Beginning with the Adoption Assistance and Child Welfare Act of 1980, when, for the first time in child welfare history, Congress required that states make reasonable efforts to prevent the removal of children from their parents into foster placement or institutional care, there has been considerable interest in applying developmental theories and clinical knowledge to public policies and federally supported programs for children in troubled, disintegrating families. In August, 1993, this interest culminated in federal legislation that effected changes in Title IV-B of the Social Security Act, which embraced the concepts of family preservation and family support and financially rewarding states for developing systems of care that promote family integrity and prevent children from entering the foster-care system without exhausting other alternatives to placement. Inherent in the new legislative policy were the assumptions that by identifying parental competencies, building on family strengths, and providing services that addressed child and family needs across functional domains, states could help families to function well enough to prevent disruption and reduce dysfunction.

The federal goals for family support and family preservation services are: (1) to enhance the ability of parents to create stable and nurturing home environments that promote healthy child development; (2) to assist families to resolve crises, access necessary and appropriate services, and remain safely in their homes; and (3) to avoid unnecessary out-of-home placement, assist in family reunification of children already out of home, and support alternative permanent living arrangements. Federal guidelines encourage Family Preservation and Support Programs to engage in community-based preventive activities to reduce stress, promote parental competencies to increase the family's ability to nurture, enable families to use available resources as needed, and create supportive networks to decrease social isolation and vulnerability. Family Preservation Services are designed to alleviate crises leading to out-of-home placement, maintain children safely in their own homes, support reunification and adoption efforts, and assist families in obtaining services as needed.

What is not made explicit in the language describing family support and family preservation services, but is implied in the references to safety, is the centrality of a clinical assessment to the decisions about whether or not it is reasonably safe for a child at risk to remain at home even when comprehensive services are being provided to the family. For those children whose physical integrity is threatened within their own families, attempts to maintain the child within the family may be far more damaging than removal to a permanent, safer environment. Whenever the circumstances of a child's life require that a decision be made whether to preserve the family for the child's sake or seek placement, there is a risk to the child's intrapsychic organization. At these important times, the child's best interest demands thoughtfulness, understanding, and a willingness to confront the limitations of our knowledge and the reality of our choices. All too often children need to be protected not from their families but from those who mistakenly believe that they are protecting them. The failure of the lay public to understand that risk is present in any decision to maintain a child in a home in which placement is under consideration has led to newspaper headlines decrying family preservation programs and spurred a national debate on their efficacy (Murphy, 1993). During 1995, well-publicized deaths of young children who were kept at home in unsafe families known to the State Child Protection Agency have led to increases in the numbers of children removed from their homes and to crowded, troubling conditions in existing foster homes, reversing the policy of prior national and state administrations. Those who reacted swiftly to curtail the use of family preservation programs failed to recognize both the importance of informed risk taking and our inability to make accurate predictions about human behavior.

PROGRAM AND CASE ILLUSTRATION

The Yale family preservation and support programs target all three domains identified by Garmezy. They offer services that are available twenty-four hours a day, seven days a week, for approximately sixteen weeks. The interventions rely on the development of a working alliance between the parent and a clinically informed team, consisting of a social worker or psychologist and a family support worker, to support and encourage changes in the child's and family's external world. The clinician is responsible for developing a psychodynamic formulation, providing individual or family psychotherapy, or making appropriate referrals for treatment for both child and adult family members. The family support worker addresses concrete issues such as entitlements, access to care, parenting skills, and interactions with other systems and bureaucracies. The child's primary needs for continuity, stability, and safety are the touchstones on which all treatment planning is based.

It is expected that changes in the behaviors of the caregiving adult will occur in the context of the working alliance. From this relationship the parent may derive satisfaction, acceptance, and validation of her self and her parental strengths. In addition, the intervention provides an opportunity to model more positive parent-child interactions. For some parents with histories of familial dysfunction, positive interactions with and acceptance by a supportive, caring adult may be occurring for the first time. For that reason the meaning of the relationship in reality and in the relation to past unrequited longings for affection, guidance, approval, and safe limits must be continually examined. The Yale family preservation program assesses and makes use of the strength of the maternal tie and the wish to succeed in the parental role as primary motivating factors that enable mothers, even those who are seriously drug-involved, to gradually accept responsibility for themselves and their children and respond more appropriately to their needs.

SONNY

Sonny is an eight-year-old Caucasian boy living with his mother and her current boyfriend. He has a long history of self-destructive and disruptive behaviors including suicidal ideation, fire setting, and exposing himself. He was hospitalized on a pediatric psychiatric service following an attempt to set his bed on fire while sitting on it and diagnosed with Attention Deficit Hyperactivity Disorder (ADHD) and posttraumatic stress disorder, resulting from previous sexual abuse. For the first two years of his life, Sonny was cared for primarily by his maternal grandmother.

Sonny's mother, Sara, is a 30-year-old hearing-impaired clerical worker; her live-in boyfriend, Nick, is ten years her senior and is self-employed as a carpenter. Although Sara maintains her home and her job, she has little time or patience for her son, whose "lack of progress" angers and frustrates her. During Sonny's hospitalization, his mother failed to attend scheduled family meetings and was viewed as unsupportive of his treatment. Sara's family history includes parental divorce when she was sixteen, maternal sexual promiscuity, sibling drug abuse and criminal behaviors, psychiatric illness, poor social relatedness, and the death of her mother, Sonny's earliest caretaker, from cancer. Sara's husband, Sonny's father, was an alcoholic who physically abused his wife and may have sexually abused his son; both he and a maternal uncle are suspected perpetrators.

At the time of referral for family preservation services, Sonny was in outpatient psychotherapy with the psychiatrist who had been his primary therapist on the inpatient service. He attended a special school and was seen by the social worker there as well. Sara and Nick were ambivalent about Sonny's return home following hospitalization and went off on vacation shortly after his discharge, leaving him with an unfamiliar caregiver. A few days later they telephoned him to say that they might not return. The intervention team, although committed to serving the family, considered the possibility of therapeutic foster care rather than family preservation services for Sonny if his mother remained unwilling to return home.

The goals of the intervention were to seek a reduction in Sonny's self-destructive and disruptive behaviors by creating working alliances with Sara, Nick, and Sonny through which attempts could be made to improve communication among the family members, control their aggression, and allay Sonny's fears of rejection and abandonment. Sonny was expected to remain in individual treatment and to continue to see his school social worker. The intervention team would also work with the adults to help them understand how they could help to manage Sonny's illness and develop more appropriate expectations for him.

During the sixteen weeks of in-home intervention Sonny's symptoms decreased and his use of psychotherapy improved as his mother and her boyfriend became able to support his recovery. The team was able to establish a relationship with Sara and Nick that offered them validation as parents and allowed expression and acceptance of their conflictual feelings and wishes about her son. The family support worker helped Sara to move away from casting him as a hopeless, bad boy and move toward a more nurturing position; the clinician helped Nick to understand Sonny's dependence on him and his fear of losing another father figure.

Preparation for termination of treatment involved not only Sonny's therapist and the school social worker but also the state child welfare worker, with each system agreeing to work collaboratively to ensure that the resources the family required would be in place. By joining with the family, accepting them, and helping them to understand each other's needs, limitations, and anxieties, the family preservation team was able to help them create a safer and more stable environment in which treatment could take place more effectively.

DISCUSSION

Goldstein, Freud, and Solnit (1979) make clear our responsibility to take clinically informed risks, some of which, because of the limitations of our knowledge and our human capacity for error, may lead to unintended consequences. These risks are essential because separating children from parents introduces discontinuity into the developmentally significant relationship between them and interrupts the child's ability to access a caregiver who is familiar to him and represents a tie to the child's extended family, his family history, and his culture. Once a child has been removed from home, the probability of experiencing more than one placement increases exponentially. Children who experience multiple foster placements may be compromised in their ability to form intimate, reciprocal relationships with others throughout the life cycle. And although there are excellent foster caregivers, the foster care system in general suffers from overutilization, lack of adequate support for caregivers, and little preparation and training to enable foster parents to help children cope with the sequelae of the significant problems with which they enter the system.

For many children such as Sonny, whose families receive family preservation services, decision making is based not on selecting an optimal choice but rather on selecting the least detrimental alternative. Although placement prevention is seen as a desirable outcome, these programs recognize that if the child's safety and well-being are severely compromised, good practice demands removal to another, expectably permanent placement.

Decisions that determine where a child will live and who will care for him are likely to have lifelong consequences. Assuming such an awesome responsibility requires a level of clinical knowledge and clinical competence not easy to communicate in legislative language. If we are to build the national consensus necessary to change the paradigm from one of removing children from their parents to one of support for families in order to prevent placement, serious efforts must be made to destigmatize and empower parents and to involve significantly those who have felt most disenfranchised by the traditional medicalized model of mental health services and who also exert considerable influence on the child's development—classroom teachers, special educators, police and probation officers, and counselors. A broader appreciation of the roles played by these professionals in shaping the child's view of himself, particularly in relation to the child's sense of opportunity, dreams, and possibilities, could add to our ability to meet the needs of vulnerable children.

An effective paradigm shift requires the involvement of well-trained clinicians in new partnerships with protective services, child welfare, drug treatment, adult mental health, day care, and school and law-enforcement systems. Collaborations that lead to shared understanding of children and their vicissitudes can extend and enhance the ability of individual systems to intervene meaningfully, offer important opportunities to share risk, and provide support to those whose professional roles make them responsible for children's safety. Collaborations that bring mental health practitioners out of the examining room and into the community may truly be in the best interests of children and their parents. However, unless the interventions of these well-intentioned community providers are clinically informed and clear in their treatment strategies, we cannot expect children and their families to be well served. In the zeal to empower parents and others, the needs of children may be subjugated. In addition, the focus on families rather than on children may obfuscate the ability to intervene appropriately when the child's interest diverges from that of the parent. To be effective, mental health clinicians and community-based caregivers, institutions, and agencies will need to renegotiate their relationships and gain increased respect for each other's professional roles (Goldstein, 1986).

Family preservation and family support services should not be overburdened by expectations of success that can only end in further frustration and disillusionment for children, parents, and system reformers. These services are useful, but they cannot ameliorate all of the environmental ills that currently plague children and families. For some children, damage may be so pervasive that, even with long-term treatment, rehabilitation and recovery may not be achievable. A rational system will add family preservation and support services to a continuum that includes more traditional services and treatment modalities as well as linkages to other community services.

As we at Yale enter into the next generation of our work, we must continue to be mindful of the insufficiency of our knowledge and our limited understanding of how family members perceive our entry into their lives. Although we may believe that we are protecting children, we may be acting in ways that continue to victimize them. Certainly we have more careful work to do to understand both the value and the potentially destructive power of our prevention and intervention strategies.

Although Anna Freud's theories of child development were characterized by Hartmann as "simplifications" (Solnit, in press), she recognized that they would become complicated in the process of application. In so stating, she was prophetic. In developing the metapsychological profile (1965) she provided a schema that yields a rich and well-integrated assessment of the data derived from consideration of the external and internal worlds of an individual child. The profile offers a means of organizing, reflecting on, and eventually responding to the child's needs. Importantly, it provides a psychoanalytically informed way of thinking. Making decisions about preserving and supporting families for children also requires consideration and integration of complex and sometimes conflicting information about the child's functioning, fantasies, and wishes and those of his family. The developmental theories and scientific achievements of Anna Freud provide a map that brings the complexities in the lives of troubled children and their families into high relief, thereby enabling us to better understand them and to intervene more effectively.

BIBLIOGRAPHY

Bowlby, J. (1953). Special problems: Problem families, neglectful parents, broken homes, illegitimacy. In *The Family: Report of the British National Conference on Social Work*. London, National Council of Social Service.

Caplan, G. (1978). Family support systems in a changing world. In *The Child in His Family: Children and Their Parents in a Changing World*. New York: John Wiley and Sons.

Freud, A. (1930). Introduction to psychoanalysis. In *Four Lectures on Psychoanalysis for Teachers and Parents*, pp. 73–90. New York: Int. Univ. Press.

——— (1965). *Normality and Pathology in Childhood: Assessments of Development*. New York: Int. Univ. Press.

Freud, A., & Burlingham, D. (1944). *War and Children*. New York: International Universities Press.

Garmezy, N. (1993). Children in poverty: Resilience despite risk. *Psychiatry*. 56:127–36.

Goldstein, J., Freud A., & Solnit, A. (1973). *Beyond the Best Interests of The Child*. New York: Free Press.

——— (1979). *Before the Best Interests of the Child*. New York: Free Press.

——— (1986). *In the Best Interests of the Child*. New York: Free Press.

Murphy, P. (1993, June 19). Family Preservation and Its Victims. *The New York Times*, p. 21.

Rutter, M., & Quinton, D. (1984). Parental psychiatric disorder: Effects on children. *Psychological Medicine*. 14:853–80.

Solnit, A. (in press). Review and Commentary. Anna Freud: A Biography. *J. Amer. Psychoanal. Assn.*

The Bereavement Process in
Children of Parents with AIDS

SETH ARONSON, PSY.D.

AIDS has left tens of thousands of children with dead or dying parents. This epidemic is forcing us to take a new look at loss in childhood, paying attention to the impact of the social and cultural forces in these children's surroundings on their internal/psychological worlds. This chapter is a preliminary attempt to examine these factors, integrating psychoanalytic concepts, the sociocultural context, and treatment issues. Clinical vignettes are used to illustrate throughout.

IN TODAY'S WORLD WE ARE CONFRONTED WITH EVER-NEW CHALLENGES TO age-old dilemmas, particularly in the application of psychoanalytic ideas to contemporary sociocultural issues. One such current problem is AIDS and its impact on children and families. The work that I describe in this paper represents a preliminary attempt to apply psychoanalytic tenets to the tragic life circumstances of children whose parents have died or are dying of AIDS.

In an address to a conference sponsored by the Yale Child Study Center, Anna Freud (1971a) described her work at the Hampstead Clinic, which provided her an "opportunity to maintain a close connection between theory and practice" and allowed her "to check constantly on theoretical ideas by practical application" to the problems of the day

Assistant director, Child/Adolescent Psychiatry, Jacobi Medical Center/Albert Einstein College of Medicine, Bronx, New York; Faculty, Yeshiva University, Long Island University, Bank Street College of Education; candidate, William Alanson White Institute.

The author wishes to acknowledge the helpful comments of Salvatore Lomonaco, M.D., on an earlier draft.

The Psychoanalytic Study of the Child 51, ed. Albert J. Solnit, Peter B. Neubauer, Samuel Abrams, and A. Scott Dowling (Yale University Press, copyright © 1996 by Albert J. Solnit, Peter B. Neubauer, Samuel Abrams, and A. Scott Dowling).

(p. 227). She insisted on always beginning "with the developmental needs of children" and advocated that "plans for children should be based on detailed knowledge about their needs and the possibility of meeting those needs" (p. 228). Her ideal psychoanalytic institute would teach candidates to observe the world outside the training center. Eventually, the knowledge gained through such observation would permit the application of psychoanalysis to the cultural, social, political, and legal arenas (A. Freud, 1971b). In her renowned Hampstead nursery for British children during World War II as well as in the famous Bulldogs Bank group home for children whose parents were killed in the Holocaust (A. Freud, 1951) she brought psychoanalytic principles to bear on the problems of the day. In each case, developmental principles and ideas about children's reactions to loss were applied to extraordinary circumstances.

Children of AIDS sufferers are placed in tragic, difficult situations for which they are often unprepared. Those who lose a parent to AIDS lack many of the necessary elements for grief work. This paper is an initial effort to understand the impact of AIDS on the bereavement process. I examine the social and cultural factors particular to AIDS through the lens of psychoanalysis, in the hope of conceptualizing treatment planning for these children based on, in Anna Freud's words, "detailed knowledge about their needs."

THE BEREAVEMENT PROCESS IN CHILDREN

Many theorists have described the bereavement process in children.[1] Caring, supportive figures are crucial for successful grief work in children who have lost a parent. Such figures provide a "holding environment" (Winnicott, 1960) and allow for the expression of feelings so necessary for working through the tragic psychological event.

Wolfenstein's study was based on clinical work similar to the work described here. The children and adolescents she examined were patients in a child/adolescent outpatient service of the same large municipal teaching hospital under whose auspices the children described here were seen. Wolfenstein's seminal work focused on the developmental preconditions for mourning, such as the ability to transfer positive feelings to the remaining adult figures in the child's life. She also noted the importance of a supportive home setting for the provision of basic needs. The new home environment, following parental bereavement, should ideally provide the child with the reassurance that he or she will

1. E.g., Pollock, 1962; Altschul, 1988; Furman, 1974; Bowlby, 1980; and notably Wolfenstein, 1966, 1969.

be cared for. At a time when children feel bereft and abandoned, it is imperative that they know that simple needs will be gratified. The new setting should also account for specific needs based on the child's level of development. As Pollock (1978), Buchsbaum (1987), and Dietrich (1989) point out, these needs may change in relation to the child's developmental stage. Thus, a young child may use parental surrogates for help with the "development of reality testing, behavioral control and tolerance and expression of affect while an adolescent may utilize the parent substitute as a harbor to venture from and measure him/herself against" (Furman, 1974, p. 112).

Ideally, the new setting should facilitate the transference of positive feelings to the new caretaker. Within the secure confines of this relationship, the child may develop constructive identifications with the lost parent that help with progressive development while at the same time successfully differentiating self from other. The safe, containing aspects of the new relationship may also allow the child to work through the heightened sense of ambivalence that often accompanies a loss to a level that is tolerable. Ultimately, it is necessary to develop a stable internal representation of the lost object so that the child may let go. As Loewald (1962) writes, "Mourning involves not only the gradual, piecemeal relinquishment of the lost object, but also the internalization, the appropriation of aspects of this object" (p. 493).

The child's ability to form attachments is also important. Many children of parents with AIDS experience significant gaps in their care as they are shifted to various relatives during parental hospitalizations. In extreme cases of permanency planning, these children may be sent to live with relatives they have never met. The children's later development is significantly affected by the confluence of these disruptions in attachment with their parents' own early attachment experiences and the possible repetition of neglect and abuse (Main, 1993; Fonagy, 1993). How the child and parent cope with such breaks in their connectedness can be critical to a more adaptive grief process.

CASE MATERIAL: THE CHILDREN

All the children described here were seen as outpatients, either in the clinic of a municipal teaching hospital or in their respective schools. Families were involved whenever possible. In effect, the child benefited from multiple treatment modalities—that is, individual treatment, support groups, and parent/family guidance.

JOSÉ

An obese, handsome five-year-old, José was brought to the clinic by his foster mother because of his aggressive, self-destructive outbursts. The most severe of these culminated in José's puncturing his arm with pins. José's mother had been imprisoned for selling drugs, and the boy's care had been entrusted to his father and paternal grandmother. He was routinely beaten for infractions of the house rules, and his daily needs, such as food and clothing, were not always fulfilled. His father, who reportedly was himself obese and unkempt, contracted AIDS through intravenous (IV) drug use. When word got out that his father was ill with AIDS, José was teased by his peers and quietly ostracized by the staff. His school was unprepared to handle the situation. Fortunately, placement with his foster family meant a move to another neighborhood, away from José's abusive, dying father and unsupportive school situation. At the time he came to the clinic's attention, his father had been dead for several months.

It became apparent that José's dramatic symptom of puncturing his arm was multidetermined and served to encapsulate his rage at and identification with his IV-drug-abusing father. José's profound feelings of abandonment and victimization seemed to result in his defensive identification with the powerful, deserting (through illness and death) parent—the aggressor. José's obesity also appeared to be in part a way of maintaining a tie to his dead father, perhaps due to a primitive identification, a result of fusion of self and object images.

José viewed himself as damaged and tainted, and he voiced concern that he would or could contract his father's illness. Treatment allowed him to begin to consolidate a clearer, differentiated sense of who he was vis-à-vis his father. His foster parents, who were genuinely concerned for the boy's well being, helped to provide a more stable, consistent, and nurturing home environment. This, in turn, led to a decrease in José's aggressive outbursts. A warm, supportive new teacher worked in unison with his therapist to provide safe outlets for José's anger while concurrently containing him.

CAITLIN AND MARY

Caitlin, age 12, and Mary, 8, were brought to treatment by their maternal grandmother, who had become their guardian following their mother's death from AIDS. Before the mother died, the girls had experienced neglect by their mother and abuse by her boyfriends. Their brother, 2, had also died of AIDS. Caitlin and Mary had begun to lie and steal. The grandmother was threatening to place them in foster care as a result, in part also because of her own unresolved anger at the girls' mother.

Sessions with the grandmother centered on helping her to see the symbolic function of the girls' behavior (Bonnard, 1961) and how this related to their sense of loss and deprivation.

Identification with the lost object is an important aspect of mourning (Freud, 1917). Caitlin's identification with her mother took on a stark, dramatic form. She immediately became entranced with her therapist's long hair, often comparing it with her own closely cropped hairstyle. Over time, she revealed that her mother had had long hair, which she had spent many hours brushing and braiding. This initial identification of her therapist with her dead mother was based more on action and on concrete, easily perceived details than on personality traits and characteristics. Gradually the therapist helped this 12-year-old to put her feelings into more developmentally appropriate words instead of keeping her memories and identification at the sensorimotor, concrete level typical of a much younger child (Buchsbaum, 1987).

Both sisters struggled with issues of identification with their dead mother. This was fostered by the grandmother's frequent complaint that they were behaving "just like their mother." Their presenting problems—lying, stealing, and truancy—were all behaviors in which their mother had engaged. During the course of treatment, the girls decided, on their own, to make two lists entitled "Ways to remember our mother" and "Ways *not* to remember our mother." Ways to remember mother included talking, crying, looking at pictures, and eliciting stories from their grandmother about the mother. Ways not to remember her included stealing, lying, cursing, playing hooky, not listening to adults, using drugs—all behaviors that they had heard attributed to their mother. Over time, the girls came to realize their pathological identification with their dead mother and began to develop identifications that were more positive, often based on stories told by their grandmother. (Incidentally, it took much work to help the grandmother understand the importance of relating stories that cast the mother in a positive light, despite her long and conflictual history with the girls' mother.)

The girls also struggled to acquire a clear, cohesive picture of their mother. They had difficulty reconciling polar views of this parent, who had once been kind and nurturing but at times also abusive and neglectful. Memories of happier times, such as birthday parties, picnics, and outings, vied with memories of their mother's neglect, drug use, and inability to protect them from her abusive partners. Complicating the girls' struggle was their insistence that they could not be angry with their mother (which represented a breach of a cultural value), especially because she was now dead and deserved their sympathy. This conflict remains a focus of their treatment to this day.

PAUL

Paul, a slightly built, freckled 10-year-old, was referred for treatment by his school guidance counselor because of his increasingly withdrawn and depressive behavior. Both of Paul's Irish Catholic parents had been diagnosed with AIDS. His father (despite continued IV drug use and alcoholism) was healthier and more robust than his mother. Although the parents were divorced, they continued to live together so that they could care for each other and Paul, their only child. Paul's father was physically and verbally abusive toward him, and his substance abuse made him an unreliable caretaker. The mother was hospitalized frequently; during these times, Paul either cared for himself or was precipitously sent off to his maternal grandparents, who lived in another city several hours away.

Paul was extremely engaging and often used his charm to avoid conversation about his parents' illness. However, he was a talented, sensitive writer and agreed to bring in some of his poems for discussion. In one poem, entitled "Home," he described his father's physical abuse of him and how his mother, weak from AIDS, slept around the clock while Paul quietly prepared his own dinner, played outside, and tucked himself into bed at night, all the while trying not to incur his father's wrath. Paul's writings led to our discussions of his facing the drawn-out experience of having a mother who was alternately present and absent, owing to hospitalization and illness. His mother's physical presence in the household was ultimately disappointing because of her unavailability. Even when she was in the next room, his mother was helpless to care for him adequately and to protect him from his father. This saddened Paul greatly and left him at the mercy of his explosive, unpredictable (and unwell) father.

Being shuttled between home and various relatives was unsettling to Paul. He was caught between his life with his dying parents and his attempts to establish a stronger attachment to his maternal grandparents, who were to be his caretakers and guardians following his mother's death. This state of being in limbo left Paul confused and feeling sapped of energy.

As the mother became sicker and increasingly unable to care for herself and Paul, it became apparent that she and Paul would need to move to the maternal grandparents' home. Paul was upset by the significant changes that would occur—a move away from his school, neighborhood, friends, and city, with subsequent loss of social support. Treatment focused on Paul's acclimating himself toward the move, acknowledging his sadness, and planning for the future. Following the move, Paul, his mother, and his grandparents kept in touch with me by phone until they were able to see a therapist closer to their new home.

MELISSA

Melissa, aged 12, was referred for treatment because of excessive fighting both at school and with siblings at home. Melissa, a pretty olive-skinned girl of Hispanic descent, was the second of five siblings. Her mother had died of AIDS five months prior to referral, after a long and debilitating course of the illness. She was blind, frail, and intermittently demented toward the end of her life. Consequently, Melissa and her siblings had gone to live with a maternal aunt, who herself had several children, many with children of their own—all of whom lived together in a tiny apartment.

In the early part of the treatment, Melissa had many questions about AIDS. She asked, for example, "If AIDS is spread through sex, if a person with AIDS has sex with a person with cancer, can they give each other the illness each has?" Even though Melissa had already attended AIDS-education training at her public middle school, she clearly was attempting to cognitively master a confusing, bewildering situation, an initial step in her bereavement (Elizur and Kaffman, 1982).

Melissa also shyly, tentatively, confided that every day after school she had been purposely walking past the cemetery in which her mother was buried. She stated she knew this was "weird" and "creepy," but she felt helpless against the impulse to do so. Discussion focused on her curiosity about her mother's death. (It was forbidden to discuss it at her aunt's house.) Together, we explored the ritual of her after-school walk as an attempt to master her sadness, anxiety, and deep feelings without concomitant shame. Melissa began to feel enormously relieved about exploring these feelings openly, away from home, where she could not bring up her mother's illness and death.

Melissa gradually began to discuss her fighting in school. She displayed disproportionate rage in various peer interactions and was particularly sensitive to the epithet "your mother." She had few ways to relieve and displace her angry feelings. However, in treatment, Melissa began to express anger and discontent at politicians who made and failed to keep campaign pledges to earmark more money for AIDS research. She often railed against the insensitivity of the doctors and nurses who had cared for her mother. Issues of her inability to ameliorate her mother's condition came to the fore, as well as the link between these feelings and her rage. Melissa also described tearfully but helplessly pleading with her mother not to shoot up. She began to weep openly over the loss of her mother and the profound changes that had occurred in her life as a result. She brought in pictures of her mother's high school graduation to help in her efforts to maintain a positive, intact, and physically healthy image of her dead mother.

Toward the end of treatment, Melissa's fighting had decreased considerably. She noted that she missed being able to share her behavioral and academic improvements with her mother. We began to discuss what it would be like at the time of her prom and graduation, events that she would be unable to share with her mother. With help, Melissa acknowledged that through each stage of her life—graduation, marriage, and childbearing—she would be thinking of her mother and would need to reevaluate the loss in light of both her own development and her mother's wishes and aspirations for her.

Discussion

Mary Lennox, the heroine of Frances Hodgson Burnett's classic novel *The Secret Garden,* is sour, contrary, and disagreeable at the story's opening. She has recently lost both parents and her beloved nursemaid to cholera and has been obliged to leave her home in India. But with her introduction into a supportive new home setting in England, where her every need is met, and with the help of loving caretakers, she emerges from her state of grief, recuperates from her tragic losses, and resumes a normal course of development. In contrast, children of parents with AIDS lack many of the necessary elements for an adaptive bereavement process.

The AIDS epidemic, as I have noted, has left tens of thousands of children with dead or dying parents. Wolfenstein (1966) and Furman (1974), among others, discuss the need for stability and support following a loss. This support provides the child with the necessary maintenance of narcissistic gratification for further development. This, in essence, is what Anna Freud provided for the children in the Hampstead War Nurseries (A. Freud and Burlingham, 1943). According to Wolfenstein (1969), the caretaker should ideally be a substitute object already known to the child, to whom the child may transfer attachment. Furman (1974) cautions against a hiatus in attachment as the child relies on the love object for maintenance of sense of self. A breach of support for a child may lead to pathological identifications as the bereaved child clings, in the interim, to an internal tie to a dead parent rather than transfers some attachment to either the surviving parent or a new caretaker.

Sadly, many of these children experience significant lapses in support as they are shuttled between relatives and foster care placements, with no time to establish attachments. These children (such as José) may be compelled to maintain a strong tie to the dead or dying parent for sheer psychic survival in the face of huge gaps in caretaking and possible ostracism by schoolmates, teachers, other family members, and societal agencies. Hiatuses in attachment make simple gratifications such as food, shelter, and clothing tenuous, leaving children in a developmental vacuum (Nagera, 1970).

Such a history has further implications for the child's quality of attachment. Fonagy (1993) has noted the significant impact of the capacity for reflection on mental states on attachment. The ability to self-reflect can be an important part of treatment, breaking what is all too often an intergenerational cycle while enabling the child to feel understood and ultimately to become more open to adaptive attachment patterns.

Furman (1974) has noted how critical it is that the surviving adults permit and tolerate the bereaved child's expression of grief. However, such expressions of feelings concerning the loss are not always permitted by the adults surrounding the child of an AIDS sufferer, especially if the dead parent was an IV drug user or a homosexual—issues that the family (and society at large) may not wish to have verbalized.

This, in turn, may contribute to denial on the part of the child. Wolfenstein (1966) describes the case of a girl who stated, "If my mother were really dead, I would be all alone" (pp. 102–103), to explain her initial denial of the loss of her mother. This terrifying notion of unbearable loneliness can be perpetuated by the surviving adults if they refuse to acknowledge and to discuss the loss that has occurred. Melissa's aunt would not condone any mention of her sister's name following her death from AIDS. Thus, for Melissa and her siblings there were no accepting adults to tolerate and empathize with their expression of pain, sadness, and longing.

The notion of identifying and being identified with a parent who has been ravaged by AIDS may be terrifying to a child who has just achieved a sense of body integrity. Jacobson (1965) discusses how the first primitive identifications occur as a result of a fusion of self and object images, at the expense of the realistic differences between the self and object. Thus, José, who identified with his AIDS-stricken father, saw himself as tainted, damaged, and shamed, and he wondered whether he would eventually contract the illness. This identification may be particularly problematic for children of José's age, who are struggling with oedipal or identification issues and with their need for superego consolidation.

The threatening linkage of child with ill parent may be further perpetuated by our cultural institutions, which often identify these bereaved children even as the children may wish to distance themselves from the illness and its ramifications of shame, secrecy, and stigma. David Kirp (1989) describes incidents in which students were expelled from school not simply because their parents had AIDS but because their mothers' *boyfriends* had contracted AIDS. This stigma by association hardly helps to further identification with positive aspects of the parent.

A history of abuse and neglect, such as many of these children experience, adds to the high-risk nature of these already traumatized children and may make the acquisition of a clear, cohesive picture of the lost parent difficult for a child struggling to integrate good and bad. Children who have been neglected or abused may feel compelled (or exhorted by relatives) to muster and display only sympathy toward a parent who was once abusive but is now weak and frail—or dead. Negotiating a reconciliation of polar views of a parent and establishing a more even-handed picture may thus be dependent not only on the child's level of achieved object relations but also on pressure to conform to cultural norms of display of affect in bereavement.

Wolfenstein (1966) describes the common finding of the child's idealization of the lost parent. The glorification in culture of the maternal imago and idealization by the surrounding family further contribute to this. However, in children of AIDS sufferers, this idealization is problematic. Memories of their mother's IV drug use competed in Caitlin's and Mary's minds with happier memories, making the normative response of idealization difficult. (It also may lead to an unconscious identification with drug use.) Additionally, children and adolescents do not always demonstrate their feelings in the same manner as adults. Family members may force children to cry and demonstrate grief at a time when the children may be feeling angry or are using another outlet for sadness. This can lead to the creation and perpetuation of a mythical parent-child relationship, affecting the children's trust and belief in their own experience.

In children of AIDS sufferers, ambivalence appears to be prominent. Anger at the parents for drug use, neglect, and abuse (either by the parents or by their partners), together with the shame and stigma of AIDS, makes ambivalence inevitable and rage a natural outcome and a predominant response in these youngsters. In fact, many of the children who present at our clinic for services are demonstrating difficulty controlling their anger at home and at school.

Shabad's (1989) concept of psychic loss is relevant to work with these children. Children whose parents have AIDS may face the protracted experience of having a very ill parent who is available and then suddenly gone, as a result of a precipitous illness or opportunistic infection requiring hospitalization. The child and surrounding family may attempt to begin the bereavement process as the parent is hospitalized for what they believe is the final time, only to find that the parent is released a few days later. Paul's mother was physically present in the household but at times unavailable to him owing to fatigue and weakness. The intermittent physical and/or psychological presence of the parent makes the experience of loss difficult for the child to comprehend and may make the child "more prone to hidden magical fantasies of restitution. . . . The idealized image of the psychically lost parent, formed during the parent's periodic physical absences, becomes increasingly difficult to maintain in the face of the very real reappearances of that same frustrating parental figure" (Shabad, 1989, pp. 108–109). The child may thus alternate between hope and disappointment for several years, making this an almost intolerable process for a youngster whose psychological resources are not yet fully developed.

In work with children of parents with AIDS, it is at times difficult to discover an adequate parental substitute. In much of the literature on grief, the situations described discuss collateral work with the remaining parent. However, for a child of an AIDS sufferer it is by no means certain there is still one caretaker alive. And, unfortunately, more often than not, the family is a single-parent one to begin with. Thus, there may not be a surviving parent or, if there is, that parent may also be stricken with AIDS. The extended-family network, then, is crucial for these children. For Paul, Melissa, Caitlin, and Mary, this network represented their future caretakers and homes. These collateral family members, when suitable, *must* be included in the treatment to facilitate the child's transition to a new household.

Family members such as Caitlin and Mary's grandmother are often angry at the dead parent for having contracted the illness or because of past behavior. For this reason, it is imperative to work with the new adult caretakers so that they do not enact their rage and grief in their relationship with the child (who may often be viewed as an extension of the parent with AIDS).

Many grandparents who find themselves having to raise young children may also be angry at the dead son or daughter for imposing this obligation on them in later life. Providing support around the difficulties of child rearing may alleviate some of their anger and anxiety over what may appear to be (in fact may be) a burden. Instruction in child development norms and how grief is manifested in children is important so that the new caretaker may be helped to understand the child's reaction to loss.

Treatment must also focus on helping the child form a positive identification with the parent. Such identification can be fostered by the child's incorporating traits and values of the parent or fulfilling the lost object's hopes and aspirations. For example, several children spoke of their deceased parents' wishes for them to finish their schooling and consequently vowed to do so. Completion of school represented both a fulfillment of the parent's wishes and dreams and an enactment of a value espoused by the lost parent.

The establishment of open communication is critical. The secrecy surrounding AIDS is difficult enough without these children's feeling that they must stifle questions or expression of affect. The therapist must also balance the child's current life situation with his or her psychological need. Thus, a child whose HIV-infected parent is doing well may not wish to discuss grief issues at that juncture in treatment. This may not be so much denial as an adaptive response (that is, attempting to enjoy what little time is left with the parent). The therapist must be careful not to impose issues and to allow the child to ask and speak freely, creating an atmosphere of trust and acceptance.

Such an atmosphere may help to diminish shame, which is a major dimension of these children's experience. Several of the children I work with describe slinking around the school corridors, trying not to draw attention to themselves. By instilling in them the belief that they are not alone, one can help these children find solace and some relief from shame.

Grief work with children of parents with AIDS is a difficult clinical challenge because there are often no immediate supportive settings, only grandparents and aunts and uncles who are themselves struggling (sometimes angrily) with the loss. Clinicians need to work harder to create healing, therapeutic environments so that these children can develop a sense of mastery and bolster their self-esteem. And unlike the ultimate reduction of the cholera epidemic in the British Empire at the time *The Secret Garden* was written, the AIDS epidemic—and its impact on children—is very much with us.

BIBLIOGRAPHY

ALTSCHUL, S. (Ed.) (1988). *Childhood Bereavement and Its Aftermath.* Madison, Conn.: International Universities Press.

BONNARD, A. (1961). Truancy and pilfering associated with bereavement. In *Adolescents,* S. Lorand and H. Schneer (Eds.). New York: Hoeber, pp. 152–179.

BOWLBY, J. (1980). *Attachment and Loss, Vol. 3: Loss.* New York: Basic Books.

BUCHSBAUM, B. (1987). Remembering a parent who has died: A developmental perspective. *The Annual of Psychoanalysis* 15:99–112.

DIETRICH, D. (1989). Early childhood parent death, psychic-trauma and organization and object relations. In *The Problem of Loss and Mourning: Psychoanalytic Perspectives,* D. Dietrich and P. Shabad (Eds.). Madison, Conn.: International Universities Press, pp. 277–335.

ELIZUR, E., & KAFFMAN, M. (1982). Children's reactions following death of the father: The first four years. *Journal of the American Academy of Child Psychiatry* 21:474–480.

FONAGY, P. (1993). Psychoanalytic and empirical approaches to developmental psychopathology: An object relations perspective. *Journal of the American Psychoanalytic Association* 41:245–260.

FREUD, A. (1951). An experiment in group upbringing. *Psychoanalytic Study of the Child* 6:127–168.

―――― (1971a). Residential vs. foster care. In *The Writings of Anna Freud, Vol. 7.* New York: International Universities Press, pp. 223–239.

―――― (1971b). The ideal psychoanalytic institute: A utopia. In *The Writings of Anna Freud, Vol. 7.* New York: International Universities Press, pp. 73–93.

FREUD, A., & BURLINGHAM, D. (1943). *War and Children.* New York: Medical War Books.

FREUD, S. (1917). Mourning and melancholia. In *S. E.* 14. London: Hogarth Press (1957).

FURMAN, E. (1974). *A Child's Parent Dies.* New Haven: Yale University Press.

JACOBSON, E. (1965). The return of the lost parent. In *Drives, Affects and Behavior, Vol. 2* M. Schur (Ed.). New York: International Universities Press, pp. 193–211.

KIRP, D. (1989). *Learning by Heart: AIDS and School Children in America's Communities.* New Brunswick, N.J.: Rutgers University Press.

LOEWALD, H. (1962). Internalization, separation, mourning and the superego. *Psychoanalytic Quarterly* 31:483–504.

MAIN, M. (1993). Discourse, prediction and recent studies in attachment: Implications for psychoanalysis. *Journal of the American Psychoanalytic Association* 41:209–244.

NAGERA, H. (1970). Children's reactions to the death of important objects: A developmental approach. *Psychoanalytic Study of the Child* 25:360–400.

POLLOCK, G. (1962). Childhood parent and sibling loss in adult patients: A comparative study. *Archives of General Psychiatry* 7:295–305.

—— (1978). Process and affect: Mourning and grief. *International Journal of Psychoanalysis* 59:255–276.

SHABAD, P. (1989). Vicissitudes of psychic loss of a physically present parent. In *The Problem of Loss and Mourning: Psychoanalytic Perspectives*. D. Dietrich and P. Shabad (Eds.). Madison, Conn.: International Universities Press, pp. 101–126.

WINNICOTT, D. W. (1960). The theory of the parent-child relationship. *International Journal of Psychoanalysis* 41:585–595.

WOLFENSTEIN, M. (1966). How is mourning possible? *Psychoanalytic Study of the Child* 21:93–123.

—— (1969). Loss, rage and repetition. *Psychoanalytic Study of the Child* 24:432–460.

Oedipal Themes in Latency

Analysis of the "Farmer's Daughter" Joke

ERIKA K. CLOWES

A sample of "farmer's daughter" jokes, gathered from archives, personal informants, and published collections, is examined in relation to the developmental progress of the latency-age boys who most often tell them. The joke texts are divided into three categories—oedipal triumph, castration, and feminization—each of which represents a different regressive fantasy. Through these fantasied scenarios, the joke teller can safely work through some of the anxieties he experiences as a result of the recent repression of the oedipal conflict. Common themes of latency fantasies such as separation from the family, confusion of gender identity, and incestuous desires are all present in the texts.

Repetition of the farmer's daughter joke not only motivates the child's individual psychological progress but also reinforces his or her awareness of taboos and socially appropriate behavior. Because the parental injunctions are internalized to help consolidate superego formation at the onset of latency and the child must now displace incestuous urges with manifestations of conscience, the retesting of values through joke telling is important during this developmental period.

IT IS WELL KNOWN THAT THE LATENCY STAGE OF CHILD DEVELOPMENT encourages the use of a newly formed capacity for symbolization. Feel-

Recent graduate of the University of California, department of English. Currently pursuing doctoral degree in English at the University of California, Berkeley.

I am grateful to Professor Alan Dundes and Dr. Teresa Doyle for their encouragement and comments on this article. Additional thanks goes to those informants who provided me with joke texts, and to contributors at the University of California at Berkeley Folklore Archives.

The Psychoanalytic Study of the Child 51, ed. Albert J. Solnit, Peter B. Neubauer, Samuel Abrams, and A. Scott Dowling (Yale University Press, copyright © 1996 by Albert J. Solnit, Peter B. Neubauer, Samuel Abrams, and A. Scott Dowling).

ings of guilt and discomfort, originating in the drives and exacerbated by the critical new superego, can now be discharged through fantasy (Freud, 1923b, 246; Furman, 1991; Sarnoff, 1971, 1987). Despite the significance of these representational fantasies, which occur in many realms of childhood activity, few studies have been undertaken to examine them outside the therapeutic context, and these few have focused primarily on the masturbation fantasy (with the notable exception of Goldings's 1974 account of the function of the jump-rope rhyme for latency girls). In this chapter I demonstrate the powerful presence of latency-appropriate themes in the "farmer's daughter" joke and discuss some of the psychological and social functions served by joke telling among children in the six-to-twelve-year age range.

Over the past two years I have culled texts from joke books, published collections of folklore, folklore archives, and tape-recorded interviews with people from a variety of age groups and backgrounds. An enormous obstacle in collecting texts during interviews was that the informants forgot their jokes. Many insisted that they had heard farmer's daughter jokes and that there must be hundreds of them in circulation but were frustrated when they could not recall a single one. I take this as an indication of the highly sensitive and age-specific nature of the jokes' symbolic content. Martha Wolfenstein has aptly pointed out that "the common tendency to forget jokes seems related to the fact that the joke makes conscious thoughts which are usually repressed. This release from repression is only momentary. Subsequently the forbidden thoughts, and the joke which gave them expression, are again excluded from consciousness" (1954, 108; see also Grotjahn, 1951). Of approximately fifty joke texts in my collection, thirty-one included enough data to indicate the age of the informant when he or she first learned the joke. None of the jokes had been learned before age 6; 58 percent were learned during the latency years (6–12); 29 percent during adolescence (13–18); and 13 percent during adulthood (19–21); 21 was the latest age recorded. The popularity of the jokes among adolescents probably reflects the resurgence of oedipal conflicts during that period. Males reported 77 percent of the jokes; many of the boys and none of the girls stated that the joke telling was a gender-exclusive activity. It is my assumption, based on the informant data, my knowledge of joke theory, and the joke texts themselves, that this joke cycle was initially intended for and promoted by latency-age boys. The fact that the jokes are occasionally found outside this participant group can be attributed to years of diffusion through retelling, and to the appeal of some of the more psychologically universal elements in the texts; incestuous desires, regressive polymorphous perversity, and the fantasy of defying the superego.

There are several versions of the farmer's daughter joke, each with many variants. In order to limit my sample to the most typical texts, I set the following guidelines for inclusion in the study: the joke must include a prohibition against sex with the farmer's daughter, and the prohibition must eventually be broken. The average text runs as follows: A traveler (or traveling salesman) needs a place to stay for the night. He stops at a farmhouse and inquires about a bed. The farmer says the traveler can stay, provided that he does not sleep with the farmer's young daughter. As the night progresses, the traveler cannot resist temptation and has his way with the daughter. The act is somehow discovered by the farmer. At this point the joke may take one of two paths: the traveler tricks or otherwise humiliates the farmer and gets away with his dirty deed, or the traveler is severely punished. Jokes that do not fit the prohibition/violation guidelines are unusual and appear to be meta-folklore; that is, they are later developments that play on the original joke pattern. For example, in one version, the traveler is ridiculed by the daughter because he *doesn't* try to seduce her; in another, the traveler finds that the farmer has a son instead of a daughter and replies, "I must be in the wrong joke." These versions were considered aberrations from the norm and excluded from my sample.

As Freud made eminently clear in his "Jokes and Their Relation to the Unconscious" (1905a), jokes exist as a convenient vehicle for the safe expression of inhibited desires (see Abrahams and Dundes, 1969). He pointed out their similarity to dreams as outlets for unconscious, repressed material. It would follow that the joke is a particularly fitting developmental tool for the latency child, who has an abundance of freshly repressed desires and the newly acquired ability to deal with those desires on a symbolic level. According to Charles Sarnoff, "The introduction of castration fear, fear of loss of love, and the incest barrier makes fantasies which involve the parent in sexual and aggressive contexts unbearable. . . . All situations which relate to or stir up the core fantasies of prelatency are resolved by the formation of seemingly unrelated conscious fantasies" (1971, 411). Freud confirmed that the latency mind is well suited to the frequent use of (joking) fantasy when he wrote: "The presence of numerous inhibited instincts, whose suppression has retained a certain degree of instability, will provide the most favourable disposition for the production of tendentious jokes" (1905a, 143).

Of special concern to the latency child is the Oedipus conflict, the recent repression of which remains somewhat insecure. There are three types of fantasies reflected in the farmer's daughter texts, each of which provides a different solution to the problematic and unshakable incestuous urges that are carried by every child unconsciously into adulthood. (It should be kept in mind that the categories provided are not absolute: the actual jokes do not always fall into one or the other and may contain numerous details that are not addressed here.) The first fantasy is the oedipal triumph, in which the father is overpowered and incestuous sex is accomplished. The second fantasy, castration, ensures that the incestuous act is appropriately punished and thus reinforces the child's obedience in the real world. In the third fantasy, feminization, the latency boy avoids the troubles accompanying heterosexual incest and castration by the parents. Here he returns to the inverted or negative oedipal position, in which he identifies with the mother and desires the father as sexual object. This entails masochistic passivity and even a kind of self-castration (via female identification), both of which prevent the trauma of having to part with the oedipal attachments in their entirety. All three fantasy types represent solutions to the oedipal conflict that are psychically simpler than the actual relinquishment of incestuous desire, recently accomplished with much difficulty by the latency child. Thus the "economy of psychical expenditure" ascribed by Freud to the joke-telling process is fulfilled (1905a). Jokes representing each of the fantasies will be examined individually.

THE OEDIPAL TRIUMPH

TEXT 1

A salesman stopped at a farm and asked for a room for the night. The farmer says OK, but the only bed is with his young, beautiful daughter. He's heard all about these traveling salesmen, so he puts up a wall of eggs between the two, and warns the salesman not to come near his daughter. During the night the salesman gets horny, and goes to make love to the girl. Of course he breaks the eggs crossing the bed, but the girl says, "Don't worry, I've got some white Will-Hold glue, and we can glue the eggs together again." So they did, but in the morning the farmer wants scrambled eggs. He breaks a couple of those empty eggs and goes for his shotgun. The salesman decides he'd better get out of there quick, and starts running. The farmer yells out to him, "Where are you running to? I want to get those roosters for wearing rubbers." (Folklore Archives, Jeffrey Landres. See also Burrison, 1989, 186–87).

A traveling salesman's car breaks down so he starts walking along a country road. He comes upon a farmer's house and asks if he can spend the night there. "Only if you don't fuck my daughter," the farmer tells the salesman. After all have gone to bed, the farmer's beautiful daughter comes into the salesman's room and propositions him. The salesman agrees to fuck her, but tells her to wait just one minute. Then he tiptoes into the farmer's bedroom and carefully plucks a single hair from his ass. The farmer doesn't wake so the salesman scampers back to his room and begins to have sex. About an hour later, he again returns to the farmer's room to make sure he isn't awake. Having plucked another hair from the farmer's ass, and getting no response, he returns to his bed for another fuck. Hours later, as the salesman is checking the farmer for about the tenth time, the farmer suddenly sits up in bed and screams, "Alright, alright! I don't really care if you fuck my daughter, but please don't use my ass for a scoreboard!!" (Folklore Archives, Kenneth Schneider. See also Randolph, 1976, 81–82, and Abrahams, 1963, 220–21).

It is clear from the beginning that the salesman is a stand-in for the listener (or teller) of the joke; he is the protagonist to whom the latency boy will relate. In the fantasy the traveler is returning home after a period of separation/estrangement from the family. This is relevant to the latency stage, when the child has just begun to declare his independence; he has his own, internalized superego and may now prefer to communicate with peers and adults outside the family (Schechter and Combrinck-Graham, 1991, 297). The decision to seek shelter with the farmer is often motivated by a storm (the harshness of the world outside) or a broken-down car (a sense of impotence or sexual inadequacy). A return to the close-knit family atmosphere, though initially comforting, necessitates a revival of oedipal confrontational situations. The farmer-father is able to provide compassion and shelter to the boy on one condition: that he obey a sexual injunction, just as in "real life." The injunction may be seen to stand for the incest taboo and also for the latency child's harsh superego in general.

The object of incestuous desire in almost every farmer's daughter joke is the sister rather than the mother. If the mother is indeed the true object, then this representation is consistent with the tendency of conscious fantasies to disguise the true identities of their characters via displacement. The daughter is usually portrayed as living alone with her father on the farm, thus implying that she is his only "mate." Another, perhaps more likely possibility is that the sister is the true love object. The Kinsey data (1953) show that brother-sister incest occurs five times more frequently than that between father and daughter.

Although Freud does not emphasize the role of the sister in the oedipal drama, it can be inferred that she is an adequate substitute for the mother, if not her equivalent. In *Totem and Taboo*, he states that a boy's "earliest choice of objects for his love is incestuous and that those objects are forbidden ones—his mother and his sister" (1913, 17). Both female figures can be seen as equally forbidden by the incest taboo and equally protected by the threatening and competitive father.

Each joke expresses the desirability of the daughter automatically, without the rationalization of a detailed physical description. She is in effect irresistible; she is pounced on in every joke, thus reflecting the absolute unavoidability of the incestuous impulse. Occasionally, as in text 2, she offers a proposition. In any case, the daughter's part in the text is shallow and short-lived; her actions and words are few, and her consent is not requisite for the joke. She merely provides a vehicle for the fantasied defiance of the father's injunction. The developing relationship between father and son, which is the true focus of the joke in every version, is set in motion by her marginal presence.

Texts 1 and 2, as imagined oedipal triumph scenarios, emphasize the child's devastating victory over the father. They flaunt the father's inability to follow through on his (implied) threat of castration or other punishment for violating his vexing taboo. In the process, the father himself is feminized. In text 2 (sometimes referred to as "The Hairy Scoreboard") the father's presentation of his buttocks rather than his intimidating phallus implies biological femininity; as a further insult to his manhood, the traveler-son plucks out his hairs. Each plucking may be viewed symbolically as castration in miniature, or more directly as a removal of the physical signs of masculinity. At the joke's end, the father begrudgingly submits to his replacement as the controlling head of the family.

In text 1, the father's injunction against incest is embodied in the protective wall of eggs. As masculine symbols, they might be seen as the father's testes, which are defiantly smashed by the young man. When the farmer finds that his "eggs" are empty, his initial concern is that his rooster (or "cock") has been using a prophylactic: in other words, that he has become impotent. He has also failed to control the sexual behavior of his family—roosters, daughter, and son.

It can be objected that eggs have a predominantly *feminine* connotation, but this is also accounted for by the characteristics of the incest fantasy. If the eggs are taken to represent the fecundity of the family, the potential for sexual productivity, then their destruction by the traveler is entirely appropriate. Any violator of the incest taboo is a threat to the productivity of a community. He defies the laws of culture, which dictate that a family must marry exogamously in order to survive and maintain successful commerce with other groups (Cohen, 1978; Lévi-Strauss, 1969; Schechner, 1971). In addition, incestuous intercourse is popularly believed to result in deformed offspring or infertility. Thus, the boy who indulges in an incestuous fantasy proudly mocks the concept of procreation. Even the traveler's vague identity as a "city boy" reinforces this notion: he represents a threatening, lawless sterility infiltrating the natural and fertile territory of the farmer. The latency boy, who has entered a period of relative asexuality, confused gender identity, and distance from his immediate family, might easily feel that he is alienated in this way.

Several other versions of the farmer's daughter joke involve the theme of the oedipal triumph. The traveler is able to humiliate and defy the farmer by taking his place, proving he's "bigger and better" and capable of adult sexual activity. In one text, for example, he gains the farmer's confidence by assuring him that his "romantic equipment" was shot off in the war, and he thus poses no threat to the daughter's chastity. When the farmer discovers them engaged in intercourse (a kind of reverse "primal scene" common to these jokes), the traveler explains that his penis *had* been shot off, but "it left a ten-inch stump" (Berle, 1989). In another version, the salesman is leaving the farm in the morning when the farmer asks, "Did you fuck my daughter?" The blunt punch line is" "Your ol' lady too!" (Folklore Archives). As the sly, victorious, incestuous Don Juan goes on his way, the preadolescent teller of the tale leaves his daydream behind. He has mastered his unacceptable libidinal urges by indulging in them symbolically and is once again ready to move away emotionally from family ties.

A second type of the joke is less triumphant and more masochistic: it allows the child to reestablish his post-oedipal security by punishing himself for his incestuous thoughts.

CASTRATION

TEXT 3

Having been stranded by a broken car, the traveling salesman asks to stay in the farmer's house. "Only if you don't fuck my daughter," he is told. "Okay, you can trust me," he tells the farmer. Late that night the farmer's beautiful daughter slips into the salesman's bed for a heavy session. But she falls asleep with him and the farmer discovers them in bed together in the morning. At gunpoint, he takes the salesman to the barn. The farmer takes the salesman's cock and puts it in a vise. He then tightens the vise down all the way before breaking off the handle. As he pulls out a large knife, the salesman stammers, "You're not really going to cut it off are you?" "No, you are," the farmer replies; "I'm just going to light the barn on fire." (Folklore Archives, Kenneth Schneider).

TEXT 4

There's this man traveling along in the countryside and he decides to stop at a farm and ask if he can spend the night there. The friendly farmer who answers the door lets him in and shows him into a room with three holes in the wall. He says, "You can spend the night here for free, just don't stick your dick into these three holes." Well, they go to bed but the man just can't stop thinking about those holes in the wall. He goes and sticks his dick into the first hole, and he hears, "Ooooooh." He sticks his dick into the second hole and he hears, "Aaaaaah." He sticks it in the third hole, and he hears, "Brzzzzz!!" [a mechanical grinding sound]. In the morning, he admits to the farmer that he stuck his dick in the three holes. "But I have to ask," he says, "what is behind that wall?" "Well," the farmer replies, "the first hole was my daughter. The second hole was my wife. And the third hole was a pencil sharpener." (Folklore Archives, Erika Katz).

TEXT 5

There were three men traveling in the countryside who needed a place to rest for the night. They decided to stop at a farmhouse nearby. The farmer there told them they were welcome to spend the night, as long as they did not fuck his beautiful young daughter. Secretly, the farmer placed a razor blade in his daughter's vagina, just in case the travelers didn't obey his rule. The next morning, the farmer had the three men line up in front of him. "Take down your pants," he said to the first man, so he took down his pants and his dick fell off. "Take down your pants," he said to the second man, so he took down his pants and his dick fell off. "Take down your pants," he said to the third man, so he took down his pants and his tongue fell off. (Folklore Archives, Erika Katz).

This last text is a particularly good example of the relative insignificance of the daughter's role. She exists only to be desired and sexually manipulated by competing males and in fact rarely speaks or consents to sexual activity in any joke. Here, the farmer's concern is clearly not for his daughter's chastity or well-being, as he assumes and almost *hopes* that she will be violated by setting a "trap" in her vagina. His true goal is to castrate the young man whose forbidden sexual attraction to his "sister" is basically inevitable.

Texts 4 and 5 involve distinct images of the *vagina dentata* that threatens to sever the traveler's penis. Although it is the vagina that castrates, it is the father who puts the castrating mechanism in place, thus ingeniously punishing his rivalrous son at the very moment of his transgression. The situation mirrors that of the oedipal child: "to begin with he does not believe in the threat or obey it in the least" (Freud, 1924, 175), and only when he becomes aware of the physical reality of the female genitals does he realize the danger he is in. Gershon Legman confirms that "the theme of castration as punishment for sexual transgression against the authority-figure's female chattels (as in harems) is particularly prominent [in jokes]" (1952, 55). The manner in which the threat is finally carried out is so overt in these examples that a detailed analysis is hardly necessary.

The final example is of particular interest because it involves the displacement of the penis to the tongue. This adds depth to the farmer's satisfying retribution: he sees through the traveler's evasive imagery and in the punch line is able to castrate even the more psychically developed rival, who uses latency-appropriate tactics of symbolization to disguise or destigmatize his desires. This may provide a stronger sense of release for the participants in the joke telling because they are able to relate closely to the third traveler and revel in the punishment he receives for his actions. Although Legman (1975) insists that the teller identifies defensively with the aggressor in castration jokes, I would argue the opposite: the emasculated protagonist is clearly the more developed and sympathetic character in the texts provided here. The purpose of the castration-theme joke is to reassure the child that the threat he so painfully submitted to in pre-latency was a real one and that he is right to squelch his remaining incestuous desires. By symbolically punishing himself for his "bad" thoughts, he may forgo actual castration and perhaps diminish his strong sense of guilt.

In text 3 we begin to see a homosexual element. The farmer comes into intimate contact with the traveler's penis, touching it as he puts it into the vise. In addition, this and many other jokes in the cycle invoke the power of the farmer's shotgun and describe the respect and passivity it inspires in the traveler. In one version of the "razor blade" text, after the men have all been castrated by the hidden weapon, the farmer actually impales them with his pitchfork. This joke was collected from a personal informant who made a revealing slip-up: "The second boy drops his trousers, and his penis is also severed. And the farmer says, 'Aha! You slept with her too!' So he impales her with a pitchfork . . . impales *him* with a pitchfork." The teller had unconsciously attributed a feminine identity to the male protagonist about to be penetrated by the father. Images like this one to some extent represent the son's happy submission to the superiority of the father's phallus, as in a normally resolved Oedipus conflict in which castration anxiety has been surmounted. This joke carries traces of negative oedipal strivings as well: although the father conveys the castration threat typical of heterosexual rivalry, it is the traveler who will be compelled to sever his own penis. Self-castration, it may be argued, represents an attempt that is homosexual in nature to escape competition with the father. As we shall see, a passive sexual attitude toward the father in fantasy is also a means of avoiding castration altogether.

FEMINIZATION

TEXT 6

Two guys break down . . . um, they're salesmen, um, they go to the farmer. Same thing, the farmer says, "Okay, you can spend the night in the barn but don't mess with my daughter." They mess with the daughter. The next day, the farmer comes out with a shotgun and says, "Okay, both of you, go out to the field and pick your favorite fruit or vegetable." Have you heard this one? Okay, and, uh . . . so one of the guys waits while the other guy goes out and picks his favorite fruit or vegetable. Comes back, he's got *all* these grapes. Then, um, the farmer sends the other guy out to pick his favorite fruit or vegetable. So while [the first guy]'s standing there with the grapes he says, "Okay, now I want you to shove every one of those grapes up your ass." And the guy starts to shove the grapes up his ass, and all of a sudden he *laughs*, and they all fall out. And then [the farmer] says, "This is not funny! I'm gonna blow your head off! You better shove those grapes up your ass right now." So the guy starts shovin' the grapes up his ass, and he gets almost to, um, to a hundred, and he laughs and they all fall out again. And [the farmer's] like, "Okay, this is your last chance. If you don't shove those grapes up your ass, I'm gonna kill you." So the guy starts shovin' the grapes up his ass, but once again, they all fall out, and [the farmer's] like, "All right. Why the hell are you laughing?" And he says, "My friend's out there pickin' watermelons." (Personal informant. See also Burrison, 1989, 187).

TEXT 7

Once a traveling salesman was passing through some of the back hills of Tennessee when he happened upon a farm. Since it was late and extremely cold, he asked the farmer for a place to stay for the night. The farmer told him that he could sleep in the farmer's daughter's room providing he promised not to fuck her. The salesman immediately promised, but, inside of an hour, the farmer could already hear the bedsprings bouncing. He raced upstairs and pulled the salesman out of his daughter's bed. Then the farmer dragged the guy outside and tied him to an upright pole while he was still nude. The farmer, pleased with himself, strutted back into the house convinced that the man would be dead by morning. The next morning, though, the farmer went out to view the body and found the man panting and sweating and in a state close to exhaustion. The farmer couldn't believe it. After staring at him in disbelief for a few minutes, he finally asked him what had happened. After catching his breath, the salesman madly yelled at the farmer, "I didn't care when the chickens pecked at my toes; and I didn't even mind the dirty hogs rubbing against my legs; but for God's sakes, doesn't that calf have a mother?" (Folklore Archives, Thomas O. Kelly).

Text 6 focuses on regressive anal-sadistic elements, which are typical of the latency-age child (Sarnoff, 1971, 393). The traveler is happiest when the farmer is punishing him with what is essentially anal inter-course; one version of the joke includes the more phallic objects of corn ears and cucumbers (Folklore Archives), while others depict the farmer himself inserting the objects (Dance, 1978, 86; Burrison, 1989, 187). Freud has established that masochistic fantasies, which often involve aggressive attacks on the exposed buttocks, are connected to the nega-tive Oedipus complex and that "the beating-phantasy has its origin in an incestuous attachment to the father" (1919, 198). This information points to the suitability of the joke's content for children in latency. The traveler's feminine passivity is strongly reinforced by his "impregna-tion" with fruit, a common symbol of fertility. The joke teller returns to his infantile conception of intercourse and birth when he fantasizes that they take place via the anal passage (Freud, 1908, 219; 1905b, 196). The traveler laughs as the fruit is released because of his joy at the concretization of a wished-for ability to bear a child to his own father (and laughs as it is inserted again because he has reversed the process of fecal loss so often mourned during the anal stage). It should be noted that not every version of this joke includes the release of the fruit. Those that do not merely avoid the unpleasantness altogether, allowing the teller to enjoy more directly the fantasies of impregnation and fecal retention.

Text 7 involves not castration but rather an identification with the phallic mother, a common tendency in the preadolescent male (Blos, 1958, 50; 1962, 63). Once again, the father's punishing actions become erotic at the moment of potential castration, when he binds the boy's nude body to an upright pole (itself graphic evidence of the superiority of the paternal phallus). This time, however, the feminized traveler takes up the maternal activity of nursing rather than impregnation and birth: the calf has mistaken his penis for the nipple of a cow's udder. The action is effective in that it saves him from the ill effects of his punishment; the resort to the negative oedipal position successfully prevents his castration or death.[1] The traveler-as-nursing-mother theme also appears in a series of jokes involving a milking machine: after making love to the farmer's daughter, wife, and/or livestock, the traveler unknowingly inserts his penis into the machine and is held captive there for the night (Folklore Archives). The experience is usually described as extremely pleasurable or painfully exhausting, as would befit a lengthy session of breast-feeding a child. Once again, the fantasy of feminization, identification with the mother, and reliance on the negative oedipal position relieves the traveler–joke teller from both the pain of castration and the difficulty of the original dissolution of the complex.

The feminization texts cited here incorporate the themes of the negative Oedipus complex: that part of the normal male psyche that yearns for identification with the mother rather than the father (Freud, 1923a, 32–33; 1921, 105–06; 1940, 190). Even during heterosexual development, relief can be sought in negative oedipal fantasies, in which dangerous sexual attraction to the mother can be neutralized and deliberate self-castration can replace the horror of castration by an angry father. Homosexuality provides a comfortable alternative to replacing the maternal love-object with another woman, to continuing rivalrous relations with the father, and to relinquishing narcissistic attachments, in addition to assurance that future lovers will retain the treasured male genital organ (Freud, 1922, 230–31). In the joke-fantasies above, the boy first engages in forbidden incestuous relations and incurs the father's wrath. When the anxiety of this situation reaches its apex and castration is about to occur, the fantasy changes course to avoid the consequences of the initial action. The participant switches from a positive to a negative oedipal position, thus enjoying the uninterrupted pleasures of each.

The resort to homoerotic experimentation is evident in the joke-telling context as well as in its text, as farmer's daughter jokes are told almost exclusively among groups of boys. Many informants made it a point to note that they would never consider exchanging such jokes

---

1. These are often conflated, in psychoanalysis and in jokes. In one variant of the watermelon text, the men die as a result of the forced anal-receptive intercourse (personal informant); in other farmer's daughter jokes, violators of the parental injunction are shot on discovery (Folklore Archives). For discussions of the relation between castration, incest, and death, see Barande, 1968, and Jeanneau, 1992.

with girls, or even with someone outside their age group (with the occasional exception of an intimate male mentor, such as a gym coach or camp counselor). Perhaps the teller, who is attempting to resolve his unconscious confusion about the Oedipus complex, finds in his young friends an unthreatening kind of attraction: they resemble neither the forbidden and castrated mother nor the strong and jealous father. The male friend, as a sexual object, permits the psychological evasion of the conflict in precisely the same way that the feminization joke does. Freud observes that, in the process of telling an obscene joke, "smut is directed to a particular person, by whom one is sexually excited and who, on hearing it, is expected to become aware of the speaker's excitement and as a result become sexually excited in turn" (1905a, 97). The teller can assume (consciously or unconsciously) that the peer group he shares his smut with will probably have sexual feelings in harmony with his own and that the joke will therefore be successful; according to Freud, the hearer should be "in sufficient psychical accord with the first person to possess the same internal inhibitions" (1905a, 151). And, in a most platonic sense, a "boys only" session of these jokes is developmentally healthy. Peer-group activities are of increasing importance to the latency child, and prefabricated, formulaic wordplay like that contained in joke cycles is a popular way to achieve stability during this period of transition.

A lack of detailed informant data has made it impossible for me to analyze these texts in specific relation to the phases *within* latency. However, it is clear that the material presented embodies many of the unconscious concerns associated with the period in general. Material involving such themes as castration anxiety, parental injunctions, and the Oedipus complex is sure to be of interest to listeners in every developmental stage, but, as the data indicate, these themes are most rigorously repressed and in need of outlet during the post-oedipal preadolescent years. Sarnoff observes that "it is characteristic of the thinking of the child in early latency that he develop a masked way of thinking and fantasizing about experiences and observations he is trying to master" (1987, 40), even more so than adolescents or adults dealing with similar struggles. He further states, "Characteristically, the unmodified (latent) fantasies in response to stress of the early latency years deal with oedipal wishes to take one parent's place in the relationship with the other" (41). He points out that fantasies of the latency period typically include fears of being alone in the world, defiant confrontations with parents, and concern about sexual identity. In an earlier article (1971, 398), Sarnoff specifically mentions "sexual relations that are abruptly interrupted by a punishing intruder" as a theme common to latency fantasies. All of these can be observed in the farmer's daughter jokes, in which a wandering, homeless "son" seeks shelter from the family, rejects the rules set by the parents, and alternates between masculine and feminine identifications in attempts to replace each parental figure. The frequency of images relating to the comparative grandeur of the farmer's phallus (he wields a shotgun, pitchfork, or pole, whereas the traveler's penis fits easily into a pencil sharpener) and to overt emasculation confirm that "the child's experience of rejection by the oedipal love object . . . revives related conflicts around sexual differences, penis envy, and castration fear" (Furman, 1991, 169). The use of fantasy to express conflicts and drives has been shown to positively affect the elaboration of cognitive controls during latency (Donellan, 1977), and through its sheer frequency of use during that period can be assumed to play a vital role in psychological maturation. The joke is an accessible and acceptable means of formulating fantasy material and provides the additional benefits of public display and reinforcement with each telling.

I would add that the farmer's daughter joke not only functions as a psychic release valve for the latency boy. It also serves the cultural function of transmitting information about taboos and appropriate social behavior. Social regulations such as the prohibition against incest, unlike legal sanctions or rules of etiquette, are passed on subtly. A mother does not sit her son down and explain that it is wrong for him to make love to her; a boy does not turn to a reference book to learn whether he may marry his sister. Instead, information about taboos is handed down through folklore (myths, ballads, fairy tales, jokes, etc.) and other cultural products like literature and film. Communal attitudes toward incest are "embedded in the organizing systems of language. . . . We have obvious unconscious linguistic triggers in such phrases as 'he's old enough to be her father.'... We have a multitude of folk, popular and country and western songs addressed to 'baby' or 'daddy' that play off the emotional spark of displaced fathers and daughters. And we have such jokes as: *Mountain Mother:* My, Billy, your prick is bigger than Dad's! *Billy:* Yes, that's what sister always says" (Twitchell, 1987, 53). The incest theme is particularly popular in myths cross-culturally. Stories and jokes that give expression to incestuous urges rather than simply denounce or deny them are effective, even therapeutic, in educating without anxiety (Bidou, 1982; Ngoma-Binda, 1976).

Text 8 is an example of a farmer's daughter joke that depicts taboo violation playfully and at the same time clearly reflects societal attitudes about the consequences of incest.

TEXT 8

This traveling salesman came to this farmhouse and asked the farmer if he could spend the night. The farmer recognized the salesman as being a feed representative for a large grain mill in the next county. He said that the man could, but that he would have to sleep with his eighteen-year-old daughter.

The farmer invited the salesman in for a little snort before bedtime, and during the conversation began to wonder if the salesman would try to screw his daughter. He decided to wrap his daughter in a sheet so the salesman wouldn't get any ideas. The salesman finally went to bed, slept the night, had breakfast with the family and left.

About a year later, this same salesman returned, but this time during the day. As he approached the barnyard, he noticed this freakish looking kid seated in a sandpile. He had one eye located where his left ear should be; his nose was in the middle of his forehead; his mouth was where his nose should have been, and one leg was growing out of his belly. "What in the hell happened to that kid?" the salesman asked the farmer.

"I don't know," answered the farmer, "but he was born after you left. To m'daughter."

The daughter came around the corner of the barn, and began to shout and rave against the salesman. "Yes, he's a freak, you son of a bitch. How would you look if you were strained through a sheet?" (Folklore Archives, Frederick L. Fuller).

The brother-traveler in this text, after daring to transcend the incest barrier (literally) established by the father, must face shocking physical evidence of his transgression. Whether incestuous relations actually result in deformed offspring is still hotly debated, but the *belief* that they do is a powerful motivation for the maintenance of the taboo. Bernos (1989) explains that the birth of an abnormal child, in fact or in lore, is often thought to be the physical manifestation of (and punishment for) the nefarious thoughts or acts of the parents. Cultural beliefs of this kind make possible the transmission of "unteachable" mores and values through folkloric tradition. Fine sums up the position well. "Sexual humor serves to establish and ratify norms and boundaries for appropriate conduct. By describing behavior considered sexually improper (and thus comical), it reveals by implication the correct forms of sexual interaction" (1976, 135). Joking is a means of reinforcing traditional values by mockingly refuting them or by disparaging those people who reject them (Powell, 1977; Vandekerckhove, 1981). The farmer's daughter joke in this light is not merely a crude bit of obscenity or a tool for individual psychological expression but a crucial means for the perpetuation of social norms.

Further motivation is provided by the threat of *aggression* involved in the actual joke performance, a factor emphasized by Freud in his 1905 work on the subject. In the case of the farmer's daughter joke, the ridicule directed at the fictive, transgressive traveler also applies to those participating in the joke exchange. Anyone present who feels tempted to explore his or her regressive fantasies will be made to understand that those who violate taboos become the butt of derisive humor, exposed before a peer group. The joke's message is: "If you give in to your desires, you too will be subject to public ridicule."

The concept of the joke as a means of social conditioning is intimately related to the latency period, because this period is initiated by the internalization of the parental injunctions (Freud, 1923a, 34–37; 1924, 176). A consequential difference is being negotiated between the personal and social understanding of taboos during this time. Because of their value to the community and to the family in almost every culture, incest taboos are imposed on the individual from outside, but they cannot be successfully maintained without the cooperation of the individual psyche. Incestuous desires are instinctual and therefore difficult obstacles to overcome. The oedipal child is "wired for sexual choice along the dimensions of proximity and similarity, encountering a society or culture that is necessarily programmed for destruction or inhibition of these natural tendencies" (Lindzey, 1967, 1056). When latency begins, with the internalization of the incest taboo, the task of making foreign prohibitions into personal beliefs has been accomplished. The knowledge of right and wrong becomes automatic once the child has developed a superego (and therefore a conscience). The internalized "punishment" provided by the conscience echoes the external one traditionally believed to accompany forbidden behaviors: Margaret Mead defines taboos as "prohibitions against participation in any situation of such inherent danger that the very act of participation will recoil upon the violator of the tabu" (1934). As the threat of punishment is internalized, the child is more easily able to understand and engage in proper behavior. The use of the joke as a reinforcement of social norms is of the utmost importance during the early years of latency, when the dissolution of the Oedipus complex is still tenuous.

Although most joke cycles are fads (elephant jokes, "little moron" jokes, "what's grosser than gross," etc.), the farmer's daughter has withstood the test of time. The earliest versions I know of date to 1900 and 1906 (Randolph, 1976, 38, 147); the most recent was remembered from 1986. Any joke can be said to have psychological resonances, but those in the farmer's daughter cycle seem to be particularly strong. Mastering the oedipal desires is from the psychoanalytic perspective

452 *Erika K. Clowes*

the most important process of a person's life, and the vital role these texts play in furthering that development is unmistakable. Through the joke a latency child can redirect his impulses when they become too uncomfortable. He can also experience punishment to resolve his unconscious guilt, act defiantly in reaction to his bitterness and fear, and experiment sexually to satisfy his desires. Joke telling for the latency child is a healthy peer-group activity that helps him to establish an identity outside of family life. And despite the popular belief that the "farmer's daughter" joke is obscene, a child's moral convictions are solidified with each telling, both in terms of individual psychology and in relation to his cultural environment.

BIBLIOGRAPHY

ABRAHAMS, R. D. (1963). *Deep Down in the Jungle.* Chicago: Aldine.
ABRAHAMS, R. D., & DUNDES, A. (1969). On elephantasy and elephanticide. *Psychoanalytic Review,* 56(2):225–241.
BARANDE, R. (1968). La "pulsion de mort" comme non-transgression (Survie et transfiguration du tabou de l'inceste). *Revue Française de Psychanalyse,* 32(3):465–502.
BERLE, M. (1989). *Milton Berle's Private Joke File.* New York: Crown.
BERNOS, A. (1989). La naissance de l'enfant anormal: Mythe et fantasme: Approche psychanalytique à partir de contes, croyances et rêves. *Topique: Revue Freudienne,* 19(43):61–84.
BIDOU, P. (1982). On incest and death: A myth of the Tatuyo Indians of Northwest Amazonia. In M. Izard and P. Smith (Eds.), *Between Belief and Transgression; Structuralist Essays in Religion, History, and Myth,* 129–151. Chicago: University of Chicago Press.
BLOS, P. (1958). Preadolescent Drive Organization. *Journal of the American Psychoanalytic Association,* 6(1):47–56.
BLOS, P. (1962). *On Adolescence.* New York: Free Press.
BURRISON, J. A., ed. (1989). *Storytellers: Folktales and Legends from the South.* Athens: University of Georgia Press.
COHEN, Y. (1978). The disappearance of the incest taboo. *Human Nature,* 1(7):72–78.
DANCE, D. C. (1978). *Shuckin' and Jivin': Folklore from Contemporary Black America.* Bloomington: Indiana University Press.
DONELLAN, G. J. (1977). Symbolization, fantasy and adaptive regression as developmental tasks of the latency period (Doctoral dissertation, California School of Professional Psychology, San Francisco). *Dissertation Abstracts International,* 38:2856–2857.
FINE, G. A. (1976). Obscene joking across cultures. *Journal of Communication,* 26(3):134–140.

FOLKLORE ARCHIVES OF THE UNIVERSITY OF CALIFORNIA AT BERKELEY.
FREUD, S. (1905a). Jokes and Their Relation to the Unconscious. *Standard Edition*, 8:3–236. London: Hogarth Press, 1960.
FREUD, S. (1905b). Three Essays on the Theory of Sexuality. *Standard Edition*, 7:125–243. London: Hogarth Press, 1953.
FREUD, S. (1908). On the Sexual Theories of Children. *Standard Edition*, 9:207–226. London: Hogarth Press, 1959.
FREUD, S. (1913). Totem and Taboo. *Standard Edition*, 13:ix–162. London: Hogarth Press, 1955.
FREUD, S. (1919). "A Child Is Being Beaten": A Contribution to the Study of the Origin of Sexual Perversions. *Standard Edition*, 17:175–204. London: Hogarth Press, 1955.
FREUD, S. (1921). Group Psychology and the Analysis of the Ego. *Standard Edition*, 18:67–143. London: Hogarth Press, 1955.
FREUD, S. (1922). Some Neurotic Mechanisms in Jealousy, Paranoia and Homosexuality. *Standard Edition*, 18:221–232. London: Hogarth Press, 1955.
FREUD, S. (1923a). The Ego and the Id. *Standard Edition*, 19:3–66. London: Hogarth Press, 1961.
FREUD, S. (1923b). Two Encyclopedia Articles. *Standard Edition*, 18:234–259. London: Hogarth Press, 1955.
FREUD, S. (1924). The Dissolution of the Oedipus Complex. *Standard Edition*, 19:173–179. London: Hogarth Press, 1961.
FREUD, S. (1940). An Outline of Psycho-Analysis. *Standard Edition*, 23:141–207. London: Hogarth Press, 1964.
FURMAN, E. (1991). Early Latency: Normal and Pathological Aspects. In S. I. Greenspan and G. H. Pollock (eds.), *The Course of Life, Volume III: Middle and Late Childhood*, 161–203. Madison, Conn.: International Universities Press.
GOLDINGS, H. J. (1974). Jump-Rope Rhymes and the Rhythm of Latency Development in Girls. *Psychoanalytic Study of the Child*, 29:431–450.
GROTJAHN, M. (1951). The inability to remember dreams and jokes. *Psychoanalytic Quarterly*, 20(2):284–286.
JEANNEAU, A. (1992). La castration comme symbole et comme représentation à propos de l'angoisse de castration. *Revue Française de Psychanalyse*, 56(Special Congress):1629–1637.
KINSEY, A. C., POMEROY, W. B., MARTIN, C. E., & GEBHARD, P. H. (1953). *Sexual Behavior in the Human Female*. Philadelphia: Saunders.
LEGMAN, G. (1952). Rationale of the dirty joke. *Neurotica*, 9:49–64.
LEGMAN, G. (1975). *Rationale of the Dirty Joke: 2nd Ser.* New York: Breaking Point.
LÉVI-STRAUSS, C. (1969). *The Elementary Structures of Kinship* (J. H. Bell, J. R. von Sturmer, Trans.). Boston: Beacon Press.
LINDZEY, G. (1967). Some remarks concerning incest, the incest taboo, and psychoanalytic theory. *American Psychologist*, 22(12):1051–1059.
MEAD, M. (1934). Tabu. In E. R. A. Seligman (ed.), *Encyclopaedia of the Social Sciences*, 502–505. New York: Macmillan.

454 *Erika K. Clowes*

NGOMA-BINDA (1976). Herméneutique de quelques interdits et structure de défoulement en société yombe. *Zaïre-Afrique,* 108:489–502.

POWELL, C. (1977). Humor as a Form of Social Control: A Deviance Approach. In A. J. Chapman and H. C. Foot (Eds.), *It's a Funny Thing: Humor,* 53–55. Oxford: Pergamon Press.

RANDOLPH, V. (1976). *Pissing in the Snow and Other Ozark Folktales.* Urbana: University of Illinois Press.

SARNOFF, C. A. (1971). Ego structure in latency. *Psychoanalytic Quarterly,* 40(3):387–414.

SARNOFF, C. A. (1987). *Psychotherapeutic Strategies in the Latency Years.* Northvale, N.J.: Jason Aronson.

SCHECHNER, R. (1971). Incest and culture: A reflection on Claude Lévi-Strauss. *Psychoanalytic Review,* 58:563–572.

SCHECHTER, M. D., & COMBRINCK-GRAHAM, L. (1991). The Normal Development of the Seven-to-Ten-Year-Old Child. In S. I. Greenspan and G. H. Pollock (Eds.), *The Course of Life, Volume III: Middle and Late Childhood,* 285–318. Madison, Conn.: International Universities Press.

TWITCHELL, J. B. (1987). *Forbidden Partners: The Incest Taboo in Modern Culture.* New York: Columbia University Press.

VANDEKERCKHOVE, L. (1981). Het fenomeen van de schuine moppen en de taboeëring van de seksuele communicatie: *quid? Tijdschrift voor Sociale Wetenschappen,* 26(4):303–315.

WOLFENSTEIN, M. (1954). *Children's Humor: A Psychological Analysis.* Glencoe, Ill.: Free Press.

Psychological Complications of Short Stature in Childhood

Some Implications of the Role of Visual Comparisons in Normal and Pathological Development

STEVEN A. FRANKEL, M.D.

*This study examines the effect of short stature on the emotional develop-
ment of a subgroup of children who were treated in psychoanalysis and
psychotherapy. These children became capable of making accurate comparisons of body size in early latency as a result of advances in cognitive
development. Recognizing their comparative smallness left them feeling
vulnerable and humiliated. They responded with envy and rage toward
normally endowed children and vindictively used their intellect to outwit
and defeat others. They acted as if their suffering exempted them from
ordinary social rules and expectations. Their preoccupation also resulted in arrests in cognitive and social development. Their distrust and
intention to deceive and defeat posed particular problems for treatment.
This outcome suggests that visual comparisons of size during early latency are implicated in pathological, and therefore in normal, development. Parallels are suggested between the subjective experience of children in this group and the experiences of children with other kinds of
physical deviations and compromising life circumstances.*

Faculty, San Francisco Psychoanalytic Institute; associate clinical professor, University
of California Medical School, San Francisco.

The Psychoanalytic Study of the Child 51, ed. Albert J. Solnit, Peter B. Neubauer, Samuel
Abrams, and A. Scott Dowling (Yale University Press, copyright © 1996 by Albert J.
Solnit, Peter B. Neubauer, Samuel Abrams, and A. Scott Dowling).

"SHORT STATURE" IS A TECHNICAL TERM USED IN THE PEDIATRIC LITERA-
ture to refer to children whose growth is at or below the fifth percentile
for their age and sex. It is one of several compromising conditions that
can alter the character of a child's developmental experience. In addition to chronic illness and physical defect, these conditions include
experiences of loss, such as the death of a parent or divorce, or in the
child's loss of an assumed biological connection with parents through
discovering he or she is adopted. In all these situations the child eventually recognizes that in some way he or she is different from and at a
disadvantage to others. There are no articles in the psychoanalytic
literature on the effect of short stature during childhood and adolescence. This lack is unfortunate since short stature is a condition that
can have profound psychological consequences for a developing child.

Cognitive decentering advances rapidly beginning at age six or
seven, during Piaget's subperiod of concrete operations. During this
period children begin to comprehend ways that they are different
from others. They are also progressively able to understand their
physical and existential limitations. For example, adopted children
may begin to comprehend the biological significance of adoption. Children with chronic illnesses or physical anomalies—like short stature—
can begin to compare themselves with others and to understand how
their conditions might impose restrictions on their lives.

Until the end of adolescence a child's discovery of deviation also
occurs within a developmental framework characterized by egocentricity and omnipotence. Children are prone to experience negative
life events as intended to affect them personally. Because of this omnipotence they also tend to feel some responsibility for causing their
plight. The discovery of difference from others may therefore take on
an irrational personalized significance apart from its actual meaning
for the child's life.

This paper is a report of a small sample of short-stature children who
were treated in psychotherapy or psychoanalysis by the author during
the past seventeen years. There were striking similarities in the academic, social, and clinical behavior of these five children.

This study supports the idea that visual comparisons of body size
from about age six play an important part in a child's conviction that he
or she is intact and physically secure. When the children to be discussed
discovered that they were much shorter than their peers, they felt
damaged and threatened, became angry at and envious of their normally endowed peers, and corrected this imbalance through fantasy
and self-assertion. Children with physical disabilities or compromising
life circumstances often follow a similar pattern. Presumably their sub-

jective experience is in ways comparable to that of short-stature children. Because of the combination of their rage, denial of physical disability or personal disadvantage, and omnipotence, psychoanalysis and psychotherapy with such children can be challenging. Also, a period of social and educational training may be required when treating these children.

I do not mean to minimize the contribution of parental attitudes to the child's discovery of his or her short stature or disability (Lussier, 1980; Bauman, 1981). The effect of these attitudes is obviously important and may determine whether psychopathology develops. For the five children discussed below, however, parenting was satisfactory at least through the beginning of latency. Short stature itself provided an adequate explanation for the children's difficulties.

The children described in this paper represent only one of many possible developmental and psychological outcomes for short stature in childhood. Also, it is clear from the literature that short stature is not necessarily pathogenic for children (e.g., see Vance, Ingersoll, and Golden, 1994).

THE PSYCHOANALYTIC LITERATURE

The psychoanalytic literature is only indirectly relevant to the study of short stature. The few loosely pertinent articles are concerned with the psychological consequences of physical defect and deformity and with the normal and pathological development of the body image and the sense of self. Specific responses to these physical deviations include ego deformation in the form of a distorted body image (Niederland, 1965); the disavowal of unacceptable aspects of the self, wishes, or thoughts (Ritvo, 1984; De Bea, 1987); a profound sense of loss as the child recognizes how he or she is different from others (Castelnuovo-Tedesco, 1981); narcissistic injury and compensation in the form of self-aggrandizement, heightened aggression (Niederland, 1965), or the requirement for constant reassurance (Coen, 1986); and the need to deal with hopelessness and disorientation as the defect is acknowledged (Coen, 1986). Physical defect or deformity can also be a potent stimulus to constructive activity and creativity (Lussier, 1960, 1980).

The development of a coherent and constant body image eventuating in "anatomical constancy" occurs during Piaget's preoperational subperiod, between the ages of approximately two and seven. This aspect of self-experience consolidates between ages five and seven. During this period the child is formulating an "awareness of consistencies and regularities in the world" (Feiner, 1987, p. 351). These developments are organized around a stable "affective core of the self" that is constant from early in development (Emde, 1983, p. 165).

This developmental process can be undermined when these children discover that, because of physical defect or deformity, they are at a disadvantage in relation to their peers. This discovery may leave them feeling worried and deceived. They may develop "hopeless feelings of unacceptibility" (Coen, 1986, p. 54). To cope with this intolerable state of mind they may need to resort to defensive denial and disavowal. The narcissistic injury may require narcissistic compensation in the form of "self-inflation, fantasies of grandiosity and uniqueness, aggressive strivings for narcissistic supplies from the outside world, impairment of object relations and reality testing, excessive vulnerability," as well as secretiveness, embellished fantasy life, and sharpened awareness of body parts (Niederland, 1965, pp. 518–533; Castelnuovo-Tedesco, 1981). Many of these children regard themselves as "exceptions" (Freud, 1916; Jacobson, 1959). To compensate for suffering, they implicitly believe that they should be exempt from the ordinary rules of interpersonal relations. For example, Jacobson describes adult women who felt "entitled . . . to rebel against the oedipal laws and to try to achieve psychical restitution through direct fulfillment of . . . oedipal desires" (p. 152).

Lussier (1960, 1980) described the psychoanalytic treatment of a thirteen-year-old boy born with very short arms who used his condition as a stimulus to productive activity and creativity. In the same way that the five small-stature children described below became preoccupied with reestablishing their sense of safety and power, his anxiety about his deformity became the focus of his life. Most of his activities were aimed at hiding or compensating for his deformity. His goal was to prove that he could do anything a normal boy could do and more—he was driven to exceed others. Lussier describes the special role of fantasy for this boy. He was vigilant about sharing and thus potentially giving up his fantasies. Lussier predicted that this boy would always "need some mechanism to deal with the psychic effect of his deformity" (1960, p. 447).

General Medical and Psychological Considerations

For studies of the psychological effects of short stature (as opposed to physical defect or deformity) we need to turn to the general medical and psychological literature. These efforts tend to be organized according to the etiology of the short stature and the height the child finally attains. In contrast to the psychoanalytic literature, which only describes pathological outcomes, the general literature studies the frequency of pathological outcomes and the predisposing circumstances.

Short stature in children that is not caused by chromosomal disorders, systemic disease, hypothyroidism, Cushing's syndrome, or malnutrition falls into three categories: (1) normal-variant constitutional short stature (C.S.S.), (2) normal-variant constitutional delayed growth (C.D.), and (3) growth-hormone deficiency (G.H.D.). Most children in the latter two categories can be expected to reach normal adult height on a delayed timetable for C.D. and if treated over several years for G.H.D. In both cases delayed growth may be detected as early as six–twelve months of age. Children with C.S.S. do not reach normal adult height (Rosenfeld and Hintz, 1983). Most short-stature children belong to the C.S.S. and delayed-growth categories, with fewer than 1 percent suffering from G.H.D. (Richman et al., 1986).

A number of reports document the psychological consequences of short stature in childhood. Some of these distinguish the characteristics of treated G.H.D. from C.S.S. Although the findings are inconsistent, the following generalizations are warranted:

(1) G.H.D. children who are treated medically tend to do better than C.S.S. and even C.D. children (Drotar et al., 1980; Gordon et al., 1982).

(2) Although significant interference with social adjustment may be detected in preadolescence and early adolescence (Holmes et al., 1982; Money and Pollitt, 1966; Stabler, Tancer, et al., 1994; Stabler, Witt, et al., 1980), a qualified but better-adjusted picture tends to emerge toward late adolescence and early adulthood for all categories of short stature.

The prevalence of disturbance among short-stature children is debated in the literature. Sandberg, Brook, and Campos (1994); Skuse et al. (1994); Vance, Ingersoll, and Golden (1994); and Voss and Mulligan (1994) report a weak correlation between short stature in childhood and school and social problems. Stabler, Clopper, et al. (1994) find the opposite. There is no consistent gender difference reported in the literature.

Mitchell et al. (1986) administered questionnaires and limited testing to seventy G.H.D. patients with an average age of twenty-six and their parents. They found that social relationships remained troublesome, but educational achievement and job history were equivalent to those of the normative groups against whom the tests were standardized. There were no discernible differences in aspects of self-concept, but the short-stature group scored lower on "self-criticism."

Because the short-stature group had been treated with long-term-growth hormone, the researchers speculated that the hormone treatment was instrumental in alleviating the effects of short stature.

Galatzer et al. (1987) studied a group of young adults who had been treated with growth hormones over a protracted period and also received counseling. This group deviated little from the normal-height group in their adjustment. Holmes et al. (1986) demonstrated that the deteriorating psychosocial adjustment of their short-stature group in pre- and early adolescence seems to ease by late adolescence. Girls appear to have more problems than boys, including in the academic area. Zimet et al. (1994) had similar findings for non-G.H.D. adults but did not find a gender correlation. In contrast with the qualified optimism of the studies just cited, Dean et al. (1986) in their longitudinal study reported that rates of employment and marriage among their short-stature subjects were significantly lower than in the general population and in the subjects' siblings.

Overall, the literature suggests that the adjustment of short-stature children and adolescents may be a function of socioeconomic status, the success of growth-hormone treatment (Clopper et al., 1986; Young-Hyman, 1986; Stabler and Underwood, 1977; Blizzard et al., 1986; Dean, 1985), and the availability of psychotherapy. Troubled short-stature children begin with a generally poor self-concept and tend to be socially maladjusted. These characteristics may be ameliorated in late adolescence or adulthood, but some studies report a tendency for persistent social difficulties, including lower rates of marriage and employment. Employment and academic success are least consistent from report to report; in these factors short-stature subjects appear to be equivalent to normal-height children in several of the studies.

(3) Although both "externalizing" symptoms such as aggressiveness and "internalizing" behavior such as shyness and withdrawal are reported, there is an emphasis on the latter (Gordon et al., 1982; Holmes et al., 1982; Richman et al., 1986; Steinhausen and Stahnke, 1976). This behavior may inhibit interpersonal relationships. Gordon et al. (1982) described short children as having "significantly more behavior problems and less self-esteem," "a general picture . . . of socially withdrawn and aloof children who express emotional concerns internally and view themselves less favorably than do their taller peers." On the other hand, in several reports academic and vocational performance of short-stature and normal-stature individuals was judged to be consistent, suggesting that academic achievement may be used as a compen-

sation for small physical stature (Abbott et al., 1982; Drotar et al., 1980; Young-Hyman, 1986).

(4) Several studies (e.g., Abbott et al., 1982; Richman et al., 1986; Rotnem et al., 1977) noted that parents had a harder time setting limits for short-stature children than for children of normal height.

In summary, these research findings seem generally consistent with the psychoanalytic reports on the psychopathology of troubled children with physical defects and deformities. The children described in both literatures may harbor a profound sense of inadequacy. They may be withdrawn or angry and unmanageable. In the case of short stature, this outcome can be ameliorated by growth-hormone replacement, psychotherapy, or maturation in the absence of treatment. Nonetheless, there still seems to be a tendency for difficulties to persist through adulthood, and to have an impact on social relationships, marriage, and employment. The research also specifies that manifest psychopathology is not a necessary consequence of short stature. The same appears true for physical defect or deformity and anomalous life circumstances (Avo and Palosaari, 1992; Kelly, 1993).

The literature reviewed offers only limited help in distinguishing the psychological consequences of short stature from those of other conditions. None of the research studies on short stature from the general literature uses the kind of personal data that are available from psychoanalysis or psychotherapy. These studies say little about the inner life of short-stature children or about developmental factors that determine when and how a child becomes meaningfully aware of his or her size. Conversely, none of the psychoanalytic case reports is specifically concerned with short stature.

THE STUDY

The study sample consists of four short-stature boys, two with C.D. and two G.H.D., and a C.S.S. girl. One boy, Joshua, was seen four times a week in psychoanalysis during three separate periods and the other children were seen in twice-weekly psychodynamically informed psychotherapy. All were treated for at least two years. Parent meetings occurred approximately monthly, and regular contact was maintained with teachers. The two G.H.D. boys have been followed through age eighteen and twenty-four, respectively; one C.D. boy was followed to age twenty; and one C.D. boy and the C.S.S. girl were followed through age sixteen. All five were referred in early to mid-latency for social problems that had begun in early latency, consisting of aloofness from their peer group and overtly aggressive and devious behavior both in school and at home.

In each case children and parents associated the onset of the child's difficulties with his or her first meaningful (as judged by the child's comments at the time) visual comparisons of his or her size with that of others. As a result of developing cognitive capabilities, the children had become aware of their comparative smallness. No previous problems with adjustment were reported for any of these children. All five were white and came from intact middle-class families where the parental contribution to the child's psychological problem was assessed to be minimal. The major discernible pathogenic event, then, appeared to be the child's recognition of his or her short stature.

Case 1, Joshua. Joshua was first seen at age six. His height was that of a four-year-old. In addition to his escalating aggressive behavior with peers, he had become impossible to control at home, especially by his mother. When she disciplined him, he became enraged. When he was sent to his room he remained defiant, stoically refusing to show any emotion. When his parents attempted physical punishment, he defied them and again showed no emotion.

In psychoanalysis he behaved similarly. Necessary attempts to contain his aggression resulted in menacing outbursts toward me. Characteristically he threatened to "punch out" my glasses, because, as he explained later, it was through my eyes that I could see his smallness. He repeatedly described or played out the humiliation and anxiety he experienced when others could see how small he was. He often stalked off or screamed that he did not want anyone looking at him. At the same time he told me about his cousin Jeff, who protected him and "could beat up anyone."

As Joshua became invested in treatment and began to play more willingly, he developed in his games the theme of a fantasied mummy hidden by its wrappings but imbued with the power to surprise and destroy anyone. He enjoyed surprising, tricking, and scaring me. He was ecstatic as I played his frightened and helpless victim.

Eighteen months passed, and Joshua's disruptive behavior at home and school abated. He still had no close friends and blamed others for his failures. The analysis became bland as his play became repetitive and less affectively charged. I found myself impatient with his self-centered monologues. This state of affairs prevailed for about two years, when circumstances in his parents' life made it necessary for them to terminate his treatment.

At age ten (grade four) Joshua returned to treatment. His behavior had deteriorated during the previous several months after a few incidents in which other children had picked on him. His height discrepancy had become painfully obvious (he was the size of a five-year-old). He again had become overbearing with peers and disruptive in class, and his school performance had deteriorated. In my office, paradoxically, he was friendly and compliant, but also detached. It took five or six months before I understood that his lack of involvement was deliberate. He revealed that he had a "secret" and that he had been "lying" to me. There were a great many things on his mind, but he was unwilling to talk about them with me.

The essence of Joshua's secret was that he had learned to use his mind as a manipulative weapon. Rather than overtly defying others, he had become an expert at deceiving and frustrating them. His parents were well aware of this as he resisted their efforts to help him improve his school performance. When he was willing to talk openly, he and I formulated that he had grown into a real-life version of the mummy he used to fantasize about. He explained that although he could not use his body to fight the humiliation he experienced, he had learned to substitute his most powerful hidden asset, his mind.

Growth-hormone treatment was started at age ten and a half. Joshua's growth rate accelerated, but he continued to remain much shorter than his peers until about age seventeen, when he reached his final height of 5 feet 4 inches.

Over the next year and a half it became clear how little influence I had with Joshua. He appeared friendly, but his private life remained entirely inaccessible to me. He enjoyed frustrating and outsmarting me and everyone else in his life. Although there were severe social consequences as other children grew to detest his aloofness, he tenaciously held to his goal of upsetting everyone. Finally, Joshua provoked so much hostility in his peers that he was forced to transfer to another school.

During the following months Joshua continued to elude me. There was no point of intimate engagement. After settling into his new school, he again insisted that he was doing well, even though he had few friends and his schoolwork was spotty. Eventually it became unrewarding to continue the psychoanalysis and again we stopped.

In retrospect it is clear that Joshua had mastered the technique of becoming personally inaccessible. Nobody could crack into his closed system. Those who tried came away battered and angry. Most people eventually stopped trying. This state of affairs continued through his freshman year at an exclusive private high school. He exuded an air of perfect confidence, remained beyond influence, and failed miserably socially and at school. He was expelled from the school at the end of the year.

For the first time in his life, Joshua was visibly shaken by an event he had provoked, his expulsion from school. At age fourteen he finally began to recognize that the consequences of his behavior could seriously hurt him. While he continued to blame others for his day-to-day difficulties, he appealed to me for help. He returned to analysis and worked with me to create a neutral ground within which to talk. In that framework we could avoid his pitched battles for control and revenge.

As we worked together, Joshua began to think about making changes. With a deliberateness that matched his calculated efforts to defeat others, he methodically considered developing a new social identity. Working within a thoughtful analytic process, he conceived of replacing the diabolical work of the invincible, brilliant mummy with a different kind of personal power. He thought of redeploying his intellect (his "weapon") to understand himself and others. Similarly, within our own work, he would become an expert on the inner life of others. He would use his power to help and advise others rather than to frustrate them. He came to understand why he could not do that earlier. By his junior year Joshua had begun to implement these ideas and as a result was starting to make friends.

Vestiges of Joshua's omnipotence and egocentricity were still evident in analysis. For example, I found his self-righteous tirades about alleged injustices tiresome. He insisted that he had the power to influence people and would lapse into monologues on that subject. He used me as an accessory to accomplish his goals and as a sounding board for his complaints about how his parents misunderstood and tormented him. However, in general he could understand me when I interpreted his sometimes frantic need to be seen and heard and in control of others as well as his rage at feeling inconsequential.

As we prepared to separate, at the end of his senior year, the interpersonal quality of our work was quite different. Joshua now had several friends. His egocentricity was disappearing, and I usually enjoyed being with him. He had become insightful. On the other hand, his belief in his abilities still exceeded his performance. In spite of his A-level ideas he got only C+ grades in school.

Case 2, Bart. Bart was referred at age ten after his psychotherapist died. He had just started growth hormone treatment and had the physical appearance of a six- or seven-year-old. In spite of his excellent intellectual endowment, he was performing unacceptably in the private school he attended and generally seemed indifferent or hostile to attempts by teachers and parents to change. He had virtually no friends and spent most of his time secretly plotting small attacks on his peers and his sister. These assaults were subtly and brilliantly conceived, and he seemed to get great pleasure out of others' suffering.

In therapy he remained equally aloof but was willing to engage around strategy games, which he invariably won and in which the element of surprise was central. Through this vehicle he revealed his fantasy of becoming "an international jewel thief" with an organizing theme of being "invisible" and "undetectable." Although he was soon expelled from his school, psychotherapy prevented his expulsion from home, where his parents began to fear that he would kill his sister. Like the other short-stature children in this sample, he became more able to cooperate only after he could comprehend his boundless hatred of those who were bigger and who had caused him to feel humiliated.

The vehicle for his understanding was our work with a transference in which he thoroughly exploited me. He was cold and ruthless as he defeated me in games. He betrayed me by telling his parents that I disparaged them. He watched me squirm when he insisted I order in a jumbo sized pizza for his birthday. There was never a sign of care or empathy for me, no interest in my analytic comments.

Still, I did not give up on Bart and he continued to come to sessions. As with Joshua the first opening for collaboration came when he needed something vital from me. His father had grown to despise him and was planning to send him to boarding school. I intervened and prevented his exile. From that point he was willing to talk. He told me he hated being pushed around. He wanted to "kill all those bastards who teased him." His father was the worst one.

First we became partners in hatred. Soon it became the past indignities that were the offenders. Finally he could see his size as the culprit and entertain the possibility that there might be alternatives to his indiscriminate rage and revenge. He then dedicated himself to the goal of being admitted to a private high school. Therapy ended on a positive note soon after he matriculated. Upon graduation from high school he joined the Navy. Before long he recognized the potential value of his old skill at plotting strategies to defeat enemies. He competed for and was selected to enter a program that will train him to be a military strategist.

Case 3, Alex. Alex, a C.D. child, was referred at age eight because of "incorrigible attention-getting behavior" that had started between ages six and seven, soon after he became aware of "looking different" from other children and being "too small for people to notice." His parents removed him from psychotherapy several months later, but he returned at age twelve, when he was about to be expelled from school. Over the next several months the full extent of his secretive, antisocial behavior was revealed. He had rewired smoke alarms, ordered expensive items to be delivered to the homes of children he did not like, set off smoke bombs in public places, and begun to collect paramilitary paraphernalia. It became clear that he had an extraordinary capacity to fool people into believing that he was honest and forthright, even though he was contemptuous and hostile. Privately, he relished the capacity to "invisibly" outsmart and upset those who he felt had humiliated and overlooked him.

Unfortunately Alex never caught on. His system for avenging his perceived enemies was too slick. He was too practiced at being dishonest. He was expelled from school after school. Finally he was sent for a year to an educational program in Africa. All during this time his parents and I frantically tried to find ways to constructively involve him. Alex was uninterested.

Therapy was terminated during Alex's second high school year. He has come back to me frequently, usually in the midst of crises. He always seems interested in talking, but he has not changed. He remains headstrong and persists in being contentious toward the world at large.

Case 4, Erica. Erica, whose short stature was due to C.S.S., ultimately followed a course similar to the boys' except in its timing. Until about age ten, Erica had removed herself from her peers and used her parents for reassurance. From age ten, she shocked her parents by becoming hostile toward them, losing interest in school, making friends with older children, and becoming sexually promiscuous. She became proficient in concocting and implementing plots to annoy girls she envied and to thwart her parents. Erica's ability to attract attention was impressive. This included flaunting her body, particularly her ample breasts. As a result of psychotherapy this desire to be looked at and impress was restructured into a fervent and eventually successful interest in acting.

Case 5, Michael. Michael was four when his mother called for a consultation. He had just been diagnosed as C.D. His small size and winning disposition had made him everyone's pet. However, his parents wanted to anticipate and mitigate the psychological consequences of what promised to be a lifetime of short stature. It was tormenting for them to watch Michael's personality reverse over the next several years. Beginning at about age six, they began to receive reports from teachers that Michael was insensitive to other children and beyond their ability to control. He would talk endlessly, and he ignored rules and discipline.

While his peer relationships had been more than adequate at age six, by age nine Michael had alienated most other children. He was controlling in all aspects of social play and became combative if he felt another child opposed him. In psychotherapy, Michael represented himself as an invincible, superpowered being. In his play his survival was entirely dependent on his ingenuity. Unlike most other children of his age, he needed to do everything himself. He gave me the machines and army men and then devised ways to singlehandedly defeat us all.

Of particular concern was the absence of emotion in Michael's play and in our personal interaction. I tried to use my words and actions to build a meaningful connection with him. Several of the challenges of therapy were like those with Joshua in that my constant task was to maintain our engagement.

The Final Treatment Task. Treatment with these children was initially conducted conventionally, with engagement and insight as the goals. As the patient and I identified and worked through their feelings of humiliation and rage, these children accepted and accommodated to their short stature. Still, their vigilance had limited their social exposure during early school years and had impeded their social and cognitive development. They remained egocentric, limited in their ability to modulate intense affects, and lacking in social judgment. They were ignorant of the expectations that governed the behavior of others. They acted as if special rules without consequences applied to them. As part of each treatment I had to address these developmental deficits (A. Freud, 1976). As much as possible I maintained a close liaison with parents and teachers. School expectations and social decorum were discussed straightforwardly in our sessions. Some children required special remedial procedures. For example, Joshua spent his sophomore year in a small private high school where he was closely monitored and received individual help.

DISCUSSION

Clinical Features. The following features were common to these five cases: (1) These children were profoundly resentful of peers who were bigger and more physically powerful than they and who actively or implicitly made them feel small and humiliated. They began to experience this resentment from about age six, when they were first able to understand how small they were as compared to others. (2) These children used their wits to secretly outthink and frustrate others. Because they were limited in their ability to compete and retaliate physically, they planned and carried out active sabotage or became stubborn and obstructionist. Any attempt to contain or discipline them was perceived contemptuously as a confirmation that they had upset their victim and an invitation for further acts of perversity. (3) This posture made it impossible for these children to engage cooperatively with peers and distracted them from learning socially and in school.

A Developmental Perspective. In order to understand these powerful responses, we need to place them in a developmental framework. (1) *Preschool:* Cognitively, these children are egocentric and unlikely to be able to make objective comparisons between their physical size and prowess and those of others. While the size and cognitive limitations of all children of this age make them feel very vulnerable, most children can take refuge in the "absolute" protection of parents and other trusted adults. They also contain their fears with primitive play scenarios—for example, by crashing cars, which allows them to turn their passive experience of humiliation and anxiety into an active experience of mastery. (2) *Early latency:* Children of this age can begin to make accurate physical comparisons between themselves and others (C. Frankel, 1989). In part this development reflects the attenuation of the omnipotence and egocentricity associated with Piaget's pre-operational subperiod. This development occurs in conjunction with the resolution of oedipal issues and the consequent early turning away from intense emotional involvement with parents (Greenspan, 1979; Feiner, 1988). Once they comprehend their limitations, children of this age characteristically seek protection by aligning with fantasied omnipotent figures such as superheroes. They take on the identity of these figures in fantasy and play (Sarnoff, 1976). Socially, reassurance is also gained from the supportive association with other children and the early development of competence in interactional play (Whiteside, Busch, and Horner, 1976). Larger children begin to feel that they have some advantage. Children may reassure themselves of their immunity from harm and humiliation by teasing and victimizing smaller or more fearful children. (3) *Late latency:* Devices that provide magical reassurance become less necessary as children gain a sense of control and power through the development of real competencies. During this period, for example, children are able to acquire real athletic skills. They can picture themselves in meaningful social roles—for example, as gymnasts or dancers. In part, these developments are facilitated by identifications with the parent and other admired figures of the same sex.

For short-stature children, however, this process may begin to fail in early latency. As cognitive decentration occurs, these children recognize that they are smaller and more vulnerable than their peers. They are reminded of their size by comments, teasing, and physical mishandling by other children. They use the same mechanisms for reassurance as normal-stature children, such as testing of physical limits and identification with superheroes. However, these maneuvers may not be enough. These children may be compelled to fight a more extreme battle. They either regress and seek the protection of other adults and children by becoming mascots (as was the case with two of the short-stature children I treated), or they endeavor to become as intimidating as their perceived and, in some cases, real tormentors. Hypervigilance and omnipotent belligerence become mandatory.

Under these conditions resolution of the competition and anxiety associated with unattenuated oedipal concerns is delayed. These children find their peers, especially those of the same sex, dismissive and physically threatening. They miss out on the intense social interaction characteristic of this age period and fail to reach the level of social competence that normal-stature children achieve by late latency. Ego development resulting in improved internal regulation and the acquisition of skills is delayed.

The psychology of the short-stature children in my sample was complex. They came to regard themselves as exceptions to social rules (Freud, 1916; Jacobson, 1959) and felt entitled to compensation because of the indignities they had suffered and believed they would always have to endure. They were certain that they never would be able to compete straightforwardly and would require exceptional protection and luck to succeed. Added to this picture were actual social and academic deficiencies. These children also experienced exquisite pleasure in their ability to torment and deceive others. Left alone, the thinking and behavior I have described would probably have consolidated as part of each child's developing character structure.

Implications for Treatment and Management. The findings of this study have implications for prevention. Short stature first becomes a problem during early latency, when children can make meaningful visual comparisons with others. Parents can help their child anticipate and prepare for this event. In addition to offering explanations, they can, for example, help the child build skills that do not depend on height or strength and that have social value nonetheless.

In treatment the short-stature children I described needed first to come to terms with their resentment about their size disadvantage. A prerequisite for this development was full recognition of their small size and sense of physical vulnerability. Reaching this goal often required months or years of work. Initially all these children held fast to the belief that they could become normal or that in some hidden way they really *were* normal (Lussier, 1960). For Joshua this hope was fueled by the promise of a cure through growth-hormone treatment.

These defensive efforts were tenacious and reminiscent of those used by children with other compromising conditions. The short-stature children I have described created an illusion of being powerful by intimidating and tormenting others and refusing to cooperate with parents and teachers. In another publication (S. Frankel, 1991) I described how troubled late-adopted children withdrew from their adoptive parents and became secretive and devious after they could understand that they had been given up by their biological parents. Children with chronic illnesses such as diabetes or cardiac anomolies typically insist that they are normal and attempt to deny and reverse their own physical limitations and to devalue other peoples' good fortune. They also disregard medical restrictions.

Once they could face their disadvantage, the short-stature children in my sample could begin to devise adaptive solutions for themselves by using their actual competencies. In some cases these tactics incorporated skills they had developed earlier to compensate for their small size and vulnerability. For example, the theme of plotting strategies that governed Bart's omnipotent defense as an adolescent became central in his choice of a military career as a strategist.

These children had an additional limitation. Their anxiety, beginning in early latency, led to arrests in areas of social and cognitive development. In treatment it was necessary to address their social and academic deficiencies directly and sometimes to guide them through their encounters with peers and in school.

Summary

The short-stature children described here showed pathology reflective of two departures from the usual developmental process. These can be traced to the early latency years. The first is a constellation involving overestimation of the potential for harm and humiliation from other children, and a defensive response characterized by attempts to control and torment others. This mental set carries with it the omnipotent and egocentric thinking characteristic of the early latency period. The second departure consists of deficiencies in social and some aspects of cognitive development, a consequence of the immense preoccupation these children have with fighting their perceived "tormentors." Remediation involves addressing both issues.

This appraisal suggests that a child's observations and comparisons of physical attributes are likely to play an important role in development beginning at about age six. These normal experiences may be a powerful, albeit silent, part of the developmental process. Ordinarily they contribute to the consolidation of the child's sense of being competent and a progressive, realistic evaluation of self and others. It is when these comparisons are negative and provoke anxiety that this developmental activity is disruptive and becomes noticeable.

Finally, the constellation consisting of envy, withdrawal from others, substitution of an omnipotent belief system, and retaliation is not restricted to troubled short-stature children. Children who feel deviant because of other problematic physical or life-related circumstances behave in analogous ways. Apparently children in all these situations share a common set of subjective experiences.

BIBLIOGRAPHY

ABBOTT, D., ROTNEM, D., GENEL, M., & COHEN, D. J. (1982). Cognitive and emotional functioning in hypopituitary short-statured children. *Schizophrenia Bulletin* 8:310–319.

AVO, H., & PALOSAARI, U. (1992). Parental divorce, adolescence and transition to young adulthood: A followup study. *Amer. J. Orthopsychiat.* 62:421–429.

BAUMAN, S. (1981). Physical aspects of the self: A review of some aspects of body image development in childhood. *Psychiat. Clinics of North America* 4:455–470.

BLIZZARD, R. M., JOYCE, S., MITCHELL, T., JOHANSON, A. J., LIBBER, S., PLOTNICK, L., & MIGEON, C. J. (1986). Psychological impact of long-term growth hormone therapy. In *Human Growth Hormone*, ed. S. Raiti and R. A. Tolman. New York: Plenum, pp. 93–106.

CASTELNUOVO-TEDESCO, P. (1981). Psychological consequences of physical defects: A psychoanalytic perspective. *Int. Rev. Psycho-Anal.* 8:145–154.

CLOPPER, R. R., MACGILLIVRAY, M. H., MAZUR, T., VOORHESS, M. L., & MILLS, B. J. (1986). Post-treatment follow-up of growth hormone deficient patients: Psychosocial status. In *Slow Grows the Child*, ed. B. Stabler and L. Underwood. Hillsdale, N.J.: Erlbaum.

COEN, S. (1986). The sense of defect. *J. Amer. Psychoanal. Assn.* 34:47–67.

DE BEA, E. (1987). Body schema and identity. *Int. J. Psycho-anal.* 68:175–184.

DEAN, H. J., MCTAGGART, T. L., FISH, D. G., & FRIESEN, H. G. (1985). The education, vocational and marital status of growth hormone deficient adults treated with growth hormone during childhood. *Amer. J. of Diseases of Children* 139:1105–1110.

——— (1986). Long-term social follow-up of growth hormone deficient adults treated with growth hormone during childhood. In *Slow Grows the Child*, ed. B. Stabler and L. Underwood. Hillsdale, N.J.: Erlbaum.

DROTAR, D., OWENS, R., & GOTTHOLD, J. (1980). Personality adjustment of children and adolescents with hypopituitarism. *Child Psychiat. and Human Development* 11:59–66.

EMDE, R. (1983). The prerepresentational self and its affective core. *Psychoanal. Study of the Child* 38:165–192.

FEINER, K. (1987). Development of the concept of anatomical constancy: Part 1. *Psychoanal. Psychol.* 4:343–354.

——— (1988). A test of a theory of anxiety about body integrity: Part 2. *Psychoanal. Psychol.* 5:71–79.

FRANKEL, C. (1989). Pilot study to assess the ability of early school age children to make accurate visual comparisons between themselves and others. Unpublished.

FRANKEL, S. (1991). Pathogenic factors in the experience of early and late adopted children. *Psychoanal. Study of the Child* 46:91–108.

FREUD, A. (1976). Dynamic psychology and education. In *The Writings of Anna Freud, Volume 8, Psychoanalytic Psychology of Normal Development.* New York: Int. Univ. Press, pp. 307–314.

FREUD, S. (1916). The exceptions. *S.E.* 14:311–315.

GALATZER, A., ARAN, O., BEIT-HALACHMI, E., NOFAR, E., RUBITCHEK, J., PERTZELAN, A., & LARON, Z. (1987). The impact of long-term therapy by a multidisciplinary team on the education, occupation and marital status of growth hormone deficient patients after termination of therapy. *Clinical Endocrinology* 27:1991–1996.

GORDON, M., CROUTHAMEL, D., POST, E., & RICHMAN, F. (1982). Psychosocial aspects of constitutional short stature: Social competence, behavior problems, self-esteem, and family functioning. *Journal of Pediatrics* 101:477–480.

GREENSPAN, S. I. (1979). *Intelligence and Adaptation.* New York: Int. Univ. Press, pp. 187–196.

HOLMES, C. S., KARLSSON, J. A., & THOMPSON, R. G. (1986). Longitudinal evaluation of behavior patterns in children with short stature. In *Slow Grows the Child,* ed. B. Stabler and L. Underwood. Hillsdale, N.J.: Erlbaum.

HOLMES, C. S., HAYFORD, J. T., & THOMPSON, R. G. (1982). Personality and behavior differences in groups of boys with short stature. *Children's Health Care* 11:61–64.

JACOBSON, E. (1959). The "exception": An elaboration of Freud's character study. *Psychoanal. Study of the Child* 14:135–154.

KELLY, J. (1993). Current research on children's post-divorce adjustments: No simple answers. *Family and Conciliation Courts Review* 31:29–49.

LUSSIER, A. (1960). The analysis of a boy with a congenital handicap. *Psychoanal. Study of the Child* 15:430–453.

——— (1980). The physical handicap and the body ego. *Int. J. Psycho-Anal.* 61:179–185.

MITCHELL, C. M., JOHANSON, A. J., JOYCE, S., LIBBER, S., PLOTNICK, L., MIGEON, C. J., & BLIZZARD, R. M. (1986). Psychosocial impact of long-term growth hormone therapy. In *Slow Grows the Child*, ed. B. Stabler and L. Underwood. Hillsdale, N.J.: Erlbaum.

MONEY, J., & POLLITT, E. (1966). Studies in the psychology of dwarfism: II. Personality, maturation and response to growth hormone treatment. *J. Pediatrics* 68:381–390.

NIEDERLAND, W. (1965). Narcissistic ego impairment in patients with early physical malformations. *Psychoanal. Study of the Child* 20:518–534.

RICHMAN, R. A., GORDON, M., TEGTMEYER, P., CROUTHAMEL, C., & POST, E. M. (1986). Academic and emotional difficulties associated with constitutional short stature. In *Slow Grows the Child*, ed. B. Stabler and L. Underwood. Hillsdale, N.J.: Erlbaum.

RITVO, S. (1984). The image and uses of the body in psychic conflict: With special reference to eating disorders in adolescence. *Psychoanal. Study of the Child* 39:449–469.

ROSENFELD, R., & HINTZ, D. (1983). Diagnosis and management of growth disorders. *Drug Therapy*, May 1983, pp. 33–48.

ROTNEM, D., GENEL, M., HINTZ, R. L., & COHEN, D. J. (1977). Personality development in children with growth hormone deficiency. *J. Amer. Acad. Child Psychiat.* 16:412–426.

SANDBERG, D. E., BROOK, A. E., & CAMPOS, S. P. (1994). Short stature in middle childhood: A survey of psychosocial functioning in a clinic-referred sample. In *Growth, Stature, and Adaptation: Behavioral, Social, and Cognitive Aspects of Growth Delay*, ed. B. Stabler and L. Underwood. Chapel Hill: University of North Carolina Press, pp. 19–34.

SARNOFF, C. (1976). *Latency*. New York: Aronson.

SKUSE, D., GILMOUR, J., TIAN, C. S., & HINDMARSH, P. (1994). Psychosocial assessment of children with short stature: A preliminary report. *Acta Paediatr. Suppl.* 406:11–16.

STABLER, B., CLOPPER, R., SIEGEL, P., STOPPANI, C., COMPTON, P., & UNDERWOOD, L. (1994). Academic achievement and psychological adjustment in short children. *Developmental and Behavioral Pediatrics* 15:1–6.

STABLER, B., TANCER, M., RANC, J., & UNDERWOOD, L. (1994). Psychiatric symptoms in young adults treated for growth hormone deficiency in childhood. In *Growth, Stature, and Adaptation: Behavioral, Social, and Cognitive Aspects of Growth Delay*, ed. B. Stabler and L. Underwood. Chapel Hill: University of North Carolina Press, pp. 99–106.

STABLER, B., & UNDERWOOD, L. (1977). Anxiety and locus of control in hypopituitary dwarf children. *Research Relating to Children Bulletin* 38:75–81.

STABLER, B., WHITT, J., MOREAULT, D., D'ERCOLE, A., & UNDERWOOD, L. (1980). Social judgements by children of short stature. *Psychological Reports* 46:743–746.

STEINHAUSEN, H., & STAHNKE, N. (1976). Psychoendocrinological studies in dwarfed children and adolescents. *Archives of Disease in Childhood* 51:778–783.

VANCE, M., INGERSOLL, G., & GOLDEN, M. (1994). Short stature in a nonclinical sample: Not a big problem. In *Growth, Stature, and Adaptation: Behavioral, Social, and Cognitive Aspects of Growth Delay,* ed. B. Stabler and L. Underwood. Chapel Hill: University of North Carolina Press, pp. 35–46.

VOSS, L., & MULLIGAN, J. (1994). The short normal child in school: Self-esteem, behavior, and attainment before puberty (The Wessex Growth Study). In *Growth, Stature, and Adaptation: Behavioral, Social, and Cognitive Aspects of Growth Delay,* ed. B. Stabler and L. Underwood. Chapel Hill: University of North Carolina Press, pp. 47–64.

WHITESIDE, M., BUSCH, F., & HORNER, T. (1976). From egocentric to cooperative play in young children. *J. Amer. Acad. Child Psychiat.* 15:294–313.

YOUNG-HYMAN, D. (1986). Effects of short stature on social competence. In *Slow Grows the Child,* ed. B. Stabler and L. Underwood. Hillsdale, N.J.: Erlbaum.

ZIMET, G., CUTLER, M., LITVENE, M., OWENS, R., DAHMS, W., & CUTTLER, L. (1994). Psychosocial functioning of adults who were short as children. In *Growth, Stature, and Adaptation: Behavioral, Social, and Cognitive Aspects of Growth Delay,* ed. B. Stabler and L. Underwood. Chapel Hill: University of North Carolina Press, pp. 73–82.

Mother's Milk

A Psychoanalyst Looks at Breastfeeding

MICHELLE E. FRIEDMAN, M.D.

This chapter examines the complex experiences and meanings of breast-feeding for women engaged in it. My review of the sparse literature to date reveals that understanding of breastfeeding has been limited largely to an oral perspective. The sociology and physiology of lactation are sketched here to provide a background for the multifaceted psychic experiences reported by breastfeeding women. Within this more complex context it can be demonstrated that breastfeeding kindles aspects of all the psychosexual stages, touching off a cascade of fantasies and feelings in the nursing woman. Case vignettes also illustrate the broad clinical utility of an interest in breastfeeding.

The question arises as to why there has been such reticence on the part of both patients and analysts regarding breastfeeding. Paying attention to this activity can yield rich and useful information about the nursing mother's unconscious attitudes. Issues of power, competence, erotism, and aggression are discussed in addition to those of orality and nurturance.

> Then said his sister to Pharaoh's daughter: "Shall I go
> and call thee a nurse of the Hebrew women, that she
> may nurse the child for thee?" And Pharaoh's daugh-
> ter said to her: "Go." And the maiden went and called
> the child's mother.
>
> —Exodus 2:7,8

Assistant clinical professor of psychiatry, Mt. Sinai Hospital and Medical Center; lecturer, Columbia University Center for Psychoanalytic Training and Research; and psychiatrist in private practice in New York City.

The Psychoanalytic Study of the Child 51, ed. Albert J. Solnit, Peter B. Neubauer, Samuel Abrams, and A. Scott Dowling (Yale University Press, copyright © 1996 by Albert J. Solnit, Peter B. Neubauer, Samuel Abrams, and A. Scott Dowling).

FOR MOST WOMEN, FEEDING A BABY AT THE BREAST IS A REMARKABLE, stirring, natural, and somewhat strange experience. Breastfeeding is an entirely elective activity that is initiated at birth and may continue for a few days to a few years. Because feeding is the paramount communicative activity between a mother and her infant, a woman nursing for the first time experiences herself and her breasts in an entirely new way.

In our field, which is so rooted in tissue–mucosal membrane–level experiences, one would expect special curiosity about nursing. It is, after all, a female adult body function that has no direct childhood precedent experiences for the little girl, who in fact lacks the necessary equipment until puberty. How does the nursing mother unconsciously make sense of feeding her baby directly from her own body? My observations suggest that the psychic experience of breastfeeding is an amalgam of fantasies evoked from successive psychosexual stages, oral through oedipal. One example, which I discuss later, is the blatant similarity between the lactating breast and the functioning penis. Both have erectile capacity, produce a powerful substance, and are a source of pride and anxiety to their possessors.

A secondary point of interest is the paucity of analytic literature concerning mothers' feelings and fantasies about nursing as compared with the copious writing on babies' experiences of feeding. Considering that adult women can provide much more accessible data, I found this especially intriguing, and I speculate on reasons for it. Paying attention to nursing mothers' inner experiences can yield insights into the developmentally layered psychology of women. Examples from my own practice illustrate the clinical applicability of these insights.

LITERATURE REVIEW

The analytic literature is replete with inferences about the effects of breastfeeding on the infant. To date, however, psychoanalytic inquiry into the maternal side of nursing is strikingly spare. This sparse literature has focused almost exclusively on the oral phase of development. Breastfeeding has been credited with reviving feelings and fantasies embedded in the nursing mother's early life, particularly in her relationship with her own mother. This is a limited view in that it ignores later developmental factors that modify and transform the oral beginnings of the breastfeeding experience.

Also rare in the psychoanalytic literature are detailed case reports of the postpartum period that specifically address breastfeeding, despite greater recent analytic interest in pregnancy. The *Guide to the Language of Psychoanalysis* (Klumpner, 1992) includes no mention of breastfeeding, although one finds an entry for both *breast* and *breast envy.* In fact, with one exception, the few clinical discussions on the subject date back several decades.

Merell Middlemore (1941), who was trained both in obstetrics and psychoanalysis, is frank about the difficulties women often have in undertaking breastfeeding and attributes them to anxieties from such sources as the mothers' own suckling experiences, which provide the basis of unconscious oral fantasies of biting and destroying. She also discusses women's anxiety about the sensual pleasure they may feel while nursing. A common expression of these conflicts, according to Middlemore, is for the mother to have misgivings about her ability to feed and to worry that the quality of her milk is "bad." In optimal circumstances, mother and child mutually adapt and form a successful nursing couple.

Helene Deutsch (1944, 1945) devoted significant attention to the influence of psychological factors, particularly aggression, on breastfeeding and weaning. She diagnosed one young mother's inability to provide milk at feeding times despite copious breast leaking between attempted nursings as stemming from her ambivalence toward her newborn. By comparing this symptom with premature ejaculation, in which the timing of fluid delivery is also a problem, Deutsch suggests a penis-breast parallel. Her lively descriptions of nursing situations include observations of the direct and primitive satisfaction of women who devote themselves wholeheartedly to nursing and often say they feel like "contented cows." Despite a fundamental commitment to the matrix of feminine masochism. Deutsch concedes that not only "feminine-passive" but also "masculine-aggressive" mothers enjoy breastfeeding. The latter group, she feels, is pleasurably motivated by the proud accomplishment of lactation and the fulfillment of the needs of the child. In contrast, if a mother feels that her ego is endangered by the baby, whom she perceives as overwhelmingly needy and devouring, she may reject the child and stop nursing.

Deutsch says that breastfeeding affects women in all cultures. She points out that the frequent idealization of mothering in primitive societies leads to a distorted notion that nursing poses few if any problems for these seemingly less psychologically complicated women. Deutsch describes magical rituals, formulas, and superstitions among all peoples to defend against the catastrophe of mother's milk drying up. She analyzes several myths involving infant exposure—the stories of Romulus and Remus and of baby Moses, for example—as incorporating mothers' efforts to protect their offspring not only from threatening father figures but also from their own destructive impulses potentially unleashed in the throes of maternal lactation conflicts.

Marie Langer (1945) offers a Kleinian perspective on women's experience of breastfeeding in that she understands the psychological problems of breastfeeding as stemming from a woman's own oral dissatisfactions. Langer feels that this conflicted position reveals the persistence of aggressive infantile attitudes toward the nursing woman's own mother, which then contribute to her sabotage of the adult responsible-mothering role.

In his classic paper on the transitional object, D. W. Winnicott (1951) regards the breast or breast substitute as the crucial first object that allows the infant the illusion of creating reality; this in turn sets the child on the road to separation from the mother. Winnicott expects that the mother's own experience of feeding will be evoked. He cites a clinical case in which a mother's awareness of her first son's intense attachment to his exclusive breastfeeding led her to use an occasional bottle with her second son, yielding a more relaxed outcome. In another paper on basic emotional development (1945), Winnicott acknowledges that breastfeeding can be difficult and entreats mothers, who after all are more mature than their offspring, to be tolerant and understanding of their babies.

Therese Benedek's (1959, 1970) discussions of breastfeeding hint at a broader view and are integrated in her theory that personality continues to develop past adolescence. She sees parenthood as a crucial developmental phase for both men and women and views mothering as a powerful, drive-motivated activity that draws on a lifelong experience of the sexual response cycle. She also emphasizes the new mother's positive feminine identification with her own preoedipal mother. Like Deutsch, Benedek points out the modern woman's conflict in establishing her identity as a mother in a confusing cultural climate that champions outwardly directed achievement (not related to motherhood) but extolls the passive and regressive aspects of mother-dependent baby care.

In his effort to correlate psychoanalytic concepts with physiological data, Marcel Heiman (1963) notes that the breast as well as the uterus is a target organ for the neurohormone oxytocin. For him as for Deutsch, suckling and coitus have bedrock biologic and symbolic interconnections. Just as the breast actively engages the infant's mouth, so the vagina incorporates the penis; thus both restore a primordial condition of unity.

Charles Sarlin (1963, 1981) views breastfeeding as a primal scene, a way of integrating nursing into the rich composite of developmental epochs. According to his intriguing schema, the nursing infant is participating in and simultaneously viewing a mutual, openly erotic relationship with the mother. This stands in distinct contrast with the more familiar situation of the phallic-oedipal period, when the child is accorded envious, spectator-only status.

Ruth Lawrence's (1994) compendium on breastfeeding, which is designed for a general medical readership, contains many insights into the maternal side of nursing. Describing the decline of breastfeeding in this century, she criticizes modern society for failing to support what she feels is a clearly superior means of infant feeding. According to Lawrence, women may have internal conflicts regarding their biological maternal role versus their other social roles. Further, they may experience anxiety at seeing their breasts as organs for feeding as opposed to sexual enjoyment. In this formulation, in which the breast is likened to the penis as a source of pleasure, nursing may represent a castration threat.

These dichotomous versions of the female bosom, the sacred maternal feeding font and the profane erogenous breast, are explored by Serge Lebovici and Evelyne Kestemberg (1993). They present a case in which a single woman whose mother died of breast cancer seduces her toddler daughter into prolonged nursing. This pathological mutual dependence on breastfeeding suppressed the child's strivings toward autonomy, to maintain the mother's oedipal attachment with the dead grandmother, and to curtail any potential romantic or erotic relationships for the mother.

Discomfort with discussing breastfeeding is certainly not limited to the analytic community. In a scholarly feminist article Linda M. Blum (1993) discusses in gender-oriented political, racial, and economic terms the difficulties breastfeeding poses. Blum points out that the feminist community has addressed more the inequities surrounding pregnancy and childbirth than the challenges posed by breastfeeding. She suggests that feminists, too, have difficulty meeting the extensive time and availability demands imposed by nursing; in pregnancy women have relative autonomy and freedom of movement, and birth is simply a far shorter event.

DISCUSSION

The meaning of nursing for a woman can best be understood by exploring it as a developmental experience that potentially enfolds and reorganizes traces of earlier libidinal and aggressive epochs. To introduce the multiple meanings of breastfeeding, I include a review of several sociologic factors and the basic physiology of lactation (Lawrence, 1994).

Among members of the college-educated, upper-middle-class group that currently comes to analysis, there is an expectation that a mother will breastfeed her baby (Blum, 1993). Whether the manifest motivation for this expectation is concern about the infant's nutrition or immune fortification, bonding, the mother's health, or other issues, cultural peer pressure to breastfeed has been a powerful influence for at least the past decade. Questions about feeding babies are inevitably discussed by mothers, and a woman who doesn't breastfeed almost invariably seems compelled to offer an explanation of her decision.

It is rare for a pregnant woman in this population to announce that she has no intention of nursing. She may articulate a revulsion for the physicality of breastfeeding or resent the impositions on her time and mobility. She may also worry that nursing will cause her breasts to lose their shape, rendering her less sexually attractive. For centuries these concerns motivated upper-class women to hire wet nurses (Fildes, 1986). Extensive research confirms that preconceived attitudes about nursing prevail in the immediate postpartum period. Uncertainty about the decision to breastfeed, lack of confidence in the ability to do so, delayed first-breastfeeding contact with the baby, and depression all contribute to early nursing failures (Buxton et al., 1991; Cooper et al., 1993).

Lactation is a remarkable physiological function. A woman who decides to nurse has made a choice, albeit a complicated one in today's industrialized society, to continue to feed the baby she nourished passively in utero. The breasts, whatever their meaning to her before childbirth—ornamental, burdensome, sexual—take on a purposeful value. The breasts' actual shape, behavior, and sensation alter dramatically. The pregnant woman usually has some breast tenderness and enlargement. Early in postpartum, the breasts produce colostrum, a high-protein, immune-fortifying precursor to breast milk, which itself generally is produced a few days after childbirth. Lactating women have bigger breasts as well as broader and darker areolae than before becoming pregnant. However transiently, the nursing mother who was not particularly full-bosomed before finally has perfect breasts, firm and full, universally idealized.

The nipple itself can become erect and elongate by as much as a centimeter when stimulated erotically or when the infant latches on to it to begin feeding. Sarlin (1963) reminds us that the only organs capable of this erection are the nipple, the clitoris, and the penis. The baby's latching on stimulates the mother's milk letdown, an oxytocin mediated reflex that allows breast milk flow to begin. These sensations along with suckling may elicit a range of physical feelings including uterine contractions and intense pain in the early days of nursing—or later if there are such complications as cracked nipples or mastitis. On the other hand, many women find nursing immensely relaxing and sensually gratifying even to the point of orgasm.

Sexual fantasies that have evolved throughout a woman's development and are usually evoked during genital sexual activities may become available during breastfeeding. One mother, for example, became aware during nursing of a familiar boredom, underwritten by a fantasy of being trapped in a cave. Analytic work clarified the connection to a familiar sadomasochistic fantasy of entrapment that was both pleasurable and confining in her sexual relationship with her husband.

A nursing mother may be disturbed to feel anything frankly erotic while so close to her baby, or she may find that this reactivity facilitates the return of her active sexual life with her spouse. The decreased sexual drive often reported by breastfeeding women may also be a result of fatigue, the hormonal changes caused by lactation, or the sense of libinal satisfaction through the exclusive "love affair" with a nursing baby.

Husbands of women who breastfeed have a variety of reactions, ranging from enjoyment of their wives' milk-filled breasts and pride in their babies' having this nourishing experience to feeling shut out and jealous. It follows that a woman's decision to undertake and continue nursing may be influenced by her husband's fantasies and attitudes (Waletzky, 1979).

Young children spend a lot of time around their nursing mothers and infant siblings. Kleeman (1971) tells us that the breast as a powerful and capable organ system is evident in children's play and fantasy. Direct observation of the hungry baby taking in a substantial portion of the mother's breast and being satisfied undoubtedly leaves a vivid impression on the spectator/sibling in contrast with the unclear notions that he or she still has of female genitalia. The exclusion of the watching child from the nursing dyad provides another model for later triadic primal scenes in which the observer is the outsider and third party. At the same time, the sight of the nursing sibling's face busily buried in the mother's breast elicits fantasies of breastfeeding as a powerful and confusing female function. The often-heard question posed by older children, "Mommy, is the baby eating you?" illustrates how comfort and feeding are mixed with cannibalistic notions. Thus, for a woman who already has children, such reactions may be factors in her decision to breastfeed a new baby.

The quality and quantity of breast milk have a multiplicity of meanings that have a prized, phallic tone. Breast milk is readily palpable, visible, can be expressed and even squirted some distance. The phallic and breast systems endow their possessors with particular power, vulnerability, and status. In his exegesis of the biblical quotation that prefaces this chapter, the medieval commentator Rashi appears to wonder why Pharoah's daughter would even risk choosing a Hebrew wet nurse. His interpretation, embedded in a complex rabbinic literature, asserts that the baby Moses refused the milk of Egyptian women (Cohen, 1966; Flashman, 1992). Rashi thus supports the notion that mother's milk has intrinsic, recognizable properties far beyond its biologically nutritive value.

The nursing mother not only is in near-total charge of her baby's nourishment and bowel function—for each feeding usually ends in a diaper change—but also she can choose to pacify distress or lull the baby to sleep via breastfeeding. At the same time, she must relinquish some freedom of movement and tolerate possible discomfort in order to be available to her baby. In fact, the common male fantasy of "use it or lose it" (referring to the erect penis) holds true for a nursing mother, whose breast milk will dwindle if she skips feedings.

The woman's experience as provider of this powerful substance evokes feelings and fantasies of competence that are usually termed phallic but resonate with all stages of psychosexual development, including oral, urinary, and anal ones. An analysand, one of my own patients, who had proudly nursed her children prior to her analysis was engaged in an intense erotic homosexual transference to me when, several months after I returned from my maternity leave, she angrily described the following masturbatory fantasy: "I imagined that milk was coming out of your breasts like a stream. I had the idea that it's like a penis that ejaculates. . . . It's the same thing, life is coming out, and it's for me." This woman's fantasies had occasionally featured her using a dildo strapped on like a penis. It seemed to me that she was suffering from a castration reaction such as that described by Lawrence (1994) and Lebovici and Kestemberg (1993). My breasts had taken on the importance of a powerful, penetrating penis that dwarfed both her now-flaccid breasts and her fantasy toy penis. Despite much interpretation, her rage at me for being unavailable when she desperately wanted my attention remained a powerful resistance. The patient's feeling of crushing loss in her competition with my child was made clear when she furiously accused me of nursing my infant during a phone call with her.

Competitiveness among friends and between generations over milk production may be undisguised in the conversations of women who bemoan with pride their leaking breasts. The nursing mother who feels a glow of pride in her milk's becoming the baby's firm flesh delights in announcing the child's weight gains and eagerly shares her unconscious fantasy of continued fusion in thinking, "It all came from me!" Breastfeeding women also express satisfaction in their babies' fecal products as they compare the yellow stools their babies make with the more malodorous brown ones of formula-fed infants. In contrast, pediatricians, obstetricians, and a host of lactation consultants are besieged by anxious nursing mothers who are not sure that they can provide the proper nutrition for their babies, especially when they compare their thin-looking bluish breast milk with the seemingly richer commercial formula. The unconscious fantasy of her milk as inferior or even poisonous was operative for one such woman who, despite her baby's adequate weight gain, discontinued breastfeeding.

The enhanced sense of bodily integrity and competence associated with breastfeeding may have important compensatory meaning for women who either have overcome serious personal medical problems or have current physical limitations. One of the women who spoke most glowingly to me of her enjoyment of nursing had conquered lymphoma as a bride and gone on to bear several healthy children. Similarly, a mother of two who was severely handicapped by early polio describes breastfeeding as one of the few physical functions she could provide for her babies.

The restorative significance of breast milk may also motivate some mothers of very ill or impaired neonates to pump their breasts. As a result of their babies' medical conditions, these mothers are deprived of most of the usual tending activities through which parents convey love and concern. Expressing her milk helped one mother of an extremely premature infant feel that she could do something special for her baby amid all the high-tech equipment surrounding him. Regularly collecting her milk helped support her fantasy that her son would soon be coming home, where he would be able to breastfeed directly from her.

A further distinction between breastfeeding and supplying breast milk is worth making because nursing and pumping and storing breast milk to be given in a bottle by another caretaker are very different experiences for the mother (Furman, 1993). Although pumping is necessary for women who wish to breastfeed but are not available for a significant number of feedings, some women who need to rely on bottle usage fantasize that formula is poison. These women refuse to use it or, if they do allow an occasional commercial bottle, can't bring themselves to purchase it in the store or to prepare it themselves.

Maintaining an abundant frozen supply of breast milk may also be gratifying for nursing women who are responding to memories of the meager emotional pantries of their own childhoods. Additional meaning may be gleaned from these neatly labeled and stacked reserve stores of breast milk as they concretize a fantasy of omni-availability of their precious body fluid. This bottled breast milk may assume a fetishistic quality if it substitutes for other, more immediate forms of nurturance that require the mother's presence. Blum (1993) warns against the trend of employers' providing breast-pumping stations, which she sees as insidiously undermining efforts toward achieving the truly needed goals of job flexibility with maternal leaves and on-site nurseries.

The triadic configuration of the nursing couple plus onlooker(s) sets the stage for the abundant exhibitionistic excitement and inhibition seen in both nursing women and observers. Larger breasts, outlines of nursing pads, and stains on clothing from leaks are among the signs of nursing activity that can evoke pride or embarrassment.

Public breastfeeding is a compelling sight and elicits wonder, tenderness, or absolute horror and disgust in onlookers. Uneasiness is probably felt by most spectators to a breastfeeding; should one look or turn away? Women who never previously bared their bosoms in public routinely describe breastfeeding their babies quite comfortably in front of their fathers, male friends, or even complete strangers. When asked about this behavior, women usually invoke the desexualization of their breasts through frequent feeding or habit, but I suspect that there is really an active excitement and desire to display their breasts. Conversely, conflicts over privacy and exhibitionistic impulses may be manifested in the woman who nurses only after dramatically arranging her garments or resentfully withdrawing to a more private room.

One new mother described her own awareness of the desire to be appreciated while "performing" when she brought her several-week-old infant to a restaurant and, while feeding him, became annoyed because everyone wasn't watching her. She became aware of feeling hurt again later, when her growing and increasingly curious baby began at around five months to glance away from her during nursing.

The desire to display both baby and competent mothering is frequently enacted in the not-so-rare phenomenon of new mothers' bringing their babies to analytic appointments. Although they may claim they couldn't find a babysitter, there is clearly a wish to show the analyst the mother's highly invested creation. An analysand "accidentally" became pregnant during her first year of analysis and seriously debated having an abortion. Her mother had accompanied the patient to her one prior abortion, which occurred early in her relationship with the man she eventually married. Although she and her husband were well off and wanted children eventually, she expressed concern about adding a further impediment to her already significant creative block. Analytic work clarified deeper worries about following in her mother's footsteps, which the patient saw as total devotion to family. The reconstructed parental legacy, however, revealed staggering neglect by both mother and father, whose self-absorption resulted in their overlooking multiple sexual-abuse situations involving my patient and her siblings. She decided to keep the pregnancy.

Two weeks following a cesarean section she returned to analysis with her son in tow, whom she placed on her clothed bosom as she lay on the couch. When the need arose, she quietly and modestly nursed and then gently rocked her baby. She was unable to verbalize much of her inner experience then, but we established over time that the critical meaning of this behavior, which continued for several weeks, was to demonstrate for me her empathy toward and attunement with her child. My patient had created a new, cozy little family of three in the office, where she was acting out a part of her fantasy of me as the analytic father of her child. For, although her husband, who was closely identified with her family of origin, was certainly the infant's biological father, the certainty that the fetus would become a baby was conceived during discussions with me.

How long a woman breastfeeds a child is a decision with many determinants. Illness in the mother, an urgent situation requiring her full-time availability, the desire to become pregnant again, and the wish to "have my body back for myself" are among the reasons given for weaning. Women who enjoy breastfeeding often express feelings of sadness at weaning. Trad (1990) describes a previously well-adapted mother who became despondent when her child initiated weaning. In this case brief psychotherapy helped to clarify the mother's fear of the disruption of their special intimacy and to relieve her guilt at feeling that she was stifling his progress for her own needs.

There is certainly a darker side to breastfeeding. Even in the best situations, nursing is hard work. Most new mothers who plan on breastfeeding have a romantic view of the experience. They are unprepared for the possible hurdles to pleasurable nursing. In addition to the problems previously mentioned, the lactating woman must empty her breasts regularly to relieve the discomfort of engorgement and to maintain her milk supply. The mutuality of the nursing couple takes on an angrier tone when the mother's comfort depends on her seemingly ungrateful infant's sucking competence, just as the baby's comfort depends on the mother's making her milk supply available. Who is the giver and who is the receiver?

The feeling of being depended on as a sole source of food oscillates between pleasurable omnipotence and fear of being depleted or even devoured by an insatiable parasite. A woman who deeply enjoyed pregnancy and breastfeeding reported a disquieting shift when her second baby was nine months old and had several teeth: "I had a sense of him eating me up. . . . I could imagine the baby's teeth cutting into my breast and mixing up my blood and milk."

Perceived nursing failures are devastating. A baby who cries inconsolably or does not gain weight is painfully disappointing to the mother invested in breastfeeding. Women who are accustomed to being high achievers and who planned on devoting themselves to their newborn babies during a finite maternity leave have particular difficulty with their perceived incompetence. Middlemore, Deutsch, Langer, and Benedek have highlighted unresolved early oral conflicts in the infancy and childhood of new mothers to explain the psychologic problems of nursing. What warrants further attention is how struggles over control, mastery, and self-esteem, more typically associated with post-oral psychosexual stages, become entangled in some nursing dramas and feed into a cycle of frustration, anger, and depression.

A young woman presented with an acute depression two months after the birth of her second child. My initial open-ended consultation yielded much valuable history, including a past eating disorder that was described in a muted, sad, and reluctant tone. Specific questioning about the baby's feeding, however, brought a flood of tears and words. The patient was excruciatingly remorseful and self-critical about having quit breastfeeding after a week when, despite her milk-filled breasts, she couldn't get the baby to latch on properly and feed adequately. She was enraged at the nursing "experts" who had given her advice that had not worked, impatient with her husband's attempts to comfort her, and embarrassed in front of other new mothers in her neighborhood, all of whom seemed to be nursing champions. Although many deeper issues clearly awaited exploration, it was clear to me that the key to establishing a working alliance with this distressed woman was to validate and further explore her experience of breastfeeding.

Another new mother, the daughter of Holocaust survivors, was struggling with overwhelming despondency and a sense of failure as her dedicated efforts to breastfeed were met with a crying, miserable infant who did not gain weight. A professional herself, who planned on returning to work part-time in several months, she was aware of intense competition with her homemaker sister, who had exclusively nursed her own four children, each for at least a year.

As the patient deliberated about her decision to wean her baby, she was struck by her intense response to a newspaper description of a stranded snowbound couple and their baby, who was sustained during the ordeal by his nursing mother. The description triggered her own fantasies of survival, such as hiding in and living off the forest, which had been honed through years of hearing family tales of underground daring and partisan heroism during the war. Analytic exploration deepened her awareness of comparison of herself not only with her sister but also with her parents, whose near-miraculous survival epics seemed to dwarf her own more prosaic odyssey of childhood.

The transference, which had been characterized by a tense, oedipal rivalry, assumed an unprecedented maternal and tender tone. The patient could now allow herself to analyze the profound vulnerability she had unconsciously felt and warded off during her pregnancy. It had been kindled into symptomatic consciousness by the birth of her helpless and dependent first baby. The patient's anger at her mother's remoteness and depression during her own early years as well as her ambivalence over entitlement to a happy family of her own creation became newly available for important analytic work.

This patient also brought her baby to a few sessions and breastfed, but, in contrast to the earlier-described woman, who nursed and soothed her baby on the couch with ease, this painful demonstration appeared to be a plea for intervention and help. She weaned her baby after nine weeks. Her rumination and anxiety about breastfeeding gradually lessened but fully abated only after she successfully breastfed a second child. Until then, she reported, albeit with rueful humor, that she felt a wistful pang whenever she caught sight of other women nursing.

Like the scant literature, interviews I conducted with women who bore and nursed babies while in analysis revealed how rarely either they or their analysts, male and female, had mentioned breastfeeding during treatment. Most of these women found nursing to be positive and rewarding, something that "felt private" or "just didn't come up" in sessions. True, there are many intimate experiences and bodily functions that analysands are reluctant to discuss in treatment. I hope the specific questions of this paper add to an understanding of the larger mysteries of privacy. I can only speculate as to why there is such analytic reticence from patients and their analysts when it comes to breastfeeding. From the patient's side, "forgetting" to discuss breastfeeding might serve to sequester a host of unconscious material, including ambivalent feelings toward the infant and fantasies that elaborate the analyst's involvement in the baby's conception. Engagement in the ongoing intimate behavior of nursing also creates another variant of the primal-scene triad, one in which the analyst is the observer excluded from the secret couple of mother and baby.

As for the reserve on the part of analysts, breastfeeding might be understood simply as one more aspect of women's experience that our field, until recently, has had trouble with. Even so, more attention has been devoted to wombs and vaginas. It may be that there is a degree of unconscious collusion by analysts of both sexes to leave unanalyzed and pure some primordial sanctuary of motherhood. For example, among writings on infancy one detects a kind of glorification of the visual attunement between mother and baby during feeding (Stern, 1977). Mothers and nursing babies do gaze at each other blissfully—sometimes. But devoted and loving mothers who extoll the pleasures of breastfeeding also talk on the phone, watch television, and read novels while they nurse. Especially during the early weeks of an infant's life, the many hours a woman daily spends nursing may be the only quiet, relatively relaxed waking time she has.

In his discussion of hate in the countertransference, Winnicott (1947) points out the parallels between the hatred an analyst eventually will feel for his patient and that which a mother has for her infant from the start. Both analysands and babies are demanding, frustrating, and even dangerous. Successful navigation of these passionate and stormy emotional waters requires that analysts and mothers be mature enough to tolerate the inevitable hate that will be generated and the uncertain wait until rewards will come.

It could be that the analytic gaze from both the analyst and analysand are averted from breastfeeding in order to avoid confronting a situation fraught with unconscious fantasies, memories, and provocative dyadic as well as triadic primal scenes. The compromise of the analyst's seeming disregard staves off such contamination and preserves some shard of a relationship that is mostly out of bounds to the sullying effects of sexuality, aggression, competition, and anger.

CONCLUSION

One need only to initiate conversation with a woman about her nursing days for her to launch into an animated discussion with all sorts of detail and implied meaning. No matter how many years have passed since the actual experience, women are eager to share their triumphs and tribulations with regard to nursing and to offer advice to new mothers with whom they have no other connection. This experience has not yet found its place in the analytic literature.

Enlarging the sphere of drive derivatives and object involvement to include all psychosexual stages available to the nursing mother illuminates a wealth of clinical situations ranging from turbulent postpartum states to more subtle experiences of ongoing parenthood. This inquiry into breastfeeding may stimulate interest in and lead to greater understanding of this aspect of womanly experience.

BIBLIOGRAPHY

ANTHONY, E. J., & BENEDEK, T., eds. (1970). Motherhood and nurturing. In *Parenthood, Its Psychology and Psychopathology* 153–165. Boston: Little, Brown.

BENEDEK, T. (1959). Parenthood as a developmental phase. *J. Amer. Psychoanal. Assn.* 7:389–417.

BLUM, L. (1993). Mothers, babies, and breastfeeding in late capitalist America: The shifting contexts of feminist theory. *Feminist Studies* (19)2:291–311.

BUXTON, K. E., GIELEN, A. C., FADEN, R. R.,BROWN, C. H., ET AL. (1991). "Women intending to breastfeed: Predictors of early infant feeding experiences. *Am. J. of Preventive Medicine* 7(2):101–106.

COHEN, A., ed. (1966). *The Soncino Chumash*, 324. London: Soncino Press.

COOPER, P. J., MURRAY, L., & STEIN, A. (1993). "Psychosocial factors associated with the early termination of breast-feeding. *J. of Psychosomatic Research* 37(2):171–176.

DEUTSCH, H. (1944, 1945). Confinement and lactation. In *The Psychology of Women: A Psychoanalytic Interpretation*, 278–293. New York: Grune and Stratton.

FILDES, V. (1986). *Breasts, Bottles and Babies*. Edinburgh: Edinburgh University Press.

FLASHMAN, A. (1992). The moment of recognition. In *The Psychoanalytic Study of the Child* 47:351–369.

FURMAN, L. (1993). Breast-feeding and fulltime maternal employment: Does the baby lose out? *J. Human Lactation* 9(1):1–2.

HEIMAN, M. (1963). Sexual response in women. *J. Amer. Psychoanal. Assn.* 11:360–387.

KLEEMAN, J. (1971). The establishment of core gender identity in normal girls. *Archives of Sexual Behavior* 1:117–129.

KLUMPNER, G. H. (1992). *A Guide to the Language of Psychoanalysis*. Madison, Conn.: International University Press.

LANGER, M. (1945). Psychological problems of lactation. In *Motherhood and Sexuality*, 225–239. New York: Guilford Press.

LAWRENCE, R. A. (1994). *Breastfeeding: A guide for the medical profession,* 4th ed. St. Louis: Mosby.

LEBOVICI, S., & KESTEMBERG, E. (1993). The breast and breasts. *Journal of Child Psychotherapy* 19(1):5–28.

MIDDLEMORE, M. (1941). *The Nursing Couple.* London: Hamish Hamilton Medical Books.

SARLIN, C. (1963). Feminine identity. *J. Amer. Psychoanal. Assn.* 11:790–816.

——— (1981). The role of breast-feeding in psychosexual development and the achievement of the genital phase. *J. Amer. Psychoanal. Assn.* 29:631–641.

STERN, D. (1977). *The First Relationship Infant and Mother.* Cambridge: Harvard University Press.

TRAD, P. (1990). The emergence of psychopathology in a previously adaptive mother-infant dyad. *Amer. J. Psychotherapy* 44:95–106.

WALETZKY, L. (1979). Husband's problems with breast-feeding. *Amer. J. Orthopsychiat.* 49(2):349–352.

WINNICOTT, D. W. (1945). Primitive emotional development. In *Through Paediatrics to Psychoanalysis,* 145–156. London: Karnac Books, 1992.

——— (1947). Hate in the countertransference, *Through Paediatrics to Psychoanalysis,* 194–203.

——— (1951). Transitional objects and transitional phenomena, *Through Paediatrics to Psychoanalysis,* 229–242.

Psychoanalytic Perspectives on Adolescent Suicide

ROBERT A. KING, M.D.
ALAN APTER, M.D.

From the beginning of the twentieth century, youthful suicide has posed both a clinical and a theoretical challenge for psychoanalysis. This paper examines several paradigmatic cases of completed suicide in order to illustrate important psychodynamic aspects of adolescent suicide. The contributions of the developmental psychoanalytic perspective to our understanding of adolescent self-destructiveness are discussed, with particular emphasis on Anna Freud's concept of developmental lines toward self-care and self-regulation. The applications of this developmental psychoanalytic perspective to clinical research on vulnerability to adolescent suicide are reviewed.

THE TRAGEDY OF YOUTHFUL SUICIDE IS A HETEROGENEOUS AND MULTI-determined phenomenon that often defies prediction despite our best clinical efforts and theoretical models. Over the past decade, the authors have collaborated in studying adolescent suicidality as seen in diverse settings in the United States and Israel, such as the military,

Robert A. King, M.D., is associate professor of Child Psychiatry, Yale Child Study Center, Yale University School of Medicine; faculty, Child Analytic Program, Western New England Psychoanalytic Institute. Alan Apter, M.D., Geha Psychiatric Hospital, is associate professor, Department of Child and Adolescent Psychiatry, Sackler School of Medicine, University of Tel Aviv.

The authors would like to acknowledge the contributions of Drs. Donald Cohen, Israel Orbach, Sidney Blatt, Shmuel Kron, Avi Bleich, Donald Quinlan, and Ada Zohar.

The Psychoanalytic Study of the Child 51, ed. Albert J. Solnit, Peter B. Neubauer, Samuel Abrams, and A. Scott Dowling (Yale University Press, copyright © 1996 by Albert J. Solnit, Peter B. Neubauer, Samuel Abrams, and A. Scott Dowling).

inpatient psychiatric and pediatric settings, youth immigrant-absorption centers, and schools. Guided by a developmental psychoanalytic perspective, our goal has been to understand the complex roots of adolescent self-destructiveness in the interaction among individual, family, cultural, and constitutional factors. The purpose of this paper is to explore the contribution of this perspective to the understanding of youthful suicide, hoping that it will shed light on aspects of the problem not addressed by other approaches. We first describe several cases of adolescent suicide to illustrate the vulnerabilities predisposing certain youngsters to suicide. We then examine the potential origins of these vulnerabilities, paying particular attention to the regulation of affect, self-esteem, and attitudes toward the body and its care.

CASE MATERIAL: THREE UNANTICIPATED DEATHS

Background. The three cases described here are drawn from our ongoing study of late adolescent suicide in the context of compulsory military service in the Israel Defense Force or IDF (Apter et al., 1993). Military service constitutes an important rite of passage for Israeli late adolescents and thus provides a unique opportunity for the study of youth suicide. Because most Jewish men between the ages of 18 and 21 are on active duty in the IDF, virtually all male suicides in this age group occur during army service. Near-universal compulsory military service and mandatory pre-induction screening offer a rich source of systematic, prospective data on successive national birth-cohorts of Israeli adolescents, thereby permitting a detailed examination of emergent forms of adolescent psychopathology, such as suicide.

With only few exceptions, all Jewish adolescents aged 16 to 17 undergo careful physical and psychological screening to determine their eligibility for service and receive extensive psychological interviews and psychometric testing to determine the most suitable assignment. Following their induction, the recruits' mental and physical health and general functioning are systematically monitored. When a suicide occurs, an exhaustive mandatory legal inquiry is made by a team of specially trained investigators, including mental health professionals. Friends, family members, teachers, and military comrades and officers are carefully interviewed, and the extensive pre-induction and active-duty information available on the recruit is thoroughly reviewed.

The richness of these data helps to compensate partially for the unavoidable absence in most suicides of information derived from intensive treatment, the usual source of our dynamic picture of troubled adolescents. Furthermore, because the majority of adolescents who kill themselves do so without ever having sought treatment, nonclinical sources of information must be relied on to study the dynamics of these youngsters who may differ in important ways from those who come to clinical attention prior to death (e.g., Runeson, 1992; Marttunen et al., 1994).

CASE I: DAVID—AN APPARENT CASE OF UNDETECTED DEPRESSION

David, aged 18, came from a family with a distinguished military background. He was very shy at school with his peers but open with and dependent on his teachers. In retrospect, he appears to have had a poor self-image during his school years, with intermittent periods of depression, insomnia, and weight loss. His teachers recommended that he be seen by a psychologist but his parents refused.

David enthusiastically looked forward to his army service, hoping that success here would redeem his low self-esteem. Significantly, he did not reveal any of this history during the pre-induction screening and denied having any psychiatric or emotional difficulties. During the screening, the psychological interviewer noted that David seemed "slightly strange" but not sufficiently so to warrant referral for further psychiatric evaluation. On the basis of his pre-induction evaluation, David was found to be highly suitable for a combat unit. He applied to join an elite commando unit but was turned down by the unit psychologist for unspecified reasons.

In the army, according to his officers, David did well in both basic and advanced combat training. Some of his comrades considered him "odd," but he was popular on the routine sociometric ratings. After advanced training, David was posted to a combat unit. He seemed to do well there but complained to his parents of being depressed, losing weight, and feeling unable to cope. His parents alerted the unit mental health officer, who examined David. During the examination David minimized his symptoms and denied experiencing any depression or suicidal thoughts but said he could not continue to serve in a battle unit. After consulting a more experienced senior psychiatrist, the mental health officer diagnosed "adjustment reaction" and had David posted to a rear echelon. However, the prospect of reassignment made David feel like a "failure". Soon thereafter he fatally shot himself.

With the clarity of hindsight and the detailed postmortem accounts of teachers and peers, David appears to have had an undiagnosed depression. The diagnosis was missed because of David's desperate denial of difficulties in the service of unrealistically high internal standards and fear of failure. Although he was not really up to the rigors of a combat unit, David strove desperately but unsuccessfully to overfunction. It appears that the army seemed to him a last chance to redeem his damaged sense of self in his own eyes and in those of his ambivalently regarded father, whose perceived success he feared he could never match, let alone surpass. The prospect of falling short of this unattainable standard felt intolerable; both prior to induction and after beginning to founder, David was unable to acknowledge his difficulties in a fashion that might have mobilized support and assignment to a less prestigious but more appropriate placement in which he had a better chance of succeeding.

CASE II: AMIT—SUDDEN PERTURBATION IN A BOY WITH POOR AFFECT MODULATION

Amit, an 18-year-old soldier, killed himself while on an advanced battle-training course a few months after induction into the army. He had grown up under conditions of moderate economic deprivation. His parents were uneducated; his mother was a housewife and his father a blue-collar worker. The father was a "weak," closed person who avoided confrontation; the mother was a warm but overemotional woman who found it difficult to cope with the running of the house and the education of her children. The atmosphere in the home was one of angry accusations from the mother and passive silence from the father.

Amit was described as "difficult" from birth; he did poorly in elementary school, had trouble concentrating, caused disturbances in class, and often got into fights. He did not drop out, however, and managed to complete vocational high school with fairly good grades. During high school, his behavior changed, and he became more compliant and eager to please. Neither his teachers nor his parents ever thought of referring him for counseling. He was described as being very close to his mother and easily hurt by such insults as being called "childish" or "mummy's boy."

Amit looked forward to his army service, feeling that it would "make a man" of him, and he asked to be sent to a frontline unit. On the psychological evaluation at induction, he denied all emotional and social difficulties. The psychological interviewer considered that he was likely to do well under battle conditions. He was a highly motivated and generally well-behaved recruit; however, he tended to become flustered under stress and to have angry outbursts against his friends and sometimes even his officers. One day he returned late from a home pass, saying that there were problems at home. Consequently his next leave was canceled. He became irritable and angry, and his performance began to suffer. He also began to complain of multiple somatic symptoms. The teaching staff on the base broached the subject of his suitability for a frontline unit, but he became upset and insisted on continuing. While he was resting after a training exercise, one of the other recruits taunted him. Amit lost his temper and attacked his tormenter. When the two were separated by friends, he ran to his tent and shot himself with his weapon.

In retrospect, Amit appears to have been an emotionally immature boy with a low frustration tolerance. His self-esteem had been dealt a severe blow by his failure to be a "good recruit," and he had developed an adjustment reaction with depressive features. The impulsive suicide was triggered by a flood of humiliated rage following narcissistic injury.

CASE III: JONATHAN—A CASE OF DEATH WITHOUT WARNING

Jonathan was a 20-year-old officer when he killed himself. His father was a well-known figure in Israeli education; his mother operated a small business. The family, which included two younger brothers, was achievement-oriented and had high moral standards. They believed in honesty, industriousness, helping one's neighbor, and public service. Their personal ideals stressed controlling one's emotions and living up to high standards. The father was revered by his family and was regarded by all his children as a role model. Any conflict in the home was seen as a threat to father's authority and was suppressed. Mother was subservient to her husband in most matters.

Jonathan's early development was described by all who knew him as "excellent." As a child, he was intelligent, curious, industrious, and persistent. He was a natural leader and was popular with his teachers and peers. He was described as "slightly arrogant" but always ready to help a weaker child. He became a senior leader in his youth group and a camp counselor. Despite his popularity, however, Jonathan seems not to have had any close friends in whom he confided, suggesting difficulty with intimacy.

In the army, Jonathan did very well and was chosen for officer training, which he completed with flying colors. He was selected as an instructor for new recruits and was sent for advanced training. Here again, he did well apart from one foul up, for which he was reprimanded. This he took in stride and finished the course. His superior commended him for his ability to perform under stress. Jonathan was thrilled by his appointment as an instructor and told his father that he was determined to become the best instructor on the base. He became totally involved in his new duties, despite some difficulties as a teacher owing to his being overpedantic and rather naive. His platoon of trainees did quite well although their overall performance rating was only average. Following the ceremony in which the new recruits received their berets and rifles, Jonathan went to his room and shot himself.

Even with extensive and detailed interviews from numerous people who lived, worked, and grew up with Jonathan, no definite diagnosis could be made. If he had not committed suicide, it is doubtful that anyone would have suspected that he was in emotional pain. Dynamically, it seems that he had narcissistic trends, a severe superego, and overutilization of repression and reaction formation.

Discussion

The three young men described here are drawn from an epidemiologic cohort of forty-three late-adolescent military suicides whom we and our colleagues studied in detail as part of an ongoing effort to prevent such tragic deaths (Apter et al., 1993). These unanticipated suicides were especially troubling as they occurred despite careful screening and the ready availability of mental health services. At the time of their entry into military service, these forty-three young men appeared by the usual measures to be above average in their psychological and physical fitness for service and well qualified to withstand the rigors of military life. On the usually highly reliable pre-induction interviews, almost all were rated satisfactory to outstanding in combat-duty suitability; their average physical fitness was well above the demanding minimum required for combat troops; and their mean intelligence scores were well above average, with 25 percent having IQ's higher than 130. As a result, the majority were assigned to frontline units, a placement that is often demanding and arduous but is widely perceived as prestigious and sought-after.

The detailed investigation following each of the suicides we studied revealed a more complicated story. Diagnostically, about half the soldiers appeared to have had a major depression, although in most cases these appeared to have been recent and reactive and had gone undetected ante mortem. A small number of the soldiers appear to have had a milder depressive condition, generalized anxiety disorder, or a schizophreniform disorder. In contrast to youthful suicides in the United States, antisocial personality was rare and substance abuse absent. In over 15 percent of the suicides, no categorical diagnosis could be made.

From examination of these unanticipated late-adolescent suicides, three patterns of suicide could be distinguished: (1) those suicides who had an undetected depression or other condition that they masked in order to cover up feelings of shame and personal failure; (2) those with isolative, narcissistic, or avoidant character traits that impaired their ability to cope and exacerbated their response to specific stressors or traumas perceived as rejection or failure; and (3) those whose suicide seemed completely inexplicable in terms of their history or the context of the suicide. A fourth type, common in youthful suicides in the United States, consisting of impulsive, often antisocial youth who abuse drugs or alcohol, was not found in our cohort of adolescent Israeli suicides.

The most common immediate precipitants of these suicides were a romantic rejection, service-related stress, financial problems, or an upsetting family event. In 10 percent of the cases no apparent precipitant could be found. None of the service-related stresses involved combat; instead, almost all of the service-related stresses involved a self-perceived failure to meet expectations or a perceived humiliation.

Few, if any, of the apparent precipitants of these young recruits' suicides were beyond the usual range of late-adolescent army experiences. Indeed, although they occurred in the often physically and emotionally arduous setting of military life, the immediate precipitants of most of these suicides were not markedly different from the experiences of many university students. Their devastating significance for these young suicides became clearer, however, in light of their maladaptive personality styles, as revealed in the post-mortem inquiry. Strong narcissistic features were apparent in a quarter of the suicides, and schizoid or avoidant personality traits in over 40 percent. Although not all were perfectionistic, many had unrealistic and uncompromising self-demands for high levels of achievement and coping, even in the face of difficulties, and a wish that success in the army would redeem earlier shortcomings or confirm a competent identity. These high self-expectations and hopes may also have made it difficult for these young men to acknowledge or bear even marginal difficulties or personal limitations that emerged during their subsequent active duty; any shortcoming was seen by them as devastating.

Another crucial exacerbating feature was the strong isolative traits that many subjects shared; these appeared to be lifelong patterns rather than a reaction to recent stress or depression. In the post-mortem inquiry, about half of the suicides were recalled by parents and teachers as having been "very isolated" children and by their unit comrades as being "very private people."

This combination of traits had several catastrophic consequences. Many of these youngsters may have felt an inordinate need to do well on their pre-induction assessment, in order to be assigned to a prestigious unit. Some, like David, appear to have denied or minimized vulnerabilities or difficulties encountered earlier in adolescence. (The very high physical-fitness scores of these young men may have reflected their also minimizing nonspecific and subjective physical symptoms, such as backache and flat feet, and/or intensive training to reach high levels of fitness prior to conscription.) Once these young men encountered perceived difficulty, shame related to their unrealistically high standards combined in many cases with an isolative style to prevent them from turning to peers, officers, or clinicians for help or support.

As a result, even relatively minor (to the external observer) setbacks could rapidly spiral into disaster as burgeoning anxious preoccupation, depressive rumination, and withdrawal further interfered with the recruit's ability to perform at the high levels he demanded of himself or to reach out to others, triggering a vicious circle of isolative decompensation, with suicide seen as the only way out. Those recruits who used achievement to substitute for the lack of real interpersonal closeness seemed especially vulnerable to this kind of catastrophic decompensation.

In many respects, these soldiers resembled Zetzel's (1970) description of cases of war neurosis whose premorbid need to deny awareness of "passivity, depression, anxiety, and realistic limitations" made them prone to breakdown in situations that unavoidably confronted them with these repudiated affects. Zetzel proposed that the apparently good premorbid functioning of these soldiers with war neurosis depended on a "type of pseudo-mastery" based on the need to deny rather than acknowledge, bear, and master painful, anxious, or depressive affects. What factors distinguished World War II soldiers who were able to fall apart, yet live, from the young men in our study, who could not, remains to be understood.

PSYCHOANALYTIC CONTRIBUTIONS TO UNDERSTANDING ADOLESCENT SUICIDE

THE EARLY PERIOD

During the early decades of this century, a perceived epidemic of youthful suicide stirred great concern throughout the German-speaking world (Neubauer, 1994). This epidemic touched many of the better educated classes, including the circle of Freud and his colleagues (Young-Bruehl, 1988). The attempts to understand and respond to the phenomenon of youth suicide paralleled in many ways those of our own epoch. Writers in the lay press blamed the schools, deteriorating social values, and faulty childrearing. Medical researchers sought physical explanations, including "hereditary taints" and the elusive *status thymicolymphaticus*.

Against this background, the Vienna Psychoanalytic Society's 1910 Symposium "On Suicide with Particular Reference to Suicide among Young Students" (Friedman, 1967) was the first detailed attempt to address this problem from a psychoanalytic perspective. The participants, who included Adler, Sadger, and Stekel, proposed various explanatory dynamics: conflict over masturbatory and homosexual impulses, revenge, guilt over hostile impulses, and masculine protest against feelings of inferiority. A few vivid aphorisms foreshadowed persistent themes in later psychoanalytic thinking on suicide. Invoking the talion principle, Stekel opined: "No one kills himself who has never wanted to kill another, or at least wished the death of another" (p. 87). Sadger, in turn, proposed the principle: "[T]he only person who puts an end to his life is one who has been compelled to give up all hope of love" (p. 76). In his published remarks, Freud cautiously reserved judgment on these speculations, noting: "we have not reached a decision on the problem that interests us . . . whether [overcoming the powerful life instinct] can only come about with the help of a disappointed libido or whether the ego can renounce its self-preservation for its own egoistic motives" (p. 140). Alluding briefly to the importance of understanding melancholia and its relationship to mourning, Freud concluded tersely, "Let us suspend our judgment till experience has solved this problem" (p. 141).

Although Freud never spelled out a systematic account of suicide, beginning with *Mourning and Melancholia* (1917) he elaborated a more complex perspective that moved beyond suicide as a refusal to accept loss of libidinal gratification or a guilty reaction to death wishes toward others. Freud extended to the problem of suicide his famous dictum: "Thus, the shadow of the object fell upon the ego, and the latter could henceforth be judged by a special agency as though it were an object, the forsaken object." Especially in the case of a thwarted narcissistic object choice, Freud proposed, the patient takes revenge "by the circuitous path of self-punishment."

> It is this sadism alone that solves the riddle of the tendency to suicide which makes melancholia so interesting and so dangerous. . .we cannot conceive how [the] ego can consent to its own destruction. We have long known it is true that no neurotic harbors thoughts of suicide which he has not turned back upon himself from murderous impulses against others, but we have never been able to explain what interplay of forces can carry such a purpose through to execution. The analysis of melan-

cholia now shows that the ego can kill itself only if, owing to the return of the object-cathexis, it can treat itself as an object—if it is able to direct against itself the hostility which relates to an object and which represents the ego's original reaction to objects in the external world. Thus, in regression from narcissistic object-choice, the object has, it is true, been gotten rid of, but it has nevertheless proved more powerful than the ego itself. In the two opposed situations of being most intensely in love, and of suicide, the ego is overwhelmed by the object, though in totally different ways (p. 252).

In terms of the topographic theory, in melancholia "the excessively strong superego which has obtained a hold upon consciousness rages against the ego with merciless violence" and "often enough succeeds in driving the ego into death" (Freud, 1923, p. 53). "[T]he ego gives itself up because it feels itself hated and persecuted by the super-ego, instead of loved. To the ego, therefore, living means the same as being loved— loved by the superego, which . . . fulfills the same function of protecting and saving that was fulfilled in earlier days by the father and later by Providence or Destiny" (p. 58).

Although later writers emphasized the *aggressive* elements of this formulation (e.g., the wish to kill, the wish to be killed, the wish to die [Menninger, 1938]), the *libidinal* strand in Freud's formulation is apparent in the notion that the attack on the self is prompted by the experienced or threatened loss of the intensely needed but ambivalently loved (and ambivalently loving) object.

Taken together with his other brief remarks on the topic, Freud's speculations on suicide were brilliant and influential. They left unanswered, however, many important questions concerning the developmental pathways to suicide and the question of why certain epochs of life, such as adolescence and old age, were particularly vulnerable.

It remained for Anna Freud (1965, 1972) and a later generation of analysts to spell out in more detail the developmental processes potentially predisposing children to depression or suicide and to explicate the risk-conferring aspects of adolescence. It is to these areas of psychoanalytic investigation that we turn next.

CONTEMPORARY PERSPECTIVES ON YOUTH SUICIDE

Current epidemiological studies of attempted and completed youthful suicide in the United States and Europe have emphasized the high prevalence of categorical diagnoses such as depression, conduct disorder, and substance abuse (Shaffer et al., 1988). Aggressive and antisocial attitudes may confer as much risk for suicide as does depression (Apter et al., 1995). Family instability and parental psychopathology or suicidality also appear to be risk factors, although the relative contribution of experiential and genetic factors remains unclear. Current biological investigations have implicated brain neurotransmitter systems believed to modulate the control of impulse and aggression (King et al., 1994).

Important though these studies have been, for the most part they have lacked a developmental or dynamic perspective and provide little insight into the inner-world quality of interpersonal relationships or the developmental trajectory of suicidal youth; neither do they help us understand why some individuals with a given diagnosis commit suicide while others with the same diagnosis do not.

In contrast, the developmental psychoanalytic perspective focuses on the vicissitudes of the child's development of important self-regulatory capacities, such as self-soothing, the capacity for bodily self-care, the ability to tolerate painful affects, and the maintenance of self-esteem.

ADOLESCENT SELF-DESTRUCTIVENESS AND THE CAPACITY FOR SELF-CARE

Anna Freud's (1965) concept of the developmental line from irresponsibility to responsibility in body management provides a paradigm of such theory building. One of the striking paradoxes of adolescence in general and suicidal adolescents in particular is that the same boy or girl who can spend hours grooming and decorating his or her body or anxiously worrying over an imagined blemish can also heedlessly endanger it in reckless behavior or deliberately seek to hurt or destroy it. Anna Freud noted that the well-nurtured young child is largely able to leave concerns regarding the care of its body and protection from harm to the mother. Under normal circumstances, the mother's investment in and attentiveness to the child's bodily care protect him or her and gradually foster the control of dangerous impulses, the understanding of realistic external dangers, and, more fitfully, "the child's voluntary endorsement of the rules of hygiene and of medical necessity" (A. Freud, 1965, p. 77). Beginning with its roots in the body ego, when all goes well, the self and its body come to be seen as being capable of and worthy of being cherished, cared for, and protected.

The question of how children gradually internalize (or fail to internalize) this important aspect of the parent is an important area of study (Khantzian and Mack, 1983). Negligent, hostile, or narcissistic parental attitudes toward the child's body and its care may all interfere with this process. In our experience in pediatric settings with young children's ingestions and accidents, lapses in maternal attention due to depression or other acute or chronic maternal difficulties appear to play an important role (Frankl, 1963; Lewis et al., 1966). We also find high rates of medical noncompliance and of suicidal and self-injurious behavior in abused and neglected children, who appear to regard their bodies with the same mixture of neglect and hostility as their parents do. What is internalized reflects, of course, not only the parents' actual behavior but the child's temperament and subjective experience as well. For example, constitutional or reactive impulsivity or hyperactivity may render a child accident-prone even in the face of expectably attentive parenting. High activity or aggression levels in young school-age children are among the most powerful predictors of subsequent serious accidental injuries (Bijur et al., 1988).

Our ongoing study of self-care in pediatric patients, whose noncompliance with medical care poses a common and potentially life-threatening problem (King and Lewis, 1994), provides a useful window on the vicissitudes of the development of the child's capacity for self-care. For the young child with a chronic medical illness, such as eczema or diabetes, parental ministrations may be experienced as restrictive, painful, or even persecutory. The parents of one suicidal, medically neglectful diabetic adolescent in our study of diabetic self-care poignantly recalled having had to chase him as a preverbal toddler about the room daily with an insulin syringe. The systematic psychoanalytic study and treatment of children with diabetes have yielded many important insights concerning the causes and consequences of the frequent medical noncompliance of these and other children with chronic medical illnesses (Moran, 1984; Moran et al., 1991). Anna Freud (1975) noted the conflictual nature of the precocious self-care responsibilities undertaken by many diabetic children, for whom such demands may be developmentally premature. She also speculated that repeated early experiences of pain may distort the development of sustaining positive libidinal ties and foster aggression directed toward the child's own body as well as toward others (A. Freud, 1972).

Counterphobic attitudes are also a potential source of dangerous, self-destructive behavior. Acknowledging realistic anxieties about the body's needs and vulnerabilities provides an adaptive impetus for appropriate self-care and protection. In adolescence, however, many children with chronic conditions counterphobically and counterdependently deny the need for vigilance or compliance with medical regimens. One young man with hemophilia, for example, defied and horrified his parents by repeatedly driving a motorcycle. These counterphobic attitudes may combine with a sensation-seeking style (Clark et al., 1990) to pose a dramatic risk for life-endangering accidents or suicidality. This paradoxical attitude toward the body is epitomized in the motto, "Live fast, die young, and leave a good-looking corpse."

ALIENATION AND HOSTILITY TOWARD THE BODY

The developmental concept of self-care helps us to understand the possible origins of the alienation and hostility that many suicidal adolescents demonstrate toward the body. As we have suggested, the child's sense of his or her body as cherished, well cared for, and a potential source of pleasure appears to be rooted in early experiences of the mother's empathic care (A. Freud, 1965, 1972). In contrast, in our study of adolescent psychiatric inpatients we find that a history of suicide attempts correlates significantly with the child's perception of parents as indifferent and/or hostile to the child's physical care and appearance. Furthermore, among attempters, the severity of their suicidal intent and the lethality of the attempt correlated with the perception of the father as having been very critical of the child (King et al., unpublished data).

Suicidal adolescents' alienation from and indifference or hostility to their bodies are manifested in several ways. Orbach and colleagues (1995) have found that suicidal adolescents have much higher pain thresholds and greater tolerance for inflicted pain than do psychiatric or normal controls or accident victims. This relative anaesthesia of suicidal adolescents resembles that seen in many self-mutilating adolescents who experience a similar dissociation from their bodies. One chronically suicidal borderline adolescent inpatient repeatedly cut her legs without experiencing pain. One day she remarked to her analyst, "You know, as I was cutting, I thought about what you said, that it was my leg, not my mother's, that I was cutting, and it started to hurt so much that I stopped."

The adolescent's body serves as the bearer and representation of many instinctual concerns and attitudes (Ritvo, 1974). Such attitudes may be explicit, as in the adolescent gang member who, with his "Born to die young" or "R.I.P." tattoo, labels himself a self-ordained walking corpse. In other cases, rather than being the vehicle for pleasure, satisfaction, and contact, the body is experienced as the source of anxiety or tension. In extreme cases, the body comes to be felt as the hated repository of intolerable longings, for which it must be attacked or even destroyed. For the anorectic, these intolerable longings may be the oral-dependent (and oral-sadistic) yearnings that she perceives tie her to her mother. The anorectic projects the image of a sadistic mother onto her own body, whose threatening, indestructible, gnawing cravings she must then savagely master and subdue, a dynamic that Selvini-

Palazzoli (1965) termed "intrapersonal paranoia." Laufer and Laufer (1984) have proposed that similar mechanisms underly certain adolescent suicide attempts. In such cases, the adolescent's sexually mature body is felt as the bearer of shameful, intolerable sexual or dependent longings; feeling otherwise helpless, the adolescent attacks and tries to render the body dead in a desperate attempt to assert control and quell these painful tensions. The body becomes "totally identified with the fantasied attacker who must now be silenced" (p. 113). Not surprisingly, anorexics have high rates of suicidal feelings and attempts (Apter et al., 1995).

THE CAPACITY FOR SELF-SOOTHING AND THE CAPACITY TO BEAR PAINFUL AFFECTS

Anna Freud's concept of developmental lines toward bodily self-care can be extended to other crucial self-regulatory capacities whose failure to develop properly may render the child or adolescent vulnerable to self-destructive impulses and acts. For example, the developing capacity for self-soothing and calming may be understood from the same perspective of interaction between libidinal phase development and object-related ego capacities. The developing child's growing capacity for self-comfort and self-soothing depends on a variety of factors including the experienced adequacy and availability of parental empathy and soothing, the child's temperament (Mayes and Cohen, 1995), and the intensity of external impingements and stresses. The outcome of this process, manifested in the capacity to bear painful affects (such as loneliness, sadness, and anxiety) and to comfort oneself in face of loss or frustration, may be viewed in part as the ability to evoke sustaining internal presences to serve as a bulwark against life's various adversities (Buie and Maltsberger, 1989; Winnicott, 1958). Schafer (1960), echoing Freud's comments on the superego as heir to the parents' caring as well as prohibitive aspects, emphasized the protective and comforting aspects of the parents instantiated in the superego. When this process goes awry, however, frustration or loss may evoke unmanageable anxiety, fears of fragmentation, or susceptibility to splitting. In his theory of working models of attachment (which may be variably secure, anxious, or avoidant), Bowlby (1973) described how these internal schemas come to regulate the child's expectations of the potential availability and attunement of the needed other. The adequacy of the child's capacity for self-comfort also has self-evaluative consequences, with the internalized unsoothing object experienced as persecutory and the inconsolable self felt as bad and worthy of punishment or annihilation (Noshpitz, 1994).

The inability to bear painful affects is an important element in the vulnerability to suicide. Escape from unbearable psychic pain appears to be the common motive in suicide (Shneidman, 1989). Not all suicide attempts, however, result from frank melancholia or depression. Although rage, guilt, shame, or desperate hopelessness may often be the trigger, other unbearable affects include intense anxiety and fear of psychotic fragmentation (Hendin, 1991). The inability to tolerate these affects may stem from a variety of sources (Zetzel, 1970). A key element in the sequence of events leading to suicidal action is the perceived inability to evoke comforting or sustaining internal objects or to elicit or make use of help from significant others. The inability to modulate or bear painful affects may also be part of a broader developmental ego deficit. Although many adolescent suicide attempters are subsequently able to articulate in detail the motives or feelings leading up to the suicide attempt, a large number of impulsive adolescent suicide attempters are strikingly unable to describe their feelings prior to the attempt: "I don't know why I did it; I was upset and just took the pills." In some youngsters this reflects a transient ego disorganization in the face of overwhelming affect; in many others, however, it bespeaks a more chronic alexithymia that renders them vulnerable to recurrent affective storms and repetitive suicide attempts. Amit is an example of a youngster whose suicidal behavior was triggered by a sudden, overwhelming affective flood, most often a combination of humiliation, helplessness, and rage, in response to an acute upset.

THE REGULATION OF SELF-ESTEEM AND THE VULNERABILITY TO DEPRESSION

Although escape from intolerable pain appears to be the common motive in suicide, the central question raised by Freud persists: how does the self come to be seen as the cause of the pain and self-expungement as the solution (Baumeister, 1990)? The study of adolescent suicidality helps elucidate the complexities of how youngsters come to see the locus of their difficulties as lying within themselves or in the external world and how these sources frequently become blurred.

Developmental psychoanalytic theory has provided important insights into the vicissitudes of superego formation and the forms of self-blame and self-reproach to which children are prone at different developmental levels (A. Freud, 1965).

Bibring (1953) observed that individuals differ in their vital aspirations that, when thwarted, lead to depression. Defining depression as an ego-state of real or imagined helplessness to preserve these cherished aspects of the self or maintain crucial relationships (real or internalized), Bibring listed the vital aspirations without which life feels unbearable: (1) the wish to be worthy, appreciated, or lovable, not unworthy; (2) the wish to be strong, superior, and secure, not weak; and (3) the wish to be good and loving, not hateful and destructive.

Clinical experience suggests that both developmental and family factors shape which aspirations are most problematic for a given child, render him or her most vulnerable to depression, and color the form self-reproach takes. In the metapsychological profile, Anna Freud (1965) emphasized the importance of assessing superego functioning with respect to the contents and concerns that typically activate the superego and the quality of the resulting superego prohibitive response or threat as experienced by the ego. For example, conflict at a given libidinal level may lead to denial or exaggeration of its corresponding aspiration, such as a grandiose assertion of self-sufficiency, an inordinate need never to be bad or defiant, or excessive self-efface-ment (Anthony, 1975).

Different patterns of perceived shortcomings may have different pathogenic consequences. For example, in a study of nonclinical subjects, children who reported suicidal feelings perceived themselves as less competent in areas important to their parents, while nonsuicidal depressed children felt less competent in areas important to peers (Harter and Marold, 1989).

Two types of depressive vulnerability, the *dependent* and the *self-critical*, each with distinctive antecedents, preoccupations, and characteristic forms of dysphoria, have emerged from the convergent formulations of Blatt (1995), Beck (1983), and Arieti and Bemporad (1980). Individuals of the dependent subtype are anxiously attached, with an overvaluation of dependent relationships and ongoing struggles with attachment figures; they are preoccupied with interpersonal issues concerning dependency and abandonment and experience helplessness in the face of perceived loss (Blatt, 1995). In contrast, individuals of the self-critical type are compulsively self-reliant and discount the importance of intimate relationships; they are anxiously preoccupied with issues of self-definition, self-worth, and autonomy and respond to perceived failure with feelings of loss of control, unworthiness, and guilt.

Among our adolescent psychiatric inpatients, high levels of self-critical or dependent concerns correlated strongly with the presence of suicidal ideation and attempts (King et al., unpublished data). Other studies using this typology suggest that dependent individuals are prone to manipulative, nonlethal, impulsive suicide attempts, while self-critical individuals are prone to more planful, serious suicide attempts (Blatt, 1995).

Paralleling Bibring's perspective, these subtypes also suggest means of predicting what sorts of stress are likely to precipitate actual depression or suicidality in different individuals. For Jonathan, the proximate cause of his suicide appears to have been a narcissistic disappointment—a level of achievement that fell short of his impossibly high standard. For other more dependent young men, a romantic disappointment serves as the final trigger. Similarly, in dependent individuals, depression is more likely to be precipitated by negative interpersonal events (e.g., rejections or losses), while self-critical individuals are more likely to become depressed in response to achievement failures (Hammen et al., 1989; Hewitt and Flett, 1991, 1993).

As our clinical vignettes illustrate, certain forms of perfectionism may be particularly malignant with respect to the potential for suicide (Blatt, 1995; Hamachek, 1978). Perfectionism may be adaptive when the individual has high but attainable goals, obtains pleasure from careful efforts, and accepts realistic limitations. In contrast, maladaptively perfectionistic individuals derive little pleasure from their achievements and dread each new task, as they are anxiously preoccupied with avoiding failure and are prone to denigrate their accomplishments (Hamachek, 1978).

Similarly, the capacity to experience guilt may be advantageous within a certain range. Studies find that children who report conscious guilt about specific, reparable types of perceived transgressions show better social adjustment than those who do not; guilt of this sort does *not* appear to be associated with increased depression (Bybee and Williams, unpublished manuscript). However, when guilt is intense and global (and hence unable to serve as a realistic guide to adaptive behavior), it becomes maladaptive and conducive to depression.

The developmental roots of maladaptive perfectionism appear to lie in a parent-child relationship in which parental approval or affection is experienced by the child as precariously conditional on his or her meeting high standards. The relentless, anxious pursuit of accomplishment may represent a heroic attempt to win the approval of a parent perceived as harshly judgmental. This anxious striving is accompanied by intensely self-critical attitudes that may persist throughout life (Koestner et al., 1991). In some families, the intactness of the family (or a parent's welfare) may seem to the child to require of him or her a particular type of specialness cherished by the family; this poses a special hazard for some talented children, who may succeed in driving themselves to great accomplishment but at the cost of an anxiously nagging sense of inauthenticity or resentment. For some such adolescents, self-inflicted death may seem the only avenue to individuation or of reclaiming a separate untrammeled self (Shapiro and Freedman, 1987; King and Noshpitz, 1991).

Why the developmental vulnerabilities to depression and suicide described above become activated at a given point in an individual's life history is not always clear. In adolescence, the process of object removal leaves the adolescent especially sensitive to loss and intensely vulnerable to romantic disappointments and other interpersonal setbacks (A. Freud, 1958; Erlich, 1978; Tabachnik, 1981). The need to consolidate a still nascent identity independent of the family orbit may give added urgency to the perceived need for achievement, with a corresponding intensity of despair over perceived failure.

CONCLUSION

The psychoanalytic developmental perspective has yielded a better understanding of the vulnerabilities predisposing youngsters to suicide and served as a fertile stimulus for clinical research. The challenge remains how best to make use of these insights to develop improved preventive and therapeutic interventions. Freud remarked that neurotics have preconditions for loving. Our goal must be to help vulnerable adolescents to have less stringent and precarious preconditions for living.

BIBLIOGRAPHY

ANTHONY, E. J. (1975). Childhood depression. In: *Depression and Human Existence*, ed. Anthony, E. J., & Benedek, T. Boston: Little, Brown, pp. 231–277.

APTER, A., GOTHELF, D., ORBACH, I., WEIZMAN, R., RATZONI, G., HAR-EVEN, D., & TYANO, S. (1995). Correlation of suicidal and violent behavior in different diagnostic categories in hospitalized adolescent patients. *J. Am. Acad. Child Adolesc. Psychiat.*, 34:912–918.

APTER, A., BLEICH, A., KING, R. A., KRON, S., FLUCH, A., KOTLER, M., & COHEN, D. J. (1993). Death without warning? A clinical postmortem study of suicide in 43 Israeli adolescent males. *Archiv. Gen. Psychiat.*, 50:138–142.

ARIETI, S., & BEMPORAD, J. R. (1980). The psychological organization of depression. *Am. J. Psychiatry*, 137:1360–1365.

BAUMEISTER, R. F. (1990). Suicide as escape from self. *Psychological Review*, 97:90–113.

BECK, A. T. (1983). Cognitive therapy of depression: New perspectives. In: *Treatment of Depression: Old Controversies and New Approaches*, ed. Clayton, P. J., & Barrett, J. E. New York: Raven.

BIBRING, E. (1953). The mechanism of depression. In: *Affective Disorders*, ed. Greenacre, P. New York: Int. Univ. Press, pp. 13–48.

BIJUR, P., GOLDING, J., HASLUM, M., & KURZON, M. (1988). Behavioral prediction of injury in school-aged children. *Am. J. Diseases Child.*, 142:1307–1312.

BLATT, S. J. (1995). The destructiveness of perfectionism: Implications for the treatment of depression. *Am. Psychologist.*

BOWLBY, J. (1973). *Attachment and Loss, vol. II, Separation.* New York: Basic Books.

BUIE, D. H., JR., & MALTSBERGER, J. T. (1989). The psychological vulnerability to suicide. In: *Suicide: Understanding and Responding*, ed. Jacobs, D., & Brown, H. N. Madison, Conn.: Int. Univ. Press, pp. 59–71.

BYBEE, J., & WILLIAMS, C. Is guilt adaptive? Relationships to academic achievement, prosocial behavior, socioemotional competence, and depression. Unpublished.

CLARK, D. C., SOMMERFELDT, L., & SCHWARZ, M., ET AL. (1990). Physical recklessness in adolescence: Trait or byproduct of depressive/suicidal states? *J. Nerv. Mental Disease*, 178:423–433.

ERLICH, H. S. (1978). Adolescent suicide: Maternal longing and cognitive development. *Psychoanal. Study Child*, 33:261–277.

FRANKL, L. (1963). Self-preservation and the development of accident proneness in children and adolescents. *Psychoanal. Study Child*, 18:464–483.

FREUD, A. (1958). Adolescence. *Psychoanal. Study Child*, 13:255–278.

FREUD, A. (1965). *Normality and Pathology in Childhood: Assessments of Development.* New York: Int. Univ. Press.

FREUD, A. (1972). Comments on aggression. *Int. J. Psycho-Analysis*, 53:163–172.

FREUD, A. (1975). On the interaction between pediatrics and child psychology. *The Writings of Anna Freud*, vol. 8, 285–296. New York: Int. Univ. Press.

FREUD, S. (1917). Mourning and melancholia. *S. E.* 14:289–300.

FREUD, S. (1923). The ego and the id. *S. E.* 19:12–59.

FRIEDMAN, P., ED. (1967). *On Suicide: With Particular Reference to Suicide Among Young Students. Discussions of the Vienna Psychoanalytic Society—1910.* New York: Int. Univ. Press.

HAMACHEK, D. E. (1978). Psychodynamics of normal and neurotic perfectionism. *Psychology*, 15:27–33.

HAMMEN, C., ELLICOTT, A., GITLIN, M., & JAMISON, K. R. (1989). Sociotrophy/autonomy and vulnerability to specific life events in patients with unipolar and bipolar disorder. *J. Abnorm. Psychol.*, 98:154–160.

HARTER, S., & MAROLD, D. (1989). A model of risk factors leading to adolescent suicidal ideation. Presented at Society for Research in Child Development, Kansas City.

HENDIN, H. (1991). Psychodynamics of suicide, with particular reference to the young. *Am. J. Psychiatry*, 148:1150–1158.

HEWITT, P. L., & FLETT, G. L. (1993). Dimensions of perfectionism, daily stress, and depression: A test of the specific vulnerability hypothesis. *J. Abnorm. Psychol.*, 102:58–65.

HEWITT, P. J., & FLETT, G. L. (1991). Perfectionism in the self and social contexts: Conceptualization, assessment, and association with psychopathology. *J. Personality Social Psychol.*, 60:456–470.

KHANTZIAN, E. J., & MACK, J. E. (1983). Self-preservation and the care of the self. *Psychoanal. Study Child*, 38:209–232.

KING, R. A., & LEWIS, M. (1994). The difficult child. In: *Consultation-Liaison Child Psychiatry. Child Adolesc. Psychiatric Clinics North Am.*, ed. Lewis, M., & King, R. A. 3:531–541.

KING, R. A., SEGMAN, R. H., & ANDERSON, G. M. (1994). Serotonin and suicidality: The impact of acute fluoxetine administration. I: Serotonin & Suicide. *Israel Journal of Psychiatry*, Vol. 31, (4), 271–279.

KOESTNER, R., ZUROFF, D. C., & POWERS, T. A. (1991). Family origins of adolescent self-criticism and its continuity into adulthood. *J. Abnorm. Psychol.*, 100:191–197.

LAUFER, M., & LAUFER, M. E. (1984). *Adolescence and Developmental Breakdown: A Psychoanalytic View*. New Haven: Yale Univ. Press.

LEWIS, M., SOLNIT, A. J., STARK, M. H., GABRIELSON, I. W., & KLATSKIN, E. H. (1966). An exploration study of accidental ingestion of poison in young children. *J. Amer. Acad. Child Psychiat.*, 5:255–271.

MARTTUNEN, M. J., ARO, H. M., HENRIKSSON, M. M., & LONNQVIST, J. K. (1994). Adolescent suicides with adjustment disorders or no psychiatric diagnosis. *European Child Adolesc. Psychiat.*, 3:101–110.

MAYES, L. C., & COHEN, D. J. (1995). Constitution. In: *Psychoanalysis: The Major Concepts*, ed. Moore, B. E., & Fine, B. D. New Haven: Yale Univ. Press, pp. 271–292.

MENNINGER, K. A. (1938). *Man Against Himself*. New York: Harcourt, Brace and Company.

MORAN, G. (1984). Psychoanalytic treatment of diabetic children. *Psychoanal. Study Child*, 39:407–447.

MORAN, G., FONAGY, P., KURTZ, A., BOLTON, A., & BROOK, C. (1991). A controlled study of psychoanalytic treatment of brittle diabetes. *J. Amer. Acad. Child Adol. Psychiatry* 30:926–935.

NEUBAUER, J. (1992). *The Fin-de-Siecle Culture of Adolescence*. New Haven: Yale Univ. Press.

NOSHPITZ, J. D. (1994). Self-destructiveness in adolescence. *Am. J. Psychotherapy*, 48:330–346.

ORBACH, I., MIKULINCER, M., KING, R., COHEN, D., STEIN, D., & APTER, A. (1995). Thresholds and tolerance of physical pain in suicidal and nonsuicidal adolescents. Unpublished. Department of Psychology, Bar-Ilan University, Israel.

RITVO, S. (1984). The image and uses of the body in psychic conflict. *Psychoanal. Study Child*, 39:449–469.

RUNESON, B. (1992). Youth suicides unknown to psychiatric care providers. *Suicide and Life-Threatening Behavior*, 22:494–503.

SCHAFER, R. (1960). The loving and beloved superego in Freud's structural theory. *Psychoanal. Study Child*, 15:163–188.

SELVINI-PALAZZOLI, M. (1965). Interpretation of mental anorexia. In: *Anorexia Nervosa*, ed. Meyer, J. E., & Feldman, H. Stuttgart: Georg Thieme Verlag, pp. 96–103.

SHAFFER, D., GARLAND, A., GOULD, M., FISHER, P., & TRAUTMAN, P. (1988). Preventing teen-age suicide: A critical review. *J. Am. Acad. Child. Adolesc. Psychiat.*, 27:675–687.

SHAPIRO, E. R., & FREEDMAN, J. (1987). Family dynamics of adolescent suicide. *Adolesc. Psychiat.*, 14:191–207.

SHNEIDMAN, E. S. (1989). Overview: A multidimensional approach to suicide. In: *Suicide: Understanding and Responding*, ed. Jacobs, D., & Brown, H. N. Madison, Conn.: Int. Univ. Press, pp. 1–30.

TABACHNIK, N. (1981). The interlocking psychologies of suicide and adolescence. *Adolesc. Psychiatry*, 9:399–410.

WINNICOTT, D. W. (1958). The capacity to be alone. In: *The Maturational Process and the Facilitating Environment*. New York: Int. Univ. Press, pp. 29–36, 1965.

YOUNG-BRUEHL, E. (1988). *Anna Freud: A Biography*. New York: Summit Books.

ZETZEL, E. R. (1970). *The Capacity for Emotional Growth*. London: Hogarth Press.

The Psychoanalyst of the
Adolescent

MOSES LAUFER, PH.D.

The adolescent who comes for psychoanalytic treatment has probably experienced a developmental breakdown—a rejection of his or her body and a distorted image of himself or herself as being male or female. A critical requisite for work with such adolescents is an understanding of one's own adolescent development.

The internal freedom of the psychoanalyst is an essential ingredient in the treatment of the adolescent. This means that the psychoanalyst of the adolescent can separate his own sexual life and thoughts from what is lived out in the analytic sessions and thus can ensure that the treatment will confront whatever is essential and that he will avoid deriving gratification from the treatment process through taking over the adolescent's body or feeling that he is secretly sharing the intimacies of the patient.

THERE IS MUCH EVIDENCE ACCUMULATED FROM THE TREATMENT OF CHILdren and adolescents that supports the view that it is during the period of adolescence that one's relationship to oneself as a sexual male or sexual female becomes normally or pathologically fixed. If this is so, the period of adolescence may be a last chance to stand in the way of crippling mental disorder.

Freud first addressed the period of puberty and adolescence in his early writings. His *Three Essays on the Theory of Sexuality* (1905) is recognized as a cornerstone of our understanding of adolescent develop-

Member and Training Analyst, British Psycho-Analytical Society; Director, Brent Adolescent Centre/Centre for Research into Adolescent Breakdown, London; President, European Association for Adolescent Psycho-Analysis.

The Psychoanalytic Study of the Child 51, ed. Albert J. Solnit, Peter B. Neubauer, Samuel Abrams, and A. Scott Dowling (Yale University Press, copyright © 1996 by Albert J. Solnit, Peter B. Neubauer, Samuel Abrams, and A. Scott Dowling).

ment and adolescent breakdown and their relationship to later mental health and mental disorder. Freud begins his third essay, "The Transformations of Puberty," with a simple but momentous observation: "With the arrival of puberty, changes set in which are destined to give infantile sexual life its final normal shape." (p. 207) This statement conveys Freud's belief that during adolescence one's relationship to both internal and external reality and, from that, to one's sexually mature body may reveal the presence of pathological processes.

Freud's statement in "The Transformations of Puberty" and the later contributions of such writers as Aichhorn (1925), Bernfeld (1938), Blos (1962), Erikson (1959), Anna Freud (1958, 1965), Jacobson (1964), Katan (1969, 1975), and Schilder (1935) have made it easier for those who treat adolescents to acknowledge and accept their essential role in the life of those who come for help. Yet there seems to be an absence of discussion of the kind of preparation required of the persons who undertake the psychological or psychoanalytic treatment of adolescents and of the stresses and anxieties that are part of such work with very vulnerable young people.

In the course of our work, all of us make mistakes of commission or judgment reflecting our own blindspots—blindspots that the analyst will not be able to acknowledge unless he can ask questions about himself and his own past and present internal world. On a few occasions, I was able to discuss this problem with Anna Freud. She believed that unless we as psychoanalysts are in touch with the meanings of our own adolescent years—the crises, the enactments, the loss of emotional contact with ourselves—we may fail to acknowledge the crucial meanings of the pathologies of our adolescent patients and may be unprepared to identify the signs of severe pathology, both in the present and the past. She also believed that careful and extended study of adolescent patients could be a critical source of information about early danger signs, which can be used in the prevention of severe psychopathology in children and young adolescents.[1]

THE MIND AND BODY OF THE ADOLESCENT PSYCHOANALYST

At the start of any therapeutic undertaking, whether it is with a child, an adolescent, or an adult, we are faced not only with the person's projections, anxieties about being ill, and denials but also with his feeling that he may be attacked and devalued by the psychoanalyst.

1. It was this interest that led to Anna Freud's readiness to actively support our work and research at the Brent Adolescent Centre/Centre for Research into Adolescent Breakdown. During the last ten years of her life, she was the Centre's honorary advisor.

The way we respond to the adolescent's fears, demands, or idealization of us is an integral and central part of the transference and counter-transference, and it is an area that is essential for us to understand and acknowledge.

In my training and development as a psychoanalyst, I found that I approached my work with the adolescent patient with more caution and anxiety than I did with the child or adult patient. At first I assumed that this was attributable to the limited knowledge available about adolescent psychopathology or to my silent belief that I would soon be confronted with serious psychopathology or risk in the adolescent's life. It took me some time to acknowledge that my anxiety also derived from the intensity of the relationship with the adolescent and from my feeling that, no matter what I interpreted, I was still far from understanding the adolescent's anxiety and my own. It took me much longer than I had expected to feel able to help the adolescent begin to understand even the superficial meaning of his pathology.

It also took me some time to begin to think about and question the optimal therapeutic involvement with the adolescent, a question that raised the issue of the balance between concern, and the sexual looking into and taking over the adolescent's body as compared to the need for a trusting, unerotic relationship. Added to this was a sense of omnipotence, a feeling that can blur insight or even destroy a treatment. But, with all this, there was also the assumption that I would soon be confronted with the serious pathology or risk that was very likely present in the adolescent patient.

I also found that, in informal discussions with some colleagues on the choice of psychoanalytic or therapeutic work with adolescents, I often had difficulty identifying the reason for and meaning of my choice. Some colleagues felt that they had a "special interest" in the adolescent, or they seemed especially able to understand and work with the troubled adolescent. But there was little if any discussion of what this meant: such as, what the dangers might be? what preparation would be advisable? and what indications might discourage some colleagues from undertaking such work?

Some of these views assume that what we know about the child or the adult can serve us adequately in our work with the adolescent and that the insights we have acquired about ourselves in our personal analyses prepare us adequately for psychoanalytic work with the adolescent. I doubt this.

What, then, are the issues in preparing for psychoanalytic or therapeutic work with the adolescent? I begin with the assumption that the adolescent who comes for treatment, especially psychoanalytic treatment, has experienced a "developmental breakdown." By this I mean that, at puberty—that is, at the time of beginning to own a physically, sexually mature body—the troubled or ill adolescent responds by unconsciously rejecting his or her sexual body with an accompanying feeling of being passive in the face of the demands coming from that body. The result is that he or she ignores or disowns his or her genitals or feels that his or her body or genitals are different from what he or she wanted them to be. Such a response signifies a breakdown in the process of integrating the physically mature body image as part of the representation of oneself.

This process of developmental breakdown specifies what the overall direction of the adolescent's treatment should be, and it defines the areas of the analyst's or therapist's internal world with which he must be comfortably aware.

Although the rejection of the sexually mature body takes place at puberty, we assume that the breakdown has a much earlier history, dating back to the time of the oedipal resolution or even to the earliest relationship to the mother—that is, before the oedipal period. This means that the rejection is expressed as a negation of the body, something that existed in the oedipal and pre-oedipal periods but that becomes active and structured at the time of having a physically sexually mature body—that is, at the time of being able to impregnate or become pregnant.

This means that the adolescent patient who comes for treatment is most likely a person who has lived and lives now with a distorted image of himself and who has or may have a history of a break with the world around him—that is, he has a psychotic-like relationship to himself and to the world. What we may see in the first instance is not the break; instead we may be confronted with the adolescent's defenses, which dictate his relationship to himself—he may experience paranoia, projections, actual attacks on his or her own body, melancholic submission, the pseudo-idealization of the body, or active efforts to destroy the body or mind via suicide.

In the early transference relationship, the rejection of the body is portrayed [lived out] in the relationship to the analyst and is expressed in the adolescent's wish to hand over his body to the analyst to reject or accept or take over. If we are to help such adolescents, we must not only acknowledge the severity of the disorder but also become involved in the psychopathology without interference from our own anxieties, rationalizations, and blind spots (Anna Freud, 1962; Laufer, 1965).

Certain questions follow from these assumptions about the nature of adolescent psychopathology: what anxieties are aroused in us when working and treating adolescents who have experienced a breakdown in their development? And what demands need to be made of those who undertake psychoanalytic or therapeutic work with such adolescents? By "demands" I mean the knowledge about psychopathology that we must bring to such work—especially insight about ourselves when treating these vulnerable patients.

The Psychoanalyst's Development during Adolescence

A prerequisite for such work is an understanding of our own adolescent development and its part in our current lives. We must also understand its meaning in terms of our attitudes toward mental disorder, toward the various ways in which humans express their wishes, gratifications, loves and hatreds, and toward the sexual behavior of others. Such understanding is critical to integrate into our lives because work with those in serious mental trouble—whose lives often include perversion, terror of sexuality, lying, promiscuity, isolation, and friendlessness—can evoke in us a reaction that is very different from helping and may include condemning, hating, and perhaps even wanting or needing to fail in our work with some adolescents. These feelings must be acknowledged as existing in all of us at times, perhaps especially in those of us who work therapeutically with the troubled or the ill adolescent.

At the same time, understanding one's own adolescent development, and those aspects of oneself that have had to be kept from becoming conscious, seems much more difficult than we may at first assume. What might this tell us about ourselves, as well as about the possible reasons for the very different pace in the development of adult and child analysis as compared to adolescent analysis?

The treatment with which I am familiar, together with the views held by many psychoanalysts who carry out the treatment of future colleagues, gives great weight, correctly, to the childhood histories and experiences of their patients. But it seems that the history of the period of adolescence, including a revival and understanding of the painful and frightening behaviors, fantasies, enactments, fears of mental disorder or illness, and out-of-control actions, may not be constructed or reconstructed during the treatment of the future psychoanalyst in ways that would allow him to own the adolescent part of his life and to understand how or why his own adolescence unfolded and was experienced in specific ways.

I see this not as a debate or difference among psychoanalysts about the technique of treatment but rather as an observation of possible events that may have contributed to the analyst's avoidance of the reconstruction and revival of a period of life which, if revived and understood, would contribute substantially to the fuller integration of a person's emotional history.

Preparation for psychoanalytic or psychotherapeutic work with the adolescent means that one's own period of adolescent life should take on emotional reality and be linked to one's present life. It means that, ultimately, as part of one's own therapeutic life, there needs to be a revival and reconstruction of the meaning of the fantasies, relationships, fears, perverse and psychotic ideas or actions of that period, the out-of-control behavior, the meaning of one's private sexual and masturbatory activities and relationships, and the thoughts of giving up or dying—in other words, the frightening and often painful experiences of one's own adolescence and how these have shaped one's emotional life and are related to one's present life or have been forgotten and need to be confronted and integrated. Without this, the period of adolescence will remain something we only hear and read about, but that it is all kept away from our emotional lives.

The danger of this work with the troubled or the ill adolescent is that we may keep a distance from the real emotional life of the adolescent in trouble and from the emotional meaning of our own adolescence. If this happens, we cannot ever become therapeutically involved with the adolescent patient but instead must repeat what we have been taught without tying these critical insights to the real emotional and troubled life of the adolescent patient.

There is also another danger. Adolescent psychopathology inevitably reaches back to the earliest experiences of our lives, when psychotic anxieties of destruction, annihilation, abandonment, of being both boy and girl at the same time, or of getting back into the mother's body as a way of stopping life or changing oneself are felt to be real and all important. Unless the psychoanalyst can give emotional meaning to these primitive wishes and fears—and that we can do only through our private experiences rather than through learning—work with the ill or potentially ill adolescent remains a theoretical exercise for the psychoanalyst rather than a vital experience for the adolescent.

The fragility of our own defenses against such memories—which remain powerful and frightening throughout our lives unless we can revive them and assign meaning to them—may explain why, for many of us, our adolescent lives remain a source of fear, causing us to struggle throughout much of our post-adolescent years to avoid recalling this period of life.

The Adolescent Psychoanalyst and the Adolescent Patient

The adolescent psychoanalyst will inevitably encounter some adolescent patients whose defenses may give the impression that they are psychotic. The manifestations in the behavior of adolescents who have experienced a developmental breakdown vary immensely, but they inevitably include physical attacks on the adolescent's own body by suicide or attempted suicide, drug taking, perverse enactments through the use of one's own body, and physical violence. At our Adolescent Centre, it became clear that the adolescent's relationship to his own body is an essential area of change and a constant vehicle for the expression of his fears about sexuality or primitive fantasy. It is through the relation to his own sexually mature body that the core of the adolescent's mental life, whether normal or abnormal, is expressed and experienced.

If this is so, the adolescent psychoanalyst needs to have the internal freedom to enable the vulnerable or ill adolescent to feel that he can begin to think of expressing anything, especially things he has never before been able to put into words, whether frightening or psychotic, perverse or destructive, intimidating or loving. But we know that a characteristic of the behavior of very disturbed adolescents is to express thought and feeling through action, with the unconscious need not to give words or meaning to their actions. Every therapeutic experience in the treatment of the severely disturbed adolescent may include long periods of: action rather than conscious thought, hatred of the psychoanalyst for expecting words instead of action, experiencing words as passive submission, fear rather than trust, despair rather than hope, and violence rather than love. He may wish or need to run away from his own mind and to believe that understanding is frightening or painful or useless compared to the omnipotence of action. It means that there is the constant risk that the adolescent patient will escape into illness rather than risk putting meaning to his primitive fantasies and his destructive relationship to his mind and his sexually mature body.

The adolescent who has experienced a developmental breakdown has rejected his physically mature body. He will experience his sexual life as wrong, bad, shameful, or frightening; he may believe that his sexually mature body houses the madness that he feels is there to attack him or humiliate him or make him "mad" and unable to be helped. This may be the adolescent's way of expressing his fear of his own sadism or aggression or his wish to murder himself, his parents, or the psychoanalyst.

INTERNAL FREEDOM

Internal freedom in the psychoanalyst is an essential ingredient in the treatment of the adolescent. I refer here not only to enabling the adolescent patient to feel ultimately free to confront anything and to add new meaning to his behavior and fantasies but rather to the essential qualities the adolescent psychoanalyst must bring to his therapeutic work. By "internal freedom" I refer to the ability to postpone judgment about the adolescent's actions and thoughts, to find personal contentment outside the therapeutic setting with the adolescent, to feel at home in acknowledging and assigning meaning to his own innermost thoughts, secrets, and wishes in ways that protect his freedom in his work with the vulnerable adolescent.

Of course, such freedom must exist in our therapeutic work with any person, whether child, adolescent, or adult. But therapeutic work with the adolescent raises or revives in the analyst primitive fears or dangers that may be very different from those revived in therapeutic work with the child or adult. For example, homosexual fantasies or attractions may have existed or may still exist for us, and therapeutic work with the adolescent may be experienced as probing the adolescent's body in a secret and sexual way. Or we may feel that work with the vulnerable or ill adolescent in an unconscious confrontation with one or both of our own oedipal parents, where we blame our oedipal parent for failure and enact our need to save the adolescent and to participate in the patient's unconscious need to destroy the oedipal parent.

THE ADOLESCENT PATIENT, THE PSYCHOTIC CORE, AND THE PSYCHOANALYST

Therapeutic work, whether with a child, an adolescent, or an adult, contains many conflicting feelings and wishes—to save, to make amends, to feel responsible for the rebirth of the patient, or to steal or spoil those qualities of the patient that evoke envy or hatred or failure in us. But a special characteristic of therapeutic work with the seriously disturbed adolescent is the need to confront and assign meaning to the psychotic core that houses the patient's pathology. This is a core that must be revived and reconstructed. The possibility of creating such a therapeutic experience for the adolescent rests wholly with the psychoanalyst and depends on his own internal freedom.

Beyond this, the adolescent psychoanalyst must have the internal freedom to value normality in adolescence and to be able to rely on his own neutrality in helping the vulnerable or ill adolescent to question his reasons for having unconsciously chosen the path toward pathology—a pathology that destroys the ability to love and to experience love through relationships and through the ownership of a sexual body. The psychoanalyst may be neutral only if he values and protects his own normality, rather than falling into the trap of either avoiding understanding the reasons for his own developmental compromises or idealizing the solutions he has unconsciously adopted in his own life, which necessarily keep him at a distance from the pain or panic that existed in his own life and may now be present in the adolescent patient's life.

BIBLIOGRAPHY

AICHHORN, A. (1925). *Wayward Youth*. London: Imago, 1951.

BERNFELD, S. (1938). Types of adolescence. *Psychoanal. Quarterly*, 7:243–53.

BLOS, P. (1962). *On Adolescence*. New York: Free Press.

DEUTSCH, H. (1968). *Selected Problems of Adolescence*. New York: Int. Univ. Press.

ERIKSON, E. H. (1959). *Identity and the Life Cycle. Psychological Issues*, momo.⊥. New York: Int. Univ. Press.

FREUD, A. (1958). Adolescence. *Psychoan. Study of the Child*, 13:255–78.

FREUD, A. (1962). Assessment of Childhood Disturbances. *Psychoan. Study of the Child*, 17:149–58.

FREUD, A. (1965). *Normality and Pathology in Childhood*. New York: Int. Univ. Press.

FREUD, S. (1905). Three essays on the theory of sexuality. *Standard Edition*, 7:125–243.

JACOBSON, E. (1964). *The Self and the Object World*. New York: Int. Univ. Press.

KATAN, M. (1969). A psychoanalytic approach to the diagnosis of paranoia. *Psychoan. Study Child*, 24:328–57.

KATAN, M. (1975). Childhood memories as contents of schizophrenic hallucinations and delusions. *Psychoan. Study Child*, 30:357–74.

KLEIN, M. (1958). On the development of mental functioning. *Int. J. Psychoanal.* 39:84–90.

LAUFER, M. (1965). Assessment of adolescent disturbances: The application of Anna Freud's diagnostic profile. *Psychoan. Study Child*, 20:99–123.

LAUFER, M. (1968). The body image, the function of masturbation, and adolescence: Problems of the ownership of the body. *Psychoan. Study Child*, 23:114–37.

LAUFER, M. E. (1981). The adolescent's use of the body in object relationships and in the transference. A comparison of borderline and narcissistic modes of functioning. *Psychoan. Study Child*, 36:163–80.

LAUFER, M., LAUFER, M. E. (1984). *Adolescence and Developmental Breakdown*. New Haven: Yale Univ. Press; 1995, Karnac Books, London.

RITVO, S. (1978). The psychoanalytic process in childhood. *Psychoan. Study Child*, 33:295–305.

RITVO, S. (1984). The image and uses of the body in psychic conflict: With special reference to eating disorders in adolescence. *Psychoanal. Study Child*, 39:449–69.

SCHILDER, P. (1935). *The Image and Appearance of the Human Body.* New York: Int. Univ. Press, 1950.

SOLNIT, A. J. (1959). Panel report: the vicissitudes of ego development in adolescence. *J. Amer. Psychoanal. Assn.* 7:523–36.

SOLNIT, A. J. (1984). Preparing. *Psychoanal. Study Child*, 39:613–32.

Psychoanalysis on the Beat

Children, Police, and Urban Trauma

STEVEN MARANS, PH.D.

Anna Freud's legacy to child psychoanalysis was her understanding and description of the complexities of development and her ability to apply her findings to the care of children both within and outside of the consulting room. In addition to her approach to consultation with nonanalytic professionals concerned with children's development and well-being, she established a model for generations of child analysts and other analytically oriented clinicians. Both of Ms. Freud's concepts of development and collaboration with other professionals have served as a basis for the implementation of the Child Development-Community Policing Program in New Haven, Connecticut. This collaboration between mental health and police professionals will be described in this paper, with particular emphasis on the application of Ms. Freud's work to attempts to intervene on the behalf of children and families exposed to urban violence.

WHILE THE SITES SHIFTED—FROM THE CONSULTING ROOM, TO THE WAR nurseries, to the care of Holocaust survivors, to the well-baby clinic and nursery school of the Hampstead Clinic—Anna Freud's gift of observation and her capacity to consider the perspective of the child remained constant. From her multiple vantage points, Anna Freud was

Harris Assistant Professor of Child Psychoanalysis, Yale University Child Study Center, New Haven.

The author is grateful to the Rockefeller Foundation, the Smart Family Foundation, the Jewish Women International, and the U.S. Dept. of Justice, Office of Juvenile Justice and Delinquency Prevention, for their support of this work.

The Psychoanalytic Study of the Child 51, ed. Albert J. Solnit, Peter B. Neubauer, Samuel Abrams, and A. Scott Dowling (Yale University Press, copyright © 1996 by Albert J. Solnit, Peter B. Neubauer, Samuel Abrams, and A. Scott Dowling).

able to articulate her findings into theories that have formed a frame of reference for the observations of several generations of child analysts. Clinical psychoanalysis, however, is not the only beneficiary of the decades of her work. In addition to developing the conceptual tools for conducting the psychoanalytic treatment of children, Anna Freud devoted much of her work to conveying her understanding of the child's experience to those other professionals whose work impacts on children's care and the course of their development. Here, as in her leadership of clinical discussions and in her theoretical writings, she attempted to bring complex formulations about the inner and outer life of the child into a language of observations that could be recognized by anyone who could bear to see and revisit life through the eyes of the child.

As such, she set two standards that are her legacy—to appreciate the complexity of the child's experience of his life and to describe the implications of that experience in ways that are accessible to those professionals whose handling and decisions have a potential bearing on the trajectory of the child's development.

Anna Freud taught her students to attend, to listen, to observe, and to apply a psychoanalytic perspective to the clinical and extra-clinical interventions that aim to maximize developmental potential.

One enduring area of such psychoanalytic concern has been the impact of various types of traumatic experiences on children at each phase of development (see Mayes and Cohen, this volume). In recent years, the problem of violence is apparent throughout the world as children are increasingly exposed to war, refugee status, and separation from families. In the United States, an increasing number of children have been exposed to familial and inner city, communal violence (Marans et al., in press; Marans, 1994; Martinez and Richters, 1993). Children living in urban centers afflicted with high rates of violence are especially vulnerable to the psychic trauma that occurs when the "actual danger" (Freud, 1926) is in the form of gunfire, wounding, and death. Traditional clinical services alone are unequal to the task of responding to the number of children whose development may be compromised as a result of their acute and chronic experiences of violence in their homes, on the streets of their neighborhoods, and at school.

In the tradition of Anna Freud's involvement with other professionals concerned about children (child care workers, teachers, pediatricians, social workers, and lawyers), child analysts at the Child Study Center have recognized the central role played by a group whose professional relationship with children has not always been appreciated:

the police. As the profession with the most immediate and frequent contact with children and families exposed to and involved in violence, police officers can have a profound impact on the ways in which children experience their increasingly unsafe, disorganized world.

The collaboration between child analysts and police, the Yale Child Development-Community Policing (CD-CP) program,[1] is based on the application of psychoanalytic concepts that provide a frame of reference for extending the observations and interventions of police officers and analytically informed clinicians in responding to the needs of children who have been exposed to or involved in violent events. Prior to the inception of the Child Development-Community Policing program, police contact with mental health professionals generally was limited to delivering psychotic or suicidal patients to the hospital emergency service. Similarly, official responsibilities and options regarding children were restricted to such acts as arresting juvenile offenders and referring abused and neglected children to social services. They did not refer the numerous children they encountered on the scenes of violent crimes or exposed to family violence for clinical services. The goal of the CD-CP program is to expand the role and options available to police officers through training and consultation and to introduce a new partnership in which psychoanalytic principles are conveyed and applied.

A major result of the New Haven Department of Police Service–Child Study Center collaboration has been the expansion of the analysts' clinical field of observation. Clinical contact is now initiated on the scene by officers and analysts, sometimes only moments after a shooting, stabbing, or beating. Child analysts thus have an opportunity to learn more about the child's experience of violence and about the various responses from parents, professionals, and the larger community that may help to mediate the overwhelming anxiety and trauma that often follows such exposure.

THE CONTEXT OF COMMUNITY POLICING

Until a few years ago, standard police practice in the United States was primarily reactive. Officers patrolled in squad cars and were dispatched by headquarters to one complaint or crime scene after another. They were generally not known by members of the communities in which they worked. In the absence of a continuous, personal

1. The Child Development-Community Policing model, developed at the Yale Child Study Center, is being replicated around the United States under the auspices of the U.S. Department of Justice.

presence in the neighborhoods, police were often viewed as ineffective or as intruders in the neighborhoods in which they responded to criminal activity. They arrived too late and left too soon. The police themselves often felt dissatisfied. In spite of their hard and often dangerous work, they felt that they had done little to make a lasting difference. They repeatedly came back to the same neighborhoods, hangouts, and homes to deal with recurrent illegal activities and tragic consequences.

Criminal justice experts have recognized the limitations of the standard model. In many cities in the United States and around the world, police practices are being reorganized around an innovative philosophy, often referred to as community-based or problem-oriented policing. Community-based policing puts officers in neighborhoods where they walk beats, develop relationships, and try to prevent crises rather than simply respond to one after another.

In the New Haven model of community policing, police are increasingly being recruited from the ethnic communities they patrol. When these officers are placed in neighborhoods and work from small substations rather than central headquarters, they observe and experience the lives of children and families much more acutely. They learn who is involved in criminal activities, where and with whom trouble is likely to occur, and why things are heating up. They see and often know the many victims of violence—not only those who are shot, stabbed, or beaten and their assailants, but the many children who witness the events in horror or run for safety. As they have become a more established and personal presence, the police place greater emphasis on developing strategies to prevent or interrupt crime and on developing problem-solving relationships with members of the neighborhoods. Officers who walk the beat understand the rhythms and underlying dynamics within their communities. This day-to-day engagement brings additional personal burdens. As officers become closer to and more invested in the people who ask for or require their interventions, they run the increased risk of being overwhelmed by the problems they confront.

This vulnerability to seeing and feeling too much is especially pronounced in officers' engagement with children at risk. They find it particularly difficult to see children caught in the spiral of inner-city violence, children who are witnesses to family battles and street crime, and those who then move from the role of victim to perpetrator. On the beat, police officers begin to feel the pain and frustration that go with a sense of impotence, and they naturally wish to have the competence and authority to intervene more effectively.

POLICE AND THE PSYCHOANALYTIC PERSPECTIVE ON CHILDREN

In contrast to police officers, mental health professionals are equipped to respond to children's psychological distress. However, the acutely traumatized children who are most in need of clinical service are rarely seen in existing outpatient clinics until months or years later, if at all, when chronic symptoms or maladaptive behavior bring them to the attention of parents, teachers, or the juvenile courts. Thus valuable opportunities to intervene at the moment when professional contact could provide both immediate stabilization and bridges to ongoing services are lost. In order to be effective in their new roles within communities, officers need to be provided with a framework for understanding children and families, and they need new partners who can help in dealing with the challenges and tragedies they encounter.

In the Child Development-Community Policing program, Anna Freud's theories about development—the ego and superego mediation of instinctual life, the interaction between conflict and defense, the concept of developmental lines and phases, the interaction between significant environmental factors and psychic reality (A. Freud, 1936, 1965)—provide a shared frame of reference. In addition, the program adopts Anna Freud's approach to consultation, relying on a process of learning about the perspectives and experience of the other professional as a basis for considering the developmental implications of their observations and actions.

The analysts have learned that to be useful to police officers they must first see the clinical phenomena from the officers' point of view. This has been accomplished through the development of fellowships for clinicians and supervisory officers. In the Police Fellowship, clinicians move into police settings by riding along in squad cars, joining police at crime scenes, sitting in on discussions of case investigations and thus learn about the tasks, demands, and professional needs of the police. At the same time, in the Clinical Fellowship, officers become familiar with mental health settings and psychoanalytic perspectives through observations of clinical activities and consultations. Also, a 24-hour Consultation Service and weekly Case Conference provide ongoing opportunities to apply developmental concepts in the field. Where each of these components serves as a basis for the continued development of the collaboration, the seminars developed by senior police officers and Child Study Center analysts and analytically informed clinicians provide the shared conceptual framework that guide observations, discussions, and interventions.

Seminars on Child Development, Human Functioning, and Policing

The central task of the seminars is to engage officers in the examination of concepts regarding: 1) basic human needs; 2) developing capacities for self-regulation and mastery; 3) phase-specific sources of danger/anxiety; 4) the link between behavior and underlying psychic processes (i.e., the relation between anxiety and defenses); and 5) individual variation with regard to potential life adaptations. Proceeding along a developmental sequence, the seminars also highlight the ways in which phenomena originating in an earlier phase of development may be observed in various forms throughout the life cycle. Seminar leaders use scenarios encountered in police work, films and videotapes about children, and cases initiated through the Consultation Service to demonstrate that a greater understanding of human functioning does not mean inaction or decreased vigilance with regard to personal safety. Rather, through being informed by our understanding of development, the goal of the seminars is to help officers to discover new ways of observing and formulating responses to children. In addition, officers have the opportunity to establish a more realistic appreciation of the impact they can have on the lives of children and families with whom they interact.

Following a first meeting in which seminar members introduce themselves and talk about their expectations of the course, discussions begin about early development. The topic of infancy is introduced by the supervisory officer who co-leads the seminar with an analyst, who describes the following scene: "You have responded to a complaint of breach of the peace and arrive at an apartment where music is blaring. You are greeted by an angry young mother, in a disordered and dirty apartment, and three children under the age of four in similar disarray. Diaper changes for two of the children appear to be long overdue. What is your reaction?" The officers often begin the discussion by expressing their feelings of despair and anger about a scene that is all too familiar. As the instructors probe these reactions, the class begins to identify concerns about the babies who are unable to fend for themselves, about the children's physical discomfort, and about the notion that the mother is overwhelmed. What emerges from the discussion is the group's awareness of an infant's physical and emotional needs and the role of the mother in mediating and responding to them. The seminar leaders ask, "And what happens to the infant if those basic needs aren't met?" The answers run to the idea that the baby will be overwhelmed with pain, discomfort, and despair because the baby is not yet equipped to feed, clothe, or comfort itself or satisfy demands of its feelings on its own. The leaders ask for more details, and the class responds by identifying the extent of the child's capacities—the absence of verbal language, motoric maturation, coordination, cognitive processes for problem-solving, and, finally, his utter reliance on the mother for physical and emotional well-being.

Attention is then focused on the young mother. How, the leaders ask, do we understand her apparent insensitivity and incompetence? The discussion must first address her surly response to the officers and their indignation. Here the concepts of displacement and externalization are introduced. The seminar leaders expand on the discussion of a young woman apparently unable to look after her children, let alone herself. They ask, "How might she feel about herself?" The answers vary. "Like a failure?" "Maybe she just doesn't care!" The seminar leaders ask, "Given either of those possibilities, how might she feel when two police officers come to her door?" Seminar participants typically reply, "Like we're going to tell her off, tell her what she should be doing, how she should behave." Leaders expand the discussion asking, "And who are you to her at that moment? Who tells *you* you're not getting it right, messing up? Parents? teachers? a critical boss or colleague?"

In one session, an officer jumped in and offered, "Right, and then when she feels criticized, she takes on an obnoxious attitude and treats us like dirt." Another officer added, "as though she already knows who you are." In this particular discussion, the clinical co-leader suggested that perhaps from the moment of their arrival, the officers represent something very familiar to the young woman. The clinician added, "Before you open your mouth, you may be the critical voice, the presentation of authority, the voice that agrees with her own self-criticism and assessment of incompetence. How does it feel to be criticized? What is it like to feel inadequate and to have someone, by his very presence on your doorstep, point it out to you? Is it possible that her surly and combative response serves a defensive function that is triggered by you but not about you personally?" And the discussion goes on, often ending with the officers' greater appreciation for the complexity of the scene and the interaction but with the residual wish to do something concrete for the babies—either to implore the woman to be a more attentive mother or to remove the children so that they can have a better home.

The Robertsons' film *John* (1969) is shown in the following session. In the discussion, seminar members describe the 17-month-old's efforts to soothe himself in the midst of a nine-day separation from his parents. They note John's attempt to reach out to the child-care nurses, cuddly toys, and the observer, and his utter despair when these efforts fail. The discussion also compares John to the other children, who have spent their entire lives in the residential nursery. Seminar members often observe that while these children seem unfazed by the limited attention and multiple changes of nursing staff, unlike John, they appear to be dominated by aggressive, driven, and need-satisfying behavior. Slowly and often painfully, as the discussion continues, the apparently simple solution of removing the child from care when parenting seems inadequate fades. The idea that removal always represents rescue is replaced by a growing appreciation of the complexity of the child-parent relationship, including recognition of the developmental significance of continuity of care and the impact of disrupting it. In addition, seminar members have a fuller understanding of the balance between the child's needs and capacities as well as the distress that follows when those needs are not met.

The link between these processes and overt behavior *and* the observers' responses and overt behavior is pursued as the seminar moves into the next session, in which the hallmarks of the toddler phase are introduced. Videotapes of normal children engaged in imaginative play allow officers to consider the child's use of fantasy, identifications, and burgeoning cognitive and physical resources to achieve aim-inhibited sources of pleasure and mastery. Failures in negotiating oedipal conflicts over competition, envy, love and hate and the often unstable, overstimulating home situations are explored in discussions of latency-age children who come to the attention of police because of their anti-social activities. Similarly, puberty is discussed in terms of the intensification of struggles over sexual and aggressive urges.

Seminar leaders introduce phases of development by asking officers to describe the most salient aspects—either observed or assumed to play a part—of a given period of life. As the discussion evolves, officers often invoke their own memories as a vehicle for understanding the behaviors they encounter on the street and as a way of becoming conscious of the complicated identifications that these interactions may evoke. For example, when discussing puberty and early adolescence, officers initially describe their concerns about the provocative, tough, drug-involved, pregnant kids and the frustration they experience when logic and warnings about consequences seem to have no impact on behavior. However, as they begin to talk about their own experiences in this phase of development, their frustration and angry dismissal of these children are substantially altered. Officers often describe aspects of their own lives or things about particular children they have met in their work that they have not been able to forget. The accounts speak to the vulnerability, anxiety, and loneliness so common in this period of development and the various means used to defend against these feelings. Stories of fighting, social isolation, school difficulties, and losses alternate with stories about best friends, first girl- and boyfriends, team sports, and the like. The discussions inevitably focus on concerns about body image, group acceptance, struggles with parents, losses, and the overreaching experience of embarrassment and urgency in the competing wishes for competent, independent functioning and the wish to remain a small child.

John Singleton's film *Boyz n' the Hood* (1991) is used as the text for seminars dealing with adolescence. Many who have seen or heard about the film assume that it is simply an action-packed story of gang warfare in central Los Angeles. As the seminar participants come to the end of the course, however, they are surprised to discover that, regardless of the setting, the story is about development in an especially familiar territory: the challenges, hopes, and dilemmas inherent in adolescence. The discussion moves from issues of race and the socioeconomics of the inner city to the internal and external contributions to the fate of two brothers in the film. One becomes a gun-toting drug dealer, the other a high school football star bound for college until he is shot dead by gang members.

As the seminars come to an end, officers increasingly refer to their responses to the scenes of violence and suffering they confront on a daily basis. Sealing over, "getting used to it," and distancing themselves as best they can or displacing their frustration onto citizens with whom they interact or family members, viewing the world dichotomously— "us versus them"—and heightening the sense of vigilance are themes that commonly emerge in the discussions. These are discussed in terms of the defensive functions they serve against unwanted feelings of fear, inadequacy, sadness, despair, and anger; and officers become aware of their inner reactions and how their work is influenced by them.

CHANGES IN POLICE RESPONSES

Regardless of the setting, the aim of the discussions for both officers and clinicians is to "place ourselves in the position of children of different ages, of different developmental phases, and of different backgrounds" (Goldstein, Solnit, and Freud, 1979, p. 137). For the officers, the opportunity to reflect on what they observe, to have a framework for ordering what might have otherwise been too overwhelming to notice and to have colleagues with whom to share the burden of responding—at any hour—has led to dramatic changes in police practices regarding children. These changes are reflected in officers regularly referring children who have witnessed and experienced violence, and, increasingly, children who have committed serious violent offenses.

Incorporating developmental perspectives, the changes are also apparent in standards of police practice that go beyond making referrals for children victimized or involved in violence. These include, for example, consideration of the ways in which parents are dealt with when issued a warrant or put under arrest. In one typical seminar discussion an officer described a high speed chase involving a man and 5-year-old boy on a motorcycle. When he finally stopped the man, he began screaming at him about the way in which he was endangering the young boy. In reporting the scene, the officer described the panic he felt that accompanied his fantasy of the motorcycle crashing and killing the boy. However, what bothered him most after this incident was that as he yelled at the man, the boy began to cry and shouted at him to stop being mean to his father. The officer pointed out that while he had justified his tirade as in the boy's best interests, he had completely left out any consideration of the boy's identification with or admiration of the father, regardless of whatever anxiety he might have felt about father's reckless behavior. In addition, the officer's wish for the boy to view the police in a positive light had in fact been undermined by his own intense emotional reaction of fear followed by anger. In retrospect, the officer decided that taking the father aside to discuss the danger about his concerns for the boy's safety in addition to issuing a ticket might have served the boy's and his own professional interests far more effectively.

Similarly, officers have become more attentive to the humiliation and greater potential for dangerous confrontation when they deal with adolescents—especially juvenile offenders—in a harsh manner. As officers have become regular fixtures in the neighborhoods, they have replaced anonymous responses to the groups of kids on the streets with interactions that are informed by familiarity and relationships with individuals. From the seminars to the streets, this contact is enhanced by officers' increased appreciation of the upheaval of adolescent development, often compounded by the despair and feelings of impotence associated with severe social adversity. As a result, wholesale condemnation, frustration, and anger are not the only responses to the provocative—and, at times illegal—behavior with which adolescents confront the police. The recognition of displacements and counter-reactions that are so often associated with police-adolescent interactions on the street has also led to a more judicious and strategic use of authority when it is based on new relationships that replace stereotypic responses of the past. In turn, police imposition of authority (e.g., clearing a street corner known for drug activity, keeping public noise down, picking up truant students, etc.) is now more frequently met with compliance rather than an immediate escalation to violent confrontation and arrest.

Where the application of developmental principles have impacted police approaches to typical interactions with youth on the streets and in schools, it has also led to interventions that are anything but standard in the traditional approach to law enforcement. Following the shooting death of a 17-year-old gang member, there was concern about retaliation and further bloodshed. In the days that followed the death, grieving gang members congregated on the corner where the shooting had taken place. The efforts at increased presence and containment were in the form of police, neighborhood-based probation officers, and clinicians spending time on the corner listening to gang members express their grief. As one senior police officer put it, "We could show our concern for their trauma by being with them, lending an adult ear to their misery. Alternatively, we could put more officers on the street, show them who's boss and with a show of force, sweep them off the corner as often as necessary. . . . We could then offer them an additional enemy and wait for them to explode." At this crucial moment, however, the police did not assume the role of enemy. They did not serve as the target for displaced rage or, in confrontation, offer an easy antidote to sadness and helplessness. Rather than turning passive into active "payback" in blood, gang members discreetly assisted the police in making a swift arrest in the shooting. As one gang member, the brother of the victim, said to a neighborhood cop, "You were there for us, that helped . . . and we were there for you."

Where arrests continue to be an essential tool for police, a new look at the range of preventative measures has been added to the repertoire of law enforcement. In New Haven, arrests of juvenile offenders involved in drug dealing, assault, and murder are often accompanied by requests for consultation from psychoanalytically oriented clinicians. In many situations, the officer's concern about the psychological status of a young offender may lead to questions about whether jail or hospitalization is the more appropriate, immediate disposition. In the context of collaboration, questions about what the child needs has expanded what the officer has to offer the child, the family, and the community beyond the arrest and detention. For example, officers now offer referrals for clinical evaluations in 80 percent of the arrests of juvenile firesetters.

As police officers have found a forum for reflecting on what they have observed and have found partners in responding, they no longer need to simply turn away from the traumatogenic events they were unable to prevent. Instead, the police are able to consider the children's unfolding experiences and needs long after they have left the crime scene.

CD–CP RESPONSES TO TRAUMA

When officers have an opportunity to expand their knowledge and repertoire of interventions, the collaboration with the police provides clinicians with a new setting in which to increase their understanding of the impact of violence and trauma. Discussions about referrals from the CD–CP Consultation Service frequently emphasize the extent to which children describe the violent events they have witnessed in terms of developmental phase-specific anxieties that are aroused. By following the unfolding stories of the children exposed to violence, clinicians in the program are able to see more clearly what constitutes the specific dangers that overwhelm the individual child, or what aspects and meanings of the event are experienced as "traumatizing." Clinicians generally assume that traumatization is related to the "facts" about violence that has been witnessed. These assumptions may have little to do with the child's actual experience of the event or the meaning that is attributed by the child in its aftermath. In turn, little attention may be paid to learning about the child in order to begin to appreciate what an experience of violence might be for the individual child in the context of his or her life—history, family constellation, phase development, defense configuration, and the like—and therefore, what interventions might be most useful. As Anna Freud pointed out: "Traumatic events should not be taken at their face value but should be translated into their specific meaning for the given child. Attributes such as heroism or cowardice, generosity or greed, rationality or irrationality have to be understood differently in different individuals, and judged in the light of their genetic roots, their phase and age-adequateness, etc." (1965, p. 139).

Consideration of the child's perspective has led to ways of diminishing the additionally traumatizing effects of how the police react to the child's situation in the wake of their exposure to violence.

Sgt. G. described Lisa, a 7-year-old girl who witnessed her beloved neighbor bleed to death after being stabbed by another woman living nearby. Believing he was protecting her from the gore of the crime scene, Sgt. G. had Lisa wait on the porch outside while officers conducted their investigation. He was haunted by the intent gaze, a mixture of despair and rage, that Lisa fixed on him when he finally invited her back into the apartment as the officers were leaving. The next day Sgt. G. went back to the house and spoke with Lisa and her grandmother, and he understood that his attempt at being helpful had backfired because he did not consider what Lisa was experiencing, what was needed, and from whom. As Sgt. G. explained in the case conference, "in the midst of so much blood and terror, what she needed was to be close to her grandmother, the most stable figure in her life, not to be stranded alone with images of the scene." Both Lisa and her grandmother eagerly accepted his offer of a referral for clinical services. Lisa's treatment revealed the extent to which frightening themes and fantasies involving extremes in love and hate dominated her inner life. Her ambivalence and uncertainty about relationships were heightened by her experience of growing up with a heroin-addicted mother who dropped in and out of her life and by concerns about her grandmother's fragile health and age. Both internalized and external conflicts were boldly underlined by her confusion of loyalties in the stabbing. While she mourned the death of one beloved and idealized maternal substitute, she anxiously told her therapist about the love letters she was writing to the assailant, now in jail on murder charges. This dangerous woman also seemed safer and more available than her inconsistent, absent mother.

Nine-year-old Mike witnessed the shooting death of an older, idolized teenage neighbor, John. The older boy had squarely beaten an opponent in a game of one-on-one basketball and was then accused of cheating. The two teenagers got into a shoving match that culminated in John's challenger pulling out a gun and shooting him twice in the chest. John died almost immediately. Mike was the only witness to the murder, and the police needed to interview him. Mike was distressed by the death of his friend, and the police decided to interview him later that day. Rather than see him at police headquarters downtown, the investigating officer asked the boy and his mother what location would be most comfortable and also if they would like a referral made to a CD–CP therapist. At their request, Mike and his mother were seen by the therapist immediately after the police interview.

In the acute phase of the intervention, the therapist invited the boy to draw pictures and he drew picture after picture in which the shooter and gun grew larger while the boy and his teenage friend shrank to mere dots on the page. Over the next days, Mike had recurring nightmares and was irritable at home and school, fought with his younger brother and peers. Although his father had abandoned them when Mike was three years old, his mother described an unremarkable developmental history prior to the shooting and said he had done fairly well in school. His mother's only concern was Mike spent too much time away from home, hours on his own or watching the older boys play basketball on the courts, where the shooting had taken place. She worried that Mike would fall under the influence of the drug dealers that were part of their public housing landscape.

During the course of the twice weekly psychotherapy that continued for eight months after the shooting, Mike's drawings and accompanying narratives grew more elaborate. In them, he revealed the central role that John had played in his inner life as a realization of a dimly remembered and highly idealized father—strong, competent, and interested in him. Mike could increasingly describe how John's attention—letting him hang out at the basketball court and occasionally teaching him some shots—had been an important contrast to his mother's nagging and worrying about his safety that made him feel like a baby. In this context, as Mike repeatedly returned to depicting the moment that John was shot, his sense of disbelief turned to grief and then to rage and guilt. As he described the enduring image of watching John fall to the ground with an expression of surprise, Mike could now put into words what constituted the essence of his traumatic moment. The figure of strength and competence with whom he so desperately identified fell like a helpless baby. He again felt abandoned and helpless. With the recognition of the link between the past and the present, associated with his longings for a father and friend who had abandoned him, Mike and his therapist could begin to make sense of the irritability and fighting that served to re-establish power, express rage, and defend against "babyish" feelings associated with longings for a father and friend who had abandoned him. Increasingly, Mike was alerted to those situations in which his sense of competence felt under attack—whether the joking of friends, teasing of a younger brother, or the concerns and expectations of his mother—and gave rise to angry counterattacks. His irritability and fighting diminished and eventually stopped as did the nightmares that captured his terror and robbed him of the safety of sleep.

Although Mike ended his treatment with a good resolution of his post-traumatic adaptation, both setting and history make Mike vulnerable to a dangerous future. How will the shooting and all of its meanings be organized and represented in the developmental phases to come?

Children referred to the CD–CP program by police give child analysts the opportunity to learn more about the ways trauma is individually defined by a convergence of current and past experience. The children's experience of overwhelming anxiety derives from the realization of nodal, phase-specific fantasies, concerns, and conflicts regarding aggressive and sadistic wishes, fears of object loss, bodily integrity and damage, or guilt and shame associated with loss of control and infantile feelings of helplessness (Marans, 1994; Marans et al., in press). Moreover, the psychoanalytic understanding of development and psychic functioning guide the process of appreciating the child's and family's experience of potentially traumatic events.

PSYCHOANALYTIC PERSPECTIVES ON VIOLENCE AND TRAUMA

The psychoanalytic understanding of trauma in families, of the impact of witnessing violence in the inner city, and of the multiple pathways that can lead children from being traumatized into becoming aggressive is an important complement of other approaches to understanding children in this era of violence (Marans and Cohen, 1993; Mayes and Cohen, 1993; Pynoos and Nader, 1989). Psychoanalytic theories stand alongside sociological, political, economic and other "explanatory" systems. In this area of research, contemporary psychoanalysts serve a special role in underlining the complexity of these various relationships—individual differences among children and families—and the distance between outer displays and internal experiences.

Anna Freud demonstrated, in her work during the blitz of World War II, that children responded as much to their parent's affects and to disruptions in parenting as to the actual dangers of bombing (1943; Hellman, 1962, 1983). These observations have been repeated wherever children are studied during warfare, as in Israel during the missile attacks in the Gulf War, when child analysts worked with children and families evacuated from their homes and in the midst of natural catastrophes (Laor et al., 1995). When children are provided an interpretive frame, when their families and they can see their exposure and suffering within the broader context of the community's shared set of beliefs and experiences, the personal trauma is transmuted. However, unlike British families during World War II or Israeli families that have endured a series of wars since the founding of the nation, the children who are exposed to violence in the inner city of the United States often have little sense of community, ideology, or, at times, cohesive family structure on which they can rely for mutative support and amelioration of trauma. It is in these circumstances that the police officer, when properly equipped and supported by acute clinical intervention, may be the first and best source of stability and containment available to the child and his family. Psychoanalytic understanding of the nature of trauma and of the importance of intellectual, interpretive, and psychosocial mediation of experiences guide all efforts in helping children caught in war and experiencing or witnessing violence.

Through acute and long-term involvement with children who have been overwhelmed by their exposure to violence, child analysts have an opportunity to extend the field of observation and inquiry into what accounts for the long-term impact of trauma. Here there is an important convergence of psychoanalytic understanding of individual differences in the processing and meaning of events, biological theories of brain functioning, and developmental theories about critical stages in development. There is thus a confluence between what the brain perceives and the mind understands. What is traumatic represents the conspiracy of both: when the protective barriers give away, presumably both psychological structures and biological structures are overwhelmed (Pynoos, 1995; Pynoos and Nader, 1989; van der Kolk, Greenberg, Boyd, and Krystal, 1985; Watson, Hoffman, and Wilson, 1988). One model of the neurophysiological mediation of stress and trauma (Southwick, Krystal, and Morgan, 1993; Perry, 1994) proposes that when the individual is unable to anticipate or defend against an experience of overwhelming danger, the central regulation of the noradranergic system—which mediates heart rate, respiration, and startle reflexes—is compromised.

In the work with the New Haven Department of Police Service, child analysts have had the advantage of observing children and adults from within minutes of their being exposed to acute episodes of violence. This proximity and timing of involvement has allowed clinicians to follow patients' responses from their acute to longer-term adaptations. Regardless of their premorbid or previolence exposure functioning, each of the children and adults seen has presented with a range of acute symptoms involving dysregulation of affect, attention, memory, and bodily functions such as sleep. Subsequently, each has shown a marked exacerbation and/or introduction of increased anxiety and new symptomatic behavior.

Integrating physiologic and psychoanalytic models may be useful in understanding the acute presentation of trauma. In the acute phase, the individual's attempts to process, anticipate, and regulate levels of excitation through typical patterns of mentation and defense may be seen in increased motor agitation—at one end of the spectrum—and withdrawal, isolation, and numbing at the other end. Subsequent hypervigilance, symptom formation, and propensity for dysregulation of basic ego functions—both generalized or restimulated by traumatic reminders—may thus reflect alterations in central neuro-regulatory capacities as well as attempts to mediate somato-psychic experiences through the reintroduction of ideational representation, signal anxiety, and subsequent defensive responses in the service of restitution and ego reorganization.

Short-term distress, as in brief separations, leads to adaptive coping, structure formation, and healthy defenses. These prime the child's psychological "immune" system, allowing him to accommodate to the experiential "viruses" of the real world. Persistent distress, as in repeated exposure to violence in the home, in school, and on the neighborhood streets, predisposes the child to failure in developing the ability to feel safe and secure with others or when alone, to enjoy reciprocity, and to tolerate normal frustrations. What constitutes a normal, "immunizing dose" and what overwhelms the mental adaptive immune system remain crucial questions for those studying children living in psychosocial adversity. They are the types of questions that represent potential areas of collaboration among child psychoanalysts, child psychiatrists, social workers, and developmental psychologists. The Child Development-Community Policing program offers a vantage point for addressing these questions.

SUMMARY

Regardless of the setting, Anna Freud invited observers to reflect on what they saw from the perspective of the child and provided a conceptual framework that served as a guide that could help to organize and increase the range of their observations. Anna Freud was not content to simply observe and learn about the inner workings of children's minds or about the paths of their development. What, she might ask, can we learn about the unfolding lives of children so that we can do the least amount of harm to them? And who must see what we have learned in order to support children's optimal growth?

Anna Freud was devoted to the notion that a greater understanding of development and of children's perspectives could inform the ways in which children are treated—in the midst of a psychoanalytic treatment, a custody dispute, a hospitalization, a routine pediatric exam, in the classroom, and in the home. Both in and out of the consulting room, her work reflected an interest in the special populations of children who had endured special, significant environmental factors that shaped internal experience and adaptations in daily life. In considering the role of the environment in children's development Anna Freud suggested: "That every single aspect of the child's personality is affected adversely unless definite sources of supply and support are made available to him has been proved beyond doubt by analytic work carried on with the children of severely disturbed parents, concentration camp and institutionalized children, orphaned children, handicapped children, etc." (1968, p. 116). In this paper, "Indications and Contraindications for Child Analysis" (1968), Anna Freud discussed the dilemma that often confronts analysts when their assessment indicates that the damage to a child's development is "caused and maintained by active, ongoing influences lodged in the environment" (p. 115). She goes on to point out that whether these negative influences either disregard and frustrate or actively oppose the normal course of development, the child victim is in need of therapeutic help. However, "in neither case is the type of help clearly indicated, nor the therapist's role in the process clearly circumscribed" (p. 115).

Anna Freud's ability to make her findings about the inner lives of children accessible to nonanalysts has helped to shape policies and practices that affect the lives of children in multiple circumstances and settings. In addition, her pioneering work introduced a model for the role played by child analysts outside of clinical hour—as consultants, teachers, and partners—translating and applying psychoanalytic principles of development to a variety of settings in which development occurs. This role has been an especially important complement to direct clinical work, particularly in those cases or situations in which the type of therapeutic help, the role of the therapist, or the needs of the child could not be adequately defined or addressed in the consulting room alone. Without the opportunity to learn from children in the clinical setting we would have little role to assume in helping others consider what children need. Without venturing beyond the consulting room, child analysts might have little opportunity to be heard or to learn more about those exigent circumstances in children's lives that so often undermine developmental potential and immobilize the efforts of adult caregivers to intervene on their behalf.

In the Child Development-Community Policing program, child analysts have found a new setting in which Anna Freud's principles of development can be applied, explored, and expanded. Through the program, the field of observation has been increased by a collaboration that requires the development of a common language in which the observations, concerns, and approaches of disparate professionals who deal with the children at greatest risk for developmental psychopathology can be extended.

For many of the children and families referred by officers trained in the program, chronic symptoms and adaptation that immobilizes progressive development may no longer be the only outcome of their exposure to violence. For the officers themselves, the availability of immediate consultation has provided an additional resource that has often allowed them to take on such understanding and to feel more effective in the face of tragedy. By brokering clinical services and attending to the emotional needs of the children involved, officers have a new way of "taking control" and becoming active in the aftermath of violence rather than simply feeling overwhelmed by it themselves, sealing over, and quickly turning away from the scene. For many of the children and families, the referrals may offer not only accessible and responsive clinical services for the first time but may also reflect a very new and different—that is, positive—experience with the police. In many of these situations, police are not viewed simply as providing too little, too late but are seen as benign figures of authority who are able to play a role in reestablishing a semblance of stability in the midst of the emotional chaos that often follows children's and families' direct exposure to violence.

As cases are followed in the weekly Case Conference, the child analysts and other analytically informed investigators and clinicians are able to explore the effects of exposure to violence on the children, their families, and the professionals who become involved with them. In turn, clinicians and officers are able to learn more about the implications of our respective interventions, as well as the potential benefits and limitations of our coordinated efforts.

BIBLIOGRAPHY

FREUD, A. (1936). *The Ego and the Mechanisms of Defense.* The Writings of Anna Freud, Vol. II. New York: International University Press, rev. ed., 1966.

——— (1965). *Normality and Pathology in Childhood: Assessments of Development.* The Writings of Anna Freud, Vol. VI. New York: International University Press.

——— (1968). Indications and contraindications for child analysis. In: *Problems of Psychoanalytic Training, Diagnosis, and the Technique of Treatment.* The Writings of Anna Freud, Vol. VII. (pp. 110–23). New York: International University Press.

FREUD, A., & BURLINGHAM, D. (1943). War and Children, New York: Medical War Books.

FREUD, S. (1926). Inhibitions, symptoms and anxiety. In J. Strachey (Ed.), *The Standard Edition of the Complete Works of Sigmund Freud,* Vol. 20. London: Hogarth Press, c1974. (Originally published 1926), (77–174).

GOLDSTEIN, J., SOLNIT, A., & FREUD, A. (1979). *Before the Best Interests of the Child.* New York: Free Press.

HELLMAN, I. (1962). Hampstead nursery follow-up studies: Effects of sudden separation. *Psychoanal. Study Child,* 17:159–74.

—— (1983). Work in the Hampstead war nurseries. *Int. J. Psychoanal.*, 64:435–40.

LAOR, N., WOLMER, L., MAYES, L. C., GERSHON, A., WEIZMAN, R., & COHEN, D. J. (1995). Preschool children under SCUD attacks thirty months later: A developmental perspective on the "protective matrix" as risk-modifying-function. In press, *Archives of Psychiatry*.

MARANS, S. (1994). Community violence and children's development: Collaborative interventions. In C. Chiland & G. Young (eds.), *Children and Violence* (pp. 109–24). Northvale, N.J.: Jason Aaronson.

MARANS, S., & COHEN, D. J. (1993). Children and inner-city violence: Strategies for intervention. In: L. Leavitt & N. Fox (Eds.), *Psychological Effects of War and Violence on Children* (pp. 218–301). Hillsdale, N.J.: Lawrence Erlbaum.

MARANS, S., BERKMAN, M., & COHEN, D. J. (in press). Communal violence: Children's development and their adaptation to catastrophic circumstances. In: B. Simon & R. Apfel (eds.), *Minefields in their Hearts: The Mental Health of Children in War and Communal Violence*. New Haven: Yale University Press.

MARTINEZ, P., & RICHTERS, J. (1993). The NIMH Community Violence Project: II. Children's Distress Symptoms Associated with Violence Exposure. In: *Psychiatry*.

MAYES, L. C., & COHEN, D. J. (1993). The social matrix of aggression: Enactments and representations of loving and hating in the first years of life. *Psychoanalytic Study of the Child, 48:*150–69.

—— (1996). Anna Freud and Developmental Psychoanalytic Psychology. *Psychoanalytic Study of the Child.* 51:117–41.

PERRY, B. D. (1994). Neurobiologic sequelae of childhood trauma: Post-traumatic stress disorders in children. In Murberg, M. (ed.): *Catecholamine Function in Post-Traumatic Stress Disorder: Emerging Concepts*. Washington, D.C.: American Psychiatric Press, 223–55.

PYNOOS, R., STEINBERG, A., & WRAITH, R. (1995). A developmental model of childhood traumatic stress. In: Ciccetti, D. & Cohen, D. (eds.) *Manual of Developmental Psychopathology*, New York: John Wiley & Sons.

PYNOOS, R., & NADER, K. (1989). Children's memory and proximity to violence. *Journal of the American Academy of Child and Adolescent Psychiatry, 28:* 236–41.

ROBERTSON, J., & ROBERTSON, J. (1969). *John, Seventeen Months, in Residential Nursery for Nine Days*. Distributed by New York University Film Library.

SINGLETON, J. (1991). *Boyz n' the Hood*. Distributed by United Artists.

SOUTHWICK, S. M., KRYSTAL, J. H., MORGAN, C. A., ET AL., (1993). Abnormal noradranergic function in post-traumatic stress disorder. *Archives of General Psychiatry*, 50:266–74.

VAN DER KOLK, GREENBERG, M., BOYD, H., & KRYSTAL, J. (1985). Inescapable shock, neurotransmitters, and addiction to trauma: Toward a psychobiology of post-traumatic stress. *Biological Psychiatry, 20:*314–25.

Watson, I. P. B., Hoffman, L., & Wilson, G. V. (1988). The neuropsychiatry of post-traumatic stress disorder. *British Journal of Psychiatry, 152:*164–73.

States of Overstimulation
in Early Childhood

DONALD L. ROSENBLITT, M.D.

*This chapter considers states of overstimulation in young children, espe-
cially those who present with symptomatology consistent with a phenome-
nologic diagnosis of AD/HD (distractible, overactive, and impulsive).
These children tend to have a history of overstimulation as well as other
common developmental factors. Characteristic aspects of the deviational
ego development of these children are described.*

STIMULATION AND OVERSTIMULATION ARE AMONG THE MANY TERMS IN
psychoanalysis that are used idiosyncratically yet about which there is a
certain agreement. Neither stimulation nor overstimulation is defined
in *Psychoanalytic Terms and Concepts* (Moore and Fine, 1990). The terms
are deceptively elusive, partly because external events are more central
to these concepts than they are for many other psychoanalytic concepts. A child is in a (pathological) state of overstimulation when his or
her capacity to engage in current tasks and to maintain a progressive
developmental momentum is compromised by the child's need to devote ego resources to the management of *internal* excitation. Pathological overstimulation may be manifested by experiences of flooding and
disorganization in the psyche, or through characterological rigidities,
ego deformations, or object-relational impairments. The hallmark of
pathological overstimulation is a transient or chronic state of func-

Training and supervising analyst in adult and child psychoanalysis, University of
North Carolina—Duke Psychoanalytic Education Program, and director of the Lucy
Daniels Center for Early Childhood.

The Psychoanalytic Study of the Child 51, ed. Albert J. Solnit, Peter B. Neubauer, Samuel
Abrams, and A. Scott Dowling (Yale University Press, copyright © 1996 by Albert J.
Solnit, Peter B. Neubauer, Samuel Abrams, and A. Scott Dowling).

tional imbalance between ego and instinct, with ego in the child under six being understood in the context of the role of the love object as a provider of an auxiliary ego function. I do not classify situations as pathologically overstimulating whereby the stimulation does not result in even a transient overwhelming of the psyche but is primarily experienced and registered by the psyche in the terms of internal fantasy, superego modification, or defensive response. This definition is intended to distinguish between situations in which the overstimulation is a central issue for the child's deviational development and those in which it is a contributory or ancillary factor. Thus, pathological overstimulation can be viewed as a variant of a traumatic situation.

Two domains of data have spurred interest in the overstimulated child. The first derives from studies of a number of preschool age children, collected at the evaluation service and the therapeutic nursery of the Lucy Daniels Center for Early Childhood. Certain features appear frequently, including states of distractibility, impulsivity, excitement, and wildness in children who otherwise vary in endowment, experience, maturation, ego development, fantasy content, and extent of superego development.

Children with the symptom triad of distractibility, overactivity, and impulsivity are presenting themselves with surprising frequency. There is a methodologically rigorous, albeit psychoanalytically uninformed, group of studies that complements such clinical observations. The information offered here comes from studies on Attention Deficit disorders that document the prevalence of Attention Deficit/ Hyperactivity Disorder (AD/HD) symptomatology. DSM-IV (1994) divides Attention Deficit Disorder into three subtypes. One subtype, called Attention Deficit/Hyperactivity Disorder, Predominantly Hyperactive-Impulsive Type, is associated with a cluster of behaviors that involve problematic conduct. A second subtype, called Attention Deficit/Hyperactivity Disorder, Predominantly Inattentive Type, is not so associated. There is also a category called Attention Deficit/Hyperactivity Disorder, Combined Type. A careful study conducted in 1988, based on the work of Safer and Krager (1988), estimated that at least 750,000 children per day were receiving psychostimulants, all for putative problems with attention and impulsive behaviors. A Johns Hopkins study, conducted continuously since 1971, suggested that the prevalence of pharmacological treatment could double every four to seven years. Today, some eight years after the 1988 estimates, with the burgeoning use of psychoactive drugs to treat children, including some under six years of age, we can assume that substantially more children are being identified and treated. Estimates of the incidence of the "disorder" itself range from 3 percent to 5 percent of the population (DSM-IV, 1994).

Does the fact that more children are being treated reflect only changes in patterns of identification and treatment? Epidemiological studies of changes (if any) in the prevalence of behavioral and emotional problems have tended to have profound methodological difficulties. One recent study, however, lends strong support to the possibility that we are seeing more children with AD/HD symptomatology because there *are* more such children. Achenbach (1993) has compared data from the Achenbach Child Behavior checklist over the span from 1976 to 1989. The Achenbach checklist is a widely used and highly validated instrument that rates the presence of a broad variety of symptoms and behaviors as assessed by parents and teachers. The results of this study were clear-cut. In 1989, children had more symptomatology and substantially less competency than they had in 1976: essentially, less autonomous ego development. The symptoms that tended to increase were characterological ones, many of the type associated with AD/HD syndromes, whereas neurotic type symptoms actually diminished somewhat.

AD/HD has been with us for some time in various nosological guises. Psychoanalysts have always cast a jaundiced eye on both of the assumptions of the currently dominant psychiatric paradigm about AD/HD: (1) that the phenomenology represents a coherent disease entity, and (2) that this "disease entity" has a primary neurobiological basis. Although many psychoanalysts believe that a small group of these children *do* have neurophysiological impairment as the predominant basis of their behaviors and symptoms, most analysts have focused on psychological explanations of the behavioral syndrome.

Over the years, children who have difficulties with attention or overactivity have presented themselves to child analysts. Except in the earliest days of psychoanalysis, analysts have not tended to derive diagnoses primarily from symptomatology. Case descriptions therefore have not highlighted the so-called AD/HD features of these children. Nevertheless, treatment accounts of children with such symptomatology are sprinkled throughout the child-analytic literature. Analysts have usually discovered that these children were suffering from neurotic conditions. Their motor restlessness has been conceptualized as a symptom that contains the usual mixture of discharge, defense, and self-punitiveness. Often, instinctual overstimulation is a prominent feature.

The distractibility of children with attentional difficulties has often been understood as the characterologic or symptomatic expression of inner preoccupation. These children are manifestly distractible; however, clinically they are selectively focused and hypervigilant, presumably in response to internally generated danger situations. It has also been recognized that activity is a mode of defense characteristic of children whose response repertoire is limited.

Jack, who began analysis at age six and a half, illustrates the classic dynamics of the overactive and distractible child. His mind flitted and his body fidgeted. Because Jack sought perfection in his activities, he was repeatedly frustrated and had given up on being a self-starting child. Seemingly intelligent, he was failing first grade and was diagnosed with a variety of learning disabilities. Evaluation revealed structuralized conflict and massive anxiety in the setting of good ego development.

Analysis began. Late in the first year, after his conflicts were engaged in the analysis, Jack developed play in which I was instructed to enact the role of a mother. He asked me to chase him around the room, demanding to be "fucked." This well-mannered boy grabbed his genitals and made a rat-a-tat noise as he proclaimed that he would "tear my cunt apart with his machine-gun dick." Within moments, he was hiding in a corner, saying he was afraid that I was going "to cut off his dick in retaliation." This play was an attempt to represent the emerging memory of baths that he had taken with his mother during his oedipal years. During those baths, he had inquired about her genital anatomy. Because of a conscious wish to not overly inhibit her son, Jack's mother allowed him to explore her genital area visually and manually. The overstimulation and the distorted oedipal development were reconstructed pari pasu with Jack's emerging abilities to transcend with representation through modulated play the trauma that he had initially represented as a quasi-play enactment. As an illustration of such modulated play, he represented the female genitalia as a black hole in space that he and I approached, backed up from, appeased, and gradually learned about the internal and external origins of its fearsome and destructive power. Learning difficulties eventually lifted, as did the overactivity and distractibility. The remainder of the analysis focused on an underlying inhibited character structure under heavy superego dominance. In follow-up twelve years later, Jack was progressing quite well.

Jack's excitement and distractibility were symptomatic of and embedded in an ego that, although inevitably skewed a bit by neurotic interference, was basically intact. This boy managed conflict through symptom rather than through pathological character formation and used metaphor, play, and sublimation in the process of recovery, while he preserved his relationships from ongoing excitement, anxiety, and aggression.

Many analysts have demonstrated the use of conceptualizing overactivity and difficulties in attentionality as neurotic symptomatology in such children as Jack. However, there are many children with phenomenological presentations similar to Jack's who require different explanatory paradigms.

Contrast Jack with Albert, a child observed in our therapeutic nursery. Albert's attentional capacities were erratic; at times he was focused and organized, at other times quite distractible. Like Jack, Albert sought perfection in his activities and was beginning to relinquish initiative. Also like Jack, this intelligent child was not mastering readiness skills, appearing superficially to have severe learning disabilities. Despite the similarity in the surface presentation of Jack and Albert, there were profound differences between the boys. Although Albert was burdened with substantial structural conflict, his neurotic difficulties were grounded in a faulty ego substructure.

One area of developmental difficulty for Albert was affect control. When angered, Albert might strike out alarmingly. He also had difficulties with basic aspects of affect processing. He often appeared not to recognize his anger before an outburst and sometimes did not recognize that he had been angry even after the event. When Albert did recognize anger, the recognition did not seem to afford his ego the relief that usually accrues from registration or verbalization. He was unable to access the usual paths to control, modulation, and mastery. Subtle integrative difficulties prevented Albert from being able to use verbalization of affect in a therapeutic manner.

There were difficulties in his object relationship as well. Albert was at one moment loving, the next moment unreachable and removed, and never in sustained contact such that his teachers felt that they "knew" him. He seemed to decathect people and things. His fluctuating attention was related to his unstable internal object investment. When invested in another person, he seemed organized and focused; when he decathected, he became distractible and susceptible to outbursts.

Albert is one of many preschool-age children who present with distractibility, overactivity, and impulsivity and who have deficits in structuralization as part of their developmental problems. On the basis of preliminary observations, there appear to be four areas of developmental interference and impaired structuralization that are regularly present in these children:

1. tendencies to seek excitement and to use excitement to support internal organization;
2. disturbances in the line of development of affect;

3. difficulties in establishing a hierarchy of instinctual aims and in achieving phase dominance; and

4. interferences in the capacity to use play for defense, mastery, and adaptation.

Tendencies to Seek Excitement. Children with attentional difficulties often seek to resolve conflict through generating excitement rather than through object interaction. When conflict develops in play, usually because an aggressive derivative is emerging, there tends to be a shift of play activity rather than an elaboration of themes, or there is a breakdown of play leading to enactments.

One child may touch an adult's body, another may lift a crayon to a wall, another may masturbate, another may go to his or her mother in the waiting room and try to attain excitement. In the group setting of the nursery, these children have learned with exquisite sensitivity how to use each other for mutual excitement. One year, for example, one member could ignite group excitement by saying the word, "penis-wenis."

Many of the interactions of these children are motivated by affect generation rather than object interaction. The child seeks diffuse excitement and uses another child or adult as the catalyst to achieve it. The excitement does not seem to actualize an object-directed fantasy, such as a sadomasochistic interchange involving tormenting and victimization.

Many wildly impulsive children do not seem frightened by their wildness. This suggests that their excessive excitement may not be a manifestation of a *regression* of ego function. In observing these children, particularly in observing their ego states after periods of excitement, I believe that what appears to the outside observer as an uncontrollability is not subjectively experienced in this way by the children. To the contrary, the excitement often seems to have a pleasurable valence and is seemingly conflict-reducing and organizing. Regressions in object relatedness, in defensive strategies, or in integrative capacities do not necessarily follow the excited times. These children seem to be responding to states of threatened internal disorganization with reintegrations that are organized around states of inattention and excitement.

It is more useful to describe these children in the aggregate as excited rather than instinctualized. There are clear elements of aggression and of libido in the excitement of all of these children. There are also elements of anxiety for most children, and for some others, of less differentiated states of tension. Children experiencing less differentiated states of tension are frequently suffering from deprivational states. For some children, the excitement may be related to excessive perceptual stimulation, a phenomenon not yet understood within psychoanalysis. The excitements appear to be complex mixtures of instinct, affect, and ego state that are unique for each child.

Difficulties with Affect Development. Children with attentional difficulties often have trouble with affect registration, affect processing, and integration of affect with defensive and adaptive ego functioning. They are stunted in their ability to verbalize affective states, the importance of which Katan (1961) and Furman (1978) have noted. These children tend to operate at the level of sensation; these sensations are experienced either pleasurably or noxiously, and sensation remains primarily a mixed somatic psychic experience. One can presume that affective experience is poorly organized intrapsychically and that affective differentiation and internal representation is deficient. The motoric and physical realm is the primary mode of affective discharge and integration rather than the internal realm of thought, feeling, and internal verbalization.

Ken is a boy who managed affect with excitement. This four-year-old, whom I had evaluated a year previously, sat in a first diagnostic session with his mother as we became reacquainted. He was interested in the rules of the office. He mentioned that he sometimes had bad days, which he described as bad behavior. At this point he was sitting quietly and listening, but his mood became more low-key. I said that it makes a guy feel bad to have bad days. At this suggestion of affect, Ken began to squirm and scratch his fingers repeatedly across the couch. He then used his fingers to vigorously stretch his face in various directions. Ken was limited to representing his pain over his bad days through somatic experience, and this was true for his other affects as well. He also illustrated the way these children master conflict through the generation of excitement. In the second diagnostic interview, for example, he drew a picture of a house with thunder and lightning outside. He said he was staying inside the house. I said it was safer to be inside when it was thundering and lightning outside. This move toward the affect associated with the thunder and lightning spurred him to frantically smell one Magic Marker after another, flooding his sensorium with stimulating odor.

Another common aspect of the difficulty with affect is an inability to use affect as a signal function. Isenstadt (1980) has noted this as an ego difficulty in "hyperactive children."

Lack of Predominating Instinctual Aim. When prelatency children with attentional difficulties are observed over a prolonged period, it becomes evident that different instinctual aims exist within these children without there being a stable phase dominance. There is a fluidity that suggests a failure of consolidation more than of a coherent alternation between a dominant progressive aim and regressive organizations. This fluidity is substantially greater than what one sees as a normative phenomenon in younger children. One of the children in the nursery, for example, looked at one moment as if he was experiencing phallic phase dominance when he insisted that the teachers look at and admire him. Moments later, appearing to be oriented by a triadic organization, he tried to fondle a teacher and expressed jealousy for time she spent away from him. Again within moments, he relinquished phallic pride, insisting on having basic things done for him. He whined as I spent time with others in the room. An anal orientation soon emerged, as he became importunate, defiant, and provocative. Aside from the dynamic links between these various instinctual expressions, it was evident that this five-and-a-half-year-old did not have a hierarchy of aims that manifested itself in an integrated organization.

Interference in Play. This interference takes many forms because there are many part-ego functions contributing to the complex ego function that supports the capacity to play. Few of the children who present with the symptomatic triad of distractibility, overactivity, and impulsivity have Jack's capacity to develop play that is at once expressive and protective of their inner world and that reveals archaic and current conflicts in a frame that simultaneously opens progressive opportunities. Some of these children cannot represent through symbols; some cannot achieve enough psychic distance to create a make-believe space; some cannot channel impulse and preserve play; some use play as another source of excited enactments; and some seem bewildered by play activities. Included in this category are the subtle disturbances many of these children have in distinguishing reality and fantasy or impulse and action.

Therefore, many of the children who are phenomenologically described as distractible, overactive, and impulsive in the currently dominant psychiatric paradigm suffer from structural deficiencies that involve impairments in the development of affect development, play, and integrative function. In addition, internal stabilization is often achieved through a compromise formation organized around states of diffuse excitement that involve cognitive and affective blurring.

For some of these children, developmental difficulties with excitement are further complicated by an imbalance of ego and instinctual forces. These children present particularly complex clinical pictures.

Sometimes their states of excitement seem to be under ego dominance, and at those times the excitement appears to serve the organizing function I have described. At other times, these same children's states of excitement appear to be associated with an overwhelming of the ego and are identifiable by the associated regressions, panic, and need for help from an external other.

Concerns about stimulation to the psyche, what the psychic apparatus could manage and what it could not manage, are as old as psychoanalysis itself. In *Project for a Scientific Psychology* (1895), Freud attempted to explain psychological processes in a neurophysiological framework involving concepts of stimulation and neuronal excitation. As Freud turned to psychological conceptualizations, the centrality of issues of stimulation and overstimulation was evident in such concepts as pathological repression of affect in hysteria, actual neurosis, the topographical model, and the seduction hypothesis. Much of the early psychoanalytic metapsychology and clinical theory was based on the assumption that the progressive development of the mind and the successful mastery of stimulation were intimately related.

The child-analytic literature contains many cases of children who were externally overstimulated, particularly sexually, in early childhood, beginning with Little Hans (1909), who slept with his parents. All Freud's major case studies for which there was a reasonable amount of history or reconstruction were of patients who were externally overstimulated in childhood. Dora's adolescent distress was, as we now appreciate, related to premature sadistic sexual pressure from Herr K (1901); the Rat Man's childhood was characterized by chronic pinworm infestations and by seduction by his nurse (1909); and the Wolf Man was presumably exposed to the primal scene in his first year (1919). The only exception to this pattern, the patient reported in *The Psychogenesis of a Case of Homosexuality in a Woman* (1920), is not really an exception because Freud felt that the anamnesis may have been incomplete in this brief course of analysis. Rangell (1950), Hall (1946), Furman (1956), Fraiberg (1952), Katan (1951), Bornstein (1946), Kolansky (1960), Buxbaum (1935), Fenichel (1930), Sprince (1962), and Sterba (1935) are among those who detail the pathogenic sequelae of sexual and occasionally aggressive overstimulation in childhood. Boyer (1956), among others, has emphasized that early massive overstimulation can interfere with ego and fantasy development.

Weil (1989) published an interesting compilation of psychoanalytic case reports involving overstimulation as well as other previously unpublished cases that had come through the Judge Baker Clinic in Boston. Focusing on symptoms and using statistical methods, he demonstrated the increased occurrence of a number of symptoms with over-stimulation, and differentiated symptomatic sequelae of aggressive and sexual overstimulation.

The histories of the young children that I have evaluated with the presenting symptom picture of distractibility, overactivity, and impulsivity are characterized by the greater-than-expectable presence of five factors.[1]

1. A dispositional vulnerability and associated significant difficulties in the early mother-child relationship. This factor is the one I have observed most regularly. In the vast majority of situations, a history of problems in infancy is obtainable either initially or as maternal amnesia clears during treatment. The dispositional vulnerability seems to take several important forms. Parents of distractible, overactive, and impulsive children will frequently describe the child's infancy as having been characterized by nonadaptability and so-called high intensity. In my group, a history of a general dysregulation during infancy has been common. These children may have been colicky or difficult to feed and may not have settled easily into patterns of sleeping and eating. Often there is a history of difficulty with the functioning of one or another sensory channel (Greenspan, 1992). Examples are children who become inconsolable when hearing loud noises, children who become disorganized when approached too rapidly, and children who avoid certain kinds of tactile experience. Sometimes, distractible, overactive, and impulsive children are described as not having liked to cuddle in the first year of life or as having avoided aspects of relationship. This is a disparate group, with individual contributants from child and mother in any particular instance. All are clearly vulnerable to a problematic early mother-child experience. These situations all involve some combination of difficulties with the equipment that processes and manages internal and external stimuli and also difficulties in the basic relationship that supports the development of the internal capacity to process stimuli.[2]

2. Overstimulation that is part of the child's object relationships. These object-relational-based overstimulations can be subgrouped as follows:[3]

1. As always, one must be cautious about inferences about causality on the basis of noting associations.

2. Although there is a great deal of ongoing research about the longitudinal implications of temperamental variations, maternal-infant fit, and so-called infant competencies, this research is limited in value because it does not attend to the unconscious aspects of the dyadic relationship.

3. I am following closely the groupings and descriptions suggested by Weil (1989).

Erogenous stimulation. This form of stimulation extends from such benign activities as the child's resting in bed with an adult all the way to the
child's being fondled, penetrated, or made to penetrate.

Anal and excretory sources of excitement. These often overlooked sources of
excitement extend from the benign wiping of the young child through
exposure to adult defecation and prolonged adult preoccupation with
bowel function, enemas, suppositories, anal rashes, fistulas or pin-
worms, and manual anal manipulation and genital penetration.

Punitive overstimulation. This extends from parental negativism or rejection, which is not necessarily overstimulating, through punitive yelling
and various forms of beating.

These issues are commonplace in clinical work. It has been my tentative impression that distractible, overactive, and impulsive children
have a somewhat greater than usual exposure to these sources of stimulation than does the clinical population as a whole. The young children
I have observed have had quite heterogeneous experiences with these
sources. Naturally, these are difficult histories to obtain, and for various clinical reasons one usually does not inquire vigorously or even
directly about such matters. Allowing for what is present but not revealed or discerned, my impression is that most of these children have
not been subjected to massive levels of object-related stimulation.
Therefore, I do not think that we can account for most of these children's disturbances *solely* on the basis of the pathological sequelae of
object relational stimulation.

3. Unprotected early exposure to cultural overstimulation. Concern about cultural sources of stimulation is in vogue. Although it is
often discussed in a trivialized way, the issue has profound implications
for a child's development.

The usual issues of the child's developmental status, fantasy organization, and internal and external object relations shape any child's
reaction to cultural stimulation. Consider, for example, television. The
younger the child, the greater the likelihood that a show will overwhelm the child's capacities to integrate the violent, sexual, and complex interpersonal relationships that may be on the screen. Yet, the
presence of the parent can alter the nature of the experience for the
child. The parent's mere presence offers dyadic support. The parent
can be further available to help the child learn the appropriate affective response to television, age-appropriate defenses, and emergency
defenses against visual and verbal stimulation and to help assimilation
by answering questions and to differentiate the real from the not-real.

Video and computer games are also powerful cultural factors, as many present the child with situations of violence, destruction, and eroticism. In one popular learning program, even learning two plus two is associated with "munching," (as does the "pac-man" video game character who "eats" his opponents) dissolution, and disappearance of numbers.

There are of course many other cultural sources of stimulation. For example, radio news is replete with frightening words, newsmagazines often have frightening, violent, or erotic pictures on the cover, and homes often have guns within a child's sight.

I have observed that children having difficulties with distractibility, overactivity, and impulsivity are often exposed to greater than expectable levels of cultural stimulation. This source of stimulation may go unnoticed because it is in the background and is not among the usual items we generally think about.

The cultural sources of stimulation can be subtle. Jim, a four-year-old-boy, was having difficulties with impulsivity and excitement. His parents seemed to protect him against excessive cultural stimulation as they screened and limited his access to television and magazines. Jim arrived for his first diagnostic interview with his favorite toy, a truck. As the truck rolled, its wheels opened in a jaw-like manner to reveal a ferocious set of teeth. The truck could also transform itself into a robot with frightening eyes and deformed clawlike appendages. As I sat with the boy, I felt increasingly jangled.

Gerry, a four-year-old, and one of the less well-defended children in the nursery, gave us some insight into the meaning of video games for some children. He was drawn to video games and was unable to master the anxiety these games engendered despite numerous repetitions. At more integrated times, particularly after he was helped to develop a rudimentary signal function, he begged his parents to protect him from the temptations he felt when he was in the vicinity of the games. He struggled with the fact that something that looked so real and interacted so directly with him did not have its own independent existence. Agitation, disorganization, and impulsivity regularly followed video-game sessions, and his problem with what was real and what was not real was aggravated by a confusing world of simulated reality.

Terry, a five-year-old, had been exposed to considerable object-relational-based sexual and aggressive stimulation in his first three years. He had great difficulty feeling safe in any situation away from his mother. At the nursery, he would respond to perceived danger with frantic counterphobic identifications with superheroes. He became preoccupied with the television show *Rescue 911*. The show re-created, often with the original people, emergencies involving rescue attempts that were usually—but not always—successful. Terry would replay 911 scenarios at the nursery with a degree of personal investment that interfered with engaging other children in the play and with a repetition that was not progressing toward sublimation or other forms of mastery. Our task of helping him to differentiate past frightening situations from his safer current life was compromised by *Rescue 911's* graphic reminders about the treacherousness of life and its encouragement of the viewer to stay dependent on the rescuer, whether it be *Rescue 911* on a derivative level or his ambivalently idealized mother in his fantasy core.

Joshua, a five-year-old, had been having a difficult week at the nursery. One moment he seemed centered and involved, the next moment he was distracted, disconnected from his activity, seeming to be internally preoccupied. Joshua's pre-existing difficulties in these areas seemed to be exaggerated. Similarly, Joshua was more susceptible than usual to sliding into states of giddy excitement, during which he would try to sensually maul his teachers or lash out at other children. After one such outburst, Joshua blurted out that penises can be cut off; he had heard it on the radio. As he was saying this, he was cutting at his pants with a scissors and poking the scissors into the fabric of the chair. Staff realized that he had heard about the well-publicized incident in which a woman had cut off her husband's penis. As Joshua was helped to make some sense out of this terrifying news report and to differentiate reality from fantasy—he was a boy who was terrified of the power of women—he became better able to settle down.

Jim's difficulty with excitement was not caused by the monster truck; Gerry's difficulty with aggression, anxiety, and ego development was not caused by video games; Terry's basic anxiety about safety and his need to repeat past traumatic events in play-like enactments were not caused by *Rescue 911;* and Joshua's castration anxiety was not caused by the news report. On the other hand, it would be reductionistic to view these exogenous elements *merely* as vehicles for externalizing internal conflicts and psychic realities. These cultural stimulations do provide opportunities for externalization of internal situations, sometimes usefully from the point of view of defense and mastery; they also often enter into a synergism with pre-existing and *emerging* problematic aspects of a child's psyche. In so doing, they can intensify and shape longstanding difficulties as well as developmental crises. We need to investigate the possibility that culturally determined stimulations can tip the balance for some children, for example, turning a developmental crisis with the potential to be transient into a more abiding neurotic or characterologic difficulty.

4. The change in child-care patterns toward care initiated earlier in the child's life and for longer periods of the day. There are multiple sources of stimulation in the daycare setting for a child. One source is other children. The child is subject to intruding impulses and fantasies from other children that tempt, threaten, and confuse. Another source of stimulation is the child's own affects and needs that are internally organized in the relationship with mother and cannot be fully discharged during the daycare session. For example, there is a daily arousal of affects and fantasies around the separation and the continued apartness. Some of the fantasy and affect are displaced to caretakers, some are sublimated, but some are suppressed, increasing the level of internal arousal.

The child's susceptibility to stimulation in the daycare setting is magnified by the strain on the ego that results from the integrative and object-relational demands of daycare. The child is asked to integrate relationships with multiple caretakers at any single time of the day and to integrate relationships with different shifts of caregivers over the day. In most daycare settings, there are frequent changes of child-care staff owing to absenteeism, and there are frequent losses of teachers owing to staff turnover. Children are asked to integrate the routine of an institution with the routine of their own bodily and psychic needs, and this further strains ego resiliency. The child is asked to integrate home and daycare environments, and for some children, two homes and a daycare environment, with different people, different rules, and different access to beloved physical objects.

The rhythms of a full day of care pose another set of problems. In the morning, the toddler's or preschooler's ego capacities have resiliency. Things change around naptime, an especially difficult time for the child in care. The child is asked to surmount the difficulties of going to sleep, without access to the primary object of separation to help with the anxiety about the separations and regressions involved in going to sleep.

The postnap afternoon finds the child progressively depleted, as one ego function after another regressively deteriorates. The regression during the afternoon has many sources, including the accumulating strains of being around other children, of having to conform to routines that engender frustration and deprivation, and of having to function with deteriorating object constancy. Some children have less than optimal internal structure to manage the regressive pressures. Their structural limitations may relate to problems in the mother-child relationship resulting from impaired mutual investments, from diminished opportunity for internalization because of the relative unavailability of the primary object, as well as from interferences with optimal internalizations resulting from the unconscious ambivalence that many of these children feel toward the primary object.

By late afternoon, children in full daycare have only a handful of options. If the children are left alone, they tend to wander aimlessly, without the capacity to invest, often exciting themselves and each other through activity or through instinctualized interplay. Children of different temperament or those with more psychic structure are able to direct their energies into maintaining basic ego functions although they relinquish planning, sublimation, learning, and organized activity. For example, they may choose simple, repetitive puzzles or numbing computer games. Sometimes, a teacher or care provider intervenes to offer calming and routinized structure. The routine of the late afternoon in such a daycare environment resembles pre-bedtime rituals, which are also meant to offer, through simplification, routine, and repetition, ego support to a depleted child who is in danger of excessive stimulation.[4]

The daycare experience, then, taxes the child's ego by heightening internal arousal, increasing external stimulation, and straining the integrative and adaptive functions. These factors foster chronic states of ego-id imbalances that affect young children to varying extents for the major portion of their waking time during most of their infancy and preschool years. What is the effect on the developing mind of this repeated experience of enduring a progressive deterioration in ego function that is mitigated only by dependence on dyadic support? This is an unexplored question. It is possible that, for certain vulnerable children, this repeated experience may help to shape the ego in directions that are expressed symptomatically as distractibility, overactivity, and impulsivity. Repeated regressive deteriorations may structure a pathway in the ego that allows these children relatively easy access to modes of regressive functioning. At times this may result in ego regression, and at other times in a reorganization of regressive modes of expression into integrated compromise formations of the form previously described here.

There are cultural patterns of response to the developmental issues posed by early child care. As an illustration of how our culture is re-

4. This idea derived from a personal communication from Erna Furman.

sponding to early child care, consider a song played on *Sesame Street*. The show appears on television around the end of the daycare day and attempts to assist children with the strain of the day. "Miss Your Momma Blues" is sung in a sad, sexy style.[5] Lillian, a daycare worker, sings to Henry that his "mom went to work." Henry wants her back and has "those boo-hoos-hoos, those miss your momma blues." When Lillian tells Henry that "your momma is comin' back at the end of the day," Henry responds, "Right now that seems a long time away," Lillian says, "Now, hold it right there, I know you feel blue, but we got great stuff, great stuff here to do; got crayons and paint, got glitter and glue, we got puzzles and books and lots of friends too." Lillian continues to urge Henry to come and play, assuring him that if he does, "those miss your momma blues will go away."

How does *Sesame Street* help the daycare child to handle the "boo-hoos"? One strategy is to jazz up the child, transforming sadness into the sexy blues. Derivatives of other affects, such as terror, rage, and profound confusion, which the young child with insufficient or marginal object constancy invariably associated with separation, are ignored. Object constancy is bolstered with reminders that Mom will return. And Mom is replaced by "great stuff"—crayons, paint, glitter, glue, puzzles, and books.

This song offers the child a path for transforming a complex affective state of anger, anxiety, and sadness into a state of sexualized excitement, suggesting the substitution of exciting inanimate objects for longed-for people. The reunion between mother and child in the show finds the child excitedly and exhibitionistically showing Mommy what he has done, free of painful affects and, best of all, having made a new friend. The message is that friends can substitute for parents.

Sesame Street offers denial of aspects of the affective reaction and support for suppression, memory, substitution of activities for relationship, and excited, self-oriented exhibitionism as a means to manage the rage and anxiety associated with reunions. This song may be offering the best of what the culture at large has to offer to the beleaguered daycare child. After all, these assistances attempt to remediate the internal imbalance between frustrated need and associated affect-filled fantasies, on the one hand, and immature ego and superego capacities, on the other hand. This problematic ego-id balance and the ego regressions limit the child's access to the more progressive restructuring and sublimatory channels available through the use of more

5. "Miss Your Mama Blues," words by Robby Merkin and music by Cathy Rosenberg, used by permission of Children's Television Workshop.

sophisticated defenses and through play. It is probably necessary to assist the daycare child with defenses and adaptive strategies that are less than optimal. For some children, this may contribute to interferences in the developmental lines of play, affect, and the regulation of excitement.

5. Neurotic entanglements between child and parent. These entanglements seem to be present in families of the most distractible, impulsive, and overactive children. I have been impressed by the protean nature of these neurotic entanglements, which seem to involve all the familiar constellations. Although the situation in which the child is enacting warded-off parental fantasies or impulses is a common one, my impression is that neurotic patterns do not seem to be specific. There seem to be some situations in which the neurotic entanglements have been highly shaped and perhaps caused by early difficulties in the child's equipment or in the match between the child's temperament and mother's competencies. There are other situations in which the neurotic interactions seem to have a more internalized and autonomous origin within the parent, usually the mother.

The case of ten-year-old Sara illustrates some of the issues discussed here in a child who has progressed into a later developmental period. Sara was described by her parents as doing quite well except for a long-standing difficulty sleeping alone; she frequently sought the parental bed for assistance. In the evaluation, I felt that Sara was a child with a triadic structure to her personality. She seemed overburdened with conflicts over aggression. There were clues to her internal life—for example, in the occasional nightmare about killing her sister that Sara was able to reveal to me. Despite these clues, I was not able to be specific about her internal life with any confidence because of what I felt to be a relative lack of inner psychological elaboration. Her affects were blunted and generally unrecognized; interest in sports and in growing up rapidly predominated. Sara had no idea what was making it hard for her to sleep and little curiosity about it despite much embarrassment. For example, she was perplexed when I asked whether she thought that worries about the nightmare could be making it hard for her to relax and go to sleep.

I also learned that the parents walked around the house nude or in skimpy underclothes. Various comings and goings during toileting or showering were common. Certain aspects of the work of one of the parents were openly discussed within the family and were of a character that conceivably could both intrigue and frighten a child. Sara could watch HBO or attend violent movies without regulation. She was beginning to attend rock concerts. There was a pattern of excessive stimulation extending back into Sara's infancy.

Sara seems to be a certain kind of boundary case. She was a child who had a good deal of solid ego development and who, for the most part, had an unimpeded developmental momentum. But there were certain limitations in her ego that were attenuated expressions of the sorts of difficulty one sees in children with the symptom triad of distractibility, overactivity, and impulsivity. These limitations in ego functioning were taking the middle-latency form of her being a bit less inward, less curious, and less able to define affects. She was also more oriented toward exciting physical activity with less access to fantasy and play than one might have in an optimally balanced defensive and adaptive repertoire.

I decided that this was not a child for whom psychotherapy or psychoanalysis was the best first option. The difficulty Sara was having was focused, and her motivation was quite limited. Action, not insight, was her way, much more so than for many other ten-year-old girls. Proceeding on the possibility that a factor in her difficulty was that her latency repressions were being interfered with by excessive current exogenous stimulation, I worked with the parents to implement a routine in which as many sources of stimulation as possible were curtailed. Her sleep problem, present since early oedipal years, disappeared rapidly. My working hypothesis was that the exogenous stimulation was aggravating internalized conflicts to the extent that Sara did not have sufficient confidence in her capacities to tolerate the regression of sleep. Her neurosis was not eliminated by external management, but the potential importance of such modification to her development should not be underestimated.

The issue for this child, as for any child, is the extent to which elements of the neurotic organizations could be integrated into a progressive developmental program. Within such a working framework, it has been my experience that rigorous attention to reducing excessive exogenous stimulation will often eliminate or substantially ameliorate symptoms of distractibility, overactivity, and impulsivity, particularly in the preschool child, and may be the most appropriate first intervention if neurotic or characterologic difficulties have not already consolidated. Manipulations of exogenous stimulation generally have somewhat less developmental and symptomatic impact after the onset of late oedipal and early latency structuralizations.

Summary. Are we are seeing more children these days who are experiencing states of overstimulation as an aspect of their psychopathology? Is this overstimulation resulting in developmental interferences in some children who might otherwise have developed relatively successfully? Is it also resulting in a greater number of complex clinical pictures in children who would be having difficulties for other reasons as well? What happens to the overstimulated young child in subsequent years? Sara illustrates one possible outcome, in her case a reasonably felicitous one, in which the superego was able to consolidate and assist the ego in re-establishing a more favorable ego-id balance. From a purely phenomenological standpoint, other common outcomes into aggressive and syndromal conditions that continue to be characterized by distractibility, overactivity, or impulsivity are quite common. Studies have consistently documented that many children with AD/HD diagnoses develop substantial difficulties beginning in adolescence, usually involving impulse disorders. (Barkley et al., 1993; Mannuza et al., 1991). There are many interesting questions about the evolution of overstimulated states. For example, the relationship between states of childhood excitement and development of later perverse organizations remains a relatively unexplored area. Psychoanalysts will need to be increasingly mindful of the effect of full daycare on children and adults. It may turn out that formative daycare experiences will not enter analyses with a great deal of representation, because caregivers are rarely deeply cathected. The daycare experience may enter the analytic work via certain affective states, defensive excitements, ego deformations, and primitive object relational conflicts—that is, *through remnants of deprivational experiences.* Analyzing these children in various phases of childhood and adulthood will continue to inform us about the interrelationships among endowment, early mother-infant experience, later structuralizations and fantasy formation, cultural influences, and states of overstimulation.

BIBLIOGRAPHY

ACHENBACK, T. M., & HOWELL, C. T. (1993). Are American children's problems getting worse? A 13-year comparison. *J. Am. Acad. Child Adolesc. Psychiatry* 32:1145–1154.

BARKLEY, R. A., FISCHER, M., EDELBROCK, C., & SMALLISH, L. (1991). The adolescent outcome of hyperactive children diagnosed by research criteria—III. Mother-child interactions, family conflicts and maternal psychopathology. *J. Child Psychol. Psychiatry* 32:233–255.

BORNSTEIN, B. (1946). Hysterical twilight states in an eight-year-old child. *Psychoanal. Study Child* 2:229–240.

BOYER, L. (1956). On maternal overstimulation and ego defects. *Psychoanal. Study Child* 11:236–256.

BUXBAUM, E. (1935). Exhibitionistic onanism in a ten-year-old boy. *Psychoanal. Quart.* 4:161–189.

Diagnostic and Statistical Manual of Mental Disorders. 4th ed. (1994). Washington, D.C.: American Psychiatric Association.

FENICHEL, O. (1930). The psychology of transvestism. In: *Collected Papers*, vol. 1. New York: W. W. Norton, 1953, 167–180.

FRAIBERG, S. (1952). A critical neurosis in a two-and-a-half-year-old girl. *Psychoanal. Study Child* 7:173–215.

FREUD, S. (1895). Project for a scientific psychology. *S.E.,* 1:283–387.

FREUD, S. (1901). A case of hysteria. *S.E.,* 7:7–122.

FREUD, S. (1909a). Analysis of a phobia in a five-year-old boy. *S.E.,* 10:5–149.

FREUD, S. (1909b). Notes on a case of obsessional neurosis. *S.E.,* 10:155–318.

FREUD, S. (1919). From the history of an infantile neurosis. *S.E.,* 17:7–122.

FREUD, S. (1920). The psychogenesis of a case of homosexuality in a woman. *S.E.,* 18:147–172.

FURMAN, E. (1956). An ego disturbance in a young child. *Psychoanal. Study Child* 11:312–335.

FURMAN, R. (1978). Some developmental aspects of the verbalization of affects. *Psychoanal. Study Child* 33:187–211.

GREENSPAN, S. I. (1992). *Infancy and Early Childhood.* Madison, Conn.: International Universities Press.

HALL, J. W. (1946). The analysis of a case of night terrors. *Psychoanal. Study Child* 2:189–227.

ISENSTADT, L. (1980). From panic to signal structure acquisition in a hyperactive boy. *Int. Rev. Psychoanal.* 7:469–481.

KATAN, A. (1951). The role of "displacement" in agoraphobia. *Int. J. Psychoanal.* 32:41–50.

KATAN, A. (1961). Some thought about the role of verbalization in early childhood. *Psychoanal. Study Child* 16:184–188.

KOLANSKY, H. (1960). Treatment of a three-year-old girl's severe infantile neurosis: Stammering and insect phobia. *Psychoanal. Study Child* 15:261–285.

MANNUZZA, S., KLEIN, R. G., BRESSLER, A., MALLOY, P., & LaPADULA, M. (1993). Adult outcome of hyperactive boys. Educational achievement, occupational rank, and psychiatric status. *Arch. Gen. Psychiatry* 50:565–576.

MOORE, B. E., & FINE, B. D. (1990). *Psychoanalytic Terms and Concepts.* New Haven: Yale University Press.

RANGELL, L. (1950). Treatment of nightmares in a seven-year-old boy. *Psychoanal. Study Child* 5:358–390.

SAFER, D. J., & KRAGER, J. M. (1988). A survey of medication treatment for hyperactive/inattentive students. *J. Amer. Medical Assn.* 260:2256–2258.

SPRINCE, M. (1962). Pre-oedipal partnership between an adolescent girl and her mother. *Psychoanal. Study Child* 17:418–450.

STERBA, E. (1935). Excerpt from the analysis of a dog phobia. *Psychoanal. Quart.* 4:138–154.

WEIL, J. (1989). *Instinctual Stimulation of Children: From Common Practice to Child Abuse.* Madison, Conn.: International Universities Press.

The Eternal Triangle across Cultures

Oedipus, Hsueh, and Ganesa

NADINE M. TANG, M.S.W.
BRUCE L. SMITH, PH.D.

In this chapter we consider the cross-cultural relevance of the Oedipus complex by investigating three "oedipal" myths from three disparate cultures: Chinese, Indian, and European. Although all three myths concern the same mother-father-son triad, they stress different aspects and proscriptions. These are interpreted as reflecting the different values that are central to the respective cultures. The relationship between these values and child-rearing practices is discussed. We conclude that fundamental psychoanalytic concepts are relevant cross-culturally, although the content of the Oedipus complex may vary from society to society.

I

ONE OF THE THORNIEST QUESTIONS IN PSYCHOANALYSIS CONCERNS THE universality of psychodynamic formulations. Of all these formulations,

Nadine M. Tang is on the staff of Mills College Counseling and Psychological Services and on the clinical faculty at Mt. Zion Hospital and the University of California, Berkeley. Bruce L. Smith is assistant clinical professor of psychology at the University of California, Berkeley, and the University of California, San Francisco; adjunct professor at the California School of Professional Psychology; a past president of the Northern California Society for Psychoanalytic Psychology and president-elect of the Society for Personality Assessment.

The Psychoanalytic Study of the Child 51, ed. Albert J. Solnit, Peter B. Neubauer, Samuel Abrams, and A. Scott Dowling (Yale University Press, copyright © 1996 by Albert J. Solnit, Peter B. Neubauer, Samuel Abrams, and A. Scott Dowling).

none is more central or more controversial than the Oedipus complex. From the time Freud (1897) first proposed it, scholars both within and without psychoanalysis have debated its existence, questioned its importance, and refuted its universality. Even such contemporary analysts as Kohut (1982) have argued that the oedipal situation is not inevitable, that conflict between generations need not occur given adequate parenting, and that, in any event, its roots are not primarily sexual or aggressive.

The most important of these debates lies in the sphere of cross-cultural psychoanalysis. To some, the Oedipus complex is an immutable component of the human psyche that transcends cultural differences in kinship arrangements, child-rearing practices, or belief systems. To others, its applicability is limited to nineteenth- and twentieth-century Western European culture. (Indeed, it seems that some psychoanalysts wish to limit it to upper-middle-class urban Viennese Jews during the first quarter of the twentieth century.) Malinowski (1929), for example, argued that no oedipal configuration could be found in the fantasies or myths of the Trobriand Islanders who raise their children in the kinship system, not in the nuclear family. Chasseguet-Smirgel and Grünberger (1986) and Spiro (1985), however, have claimed that Malinowski's own data demonstrate clear oedipal themes.

The debate over the universal applicability of psychoanalytic concepts in general and the Oedipus complex in particular has been hampered by a failure to differentiate adequately between form and content and by an unnecessarily narrow and literal interpretation of the oedipal situation. Weiss (1985) draws a similar conclusion from his consideration of Freud's treatment of the original oedipal story.

It is our contention that the triadic relationship of mother, father, and son[1] presents certain inescapable psychological dilemmas. Incestuous, aggressive, and competitive impulses are inevitable components of family life and the process of maturation. How these are expressed, understood, and ultimately resolved, however, varies with what a given culture considers the tasks of development, the ideal mature adult, and the ideal relationship between father and son, mother and son, and father and mother.

We examine here alternative "oedipal" myths from three disparate cultures to compare the psychodynamic patterns of these cultures and thus the relation between culture and psyche. Because individual per-

---

1. In this chapter, we consider only the Oedipus complex involving the male child. A similar analysis can of course be made for the Electra complex.

sonality is expressed within the context of a culture and cultural forms in turn are mediated by individual expressions, the study of cultural differences in psychological makeup is difficult. Careful consideration of myths and legends can yield rich rewards in understanding cultural differences and psychological universals. As psychoanalysts, we take it as axiomatic that myths represent the crucial psychological truths that are passed down through the generations in a given society. Although it may be argued that ancient myths bear little relevance for modern society—given the myriad social upheavals over the millennia—we believe that certain myths have survived because they express timeless truths. The plays of Sophocles move modern audiences because we recognize something of our own experience in them. Each of the myths we have chosen remains alive within its culture to this day. We examine, in addition to the classical Greek myth of Oedipus, the Indian legend of the god Ganesa, and the Chinese tale of Hsueh.[2] These are not of course the only myths in their respective cultures with oedipal themes. We have chosen them because we feel that they illustrate our thesis clearly.

OEDIPUS

The Oedipus of mythology is not the Oedipus of psychoanalysis. Freud focused on Oedipus himself, as portrayed in Sophocles' tragedy *Oedipus Rex*. In this play, told from the perspective of Oedipus, his past gradually unfolds as it might in an analytic treatment. Indeed, in Freud's first published reference to the Oedipus complex (1900), he makes this observation: "The action of the play consists in nothing other than the process of revealing, with cunning delays and ever-mounting excitement—a process that can be likened to the work of a psychoanalysis—that Oedipus himself is the murderer of Laius" (p. 262).[3] Freud's interest was in the meaning of the oedipal situation *from the perspective of the son.* He paid scant attention to the roles of the parents, Laius and Jocasta, or to the conflict from the perspective of the parents, and none whatsoever to the multigenerational context in which the drama occurs.

In Sophocles' drama, Laius, king of Thebes, and his wife, Jocasta, are warned by the oracle that Laius is destined to be murdered by his son

2. The authors gratefully acknowledge Coonoor Kripalani, M. Phil., of Hong Kong University, who first suggested to us the relevance of the myth of Ganesa to a study of oedipal dynamics.

3. This has led James Grotstein (personal communication) to suggest whimsically that *Oedipus Rex* is the only mystery story in which everyone knows the identity of the murderer except the culprit himself.

and that this son will then commit incest with his mother. To avoid this fate, Laius and Jocasta pierce the feet of their child Oedipus, and Jocasta gives him to a shepherd with instructions to abandon him to his death on Mount Cithaeron. The shepherd is unable to abandon the child and instead gives him to a fellow shepherd, who resides in Corinth. Oedipus grows to manhood believing that he is the son of the Corinthian king, Polybus. Learning of the curse that he is fated to murder his father and commit incest with his mother, he flees Corinth. At the crossroads outside of Thebes, he is rudely treated by Laius' guards. In anger, he kills all four guards and Laius. He enters Thebes and is able to answer the riddle posed by the Sphinx, thereby saving the city from disaster. The grateful people proclaim him king and award him the hand of the queen. He and Jocasta subsequently have four children, two sons and two daughters.

About eighteen years later, the city is once more beset by disaster, this time a plague. (It is at this point that Sophocles' play actually begins.) Oedipus consults the oracle and learns that the plague will abate only if the murderer of Laius is found. Though dissuaded by Jocasta and her brother, Creon, he pursues information about the death. Eventually he finds the shepherd who had been charged with abandoning him and learns the truth. Jocasta commits suicide, and Oedipus blinds himself with her shawl pins.

In the original Greek myth, however, Oedipus' tragedy is but the culmination of a series of curses on the family of Cadmus, founder of Thebes. Cadmus and his line were cursed by Ares, the god of war, for slaying his sacred giant serpent. Cadmus himself was driven out of Thebes and ultimately, along with his wife, was changed into a serpent. His great-grandson Laius was raised by a stepfather, Pelops. Laius fell in love with Pelops' son Chrysippus, seduced him (thus inventing homosexuality), and was cursed by Pelops: Laius' son would kill him, and his line would end. Thus, Oedipus' crime is the fulfillment of the curses on his father and his great-great-grandfather. Indeed, the curse continued beyond Oedipus. As chronicled in Sophocles' play *Oedipus at Colonus*, Oedipus' own sons are destined to slay each other in the battle for the throne of Thebes, and all male descendants of Cadmus are destroyed.

HSUEH

The story of Hsueh, a warrior and soldier of fortune, takes place during the Tang dynasty (A.D. 618–906) and is set forth in the Peking opera *The Bend in the River Fen*. Hsueh is a humble farmer who achieves high military rank because of his martial skills. He receives an imperial commission and leaves his wife behind. After eighteen years he is allowed to return home to visit his wife, who had been pregnant when he left.[4] At the river close to home, he sees a boy who is shooting geese with a bow and arrow with great skill. Hsueh boasts that he can bring down two geese with one arrow.[5] When the boy asks him to demonstrate, Hsueh fells him with an arrow, and the boy's body is carried away by a tiger. Hsueh rides away singing: "I could have spared the boy, but a soldier like me could not let another live if he was a superior in marksmanship with the weapons in which I excel."

He returns home to his wife and at first denies his identity, saying only that he has a message for her. Ashamed of her shabbiness (even to an unknown messenger), she too denies her identity and asks him to leave the message. He declines, and she then confesses who she is. To test her fidelity, he claims that he knew her husband and that he was to take her in lieu of some money he was owed. She refuses his advances, and he then reveals his true identity. She prepares a meal to welcome her husband, but Hsueh finds a pair of men's shoes under the bed and accuses her of infidelity. She teases him by saying that the wearer of the shoes has remained close to her side for eighteen years. Eventually she reveals to her jealous husband that he has a son he has never seen. She tells him that the boy went to hunt geese by the river, and her husband realizes that he has killed his son. The story ends with husband and wife going off to seek their son's body.

GANESA

Ganesa, son of Siva and Parvati, is an important Hindu deity. There are numerous versions of his birth and life, but according to Courtright, who published an encyclopedic study of the god (1985), the most widely accepted is the following: Parvati, wife of the god Siva and a powerful goddess in her own right, wants a son but is unable to persuade Siva to come down from his meditations on the mountain. As Parvati bathes in the river one day, she, using her powers as a goddess, forms a young man, Ganesa, out of the scrum of her body and breathes life into him. Parvati then charges Ganesa to keep intruders from her bathhouse. One day Siva returns and demands entry to Parvati's bath.

---

4. Interestingly, as was pointed out by Albert J. Solnit (personal communication), this parallels the eighteen years of Oedipus' reign as well as the most common age of majority in today's Western cultures.

5. "Killing two geese with one arrow" is an old Chinese saying, equivalent to the English "killing two birds with one stone." In this case, the "two geese" undoubtedly refer to the boy as military rival and oedipal rival.

Ganesa refuses him entry, a battle ensues, and Ganesa is beheaded. Parvati emerges from the bath house, horrified and angry, informs Siva that the young man was her son and threatens to destroy the universe unless he is restored to her. Siva, now remorseful, sends his minions to seek the head of the first animal facing north, the direction from which good things come. They return with the head of an elephant, which is then placed on the shoulders of Ganesa, who is brought back to life. Siva agrees to recognize Ganesa as his own son and commands the other deities to offer sacrifice to him before undertaking any venture or journey. Ganesa remains one of the most popular Hindu deities. He is known as the Lord of Beginnings, who overcomes all obstacles. It is of interest that Ganesa has one broken tusk, and although there are several versions as to how this came about, the most popular seems to be that he broke it off to serve as a crutch.

II

All three myths concern the fundamental triad of mother, father, and son, and, in particular, some form of conflict between father and son. As such, all can properly be termed oedipal. The most striking difference is that the Oedipus story involves the crimes of parricide and incest, whereas in both the Hsueh and Ganesa stories, the crime is infanticide. How can this difference be understood? Clearly the taboos against incest and parricide are extant in Chinese and Indian cultures, as they are in the West (indeed, "fuck your mother" is as powerful a curse in Cantonese as its equivalent is in English). So too is the sanction against killing one's son in European culture. To some extent this difference is more apparent than real, a consequence, in part, of the exclusive focus on the Greek myth from Oedipus' perspective. As noted above, the complete story is multigenerational; even Sophocles' version begins with an attempted infanticide. The mother-father-son triad involves inevitable conflict and jealousy. The son's first (and for some time only) love object is his mother, but he gradually becomes aware of the intrusion of his father as the Third, the primary object of his mother's desire. This awareness is a cruel, narcissistic blow, as the fantasy of a perfect mother-son Eden is disrupted by an interloper. As Chasseguet-Smirgel (1986) has pointed out, this is primarily a narcissistic injury, because as the child becomes aware of his rival, he also becomes aware of his competitive disadvantage—the impossibility of his satisfying his mother or defeating his father. Rage at the father, fury at his own impotence, and compensatory fantasies of ridding himself of

the rival are the result. At the same time, however, jealousy, competitiveness, and the wish to be rid of the rival are aroused in the father as
well. Although most analysts tend to overlook the "Laius complex" (the
work of Ross [1982] is a notable exception), it is nevertheless a profound element of the oedipal drama. As Erikson noted, "We have
forgotten to ask what made Laius believe the oracle and act upon it. We
know much more about the fear of the son and his hate of authority
than we do about the mistrust of the father and his propensity for
sacrificing his son for his beliefs" (1971, p. 744). Thus, the proper
question is not why infanticide is not part of the Oedipus myth, but why
we focus exclusively on the wish to kill the father, whereas the Eastern
myths seem more concerned with homicidal wishes toward the son.

The answer to this more circumscribed question lies both in the
sphere of social organization and in child-rearing practices. In Chinese
society the transcendent unit is the family, seen as a multigenerational
entity of which individuals are but a part. To a large degree, the individual attains his sense of identity from the family and defines himself
principally in terms of his roles vis-à-vis other members of the family
system. In development and child rearing, the overriding emphasis is
on filial piety—obedience to and caring for one's ancestors. Indeed,
the *Twenty-Four Examples of Filial Duty*, from the Ming dynasty (A.D.
1368–1644), and the older *Hsiao Ching* or *Book of Filial Duty*, from the
fifth century B.C., make it clear that the son's only requirement is to
sacrifice his own well-being, his flesh, and, if need be, his own son in
order to preserve his parents. The true measure of a mature man in
traditional Chinese society is his willingness to obey and conform to his
role requirements. The most important of these is his filial duty. Only
in acknowledging his own unimportance can he become a man. This
contrasts sharply with the emphasis on autonomy, independence, and
"becoming one's own man" in the West. Consideration of the characters
of the sons in the three myths bears this out.

Each of the sons in the stories has different attributes. Little is known
of Hsueh's son other than that he is filial because he has stayed close to
his mother and helped provide for her. He has developed his archery
skills to a high degree. Ganesa, too, is protective of and loyal to his
mother and guards her in the bathhouse even after Siva identifies
himself. Yet he is also mischievous and playful and not terribly concerned with the notion of self-cultivation. Oedipus, on the other hand,
is brilliant and powerful and much older than the other two. He is a
man of action, and in spite of his fate, he rises heroically above his
helpless stance. First, he destroys his eyes and then says:

"Apollo, friends, Apollo—
he ordained my agonies—these, my pains on pains!
But the hand that struck my eyes was mine,
mine alone—no one else—
I did it all myself!   (1467–1471)[6]

It is almost with triumph that he beckons the chorus to touch him, asserting: "Do. Don't be afraid. My troubles are mine / and I am the only man alive who can sustain them" (1548–1549). Clearly, then, Oedipus demands some autonomy and freewill in his life, even if only by bringing on his own suffering and to bear it.

Yet another element may be found in the different approaches to child rearing in Western and Eastern cultures. As Tang has pointed out elsewhere (1992), the Chinese mother typically has far more physical contact with her infant and for a longer period than does her Western counterpart. The infant commonly sleeps between his parents until the birth of the next child. The effect of this difference on the process of separation-individuation has already been described (Tang, 1992); we would suggest that there is a similar impact on the father-son relationship. Whereas the prototypic Western son has been supplanted by his father (physically) long before he is aware of his oedipal strivings, in the East, it is the father who may feel the need to forcibly reclaim what is rightfully his (the mother's body). It is this recapture that is symbolized by the return of the absent fathers, Hsueh and Siva.

What then of the fathers? In the story, *At the bend of the River Fen*, we are introduced to a man of humble origins, a mere peasant. Though he is ambitious and successful as a soldier, the Chinese culture tends to laud the intellectual achievements, not military ones. Both Ganesa and Oedipus are of royal blood, Ganesa the child of a god and goddess and Oedipus descended from a long line of kings. While Parvati has her own bathhouse, Jocasta and Oedipus their palace, Hsueh and his wife live in a hovel. We argue that it is the royal families who are the ideal for those cultures. They represent power, the early ideal family, which was omnipotent, only to be struck by tragedy. Hsueh, who represents the common man, poor and powerless, is much more easily and realistically identified with. Unlike Siva, he cannot undo what he has done. The only magical element in the story is the removal of the boy's body by the tiger. There are otherwise no gods, oracles, or resurrections. In some ways, it would seem that the Hsueh story is more plausible, that

6. All references to *Oedipus Rex* are to the translation by R. Fagles, Viking Press (1982).

the feelings of competition with the unknown and young son are more clearly recognized.

In neither Asian story is there any indication of the son's wish to compete with the father. There seems to be a denial of any such striving. For Ganesa, it is only with Siva's blessing that he can become an important deity. Hsueh's son is simply an unknowing victim of a stranger by the river. Oedipus becomes king only by killing his own father. These differences point to the central questions raised by these stories: What are the culturally sanctioned ways that a boy may become a man, and what is the proper relationship of father to son? Only in the Greek myth are violent urges against the father recognized clearly. It is only by parricide that Oedipus can become a man/king. This mirrors the break to independence, the need to "kill" the influence of the father and become one's own man—which Western culture so values. The story of Ganesa suggests a different route. It is with the mother's intervention that Ganesa is restored to life. But it is the father who allows the child to live and to become a god. Only when Ganesa is taught vulnerability—after all, he is killed by Siva and his minions first—can he attain adulthood. The father's acquiescence here is of great importance. For Hsueh's son there is only the role of passive victim. He has remained a filial son, but his father controls his life and death. Indeed, "the good father was aloof, strict, and authoritarian. To befriend a son was to be a bad father, neglecting one's duties. Conversely, to thrash a son, to order him about, to command his awe, to decide what was good for him were the acceptable forms of paternal caring" (Lord, 1990, p. 94). Hsueh's son does not challenge or question this. He obediently agrees to a challenge, only to be cheated and killed. In a sense, this is the posture that traditional Chinese demand of their sons: complete obedience and respect.

In the cases of both Hsueh and Ganesa, the father is ignorant of the birth of a son. This is not the case for Laius, although he is ignorant of Oedipus' ultimate survival. The circumstances of Ganesa's birth are intriguing because they also deny the sexual nature of conception. Indeed, Ganesa's birth, by parthenogenesis, is paralleled by his rebirth, entirely brought about by the father. Thus, as an adult he is the product of both parents, but not of their sexual union. Ganesa is characterized as a rather plump deity, lovable but immature, who indulges in sweets. He is not a sexual being but a son who remains forever a prince by his parents' side. The stories about Ganesa's antics abound in references to his childish jokes and to his overindulging in candy. Indeed, one might see Ganesa's physical self as exemplary of this status, his elephantine head with its trunk a massive but detumescent phallus, his broken tusk mute testimony to his eternally unrealized potency. In contrast, both Oedipus and Hsueh's sons are noted for some prowess—the former as a great king and ruler, the latter as a skilled archer. Both are clearly seen by their mothers as sexual or potentially sexual beings. This is implied in the teasing to which Hsueh is subjected by his wife when he discovers his son's slippers under the bed. For Jocasta, of course, it is far more overt. One possible explanation for these different outcomes may relate to the degree to which the son is indeed a sexual rival to his father. Ganesa remains alive for eternity, but always as a child in his parents' company.

In the panoply of Indian deities, there are also figures of powerful women—Parvati, Kali, and other manifestations of Devi come to mind—but no such parallel figures are found in Chinese mythology or folk tradition. These differences reflect, we believe, differences in social structure and the role of women, and in turn they profoundly affect the nature of the oedipal conflict and its resolution in the respective societies.

The women in the stories differ greatly as well. Both Jocasta and Parvati are queens with particular powers. Hsueh's wife is a more passive, poor, and humble woman. Her virtues are her fidelity to her husband and her dignity in not wanting to be revealed as shabby before the messenger. The latter virtue would likely relate to saving her husband's face. She is a good, faithful wife who conforms to the dictates of her society. Jocasta and Parvati are more active, even rebellious. Jocasta urges Oedipus not to heed the oracle, rules as an equal to her husband and brother, and clearly ranks as a powerful person. To save her husband, Laius, she is willing to sacrifice her son. So, too, Parvati, who is able to create a child out of her own skin. Her fury leads Siva to bring her son back to life. She alone has claim to the son until Siva participates in his rebirth and then adopts him. The Chinese woman is seen as the least powerful. She is shabby and pathetic, and though he accuses her of infidelity, nothing portrays her as a particularly seductive woman. Parvati is powerful yet clearly not seductive enough to persuade Siva to impregnate her with the child she so desperately wants. Only Jocasta has the power to seduce men.

The differences among these women may well reflect the different ways that women are viewed in their respective cultures. They would appear to be the least threatening in the Chinese culture, powerful but in a limited fashion in the Hindu society, and almost omnipotent in the Greek. Jocasta is the only character who appears to be utterly ruthless. It has been argued that Jocasta knew the identity of Oedipus at his appearance (Steiner, 1985) and also knew that he had murdered his father, yet she chose to ignore all the evidence. Earlier, she had been willing to cooperate in the murder of her own infant. Jocasta is the most sinister and blameworthy of all characters in the drama. This is in keeping with the Western image of Woman as Temptress, exemplified in such mythological figures as Eve, Helen, and Lilith.

Slater (1968) has argued that the role of women in Greek mythology reflects a profound ambivalence on the part of the male. On the one hand, there is an intense erotic attachment and on the other a correspondingly intense fear of the power of the mother figure. The result is unbridled aggression toward the mother as the source of this ambivalence. It is interesting to recall that although Oedipus blinded and exiled himself as expiation for his crimes, Jocasta had to suffer more severely; she hanged.

Another difference among these myths is in the role played by minor figures. No figures of consequence are introduced in the tale of Hsueh save for the mysterious tiger; the story takes place entirely within the nuclear family. There are other figures in Ganesa—Siva's men—but they are of little importance. Only the drama of Oedipus occurs within a complex social context. Although there are multiple reasons for this state of affairs, we wish to focus on one aspect, the role played by these secondary characters as objects of identification. Oedipus' relationship with the blind soothsayer, Tieresias, is particularly noteworthy. It is from Tieresias that Oedipus first seeks the truth about the slayer of Laius. It is in part through the riddles of Tieresias that Oedipus finally comes to accept his own guilt, and it is in partial identification with Tieresias that Oedipus blinds himself. (Michels [1986] suggests that this identification is a prototype of a negative therapeutic reaction.) In becoming "his own man," Oedipus moves through a series of shifting identifications. For much of his life he believed himself the son of Polybus of Corinth, only to learn that Laius was his father. Ultimately, he emulates Tieresias, as one might a mentor, in coming to an identity that will allow him to live with his fate. This parallels the process of adopting heroes, which is prevalent among adolescents as they struggle to form the adult ego ideal.

The notion of significant figures outside the family and the process of developing one's own identity through self-knowledge are peculiarly Western. In the Chinese culture one does not turn outside the family to resolve conflicts within the individual. To quote Confucius, "If anyone does not love his parents, but others, he is a rebel against virtue; and if anyone does not respect his parents, but others, he is also a rebel against the standard of rites" (*Hsiao Ching*, p. 24). Indeed, as has been pointed out earlier, the ego ideal consists chiefly of the sense of self as part of a larger whole, a link in a chain that stretches backward many generations and forward to generations yet uncounted. It is thus not through self-knowledge or the establishment of an independent identity that one becomes a man in Chinese culture; rather, it is through acceptance of one's role and loyalty and obedience to one's superiors. Again, quoting Confucius: "Our body and hair and skin are all derived from our parents, and therefore we have no right to injure any of them in the least. This is the first duty of a child. To live an upright life and spread the great doctrines of humanity must win good reputation after death, and reflect great honour upon our parents. This is the last duty of a son" (*Hsaio Ching*, p. 16).

The acceptance of fate and role has led many Western observers to see Chinese men as passive and feminine. But what is involved is a radically different notion of masculinity, of what it means to be a man. Whereas in the West the essence of manhood is independence, autonomy, and action, in the East loyalty, the capacity to bear hardship or emotion without outward display, and conformity to one's role requirements are masculine virtues.

A striking feature common to all three stories is the fact that much of the action takes place at a boundary or threshold: the crossroads outside the gates of Thebes, the River Fen (rivers typically represent a boundary in Chinese art), and the door to the bathhouse. In each case, the mother is within the boundary or gateway. We believe that the fact that the action of the stories occurs outside (of the city, dwelling, or bathhouse) symbolizes the battle for possession of the maternal body. In a fascinating study, Chasseguet-Smirgel (1986) observed that virtually all literary descriptions of utopia depict a place set apart, an isolated island, or a city behind high walls. This represents, she argues, the fantasy of a reunification with the smooth maternal body—that is, the body emptied of all its contents (feces, children, and, most important, the father's penis). If we apply this metaphor to the myths under consideration, we find that in the case of Oedipus, the father possesses the mother's body until the son's return, whereupon the son seizes it, destroying not only the paternal phallus but the negative maternal introject (in the form of the Sphinx) as well. By sharp contrast, in the two other myths, it is the son who has exclusive union with the mother while the father is absent. The return of the father in each case provokes the confrontation that leads to the son's death. We should say the *appearance* of the father, as in both cases father and son are ignorant of each other's existence. Indeed, the water that plays a central role in these two dramas (the bathhouse and the river) may be seen to represent the amniotic fluid, and the confrontation, the trauma of birth.

It is, of course, well known that the incestuous wishes of the oedipal child have significant preoedipal elements as well. Thus, the wish to possess the mother sexually is simultaneously a wish to reunite with her in an undifferentiated duality. The wish to be rid of the father as a rival is also the wish to be rid of him as a representation of external reality, of a world outside the mother-son union. The oedipal struggle, then, is nothing less than a struggle over the reality principle itself.[7] Seen in this context, the story of Ganesa is particularly fascinating, for even though he is beheaded and resurrected he is destined to live for eternity with his mother as a presexual, preadolescent boy. As the Lord of Beginnings and overcomer of obstacles, he embodies the fantasy of a successful union with the smooth maternal body. In this context, it is interesting to note that anthropological studies consistently report a much closer and more intense mother-son relationship in India than in European cultures (Spiro, 1985).

III

That the Oedipus complex is universal appears to us to be unassailable. In making this claim, however, we are using the term in its broadest sense.

That is, the oedipal drama is a drama of the family, involving equally the desires, defenses, and fantasies of the *parents* as well as of the son and including what is brought to the current triad from preceding generations. In this we fully agree with Weiss (1985) and Lidz and Lidz (1989), who stress that the oedipal situation must be seen as a complex set of interpersonal dynamics embedded in a developmental line, rather than as the fantasies of a single individual at a single stage of development. This analysis of the three myths reveals clearly that rivalry and competitiveness between father and son for exclusive possession of the mother are common to all cultures. So, too, is murderous rage. These dynamics and desires we take as inevitable consequences of the fact that all men, regardless of their cultural background or historical epoch, begin life in a prolonged state of helpless dependency, reliant on the mother (or mother substitute) for their continued existence, pass through an even longer period of childhood during which they are repeatedly confronted with their immaturity and impotence vis-à-vis the adult world, must learn what it means to be a man in that

7. It is interesting to note that the fantasy of a fatherless Eden is seen cross-culturally. Plato's claim in *Republic* that sons shall not know their fathers is echoed in the words of the ancient Chinese philosopher Mencius, who cautioned that fathers should never teach their sons.

place and time, and can do so only by identifying with the significant adult figures in their lives. Only gradually and with great difficulty does the boy become a man, whether he is the son of a Trobriand Island fisherman, a Chinese farmer, or an English industrialist. Similarly, all parents face the conflicting wishes and fears brought about by confrontation with their children, including their own unresolved conflicts with their parents and the specter of their own mortality.

Where there are differences is in the form the oedipal conflict takes and in the precise nature of the outcome. The most important differences highlighted by the myths studied here lie in the effect of the preoedipal mother-child relationship on the form and content of the oedipal configuration and the nature of the "successful" resolution of the conflict.

That preoedipal differences in child rearing among cultures may lead to somewhat different oedipal configurations gets some intriguing support from a study of the psychodynamic themes of Japanese folk tragedies. Kitayama (1985) found that although some tales had clear-cut oedipal themes, most revealed mother-infant conflicts of a clearly dyadic or preoedipal nature. It has been observed that the Japanese man's ideal woman is a maternal figure as opposed to the youthful erotic figures typical of American fantasies (Baruma, 1984). In the aforementioned folktales specifically, tragic consequences accrued to the protagonist as a consequence of his absolute and excessive dependence on the maternal figure and his violation of a taboo *not to look*.[8] One is reminded here of the emphasis on sight and blindness in *Oedipus Rex* as well as similar concerns in numerous Indian myths, including some about Ganesa. Typically, looking (at the maternal figure) in violation of the prohibition revealed the animalistic nature of the object (portrayed as a serpent, a maggot-ridden corpse, a crane, and so on). What was seen, in fact, was the incestuous wish that lurks behind the preoedipal fantasy of the conflict-free union with the mother; that is, the mother is revealed as a sexual being, and the son is thrust into the world of the reality principle where impulses, conflicts, and rivals must be confronted. The fact that the dominant theme in Japanese folktales appears to be the shattering of the blissful mother-son dyad by the initial awareness of oedipal strivings supports our contention that there are cultural differences in the relationship between oedipal and preoedipal dynamics and is entirely consistent with what we would expect in a society in which a long period of close physical contact

8. One of the Japanese tales, "The legend of the Dojo Temple," appears to be a direct parallel to the Greek myth of Orpheus and Eurydice, in which the hero must refrain from looking at his lover if he is to rescue her from the land of the dead.

between mother and infant is normative. A similar argument is made by Lidz and Lidz (1989) in their study of initiation rites in Papua New Guinea. In these societies, violent initiation rites that include bloodletting and fellatio are understood to be necessary to break the bond between mother and son, a bond that is created by the absence of the father during the first six years of the boy's life.

As we have stressed, the notion of becoming "one's own man" as the epitome of successful development is peculiarly Western. Compare Freud's characterization of the successful Oedipal resolution:

> the human individual has to devote himself to the great task of detaching himself from his parents, and not until that task is achieved can he cease to be a child and become a member of the social community. For the son this task consists in detaching his libidinal wishes from his mother and employing them for the choice of a real outside love-object, and in reconciling himself with his father if he has remained in opposition to him, or *in freeing himself from his pressure if . . . he has become subservient to him.* (1917, p. 337, emphasis added)

with that of Confucianism:

> since "filial piety" is a cardinal value in Confucianism, a salient feature of the father-son relationship is the unquestioned obedience of the son to the authority of the father. For the son to cultivate himself, in this view, he must learn to suppress his own desires, anticipate the wishes of his father, and take his father's commands as sacred edicts. (Tu, 1985)

For Freud, one consequence of the successful resolution of the Oedipus complex is the projection of the need for an all-powerful father elsewhere, typically onto the figure of an omnipotent and omniscient Father God, which is ubiquitous in Western religion. The lack of independence from the father and the premium placed on continued obedience to him in traditional Eastern societies may at least in part explain the fact that Eastern religions stress typically not the role of the Father but rather the union or merger with the maternal principle (expressed as Nirvana, Satori, Tao, cosmic consciousness, and so on). What is projected in this instance is the return of the prolonged close mother-infant relationship that preceded the oedipal engagement. Hanly and Masson (1976) have suggested that this element of traditional Indian philosophy represents a wish for the most profound regression: "In throwing off what we must regard as a secondary (and precious) acquisition of the child, the ego, it follows that the regression will be to an even earlier, undifferentiated state of primary narcissism" (p. 58). We are inclined to interpret this primary state more in terms of a fusion with the undifferentiated mother, a fantasy of a return to a conflict-free state. To quote from the *Upanishads*, the oldest of the

Hindu texts: "It is as when a man is tightly embraced/ by the woman he loves and he knows nothing/ of the outer world or of the inner world" (Hanly and Masson, 1976, p. 59).

IV

There is no doubt that the study of culture is enriched by the psychoanalytic perspective. It is equally true, we believe, that the study of psychoanalysis is enriched by a consideration of cultural differences and similarities in the nature of psychological conflicts. Although the content of many psychoanalytic journals today might lead one to believe that our science is only of individual psychopathology, it is good to remember that Freud initially conceived a far broader scope for the science he founded.

Freud's approach to the application of psychoanalysis to the study of culture was based on his assumption that the requirements of society were inimical to the needs and desires of the individual. In particular, he was concerned with the conflict between the sexual and aggressive drives and the necessities of smooth social functioning. He conceived of the development of civilization as the development of the varieties of sublimation in a given society (1930). As such, culture became almost synonymous with the superego, the prohibitions against unacceptable sexual (incestuous) and aggressive wishes that develop in the crucible of the Oedipus complex. This has led to an essentially reductionistic approach to much of the psychoanalytic study of society, a search for oedipal (and occasionally preoedipal) themes in disparate cultures. Folklore as diverse as the myths of ancient Persia (Omidsalar, 1987) and James Joyce's *Ulysses* (Blos, 1985), from societies as distinct as Plains Indians (Omidsalar, 1983) and traditional Japan (Kitayama, 1985) have been analyzed from this perspective.

It is clear, however, that there are important psychological differences between cultures that cannot be explained solely as superego phenomena; differences in aesthetics are one example. Thus, a more encompassing model is called for. Winnicott (1971) has suggested that cultural experience lies in the intermediate zone variously referred to as the "area of illusion" or the "potential space," the structural heir to the transitional object. He defines culture as an "inherited tradition" (p. 99) to which all members of a culture contribute and from which all draw. All experience, then, is an indivisible amalgam of individual creative and common traditional elements. By linking cultural experience with transitional phenomena, Winnicott stresses the preoedipal elements, as contrasted with the oedipal elements emphasized by classical theorists. Indeed, the epigraph for Winnicott's paper is a couplet by the Indian poet Tagore: "On the shoreline of endless worlds, / children play." As Winnicott notes, the sea may represent the maternal body and the sand the external world of the reality principle. It is on the shore, the boundary, that play (and, Winnicott argues, cultural experience) occurs. This interpretation resonates with our observations about the importance of the threshold or boundary in the three myths discussed here.

We conceive of culture as having a pervasive influence on all phases of development. Further, we see the influence at one stage as having a profound effect on the structure and outcome of the next. Thus, the differences in the early mother-infant relationship among the three cultures have significant implications for how the oedipal conflict will be experienced by all participants.

Psychoanalysis has been frequently attacked as a theory relevant only for Western industrialized society. In response, too many analysts have redoubled their reductionistic efforts, insisting stubbornly that cultural differences are irrelevant because they are illusory, that all human experience can be understood in the same terms, and that the patterns of development laid down by Freud are invariant. Others, especially in America, have narrowed their focus still further to the minutiae of clinical experience, totally ignoring larger social questions. A half-century ago, Fenichel and others within psychoanalysis were decrying the lack of attention paid to cultural factors. He complained in 1945, "Today analysts know neither anthropology nor history" (quoted in Jacoby, 1983, p. 110). This state of affairs has, unfortunately, only worsened with time. The problems caused by the clash of cultures in the United States and elsewhere beg for thoughtful understanding and informed solutions, the kind of perspective that psychoanalysts can bring. Psychoanalysis has much to say about the nature of cultural forms and expressions. Conversely, a consideration of the role of culture in the psyche can only deepen the psychoanalytic discourse.

BIBLIOGRAPHY

BLOS, P. (1985). *Son and Father.* New York: Free Press.
BARUMA, I. (1984). *Behind the Mask.* New York: Penguin Books.
CHASSEGUET-SMIRGEL, J. (1986). *Sexuality and Mind.* New York: New York University Press.
CHASSEGUET-SMIRGEL, J., & GRÜNBERGER, B. (1986). *Freud or Reich? Psychoanalysis and Illusion.* Trans. C. Pajaczkowska. New Haven: Yale University Press.

COURTRIGHT, P. (1985). *Ganesa: Lord of Obstacles, Lord of Beginnings*. London: Oxford University Press.

ERIKSON, E. (1971). Words at Delos. In *A Way of Looking at Things: Selected Papers of Erik Erikson, 1930–1980*, ed. S. Schlein. New York: Norton, 1987, pp. 743–744.

FREUD, S. (1897). Letter 71 to W. Fleiss, October 15, 1897. *S.E.* 1:263–266.

FREUD, S. (1900). The interpretation of dreams. *S.E.* 3.

FREUD, S. (1917). Introductory lectures on psychoanalysis. *S.E.* 16.

FREUD, S. (1930). Civilization and its discontents. *S.E.* 21:59–145.

HANLY, C., & MASSON, J. (1976). A critical examination of the new narcissism. *Int. J. Psycho-anal.* 57:49–66.

Hsiao Ching or *Book of Filial Duty* (c. 400 B.C.). Trans. I. Chen. London: John Murray, 1908.

JACOBY, R. (1983). *The Repression of Psychoanalysis*. New York: Basic Books.

KITAYAMA, O. (1985). Pre-Oedipal "taboo" in Japanese folk tragedies. *Int. J. Psycho-anal.* 12:173–186.

KOHUT, H. (1982). Introspection, empathy, and the semi-circle of mental health. *Int. J. Psycho-anal.* 63:395–408.

LIDZ, T., & LIDZ, R. (1989). *Oedipus in the Stone Age*. Madison, Conn.: International Universities Press.

LORD, B. B. (1990). *Legacies*. New York: Alfred A. Knopf.

MALINOWSKI, B. (1929). *The Sexual Life of Savages*. London: Routledge.

MICHELS, R. (1986). Oedipus and insight. *Psychoan. Q.* 55:599–617.

OMIDSALAR, M. (1983). Oedipus in Kansas: A version of Aarne-Thompson tale type 569 among the Potowatomi Indians of Kansas. *Amer. Imago* 40: 2:159–174.

OMIDSALAR, M. (1987). The dragon fight in the national Persian epics. *Int. R. Psycho-anal.* 14:343–356.

ROSS, J. M. (1982). Oedipus revisited: Laius and the "Laius Complex." *Psychoanalytic Study of the Child.* 37:169–200.

SLATER, P. (1968). *The Glory of Hera*. Boston: Beacon Press.

SPIRO, M. (1985). *Oedipus in the Trobriands*. Chicago: University of Chicago Press.

STEINER, J. (1985). Turning a blind eye: The cover up for Oedipus. *Int. J. Psycho-anal.* 12:161–172.

TANG, N. (1992). Some psychoanalytic implications of Chinese philosophy and child-rearing practices. *Psychoanalytic Study of the Child.* 47:371–389.

TU, W-M. (1985). Selfhood and otherness in Confucian thought. In *Culture and Self*, ed. A. Marsella, G. DeVos, & F. Hsu. London: Tavistock Books.

WEISS, S. (1985). How culture influences the interpretation of the Oedipus myth. Reprinted in *The Oedipus Papers*, ed. G. Pollack & J. Ross, Madison, Conn. International Universities Press, 1988, 373–385.

WINNICOTT, D. (1971). The location of cultural experience. *Playing and Reality*. London: Tavistock Press, 1982, 95–103.

Lie as Narrative Truth in Abused Adopted Adolescents

SALLYE WILKINSON, PH.D.
GEORGE HOUGH, PH.D.

Two case examples of abused adopted adolescents are discussed to high-light tension within the treatment relationship when the therapist is expected to accept without question a clearly unbelievable story. These examples illustrate how the lies of such youths can function as narrative truth. The unbelievable tales that emerge in the therapeutic work effectively alter the adolescents' perceptions about the perplexing loss of conti-nuity, both internal and external, that occurred when they were removed from their homes. Characters in the stories represent fragmented self- and object-representations as victim, abuser, rescuer, and passive on-looker. Counterparts to the patient as victim, abuser, rescuer, and pas-sive onlooker can be recognized in the therapist's subjective responses. If the therapist can use countertransference to inform an understanding of the treatment process, an appreciation emerges that the truth of the lie is in its impact. Decisions about how to intervene can then be crafted. The second separation-individuation intrinsic to adolescent development is understood to provide a ripe opportunity for this working-through pro-cess.

Sallye M. Wilkinson is the Ishak Ramzy Professor at the Karl Menninger School of Psychiatry; staff psychologist at the Menninger Clinic; and advanced candidate at the Topeka Institute for Psychoanalysis. George Hough is in private practice in Topeka, Kansas, and an advanced candidate at the Topeka Institute for Psychoanalysis.

Presented at the International Psychoanalytic Studies Organization Meeting in San Francisco on July 30, 1995. We are grateful to Drs. Glen Gabbard and Irwin Rosen for their thought provoking questions.

The Psychoanalytic Study of the Child 51, ed. Albert J. Solnit, Peter B. Neubauer, Samuel Abrams, and A. Scott Dowling (Yale University Press, copyright © 1996 by Albert J. Solnit, Peter B. Neubauer, Samuel Abrams, and A. Scott Dowling).

THE TWO TREATMENT PROCESSES TO BE DISCUSSED HAVE TAUGHT US THAT clinical approaches to lying in abused adopted adolescents must first be formulated in the context of the adoptive idiom. Continuity was a casualty in the life of these youths. Strangers stood where mommy and daddy were available before. Reference points for the definition of self, both internal and external, had to be recalibrated—reassigned. Because the adoptions of our two patients also were based on neglect and abuse they experienced this disruption in the extreme. Sensitive to their adoption histories, we anticipated the plea inherent in their internal dialogues: "What's going on? What I knew of myself and others just a short time ago no longer holds true! What's going on?" Their fear of repeated loss and abandonment was evident in the prohibitive reply: "Don't ask! If it happened before, it could happen again—don't ask!" They approached the treatment process with suspiciousness and presumably tried to gain the upper hand by the production of numerous, unbelievable stories. What we had not anticipated was our own internal questioning about what was going on within the therapeutic relationship. As we describe our efforts to understand these tale-spinning, adopted youth, we will use the word "lie" *descriptively* to denote unbelievable stories that our patients insisted we believe unquestionably.

For consideration, some case material is offered:

THE CASE OF THE "GENETIC SPLICER"

Tom, a fifteen-year-old boy, had been taken away from his teenage mother at the age of four months due to severe neglect and failure to secure adequate medical attention. During months of foster care prior to adoption, he suffered from failure-to-thrive and required several hospitalizations. He knew only that he had been adopted at two years of age.

After thirteen placements at various hospitals, residential facilities, and foster homes in a single year, Tom, at age 15, was transferred to the residential program where the treatment reported here took place. In the first session, he informed his therapist of his treatment history and announced that he had no intention of returning to his adoptive family. He then revealed his interest in Beethoven and handed the therapist an LP of Beethoven selections. He mispronounced the names of several compositions that he claimed were his longstanding favorites. The therapist noted that he seemed to have memorized the titles listed on the album cover. He next described having been molested by an older woman for whom he performed various sex acts in the days prior to this admission to the residential program. He hinted that he had reluctantly participated but seemed proud of his sexual prowess. There was reason to believe that no such liaison took place. He then said that he had read a number of professional books that he noticed in the therapist's office. His list was incredible, particularly his story of having read "that Mode Ren [sic] Clinical Psychology book. I didn't read the mode ren part, only the clinical psychology part." He was referring to a book entitled *Modern Clinical Psychology*. The therapist was intrigued by this session, in which little of what was said could be verified.

On the residential unit, Tom quickly developed a reputation as a liar. Nursing staff repeatedly complained that he evaded the truth whenever he thought he was about to get in trouble. He seemed to be using others for personal gain. But in the therapy process, his tales took on another quality as he expounded on his special relationship to a science teacher in his small Midwestern high school. He claimed that she had taken a special interest in him and frequently allowed him to stay after school to do genetic splicing in the lab. Tom also brought in numerous short stories he had written that were filled with intrigue and death. They were well written and suspenseful but were vaguely familiar. His adoptive father asserted that he had plagiarized Stephen King and Dean Koontz. Tom maintained that his adoptive father had hit him with a baseball bat, a charge his father adamantly denied. Who was this boy?

Tom expected the therapist to respond to the content of his stories. Interestingly, the therapist's experience was akin to that of playing an interactive video game in which the characters and action come from a menu and achieve only two-dimensional status.

Another patient, Susan, presented her tales expecting only occasionally her therapist to actively affirm their content. More often, Susan was absorbed in her story and inattentive to the therapist's response. In this manner she apparently sought to re-create a situation in which she had been rejected, but this time she had a sense of active mastery.

CASE OF THE "WHOPPER KID"

Thirteen-year-old Susan had been told that she was removed from her biological parents' home when she was eighteen months old. She had suffered severe physical abuse and appalling poverty. Often neglected to the point of starvation, she stole biscuits out of the dog's dish. Despite the best efforts of her resourceful adoptive parents, Susan displayed numerous adjustment problems in her new home and later, when she entered school. Impulsive and mischievous, she repeatedly alienated teachers with her demands for attention and her daily outpouring of tall tales. Other children called her the Whopper Kid. Exasperated by their inability to trust her, her adoptive parents brought her for psychotherapy.

In the early months of treatment, Susan frequently told her therapist fantastic tales embellished with great detail and emotional enthusiasm. All of her stories began as stable and positive situations that turned into towering catastrophes—with Susan always the rescuer. For example, she described how she had been on a leisurely drive with her family when a gunman jumped in front of the car and ordered them to get out. Reacting quickly, she deftly kicked the gunman in the genitals and wrested away his weapon. Thus she had used her seventy-five-pound-frame to save the entire family from harm.

In her stories, Susan repeatedly subdued cruel abusers and compensated for neglectful caretakers. As a result, passive onlookers, like her adoptive parents and presumably the therapist, would offer their loving attention to her.

The accounts of these two young people did not reflect a formal loss of reality testing or an encapsulated schizoid fantasy. Rather, they expressed the strong wish for a particular kind of interaction with their therapists (and parents). By using the term "lie" to describe the exchange, we attempt to capture some of the tension experienced by the therapist when asked to accept a clearly unbelievable story. For example, the claims of both the Genetic Splicer and the Whopper Kid were greeted with a silent "Oh, sure!" The therapists debated internally about how much to congratulate, to hold in reserve, or to confront the patient. Or, as a compromise, should these youths be complimented for their sheer creativity? Formulating interventions was a constant struggle throughout these treatment processes.

Over the next two years Susan was seen once weekly. Her borderline level of ego functioning was marked by passive-aggressive and histrionic features. Because she was impulsive and spirited, the therapist had to actively work to express empathy and set limits.

As the treatment relationship developed, Susan discovered, contrary to her expectations, that the therapist tolerated her stories. Susan ritualistically began her after-lunch appointment saying, "I'm so hungry!" A walk to a nearby convenience store to purchase a cookie became routine. The therapist's invitations to Susan to consider her expression of other kinds of hunger were ignored. Yet

Susan at times communicated those "hungers" by breaking up her cookie and eating it off the floor. On other occasions she wanted to be fed by the therapist like a baby. The therapist's reactions were multifaceted. Revulsion over the patient's doglike behavior was mingled with heartrending empathy for her unimaginable deprivations. The therapist wanted to help her stop acting like a dog and behave as a girl.

When doglike behavior was replaced by conversation, the therapist was relieved by a sense of progress. However, that countertransference relief proved illusory when Susan told more unbelievable stories. For example, she might emphatically describe rescuing some baby squirrels from a hawk. Then she would insist that the mother squirrel had spoken to her in gratitude. By not challenging her about these "facts," the therapist facilitated the unspoken rapport developing between them. Although disbelieving Susan's tales, the therapist was mindful of protecting their fragile rapport. In sharing accounts of her rescues, Susan could be the hero twice, once in the tale and once in the telling.

The content of Susan's stories began to suggest that the therapeutic alliance was growing. In this context, her persistent request for a Christmas present was understood as a request for greater closeness. She repeatedly referred to an inexpensive doll that she wanted but refused to allow the therapist to ask about the meaning of the doll. So another variation on the dilemma of "What's going on here?" "Don't ask!"—came into the process. When the doll was presented to her as a new consulting-room toy, she would have nothing to do with it, saying that she had lied about wanting it. She alluded to something else that she "really" wanted but refused to say more.

Susan rejected the therapist's efforts to transform the disjointed meanings inherent in her behavior and statements into a narrative history that connected her early life with her present experiences. Thus standard intervention strategies were not useful. No clear threads seemed to emerge based on verifiable facts or mutual consensus. The therapist, confused and frustrated, noted countertransference urges to rescue or attack. Would insistence on truth telling reenact Susan's earlier traumas?

Susan wanted and needed the therapist to be a witness who testifies to the happy ending of her stories—despite the recurring theme of a mother's inability to care for her baby. Susan's increasingly urgent demand for the perfect doll presumably reflected an unconscious fantasy that mothers leave if they do not get the perfect baby. Her absolute exhortation evoked in the therapist a sense of emotional blackmail. The therapist's resulting helplessness and frustration when Susan rejected the doll was understood as an expression of the patient's experience as the discarded baby.

Although the introduction of the doll into the office could be debated, in terms of both technique and dynamic implications, our intention is to illuminate how the identity foisted on the therapist is a jumble of concordant and complementary identifications (Racker, 1957). The confusion, frustration, and tumult sparked by Susan's withdrawn request had begun to create an altered atmosphere (Bion, 1970). Exchanges between Susan and her therapist were not what they seemed. Smith (1968) writes about this alteration with respect to how it fits with regular development and the mother's discovery of the first lie. In that moment, aspects of her identity involving mother-infant oneness are shattered. Although the child has reached a developmental moment at which it is possible to play with separateness through manipulation of the truth, the mother must accept the loss of the old style of attachment in favor of the new. In this manner, developmental advances in identity formation are negotiated by both mother and child. The abused adopted adolescents we describe here also created unbelievable stories in an attempt to consolidate identity. But what was manipulated was not so much the boundary between self and other, as when the child tells the mother the first lie. Rather, the manipulation involved the assignment and reassignment of fragmented self- and object-representations as abuser, victim, rescuer, and passive onlooker, which could fluidly be exchanged with the therapist in an effort to prop up an identity founded on an inaccessible and unknowable history.

Whereas the altered atmosphere created by tales such as Susan's could be understood to have a settling effect for her, it was unsettling for the listener. Like the mother hearing the first lie from her child, the therapist also suffered a loss on discovering the presumably secure working alliance to be an illusion. We noticed that once we began to question internally whether reality was predictable in relation to Susan and Tom, we were primed for identifying with their projected self- and object-representations involving trauma and abandonment. Concordant identifications inducing fears of abandonment and victimization in us were consciously experienced as being deskilled. We noted that a countertransference reaction to the loss of control was to insist on the truth, which at best promised to rescue the therapeutic pair from anxiety-provoking mistrust, and at worst threatened to enact a complementary identification with the abuser.

These adolescents' efforts to project a painful inner world and build a fantasied sense of mastery over past disappointments and trauma differed sharply from the function of fantasy in less-troubled adolescents, whose imaginings are anchored in reality, serve as trial action, and lead to doing (Chetnik and Fast, 1970; Chetnik, 1986). Such anticipatory ego capacities fuel the separation-individuation process reawakened in adolescence. Yet, because the patients described here employed fantasy, not for anticipation in the building and maintenance of attachments but to manage inner pain and terror, separation and individuation were stunted. To help these youths get back on track developmentally, we had to relate to them in an unanticipated fashion.

Toward this end, silent trial interpretations paved the way toward a more open dialogue about central fantasies and primary identifications (Gabbard and Wilkinson, 1994).

> Tom was seen in a supportive-expressive psychotherapy process three times a week for the eighteen months he lived in the residential program. His borderline level of ego functioning often propelled him toward testing the limits by his impulsive and self-centered actions. His therapist noted feeling dramatic pulls either to protect Tom from himself as he damaged relationships right and left or to take him to task for his defiance.
>
> Tom's eventual admission that his adoptive father had never actually harmed him signaled that he was ready to use treatment in a new and meaningful way. At roughly the same time, his hygiene deteriorated, and a great deal of attention on the unit was devoted to his body odor. In sessions he complained of being "erased" when his adoptive family built a new home without a bedroom for him. He also insisted that he needed round-the-clock attention from his therapist. Lack of attention and erasure were conveyed as the causes for his poor hygiene; his odor was not his fault. Much later in the treatment it was learned that his biological mother had left him for lengthy periods in diarrhea-filled diapers.
>
> The therapist began to question what was "stinky" in Tom's past. Although he called such questions stupid, Tom began to map what he termed his "attention-getting cycle"—at the first hint that he was "messing up," he would launch into increasingly provocative behavior and lies. By making mistakes and irritating others first, he would be in greater control of their anger and rejection. Much review and confrontation of this cycle in the therapy did little toward altering his behavior. Perhaps he did not want to know what was going on.

Silent analysis and interpretation of this impasse led to the therapist's realization of feeling extraordinarily isolated. It was only when the therapist described a parallel cycle depicting the impact of Tom's provocative behavior on the therapist that Tom was able to change. The therapist described how the more elusive and provocative Tom became, the more helpless and irritated the therapist felt. Although Tom was not surprised by this aspect of the therapist's response, he had not anticipated that the therapist felt rejected by him at the same point in the cycle that he felt rejected by the therapist. This realization had a profound impact on him and contributed to the alleviation of his hygiene problem.

In the following months, Tom's lying decreased, and he began to bring in to the therapist a series of stories he had written. The characters were all plagued with misery linked to their evil and aggressive traits. As Tom's characters assumed more accountability for the internal sources of their problems, he began to consider that he was not so bad. With growing conviction that he had qualities ranging from good to bad, he began to appreciate that others would not automatically reject him.

Confronting Tom's solipsistic attention-getting cycle had only led him to entrench defensively. He did not want to know what was going on. But once the therapist was able to be with him in a way that allowed for the acknowledgment of mutually experienced isolation and anger, Tom's "Don't ask" prohibition disappeared. As a result, he could begin to be curious about his thoughts and feelings. His individuation allowed for a sense of continuity both between him and his therapist and within his inner world.

Tom's critical advances in individuation could have dead-ended in an adolescent pseudomaturity. Without concurrent separation from infantile objects and cessation of incestuous object choices, any teenager can achieve developmental milestones that risk being narcissistic inflations. Separation is a challenging process for the adolescent even under the best of circumstances in a relatively intact family. For the patients we discuss here, separation evoked the absence of the earliest objects. Luckily, there was a developmentally driven uncovering of the earliest separation issues. A ripe opportunity to rework difficulties stemming from abuse, victimization, rescue, and neglect became available.

At the same time, for Tom and Susan rediscovery of the earliest objects within their inner world necessitated some measure of creating those objects. They could not give a verbal account of the trauma and abandonment that occurred before they could speak or of the disbelief and anguish embodied in the question about what is going on. Yet they were able to evoke that dilemma in the therapist by expecting that everything they say should be believed without question. By observing the countertransference dilemma and silently examining the countertransference debate over whether or not to ask for absolute truth, the therapist could finally articulate the question about what was going on. Unearthing the question within the transference-countertransference process allowed a narrative truth about earliest experiences to emerge.

We believe that the questions provoked by the telling of unbelievable stories must be answered within the treatment relationship to provide a foundation for adolescent separation and individuation. To explain this perspective on the use of countertransference, we refer to two points of view on the dynamics of lying described in the literature, specifically its impact on self in relation to others. Greenacre (1958), noting the universal longing to return to a state of infantile omnipotence, wrote about the repetition compulsion inherent in habitual lying. She felt that the liar presented a falsely embellished self for acceptance by the other, who substituted for an idealizing mother. What answered, encouraged, and sustained this wishful behavior was a complementary wish in the other to be duped by a charmer, thereby vicariously savoring omnipotence. By highlighting pathological distortions of an expectable, loving exchange between parent and child, Greenacre underscored an interpersonal process in which the liar's need to deceive dovetailed with the spectator's need to be deceived. Because the spectator is entertained, the question—"What's going on?"—has minimal urgency. This can be illustrated by the concerns expressed by Tom's and Susan's parents (and subsequently by Tom's nursing staff) that their lies could not be tamed. Behind the frustration and anger at these youths lurked an appreciation of the magnificence of their talespinning capacities. The wrestling over truth telling prevented all the parties from contemplating the dynamics involved. Action and reaction prevented a loving give-and-take between caretaker and child.

The parents' frustrations over Tom's and Susan's lies parallels the literature written on whether liars are suitable for analytically oriented treatment (Fenichel, 1937; Deutsch, 1982; Weinshel, 1979; Blum, 1983; Chagoya and Schkolne, 1986; Gediman, 1985; O'Shaughnessy, 1990). Perhaps as a result relatively little has been written about the intrapsychic process in which the liar's need to deceive coincides with the internally represented spectator's need to be deceived. Mention is made of the lie's reactivation of unconscious memory traces of real experiences (Deutsch, 1982), particularly those surrounding the oedipal drama (Weinshel, 1979), but little is said about the role of the internally represented spectator. To explore the relation between the lie and the internal spectator, one has to consider the literature on perversions. McDougall (1980), for example, describes how one part of the psyche splits off in an effort to deceive and control another because of the pervert's need to deny anatomical differences. As the pervert attempts to offset what cannot be symbolized in the internal world, a compulsive ritual develops through repetitive reenactment of a perverse sexual scenario. The question—"What's going on?"—has value only as long as the internal spectator can be duped repeatedly. Consider how Tom behaved as if he did not want to know what was going on. As long as he could compulsively assert that he could do genetic splicing if he so desired, he convinced himself that his fears carried no weight. Yet the success of his effort at internal deception depended on repetitive lying.

We must distinguish our position from those represented by Greenacre and McDougall. For Greenacre, the actual other helps smooth over troubling interpersonal discontinuities in the role of the idealizing mother, who, as in the case of our patients, may be drawn into a power struggle. For McDougall, the internal other helps smooth over troubling symbolic discontinuities by colluding with the obliteration of differences. In both instances, it is undesirable for the liar to fully answer the question about what was going on. We differ by taking the stance that the question must be answered. Recall how useful it was to Tom when he could finally examine how his cycle affected the therapist while fending off internal anxieties.

> For Susan, answering this question was impossible: During the next year, Susan's insistence on the veracity of her tales continued within treatment, as well as at home and at school. Her mother frequently asked the therapist, "What is going on?" This parental pressure added to the therapist's countertransference reaction of frustration and impotence. In this context, Susan refused to return for ongoing treatment. Only in the company of her parents would she come to say her goodbyes after two years of treatment. She explained, "You tried too hard to get to know me. Besides, I wanted to leave a long time ago." Her exit line underscored how desperate she felt: "Not you—not anyone—will ever see who I really am!"

Defeated, angered, concerned, and saddened, the therapist was left to ask, "What's going on?" A reversal had occurred that left the therapist feeling abandoned and helpless. Thus the therapist remained a participant in a dramatic enactment of Susan's earlier trauma. Her departure sustained her illusory sense of control. The therapist's efforts to "get to know" her were apparently perceived as a forceful exposure, not only of her innermost fears and anxieties but also of her imperfections. Weighed down by her unconscious fantasy that mothers leave if they do not get the perfect baby, Susan could not tolerate the potential rejection.

Tom had a slightly more differentiated capacity, hard won through his residential treatment, to conceptualize the core problem as existing within his subjective experience. As a result, he was more available to consider the questions and prohibitions embodied in his lying.

> Tom complained bitterly about his biological mother's "mistake" of having borne several children by the time she was seventeen years old. With greater bitterness, he insisted that he, too, was one of her mistakes. He considered her "a loser and a slut" and speculated that she had probably died of AIDS. The therapist interceded to clarify that Tom's mother's mistakes did not mean that *he* was a mistake. A child's inability to sort out such things was gently observed. In the following sessions, Tom shared poems he had written about the pain of not having any early memories or even baby pictures. He also spontaneously generated insights into connections between his maladaptive behavior and his self-proclaimed identity as a mistake. He revealed his belief that fear was the basis for happiness; and said that he felt unwanted by his adoptive family and his treaters. He dreamed about sitting alone in a dead world. He drew pictures of events he imagined had happened in his infancy and shared those drawings with the therapist as another child might share a baby album. Finally, in a reparative gesture, he acknowledged to his adoptive parents that he had been a difficult child. He began the phase of working toward a mutually agreed-on discharge from the residential unit.

Tom's unbelievable stories did not totally cease. However, his need to use these tales to reduce others to need-gratifying objects who repetitively enacted derivatives of abuse, abandonment, rescue, and indifference had dramatically diminished. Rather than engage others to be containers for intolerable tensions through projective identification (Ogden, 1982) sparked by his lies, Tom had developed sufficient ego strength to do some of that for himself. Among his gains was a greater conscious awareness of his rage over being given up for adoption by his neglectful parents. The lying behavior that persisted as he entered outpatient treatment had a more deviant, entitled quality than his earlier adventures in genetic splicing. At this point, the lying had an easily identifiable function of compensation and revenge that signaled he was on the threshold of the mourning he had never been able to complete.

THE FACILITATING MOMENTUM OF ADOLESCENT DEVELOPMENT

We have pointed out how the tales told by Tom and Susan departed from the developmental function of such stories in typical youngsters. For example, the tales served to assign and reassign fragments of self- and object-representations as abuser, victim, rescuer, and passive on-looker. The behavioral thrust was to help Tom and Susan cope with inner pain where less disturbed adolescents might employ the same behavior to accomplish the primary task of adolescence—separation and individuation from parental figures (Blos, 1967).

Under the best of circumstances, teens navigate a bumpy course of comparing and contrasting themselves with peers while asserting their independence from or allegiance to authority figures. Through this barter between their internal and external worlds they begin to consoli-date identifications and psychic structures. Deutsch's (1982) observa-tion that at puberty, before definite object choice and before sexual activity, the whole sexual life of the child takes place in fantasy con-tinues to be generally accepted. Early conflicts are reawakened, and maturation requires a shift away from infantile fantasies and infantile object choices. The reworking of fantasies, as an effort to master reality in a new way, may become a point of departure for lies. Presumably, as Susan and Tom worked toward maturation, they spun roles for them-selves that included the desired traits of competence, attractiveness, and sexual experience. Thus, as noted by other writers, we infer that the dynamics and self-regulatory functions of their unbelievable sto-ries had relevance for the developmental tasks before them (Deutsch, 1982; Chagoya and Schkolne, 1986; Ford, King, and Hollender, 1988; King and Ford, 1988; Stouthamer-Loeber and Loeber, 1986). In fact, the momentum of adolescent development allowed Susan and Tom to articulate abandonment anxieties that previously were not available.

Susan's and Tom's improbable stories seemed to mobilize their self-experiences, both past and present, to create new permutations of self- and object-representations. When taken to the extreme, such permu-tations of self- and object-representations are pathological. After all, Susan did not rescue her family from carjackers, and Tom did not do genetic splicing. But on a modest scale developmental tasks are served; consider how manipulating what is verbally disclosed enables youths to prove to themselves the limits of what the other can know about their thoughts and feelings (Ford, King, and Hollender, 1988). Not only are interpersonal boundaries tested, but ego boundaries are also defined and enhanced vis-à-vis the internal spectator. By creating havoc through unbelievable assertions, typical adolescents may extract some degree of control, pleasure, and even revenge over the adult world about which they feel so ambivalent (Chagoya and Schkolne, 1986). Their wish to claim their future while struggling with infantile conflicts may generate the message: "You are supposed to see things not with your own eyes, but in the way I am showing them to you" (Chagoya and Schkolne, 1986).

The unbelievable stories of Tom and Susan had a slightly different developmental (and defensive) function from the lies of better-adjusted adolescents. For them, the notion that adults are supposed to see only what they are being shown has particular significance. In addition to all the other separation-individuation challenges inherent in adolescence, their early conflict embodied in "What's going on? Don't ask!" had been reawakened. They could neither separate nor individuate from a relationship that did not blossom and was not clearly represented internally. Their internal others, as represented by their biological parents, were shadowy at best. What "cannot be seen" may be vestiges of horrible deprivation and trauma. From this vantage point, Susan's and Tom's lies could be understood as an effort to create memories out of affective impressions, to control the repercussions of those memories and to establish a continuous sense of self in relation to other. Unconsciously, their answer to the question "What's going on?" may be, "I'm creating memories because I have to master where I came from before I can know where I'm going. I don't have to ask consciously about such things because I 'know' through my lies."

Yet such efforts to establish an internal sense of continuity created an experience of discontinuity with others involved with them. Lies may have assuaged Tom's and Susan's need to ask "What's going on?" but they had the opposite effect on the people hearing them. Thus the question that was too dangerous to be asked internally was evoked externally. The frustration and annoyance evoked in others hindered subsequent individuation. Consider the reactions of parents, teachers, and nursing staff to the unbelievable tales of Tom and Susan, tales that caused them to be discredited and denied developmentally appropriate autonomy. Thus the efforts of Tom and Susan to round out their personal history to facilitate growth had the effect of engaging others in regressive relationships. An opportunity was needed to forge an internal sense of continuity in a context where the external discontinuities engendered by the lie can also be explored.

TREATMENT IMPLICATIONS: THE UTILITY OF COUNTERTRANSFERENCE AWARENESS

The treatment processes of Susan and Tom invite a clinical perspective that employs an understanding of projective identification (Ogden, 1982; Gabbard and Wilkinson, 1994) in which the question of whether the patient should tell the truth about events or the self becomes less strident. The internal and interpersonal turbulence created by the scenarios assumed a greater clinical importance. Both Tom and Susan claimed the role of omnipotent rescuer to the therapist's passive onlooker. Understanding the connection between such roles and the legacy of adoption is not difficult. Furthermore, Susan's stories, in particular, graphically added the characters of abuser and victim to round out the list of internal objects commonly operating in the inner world of an abuse survivor—abuser, victim, rescuer, and passive onlooker (Davies and Frawley, 1992; Gabbard, 1992; Gabbard and Wilkinson, 1994). If the therapist can learn to recognize what is being enacted, then roles cast by the tall tales such as passive onlooker can be understood in a dramatically different way. The therapist's urge to dismiss as untrue now becomes a signal to sit up and take notice. A drama involving abuse and abandonment is being enacted, and, without thinking, the therapist could reenact the role of the denying, neglectful parent. Establishing veridical truth becomes secondary to the question of how to tolerate and transform the perplexing dilemma of the adopted child as understood through the countertransference.

Yet the therapist must also question how best to help such patients learn the degree to which their stories reduce others to need-gratifying objects who repetitively enact derivatives of abuse and abandonment. If we are correct in our formulation, the unbelievable story takes on the status of an internal object relationship. The Genetic Splicer rewrites his genetic script, presumably to introduce a new and improved family. The Carjacking Rescuer exudes affiliation with omnipotent, protective, and need-satisfying figures. Taking away such self-sustaining internal object relationships could be experienced by the adolescent as a threat. Yet developmental progression would necessitate exactly this.

The unbelievable stories of Tom and Susan functioned to alter their *perceptions* of their perplexing loss of developmentally appropriate, need-satisfying objects, both internal and external, on being removed from the home. For example, Tom's culturally refined appreciation of Beethoven and Susan's superhero capacity to rescue the weak and endangered implied superior lineage. Such altered perceptions exemplify Fenichel's (1937) observation: if that which is untrue seems real, then that which is true may be unreal. An illusory link with the past is created and separation traumas are neutralized.

Deutsch, in writing about fantasy lies or pseudologia fantastica, emphasized the psychological truth in the lie by noting the unconscious reactivation of repressed objects and experiences in her patients. Roazen (1982) elaborated her ideas by noting that pseudologia fantastica "is realistically harmless yet has its purposefulness. The pseudology is a defense apparently full of conflict, yet as a self-creation it is free of anxiety; at the same time it is a protection against present-day reality" (p. 372).

The repressed object had a peculiar quality in the inner world of our abused adopted patients. Foremost, the earliest caretakers mistreated Tom and Susan, setting the stage for removal from the home. In their troubled environment, cognitive-perceptual development had advanced enough for bits of affectively laden experiences of self and other to be encoded in memory. These fragments of trauma and loss were never fully symbolically elaborated but instead were enacted through unbelievable tales. The therapists repeatedly were perplexed about what was going on. From this perspective, the sadistic, coercive, and masochistic elements of Tom's and Susan's lying behavior could be understood as rooted in early traumatic losses. The vestiges of their abuse were further transmogrified by the ever-present absence of the earliest objects. We consider the psychological truth of the fantasy lie, as described by Deutsch and others, as a starting point. However, the emphasis placed on the capacity of the lie to evoke a former real experience requires a second thought when abused adopted adolescents such as Tom and Susan are considered. They could not call on experiences with actual caretakers. At the very most, their memories were static, pained, but certainly not based on a lifetime of shared experiences. No party involved in the treatment process—adolescent, adoptive parent, or therapist—had access to Tom's and Susan's "real" stories. For these youths, uncovering the earliest objects within their inner world required some measure of creating those objects. Thus we add to Deutsch's understanding of the fantasy lie as an act of refinding a relationship an appreciation for the lie as an act of creating a relationship. In this fashion, the therapist-spectator is nominated through the lying interaction to flesh out shadowy inner objects and piece together a narrative that had never existed.

O'Shaughnessy (1990) pointed out that to be themselves, liars must lie. We have tried to demonstrate, as have others (Weinshel, 1979; Blum, 1983), how the lie can reveal as much as it conceals. However, because of the countertransference challenges of tolerating the inconsistencies among observations, hypotheses, and formulations with such patients as Tom and Susan, treaters have to work very hard to appreciate the clinical yield. The payoff, once achieved, allows treaters to recognize the adopted child's lies as an anguished plea for interaction. The truth of the lie is in its impact. Recognition of this clinical process permitted the narrative truth in Tom's and Susan's experience finally to be articulated.

BIBLIOGRAPHY

BION, W. R. (1970). *Attention and Interpretation: A Scientific Approach to Insight in Psycho-Analysis and Groups.* New York: Basic Books.

BLOS, P. (1967). The second individuation process of adolescence. *Psychoanal. Study Child* 22:162–186.

BLUM, H. P. (1983). The psychoanalytic process and analytic inference: A clinical study of a lie and loss. *Int. J. Psycho-Anal.* 64:17–33.

CHAGOYA, L., & SCHKOLNE, T. (1986). Children who lie: A review of the literature. *Can. J. Psychiatry* 31:665–669.

CHETNIK, M., & FAST, I. (1970). A function of fantasy in the borderline child. *Am. J. Orthopsychiatry* 40:756–765.

CHETNIK, M. (1986). Levels of borderline functioning in children: Etiological and treatment considerations. *Am. J. Orthopsychiatry* 56:109–119.

DAVIES, J. M., & FRAWLEY, M. (1992). Dissociative processes and transference-countertransference paradigms in the psychoanalytically oriented treatment of adult survivors of childhood sexual abuse. *Psychoanalytic Dialogues* 2: 5–36.

DEUTSCH, H. (1982). On the pathological lie. *J. Am. Acad. Psychoanal.* 10:373–386.

FENICHEL, O. (1937). The economic aspect of pseudologia phantastica. *Int. J. Psycho-Anal.* 18:81–82.

FORD, C., KING, B., AND HOLLENDER, M. (1988). Lies and liars: Psychiatric aspects of prevarication. *Am. J. Psychiatry* 145:554–562.

GABBARD, G. O. (1992). Commentary on "dissociative processes and transference-countertransference paradigms" by J. M. Davies and M. G. Frawley. *Psychoanalytic Dialogues* 2:37–47.

GABBARD, G. O., & WILKINSON, S. (1994). *Management of Countertransference with Borderline Patients.* Washington, D.C.: American Psychiatric Press.

GEDIMAN, H. K. (1985). Imposture, inauthenticity, and feeling fraudulent. *J. Am. Psychoanal. Assoc.* 33:911–935.

GREENACRE, P. (1958). The relation of the impostor to the artist. In *Emotional Growth. Psychoanalytic Studies of the Gifted and a Great Variety of Other Individuals,* vol. 2. New York: Int. Univ. Press, 1971, 533–554.

KING, B., & FORD, C. (1988). Pseudologia fantastica. *Acta Psychiatrica Scandinavica* 77:1–6.

McDOUGALL, J. (1980). *Plea for a Measure of Abnormality.* New York: Int. Univ. Press.

OGDEN, T. (1982). *Projective Identification and Psychotherapeutic Technique.* New York: Jason Aronson.

O'SHAUGHNESSY, E. (1990). Can a liar by psychoanalysed? *Int. J. Psycho-Anal.* 71: 187–195.

RACKER, H. (1957). The meanings and uses of countertransference. *Psychoanal. Q.* 26:303–357.

ROAZEN, P. (1982). Introduction [On the pathological lie, by Helene Deutsch], *J. Am. Acad. Psychoanal.* 10:369–373.

SMITH, J. H. (1968). The first lie. *Psychiatry* 31:61–68.

STOUTHAMER-LOEBER, M., & LOEBER, R. (1986). Boys who lie. *J. Abnormal Child Psychol.* 14:551–564.

WEINSHEL, E. (1979). Some observations on not telling the truth. *J. Am. Psychoanal. Assoc.* 27:503–531.

Index